Praise for *Building Clustered Linux Systems*

"The author does an outstanding job of presenting a very complicated subject. I very much commend this work. The author sets the pace and provides vital resources and tips along the way. The author also has a very good sense of humor that is crafted in the text in such a way that makes the reading enjoyable just when the subject may demand a break. This book should be a requirement for those that are clustering or considering clustering and especially those considering investing a great deal of financial resource toward that goal."

—Joe Brazeal, Information Technician III, Southwest Power Pool

"There are no books that I know of currently that describe in this much detail the process of creating a complete cluster solution. In effect, the author has set a precedent in the design and integration process that is lacking in the industry today."

—Stephen Gray, Senior Applications Engineer, Altair Engineering, Inc.

"This book is for Beginner and Intermediate level system administrators, engineers, and researchers, who want to learn how to build Linux clusters. The book covers everything very well."

—Ibrahim Haddad, Senior Researcher, Ericsson Corporate Unit of Research

"Nothing that I know of exists yet that covers this subject in as much depth and detail. The practical 'hands-on' approach of this book on how to build a Linux cluster makes this a very valuable reference for a very popular, highly demanded technology."

—George Vish, II, Linux Curriculum Program Manager and Senior Education Consultant, HP

"In my opinion there is a significant lack of literature on this subject. Most of the currently available books are either dated or do not address the complete picture of the range of decisions that must go into building a Linux cluster. I feel comfortable recommending this to anyone interested in building a Linux cluster to better understand both the technical aspects of building and designing a Linux cluster, but also the business aspects of the same."

—Randall Splinter Ph.D., Senior Solution Architect, HP

Hewlett-Packard® Professional Books

HP-UX

Cooper/Moore	HP-UX 11i Internals
Fernandez	Configuring CDE
Keenan	HP-UX CSE: Official Study Guide and Desk Reference
Madell	Disk and File Management Tasks on HP-UX
Olker	Optimizing NFS Performance
Poniatowski	HP-UX 11i Virtual Partitions
Poniatowski	HP-UX 11i System Administration Handbook and Toolkit, Second Edition
Poniatowski	The HP-UX 11.x System Administration Handbook and Toolkit
Poniatowski	HP-UX 11.x System Administration "How To" Book
Poniatowski	HP-UX 10.x System Administration "How To" Book
Poniatowski	HP-UX System Administration Handbook and Toolkit
Poniatowski	Learning the HP-UX Operating System
Rehman	HP-UX CSA: Official Study Guide and Desk Reference
Sauers/Ruemmler/Weygant	HP-UX 11i Tuning and Performance
Weygant	Clusters for High Availability, Second Edition
Wong	HP-UX 11i Security

UNIX, LINUX

Mosberger/Eranian	IA-64 Linux Kernel
Poniatowski	Linux on HP Integrity Servers
Poniatowski	UNIX User's Handbook, Second Edition
Stone/Symons	UNIX Fault Management

COMPUTER ARCHITECTURE

Evans/Trimper	Itanium Architecture for Programmers
Kane	PA-RISC 2.0 Architecture
Markstein	IA-64 and Elementary Functions

NETWORKING/COMMUNICATIONS

Blommers	Architecting Enterprise Solutions with UNIX Networking
Blommers	OpenView Network Node Manager
Blommers	Practical Planning for Network Growth
Brans	Mobilize Your Enterprise
Cook	Building Enterprise Information Architecture
Lucke	Designing and Implementing Computer Workgroups
Lund	Integrating UNIX and PC Network Operating Systems

SECURITY

Bruce	Security in Distributed Computing
Mao	Modern Cryptography: Theory and Practice
Pearson et al.	Trusted Computing Platforms
Pipkin	Halting the Hacker, Second Edition
Pipkin	Information Security

WEB/INTERNET CONCEPTS AND PROGRAMMING

Amor	E-business (R)evolution, Second Edition
Apte/Mehta	UDDI
Chatterjee/Webber	Developing Enterprise Web Services: An Architect's Guide
Kumar	J2EE Security for Servlets, EJBs, and Web Services

BUILDING CLUSTERED LINUX SYSTEMS

Robert W. Lucke

PRENTICE
HALL
PTR

PRENTICE HALL PTR
UPPER SADDLE RIVER, NJ 07458
WWW.PHPTR .COM

Library of Congress Cataloging-in-Publication Data

Lucke, Robert W.
  Building clustered Linux systems / Robert W. Lucke.
      p. cm.
  Includes bibliographical references and index.
  ISBN 0-13-144853-6 (pbk. : alk. paper)
  1. Linux. 2. Operating systems (Computers) 3. Embedded computer systems--Programming. I. Title.

  QA76.76.O63L838 2004
  005.4'32--dc22

                                                                    2004014016

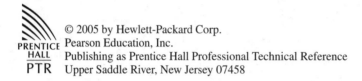

© 2005 by Hewlett-Packard Corp.
Pearson Education, Inc.
Publishing as Prentice Hall Professional Technical Reference
Upper Saddle River, New Jersey 07458

Prentice Hall books are widely used by corporations and government agencies for training, marketing, and resale.

Prentice Hall PTR offers discounts on this book when ordered in quantity for bulk purchases or special sales. For more information, please contact: U.S. Corporate and Government Sales, 1-800-382-3419, corpsales@pearsontechgroup.com. For sales outside the U.S., please contact: International Sales, international@pearsoned.com.

Other company and product names mentioned herein are the trademarks or registered trademarks of their respective owners.

Printed in the United States of America

First Printing

ISBN 0-13-144853-6

Pearson Education Ltd.
Pearson Education Australia PTY., Ltd
Pearson Education Singapore, Pte. Ltd.
Pearson Education Asia Ltd.
Pearson Education Canada, Ltd.
Pearson Educación de Mexico, S.A. de C.V.
Pearson Education—Japan
Pearson Education Malaysia, Pte. Ltd.

This book is dedicated to family and friends, whom I foolishly took for granted—until November 24, 2002.

Most important of all, this book is dedicated to my wonderful wife and best friend, Teri. Without her love, support, and understanding, I would not be where I am today. Thank you for coming into my life!

It is not his mistakes that define the man, but how he handles them.
— Robert W. Lucke

CONTENTS

LIST OF FIGURES

LIST OF TABLES

PREFACE

Welcome! This book will introduce you to building computing solutions from groups of interconnected systems running the Linux operating system. If you want to learn practical information about building this type of solution, often called a *Linux cluster*, read on!

I am writing this book because I believe the time has come for Linux cluster solutions to move into the mainstream information technology (IT) world from their current homes in universities and research institutes. This cannot happen until Linux clustered solutions, or "clusters," are introduced and demystified for mainstream system administrators and IT solution architects. If this information is what you are looking for, read on!

In this book we examine some of the architectures, processes, and collections of technologies that may be used to build clustered Linux systems. We examine the reasons that Linux may make the best choice as the base operating system for a cluster. We do this while attempting to avoid the assumptions and jargon that currently make building Linux clusters the domain of a small club of high-performance computing specialists. If this approach is what you are looking for, read on!

Learning to build Linux clusters is a journey, like learning any other complex technical task. One of the most difficult parts in any journey is just getting started. There is a folk saying that goes something like, "A map does you no good if you don't know where you are." This book will pick a starting point, identify some of the opportunities for Linux cluster solutions, define a process for creating a cluster solution, introduce you to some of the necessary components, and give concrete examples of cluster design and construction.

Let's begin the journey, shall we?

About This Book

The intent of this book is to provide an introduction to clustered Linux systems for an audience that may not have any experience working with this type of solution. A cluster comprises multiple physical systems, interconnected and configured to act in concert with each other as if they were a single resource. Throughout, I assume a basic understanding of computer hardware, network, and operating system concepts or the ability to research required topics. I do not, however, assume previous experience with clustered systems.

This book is not intended to be an introduction to Linux system administration or Transmision Control Protocol/Internet Protocol (TCP/IP) network administration. I make every attempt to point you to appropriate reference books and external sources of information as we proceed. Experience with administering Linux or UNIX systems and an understanding of network connections is essential to getting the most useful information from this book.

This book attempts to tie together the "big picture" for those system administrators and system architects who already understand the individual elements of that picture. My goal is to teach you how to configure and use Linux subsystems and tools on multiple physical computers to create the appearance of a single-system "clustered" solution. This is a potentially complex endeavor that relies foremost on understanding the basic operation of the Linux operating system and subsystems, which may involve network connections.

Notation and Conventions

Throughout this book we examine clusters based only on the Linux operating system. Indeed, that is why the title of the book is *Building Clustered Linux Systems*. To avoid the constant repetition of the phrases "Linux clusters" and "Linux cluster," wherever I use the term *cluster*, I am referring to a Linux cluster, unless specifically noted otherwise.

Whenever I need to illustrate Linux commands, subsystem names, command-line options, or URLs for Web sites, I use `Courier` font to set the information apart from regular text. I use the `Courier italic` font for text that requires specific values to be substituted, such as `<ip-address>-kickstart`. *Italic* is used in the text for emphasis.

Using This Book

Part I introduces the concept of a cluster, defines the term *cluster* as we will use it, and outlines a general process for building a cluster. Part II introduces the hardware components that make up a cluster, along with an architectural model that shows the relationship between the individual hardware components in various types of clusters. Part III applies Linux and open-source software to the software architecture of a cluster, pointing out available solutions and approaches. Part IV discusses the economics and physical construction of cluster hardware, detailing the design and implementation details (cables, power, cooling, and so on).

Part I is the key to understanding the process and components involved in building a clustered Linux system—you should start with the chapters in this section. If you are new to the hardware and software components involved in a Linux cluster, you should proceed linearly through the remaining parts of the book. After completing Part I, experienced system architects who are anxious to dive right to the Linux software portion of building clusters should read the material in Part III, followed by Part IV. Experienced Linux system administrators may wish to read Parts II and IV, then skim over Part III.

Production Information

A number of software tools were used in the production of this book and its illustrations, including

- Microsoft Visio 2000, for rack and network diagrams. (Despite my focus on Linux, Visio is still unequaled in terms of its ability to create design drawings and realistic pictures of racks and cluster configurations. In addition, I used Hewlett-Packard-specific templates and Visio stencils because they are freely available for Hewlett-Packard equipment and racks, not because Hewlett-Packard equipment is the only solution.)
- Many of the figures in the book use Hewlett-Packard hardware and network equipment stencils for Visio, and are used with the permission of Hewlett-Packard and VSD Grafx, Inc. These stencils are available (currently for free) from `http://www.visio-cafe.com`.
- Additional network equipment stencils (specifically for Cyclades port servers and Myrinet switches) for Visio are used in several figures with permission of Altima Technologies Inc. These stencils are available by subscription from `http://www.netzoomstencils.com`.
- Adobe Illustrator 10, for figures and illustrations
- Adobe Framemaker 7, for the text and layout
- Adobe Acrobat 6.0, for output to the printing process

All these tools made the writing, formatting, and production of this book easier than it might have been without them. After just one production of this nature, I am beginning to understand the amount of manual labor invested by Gutenberg.

ACKNOWLEDGMENTS

My journey through the cluster world is still continuing. I gratefully acknowledge the people who started this journey for me: Scott Studham, Eduardo Apra, Dave Cowley, Evan Felix, Scott Jackson, Bill Pitre, Gary Stouson, Tim Witteveen, Ralph Wescott, and Ryan Wright, all of those at the Molecular Science Computing Facility in the William R. Wiley Environmental Molecular Sciences Laboratory at the Pacific Northwest National Laboratory (PNNL) in Richland, Washington (see `http://www.mscf.emsl.pnl.gov` for more information).

At the time of this writing, phase 2 of the Linux-based Intel Itanium 2 supercomputer at PNNL has just "gone live" with 11.8 TFLOPs, premiering as the fifth-fastest computer system in the world, based on peak floating-point performance. Congratulations, Scott and team!

Additionally, I would like to thank Jim Gianotti, Dann Frazier, Paul Martin, Stephen Gray, Randy Splinter, Ph.D., Kevin Carson, Rudy Anderson, Chris Maestes, George Vish II, and David Mosberger of Hewlett-Packard; Duncan Roweth, John Brookes, and Dan Kidger of Quadrics Inc.; Chris Schafer (the man from Maui); Dave Norton of Linux NetworX; Roger Goff of Dell Computer Inc.; and Rick Scott of SGI—all of whom have contributed in some way to my cluster knowledge.

Finally, I would like to thank my editor, Jill Harry; my production project manager, Lara Wysong; and my copyeditor, Cat Ohala. Without their help, this book would not have happened, would not have been as organized, and would not have been as readable.

INTRODUCTION

Early in 2001, I was asked by my employer at the time, Hewlett-Packard, to become involved in a large cluster delivery at the Pacific Northwest National Laboratory (PNNL) in Richland, Washington. The request was based on my experience with Linux, knowledge of Itanium processors, computer architecture skills, large-scale system administration experience, and of course, knowing Hewlett-Packard products. (Another reason for my involvement was my proximity to the PNNL site, which is adjacent to the old Hanford nuclear reservation, which was intentionally placed in a remote desert location. Richland is a three-hour drive from my home in Portland, Oregon.) My previous experience, although very useful, did not completely prepare me for what was to happen during my involvement with the PNNL project.

The prototype and phase 1 clusters were built with preproduction Intel Itanium 2 hardware and as-yet-unreleased versions of the IA-64[1] Linux kernel. I was introduced to high-speed interconnects, in the form of Quadrics QsNet, reintroduced to FORTRAN, exposed to the message-passing interface and associated tools, and dragged kicking and whimpering into a whole host of strange and wonderful Linux and IA-64 "-isms" that were entirely new. To say that it was like drinking from a firehose, would be an understatement. It was more like drinking the Colombia River, which runs extremely close to the PNNL site before disappearing downstream into the mile-deep and two-mile-wide Colombia Gorge, before finally reaching the Pacific Ocean. If you want to find this area on a map, ask any serious windsurfer or kitesurfer. They all know about the Colombia Gorge.

---

1. A brief word about the IA-64 versus Itanium terminology. The term *IA-64* designates a 64-bit processor architecture from Intel, just like IA-32 designates the architecture of Intel 32-bit processors (along with the less-formal term *x86*). The term *Itanium* designates a particular family of IA-64 processors, just as Pentium and Intel Xeon designate families of IA-32 processors. The term *Itanium 2* designates the second generation of the Itanium processor family. The IA-64 Linux kernel is designed to execute on the 64-bit IA-64 architecture from Intel.

After helping implement the PNNL phase 1 cluster, which was 128 Intel Itanium 2 systems (256 processors), my involvement with the project ended and I moved on to other assignments. Reflecting on the experience, I realized that there was a huge opportunity to make clustered systems more "mainstream." I have noticed that today's leading-edge scientific technologies tend to be adapted and become tomorrow's leading-edge information technology (IT) or consumer solutions, given proper time to evolve and mature. (One modest example of this phenomenon is the World Wide Web, Hypertext Markup Language, and the whole concept of a Web browser.) This evolution involves standardization in the form of processes and architectures, along with what is today called *commoditization*.

With the realization that large, expensive, proprietary supercomputers are being replaced by clusters of commodity boxes running Linux, at a fraction of the cost, it is not too much of a stretch to see applications of this type of technology widespread in the engineering and traditional IT world. The availability of commodity clusters makes it possible for small research organizations, IT departments, and engineering groups to have their own supercomputers at a fraction of the cost previously required for the equivalent computing capability. A large percentage of these newly implemented, commodity-based supercomputers are running the Linux operating system.

Today, most of the clustered systems delivered are still hand-crafted, custom implementations that require intimate knowledge from the small, specialized groups of people that deploy and support them. Although a lot of experience and knowledge about clusters exists today inside universities and scientific installations, for clustered systems to become mainstream, this knowledge has to be opened up and shared in a way that traditional IT and engineering organizations can apply it.

Because there are as many ways to implement Linux clusters as there are people willing to design them, you should note that I am not claiming to have *the* absolute answer to how to design, build, and support a Linux cluster. Far from it—I am still learning new methods, new components, and new solutions to issues every day. My intention is to introduce the concepts and suggest ways of getting started. With the rapid development of Linux and open-source software, any suggestions I might make are aimed at a very rapidly moving target.

I believe the benefits of clustered systems inevitably will spill over into traditional IT organizations as solutions like Oracle 9i RAC (real application cluster) move into the "mainstream" IT world. Other areas, like graphical visualization, reservoir simulation for oil and gas companies, and thermal and structural simulations for mechanical engineering are all areas where clustered Linux systems may be readily applied today. There will be many more areas of application in the future.

I believe that we could be on the cusp of a major technological change—some would say revolution. Maybe our motto should be, "A Linux cluster in everyone's computer room."

## PART I

Introduction to Cluster Concepts

Parallel Power: Defining the Clustered System Approach

Chapter Objectives

- Define the term *cluster*
- Detail the evolution of a clustered solution
- Provide examples of parallel cluster applications
- Introduce several classes of clusters

This chapter examines the term *cluster,* the evolution of a clustered approach to applications, and the hardware that executes them, and provides a high-level description of several general classes of clustered system. A description of several parallel applications leads to a refined definition of a cluster and prepares for a description of the hardware and software components in a clustered system.

1.1 Avoiding Difficulties with the Word *Cluster*

Before we progress any further, we need to define what is meant by the word *cluster* when we use it in the phrase "clustered system." You may have noticed that up to this point I have used "cluster" and "clustered system" interchangeably. To save a lot of repetition, let's agree to use the term *cluster* in place of the more lengthy and awkward "clustered system" or "clustered computer system" or even "clustered Linux system." I feel better already.

Now it remains for us to attempt to define the term "cluster" as it will be used in this book. We'll start with a simple definition, examine some example uses of cluster technology, then progress to a more refined definition.

1.2   Defining a Cluster

Most of us will have an instinctive feel for what is meant by cluster when we use it to describe computer systems. We can all visualize a group of systems that are somehow related to one another. The systems may be sitting in a rack, sitting on the floor in someone's cubicle, or even sitting in a computer room where we can't see them. It is *how* the systems are related, how they are accessed, and what type of application they are running that determines whether they are a cluster.

One issue with throwing the word cluster about, as we shall see, is that the term is "over-loaded"[1] and has different meanings to different groups of people. If you were to use cluster in a scientific computing discussion, it would paint a very specific picture—one quite different from what would be invoked in a high-availability or transaction processing discussion. In other words, the type of cluster, dictated by its use, will determine what the term *cluster* really means in a given conversation.

Let's defer the full, formal definition of a cluster until after the following sections, but we *will* make adjustments along the way. Looking at how a cluster solution evolved from available technology, and what its characteristics are, will help us craft a more usable definition. For now, let's start with the following definition.

> A *cluster* is a collection of closely related computer systems, providing a common service or running a common parallel application.

1.3   The Evolution of a Clustered Solution

It took improvements in technology, reduction in the price of components, invention of high-speed networks, and other advances to create today's clusters as a computing solution. But it also took the limitations in today's symmetric multiprocessor (SMP) systems to *enable* the solution. Essentially, most large SMP machines are expensive, proprietary, have single points of failure, are not highly available, and suffer from scalability limitations in terms of central processing units (CPUs) and random access memory (RAM) capacity.

To address the large, leading-edge problems that they must solve, universities and US national research labs have been working to expand the computing capabilities available to them. To do this they needed to find ways to address the limitations of SMP systems. For this reason, much of what is happening with clusters was enabled by research done at universities, corporations, government research facilities, and, more recently, in the open-source software

---

1.   The term *overloaded*, in this sense, is an object-oriented programming term referring to functions that have the same name, but may behave differently depending on the data types that are passed to them. For example, a function named "add" must perform different operations on integers, floating-point, arrays, complex numbers, vectors, or other data types. The object-oriented language's compiler or runtime environment determines the correct action, based on the actual data type being processed.

development (OSSD) community. Let's trace some of the architectural evolution in the next sections, just to build a mental picture of how the concept of clusters got to its current state.

1.3.1 Uniprocessor Systems (UPs)

The simplest architecture, and the first to appear, was the UP, similar to the hardware configuration shown in Figure 1–1. A single CPU, a RAM controller, and an input/output (I/O) bus converter are all attached to a central system bus. Each device has to assert control on the system bus to send data to another, potentially waiting for any conflict to be arbitrated.

In this arrangement (as in the others to follow), it is the job of the operating system to allow programs to share the resources of the system and to give each application the appearance of a dedicated CPU and memory resource. This was the basis for the time-share/batch systems on which some of us started our early careers. Please forgive me the similarity to the "First the earth cooled. Then the dinosaurs came, but they died" type of history used in the movie *Airplane*. We don't want to wander down memory lane too far and get lost.

Today's UP systems are fast, inexpensive, and comprise special mass-produced chip sets and application-specific integrated circuits (ASICs) that implement the functions that would once take tens of cubic feet of discreet components like resistors and transistors. Devices like graphical interfaces, universal serial bus (USB), peripheral component interconnect (PCI), built-in Gigabit Ethernet (GbE) network interfaces, and disk interfaces like small computer system

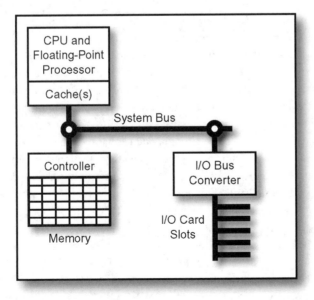

Figure 1–1 Generic UP system diagram

interconnect (SCSI) and integrated drive electronics (IDE) advanced technology attach (ATA) are all integrated onto the system's motherboard.

Floating-point processors, which were an expensive option on original "discrete" computer systems, are now commonly integrated on the same die as the CPU. Because CPUs tend to run at a higher clock rate than memory subsystems, the CPU may have one or more levels of fast cache memory between it and the main memory. The cache serves to reduce the access time to frequently accessed data or instructions by keeping them "close" to the CPU. Cache may be "on-chip" if it is part or the CPU chip, or "off-chip" if it is external.

Modern operating systems are better at providing the illusion of dedicated resources to each application or user. Anyone who lived through the early years of time-sharing knew that the huge monsters in the computer room were great at cutting the resources into smaller and smaller shares as more people joined the party. As the computer slowly (or sometimes rapidly) got slower and slower, we all reflected on the negative aspects of sharing central resources.

Today we all expect to have unrestricted access to our own dedicated computer resources, within reason and budget, and don't like to share anything if we can help it. Sharing resources is an important aspect of a cluster, whether it is RAM, CPU cycles, or availability. We will revisit this topic when we discuss the types of clusters later in this book.

1.3.2   SMP Systems

What do you do when your application runs out of CPU or RAM resources within a UP computer system? (One of the fundamental laws of computing is: "A program will expand to fill all memory or use all possible CPU cycles.") One answer to this question involves another step in the evolution of computer systems, culminating in the arrival of SMP systems. SMP systems add one or more processors into the system architecture, as depicted in Figure 1–2.

A computer system is referred to as "symmetric" if all processors are equally capable of accessing global shared memory. The operating system software on an SMP machine requires the protection of data and other resources that might be accessed by multiple processors at once, and is therefore more complex than an operating system for a UP system.

An SMP system also may require a more complex hardware infrastructure to support multiple CPUs. The system bus, which is one of the points of contention between the elements of the system, must support full-speed access to RAM and I/O for both (or all) processors, or system performance and scaling may suffer. The practical scaling of an SMP system is limited by the central system bus or crossbar connection between the CPUs, memory, and I/O subsystems. As we shall see, scaling is also a very important aspect provided by clusters.

In larger SMP systems, the system bus is sometimes replaced by a crossbar switch to improve performance. A crossbar is essentially a nonblocking switch that allows direct, high-speed connections between multiple ports simultaneously. Each connection is dedicated, allowing transparent access between CPUs, memory, or I/O up to the maximum number of connections and the bandwidth of the crossbar.

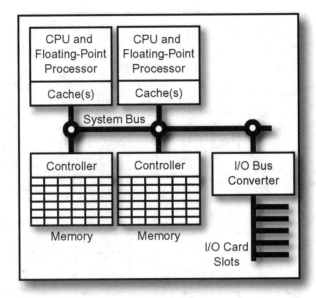

Figure 1–2 Generic SMP system diagram

An example SMP system with a crossbar is shown in Figure 1–3. Crossbars, as you might guess, add to the cost of SMP systems. Systems with crossbars are rare in clusters that are built from "commodity" systems, mainly because of cost—although there are notable exceptions, which we will see later.

1.3.3   Networks of Independent Systems

Individual SMP (and UP) systems all have limitations in terms of the amount of RAM they can hold and the number of processors that are usable without saturating the system bus. This may be a physical limitation of the hardware design or a consequence of the physical RAM addressing ability of the processor, or both. An application that needs more RAM or more CPU resources becomes limited by the physical boundaries and capabilities of the system packaging.

What is the next logical step to expand the resources available to an application if it cannot grow beyond the boundaries of a single system? Three major things happened technologically and economically to help answer this question. These advances were

- Introduction of the microprocessor
- Development of networking technology
- Remote procedure calls (RPCs)

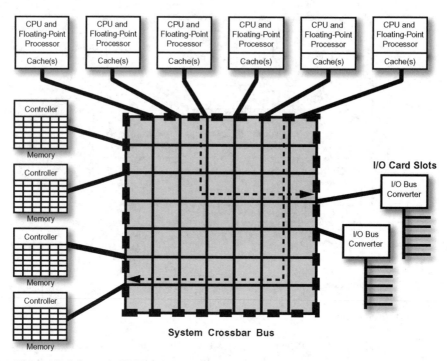

Figure 1–3 Generic SMP system with a crossbar

An individual book could be written about the history and technologies involved in each one of these separate developments, but we pursue only a brief overview here, because it helps prepare us for some of the software aspects of clusters.

1.3.3.1   The Introduction of Microprocessors

Prior to the invention of the integrated circuit, computer systems comprised cabinet after cabinet of circuit boards containing discrete electronic components. The primary components were originally vacuum tubes, but became transistors as that technology advanced. These early computer systems were difficult to design, manufacture, and support. They were priced far beyond the reach of small organizations or individuals, and required a special cooling infrastructure and power connections. The systems, however, did the work of hundreds or thousands of people, so the economics justified the expense of purchase, programming, and support.

The invention of the solid-state transistor, and the need for miniaturization in electronic devices, drove the invention of the first "integrated circuits." Following on the heels of IC development, generalized CPUs, called *microprocessors*, appeared.

Along with these mass-produced, standardized processing units came related infrastructure support ICs that implemented external I/O device interfaces, memory interfaces, and communications devices. These enabled the mass-production of even more compact, lower cost systems. The IBM personal computer (PC) made computing available, at an affordable price, to individuals in a package that could run on (or beside) a desktop. Microcode and complex instruction-set computing (CISC) gave way to reduced instruction-set computing (RISC), even in institutional-size machines. And we now have explicitly parallel instruction-set computing, EPIC, implemented in the Intel Itanium processor family.

Because the technology continues to advance, following "Moore's Law,"[2] a wide range of prices, performance ranges, and capabilities are now available in individual computer systems, from 128-way SMP systems to portable UP laptops, and even hand-held devices. Improvements in IC technology continue to put more and more computing power into smaller and smaller packages. Systems and their processors are now edging into the 64-bit world, allowing access to petabytes (or 2^{50} bytes) of RAM. The trends are continuing to push the cost of computing resources lower and lower per unit of computing power. Alongside the advances in processor and system technology, came advances in networking.

1.3.3.2   Evolution of Network Connections

Initially, networking technologies were based on proprietary connections and software. Interoperability between the various manufacturers was difficult, if not impossible. Connecting two or more machines was difficult and unlikely, given the expense of a single system and the interconnection hardware. Technologies like Ethernet not only enabled relatively inexpensive communication between separate systems, but enabled *standardized* interfaces, cables, and software protocols.

The development of inexpensive, low-latency network switching components is helping push today's implementation of computer networks (and clusters) forward. Connection to a common network enables multiple independent systems, and software components within those systems, to communicate with each other and share information and resources. The continuing trend is faster interconnections at lower per-port cost for the switching equipment.

Multiple interconnected SMP systems are shown in Figure 1–4. Notice that theoretically a direct connection between the CPU and memory resources in the systems exists via the network interfaces. This connection, however, is not possible without the operating system, network drivers, and some way for the software components to communicate across the network links.

Another important network development occurred when networks started incorporating nonblocking switches into their infrastructure. Instead of the old collision mechanism used by Ethernet hubs (or direct "vampire" attachments), a switch can make a direct connection between any two ports without waiting for the entire network packet to arrive. The net result is independent delivery of messages to the proper port, and lower latency for message transmission.

---

2.   The law, stated in 1964 by Gordon Moore, one of the founders of Intel, is that the device density of integrated circuits follows the curve described by $2^{(\text{Year}-1962)}$. The period of doubling is closer to eighteen months today.

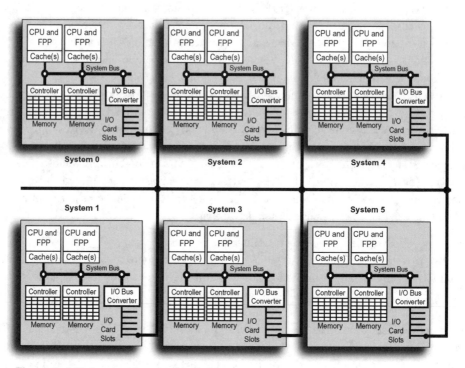

Figure 1–4 Networks of computer systems

1.3.3.3   Remote Procedure Calls

Shortly after it became possible to connect multiple systems to a network economically, researchers began looking for a good mechanism to share data between multiple systems *over* the network connection. One mechanism that arose was the network file system (NFS). This was the natural extension of the local data access model provided by the operating system.

Operating systems like AT&T and Berkeley Software Design, Inc. (BSD) UNIX, Digital Equipment Corporation's VMS, and Apollo Computer's DOMAIN/OS developed file systems that allowed remote computer clients to access information in a server's file system as if it were local. There were winners and losers in the ensuing technological competition to produce a usable, popular networked file system. One big winner in this development contest was the network file system (NFS) from Sun Microsystems, which is an industry standard that is still widely used and extended today.[3]

---

3.   File systems like Microsoft's server message block (SMB) also became widely used, based on sheer numbers of users. The SMB protocol, with additional functionality, was proposed to the Internet engineering task force (IETF) as a standard called the common internet file system, or CIFS.

A networked file system hid (well, mostly anyway) the network-specific details of the connection between the client and the server system underneath the operating system's standard file system calls (read, write, open, and so on). This allowed existing software to use remote data with a minimum of modification. The approach, and the software and experience that sprang from it, enabled more generic ways for programs to share information and resources across a network without using the file system metaphor.

Hidden in the lower layers of all the early networked file systems lay a common class of interface that came to be called a *remote procedure call*, or RPC. An RPC allows a program to call a special interface routine that appears to be a local procedure. That routine then handles data translation, error processing, and network communication to a remote program component that performs processing on behalf of the caller. RPCs were used by networked file systems to perform remote reads, writes, opens, closes, and other common file system operations on behalf of the client.

It took a while for the designers of networked file systems to realize that they had a generalizable technology buried in their hand-tuned file system code. As an example, the RPC mechanism from the Apollo Computer distributed file system became the network computing system (NCS) and was used by the Open Software Foundation (OSF) as the distributed computing environment (DCE) RPC mechanism. At this stage, Apollo Computer, the OSF, and DCE have all but faded into computer history.

This "action at a distance" enabled with an RPC gives the *appearance* of a simple local procedure call and return to the program component making the call. The local RPC "stub" and the RPC library hide the complexities of dealing directly with underlying network connections, implementing security, transport protocols, and error recovery. One of the major differences, of course, is the length of time the RPC and return take with respect to a local procedure call. An example of an RPC call is shown in Figure 1–5.

Figure 1–5 details the major steps required to initiate and complete an RPC. What is not detailed in the diagram is the conversation with a directory service of some kind to *locate* the remote service and to determine its communication information, such as port number, encryption mechanism (if any), and other details required to initiate the conversation. The individual, high-level steps in this communication process are as follows.

1. The local program makes a procedure call, passing a list of parameters and expected returns to what it thinks is a local subroutine, but is actually a "procedure stub." The "procedure call stub" "marshals" the parameters and call information into a packet containing a network-neutral data format. The procedure stub then passes the information to the RPC library for processing.
2. The RPC library, which forms the interface to the underlying network transport service (TCP, UDP, or something else), creates and sends the encapsulated RPC information to the remote host. The library layer handles retrying the request, propagating error

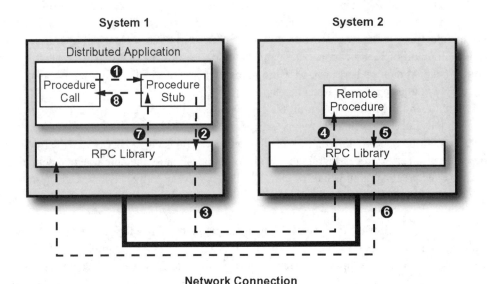

Figure 1–5 RPC example

returns such as signals or "catch/throw" semantics to make the network behavior invisible to the local program.

3. The physical network media transports the frame or packet to the remote host system.

4. The remote RPC library receives the frame or packet, extracts the RPC information, unmarshals the parameter information, converts the network-neutral data format to the local host's format, creates the required local stack frame, and calls the requested procedure "attached" to the RPC request type. In some cases there may be a local procedure stub that is executed by the RPC library to perform operations similar to those of the RPC stub on the requesting system.

5. The remote RPC procedure performs the requested operations and returns any requested values to the RPC library.

6. The RPC library marshals the return values along with any error returns (signals or catch/throw conditions) and transmits the frame or packet containing the RPC message back to the requesting host.

7. The physical network media transports the frame or packet to the requesting system.

8. The requesting host's RPC library receives the remote reply, recreates any error conditions, and passes the RPC return information to the RPC procedure stub.

9. The RPC procedure stub recreates a "normal" procedure return stack frame, and returns to the calling program's requesting subroutine.

There are several things to note about RPC behavior. First, there are several components to the time period required to generate and receive a response: the software marshaling time on both ends, the time spent in the RPC libraries, the network transmission time, and the length of time spent performing the remote computation on behalf of the requesting system. Second, although the network behavior is "abstracted away" from the requesting program and the remote RPC client, the program still needs a way to deal with a different class of errors that may be injected by the presence of a network between the program components—it is difficult to write "non-RPC aware" software for this type of environment and have it be robust.

The RPC code was extracted and generalized. The result was a separate set of RPC libraries, application programming interfaces (APIs), and other components like directory services to locate remote components in the network. The early RPC packages were available from Sun Microsystems (transport-independent RPC, or TI-RPC), Microsoft (DCOM), and the OSF (distributed computing environment, or DCE RPC). The concepts involved with RPC mechanisms continue to evolve, and exist in many forms in Web-based software being developed today.

1.3.3.4 Tying Everything Together

The three previous sections describe an evolution of some of the technology that has contributed to today's clusters. The microprocessor, network connections between systems, and the availability of RPC and communication libraries are technological and *economic* factors that we use to create cluster solutions from separate technologies.[4] The evolution we are following is arguably a much simplified view, but my intent is to show broad avenues that have led to today's cluster configurations.

It did not take researchers and entrepreneurs very long to begin applying the three technologies to unique applications and hardware solutions that jumped the resource barriers between separate systems. The application of RPC mechanisms involves other components, like directory services to locate remote services, scheduling services, and resource location (load-balancing) services. A solution involving RPC calls and a distributed program is a fairly complex endeavor, but "toolkits" are available that make design and implementation of these solutions easier.

Figure 1–6 depicts a distributed application,[5] comprising a master program and five slave tasks, all tied together by network RPC calls. What is not shown are the other required services like name lookup, component directory services, scheduling, and load balancing. Writing, debugging, and supporting this type of distributed application is not necessarily an easy task, but distributing the computation to take advantage of specialize hardware or to avoid resource limi-

---

4. A technology is a very useful thing, but in and of itself it may not perform any useful work. The technology must be applied to a real-world problem before it becomes a usable solution. This may take programming or simply the proper configuration. It still involves extra work above and beyond producing or acquiring the technology.

5. A distributed application may or may not be parallel. The term *client–server* describes a distributed application, with three components (graphical user interface [GUI], application logic, and data access logic) running on separate systems, but not necessarily performing parallel computations.

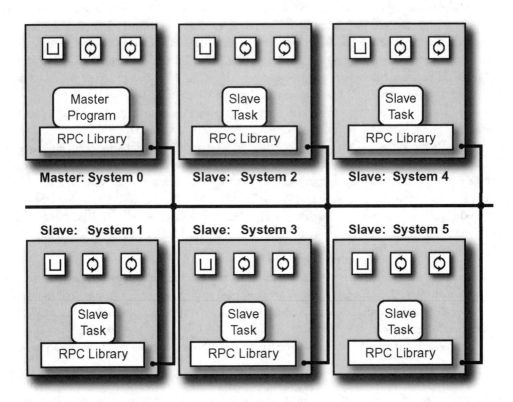

Figure 1–6 Distributed application using RPCs for communication

tations is a useful thing to do. In many cases, the computation could not be done on a single system alone.

An early example of the type of application in Figure 1–6 was a Mandelbrot[6] set "browser" that graphically depicted the output from a mathematical equation on a graphics screen. Moving the viewpoint around on the graphics display caused the master program to redisplay the image by breaking it into pieces and sending the computation to the slave tasks on remote machines. Because the computation involved used floating-point calculations and multiple iterations per graphics pixel, the more slave systems available, the faster the display was assembled.

What is required for this type of problem is that it may be broken into pieces that are computationally *independent* from system to system. The master program breaks the problem into pieces, distributes it to the slave tasks, and receives the results back. If work remains to be done,

---

6. First described by Benoit Mandelbrot. See http://www.olympus.net/personal/dewey/mandelbrot.html for a good introduction to the Mandelbrot set and associated mathematics.

the master program sends a new piece of work to an available slave task. Dependencies between the data sets given to the slave systems would require the slaves to share data back and forth until the computations were completed.

The master system may scale the size of the display given to the slave systems. The more slaves that are available for the calculations, the smaller the data set that is sent, and presumably the faster the display is created. How well the application really scales depends on a number of factors, including the type of network used, the capabilities of the slave systems, and the robustness of the communication code and pathway.

As we shall see, independent versus dependent data sets is an important distinction for the hardware and software design of a cluster. Several observations about this example are in order.

- As mentioned, the data set and computation in this example are independent of one another, so no interaction between slave components is needed.
- Each slave system has two CPUs, so it could be possible to run two instances of the slave task per slave system, provided they don't interfere with each other by saturating the system bus.
- The length of time it takes to move data and results back and forth between slave tasks and the master program (latency) is important. The time needed for calculations needs to be large in relationship to the latency between systems for the computation to be efficient.
- Because the slave tasks are running on separate systems, they are not sharing CPU or RAM resources, and the net effect is that the work gets done faster.
- This example uses RPCs as a communication method. There are other protocols that use the "socket" libraries to perform the communication.

The early hardware participants in this type of application tended to be low-cost workstations (sometimes referred to as a *carpet cluster*), in an attempt to "capture" unused CPU resources on multiple desktops or servers. (My experience has shown that when a usage survey is done, that desktop resource [CPU and RAM] utilization is usually in the 11 to 25% range. The vast majority of the results indicate that the 11% utilization factor is more realistic.) When users complained about slow response time or the inability to use their machine at all, system managers started looking at dedicated resources for the "slave" portions of the applications. An example of an informal "carpet cluster" is shown in Figure 1–7.

1.4 Collapsed Network Computing for Engineering

The client–server model for applications is a familiar division of compute tasks between potentially distributed components. (They can all actually run on the same system if there are sufficient resources.) A three-tier client–server (3TCS) application, for example, comprises three logical components: the GUI, the application logic (computation), and the data access logic (file or database server). The three components may each run on specially tuned hardware and com-

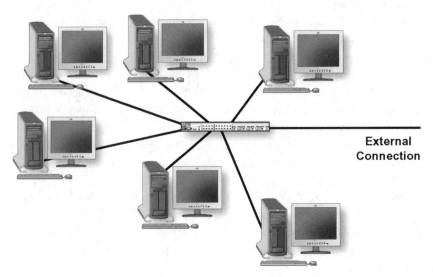

Figure 1–7 An informal or carpet cluster of workstations

municate over a network to increase the overall application's performance. We provide more analysis on this architecture in Chapter 3.

In the preceding sections, we followed a progression of software and hardware developments that may help us to visualize one type of cluster, but we are not quite to our final destination yet. We have used an example of a distributed application that uses RPCs or socket communications to operate on data or processing problems with few interdependencies.[7] This type of application and hardware model fits areas such as database transaction processing, Web page distribution, and graphics rendering, for which there are "clean" ways to break up the data or the computation.

The scientific computations performed on clusters, however, have different underpinnings than are covered by this example. We examine these differences in the next section.

1.5   Scientific Cluster Computing

Our previous examples of software that used parallel compute resources involved problems with little or no interdependencies. This type of relationship between computations is called *loosely coupled* in the case of few dependencies, or *independent* in the case of no interdependencies. Not all problems fall into this area.

---

7.   Some problems, when they fall into this class, may be called *embarrassingly parallel*, as if someone is abjectly disappointed that they are not more difficult. The data handled by the search for extraterrestrial intelligence (SETI) "SETI@Home" screen saver falls into this type of problem. See http://www.seti.org/seti/ other_projects/seti_at_home.html for details about this project.

When there are dependencies between pieces of a distributed or parallel application, it is referred to as *tightly coupled*, implying a close relationship between the individual pieces and the data that they share. The programming models may be different for tightly coupled problems, and the underlying hardware must support high-speed, low-latency connections between all the systems in a cluster to support rapid communication.

In this type of problem, you may think of all systems in the cluster sharing a global array (or arrays) of data, much like what occurs in a large SMP machine. Instead of automatic, transparent access to the shared data, however, the cluster software and hardware architecture must "simulate" the shared access. An example will serve to illustrate what is meant when we talk about a tightly coupled problem with data dependencies.

1.5.1   An Example Parallel Problem

Before we start, let's agree that this first example will not be a *real* problem. It is only a visualization tool to allow us to understand some of the needs dictated by problems with data dependencies. Figure 1–8 shows four tasks sharing a data array across four UP systems. Each system is capable of running one computational task in addition to the operating system.

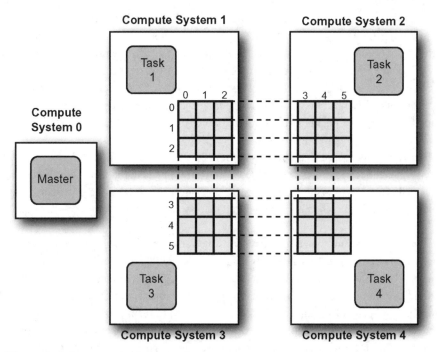

Figure 1–8 An example distributed array

In reality, a 36-element array is not large enough to warrant the complexity of splitting it across four systems. Suffice it to say that there are problems and data sets for which the amount of memory required dwarfs the physical RAM available in a single machine, or the computation requires many CPUs, making the effort worthwhile.

Let's say that our parallel application will sum each row and column of the array, and make the information available to a master process, which will produce a total sum of all row and column elements as the output. Several questions arise.

- How are the actions of the tasks synchronized?
- What actions should the individual tasks perform?
- How is the information shared across the systems performing the calculations?
- How is the computation broken up between the individual systems?
- What type of hardware and software supports the communication between tasks?

A parallel application developer needs to answer all these questions, and the standard consultant's answer, "It depends," holds true. The answers to our questions depend on the problem, the data, the algorithm being used, and the underlying hardware. Our parallel application development slate is blank.

We could, as the designers of this application, choose to have the slave tasks send their arrays to the master and let the master do all the work. This, of course, becomes impractical as the array gets very large. It also does not use the extra CPU and memory resources available to us very efficiently. The aim, after all, is to get some gain from the hardware we just bought.

We'll design our application so that task 1 will sum the row elements it "owns" and send the three results to task 2. Task 2 will incorporate the sums with its continuation of the array rows and send the three results to the master. Task 3 and task 4 will perform similar row operations, with task 4 sending the three lower row results to the master.

The master task receives the results from tasks 2 and 4 (at different times) and totals them in a local value called `row_total`. The column operations take place in a similar fashion, with tasks 2 and 4 returning totals to the master, which calculates a total in `col_total`. This is diagrammed in Figure 1–9. When all is said and done, we hope that the two totals are equal to each other.

The master program, when run, is responsible for starting the subtasks. (How the hardware resources are allocated for the whole job, what handles scheduling the subtasks, and how other setup activities occur are discussed later.) Right away, you may notice that there will be some synchronization issues. Task 2 must wait for the row results from task 1; likewise, task 4 must wait for the row results from task 3. Because the hardware resources are independent systems, there must be a way of coordinating the various pieces of the application, waiting for results to arrive, and communicating between the components. See Figure 1–10 for one graph of time relationships for our example problem.

Even with this simple, unrealistic example, there are many ways to coordinate the components and arrive at the answers. Some approaches make better use of the parallel resources than

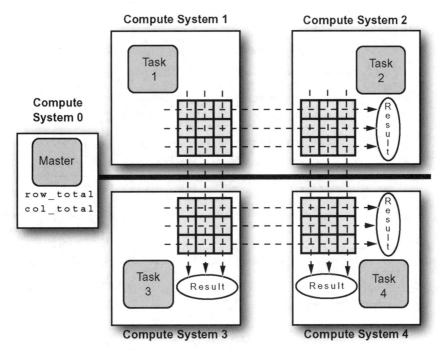

Figure 1–9 Parallel array row and column addition example

others, some take minimum time, some are easier to implement, and some are more resistant to failures. For example, notice that the master program in our example can tell all the slave tasks to start summing their local arrays at the same time, which makes better use of the parallel hardware than inserting wait time. This takes implicit knowledge of how the problem and data may be divided between the cluster's systems. Parallel application development is still high art at work. It takes a special mind to visualize and develop parallel algorithms, partition the data, and then map the solution to a particular parallel hardware configuration, using it to solve complex problems.

1.5.2   Refining the Parallel Example

Now let's assume that our compute systems are dual processor and are capable of running two computationally intensive tasks simultaneously. Each system will have a task processing both the row and column totals for the local array at the same time. This arrangement is shown in Figure 1–11.

Because we are able to do the rows and columns on each system at the same time (we are ignoring scheduling delays and communications differences between systems), the overall job gets done in roughly half the time. The modified timing diagram is shown in Figure 1–12.

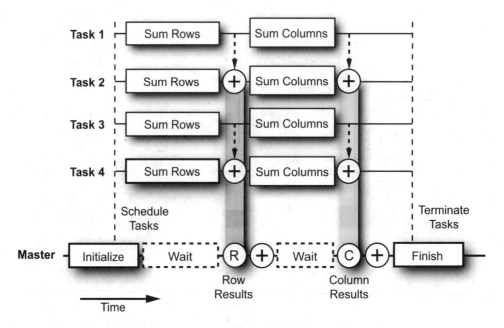

Figure 1–10 Timing aspects of our example application

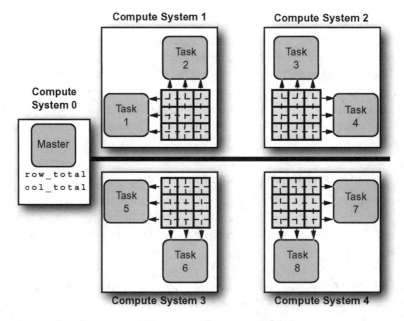

Figure 1–11 Parallel array addition example with dual CPUs

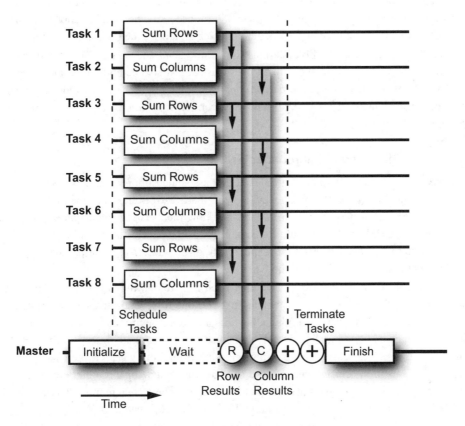

Figure 1–12 Parallel array addition example with dual-CPU timing

1.5.3   Software Communication Facilities

The software "glue" that holds many parallel applications together is a communication API that presents a particular resource model to the parallel application components. One such model is based on message passing. There are several standardized and widely available message-passing libraries, like parallel virtual machine (PVM) or the message-passing interface (MPI). The MPI environment has its origins in client–server applications running on distributed systems, much like our previous discussion of RPC-based applications.

Research into improved implementations and new programming models continues, particularly in the area of efficient use of large multi-CPU, shared memory systems. One area of standardization involves compiler directive-based tools, like open multiprocessing (OpenMP), which is available for large SMP systems that support shared memory configurations and threads. The memory in a shared-memory system does not necessarily need to be in one huge "lump." Access to local memory and large amounts of nonlocal memory may be handled by the underlying hardware with no explicit programming necessary. One type of system in this category is called a *ccNUMA architecture*, or a *cache-coherent nonuniform memory access system*. In this type of system, there is a penalty to be paid for accessing nonlocal memory, but the hardware still maintains the correct access patterns, which simplifies the programmer's job.

At the lowest level, the libraries must be able to *send* and *receive* or *get* and *put* values from one system or area of memory to another. Tasks must also be able to tell how many other tasks or threads are involved in the parallel application and must be able to identify a specific task (like the originator of a message) with an identifier. How this is implemented depends on the specific library being used.

1.5.4   High-Speed Interconnect (HSI)

Underneath the software communication API and associated library routines, there are drivers that interface to a high-speed, low-latency network that we will refer to as the high-speed interconnect, or HSI. Depending on your budget, and how much latency your parallel application will tolerate, the HSI hardware could be Gigabit (or 10 Gigabit) Ethernet, Myrinet from Myricom, Infiniband, or Quadrics QsNet-II. The ability of the cluster to scale parallel applications may be tied to the characteristics of the HSI.

At this stage of our discussion, we only need to note that the HSI is one of the defining characteristics of some kinds of clusters and may be one of several physical networks that are present in a cluster. (Interestingly enough, the Oracle 9i RAC environment uses an HSI to enable cache coherency and communication between cluster systems. Thus, the presence of HSI hardware is not tied only to clusters supporting scientific computing.) The HSI allows sharing data between systems in the cluster, and may be used in "raw" mode or through the communication (message passing or shared memory simulation) libraries. There are a number of specialized networking technologies and topologies used by the available HSI technologies.

Bandwidth, latency, topology, and cost are all important factors in choosing the HSI for a given cluster. We cover these technologies more in depth later, because the HSI characteristics may affect the performance of the cluster and its applications.

1.6   Revisiting the Definition of *Cluster*

As you may recall from earlier in this chapter, we defined the word *cluster* as follows.

> A *cluster* is a collection of closely related computer systems, providing a common service or running a common parallel application.

This definition, however, does not completely capture the true nature of a cluster, because it is equally applicable to a widely distributed network or workgroup. We need to adjust the definition so that it more accurately describes the specialized hardware and software environment that we continue to describe. A more refined definition of *cluster* might be

> A closely coupled collection of computer systems that shares a com-

mon infrastructure and provides a parallel set of resources to services
or applications.

We may yet adjust the definition further.

1.7 Commercial Cluster Computing

A growing number of systems in the commercial world are clusters of commodity computers.
These clusters provide scalable Web services, database serving, and high-availability environments for business-critical applications and services. The parallel nature of cluster hardware and
software can not only allow scaling beyond the capabilities of a single SMP system, but can also
provide immunity to failure to the applications using the cluster. The high-availability nature of
a cluster is one of the driving forces in the adoption of clusters in the traditional information
technology (IT) environment.

It is important to note that the architectural evolution leading to clusters in the scientific
and traditional IT environments has taken different paths as a result of different user requirements, *but many of the underlying hardware characteristics are the same*. Although the underlying hardware and software architecture may be similar, the types of applications differ from the
scientific and engineering cluster environments.

1.8 High Performance, High Throughput, and High Availability

Cluster configurations may be grouped into three general categories, based on the usage patterns
and services they provide. A high-performance cluster provides one or more parallel applications with shared levels of CPU and RAM resources that would be impossible in a single SMP
system. (The Pacific Northwest National Laboratory [PNNL] Linux cluster, for example, in
aggregate provides 11.8 teraflops of compute power and has 1.6 terabytes of RAM available for
parallel applications.) High-throughput clusters provide the ability to execute large numbers of
independent jobs in parallel. High-availability clusters provide guaranteed access to services
with parallel (redundant) resources and fail-over capabilities for hardware and services.

Because the world is never as simple as we would like, we may well have to perform a
thorough analysis to find out the type of cluster with which we are dealing in any given situation.
It is likely that any cluster we examine will focus on one of these three major areas, but may
share some characteristics with one or more of the other types. A particular configuration of a
Web-serving cluster, for example, may be viewed as both a high-throughput cluster *and* a high-
availability cluster.

I will provide more details and we look at some example configurations in Chapter 3,
Underneath the Hood: Cluster Hardware Components and Architecture.

1.9   A Formal Definition of *Cluster*

A central premise to the concept of the word *cluster* is sharing resources: compute cycles, memory, data, or services. We have seen that several different disciplines of computer users have used groups of specially configured systems to break through resource or availability barriers associated with large SMP systems.

In light of our current explorations, a more refined definition of the term *cluster* might be

> A closely coupled, *scalable* collection of interconnected computer systems, sharing common hardware and software infrastructure, providing a parallel set of resources to services or applications for improved performance, throughput, or availability.

This definition will frame our further discussions of clusters.

1.10 The Why and Wherefore of Clusters

We have covered the "what" of clusters to a certain level of details, but the question of "why" still remains. A single, large SMP system is arguably easier to purchase, install, and maintain than a collection of smaller systems tied together with specialized networks. Why in the world would somebody choose a cluster over a large SMP?

One reason is scalability. Today's largest SMP systems will scale "up" to approximately 128 CPUs in a single "complex." (I use the term *complex* because the largest SMP systems are really collections of "cells" or smaller units, each of which contains CPUs and local RAM. These units are put together with an infrastructure like crossbar switches and toroidal interconnects to create larger collections of RAM and CPUs. It becomes very expensive to maintain cache coherency across a system like this, but it is being done today in complexes as large as 128 CPUs.) Large systems such as this are essential for scaling large applications that do not lend themselves to parallel environments. But once you reach the "ceiling," in terms of the maximum number of CPUs, you have nowhere to go but to split the application, or data, or both, into smaller pieces. A cluster potentially scales "out" to more CPUs than is currently possible in even the largest SMP system.

Another reason is total available physical RAM. In addition to the physical limitations on the number of CPUs in a large SMP system (usually dictated by maximum system bus throughput), there is usually a limit on the maximum physical RAM that can be added to a single complex. Some problems being solved today require terabytes of RAM—there aren't very many systems that allow this much physical RAM to be present in a single system. By breaking a problem up and spreading it across multiple systems, the total available RAM becomes N times the maximum physical RAM possible in the cluster's member systems. This is most often larger than that available in a single SMP system.

One final and frequently used argument is reduced cost. It *may* be cheaper to build a cluster of smaller SMP systems rather than attempt to concentrate all the resources in a single, large

SMP system. The use of commodity compute components allows lower hardware cost in a cluster solution.

Taken together, the scaling of CPUs, the breaking of the physical RAM barrier, and the potential for reduced costs are powerful factors that are driving the adoption of commodity clusters. The use of a cluster in a given situation, however, is predicated on having an application or service that can make use of parallel resources. It pays to do careful research into the capabilities of your application software or services before you assume that a cluster is the correct solution for you.

1.11 Summary

We have taken a brief and shallow cruise through some different cluster architectures, and the evolution of both scientific and commercial IT clusters in this chapter. While touching on parallel problems, both with and without data dependencies, we encountered the need for tightly coupled cluster configurations with HSIs to share data between "compute slices" in the cluster. A brief diversion into some of the simpler aspects of parallel applications, such as the message-passing libraries, helped us think about the distribution of processing tasks in a parallel cluster environment.

Introduction to the three basic types of clusters—high performance, high throughput, and high availability—will help us to understand the underlying hardware and software characteristics of the solutions that we are building. Our formal definition of a cluster takes multiple cluster types into account and serves as a basis for further refining the design requirements for each cluster type.

We stand at an interesting point in cluster history. Economic and technological forces are making clusters affordable, high-performance alternatives to large SMP systems for the types of applications that can use their parallel resources. Clusters with the capabilities of large SMP computer systems that were once tens or hundreds of millions of dollars are now affordable and available to small organizations.

It is as if the technological pasture gate has been left open, and the specialized animals we call clusters have escaped into the world at large. Let's try and herd one into *your* computer room. The chapters ahead cover hardware and software components of the cluster in more detail.

One Step at a Time: A Process for Building Clusters

Chapter Objectives

- Detail the high-level steps involved in designing and deploying a cluster
- Propose a formal process for implementing a cluster project
- Discuss required information for large projects at each stage of the implementation

Getting a cluster out of the back-of-the-napkin stage and into the computer room involves a sequence of interrelated steps from design to rollout. The larger the cluster and the tighter the time schedule, the more organized the implementation process needs to be. Even small clusters may benefit from an organized approach such as the one presented in this chapter.

2.1 Building Clusters as a Complex Endeavor

Creating a reliable cluster from scratch can be one of the most difficult system engineering exercises in the computer world. Believe me when I tell you that I am not trying to sound discouraging. After all, the purpose of this book is to *encourage* you to build a cluster and to *help* you do so. It is best, however, to adopt a realistic approach and to know ahead of time what is required.

The major issues begin to arise from the increase in complexity as a cluster grows larger. Let me say something that is not immediately obvious: The larger the cluster gets, the more difficult it will be to build. One would think that this is intuitively obvious, but again and again I have confronted the mistaken belief that a large cluster should somehow be easier than a small one. A frequent question is: Isn't there economy of scale for building larger clusters? Large clusters are more complex and difficult than smaller ones for a number of reasons.

- There are more hardware and software components involved in larger clusters.
- Switches used for network and HSIs have "natural" break points in the numbers of available ports, above which cascading the switches becomes necessary.
- The more components in the cluster, the more interconnections are needed, and the more interrack connections are needed.
- The more applications the cluster is expected to run, and the more complex the application, the more complex the underlying hardware and software infrastructure.
- Operations that take small amounts of time on a per-system basis scale up dramatically in large clusters. For example, manually powering off all systems in the cluster may take ten seconds of holding in the power switch after the operating system has shut down. In a 32-node cluster, this is 320 seconds (5.33 minutes) and can be handled manually. In a 750-node cluster, this is 7,500 seconds (125 minutes, or roughly two hours). It is obvious that an automated (and parallel) approach is needed for a larger cluster, increasing the software complexity.
- Just tracking and documenting the work in a large cluster becomes a significant portion of the overall effort.

A cluster is the integration of hundreds of physical parts and hundreds or thousands of virtual software components. To be successful, all the components must function as if they belonged to a single, well-behaved system. A large cluster may be thought of as an entire enterprise computing environment or workgroup disguised as a single computer system.

This is not to say that dealing with such complexity is impossible. Any complex endeavor can be (and frequently *must be*) broken down into subordinate steps that appear to make the overall activity less complex. Breaking a complex action into multiple pieces does not make the overall activity simpler; it allows for assignment of the tasks to multiple people and divides the complexity between multiple subtasks. *"Divide et impera"* (divide and conquer) as a means of solving complex problems has been known since the time of ancient Rome.

For example, to automate a complex system administration procedure requires a human to perform the steps manually at least once, documenting all actions taken and configuration changes made. It also helps to keep track of all the failure modes along the way. Automating this process then requires writing the scripts or programs to perform the actions for the system administrator, covering possible error procedures, and accounting for every action the script may take. Once the automated process is created, it may be documented, tested, expanded, improved, and measured against the original objectives.

The process of creating a cluster is two parts physical assembly and eight parts software configuration and integration. There are, I believe, distinctly discernible "break points," where one part of the process gives way to another. Recognizing these patterns while building a cluster and taking advantage of them for organizing the work is very useful. This chapter proposes a cluster creation process with steps or elements that are geared toward making the job of building a cluster more structured and manageable—with an eye toward the word *repeatable*.

It is important to note that this proposed process is not the only possible approach to building a cluster. It is only a potential starting point for your own process if you decide to create one. Some kind of process, either formal or informal, is necessary if you are going to build multiple clusters, build large clusters, or build clusters for paying customers. It does not matter whether you are an IT department creating clusters for your internal customers or a hardware/software integration company creating clusters on behalf of a hardware manufacturer for your customers. The important point is that your customers will expect a certain level of performance, reliability, documentation, and consistency from you *and* the cluster you build.

A process or well-defined, planned approach is also necessary to deal with the increased complexity in larger clusters. This point is often missed by sales and marketing people who, along with some customers, subscribe to what I have come to call the "lump o' hardware" mentality. Order most of the correct pieces and pile them up, and they will magically self-assemble into a complete cluster solution in a remarkably short period of time, with no project management or planning.

2.2   Talking about the "P Word"

First, a brief comment on the "p word"; that is, *process*. I have used "process" several times already in this chapter, and some of you are probably already cringing. Most technical people, myself included, have come to hate the word *process* with a passion (another "p word"). One of the biggest insults that a technical person can hurl at another is, "Oh, he is so *process* oriented," meaning that the person is inflexible and robotlike in their approach to problem solving. This is sometimes because "the process" has been lorded over the members of a project team as a political tool, to the point of stifling all possible creativity (and, by the way, improvement). It should *not* be that way.

A process of some kind, however, is necessary to ensure that actions are repeatable to some degree of certainty and to make sure that certain requirements or standards are met during the action covered by the process. This is especially important when different groups are responsible for implementing different phases of the cluster under construction. Each phase needs to be in a well-defined state before the next phase, and responsible group, takes over.

However, any usable process must have ways of recognizing and incorporating changes, along with adapting to new and better ways of performing the actions that it captures. When things seem to go awry is when the process becomes rigid, inflexible, and most of all, political. So let's agree that our cluster process is not cast in concrete. It is just a tool for us to use in becoming better at building consistent clusters.

Also, remember that applying a process to your work depends on what you are building. It is all but impossible to have a process for random, custom-built cluster projects. If you are never building the same thing twice, it is difficult to see patterns or to attempt improvement in the steps involved. It may be possible, however, after building several clusters, to recognize similarities and to create a process using the 80/20 rule. In this case, roughly 80% of the steps are common between any given effort.

2.3   Presenting a Formal Cluster Creation Process

Although larger clusters may require a formalized implementation process, smaller clusters may benefit from an organized approach as well. The process documented here is based on observations and experience with larger cluster projects. Pick and choose the portions of the process that will apply to your particular situation.

The entire process is diagrammed in Figure 2–1, Figure 2–3, and Figure 2–4. You can think of the process as being divided into three phases: cluster design, cluster installation, and cluster testing. Each step in the process has a set of deliverable items as its output, and requirements as inputs. The individual phases and the substeps in the process are explained in subsequent sections.

2.3.1   Phase 1: Cluster Solution Design

The first phase of producing a functional cluster involves identifying and understanding the computational problem to be solved, and placing bounds on the type and number of systems participating in the cluster. From this flows many of the physical characteristics of the cluster, such as number of systems, number of racks, switch requirements, and construction cost and time estimates. The design also includes choosing the expected software architecture and components.

Without understanding the external requirements for the cluster, it is not possible to design the final solution. The steps involved in this part of the process are by nature iterative and driven by customer requirements such as performance and cost. Start by understanding as much as possible about customer requirements and the cluster's physical "context" (physical surroundings). It is very dangerous to start ordering systems or building the cluster without a thorough understanding of just what it is that you are building. Figure 2–1 shows this phase and the three substeps.

2.3.1.1   Technical Analysis

Systems analysis does not need to be a lost art—and it is absolutely essential in building a cluster. Before embarking on a cluster project it is necessary to understand how (and whether) this type of solution fits the problem and to determine the best components for the new cluster. Remember that a cluster may not automatically be the correct answer for whatever question your users might be asking.

So many questions to ask. What are the requirements for the cluster solution? Is the cluster to run a single application, such as a parallel database, or is it to be a general-purpose resource for multiple, parallel applications? Defining the problem to be solved and the expectations about performance will help determine the total number of necessary systems, the number and type of CPUs required in each system, the type of HSI, and other important design criteria.

Rough cost estimates for the cluster are possible once the performance requirements are defined and the number of compute slices is determined. Running benchmarks on singular instances of the compute slices may be necessary to determine memory speeds, I/O characteris-

Phase One: Cluster Solution Design

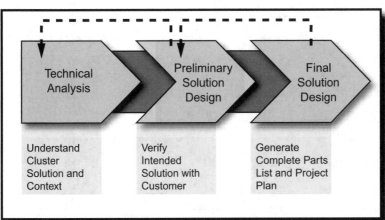

Figure 2–1 Cluster solution design phase

tics, and floating-point or integer performance of the CPUs. Testing the performance of the interconnect cards and switches in conjunction with the expected software is another frequent up-front activity.

An example list of deliverable documents for this portion of phase 1 is

- Technical analysis of system requirements
- Business and cost analysis
- Performance requirements
- Acceptance requirements
- Benchmarking plans
- Cluster test plans
- Cluster context diagram

Understanding the physical "context" for the cluster is also an important part of the design phase. Are there constraints for space, power, or cooling? Are raised floors available in the proposed location for running cables? Is there enough available space for all the anticipated racks? What are the external networking connections required to make the system visible to its users?

Because the cluster's relationship with the outside world may be complex, I tend to draw a good, old-fashioned context diagram (The top-level diagram for a software system using a number of structured analysis, structured design tools from the "old days") detailing all the physical inputs and output for the cluster. The whole exercise is intended to identify all external influences on the cluster and to ensure that the design and project plan will address them. This is one of the deliverable items in the list for this phase. Figure 2–2 shows an example context diagram.

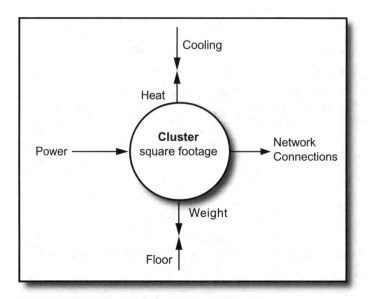

Figure 2–2 An example cluster context diagram

2.3.1.2   Preliminary Solution Design

The technical analysis step produces information needed to prepare a preliminary solution design for the cluster and then creates a first-pass design. It is important to realize that the first two steps in this phase of the process are iterative and will involve multiple trips back to the users of the cluster and its proposed physical location. Figure 2–1 shows dotted lines leading back to earlier steps in the process for a very good reason: Attempting to build a cluster before the design and expectations are completely set is a recipe for disaster (political, professional, and financial).

Sometimes it is necessary to estimate things like number of systems and racks to get an idea if a proposed system is feasible. This is an important part of moving the process forward. At each major stage, however, if there are design issues that are not resolved, it is imperative to revisit them before moving on.

Adjustments will be made to the number of compute slices, head nodes, switch ports, physical layout of the cluster racks (and therefore cable lengths), and other critical design parameters as this step progresses. It may be necessary to perform additional technical analysis to solve issues with the preliminary design. I haven't worked on a project yet in which the pre-liminary design didn't undergo lots of change. This is natural, and it is important to involve the end customer in the design to verify the decisions that are being made. Nobody likes last-minute surprises.

The preliminary solution step should generate a set of documents that may be refined and finalized in the final solution design step. The list of potential deliverable items from this step to the next is

- Requirements document
- Cluster structural design (floor plan)
- Cluster racking design
- Cabling design
- Site preparation document (power distribution and conditioning, cooling, and so forth)
- Network design (management and data local area networks [LANs])
- HSI design
- Software "stack" design
- Storage design
- Management and security design
- Preliminary project plan

As you can see, there may be a large amount of design work necessary. This is particularly true of large clusters (more than, say, 64 systems), but similar design work is also needed for small clusters. If you are providing the cluster to yourself, then this amount of formal documentation may not be needed. If you are building the cluster for a customer, it is essential to provide the documentation required to support and manage the final cluster.

A word about drawings and cable diagrams is in order. There are a number of tools available for creating realistic designs of clusters, and Microsoft's Visio is the best that I've found. In addition to front physical views of the racks, there are certain types of equipment, like network switches and serial port concentrators, that face *backward* in the racks. These devices add the requirement of a rear physical view of the equipment racks. These are in addition to logical views and cabling diagrams.

2.3.1.3   Final Solution Design

The third and final step in phase 1 takes the documents from the preliminary solution design step and further refines them to their final state. A slowing down or cessation of the constant changes and iterations in the design is one way to know that you should move from the preliminary design to the final design step (yeah, like this is ever really an obvious point in the process). Another sign is that your customer (and construction team) is satisfied with the preliminary work and is willing to move on.

At this point you should know enough about the cluster to begin ordering hardware, start planning any changes needed to the physical location (for power, cooling, and so on), and arrange the other resources to construct the cluster. You often will not be able to finalize the project plan until vendors, contractors, and craftsmen respond with things like hardware lead time and crew availability. This is when reality starts creeping into the project plan and time line.

A list of deliverable items from this step is

- Final versions of the design documents listed in the previous step
- A complete parts list by vendor
- Hardware and software orders
- Finalized project plan, with adjustments resulting from hardware lead times
- Hardware and software test plans

Even though we talk about "final" solution design in this step, the design will almost certainly need adjustment during the installation and test phases of the process. There is no better way to test design assumptions than by actually implementing the design and using it. Areas in which you have little experience with the software obviously contain the most risk.

2.3.2   Phase 2: Cluster Installation

Once a final design is completed for the cluster, it is time to begin the physical assembly of the whole system. The three steps involved in actually installing the cluster—site preparation, physical hardware assembly, and software installation and configuration—are diagrammed in Figure 2–3. The phase 2 activities are now focused mainly on the physical activities of assembling and verifying the hardware (including all cabling) and getting all the individual systems, racks, cables, and assorted pieces into their proper place within the cluster.

Note that there is a potential link *back* to the design phase (documentation) from the installation portion of the process. Say, for example, your customer specified a particular brand of Ethernet switches be used in the cluster, and during installation it was discovered that those switches simply would not work with the Ethernet interfaces in the compute slices. The switches would need to be replaced, the design documentation updated, and the entire forward portion of the cluster installation process reevaluated for issues. (Lest you think this is an artificial example, it comes from the direct experiences of a close friend.)

2.3.2.1   Site Preparation

Wherever the finished cluster will eventually "live," and whatever its size, there must be power, cooling, and space allocated for it. Ensuring that there are adequate resources to support the physical needs of the cluster is essential to its success. Bigger clusters require more effort to prepare for their installation. The Itanium Linux cluster at PNNL, for example, required building additions to deal with power and cooling requirements amounting to around 2.2 million BTUs.

Each site preparation step may be a unique exercise, but here are some lessons learned that may help.

- Have your power and cooling facilities professionally designed or evaluated according to local codes. Don't cut corners.
- For large clusters, run thermal simulations to verify heat flow, cooling requirements, and rack placement.

Phase 2: Cluster Installation

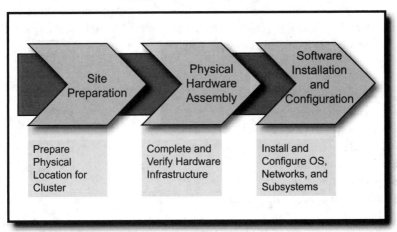

Figure 2–3 Cluster installation phase

- Remember that individual systems will draw more power when they are working than may be indicated by the vendor's nominal power ratings. For example, most CPUs will produce more heat during floating-point calculations than during regular integer operations.
- Don't underestimate the weight of a fully loaded rack of hardware and its effect on your computer room floor.
- Allow enough floor space for the racks, their doors, and proper access (ladders, crash carts, system removal, troubleshooting, and so forth) to the systems and cables.
- Leave the top and bottom rack spaces (1 EIA unit, or 1U) vacant to deal with access and cable issues, or other unexpected clearance issues.
- *Don't skip the planning for this phase because "everything will work out all right."*

This step in phase 2 tends to be on the critical path for your project. If the facility is not physically ready for the cluster, you may not have the space to start installing it. (What are you going to do with all the boxes, anyway?) One way to gain project time in this case is to perform the next step—physical hardware assembly—in another location, or to have someone do the rack-level integration for you. Deliverable items from this step include documents for

- Verification of physical placement against floor plan
- Verification of power distribution installation against plans
- Verification of cooling installation versus plans

2.3.2.2   Physical Hardware Assembly

Your experiences during this step will depend a lot on the vendor's rack design and the mounting rails, along with any cable management hardware used. Direct experience with the vendor's rack mounting hardware is essential to planning the amount of time for this activity. See Chapter 18 for an example breakdown of physical assembly steps.

The high-level steps involved in physically assembling the cluster hardware are

- Component unpacking
- Individual system assembly
- Individual system racking
- Individual system cabling
- Rack-level installation
- Interrack cabling
- Hardware and network verification

If you bought a do-it-yourself kit for your cluster, you may end up unpacking systems, interface cards, RAM, mounting rails, and cables for each system from their shipping containers. Just unpacking the components may consume a considerable amount of time and space. Then there is the disposal (recycling, right?) of the individual cardboard boxes to consider. Having enough room and the proper equipment (hand trucks, and so on) for the unpacking activities is important.

After unpacking, each separate system needs to be assembled from the individual components such as disks, additional RAM, and interface cards. If you are using an HSI, you will be integrating third-party interface cards. (Many full-service hardware vendors and system integrators will gladly integrate the hardware components for you for an extra charge.) This, of course, requires opening the computer's case for each system, in an area designed to control electrostatic discharge, to install internal components. Additionally, you may need to perform basic input/output system (BIOS) or other firmware upgrades at this point.

While the system is still out of the rack, it is a good idea to check that it is functional before you place it in the rack and cable it. This can save putting the system into the rack, cabling it, and *then* discovering that it is misconfigured or nonfunctional. If the system arrives from the manufacturer with an operating system installed, booting the system allows a functional check. This is also a good time to record serial numbers, network media access control (MAC) addresses, and other essential system characteristics, along with configuring any network-enabled management cards built into the system. To support these activities, the assembly area should provide power, console facilities, and network access for the system being integrated.

Once the systems are assembled, the rack-mounting hardware may be installed and the systems placed in the racks. Most racks with sliding mount rails also have some form of cable management "arms" that allow the cables to follow the system as it slides out of the rack on the mounting rails. Those arms may need to be installed into the rack along with the system. Some form of strain relief for the cables is absolutely necessary—do not scrimp!

With the system installed in the rack, you may install the power, network, HSI, serial, and other cables between the systems and the infrastructure. Placement of the switches, power distribution units, and other items with intrarack connections is important to cable management inside the rack itself. Along with all the cables comes the need for a system of tracking the cables and connections, especially if interrack connections are needed. See Chapter 19 for a suggested cable-labeling scheme.

If there are multiple racks involved in your cluster, then there will undoubtedly be interrack connections needed along with the intrarack connections. The physical placement of the racks, along with any cable length limitations, determines where and how these connections are placed. Once a rack is completed, it may be placed in position, attached to power, and cabled into the rest of the cluster. The most likely cable-length limitation involves the cables for the HSI and any SCSI connections for local disks. Note the circular dependency: Physical rack placement drives cable length, and cable length also drives physical rack placement. The design steps of the process should have detected and satisfied all these requirements.

When all the racks are placed and cabled into the cluster, it is time to start verifying all the connections. The tendency is to get excited at this point, power everything on, and start trying to use the cluster (especially if you foolishly allow your users to be breathing down your neck during this phase of the project). All in good time. It is a better approach to double-check all the cable connections, system labels, and rack labels against the documentation, to save troubleshooting time down the road. Verify that the physical configuration is really what you *think* it is and that it matches the documentation before you proceed.

Now comes a chicken-and-egg problem: Verifying the network connections relies on having the network hardware properly configured *and* on having some level of a functional operating system on each of the compute slices in the cluster. If you configure the default operating system image's network for testing, you will throw away that effort when you install your own image, assuming that the system image present is not custom installed for you. Some vendors will do custom image installation as part of the manufacturing process; others will automatically and inflexibly ship you Microsoft Windows Server (and charge you for the license) no matter what you really want. If you wait to verify the networks until all the systems are installed, you may be debugging network issues when you should be concentrating on the next step in the phase: software installation and configuration.

One approach is to concentrate on incrementally setting up the server systems (or head nodes) that will be used to provide system images and configuration information to the cluster's compute slices. This will also involve setting up infrastructure services such as Dynamic Host Configuration Protocol (DHCP), the Domain Name Service (DNS), or the Network Information Service (NIS) to provide boot-time information to the client systems and to support either the `kickstart` or `SystemImager` installation process. Once the minimal infrastructure is in place and one of the compute slices is installed with a best-guess operating system configuration, you may use the operating system image installation as a network verification and debugging tool. Deliverable items from this step in phase 2 are

- A list of outstanding hardware orders and plan for correction
- An amended project plan
- A completed floor plan that matches physical installation
- Completed rack diagrams that match physical installation
- Completed cable documentation that matches physical installation
- Completed network diagrams for all networks and interconnects
- A catalog of all system attributes (serial numbers, MAC addresses, and so on)

The complete physical state of the cluster should be documented at this point in the process. It may be necessary to engage another team for the next steps or to hand the completed hardware over to your customer for the next step in the process: software installation and configuration. Ask yourself, What information and documentation would I need to complete the job if *I* were on the software integration team?

2.3.2.3   Software Installation and Configuration

The final step in phase 2 of our cluster manufacturing process involves the installation and configuration of the software required to operate the cluster. This software "stack" is the most complex (and invisible) portion of the cluster. It is also the most difficult to get running consistently. Some of the major classes of components involved in the software stack are

- The operating system and device drivers
- Compilers and application development libraries
- Runtime libraries and interfaces to the HSI
- Loadbalancing and job scheduling
- Infrastructure services
- Authentication and security services
- Cluster file system
- System management tools
- Applications

There are numerous software subcomponents to each of the major items listed here. All software subsystems and components on each system in the cluster must be configured to operate as if the system resources in the cluster were available from a single, large system. The larger the cluster, the more difficult the task, because the number of possible virtual dependencies in the cluster grows exponentially as the size increases.

It is very important to avoid building the hardware, *then* locating the proper software to make the cluster function. Part of the design steps in phase 1 is to research possible components of the software stack and to provide a design document. This is to avoid nasty surprises during the software implementation. This is not to presume that nasty surprises can always be avoided.

The list of deliverable items from this step is usually the largest in the whole process.

- Documented operating system images for all system classes in the cluster
- Documented installation and system replacement procedure
- Configuration documentation for all software subsystems
- Security configuration and test documentation
- Documentation for parallel system administration processes
- Documentation for all host names, Internet Protocol (IP) addresses, and MAC addresses
- Documentation for account management and authentication
- Documented power-on and power-off process
- File server and file system configuration documentation
- Network switch management and access documentation
- Job queue and scheduling configuration documentation
- Revisions to design documents based on configuration changes

Although the design documents should outline the high-level structure of the software components and subsystems in the cluster, the deliverable documents from this step in the process actually capture the configuration information for each subsystem or component. This documentation is the basis for changes to the cluster configuration and, more important, any system administration procedures that your customer will develop to support the cluster.

2.3.3   Phase 3: Cluster Testing

The steps in phase 3 of the process involve verifying the cluster's operation as a single resource and meeting performance and stability goals for releasing the system to its users and system managers.

2.3.3.1   Cluster Operational Testing

Operational testing is the first point at which the cluster is expected to function as a complete system. This means that a limited set of users are allowed to log in, submit jobs, and verify results. At this point there may be additional benchmarking activities on the cluster, in a larger set of systems than was originally available. The phase 3 steps are shown in Figure 2–4.

The goal of phase 3 is to find major issues with infrastructure like job scheduling, interconnect performance bottlenecks, authentication, security policies, and general operation of the system environment. Issues are almost always uncovered during this step that require modification to the software configuration and the appropriate documentation.

Even with appropriate up-front research and design efforts, you may discover that some software components of the stack will not scale to the size needed by your cluster. As an example of software scaling issues, consider the system image installation facility. If there are contractual or practical requirements for total cluster reinstallation time (say, one hour), network limitations or disk saturation issues on the installation server may require a different approach to

Phase 3: Cluster Testing

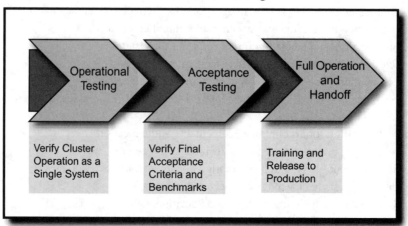

Figure 2–4 Cluster testing phase

installation than originally planned. Solutions may include choosing another installation method, using multicast installation tools, or adding more installation servers to meet the requirements.

One of the major activities in this step is the verification of application operation and performance. Performance tuning of the applications, the file system, the HSI libraries, network, or other components may be needed to meet criteria in the next step, when the cluster is "accepted" by the customer. Scheduling jobs, running them, and verifying acceptable levels of performance may involve repeated adjustments to the cluster and its components.

The cycle of test, fix, test may take a substantial amount of time. The more applications that the cluster must run, the more complex the testing and the more issues that are likely to be discovered. Usually, before the process can move to the acceptance step, some set of prearranged acceptance criteria must be met, usually based on performance, stability, or other very specific requirements. Deliverable items from this step include

- Documentation of performance tuning activities
- Documented verification of all parallel application operation and performance
- Adjustments to system administration procedure documents
- Documentation adjustments for design changes

2.3.3.2   Cluster Acceptance

This step in phase 3 verifies that the cluster meets or exceeds all the customer's acceptance criteria. There may or may not be a formal "acceptance period," during which the cluster must demonstrate normal operation within guidelines for performance, stability, and availability. Having agreed-on acceptance criteria is essential to "knowing when you are finished" with the implementation of the cluster. Deliverable items from this step include

- Finalized documentation from preceding phases and steps
- Test results from testing and acceptance steps
- Training and support plans

2.3.3.3   Full Operation and Release to Production

The preceding steps in our cluster production process should result in a fully operational, fully documented cluster solution. At this stage of the process, the cluster is released to the general user community and the system administrators. The cluster construction group must ensure that the system administrators and users of the cluster are adequately trained in its use before the turnover is completed.

Full turnover to production usually occurs after any formal acceptance steps are certified by the customer. There may or may not be official document signings, ribbon-cutting ceremonies, visits by corporate dignitaries, parades, or other joyful activities. Great care must be taken at this step not to overindulge during any acceptance/release celebrations that may occur.

2.4   Formal Cluster Process Summary

Your cluster construction project may not require such a formalized, rigorous process as described here. The overall process of producing a complete cluster solution, however, will be a lot easier if you have *some* form of process in mind when you start, and some way of knowing when you are finished. Hopefully, some of the structure described here can be adapted to your specific situation.

## PART II

Cluster Architecture and Hardware Components

Underneath the Hood: Cluster Hardware Components and Architecture

Chapter Objectives

- Examine the underlying hardware components of a cluster
- Categorize some of the of components used in a cluster hardware
- Examine several cluster architectures taken from real-world designs
- Explore differences in hardware configurations for different cluster types

Before we can begin to design software environments for a specific parallel application, we need to understand the individual hardware components used to create a cluster and how to provide a parallel hardware environment that supports the software. In this chapter we examine types of hardware in the cluster, and the individual hardware components that compose a cluster.

We have seen that there are several specific types of applications that might run on a cluster, and that they have different characteristics. Because the underlying computer hardware often mimics the architecture of the software using it, we would expect to find different cluster hardware configurations for different application types. This is indeed the case, but only to a point. Besides the presence or absence of an HSI, differences often have more to do with manageability and design choices than the application environment itself.

3.1 Hardware Categories in a Cluster

A major hardware category in a cluster may be thought of as the "passive" hardware elements. Passive hardware elements comprise racks, cables, power distribution units, mounting rails, cable management systems, screws, and other "glue" that physically and electrically hold the

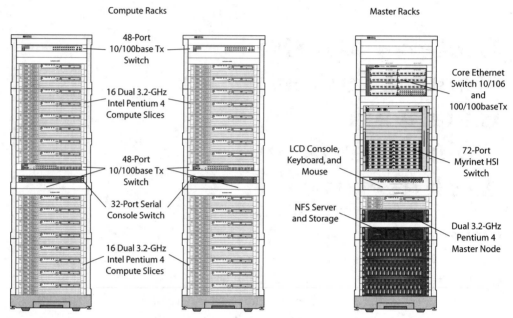

Figure 3–1 Rack diagram of cluster hardware components

cluster together. Active elements, like network switches, compute slices, disk arrays, and HSIs, are certainly more of an intellectual challenge than a cable, but both categories require close attention during the design of your cluster hardware. An example set of cluster racks is shown in Figure 3–1.

3.1.1   Passive Hardware Elements in a Cluster

Words that come to mind for the passive elements in a cluster are boring, unexciting, and tedious. The very word *passive* reeks of boredom. Passive hardware elements don't solve computing problems, you can't talk to them with network protocols, and they don't appear to require much thought—but, they physically support systems, help dissipate heat, and carry essential signals throughout the cluster. They also can fail, taking the entire cluster with them. So, however much you would like to jump immediately to the fun stuff, don't ignore selecting the proper passive components required to build your cluster.

The proper hardware rack selection (if it is not dictated by your computer hardware vendor) can make your life easier. The power distribution and cable management systems in the racks will help determine how easy it is to wire, maintain, and troubleshoot your cluster. Rack capacity, airflow, and power distribution are also particularly important characteristics. If you plan on assembling and shipping your cluster racks to another site, make sure that the rack

Table 3–1 Passive Components in the Example Cluster

Hardware Component	Quantity
Cables	385[a]
Mounting rails	160
Power distribution units	9
Racks	3
Total passive elements	567

a. Plus or minus about twenty.

equipment is designed to allow shipping fully populated racks—not all vendors (or rack designs) support this type of loading and stress.

Don't scrimp on slide mounting rails for hardware in your cluster. The ability to slide an active element out of a rack for repair is a big advantage when compared with physically unracking and removing it for access. Most hardware vendors have slide mounting kits and telescoping cable management systems available for their hardware and racks. If it is available, seriously consider using it—despite the extra cost.

By far, the largest number of passive elements in a cluster is represented by cables. Cable management, cable labeling, and cable *minimization*[1] during design are details that must be attended to—no matter what the size of your cluster. See Chapter 19 for a discussion of cables in a cluster. I do not cover the subject further here. A list of passive components for our example cluster is shown in Table 3–1.

3.1.2 Active Hardware Elements in a Cluster

Mention the word *cluster*, and most technical people will right away visualize racks of system hardware, all nicely racked and stacked. Just like flashing lights and reel-to-reel tape drives stood for the word *computer* in early television and movies, the racks of "worker nodes," "compute slices," or just "nodes" or "systems" tend to represent *cluster*.[2] This is not as out of line as

---

1. It is not obvious at first, but the number of cables in a cluster directly affects the amount of time it takes to construct the cluster, and also can affect troubleshooting and reliability. Minimizing the number of cables, particularly those that span racks, is a good design goal.

2. One has to be careful with terminology. Large ccNUMA systems like Hewlett-Packard's Superdome and SGI's Altix Supercluster may use terms like *cell*, *domain*, and *node* in different ways. As I use it, the terms *compute slice* or *node* refer to a single, independently packaged system integrated into a cluster.

Table 3–2 Active Components in the Example Cluster

Hardware Component	Quantity
Compute slices	64
Data network switches	4
Storage arrays	2
Console serial switches	2
Management switches	2
HSI switch	1
Core network switch	1
Master node	1
File server	1
Total active elements	78

you might expect. In most clusters the compute slices *are* the most numerous and immediately visible elements (besides cables) in the cluster.

Figure 3–1 shows a rack diagram of an example cluster's hardware. Although this is a rack configuration for a fictitious cluster, it is a fairly accurate representation of the active hardware and communication components present in a real cluster of this size. A list of the active components in this example cluster is shown in Table 3–2. There are 64 dual-processor compute slices (128 processors), 10/100base-TX switches for a management LAN, 100/1000base-TX switches for a data LAN, serial port console switches, a core Ethernet switch, a Myrinet HSI switch, an NFS server and associated storage arrays, and a single master or head node.

A cluster may have a number of system categories, or classes, involved in its operation. A typical reason for separating out some of the cluster's functionality is to avoid interference between compute or I/O-intensive operations and time-sensitive ones like HSI communications. It is also possible that services may be placed on separate systems to provide increased security or to enable high-availability features to protect those services.

You are likely to find one or more of the following active system elements in a cluster:

- Master or "head" node—used for user access to compute resources, job scheduling, and cluster/local storage
- Compute slice—performs the computational tasks on behalf of a portion or piece of a parallel job, or provides one "unit" of a scalable service (such as a database instance)
- Administrative node—provides administrative services, such as performance monitoring or event generation for the cluster's system administrators

- Infrastructure node—provides essential services to the cluster, such as license serving, authentication services, or load balancing and scheduling
- File server or I/O node—provides access to the cluster's storage for the applications and users

The picture of the cluster's physical hardware in Figure 3–1 doesn't tell the whole story of the example cluster's hardware because it doesn't show either logical or physical interconnections. I chose this example to illustrate the multiple networks (and their physical connections) that may be present in a cluster: HSI, management LAN, data LAN, and the serial console switches.

A combination logical and physical diagram is shown in Figure 3–2. There are several things to notice about the details of this diagram. First, the compute slices are segregated into groups or "pods" of 16 systems. This allows segregating the various networks to preserve security (when required) between the data and management LANs, and to increase bandwidth between the rack and the core switch (at the cost of an extra level of switch latency.) This approach also allows minimization of interrack cables. Additionally, the two compute racks are identical to simplify manufacturing,[3] with the common equipment segregated to a "management" rack.

The head or master node belongs to all the networks in the cluster—management, HSI, serial console access, and data. The master node is where management and monitoring software runs and where users log in to the cluster. I discuss the user's view of the cluster in the next section.

3.1.3   Cluster Resources and the "Outside" World

If a cluster was just a group of systems on "the network," then it would be very difficult to manage the systems and their resources. Users who have access to network resources could log in to a particular system or group of systems, and tie them up with their jobs. For this reason, a cluster typically "hides" the compute resources behind the master or head nodes, making the entire set of resources appear as a single system.

Furthermore, the "normal" user is only permitted to access certain resources inside of the cluster environment. A user's login may permit him to access his files, submit jobs to the cluster, and do normal "user space" activities. Access to resources like system logs, consoles, power control scripts, and configuration utilities are reserved for cluster administrators. Most of this protection is at a software and operating system level.

---

3.   The compute slices in this example cluster are one Electronics Institute of America (EIA) unit (a standard unit, or U, is 1.75 inches) high, which means that up to 41 would fit in the example racks. Using the full 41 units for compute-slices, however, would increase the number of interrack cables, because the serial port console connections, management LAN connections, and data LAN connections would all need to exit the rack.

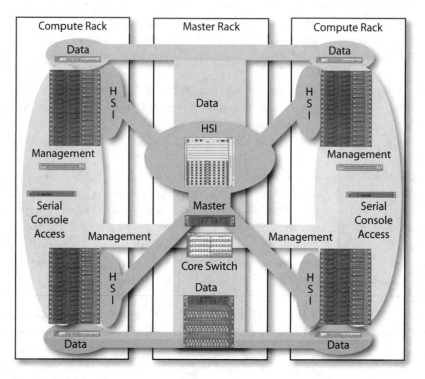

Figure 3–2 Logical and physical cluster diagram

The internal networks and resources of the cluster are normally configured to be "private" and invisible, except to the access points to the cluster: the master nodes and the management nodes. Users may log in to the cluster access points (master nodes) and submit jobs. They do not know which specific portions of the cluster actually execute the job, only that the job's resource requirements will be met and that the job will be scheduled.

The cluster may be visible to the outside world as a single system name registered in the name lookup service DNS. The DNS host name may be configured with "round-robin" access to load balance user login access between multiple master nodes. The master nodes themselves may need to be highly available, in which case there must be redundant hardware and fail-over software configured. If a single master node becomes unavailable, access to the cluster is blocked. Providing multiple master nodes, or a node that can act as a temporary master in the event of a failure, makes the cluster access more highly available in the event of a failure. If there are multiple master nodes, then round-robin DNS may point a user trying to log in to a "dead" master. In this sense, "highly available" may include mapping the dead node's IP address to a "live" machine to minimize the inconvenience caused by a hardware failure.

Figure 3–3 shows an example configuration, along with two users accessing the cluster's hardware and software resources for their jobs. Similar configurations may be used for database

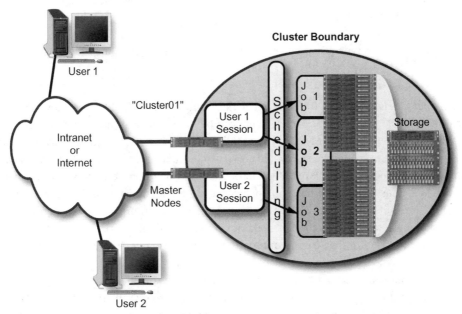

Figure 3–3 Cluster resource hiding

servers, Web servers, and other commercial cluster configurations, but the master nodes are either absent, as in the case of a parallel database cluster, or replaced by load-balancing "director" systems in the case of a parallel Web server.

For the parallel Web or database servers, the user authentication and access are performed by client software running on the user's system. Instead of logging in to a master node in this circumstance, users authenticate themselves to the client software, if required.

3.2   A Survey of Cluster Hardware Configurations

As we have noticed, there is some confusion over just what is referred to when we hear the word *cluster*. This is partially because there are a number of different configurations and uses that share similar hardware arrangements, but each has differing software architectures, user expectations, and objectives. A brief survey of some of these configurations will lead us to a generalized hardware architecture for a cluster, and will identify some of the common hardware elements used to build a cluster.

3.3   High-Throughput Cluster Configurations

One class of clusters is a *high-throughput* configuration, which has the following characteristics and goals:

- Data independence of individual jobs
- Intersystem latency not a big issue

• Individual job resources possibly constrained to a single compute slice
• Goal of completing the highest number of jobs in the shortest possible time

Some examples of this type of hardware configuration are discussed in the following sections.

3.3.1   A "Carpet" Cluster

The term *carpet cluster* comes from the experiences and stories of building your own cluster in your office cubicle, on the floor carpet, unnoticed by your boss and the IT department. Every computing environment has hardware that has fallen off the performance curve, may be destined for disposal or the recycling bin, and would cause no questions if it were to disappear. (Although this may seem to be a joke, I have visited numerous sites that don't officially permit Linux in their network. This prohibition has not stopped the system administrators, engineers, or other personnel from building a Linux cluster underneath their desks from throw-away hardware.)

Carpet clusters were attempts to break the bounds of a single workstation or PC, and they still allow users to do just that. They work for a low number of users, typically close to one, and take a minimum amount of effort, expense, and management. This was probably one of the starts of the whole commodity cluster "phenomenon"—underneath someone's desk.

Although this type of configuration was the original source of the term *carpet cluster*, today a carpet cluster denotes more of an air of informality: no special cooling, no special power requirements, inexpensive network connections, and small numbers of low-cost (possibly throw-away) hardware. There are quite a few useful clusters being built out of what yesterday would have been called "improbable" hardware.

Throughout this book, most of the diagrams of clusters are focused on racked configurations. This is simply a practical matter of space and controlling access, heat, power, and noise generated by a *larger* group of systems. It is certainly possible that a cluster may be built from individual PC or workstation enclosures. In fact, this is done all the time. Larger configurations, and configurations that must provide more manageability features, dictate a more compressed physical configuration—one that is best racked and placed in a computer room.

Hand-held devices and other commercial off-the-shelf (COTS) systems, when coupled with low-cost Ethernet switches or wireless networks, may be used to do useful work in specialized situations. A carpet cluster may be used to prove a point or conjecture about a particular solution, without costing a large sum for hardware.

A cluster of this type may be used to handle parallel compiles for a small group of developers, or to run embarrassingly parallel[4] applications like SETI@home, Folding@home, or

---

4.   This term refers to the extremely low level of difficulty required to break the problem into parallel pieces. I have
        run across it in several industries, including in the oil and gas industry, where it is used in a serious sense.

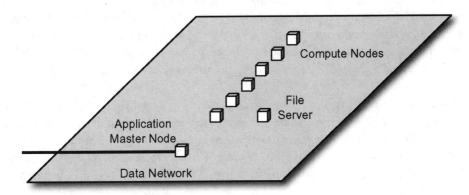

Figure 3–4 Carpet cluster hardware architecture

Genome@home[5] software by home computing enthusiasts. The architectural components present in a carpet cluster are

- Compute resources (systems)
- Possibly a file server
- Data and compute networks (collapsed to one physical network)

An example carpet cluster architecture is shown in Figure 3–4. The single network interconnect (most likely Ethernet) connects all the components of the cluster. The cluster is built out of "left-over" or discarded hardware and probably sits "on the carpet" in someone's cubicle.

There is a single, shared network for the data, management, and HSI. This type of configuration works fine in a smaller cluster, but sharing the network between multiple functions, although it saves money, can impact performance, particularly if bulk data transfers and time-sensitive HSI traffic are operating on a shared network connection. Clusters really don't get too much simpler than this.

3.3.2   Compute "Farms and Ranches"

As with most terms that have a marketing origin, it is difficult to tell the difference between a *compute farm* and a *compute ranch*. The difference is somewhat fuzzy, but (as you would expect from the metaphor) is one of scale. (Both terms, however, seem to be a variation of the same "marketechture.") When the number of independent tasks outgrows a single workstation, a logical approach is to provide back-end racks of equipment that can be scheduled to do lots of independent jobs at the same time.

---

5.   See both `http://genomeathome.stanford.edu` and `http://foldingathome.stanford.edu` for more information on the Genome@home and Folding@home projects.

In a way, you can view this as a formalization of the "carpet cluster" approach. Because of heat, power, and noise, however, the scale of this type of solution is typically larger than can be sustained in someone's cubicle. Application areas that come to mind immediately are software compilation for large complex source code and electronic design automation (EDA) circuit verification. By the time a group of systems reaches this size, they can no longer be financially (or physically) hidden.

Some resourceful systems architects have discovered that by dividing their networks into two tiers (one for the GUI on the desktop and one for the application and data), the heavy data traffic can be localized to the computer room, where high-speed networking may be inside or between racks within close proximity of each other. This represents a large step toward what would be called a "full-blown" cluster, and it "collapses" several of the networks involved into closely located racks.

It is less expensive to pull a fiber between two racks in the computer room than to run fiber between the computer room and all desktops in the environment. The desktop's primary function in this type of environment becomes access to back-end resources on servers located in a computer room. Front-end GUI technologies, multiuser operating systems, and remote login and authentication all enable this configuration.

At the same time, "pushing pixels" to the desktop system requires less bandwidth than the remote access to ever-growing data files. For applications that require bit-mapped graphics, display "projection" technologies like the X Windows system, Citrix, Remote Desktop Protocol (RDP), and virtual network computing (VNC), among others, enable remote graphics display from systems "out there" in the network.

Figure 3–5 shows an example of this multitier architecture, which may be called *collapsed network* computing. This label is the result of "collapsing" the major portion of the entire two-tier network into the racks located in the computer room. The compute resources in this type of arrangement are either grabbed by users in an ad hoc manner[6] or are parceled out via a load-balancing service, such as the products from Platform Computing or from Altair Grid Technologies. (There are many more load-balancing, batch-queueing, job-handling packages, and I will cover several of them later in the book.)

Using a load-balancing layer between the client systems and the compute resources allows tasks to be submitted without the knowledge of where they execute, only that the correct, available resource will be reserved and used. This, in turn, allows the system administrators to add, subtract, or modify the types and amounts of resources available without directly affecting the users. This type of architecture is very well suited to project-oriented environments in which projects are created, destroyed, or moved on a frequent basis.

When using a load-balancing service, if the number of tasks trying to run exceeds the available resources, a queue is created and managed by the software. As resources become avail-

---

6.   Something I call "hunter–gatherer" scheduling. Note that the tendency is for users to hunt, gather, and consume, but not to return the resources.

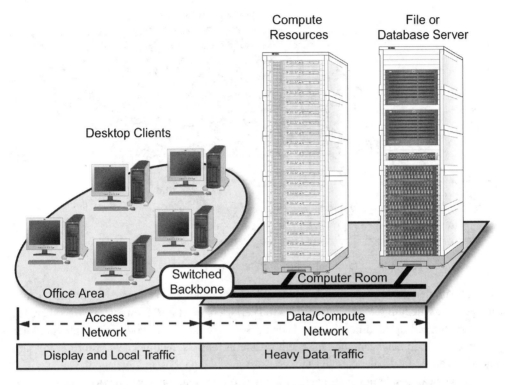

Figure 3–5 Engineering compute "farm" or "ranch" functional diagram

able, new tasks are assigned and executed on the proper compute resource. This is a preferred method of operation,[7] and we shall see that load balancing and job scheduling are important services in a general-purpose cluster. Task types that require multiple, simultaneous compute resources may also be handled by the load-balancing software, which will reserve the required number of systems or processors for the task's execution.

The amount of network resources from the client system (user's) point of view can appear to be infinite—to the limit of the back-end resources. Every time a user requests execution of an application from a menu, icon, or command line, a "thread" of resources is created for her by the load-balancing service, which reserves the compute resources and starts the application. Each application, its associated GUI windows, and the allocated resources may be viewed as a "virtual computer" within the compute environment. This is a useful way to think about resources, and we will use it in the future.

---

7.   The issue becomes one of ensuring that enough compute resources are available to handle peak demand within a reasonable completion time.

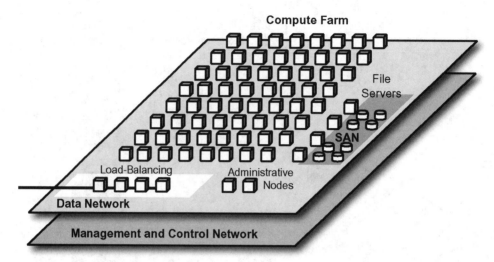

Figure 3–6 Compute farm hardware architecture

The proper use of groups of resources, like a compute farm or ranch, entails proper management and scheduling of those resources to keep users from interfering with each other. This task is performed by load-balancing, queueing software. A user's workstation runs the client portion of the load balancer, allowing them to submit jobs—sometimes lots of jobs at the same time. Centralized load-balancing master systems schedule the jobs and manage the queues.

As you can see, both the size and complexity of this solution have grown, when compared with the carpet cluster's architecture. It now will take appreciable amounts of design, implementation, and system administration effort to support the hardware and operating environment.

Another architectural addition is the "administrative node." This type of system runs services, like load-balancing that need to be highly available and "out of the way" of competition for resources with applications and users. Indeed, the separation of data and management network functionality is to avoid interference, as well as to provide added security. In this type of cluster architecture there are lots of independent compute resources that probably share data through one or more file servers. The file servers provide data from a storage area network (SAN) containing high-density storage devices. This architecture is shown in Figure 3–6.

A compute farm may have a mixture of different hardware and operating system types to support different application revisions that execute in it. The job-scheduling service is able to pick the correct (and best) location to run a given job, based on the job type. The flexibility to hide the details of resources from users is a major advantage of this approach.

Because of the hardware density implied by the *ranch* term, it is likely that there are many racks of equipment. Architectural components present in a compute farm/ranch are

- Compute resources (systems)
- Data network
- File servers and SAN
- Administrative nodes
- Possibly a management network for console access and monitoring

This hardware architecture of a compute farm is almost identical to that of a Linux virtual server (LVS) configuration used for a scalable Web server and is shown in Figure 3–6.

3.4   High-Availability Cluster Configurations

Although all clusters have some measure of reliability and availability required, this may not be their primary design goal. The scalable nature of commodity clusters, coupled with service requests that are independent of each other, allows us to use a cluster environment to provide highly available Web services, database servers, and other types of "traditional" services. High-availability clusters have the following goals:

- Maximum service availability
- Sustained performance

A good portion of the reliability in this type of cluster is provided by software that detects hardware and service failures, triggering alternate resources. This software is covered later, but there are also hardware aspects required in a highly available design, such as ensuring that there is no single point of failure (SPOF) in the hardware design. Several examples of highly available hardware architectures follow.

3.4.1   An Example "Virtual" Web Server

Businesses wishing to provide information and services over the Internet require solutions that are both highly available to their customers and highly scalable to meet peak demands. One approach to meeting both these requirements is to use a cluster of systems to run Web services for Web-based Internet clients. Figure 3–7 depicts a cluster operating as a virtual Web server.

This configuration is referred to as a *virtual server*, because client systems make requests to a single network address held by a load balancer, or "director," system. The director system redirects the request to one of several virtual servers that perform the work on behalf of the client system. The client is virtually unaware that its request has been redirected because the virtual servers remain hidden "behind" the director system.

To maintain availability, the primary director system has a standby replacement available. The two systems share "heartbeat" information to ensure that the primary director is available to clients. If the heartbeat information ever indicates that the primary director has failed, the secondary director takes over the IP address and host name of the failed system, taking over any new requests from client systems.

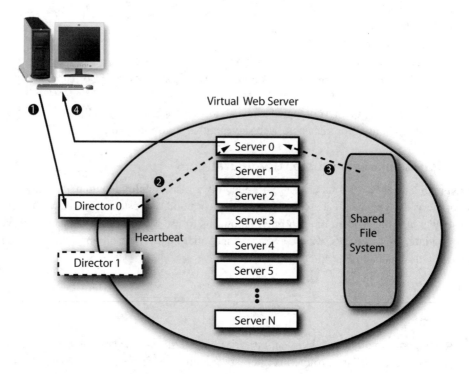

Figure 3–7 A virtual Web server functional diagram

In this configuration,[8] each client request is independent of other requests, so there are no data dependencies between the compute slices in the cluster. Data *is* shared, however, through a highly available file system that presents all clients with the same view of common file system data. In the case of Web data, which may not change very frequently, the clients do not need to worry about inconsistent views of the data that would be caused by clients writing changes to the file system. Not all cluster configurations share this simplicity.

The shared file system, or cluster file system used by the cluster compute slices, may be one of several highly available cluster file systems, such as InterMezzo (`http://www.inter-mezzo.org`), Lustre (`http://www.lustre.org`), or IBM's cluster file system, the general parallel file system (GPFS). Sometimes, because of its wide availability and relative simplicity, a cluster will use NFS for shared data.

In our example configuration, the file system needs to be highly available to all members of the cluster, even though the data is read-only. It should be noted here that multiple file servers

---

8.   The LVS project provides software and instructions for this type of configuration at `http://www.linux-virtualserver.org`.

may be unnecessary if each node in the cluster has a SAN connection to storage devices. The data is exported directly to the nodes, via the SAN, instead of over another type of network via a network attached storage (NAS) protocol like NFS. Whether there are dedicated servers to manage locking and meta-data for the file system depends on the particular configuration.

The cluster file system, as it turns out, is a common component in almost all types of clusters, whether scientific or commercial. The requirements and usage of the cluster file system may be different, but the need for a single view of common data is almost universal in a cluster environment. We will be hearing a lot more about cluster file systems as we proceed. An example hardware architecture for a virtual Web server is shown in Figure 3–8.

3.4.2   A Parallel Database Server

Our previous example of a parallel Web server introduced us to a cluster solution that had no data interdependencies and yet shared data in the "back end" of the architecture. One commercial cluster solution that *does* have data interdependencies is a parallel database, such as Oracle 9i RAC. Because databases are, by nature, read/write solutions, it is natural to expect that a cluster database solution must maintain data consistency between the disk storage and memory contents of individual compute slices in the cluster.

Because multiple clients may attempt to read or write the same data in the database, consistency must be maintained by the database and file system software. In addition to preventing destructive interference from multiple writes, the database software must maintain performance across the cluster by minimizing the number of physical reads performed against the storage. To

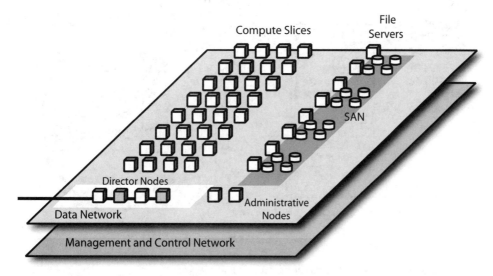

Figure 3–8 Virtual Web server hardware architecture

do this, the database software shares storage blocks between compute slices in the cluster using an HSI such as Myrinet, Infiniband, or GbE.

Along with data consistency and scaling across the cluster, the parallel database software must maintain high availability for the client applications. Some database systems provide their own high-availability software for cluster configurations, although there are also hardware and file system vendor-specific versions available. A cluster that is capable of running a parallel database configuration like Oracle 9i RAC shares many of the same underlying hardware components as a scientific cluster, although for different reasons.

Figure 3–9 shows a simplified diagram of a parallel database server at work. Each compute slice runs an instance of the same database, and consistency is maintained by a global cache and lock managers. A read request from a client results in a database block being read from the parallel file system that contains the database tables into the local cache on the compute slice. A subsequent write request to the same data causes the cache manager to transfer the block from one compute slice to another over the HSI. The data is written to the block, which is then flushed to the storage.

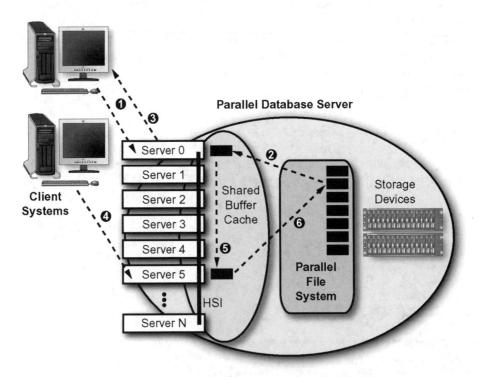

Figure 3–9 A parallel database server functional diagram

An example hardware architecture for the highly available database cluster is shown in Figure 3–10. In this architectural diagram, I introduce some new components: the SAN, replacing the "data network"; and test and spare nodes for the cluster. The choices between LAN and SAN, as well as the number of test and spare nodes, are design considerations for your cluster, based on its type and application.

3.5   High-Performance Cluster Configurations

High-performance computing (HPC) is a common term used for scientific clusters, but high-performance clusters are not just limited to scientific applications. The scientific HPC cluster runs large jobs that simultaneously need lots of aggregated compute power, lots of aggregated memory, or both. The tendency in HPC is to push the limits of performance, trying to do bigger and more complex computational challenges.

Scientific problems running a on high-performance compute cluster may be referred to as *grand challenges*, for the simple reason that the research is truly ground breaking—results may have never been produced before. Just trying to run this type of job, and getting it to complete, is an accomplishment. There are profound reliability issues with this type of cluster environment. You will find that many parallel applications that run for long periods of time are capable of "checkpoint and restart." The current state of the computation is saved across all parallel nodes and may be resumed in the event of a failure. Performing a complete checkpoint across the clus-

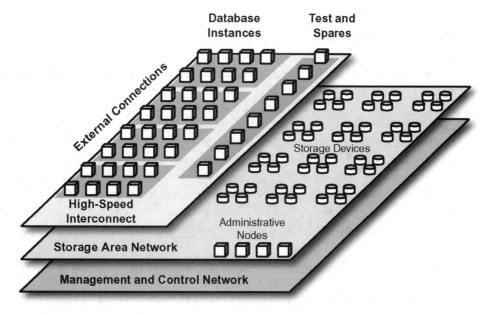

Figure 3–10 Parallel database cluster hardware architecture

ter in a specified period of time sometimes determines the required I/O bandwidth value to the cluster's file system.

It may take teraflops of compute resources and terabytes of RAM just to run the application to the desired resolution or accuracy, and the job may not complete for weeks (or longer). As soon as the cluster's resources are expended, the users will increase the resolution of their computations to fill them. It seems that a (simulated) digital gas expands to fill the available container.

Once computations are done, it is often useful to generate three-dimensional (3D) renderings and movies that represent the data over time. Data "visualization" and rendering are natural applications of HPC clusters, particularly if real-time display is desired. This type of computing is also used by the automotive industry for crash analysis, the engineering community to check three-dimensional assemblies for accuracy before they are built, and in numerous other industries and application environments.

Most times, the visualization cluster is a separate section of the HPC cluster, or even a separate cluster entirely. Having two separate environments means the data must be moved between them, which may be a large effort. There is a trend to use portions of the same cluster, or dedicated sections of the same cluster, as the visualization hardware.

Using clusters as real-time visualization and display tools is starting to enter the commodity world as the price for the specialized display equipment and associated cluster hardware drops. Let's start with visualization examples first, then progress to HPC clusters.

3.5.1   A Visualization Cluster

Real-time generation of 3D objects is an exercise in floating-point performance. If you look at the hardware characteristics of any commodity 3D graphics card, you will find one or more devices, sometimes digital signal processors (DSPs), that are capable of very fast floating-point operations. The NVIDIA Quadro FX (see `http://www.nvidia.com/page/quadrofx.html`), for example, is capable of full 128-bit floating-point calculations on the card itself.

The graphics application manipulates 3D objects in its own internal numerical format. Once the objects are properly described, the application uses graphics interface software, like OpenGL, to describe the 3D objects to the graphics interface, along with attributes like their location in 3D space, colors, shading, reflective properties, and effects from any light sources. This application uses the graphics application programming interface (API), such as OpenGL, that specifies data types with a standardized graphics communication protocol that the interface card can understand.

The graphics card then takes the digital description of the objects and "renders" them *visually* into its graphics memory. What may have been a wire-frame representation of the object, along with attributes, becomes a fully lighted, colored, and shaded 3D object in the graphics card's video memory. The video memory is then is output by the card as a "frame" to a display device via a digital-to-analog convertor (DAC) for monitors, or digital visual interface (DVI) for displays that can handle digital information directly.

Multiple frames per second in the graphics output create the illusion of motion, and even stereo vision with the appropriate goggles or glasses. If the 3D objects in a scene are moving, displaying requires floating-point calculations to determine or "translate" the new position of the object in relation to its previous position. The more objects in the scene and the more complicated their attributes, the more compute power it takes to produce the output, both from the graphics card *and* from the computer running the 3D application. The graphics card, in and of itself, may be considered a specialized supercomputer on a board.

Although graphics card capabilities and performance are continuing to advance, there is a *size* limit to the scene that can be rendered from a single card, along with a limit on the number of shaded triangles per second that may be displayed. The NVIDIA Quadro FX, for example, can go up to a display resolution of 3840 by 2400 pixels for a single DVI output. As large as that might seem, for very detailed, complex objects or for "immersive" environments like "caves" or "coves," it takes larger amounts of total display area and resolution. (A cove may be thought of as immersing the user in graphics by displaying in front and to the right and left portions of the visual field. A cave is more immersive, with front, right, left, top, and possibly bottom displays.)

How do we break through the single-card limitations? The solution, of course, is to "parallelize" the graphics display operations. To provide more output, we need more cards; to supply the multiple cards with processing power and parallel data, requires parallel hardware and versions of the graphics interface software that can assign portions of a scene to different systems and their graphics cards. A parallel path for graphics data may be referred to as a *graphics pipeline*, and there may be multiple, active rendering components in each pipeline.

When the scene is broken apart and rendered into a flat block of pixels by separate graphics pipelines, it must be visually assembled for viewing. How this is done depends on the destination display type and characteristics, but there are hardware "blenders" or "compositors" that take multiple digital or analog graphics outputs and generate a single viewable output. Direct, multichannel input to a display device is also possible. The final display device may be multiple projectors for a flat screen, a "tiled" wall consisting of multiple discreet display devices, or something more exotic. (See http://www.panoramtech.com for some examples of this type of equipment. Wouldn't it be nice to have one of these babies in your media room?)

Interface cards are also becoming available that take a DVI input and use an HSI to share rendered pixels, including the depth information, along a processing chain or pipeline. Each card adds its own scene components to objects rendered earlier in the chain and passes the result to the next interface card. The end card in the chain directly drives displays, compositors, or projectors to produce the final images. This architecture may be described as having a graphics compositor present on every system, as opposed to a single-output compositor as shown in Figure 3–11.

As you might imagine, the individual systems in a graphics cluster must all be synchronized to produce their frame components to provide a meaningful, nongarbled output. Much of

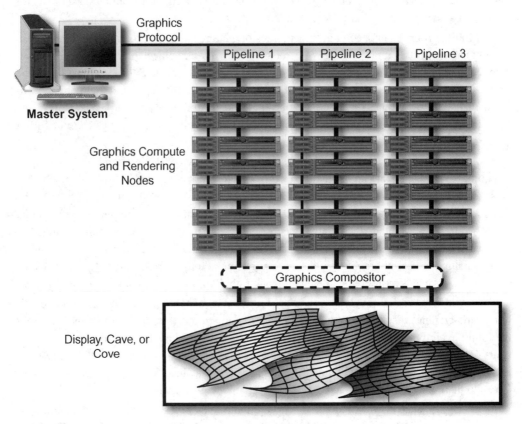

Figure 3–11 Visualization cluster functional diagram

the synchronization work is handled by both software and hardware components in the visualization cluster. An example of a commercially available software package that performs the parallelization of graphics operations may be found at http://www.modviz.com. A functional diagram of a visualization cluster is shown in Figure 3–11. A diagram of the hardware components is shown in Figure 3–12.

Another type of visualization cluster does not make use of individual graphics cards in the compute slices. Instead, the rendering or graphics computations are performed on the individual systems in the cluster and are presented to a central system for external display. This type of architecture might be used for volumetric rendering (3D volumes) for applications like oil and gas exploration or medical imaging.

A key differentiation is the separation (or sharing) of the compute portion of the application and the visualization hardware. The hardware for the two pieces of the process may be used simultaneously, or serially, depending on the amount of computation and the size of the data being rendered and displayed. The amount of data being moved between the visualization clus-

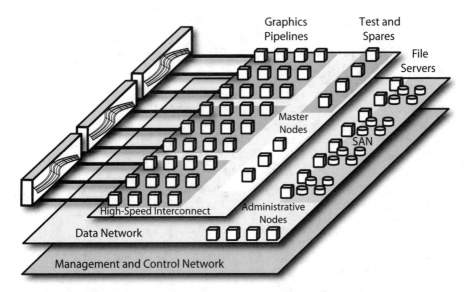

Figure 3–12 Visualization cluster hardware architecture

ter and the cluster that generates the graphics data will also help determine whether the two clusters are collocated in the same infrastructure and share the same storage.

3.5.2 High-Performance Parallel Application Configurations

We have been moving up the scale in terms of hardware complexity and associated capability. The HPC parallel applications run in the scientific world live at the very pinnacle (and leading edge, to mix a metaphor) of the commodity cluster world. It is the trickle-down effect from the scientific community's advanced research that is helping smaller organizations build their own commodity clusters. Let's look at HPC clusters by examining the hardware required to run a leading parallel application in computational chemistry.

An example of scientific HPC parallel application software is NWChem from the PNNL Environmental Molecular Sciences Laboratory (EMSL). A description of the software may be found at http://www.emsl.pnl.gov/docs/nwchem/nwchem.html. I will leave it up to you to take a look at the software's capabilities and increase your vocabulary. (Although this particular example is from computational chemistry, sometimes working with HPC clusters is, indeed, "rocket science.")

The hardware environment that runs the software, however, is within the realm of our current understanding. To quote from the EMSL Web site,

> NWChem is available on almost all high-performance computing
> platforms, workstations, PCs running LINUX, as well as clusters of
> desktop platforms or workgroup servers. NWChem development has

> been devoted to providing maximum efficiency on massively parallel
> processors. It achieves this performance on the 128-node Hewlett-
> Packard Linux system in the EMSL's MSCF. It has not been opti-
> mized for high performance on single-processor desktop systems.
> [PNNL EMSL 2004]

From `//http://mscf.emsl.pnl.gov/`, as of January 10, 2004:

> The Pacific Northwest National Laboratory's supercomputer has
> been ranked No. 5 on the top 500 list of the fastest computers in the
> world that was released yesterday. The HP system installed at PNNL
> was designed specifically for complex computational environmental
> and biological sciences.

> The latest list represents the first time the 11.8-teraflop supercom-
> puter was ranked based on its full power. The machine consists of
> nearly 2,000 1.5GHz Intel Itanium 2 processors. The Top 500 list
> ranks computers based on their performance running a benchmark
> called Linpack, which is a method to measure a machine's ability to
> solve a set of dense linear equations. [PNNL EMSL 2004]

The same laboratory, PNNL, that maintains the NWChem code also has constructed one of the
world's largest and fastest HPC clusters using Linux. It is interesting to consider the characteristics of the cluster hardware and software that support such a world-class parallel application (as
well as others). Using this cluster as an example will not only help us understand a generic, leading-edge HPC cluster and its architecture, but it will serve as an explicit example for other calculations and observations that we make later in this book.

As of this writing, the hardware and software configuration of the PNNL Mpp2 (phase 2a)
cluster is:

- 1960 Itanium 2 processors
- Hewlett-Packard/Linux for 64-bit Itanium
- 980-node/1,960 Itanium 2 processors (1.5 GHz) two configurations, "fat" and "thin"
- 566 nodes are "fat," with 8 GB of RAM and 430 GB of local disk
- 414 nodes are "thin," with 6 GB of RAM and 10 GB of local disk
- Quadrics QsNet HSI[9]
- 11.8 TFLOPs peak theoretical performance
- 6.8 TB of RAM

---

9.   MPP2 will be upgraded with the faster Quadrics QsNet-II interconnect in early 2004.

> • 450 TB of local scratch disk space
> • 53 TB shared cluster file system, using Lustre

You can see a 3D, color, rendered picture of the system in its computer room at `http://mscf.emsl.pnl.gov/images/hardware/hpcs2_rendered.jpg`.

3.6 Common Cluster Hardware Architecture

The survey of various cluster configurations has introduced us to the common building blocks found in the hardware architecture for clusters. Just as an artist has her palette of colors, we can paint our cluster designs with a broad brush from this list of components. The common hardware pieces of a cluster we have reviewed are

> • Compute slices
> • Master nodes
> • Administrative nodes
> • HSI
> • Management, control, and data networks
> • File servers
> • Storage

Additionally, there may be test and spare nodes in the cluster that duplicate compute slices. A generalized functional diagram of a cluster, with all architectural elements present, is shown in Figure 3–13.

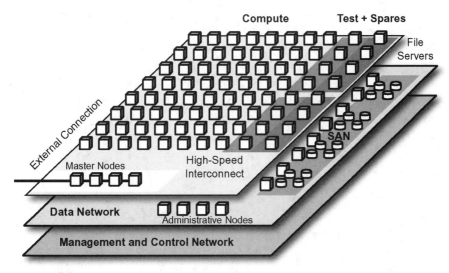

Figure 3–13 Cluster hardware and network model

3.7   Cluster Hardware Architecture Summary

In this chapter we have examined three basic classes of clusters: high performance, high throughput, and high availability. We have also studied the functional architectures of these classes of clusters to survey the varying hardware components and levels of complexity.

Not all clusters contain all the hardware components that we encountered in our examples. For us to begin designing clusters using the various elements we encountered, we need to examine the characteristics of the hardware building blocks. In the next chapters, we look at the information we need to choose the proper hardware for our cluster design.

## CHAPTER 4

Any Way You Slice It: Work and Master Nodes in a Cluster

Chapter Objectives

- Examine the characteristics of "worker nodes" or "compute slices" in a cluster
- Discuss criteria for choosing a compute slice
- Describe several example system architectures[1]
- Analyze expected performance and potential bottlenecks in a given system

T he individual systems in a cluster that actually perform parallel work may be viewed as "slices" of a larger computer. Because each of these systems is usually in an individual package that includes a motherboard, CPUs, RAM, internal disks, and other components, it is important to consider what characteristics make a particular system suitable for use in a given cluster. This entails understanding underlying hardware "compute slices" and their architecture, and then being able to apply that knowledge to the cluster applications.

4.1 Criteria for Selecting Compute Slices

There is a wide range of systems available that are suitable for use as compute slices in a cluster. Which system you select depends on your budget, the desired characteristics for your cluster,

---

1.   To do the level of analysis performed in this chapter, you need to have some familiarity with the hardware manufacturer or perform the necessary research into the hardware designs. I chose example hardware that I had previously encountered, to provide realistic approaches and information. For this reason, you will find that I focus on hardware from Hewlett-Packard, which I actually used to build clusters. This is a matter of practicality, and not a fixation on a particular vendor.

and the applications it will run. There are a number of system characteristics that should be considered when selecting the proper vendor and model for your cluster's compute slices:

- Total cost per individual system
- Number and type of CPUs
- CPU floating-point and integer performance characteristics
- Transaction processing capabilities
- Maximum supported RAM
- Error check/correct (ECC) memory
- 32-bit versus 64-bit memory addressing capabilities
- Memory to CPU bandwidth
- Memory to I/O bandwidth
- Internal disk subsystem performance
- Hot-plug disk support
- Number of available I/O slots
- Presence of serial port for console management
- Built-in system management capabilities (remote power on/off)
- Power and heat ratings
- Built-in LAN capabilities
- Operating system support for hardware and accessories
- Overall system design quality

These characteristics may be grouped into performance-related, capacity-related, quality-related, and management-related groups. Which sets are more important depends on your application performance expectations, budget, cluster availability, and reliability requirements for the whole cluster.

4.2   An Example Compute Slice from Hewlett-Packard

The example clusters shown in Figure 3–1 and Figure 3–2 are built with compute slices from Hewlett-Packard: the Proliant model DL-360g3 server. As of this writing, this system is available with dual Intel 2.4/2.8/3.06/3.2 GHz Pentium 4 Xeon processors (IA-32 or "instruction architecture-32," meaning 32 bits) with 1-MB level three cache, and up to eight gigabytes of system RAM in a 1 EIA unit (1U) package. (See `http://www.hp.com` for more information on this product family.)

Understanding the capabilities of the compute slices in your cluster includes taking a close look at the packaging and built-in connections. In the case of the DL-360, which is shown in Figure 4–1, there are two integrated 10/100/1000base-TX network connections, a serial port, either PS-2 or USB keyboard and mouse connections, and an integrated ATI Rage XL graphics controller with VGA graphics output. (VGA is a legacy output format that is supported by most Windows and Linux-compatible hardware platforms. It allows you to treat the graphics device as

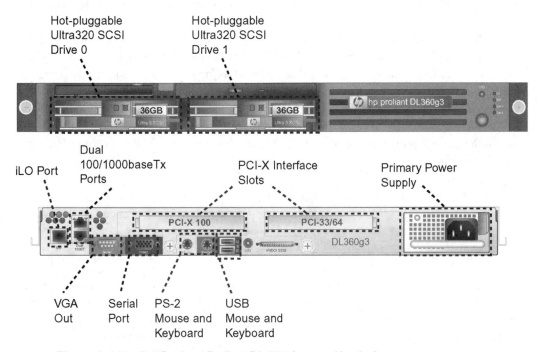

Figure 4–1 Hewlett-Packard Proliant DL-360 front and back view

an 8-column by 24-row character device with character attributes like color, underlining, inverse video, and so forth.) Two hot-plug disk bays are attached to an internal redundant array of independent disk (RAID) array controller (capable of RAID mode 0 or 1—striped or mirrored—operation) with a 64 MB cache. The disk bays may contain two 18/36/73/146-GB disk drives.

There are two PCI interface slots available: One is taken if the optional redundant power supply is installed. The interface slots are PCI-X compatible. One is backward compatible to older PCI standards, which enables 133-MHz 64-bit I/O with burst rates of more than one gigabyte per second. It is important to look at the system block diagram to see where bottlenecks might exist in the I/O path.

A very useful feature is the integrated lights-out (iLO) management port, which allows connecting the system to an out-of-band management network for monitoring and management. This enables a secure, text-based console and remote power on and off, along with BIOS upgrades with the associated software tool. Most hardware vendors have some models with integrated management capability, and the software to do basic operations may be free. You need to check on the availability of Linux management software and Linux agents to enable full functionality for your systems. In the case of Hewlett-Packard, the software package for the Proliant server family is called "Insight Manager." A basic feature that you should look for in any package is the ability to perform unattended BIOS upgrades via the management tool. This can save an immense amount of time, even if you have to use a proprietary software package.

The eight gigabytes of main memory is PC-2100 ECC 266-MHz double data rate (DDR) synchronous dynamic random access memory (SDRAM) and is 2:1 interleaved. Interleaving is a very important feature that can increase the bandwidth of memory access and relieve potential conflicts between multiple processors on the same memory bus In this case, the memory to the processor bus is called the *front-side bus* (FSB), and runs at 533 MHz. Most modern processors access memory in units of a cache line. The size of the cache line varies by processor type and system design. Memory accesses to sequential cache lines are spread across two independent memory channels.

T I P   Memory bandwidth is an important feature for performance, no matter what the number of processors in the compute slice or whether it is a technical or commercial cluster. Memory performance becomes increasingly important as the speed and number of CPUs, or the amount of floating-point computations, increases.

The single power supply is rated at 325 W. In evaluating the power utilization for a given system from *any* manufacturer, you need to be careful with the published specifications. The rating may be the absolute maximum for the power supply input, it could be a minimal configuration of RAM and disk, it could be for a fully loaded system, or it could just plain be wrong. It is very likely that you will get conflicting and inconsistent information. If possible, *measure* the actual power utilization of your final configuration under full load. (Strange as it may seem, a CPU that is performing intensive floating-point calculations may run hotter than one that is running the operating system's idle loop. I swear I am not kidding.)

This is not intended as an advertisement for this particular system, only an example of the kinds of specifications you are likely to wade through in choosing the proper compute slice for your cluster. This system is intended for use as a small to medium sized business server, so it has features that you may not need (the RAID controller, for example), which add to the complexity and cost. Remember that cheapest is not always best. It is a false sense of savings, for example, to buy the cheapest systems that frequently fail because they were not designed to withstand the extra heat of a racked configuration.

4.2.1   Analysis of the Example Compute Slice

Let's take a quick look at a schematic of the "guts" of a dual-processor Intel Pentium Xeon server. This is a fictitious design, based on architectural information on the Broadcom Server-Works GC-LE dual-processor server chip set and the Hewlett-Packard specifications for the Pro-liant Model DL-360. This is only an approximation as to what is really inside the system on the motherboard, so don't hold me to the details too closely. For the sake of this analysis, let's just assume that we started by looking at this system because we were familiar with the particular vendor.

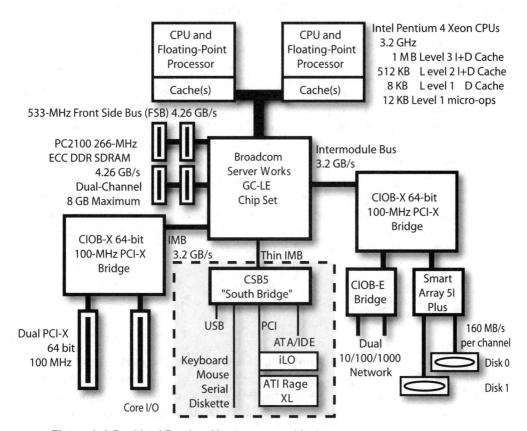

Figure 4–2 Dual Intel Pentium Xeon server architecture

Figure 4–2 details the major components and buses that tie them together. You should notice the similarity between this figure and the generalized SMP system architecture pictured in Figure 1–2. Looking at the internal design of a system in this way may be instructive. It can help gauge expected performance of the compute slice or explain observations about performance characteristics.

Whether you want raw floating-point performance for scientific computing, or high levels of integer performance and I/O for transaction processing, there are common, desirable design characteristics. I typically look at the design of the system components and interconnects, examining the following.

- Are there any obvious bottlenecks?
- What is the CPU-to-memory bandwidth?
- What is the disk-to-memory bandwidth?
- What is the I/O-to-memory bandwidth?

- What is the maximum memory capacity and controller configuration?
- How many I/O slots are available in the system?
- What is the network I/O capacity?

When examining this system, you can see that there is a lot of capability built into a 1U package. There are no obvious problems with the configuration (such as bottlenecks between the network and RAM). The next step is to begin characterizing the system's performance and compare it with alternatives. This is unfortunately easier to do for technical applications than for commercial processing.

One measure of system floating-point ability is the "theoretical peak" floating-point performance. This is simply calculated by multiplying the CPU instruction clock rate by the number of floating-point instructions that may be completed per cycle. It sets an upper bound on what is possible for the CPUs in the system and allows us to determine the efficiency of the system implementation. For our example, a dual 3.2-GHz Pentium Xeon compute slice, the calculation for theoretical peak floating-point operations per second (FLOPS) is

$$\text{Theoretical Peak GFLOPS} = 3.2\ \text{GHz} \times \frac{2\ \text{FLOPS}}{\text{Hz}} \times 2\ \text{CPUs} = 12.8\ \text{GFLOPS}$$

In reality, however, the system performance on benchmarks such as Linpack,[2] which is a measure of CPU-bound floating-point performance, is likely to yield somewhere around 8.53 GFLOPs. Why? The location of the potential bottleneck is left as an exercise for you, the reader, but a good guess is probably the memory subsystem.[3] In other types of benchmarks, such as Web serving or transaction processing, the likely bottlenecks are elsewhere in the system.

---

2.   The Linpack benchmark, developed by Jack Dongarra, currently at the University of Tennessee at Knoxville, is a solver that operates on an N by N matrix representing a dense system of linear equations. For vendor-specific benchmark values, see http://performance.netlib.org/performance/html/pds-browse.html. The top 500 computers in the world are rated using this set of benchmarks and a parallel variation, and may be viewed at http://www.top500.org.

3.   Paraphrasing one of the many laws attributed to Gene Amdahl, "There must be one megabyte per second on the system bus for every MIP (million instructions per second) of CPU power." Because a double-precision floating-point calculation moves 16 bytes between the floating-point processor and main memory, we can restate the law as, "For every megaFLOP, there must be one megabyte per second on the system bus."

A similar calculation for the Hewlett-Packard dual 1.5-GHz Itanium 2 processor system shown in Figure 4–3 is

$$\text{Theoretical Peak GFLOPs} = 1.5 \text{ GHz} \times \frac{4 \text{ FLOPs}}{\text{Hz}} \times 2 \text{ CPUs} = 12 \text{ GFLOPs}$$

The system in question, a Hewlett-Packard rx2600 (similar to the workstation version, the zx6000) examined in the next section, yields 11.42 GFLOPs peak in benchmarks. This is because the memory is multiple banks of interleaved dual in-line memory modules (DIMMs), with a bandwidth of 6.4 GB/s to each bank.

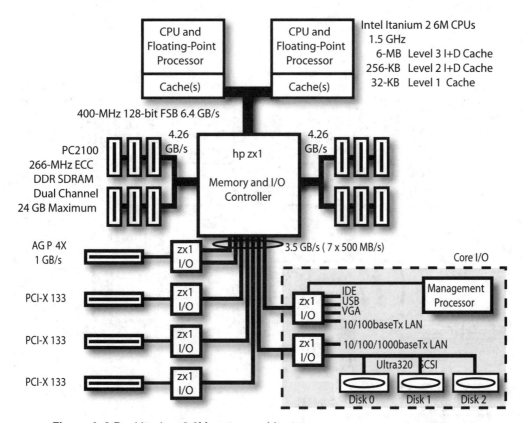

Figure 4–3 Dual Itanium 2 6M system architecture

The theoretical peak calculation for the dual-processor 2.0-GHz Opteron system is

$$\text{Theoretical Peak GFLOPs} = 2.0 \text{ GHz} \times \frac{2 \text{ FLOPs}}{\text{Hz}} \times 2 \text{ CPUs} = 8 \text{ GFLOPs}$$

This system is interesting because each CPU has its own integrated memory controller and local RAM. A system with RAM distributed in this manner has a penalty to be paid for accessing non-local RAM on another processor. Taking full advantage of this architecture would seem to require an operating system that is ccNUMA capable. The fact is, the details of memory location are hidden by the hardware of the memory controller. The question to consider is: Just what *is* the system memory bandwidth for a hardware configuration like the system shown in Figure 4–4?

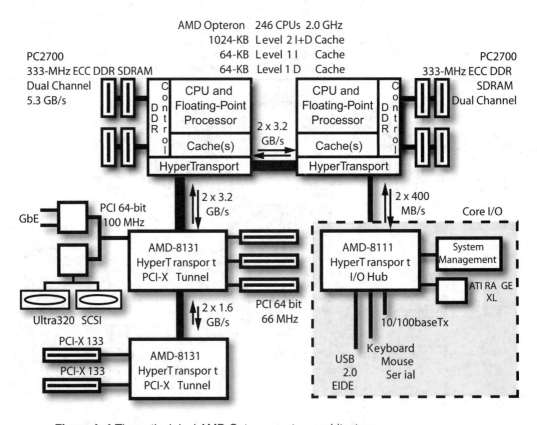

Figure 4–4 Theoretical dual AMD Opteron system architecture

The "it depends" answer applies to this situation. Note that bandwidth-to-local processor memory is 5.3 GB/s across two channels and to nonlocal processor memory is 6.4 GB/s. Looking closer, you can see that the 6.4 GB/s is actually divided between separate read and write channels between the processors. So, for a problem that fits into the local RAM, you can expect local bandwidth and latency, and for problems that span local and remote RAM, you can expect a mixture of local and remote performance characteristics. Indications are that the architecture scales well to at least four processors. (Because this configuration is so new, I could not find any four-processor systems using the Opteron processor. They are sure to appear two days after this book is published.)

As we have seen, looking at the system hardware diagrams *can* sometimes make a difference when it comes to understanding benchmark numbers. Note that the theoretical peak performances for the Itanium and Xeon systems are roughly equivalent, even though the Itanium system operates at less than half of the clock rate of the Xeon system. Clock rates alone are not a good performance comparison point. The other surprise is the memory configuration of the Opteron system.

4.2.2   Comparing the Example Compute Slice with Similar Systems

One way of comparing systems is to examine the performance characteristics that are important to your application. The major categories of performance are integer and floating point when looking at a particular CPU and system configuration. Some representative numbers for the systems we are examining are shown in Table 4–1. We need to make sure that the numbers we are examining are "apples-to-apples" comparisons, and that they have something to do with the real world.

Table 4–1 Price and Single CPU Performance for Three compute slices

System Type	Base Price[a]	Final Price	SPECint_2000[b]	SPECfp_2000
Hewlett-Packard rx2600 1.5-GHz Itanium 2 3M	$5,730	$22,990	1322	2119
Hewlett-Packard DL-360g3 3.2-GHz Pentium Xeon	$4,448	$7,546	1319	1197
IBM eServer 325 2.0-GHz AMD Opteron	$5,959	$8,746	1226	1231

a. Base and final prices are U.S. list prices from the respective manufacturer's Web site as of December 30, 2004.

b. All SPEC values are from the SPEC Web site as of December 30, 2004.

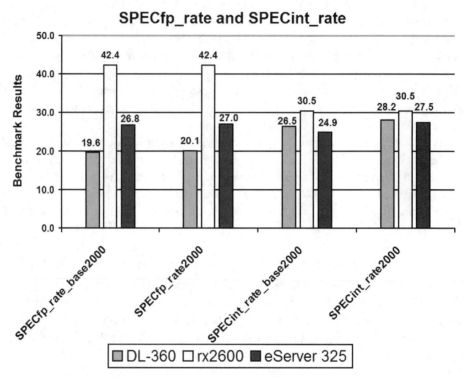

Figure 4–5 Performance for three dual-processor compute slices

A very important parameter in the choice of compute slices is total system cost. After all, you are building a cluster from multiple (tens to hundreds) of individual systems. Three individual systems were configured and priced: a 2U Hewlett-Packard dual 1.5-GHz Intel Itanium 2 6M, a 1U Hewlett-Packard dual 3.2-GHz Intel Pentium 4 Xeon, and a 1U IBM dual-2.0 GHz AMD Opteron 246 system. Each system was configured with dual 36-GB disks, 4 GB of RAM, two processors, and a RAID controller (if available). The relative performance in terms of floating-point and integer performance is shown in Figure 4–5.

The system list prices[4] are shown in Table 4–1, along with single-CPU performance numbers from the Standard Performance Evaluation Corporation (SPEC) CPU2000 benchmark.[5]

---

4.   All prices are list values from the associated company's Web site as of December 30, 2003. Actual prices may vary with time and other factors. Every effort was made to compare similar configurations.

5.   Competitive benchmark results stated in the comparison reflect results published on www.spec.org as of December 30, 2003. The comparisons presented are based on the best performing systems currently shipping by Hewlett-Packard and IBM. For the latest SPEC CPU2000 benchmark results, visit www.spec.org.

Table 4–2 Multiple CPU Performance for Three Compute Slices

System Type	SPECint_rate_2000	SPECfp_rate_2000
Hewlett-Packard rx2600 1.5-GHz Itanium 2 6M	30.5	42.4
Hewlett-Packard DL-360g3 3.2-GHz Pentium Xeon	28.2	14.0
IBM eServer 325 2.0-GHz AMD Opteron	27.0	27.5

The SPECint_2000 and SPECfp_2000 benchmarks are subcomponents of the SPEC CPU2000 benchmark.

The SPEC CPU2000 benchmark includes the CFP2000 and CINT2000 benchmarks, both of which contain single-CPU benchmarks (SPECint_2000 and SPECfp_2000) and multi-CPU benchmarks (SPECint_rate_2000 and SPECfp_rate_2000). The CINT2000 benchmark is a composite of 12 individual application benchmarks and the CFP2000 benchmark comprises 14. (Just to make things more interesting, there are also "base" benchmarks, such as SPECfp_base2000 and SPECfp_rate_base2000, that have stringent rules on compilation options and other environmental factors. Numbers are reviewed by the SPEC organization before they are published.) Multi-CPU versions of the benchmarks are presented in Table 4–2. Multi-CPU benchmarks run multiple copies of the individual applications and measure the relative system scaling.

We have the price and we may calculate price performance ratios for the three compute slices to compare the relative costs. This represents how much you pay for a given unit of performance, either integer or floating point. The calculation also works for transaction processing and Web operations, and some industry benchmarks specify their results in dollars per transaction per second.

So how did our three example systems compare? As you can see in Table 4–2, the Itanium 2-based system from Hewlett-Packard wins in terms of highest integer and floating-point performance overall, based on the SPECint_rate_2000 benchmark. The IBM eServer 325 Opteron 246-based system[6] outperforms the Hewlett-Packard Xeon-based system in terms of floating-point performance, but is almost identical in terms of integer performance. The integer performance of all three systems is pretty close, but there is a substantial difference in floating-point performance when the Opteron and Xeon are compared with the Itanium 2 system.

Figure 4–6 shows the price-to-performance ratios for the systems, based on list price and the SPECint_rate and SPECfp_rate benchmarks. Notice that the high cost of the Itanium system

---

6. Information on Opteron may be found at http://www.amd.com. Additional information from presentation titled "AMD Opteron: Performance Issues, Application Programmers [sic] View" [Rich and Cownie 2003]

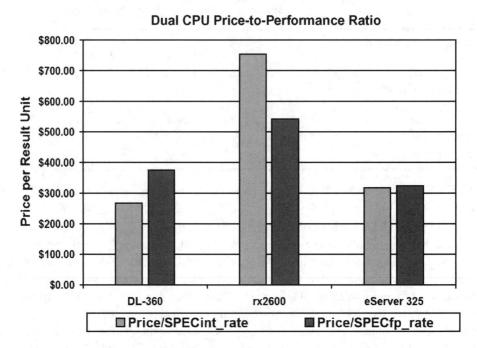

Figure 4–6 List price-to-performance ratio for three example compute slices

drives the cost per operation up for both floating-point and integer operations. There are some reasons for the extra cost in the Itanium system.

The EPIC processor is new and fundamentally different from the other reduced instruction set computing (RISC) systems, the system is 64-bit and 32-bit capable (as is the Opteron), and the maximum RAM capacity is 24 GB. The memory latency and bandwidth, along with the I/O capabilities make the system the fastest compute slice available when coupled with the Quadrics HSI. There are specific applications and situations when the Itanium systems are simply unparalleled (please excuse the pun). The price-to-performance ratio of the Intel Xeon system is lower than the AMD Opteron for integer performance, but is higher in terms of floating-point performance. The choice, based solely on performance or price-to-performance is not clear-cut.

4.2.3   Example Clusters Using Our Compute Slices

Up to this point, we have taken a look at single systems and their architecture and performance characteristics. But before we jump into a choice of compute slice for our cluster, we need to compare some other factors using *all* the compute slices. But just how many is that?

Let's say we have a requirement to provide one teraflop of floating-point performance in our cluster. How many compute slices would that be? Now we run into a little "issue" with benchmarks.

We have been comparing systems based on their SPEC performance characteristics, but the SPEC benchmarks don't map cleanly to teraflops. The Linpack benchmark, however, does map to teraflops, provided someone has run the benchmark for the particular processor and system you are evaluating. In our case, two of the systems did not have current Linpack numbers as of this writing.

Another factor to keep in mind is that benchmark and application scaling across the cluster is not perfect. The numbers in Table 4–3 are for single systems. To get one teraflop across the cluster, we would need to measure the actual performance and adjust the number of systems in the cluster. If 80% scaling across the cluster is good (80% scaling is darned good), then we would actually need 102 Itanium 2 systems, 144 Pentium Xeon systems, and 185 Opteron systems to meet our goal. This increases the size of the cluster to seven Itanium compute racks, five Pentium Xeon compute racks, and six Opteron compute racks.

To make the best choice for a given cluster, we would have to examine other factors like the status of 64-bit applications, total memory capacity in the system, the cooling "budget" for the cluster's location, vendor price discounts, and integer versus floating-point performance requirements for *real* applications.

Table 4–3 Calculations for a One-Teraflop Cluster

System Type	Theoretical Peak GFLOP	2 CPU Linpack NxN GFLOPs	Number of Systems for One TFLOP[a]	List Price	Racks[b]
Hewlett-Packard rx2600 1.5-GHz Itanium 2 6M	12.0	11.83	85	$20,346,150.00	6
Hewlett-Packard DL-360g3 3.2-GHz Pentium Xeon	13.6	8.38[c]	119	$897,974.00	4
IBM eServer 325 2.0-GHz AMD Opteron	8.0	6.50[d]	154	$1,346,884.00	4

a. Rounded up to nearest whole system.
b. Compute racks, using 32 EIA units per 41U rack.
c. Estimated from 3.06 GHz Linpack numbers.
d. Estimated from 81% of 8 GFLOPs.

4.3   Thirty-two Bit and 64-Bit Compute Slices

It is important not to get confused about the 32-bit versus 64-bit functionality when considering compute slices. Many modern 32-bit systems and their processors already incorporate features that can be considered 64-bit in nature: wide internal data buses, wide registers, and extra physical memory address lines. Many of these features have been in 32-bit hardware for years now. We need to pay close attention to what is being discussed when "32-bit" and "64-bit" are used as adjectives.

4.3.1   Physical RAM Addressing

If you go back to Figure 4–2, you will notice that the two, 32-bit Intel Pentium Xeon processors in the system are capable of addressing a total of eight gigabytes of physical RAM. For this system to be an SMP system, the processors need to share uniformly all eight gigabytes of physical system RAM (in other words, have a uniform addressing scheme). This requires at least 33 hardware address bits on the memory bus for both processors, because the maximum value of a 32-bit binary number is 4,294,967,295 (or 2^{32} minus 1) or four gigabytes.

Intel 32-bit processors incorporate physical address extension (PAE) features to allow the system hardware to address up to 64 GB of physical RAM. This means that there may be up to 36 bits in the physical RAM address used by the processors, if the extra lines are implemented by the hardware designers on the system's motherboard. This hardware feature allows a system's hardware to accommodate more that the four gigabytes of physical RAM that would be possible with 32 address bits.

So, to provide more than the four gigabyte physical RAM that is addressable by a 32-bit processor, the underlying processors and chip set must support a larger physical address with more than 32 address lines, *and* the hardware designers must take advantage of this by implementing the extra address lines. The operating system also must be able to manage the larger amount of physical RAM and properly parcel it out to 32-bit processes.

Even the two example compute slice systems that have 64-bit-capable processors (the Itanium 2 and the Opteron) do not fully implement the complete 64 possible hardware memory address lines, mainly for practical reasons of cost. The Opteron systems, for example, allow up to 40 bits of physical memory address (taking up space on the motherboard as circuit connections), which allows addressing up to one terabyte of physical RAM. This amount of RAM, even at today's prices would be very expensive, and would fit into any system enclosure only with great difficulty. (This would be 512 DIMMs at two gigabytes each. That's a lot of memory slots on the motherboard!)

The 64-bit processors can address up to 16,535 (2^{14}) petabytes (2^{50} bytes) if the full 64 bits were used for physical RAM addresses, but because of physical constraints, hardware designers usually implement only a subset of the possible address bits. Once the hardware can address all the physical RAM, it is up to the operating system's virtual memory system to provide a "virtual address space" to execute a process.

4.3.2   Process Virtual Address Space

It is the job of the operating system and its virtual memory subsystem to manage physical memory assigned to a given process. This is done by dividing physical memory into fixed-size "pages" that are allocated to processes when needed from a page pool in main memory. The operating system keeps track of which physical page is associated with a particular "virtual" page being used by a process and manages the system's page pool. Once this relationship is determined, the hardware keeps frequently used physical-to-virtual page translations in a set of registers called the *translation lookaside buffer* or TLB.

How large a program can get, in terms of code and data size, is determined by the maximum virtual address space available (32 or 64 bits) from the hardware and the operating system. The total number of *processes* that may run on the system simultaneously, without "bumping" another process' physical pages, is determined by the total size of physical RAM. Two processes running on a dual-processor system, each requiring four gigabytes of memory, will not interfere as long as the system has eight gigabytes of physical RAM or more (ignoring operating system memory requirements).

The IA-32 architecture uses four kilobyte (2^{12} bytes) physical pages. With four gigabytes of physical RAM, this yields a total of 1,048,576 pages (or 2^{20} pages). Notice that

$$2^{12} \times 2^{20} = 2^{(12+20)} = 2^{32} = 4\,\text{GB}$$

An address consisting of 32 bits may be divided into a page number (20 bits) and an offset into that page (12 bits). The IA-64 architecture supports multiple page sizes, but the Linux kernel may be compiled to use one of 4, 8, 16, or 64 kilobyte pages.

Not all pages in a given process' "virtual address space" need to be allocated or "mapped" to physical pages, but the total number of pages that a process can access in its virtual address space, fully mapped or not, differs between a 32-bit and a 64-bit process. A 32-bit process can address *at most* four gigabytes of virtual memory divided between instruction code and data. A 64-bit process may address multiple petabytes of virtual memory divided between code and data.

Figure 4–7 shows two situations: The first is a system with two four-gigabyte process address spaces sharing four gigabytes of physical RAM, and the second is the same two processes sharing 12 GB of physical RAM. In the first case, there are not enough physical pages available to satisfy the two processes completely, so virtual memory "paging" will occur. In the second case, the 12 GB of physical RAM completely fills the needs of both processes' address space, so some physical pages are left over. In both cases, the operating system pages mapped into the processes address space are shared through the magic of virtual memory.

If you are going to run multiple processes on your compute slices, then it is important to have enough physical RAM to allow the processes' to coexist without "fighting" for physical pages. If the operating system and the virtual memory system have to share physical pages

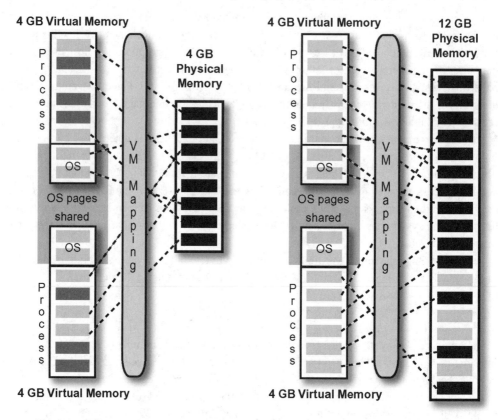

Figure 4–7 Processes sharing physical memory

between processes, virtual memory "paging" occurs. Performance suffers greatly when a system begins paging.

Before your eyes glaze over completely, let's discuss why all this is important in choosing a compute slice for your cluster. If you are processing chunks or pieces of data that will never grow beyond the four-gigabyte limit imposed by 32-bit process virtual addresses,[7] then you don't need 64-bit hardware, 64-bit operating systems, or 64-bit applications. If, however, you are going to be working with extremely large data sets (beyond four gigabytes) on a per-process basis, then you have no option but to use a 64-bit application, operating system, and hardware or to subdivide the problem into smaller pieces.

---

7.   Because the maximum number of bytes addressed with 32 bits is 4 GB, this is the absolute maximum available to a process, unless the operating system can "play games" with the virtual address space. What this means is that the space is shared between the three major sections in your application: code, data, and the stack. If the combination of code + data + stack is larger than 4 GB, you are out of virtual address space (and luck).

4.3.3   Software Implications of 64-Bit Hardware

The hardware compute slice and effects on the software applications you will run are not independent of each other. For example, both the Opteron and the Itanium processors in our example compute slices are designed to allow *both* 32- and 64-bit applications to coexist. Just because the hardware is capable of this behavior does not mean that it will be available in your chosen environment. The operating system must also provide facilities to support simultaneous 32- and 64-bit operation.

But why would you want to be able to run both "flavors" of applications on the same hardware? There are a number of answers, including legacy code, that cannot easily be ported to 64-bit operation. Making an application "64-bit clean" is not an easy task, particularly if the original programmers did not adhere to portability standards.

Several things happen in 64-bit code that do not occur "naturally" in 32-bit code.

- Code becomes larger because of "immediate" values.
- Data becomes larger, because data types like pointers become 64 bits instead of 32 bits.
- The operating system must provide both 32- and 64-bit versions of libraries and interfaces, and applications must be linked against the proper libraries.

If you have complete control of your application and the source code, then it becomes your job to port to any new environment. If you use third-party applications, you must check to ensure that the application is available for the type of environment (and compute slice) you are choosing.

In addition to the issues we have discussed so far, there is the additional consideration of the programming model chosen by the operating system. In the integer-long-pointer 32-bit (ILP-32) model, the data types integer, long, and pointer are represented by 32-bit values. There are two competing models in the 64-bit world: integer-long-pointer 64-bit (ILP-64) and long-pointer 64-bit (LP-64). In the first, integer, long, and pointer data types are all 64-bits in length. This can tend to break code that was originally written to the ILP-32 model, because the integer type changes size from 32 to 64 bits.

The LP-64 model represents long and pointer data types as 64 bits, and leaves integers at 32 bits. Although this model does not guarantee trouble-free 64-bit porting efforts, it minimizes the number of changes made to the original 32-bit programming assumptions. Which hardware and operating system you choose for your compute slice will determine whether you have this issue.

As of this writing, the IA-64 Linux maintainers have decided that it is not necessary to use the hardware's ability to run 32-bit Itanium applications at the same time as 64-bit applications. You will need to compile your code for 64 bits for it to perform on this hardware. The Itanium hardware allows execution of 32-bit IA-32 (Pentium III) code, and Linux provides this functionality only to a limited extent. A good deal of performance is given up in the process, and code compiled for later Intel processors may not run under this facility. This attitude may change in the future; we will see. We do not discuss the software issues further here.

4.4 Memory Bandwidth

Commodity systems are based on widely available chip sets and other standardized parts, and RAM is no exception. There are a wide range of manufacturers and sources of system RAM, but the type and speed of the RAM will dictate its performance to a large extent. In addition to a plethora of types and speeds, there are different packages: dual in-line memory modules (DIMMs), single in-line memory modules (SIMMs), ad infinitum. We won't go any deeper into memory terminology, because we need to stay awake and focused.

For purposes of discussion, the types of RAM we have been encountering in our example compute slices is ECC DDR SDRAM.

The ECC designation means that the RAM has extra bits available that are used to detect and correct single-bit errors, and to detect multiple-bit errors in the RAM. This is an essential feature of RAM that is to be used in production systems. We would not want a stray bit error to cause improper results in the cluster's calculations. The message is: Don't buy systems without ECC RAM. Most of the example compute slices have RAM buses that are 128 bits wide for data outside the RAM controller, but have a total of 144 bits between the DIMMs and the controller. The extra 16 bits are being used for ECC check bits by the controller.

The SDRAM uses a clock (the S stands for synchronous, meaning in time with a clock signal) to determine valid times to read data from and write data to the storage devices in the RAM chips. DDR indicates that data may be moved at two times the clock frequency, as opposed to "single data rate" RAM.

To understand the designators for the RAM we are using in our compute slices, examine the following calculations and then look at Table 4–4:

$$PC1600 \ = \ 200 \, \text{MHz} \times \frac{8 \, \text{Bytes}}{\text{Hz}} \ = \ \frac{1600 \, \text{MB}}{\text{Second}}$$

Notice that the data rate, 1600 MB/s, matches the numeric part of the "PC1600" designator. But this is *double* data rate RAM, so the calculation is really

$$PC1600 \ = \ 200 \, \text{MHz} \times \frac{16 \, \text{Bytes}}{\text{Hz}} \ = \ \frac{3200 \, \text{MB}}{\text{Second}} \ = \ 3.2 \, \text{GB/s}$$

See Table 4–4 for more calculations—and you thought this was mysterious, right? So did I, until I started researching this book. Well, before we get overconfident, notice the rounding that takes place with PC2100 and PC2700 RAM. Oh, well, it was the thought that counts.

Table 4–4 Dual-Channel DDR SDRAM Peak Performance

RAM Designator	Clock Rate	Data Width[a]	Data Rate	Peak Bandwidth
PC100	100 MHz	64 bits	SDR	800 MB/s
PC133	133 MHz	64 bits	SDR	1.1 GB/s
PC1600	200 MHz	128 bits	DDR	3.2 GB/s
PC2100	266 MHz	128 bits	DDR	4.2 GB/s
PC2700	333 MHz	128 bits	DDR	5.3 GB/s

a.   The data width used here does not include ECC bits.

4.5   Memory and Cache Latency

Memory latency is another factor we need to look at if we are going to be performing lots of memory-intensive computations with our compute slices. An extra nanosecond here and there for each memory access tends to add up when you are performing billions of calculations a second over long periods of time. Although memory latency may be less critical for commercial computing, it is still important for the overall performance of the system.

Everything, of course, starts with main memory. Information like that covered in the last section can help understand the overall memory architecture and the bandwidth available to supply the processor caches. Some example main memory latencies are supplied in Table 4–5 and some specific values for the Itanium 2 processor (1.5 GHz) are shown in Table 4–6.

If your application is sensitive to memory latency, you will need to investigate the characteristics of the candidate hardware. A good place to start is by finding diagrams or descriptions of the processor caches and system chip set characteristics. It turns out that today's processor memory architecture is a hierarchy, potentially with many levels of caches. A diagram of this hierarchy for the processors in our example compute slices is shown in Figure 4–8.

Table 4–5 Main Memory Latency Examples

System Type	Main Memory Latency
Two-processor 1.5-GHz Itanium 2 6M (HP zx1)	110 ns
Two-processor 3.2-GHz Pentium Xeon	243 ns
Two-processor 2.0-GHz Opteron 246 (1 "hop")	89 ns
Two-processor 2.0-GHz Opteron 246 (2 "hops")	115 ns

Table 4–6 Itanium 2 1.5 GHz Cache Latencies[a]

Description	Latency in Cycles	Latency in Nanoseconds[b]
Level 1 Instruction and data cache	1 cycle	0.67
Level 2 Integer	5 cycles	3.33
Level 2 Floating point	6 cycles	4.00
Level 3 Integer	12 cycles	8.00
Level 3 Floating point	13 cycles	8.67

a.   These are estimates only. There are exceptions and special cases not shown.

b.   At 1.5 GHz, a single cycle is 0.67 nanoseconds.

As you can see from Figure 4–8, there are several cache levels involved, and each architecture has a different approach to keeping the processor "fed" with instructions and data. Keeping

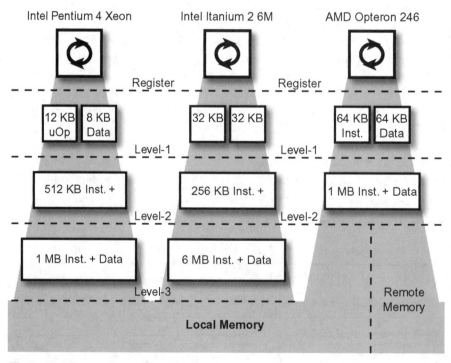

Figure 4–8 Processor memory hierarchies

the processor supplied with instructions and data is important. "Processor stalls," or pauses in processing, occur when the processor must wait for items to be fetched from main memory. Notice that the Opteron processor must deal with both processor local and "remote" memory, which means that there are two "main" memory latencies involved. This detail is "hidden" from the caches and the processor by the memory controller.

Each level of the memory hierarchy has its own penalty for a cache "miss," which occurs when the needed item is not present. The miss information is usually specified in terms of cycles, so you need to know the specific frequency at which the particular cache is running. Because this changes with every generation and tweak of the processor, it can be difficult to find current information. Caveat inquisitor.

4.6 Number of Processors in a Compute Slice

A common number of processors found in a compute slice for scientific and engineering clusters is two. This may be due in part to packaging issues for high-performance processors (it is hard to fit four or more processors and RAM into a 1U or 2U package within a heat budget), but most likely is a result of the demand placed on the system bus by scientific computation. More than two processors on today's commodity buses tend to run out of memory bandwidth for scientific applications.

TIP   If you find a commodity SMP system with more than two CPUs that provides the proper scaling for your application, take a closer look at it. More CPUs per package reduces the number of compute slices to manage, and may also reduce the power and heat requirements for your cluster.

A cluster for Web serving or database serving may benefit by using compute slices that have more CPUs and a larger physical RAM capacity. There are newer architectures, like Opteron, that show promise of good scaling beyond two processors per system. In addition to the ability to add more physical RAM, larger packages also tend to allow more I/O connections to peripheral devices.

4.7 I/O Interface Capacity and Performance

Data I/O to peripherals is an important performance criterion for your cluster's compute slices. If your compute slices have local scratch disks, or if you are using an HSI, the I/O capabilities and performance will be important to the overall performance of the cluster. The ability to move data efficiently to and from device interface cards and main memory involves the direct memory access (DMA) controller, PCI bus controller, and the PCI interface card itself.

Care must be taken to select a compute slice that is capable of sustaining the necessary I/O rates for the type of work your cluster performs. The most common interfaces in commodity computer systems are built around the PCI standard. Along with the I/O rates, the number and type of the PCI interface slots must be sufficient to allow adding interface cards for the HSI and other required peripherals.

We must be wary of relying on the I/O performance of "core I/O" devices, because these devices tend to be low-cost PCI interfaces that are integrated on the system's motherboard. Although integrated devices may save on PCI slots, an analysis of the compute slice's core I/O architecture may be necessary to avoid encountering bottlenecks. In some cases, it may be better to add an interface card, if there are available slots, rather than use the built-in functionality.

4.7.1   PCI Implementation

We can think of the PCI bus as being implemented by an I/O convertor or bridge with a 64-bit input bus running at 66.6 MHz. At this speed, the maximum throughput to the bridge is 532 MB per second. Underneath the bridge (no, we aren't looking for trolls) there may be individual buses running 32 bits at 66.6 MHz or 64 bits at 33.3 MHz. The throughput on these buses is 266 MB per second.

The peripheral component interconnect express (PCI-X) allows for a 64-bit main bus running at 133.33 MHz, yielding a throughput of 1.06 GB per second. Subbuses are specified at 66.66 megahertz. A PCI-X interface card is backward compatible with PCI, but the data rate will drop to the 33.33 MHz value associated with the PCI 64-bit bus. PCI bus data rates are shown in Table 4–7.

In addition to the PCI interface bus type, there are two *sizes* of PCI interface cards defined: full-size and short (sometimes called *half size*). You should make sure which types of slots are available in your compute slice hardware before making assumptions about interface cards. Sometimes one or more of the available PCI slots are half size, and this can really cramp your I/O style.

For examples of PCI bus implementations and speeds, see the example systems in Figure 4–2 through Figure 4–4. All three of these systems have PCI-X interface slots and use PCI for internal core I/O devices.

Table 4–7 PCI and PCI-X Data Rates

Bus Type	Data Size, bits	Clock Rate, MHz	Data Rate, MB/s
PCI main	64	66.66	532
PCI	32/64	66.66/33.33	266
PCI-X main	64	133.33	1066
PCI-X	64	66.66	266

Table 4–8 Accelerated Graphics Port Data Rates

AGP Interface Type	Clock Rate, MHz	Data Rate, MB/s
AGP 1x	66.66	266.6
AGP 2x	133.33	533.3
AGP 4x	266.67	1066.6
AGP 8x	533.33	2133.3

4.7.2   Accelerated Graphics Port

If your cluster is doing graphics rendering, then you may wish to investigate compute slices with an accelerated graphics port (AGP) slot. An AGP bus provides 32-bit data at various clock rates. AGP was originally intended to provide higher throughput than that of the first implementation of the PCI bus, to support high-performance two- and three-dimensional graphics interface cards.

The AGP 1.0 standard was introduced in 1996, and it provided for both AGP 1x (264 MB per second) and AGP 2x (528 MB per second). The AGP 2.0 standard provides AGP 4x (one gigabyte per second), and the more recent AGP 3.0 specification allows AGP 8x at two gigabytes per second. The "speeds and feeds" for AGP are listed in Table 4–8.

4.8   Compute Slice Operating System Support

Because this is a book about building Linux clusters, any hardware we discuss must be capable of running the Linux operating system. Intel processors, including Itanium, all run versions of Linux, as does the Opteron processor family. Don't automatically assume, however, that a particular distribution or version of a distribution supports your choice of compute slice hardware.

4.9   Master Node Characteristics

The master nodes in a cluster are the access points for users. As such, the master nodes must be multiuser systems, with enough resources to support the expected number of simultaneous cluster users. In addition to the multiuser aspects of the master nodes, it is likely that the master node needs to be highly available to allow users uninterrupted access to the cluster resources. The loss of an unprotected master node will make the cluster unavailable until it is repaired or replaced.

Because it is a highly available, multiuser system, the master node will most likely be a different system model from the compute slices in your cluster. It will need more RAM, potentially more CPUs, and also more I/O slots to support redundant peripheral connections. How much you need to scale up the resources in the master nodes will depend on the number of simultaneous users expected and the activities that are allowed.

Another point worth mentioning is in regard to using a master node as a file server for the cluster. The tendency is to allow users to store data and software local to the cluster, to avoid the necessity of copying information to and from the local storage and external file servers. Because of this, and cost constraints, the temptation is merely to attach the cluster's storage to the master nodes and export it, via NFS, to the remainder of the compute slices in the cluster.

The performance of an NFS server, much like a disk array, is dependent on its ability to cache frequently used data in the system page cache to prevent physical I/O to the disk. By sharing memory and CPU resources between NFS and the users on the master node, the NFS performance to the whole cluster will be severely reduced. Although we will look at file system issues later in this book, it is best to keep a separate set of master and file server nodes in mind when choosing the hardware.

T I P   Do not *ever* seriously consider using the master nodes in your cluster as NFS file servers. This is bad, bad, bad. The quickest way to impact the performance of the *whole* cluster is to "save money" by combining the master node and the NFS server.

Figure 4–9 depicts a possible hardware choice for a master node in our example cluster. This particular system is a Hewlett-Packard DL-580, which incorporates up to four 2.8-GHz Xeon processors, 32 GB of RAM, dual hot-plug power supplies, redundant fans, and six PCI-X slots. Interesting hardware features of this system include on-line spare memory and the possibility to mirror memory (in other words, 16 GB replicating another 16 GB).

This hardware configuration is possibly overkill for smaller clusters. In large clusters that require high availability on the master nodes, the PCI slots become a limiting factor in providing the necessary redundant connections. Support for additional processors and memory to accommodate multiple users is another important feature.

T I P   Choosing a different processor type for a cluster's master node versus the compute slices can lead to issues. If software development is done on the master nodes, remember that many compilers default to compiling and optimizing *for the type of system on which they are currently executing.*

Although more expensive than a compute slice by a factor of ten, this system provides enough PCI connections to allow redundant network connections to the external network (two dual-GbE interface cards), and redundant connections to the internal management and data networks. It would also be possible to add a storage area network (SAN) connection for management purposes.

4.10 Compute Slice and Master Node Summary

What type of hardware you select for your cluster compute slices and master nodes will depend to a certain extent on what type of cluster you are building. CPU, memory, and I/O capabilities,

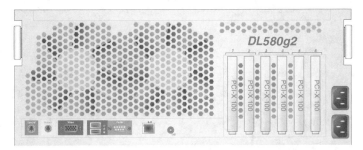

Figure 4–9 An example master node from Hewlett-Packard

and I/O performance are important to all types of clusters. Understanding the design strengths and weaknesses of a particular system's hardware can help avoid surprises and disappointment.

T I P   I need to make one very important point about cluster hardware: If you don't need something, leave it out of the systems you select. Extra hardware in the form of RAID controllers, graphics cards, dual power supplies, disks, and other unused hardware consume power and generate heat. For a single system, the additional usage may be negligible, but when you multiply the effects over tens, hundreds, or thousands of systems, it becomes a substantial liability. Extra hardware also conspires to lower the reliability of your cluster. When in doubt, leave it out.

System specification alone cannot guarantee that a particular hardware choice will be the correct one, but the more you understand about your application and its requirements, the better. Whenever possible, you should learn from the experience of other cluster users, and run your own benchmarks if possible. The information in this chapter can help you understand some of the issues involved in selecting the proper compute slice and master node hardware for your cluster.

CHAPTER 5

Packet In: Cluster Networking Basics and Example Devices

Chapter Objectives

- Discuss basic Ethernet network technologies and topologies
- Introduce the Ethernet hardware components in a cluster
- Cover the design of Ethernet networks in a cluster

A ctive elements in a cluster are tied together by communication networks that allow the sharing of data and control information. A cluster may have one or more networks, each with their own characteristics. A given cluster may have management and control, data, SANs, and the HSI. This chapter covers the information needed to begin the Ethernet network design discussion in the next chapter.

5.1   A Short View of Ethernet Networking History

Today's low-cost network switching components provide us with a lot of design choices for connecting cluster components. Ethernet is one of the primary network types used for management, data, and inexpensive high-speed connections between compute slices, file servers, administrative nodes, and master nodes. The commodity status of Ethernet networking equipment makes it a prime candidate for low-cost, high-performance networks, and hard to ignore unless there are other criteria being considered.

From a humble beginning in teletypes, acoustic modems, proprietary RS-232, RS-422, and other serial physical links running synchronous data link control (SDLC) and high-level data link control (HDLC) protocols, networking technology has settled on Ethernet as one of the primary interconnect standards. Gone are the proprietary serial point-to-point links that had more to do with interfacing to RS-232 terminals, papertape readers, and card punches than connecting peer-to-peer systems. (Ah, the days of Heathkit terminal kits, extra charges for read-only memories [ROMs] containing the upper-case character set, and point-to-point terminal cables running at a whopping 1200 Baud [with the wind at their backs].) Except in a very limited and aging technical population, they shan't be remembered.

Ethernet is a LAN technology based on a contention protocol called carrier detect multiple access with collision detect (CDMA/CD). The original protocol was developed for Aloha Net in the 1970s, which used a packet radio-based networking link to communicate between mainframe computers at the University of Hawaii, over the "ether."

Ethernet was developed by DEC, Intel, and Xerox in 1976. The original network was a bus or star topology that supported one megabit per second. Connections to the cable were made with "vampire" taps that pierced the coaxial cable's insulating jacket with pointed contacts that even looked like "fangs." The ten megabit-per-second version of Ethernet technology became an Institute of Electrical and Electronics Engineers (IEEE) standard, designated 802.3, in 1983.

Current Ethernet standards support 1-Mb, 10-Mb, 100-Mb, and 1000-Mb (GbE) per-second data rates full or half duplex over both fiber optic cable and copper shielded twisted-pair physical connections. At the time of this writing 10 GbE is available and becoming a standard.

One may take the view that today's networking technology inhabits a twilight zone between software and hardware. It is hard to distinguish where the software influence stops and hardware takes over. Once a packet is created by a software protocol stack and is given to the network interface, the intervening hardware delivers it to the destination interface as if by magic.

Just to complicate things, complete Transmission Control Protocol/Internet Protocol (TCP/IP) software "stacks" are now available implemented in hardware. The addition of protocols like remote direct memory access (RDMA), which allows low-latency movement of data between individual systems, also blur the line. Because it is hard to draw a direct line between hardware and software in the networking world, we cover a mixture of both in this chapter.

5.2   The Open System Interconnect (OSI) Communication Model

The hardware and software composing one side of a network link may be viewed as a series of layers. The most common model is the open system interconnect (OSI) model, originated in the early 1980s, which comprises seven levels. This model is shown in Figure 5–1 along with the associated TCP/IP layers.

The models are useful in helping us to discuss *where* particular actions are taken in the sequence of sending frames, network packets, or datagrams from one system to another. The OSI model includes both hardware and software aspects of the communications interface in its layers. Most of our discussion about networking equipment will be associated with levels 1, 2, and 3.

5.3   Ethernet Network Topologies

The original Ethernet network was a single segment of cable, and true to the nature of a bus, only one station could be transmitting data at a time. To send a frame (OSI level 2) across the

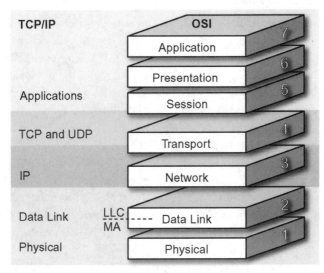

Figure 5–1 The seven-level OSI communication model

network medium (OSI level 1), a station began to broadcast the frame, then checked to see whether there was a collision with another station. If a collision was detected, then stations would *both* "back off" for a random period of time and then try again.

It is not hard to see the packet radio origins of the original Ethernet technology and CDMA/CD protocol. The more systems on the bus, and the busier those systems become, the less likely that a particular station's data will make it through to its destination. The term *broadcast storm*, describing the complete overload caused by too many networked systems trying to send data at once, soon appeared in the networking dictionary.

New interconnection devices appeared as the limitations of a single physical cable became obvious, which allowed extending the number of physical connections and the area of coverage. The active and passive hubs were developments that extended the reach and scope of the LAN. As Ethernet transmission became possible over twisted, shielded-pair cables, the scope and breadth of the network grew.

Early networking devices performed their duties at OSI level 1, the physical layer. They merely replicated the properly conditioned electrical signals to multiple attached physical media. You should note that stations (or interfaces) attached to the Ethernet segment or LAN receive all the frames being sent across the it. The frame is discarded by all stations that do not match the destination address for the frame. This is the default behavior, although it is possible to put an Ethernet interface into "promiscuous" mode, which captures all frames from the segment to which it is attached.

5.3.1   Ethernet Frames

Ethernet frames in a LAN are addressed between media access control (MAC) addresses that are unique for every Ethernet interface on the LAN (or had darned well better be unique to avoid nasty problems). IEEE 802 networks further divide the OSI "link level" into two sublevels: link level control (LLC) and MAC. The LLC sublayer sits on top of the physical layer and handles frame detection, flow control, and error checking. The MAC sublayer sits below the LLC sublayer and controls access to the network medium and the interface's ability to transmit data.

An Ethernet MAC address is 48 bits wide, and usually is specified in hexidecimal digits, such as `0x00010203EB9B` (the `0x` prefix specifies a hexidecimal number), or in pairs of hexidecimal digits, like `00:01:02:03:EB:9B`. The first 24 bits of the MAC address are unique to a manufacturer, being the IEEE organizationally unique identifier (OUI) assigned to that organization. There may be more than one OUI associated with a given manufacturer as a result of the mergers, acquisitions, and running out of space in the remaining 24 bits. The Ethernet interface's MAC address is only valid and "visible" on the LAN segment to which it is directly attached.

An Ethernet frame propagating across a physical LAN segment is shown in Figure 5–2. When viewed at OSI level 1, the frame is a set of signals propagating across the media (ether, copper cable, fiber-optic cable, and so on). At OSI level 2, the frame contains start and stop information that "frames" the actual data, a header that contains source and destination MAC addresses, a data "payload," and a checksum for error detection. The maximum data payload, also called the *maximum transmission unit* (MTU), is normally 1500 bytes for Ethernet. A nonstandard MTU size is implemented by some networking equipment vendors. Called *jumbo frames*, it allows data payloads of up to nine kilobytes per frame.

Ethernet frames are capable of containing or "encapsulating" data packets (datagrams) from other protocols like TCP/IP. Once a frame is received from the Ethernet network, the computer's operating system "network stack" will remove the Ethernet-specific information. The operating system kernel then examines the content of the data from the frame and determines the proper *software* destination for the information.

Some of today's modern Ethernet interface cards allow the interface's MAC address to be changed or programmed by the operating system software or driver. This feature allows one interface to take the place of another at the network link level (OSI level 2). This ability is used by high-availability software that allows one server system to assume transparently (to client systems) the identity of another.

5.3.2   Ethernet Hubs

Hubs allowed extending the number of LAN connections and the area covered by the network, but also extended the "collision domain" to the connected segments. A passive hub merely broadcasts Ethernet frames received to all attached ports. An active hub performs signal amplification before broadcasting the frames. Hubs perform the signal regeneration and broadcasting at the physical level of the network.

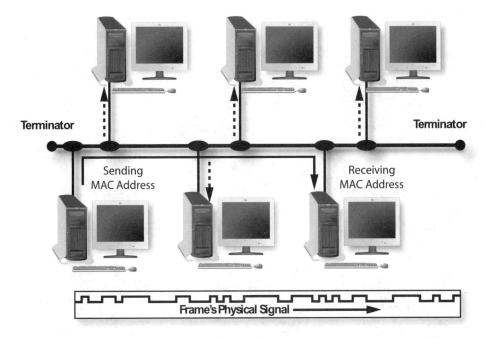

Figure 5–2 Single-cable Ethernet LAN segment

In some literature, passive hubs and active hubs may also be called *concentrators* or *repeaters* respectively. As the number of ports available on hubs increased, the ability to control the port parameters and to monitor behavior of the network and the hub itself became more important. A hub transmits a frame on all connected LAN segments, as shown in Figure 5–3.

Ethernet hubs are still available and are low cost, but they are not suitable for high-performance cluster networks because of their collision domain characteristics. The next technological breakthrough was the network "router."

5.3.3   Network Routers

Hubs allowed expanding the number of shared *segments* in a single physical LAN, but they also extended the LAN's collision domain. As the number of network segments and attached systems in a LAN grows, the collisions take their toll. Systems spend more and more time *trying* to communicate than *actually* communicating. Because sharing data is the primary reason that networks exist, a solution was needed.

The network router appeared in the late 1980s. It extended the rudimentary filtering abilities of hubs and provided the ability to isolate traffic and separate LAN segments from each other. Isolating LAN segments effectively reduced the size of the collision domains, reducing the number of systems per physical segment.

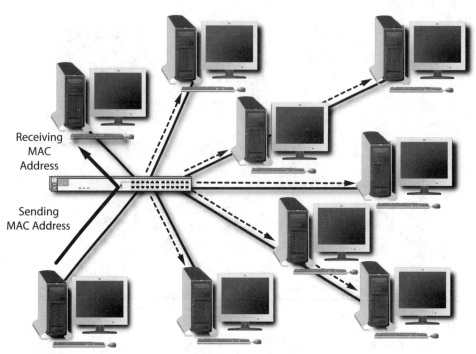

Receiving
MAC
Address

Sending
MAC Address

Figure 5–3 Ethernet hub and attached LAN segments

Routers also provided (and still provide) additional protocol and media interface capabilities beyond just Ethernet. Thus, connections to different network media types are possible with routers, and this can enable LAN data to be sent over longer distances—the *wide area network* (WAN). Routers are still commonly found at the "edge" of a network, where either protocol or physical medium translation, or both, is needed.

Figure 5–4 shows multiple LAN collision domains isolated by a router. The router in the diagram also provides a connection to the WAN along with a path between collision domains or separate LAN segments belonging to the same LAN. This was the first point in the evolution of LAN topology where a LAN could span multiple isolated segments separated by an arbitrary distance.

A router works its magic at OSI level 3 or higher. Notice that this level is above level 2 in the OSI model. If this is the case, we have a slight issue when talking about communicating between physical Ethernet segments. How does an Ethernet interface with one MAC address, on an electrically and physically isolated segment, communicate with an interface and MAC address on another?

The answer is that it can't and it doesn't—directly. The communication takes place at a higher level in the OSI model, facilitated by the router, using a protocol and *datagram*, or "packet" format defined for just that purpose. The Ethernet frame's information is encapsulated

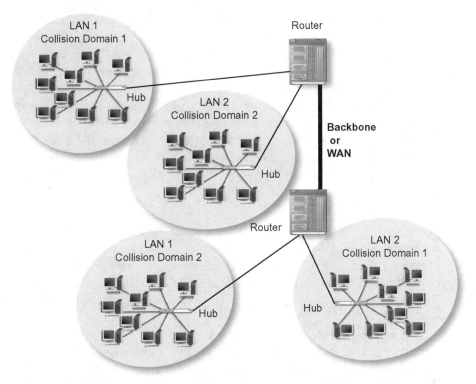

Figure 5–4 LAN collision domains connected by a router

in a datagram sent or "routed" to the proper destination across the network "backbone" or WAN to its final destination, where it is placed into an Ethernet frame to continue its journey. The Ethernet communication no longer relies on a direct, electrical connection to a LAN segment to be properly delivered.

A router also implements packet filtering. It does this by inspecting the contents of the datagrams it receives from the attached networks. The need to start looking into the payload of the datagrams increases the overhead on a per-datagram basis and can slow transmission even when this behavior is implemented in hardware. In other words, there usually is both a dollar cost and performance price to be paid for the generality of a router.

Up to this point we have avoided details of the protocol that is used to transport data between networks and physically separated segments. To continue our discussion, however, we must cover some of the basics of this "internetwork" protocol.

5.4   Internet Protocol and Addressing

As you will recall, the MAC addresses used to send and receive Ethernet frames are only meaningful and "visible" on the physical LAN segment to which the interface is connected.

Referring to Figure 5–4, notice that for a system in LAN 1 to communicate with a system in LAN 2, there must be a protocol to bridge the addressing between the MAC addresses on separate LANs.

Also, remember that we separated the LAN collision domains with "smart" hubs, and then routers, to cut down on the intersystem "chatter" or broadcast storms caused by normal Ethernet behavior. However, this does not mean that we want to filter all packets traveling between the LANs or collision domains. We need a way for useful packets to travel between networks—a method that augments the MAC addressing used in the LAN.

The TCP/IP is the most widely used protocol that allows addressing and routing packets, or datagrams, between networks. There are several good books on the TCP/IP protocol, so I cover only the fundamentals here.

5.4.1   IP and TCP/UDP

The IP specification defines a datagram or "packet" format, an address format, and rules for routing packets between IP addresses on separate networks. Looking back at Figure 5–1, you can now see the correlation between levels in the OSI model, and the model used for TCP/IP. The IP corresponds to the network layer (level 3) of the OSI model. The two other protocols shown, TCP and user datagram protocol (UDP), correspond to the transport layer (level 4) of the OSI model.

The TCP specification defines a connection-oriented method of exchanging packets, with provisions for flow control, error recovery, and out-of-order packet arrival. These features are most useful for unreliable connections, connections that may route data across multiple pathways, or connections that have low bandwidth and long delays—the WAN or Internet.

The UDP protocol specification defines a mechanism that is not connection oriented and has no flow control, error recovery, or provisions for out-of-order arrival. UDP does have a packet-level checksum available to detect packet corruption. UDP is most suitable for reliable LAN traffic, low-overhead communications, or as a low-level transport for services that are willing to implement their own error detection and recovery mechanisms. It does not have the extra "overhead" associated with TCP, but neither is it a reliable transport.

5.4.2   IP Addressing

A TCP/IP address is 32 bits, which is usually specified as four eight-bit decimal numbers (or "octets") between dots. An example of this IP address notation is 192.168.0.103,[1] which may be called a *dotted quad* or *dotted octet* notation. Originally, a TCP/IP address was envi-

---

1.   Please notice the absence of any leading zeros in these decimal numbers. On a UNIX or Linux system, any number that starts with a zero is interpreted as an octal number. Thus if a misinformed system administrator enters 015.026.102.34 as an address, it will most likely be interpreted as 13.22.102.34, which is not the intent.

sioned as belonging to one of three "classes"—A, B, or C. This was to make it easy to determine the network address portion from the system address portion for routing purposes.

A class A address had one byte of network address content and three bytes of system address content. The high-order bit in a class A address is set to 0, allowing a range for the first octet from 0 to 126 (the 127 network is reserved). This allows 127 networks of 16,777,214 host addresses. (The host address that is all zeroes is the network address, and the host address with all ones is the broadcast address. This subtracts two from the total number of available hosts.)

A class B network had two bytes of network address and two bytes of system address. To identify a class B address, the two most significant bits in the first byte were set to 10, yielding first octet values from 128 to 191. Two bytes of network address, ranging from 128.0 to 191.255 allows 16,385 networks of 65,534 hosts.

A class C address had three bytes of network address and one byte of system address. The first three bits in the highest byte were set to 110, which meant the first octet values ranged from 192.0.0 to 223.255.254. This arrangement produced networks of 254 hosts.

If you look at these conventions, you will see that the binary prefix (the first binary bits of the first byte) for class A addresses is 0, for class B addresses is 01, and for class C addresses is 011. Are there more classes? The answer to this question is yes: Class D addresses, those with a prefix of 1110 are used for multicast addresses, and class E addresses, with a prefix of 1111, are reserved for future use. We will not explore any further classes, but we will revisit the term *multicast* later. The three network classes and their address ranges are shown in Figure 5–5.

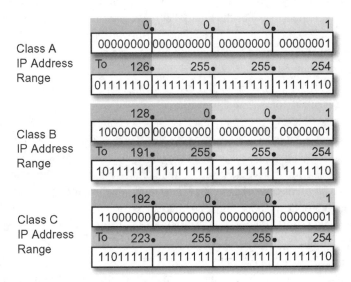

Figure 5–5 IP network classes and address ranges

This class-based division of IP addresses worked well enough in the early days of the Internet, but the allocation scheme eventually started to show strain with the growing number of connections. For example, the practical number of systems that could be attached to a physical Ethernet segment is certainly less than 1024, but a class B network allowed more than 65,000 system addresses. It was, therefore, difficult to use all the system addresses in an assigned class-B network efficiently. The network address space became fragmented with used and unused addresses, reducing the actual number of available addresses. (The network address space is the range of all possible network and host addresses contained in the allowed 32 bits. Without the reserved addresses, this would total 2^{32} or 4,294,967,296 addresses.)

5.4.3   IP Subnetting

To solve this issue, IP "subnetting" was introduced in 1984. Subnetting allowed specifying a "subnet mask" that divides a class A, B, or C network into smaller pieces by masking the address into two pieces that are not constrained by the byte boundaries of the original class-based addressing scheme. The bits in the left-hand portion of the subnet mask are set to 1 to specify the corresponding network portion of the IP address, and the remaining 0 bits specify the host portion of the address.

To find the network portion, perform the logical "AND" of the binary value for the address and the binary value of the net mask. To find the host portion of the address, you first perform the one's complement of the binary net mask, exchanging zeros for ones and ones for zeroes, and then perform the logical "AND" of the net mask and the IP address. To find the broadcast address, perform the logical "OR" of the binary net mask and the binary IP address.

These calculated values are not always straightforward and intuitive, so be careful. You can think of the subnet mask as being "implied" by the byte positions in the earlier class A, B, and C address class schemes. If you need a refresher on binary arithmetic, there are a number of good references on the Internet, such as `http://www.learntosubnet.com`. A very useful network address calculator is available at `http://www.telusplanet.net/public/sparkman/netcalc.htm`.

As an example, let's take a class A network: `15.0.0.0`. This network allows three bytes, or 24 bits, of host address—that's more than two million hosts, ranging from `15.0.0.1` to `15.255.255.254`. To make efficient use of this address range for a large, distributed enterprise with multiple physical networks, we may wish to divide the address into subnets, each with a more usable number of hosts. If we chose a subnet mask of `255.255.248.0`, we would produce 8192 networks (13 bits) that may have 2048 hosts (11 bits) each. This example, and the next, are shown in Figure 5–6.

As another example, let us return to our class C IP address, `192.168.0.103`, which has a network address of `192.168.0.0` and a system address of `103`, based on the implied, class-based net mask of `255.255.255.0`. Another common notation for the address and network portions is: `192.168.0.103/24`. The `/24` indicates that the first 24 bits of the IP address

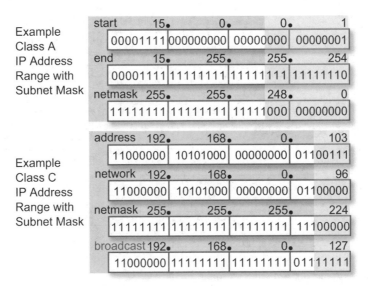

Figure 5–6 IP subnetting example

specifies the network portion. The network portion of this example address is 24 bits, and the system portion is eight bits, using the class C scheme, allowing 254 hosts.

We may decrease the number of hosts and increase the number of subnets available in this class C address by using a subnet mask of 255.255.255.224. With this choice, the IP address is divided into eight networks (with decimal addresses in the fourth octet of 0, 32, 64, 96, 128, 160, 192, and 224) with 30 hosts each. Another way of specifying this address scheme is 192.168.0.0/27, and the example is shown in Figure 5–6. The IP address 192.168.0.103 would have a network portion of the address of 192.168.0.96 and a system portion of 7. (By subnetting in this way, we have actually decreased the potential number of hosts from 254 [2^8 minus 2] in the pure class C scheme to 240 or 8 times [2^5 minus 2], because of reserved broadcast and network addresses.) The network broadcast address would be 192.168.0.127.

The pure, class, and subnet approaches to addressing were modified in the early 1990s, and were replaced with classless interdomain routing (CIDR), which specifies the network portion of the IP address as a bit prefix, which is easier for networking equipment to route. Based on a given network prefix in the IP address, the datagram may be routed to a single location by a global Internet router, for which the local internet service provider's (ISP) routers determine the correct "local" or "internal" destination. This simplifies the global routing tables by treating the addresses as if they were hierarchical.

Example Class
C
IP Networks
with
Supernetting

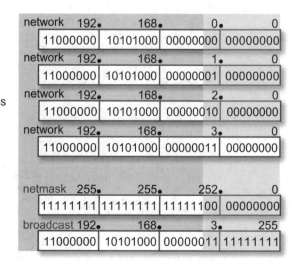

Figure 5–7 An IP supernetting example

5.4.4   IP Supernetting

With the net mask freed from the byte boundaries defined by the IP address classes, it is now possible, using CIDR, to have subnets that contain more addresses than allowed by the more restrictive class scheme. Combining four class C networks—192.168.0.0, 192.168.1.0, 192.168.2.0, and 192.168.3.0—along with adjusting the net mask to 255.255.252.0 or /22 allows a single network with 1022 hosts (2^{10} minus 2). This combined set of networks is called a *supernet*, and the process is called *IP supernetting*.

Supernetting allows the aggregation of smaller network address spaces into larger, more usable address space. This address space aggregation also allows a decrease in the complexity of global routing tables, because where there would have been multiple entries, there need only be one. Although it is unlikely that we will use supernetting, per se, in the design of clusters, it does help us understand the networking tools that we are likely to use.

5.4.5   Ethernet Unicast, Multicast, and Broadcast Frames

Ethernet frames may be categorized into three types: unicast, multicast, and broadcast. Each type of frame serves a different purpose and is accepted by a different number of systems. Unicast frames are the most restricted in terms of target audience, with broadcast frames being the least restrictive. The sending interface places its own MAC address into the Ethernet frame, in the source address field of each of the three frame types.

A unicast frame is used to send an Ethernet frame from one system to a single destination system. The frame is placed on the Ethernet medium with the destination MAC address of the target interface as part of the frame's header. Although every attached station on the LAN can "see" the frame, other interfaces will ignore the frame if the destination MAC address does not match theirs. Unicast traffic is a "one-to-one" communication.

Multicast frames are somewhat more complicated than unicast or broadcast frames, and are beyond the scope of this discussion. Suffice it to say that systems may participate in multicast traffic, and frames are sent to all participants. Multicasting is a useful feature, particularly when sending installation data to multiple systems at once. Multicast traffic is "one-to-many" communication. Multicasting is similar to broadcasting, but systems must "subscribe" to a multicast channel on an interface to receive the traffic. This allows the network interface to ignore multicast traffic if it is not information that the system has explicitly requested. This is in contrast to broadcast traffic.

A broadcast frame on an Ethernet segment contains a destination MAC address consisting of all (48) one bits. An Ethernet interface that detects a frame with the broadcast address will accept it, passing the frame contents up the network stack to be interpreted. All physically attached interfaces have access to broadcast frames. A broadcast frame may be considered a "one-to-all" communication.

5.4.6   Address Resolution Protocol (ARP)

Once a system has an IP address associated with its Ethernet interface, it must be able to determine the system with the desired destination IP address. On an Ethernet segment, the ARP provides the translation mechanism. A system on an Ethernet segment that wishes to send a datagram to another sends a broadcast Ethernet frame that contains the IP address of the desired target.

The ARP request frame is seen by all systems and devices directly connected to the physical Ethernet segment. Only the system that owns the desired IP address sends the reply frame directly to the requestor. The sender will cache the ARP information in the system ARP cache for a period of time, "killing" them in a preset amount of time.

A network device connected to the Ethernet segment may answer the ARP request with its own MAC address if the sender's data needs to transition between network segments. The sender makes an ARP request and the router responds with its own information. The sender then transfers its data to the router's interface, and the packet "escapes" the local segment into the willing hands of the router.

5.4.7   IPv4 and IPv6

The current version of the IP protocol, IPv4, is rapidly running out of available address space. There are several stopgap measures that have prolonged exhausting the available 32-bit IP addresses provided by IPv4. Supernetting, reclaiming unused addresses, Dynamic Host Configuration Protocol (DHCP), and network address translation (NAT) have all been used to prolong the inevitable.

T I P   Do not use IPv6 addressing inside your cluster unless you have a good reason for the added complexity.

A new version of the IP protocol, IPv6, is making an appearance in the networking world. Many systems, Linux included, support features of IPv6 as they become available. It is expected that network devices, such as routers, will also begin supporting the new protocol. The IPv6 protocol provides the following features and advantages (among others):

- 128-bit IP addresses
- Additional security (IP Security Protocol [IPsec] is required)
- Help with routing scalability

The availability of IPv6 is something of which we must be aware, just in case we need a cluster to attach to an IPv6 network. For a treatise on IPv6, see Loshin [2004] for an in-depth analysis. I consider IPv6 beyond the scope of further discussion.

5.4.8   Private, Nonroutable Network Addresses

Several network address ranges within each class (A, B, C) are reserved for private, nonroutable networks.[2] These network address ranges are considered unavailable for public use and may not be registered by any person or company. Any routing equipment is designed to drop the packets using these addresses.

T I P   Using private, nonroutable network addresses inside your cluster will help to "hide" the internal resources from the outside world. This adds to security and the illusion that the cluster is a single entity.

The private, nonroutable networks are: class A addresses `10.0.0.0` to `10.255.255.255`, class B addresses `172.16.0.0` to `172.31.255.255`, and class C addresses `192.168.0.0` to `192.168.255.255`. We will be using a selection of these special addresses for the internal cluster networks.

---

2.   There is a specific request for comment (RFC) that defines these networks and their use. Please see RFC 1918 at `http://www.ietf.org/rfcs/rfc1918.txt` for the complete definition.

5.5 Ethernet Switching Technology

The Ethernet switch was introduced in the early 1990s. Ethernet switches are low-latency, high-bandwidth, learning bridges that switch frames at the MAC level (OSI layer 2). The switch may be thought of as providing a direct hardware connection between any two ports that are communicating, with no collisions. A switch allows multiple connections between ports to be active at the same time without interference, and because the switching is done at the MAC level, they are protocol independent.

The switch maintains a table of MAC address and port relationships, and will send frames to the appropriate port or ports on the switch based on the destination MAC address and the MAC addresses in the table. Any frame containing a destination that is not in the table is forwarded to the switch's backbone port. Frames arriving from the backbone port are checked against the local switch tables and are forwarded to the correct local port if appropriate.

To handle multiple simultaneous connections, the switch's backplane is typically rated in terms of tens to hundreds of gigabits per second. Much of the switching functionality is implemented in hardware to maintain high throughput. To support frame switching, MTU conversion, flow control, and other features, a switch usually incorporates an intelligent switching matrix and a shared-memory architecture, along with specialized firmware.

Some switches share some packet routing capabilities with routers and are able to route packets at OSI level 3. A fully switched LAN allows moving slower, more expensive routers to the "edge" of the network. (There is considerable confusion between terms like *layer-2 router* and *layer-3 switch*. These terms were introduced when filtering and "learning" technology was added to layer 2 bridges in an attempt to differentiate the new product from the more limited bridging technology. The confusion is still rampant.) You will rarely, if ever, find a router in the midst of a cluster. Note that a LAN is formed by devices connected at OSI levels 1 and 2 (hubs and bridges). Once a router is involved, the LAN ends.

5.5.1   Half and Full Duplex Operation

One feature inherent with switched Ethernet was the ability to allow simultaneous sending and receiving of data on the same connection. The original Ethernet CDMA/CD protocol, which allowed transmission by one interface in one direction at a time, is now termed *half duplex* and is still supported by switches for backward compatibility. The ability to send and receive data on the network link simultaneously is called *full duplex operation*.

There are obvious performance advantages to full-duplex operation. Half-duplex operation requires the line to be "turned around" to transmit data in the opposite direction. If collisions are present on a link, then it is in half-duplex operation. Collisions and one-way traffic reduce the potential throughput on a link, so full-duplex operation is desirable and may provide a substantial performance improvement.

During link initialization, information may be exchanged between the link client and the switch regarding the capabilities of each entity and the desired mode of operation. It is possible to set the speed and duplex of a particular link explicitly at either or both ends, or to allow the switch and network interface card (NIC) to "autonegotiate" the behavior. Ensuring that both the switch and the client interface agree is important to proper operation of the network link.

Although it is usually best to allow autonegotiation to handle the link configuration, it is not always successful. The standards for various implementations of Ethernet define how the auto-negotiation process works, and determine the default behavior in the event of disagreement between the switch and client NIC. The link components must be able to pick an operating mode for the physical link successfully, even if the capabilities of the NIC are not the smartest.

For unknown reasons, some 100base-TX Ethernet links seem to have inherent autonegotiation problems. I have seen frequent disagreements between the switch and the client NIC regarding the current operating mode of the link. When one party thinks it is in half duplex and the other thinks it is in full duplex, data errors occur on the link. If I had a nickel for every link (and associated unexplained performance issues) I have encountered in this state, I could retire.

Some Ethernet implementations, such as GbE, are inherently full duplex. In other words, the standard specifies two sets of fibers or shielded twisted pairs, one set for transmit and another for receive.

5.5.2   Store and Forward versus Cut-through Switching

Two major classes of data switching are circuit switching and packet switching. In circuit switching, a control packet creates or destroys the circuit. Once established, data flows along the established circuit. If a port is allocated to a circuit, then it will block other attempts to create a circuit, using it as an end point until the existing circuit is destroyed.

In packet switching, packets are routed based on their header contents. Two classes of packet switching are "store and forward" and "cut-through." A store-and-forward device first receives all portions of the frame, checks the frame for validity, then sends it to the destination ports. Checking for a complete and valid frame eliminates the forwarding of malformed frames, but also increases the switch's latency.

A cut-through switch will detect the incoming packet and immediately begin sending it to the destination ports as soon as the destination address is be detected. Busy ports may force even a cut-through switch to buffer the packet. (Some vendor's switches will not buffer UDP packets by default, instead dropping the data if the switch gets congested. Although UDP has no built-in guarantee of datagram delivery, the acronym should not stand for "U Drop Packets." This behavior is a particular issue if you are using UDP as the primary transport for NFS traffic.)

5.5.3   Collision Domains and Switching

A switch with ports dedicated to a single system creates a collision-free "switching domain." Connecting switches together, with a backbone, enables systems with the same LAN addresses to communicate, even if they are not on the same switch. Again, this communication takes place without collisions.

An example of four LAN segments, physically separate and located on two different switches, is shown in Figure 5–8. Each switch allows systems belonging to the same LAN to

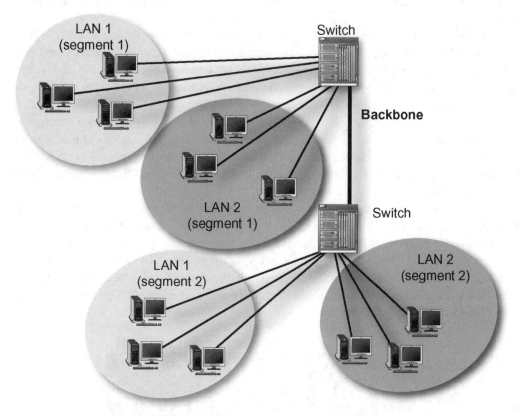

Figure 5–8 A multiple switch domain

communicate with each other, even though they are not on the same physical LAN segment. Any packet destined for a system not on the current switch is routed across the backbone to the other switch in the switching domain.

To allow connections between switches without creating bottlenecks, higher bandwidth links than the switch connections themselves are needed. Additionally, high-bandwidth connections to servers and other local resources may require more bandwidth than a single switch port. We look at the method for interconnecting switches with higher bandwidth links in the next section.

5.5.4   Link Aggregation

The ability to "gang," "team," or "aggregate" multiple network links together is a way to increase available bandwidth and network availability. Multiple full-duplex links operating in parallel provide the aggregated bandwidth of the component links. If one of the aggregated links should fail, the remaining links continue to operate, with the overall link operating at reduced capability.

Four, full-duplex 100base-FX links, for example, provide the equivalent of a single 400-Mb link—400 Mb in each direction. Another term for this functionality is *trunking*. The ability to aggregate ports originated with proprietary protocols and functionality from several switch vendors. Today, the IEEE 802.3AD specification defines an industry standard way of aggregating switch ports.

There is typically a limit to the number of individual links that may participate in an aggregate, which may depend on the switch's manufacturer. To the systems using the link, it must behave just as if it were a discrete link, with its own MAC address and network behavior. The switch must be able to balance traffic across the link transparently, and there are several load-balancing approaches.

An example of link aggregation is shown in Figure 5–9. Two core switches are linked together by four 10-GbE links, providing 40 Gbps in each direction. One of the core switches is tied to an edge switch with four one Gbps links, providing four Gbps in each direction.

Link aggregation will be an important ability for the switches that we choose to design our cluster's network. Without this capability, we would be unable to provide a network without inherent bottlenecks resulting from bandwidth imbalances between switch ports and uplinks. We delve deeper into aggregation later.

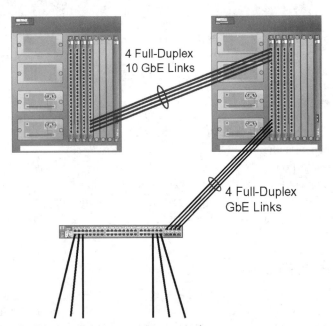

Figure 5–9 An Ethernet link aggregation example

5.5.5 Virtual LANs

An Ethernet switch will normally forward, or "flood," all broadcast and multicast frames it receives to all ports. The larger a switched LAN grows, the more this type of flooding occurs across ports on interconnected switches. The ability to control which frames arrive at a switch's ports is an important switch capability.

Switches with virtual LAN, or VLAN, capability allow a system manager to assign individual switch ports to one or more numbered VLANs. The port's VLAN assignment determines which broadcast and multicast frames are sent to the port by the switch. The switch maintains a table that maps MAC address and port location to the VLAN.

Broadcast and multicast frames are kept within their port's originating VLANs by the switch. Ethernet frames are tagged with VLAN information so that VLAN-capable switches can properly deliver them to participating ports. Using VLANS can

- Provide extra security by limiting the ports that "see" restricted frames
- Improve performance by limiting switch broadcast domains
- Isolate multicast participants from the rest of the LAN
- Drive you crazy configuring them without software help

Not all switches are capable of handling VLANs. Even though there is an IEEE standard, 802.1Q, that defines operation of VLANs, there are many proprietary features and potential interoperability issues. You should carefully check the capabilities of any switch before committing to it. An example network with switched VLANs is shown in Figure 5–10.

Systems that are members of one VLAN are not able to communicate with systems in other VLANs without the intervention of layer 3 routing. This is one reason that some switches implement both layer 2 switching along with layer 3 routing. The routing capability is needed to interconnect VLANs, just as if they were physically separate LAN segments.

5.5.6 Jumbo Frames

The default MTU, or data payload, for Ethernet frames is 1500 bytes, but some switches allow this value to be increased to as much as nine kilobytes. One term applied to this feature is *jumbo frames*, and it can increase the performance of bulk data transfers between Ethernet devices. Increasing the size of the data payload in each frame reduces the amount of fragmentation that occurs when sending large streams of data. Jumbo frames are extremely useful for file server connections over Ethernet, especially for NFS.

It is extremely important to ensure that both the switch and the NICs are capable of handling jumbo frames before enabling this functionality. Along with the hardware capabilities, the operating system, drivers, and utilities must be able to handle jumbo frames. A lack of complete support will make the use of jumbo frames difficult or impossible.

In some switches, a system manager may use the device management interface to create a VLAN within which jumbo frames are used. Ports assigned to that VLAN must usually be

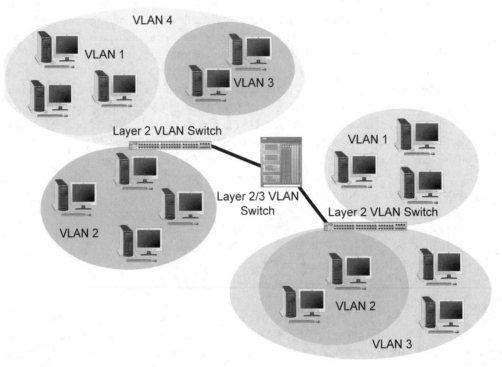

Figure 5–10 An example switched VLAN

attached to NICs that have jumbo frames enabled. To interface with devices that cannot support jumbo frames, the switches in the network must be configured to fragment and route the traffic to ports in VLANs outside the "jumbo frame" VLAN. Careful consideration is needed to trade off the additional complexity against the potential for performance increases.

At the time of this writing, there is no standard for implementing jumbo frames across all hardware and software that might be involved, so each switch vendor has implemented it in their own special ways. One would hope that all implementations would interoperate, but this may or may not be the case. Carefully investigate all capabilities before committing to, or depending on, this functionality.

5.5.7   Managed versus Unmanaged Switches

As switches get more complicated and add more features like VLANs, they become more diffi-cult to monitor and manage. Most modern switches have some level of management interface, including Web-based interfaces, serial port consoles, or Simple Network Management Protocol (SNMP). This is not to say that "dumb" unmanaged switches are not available.

Remember that your ability to debug the behavior of switch issues like autonegotiation conflicts, VLAN assignments, routing tables, and other essential switch information will depend on your ability to access the internal switch information with some form of interface. It is essential to select switches that may be configured and monitored remotely for your cluster.

T I P   Use only managed switches in your cluster. The ability to examine and control the operation of individual ports and global switch parameters is essential to proper administration (and debugging) of your cluster's networks. Selecting unmanaged switches to save money is a false economy.

5.6   Example Switches

As a final examination of switched Ethernet, let's examine two example switches, both made by Hewlett-Packard in their ProCurve line. One switch is a 1U "edge" switch and the other is a "core" switch, meaning it is intended to be a central switch. Both switches have a good price-to-performance ratio.

5.6.1   A GbE Edge Switch

First, let's examine the Hewlett-Packard ProCurve Switch 2848, shown in Figure 5–11, which provides 48 ports of 10/100/1000base-TX. (This is not to be considered an endorsement of this particular manufacturer or product, it is used only as an example.) Other features include

- Secure shell (SSH) command-line interface
- Secure socket layer (SSL) encrypted Web management access
- 96-Gb-per-second backplane
- Optional redundant power supply
- Support of up to 60 port-based VLANs
- Support of the Simple Network Time Protocol (SNTP)
- DHCP relay
- Serial RS-232 out-of-band management port
- Cisco fast ether channel (FEC)
- 802.3AD link aggregation
- Latency of 11.8 microseconds for 100 Mb per second, 4.4 microseconds for 1000 Mb per second
- Support of remote monitoring (RMON) and extended RMON for switch statistics, alarms, and events

These features, and many others, give us a very flexible switch for data connections or even for HSIs. The number of ports on the switch supports an expected number of 1U or 2U systems installed in a 42U rack, while taking only 1U.

One way of measuring the price performance of a switch is the cost per port. This gives one way of evaluating the switch characteristics for making design decisions. Based on the list price for this switch (as of January 19, 2004), the cost per port is $82.99, which is quite reason-

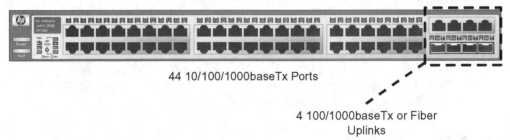

44 10/100/1000baseTx Ports

4 100/1000baseTx or Fiber
Uplinks

Figure 5–11 An example edge switch

able for the performance. There is also a 24-port version, the ProCurve 2824, with a per-port cost of $84.66.

One thing to steadfastly avoid is using a switch in which the backplane is "oversubscribed." This means that the sum of the port bandwidths exceeds the backplane performance. For this switch, the backplane throughput is 96 Gb per second which equals the total bidirectional bandwidth of all 48 ports (one-Gb-per-second input and one-Gb-per-second output in full-duplex 1000baseTX operation).

One issue with this switch is the possibility of the four uplinks becoming a bottleneck. The sum of the 44 port bandwidth is 88 Gb per second, whereas the four uplinks are only capable of handling a total of 8 Gb per second.

5.6.2   Ethernet Core Switches

A "core" Ethernet switch can be thought of as a collapsed network backbone. It is a central connection point for the edge switches in the cluster's racks, which connect directly to devices like compute slices. Depending on the size of the cluster, we can choose a switch with sufficient ports for direct connections to the systems in other racks, or for the trunked connections, or for "uplinks" from the edge switches in individual racks.

The core switch needs to have routing capabilities to tie together any VLANs in the cluster. It should also be able to sustain the level of data transmission necessary to keep all attached ports active simultaneously. As a cluster grows in size, the requirements for the core switch also grow.

Let's examine two switches with more capabilities than an edge switch. As with the edge switch in the previous section, the switches are Hewlett-Packard ProCurve switches. First, let's take a look at the 5304xl and 5308xl switches. The first model, shown in Figure 5–12 is the model 5304xl. This switch has four slots that accept modules providing various types of network connections. Our example switch has four 20-port 10/100/1000base-TX modules.

Some of the other features of this switch are

• Layers 2, 3, and 4 (TCP/IP port-based) routing
• 76.8 Gb-per-second backplane

Figure 5–12 A small core switch

- Hot-swappable modules
- Static NAT capability
- Secure management with SSH and SSL
- Up to 256 simultaneous VLANs
- Link aggregation with Cisco FEC and 802.3AD
- Optional redundant power supply

The support for VLANs and link aggregation, among others, allows us to connect uplinks from the edge switches in our cluster, and provides aggregated links for file servers. Routing capabilities allow connection of any VLANs that we might define.

As with other switches, we need to be careful not to oversubscribe the backplane. The current configuration, with 80 GbE ports, could require 160 Gb per second if all ports are operating simultaneously in both directions. This configuration is certainly suitable for smaller clusters.

Finally, let's look at a much larger switch chassis, the ProCurve 9308m. The switch chassis shown has eight slots available for switching "blades." The configuration in Figure 5–13 shows six 16-port 10/100/1000base-TX blades, and a dual 10-GbE blade. This switch comes in a smaller four-slot version and a larger 15-slot chassis.

Some of the switch features are

- 256-Gb-per-second backplane
- Less than 7-microsecond latency
- Hot-swappable modules
- VLAN support
- 802.3AD link aggregation

The ability to handle larger numbers of direct connections, or trunked links, makes this switch a choice for larger cluster configurations. If the number of connections in a chassis is exhausted, the switches may be trunked together to provide an internal backbone for all the Ethernet networks in the cluster.

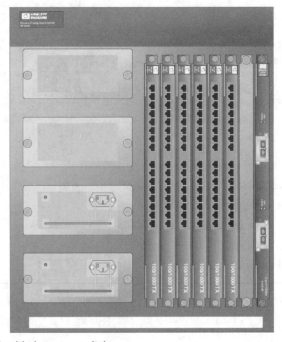

Figure 5–13 A mid-size core switch

5.7 Ethernet Networking Summary

In this chapter we covered some networking basics that will be used again and again as we design the internal networks of a cluster and make system administration choices about the network configurations. We covered the various networking technologies associated with Ethernet and Internet routing. Finally, some example hardware from Hewlett-Packard provided examples of features and configurations available in various sizes, and prices, of network switching hardware. The products from other switch manufacturers, like Extreme Networks and Cisco Systems, also have an abundance of features and price points, and make good choices as networking infrastructure for clusters.

## CHAPTER 6

Tying It Together: Cluster Data, Management, and Control Networks

Chapter Objectives

- Provide an example of serial port console management equipment
- Describe remote system management cards and their features
- Investigate the design of management and data networks

In addition to the HSI, there may be one or more Ethernet networks in a cluster. Here I present some of the design characteristics and choices for these networks, along with an example IP addressing scheme for a cluster.

6.1   Networked System Management and Serial Port Access

There are at least two classes of management access possible with compute slices, network devices, and other active elements in your cluster. How you access the devices will depend on their capabilities and the software support for their remote interfaces. Because of operating system limitations, some devices may have a very nice automated management interface for Microsoft Windows that is not available on Linux.

Irrespective of the availability of graphical remote tools, the device itself may allow out-of-band management via a network port, access to a character-based interface via a serial port, Web-based access, secure shell (SSH) access, or a combination of all these methods. ("Out-of-band" management typically means the device provides a completely separate network connection that is used only for management purposes.) The cluster's designer may wish to restrict access to management devices associated with systems, switches, and other manageable devices. The most secure way is to use a separate network to access only the management devices.

Careful planning of the management network details like addressing, default routes, which devices need to be attached, and attachment methods can save a lot of issues later. Because Ethernet switches flood all packets to all ports (unless VLANs are used), multiple logical networks may exist on the same physical network without too much effort. In some security-conscious environments, a physically separate, secure network for management access is an absolute design requirement.

6.1.1   Remote System Management Access

Selecting a compute slice that has a built-in system management interface can add to the manageability of your cluster. A system that is designed as a stand-alone server is more likely to have this functionality. Management or remote access devices, whether built in or added as separate PCI interfaces, allow functionality like remote access to the system console in graphics mode, remote power on and power off, and the ability to upgrade firmware and BIOS remotely, among others. The usefulness of these features becomes apparent the larger your cluster becomes.

The remote management capabilities are usually available from a separate, "out-of-band" network port integrated into the system. This means that the management capability is available from the external port, but the network is not available to the operating system. Think of the management device as having direct access to the state of the system hardware (even with the system shut down in some cases), but with no direct access from "inside." An example of a built-in management interface is the iLO available in the Proliant servers from Hewlett-Packard. The network connections will normally support 10/100base-TX connections.

In addition to the integrated management interfaces, there are third-party PCI interface cards that provide system management capability. The software and drivers for these cards tend to be more focused on the Microsoft Windows operating system, rather than Linux, so beware of assuming driver support. Investigate the availability of drivers and functionality carefully before choosing a particular vendor's management interface card. Also, be aware that the add-in card may take up a much-needed PCI slot in your compute slices.

The management interface on each system will most likely need to be configured with an IP address before it can be remotely accessed over the management network. There are various approaches to configuring the management address, depending on the manufacturer. As shipped from the factory, the device may come with a default password and IP address. For security's sake, *never* use the default configuration shipped from the manufacturer.

Many of the more intelligent management devices are capable of getting their address and network information from DHCP. Collecting the device's MAC address for the DHCP configuration and setting the access password will still require an initial connection to the device. You should plan on making a temporary connection to each device through its serial or network port to configure the IP address and the management password.

Once configured, the management interface to the system will allow operations like remote power on and off, console access, BIOS configuration and updates, and monitoring of system parameters like chassis intrusion, fan speeds, and internal temperature. Some of the more advanced system management interfaces allow access to the integrated graphics device in the system via a Web-based Java interface.

6.1.2   Keyboard, Video, and Mouse Switches

The lowest common denominator for accessing a system console in graphics mode is video graphics array (VGA), which is supported to some level by virtually all PC graphics adapters. This minimal level of support still gives installation and configuration utilities a usable ability to present their interfaces in text, color, and even graphics. Some systems include reasonable integrated graphics capabilities such as the ATI Rage XL device shown in Figure 4–1, which depicts a Hewlett-Packard Proliant DL-360 system.

A VGA interface allows 720 pixels by 400 pixels in graphics mode, which is sufficient for a bit-mapped 25-line by 80-character display. In graphics mode, VGA displays may be 640 pixels by 480 pixels with 16 colors (from a palette of 262,144 colors) or 320 pixels by 200 pixels with 256 colors. There are other graphics modes such as super VGA (SVGA) that we will not cover here. What graphics functionality is available, and whether you can access it via the remote management card, depends on the system's manufacturer.

To allow graphics access to the system consoles in a cluster, a single keyboard, mouse, and graphics monitor may be shared between multiple systems with a keyboard–video–mouse (KVM) switch. Doing this requires a connection between the KVM switch and the VGA output, keyboard input (PS-2 or USB), and mouse input (PS-2 or USB) on each system. Because of the number of connections (three per system), distance limitations for cables, and KVM limitations, this should be limited to the master nodes or other important systems that need local access in the computer room.

6.1.3   Serial Port Concentrators or Switches

Many commodity server systems still have serial ports that allow access to external, character-based console I/O. This feature may be intended to have a character-based RS-232 terminal with a keyboard directly attached to it for use as a system console. The vast majority of systems in a cluster, however, will not have physical consoles attached to them.

Because system console access is necessary for troubleshooting and reporting purposes, a way of getting minimal connection to the console (and logging console output) is needed. Connections may be made via a "crash cart," which has a terminal, monitor, keyboard, and mouse available for direct *temporary* connection in the event of a problem. The crash cart is wheeled up and the connection is made to the system via PS-2, USB, VGA, or serial connectors.

The console output from a system is very useful in tracing kernel panics, application errors, power-on self-test (POST), and operating system boot history. To collect this information requires a permanent connection to the serial port and a way to access the output. Additionally, it is not possible to get "in-band" management information from the system's built-in network interfaces, because a live operating system is required for these to be active.

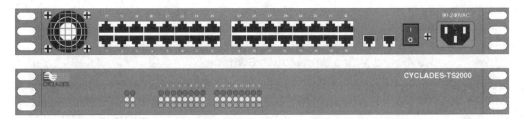

Figure 6–1 Cyclades TS-2000 serial port switch

What is needed is a connection to the serial port from an external device that can access and log the information. Serial port concentrators, sometimes called serial port switches, can provide this access over a network connection. An example serial port switch, the Cyclades TS-2000 16-port Console Server is shown in Figure 6–1. (Information on the complete set of products is available at `http://www.cyclades.com`.)

This device runs Linux as the internal operating system and has a number of very useful features for our purposes:

- Secure SSH access via an in-band or out-of-band network connection
- Event notification tied to console output
- Remote output buffering
- 8-, 16-, 32-, and 48-port configurations, 1U rack utilization
- Support for trivial file transfer protocol (TFTP), DHCP, and network time protocol (NTP) protocols and functionality

With this device, we can monitor and log the output of the compute slice's serial console to either the "syslog" daemon or an NFS mount point on a remote system. If necessary, a login to an attached system's serial console is possible by accessing the switch via SSH.

We can eliminate the need for crash carts or physical access to the systems, by controlling *who* can access the management ports of the compute slices and Ethernet switches. At the same time, a single Ethernet connection gives us access for as many serial port consoles as are attached to the device. Although this level of management access is not needed for every cluster, the larger the cluster becomes, the more the system managers require this type of functionality.

6.2   Cluster Ethernet Network Design

To begin making design decisions about your cluster's Ethernet networks, you must first decide *which* networks will be present from the possibilities of data, management, and HSI. The size of your cluster will dictate whether you have a management LAN that is physically or logically separate from the data network. You might also be using Ethernet as the HSI for your cluster to save cost.

Whether you separate the networks into discrete management, HSI, and data networks will depend on your budget and the required performance of your cluster. Time-sensitive HSI communications, bulk data transmissions for the NFS or cluster file system, and console logging and management traffic do not necessarily play well together on the same physical link. Depending on your security considerations, it may be a requirement that the management network be physically separate in terms of links, switches, and access points.

The first step is to gather all the user requirements for security, access, and performance together in one place. With this information collected, you will have a clear picture of which types of networks are required and how to implement them with Ethernet devices. We look at specialized HSI networks in a separate chapter.

6.2.1 Choosing a Clusterwide IP Address Scheme

Having an idea of how many networks are required and what IP address ranges to use for your cluster's Ethernet networks is a good starting point. The size of the cluster, coupled with any plans for future additions, will help you to select the proper type and range of IP addresses. Choose wisely, because it is very difficult to change IP addresses once the cluster goes "live."

Using the class-based IP scheme as an example, it would be a disaster to choose a "pure" type C network address and subnet mask for a cluster of 1024 nodes, unless you want to deal with subnetting within the cluster. Because a class C address is limited to 254 hosts, you might choose supernetting. You should carefully consider the impact on system administration effort.

Like it or not, we all think, and a lot of software is still written, to display and assume the old "pure" class-based schemes, with network and host addresses divided evenly on byte octet boundaries. Clean address boundaries and subnets make it easier to picture, and therefore administer, the networks.

6.2.2 IP Addressing Conventions

No matter what networking scheme you select, the host address with all zeros and the address with all ones in the host portion of the IP address are reserved. The network address (at the low end of the range) and the broadcast address (at the high end of the range) flank the set of available host addresses.

To make automation of system administration easier, you can choose a set of conventions for the remaining address range that divides it into two or more "blocks" of addresses assigned to specific types of equipment. Allowing scripts (and system administrators) to make assumptions about important addresses can lead to improved automation of administrative and start-up tasks.

One example of this is to use high addresses on a subnet to represent devices like switches, assigning them in a decreasing order. The lower range of addresses would then be reserved for connections to systems, reserving them in an increasing order. The default gateway for the subnet might always be the broadcast address minus one.

6.2.3   Using Nonroutable Network Addresses

To "hide" the internal networks in the cluster, you can choose network addresses from the private, nonroutable networks. Refer to Section 5.4.8 for more information on the available nonroutable network address ranges. By making the master nodes in the cluster the access point, and by disabling routing between any internal networks and the external network, you can prevent packets from "leaking" to the outside world.

Using the nonroutable private addresses does not necessarily guarantee that packets with those addresses won't "escape" the cluster. Most routing equipment is designed to drop any packet it sees with the special network addresses. Additional security measures may be necessary to prevent access to internal cluster resources from the "outside" world. Some of the internal cluster networks are shown in Figure 6–2.

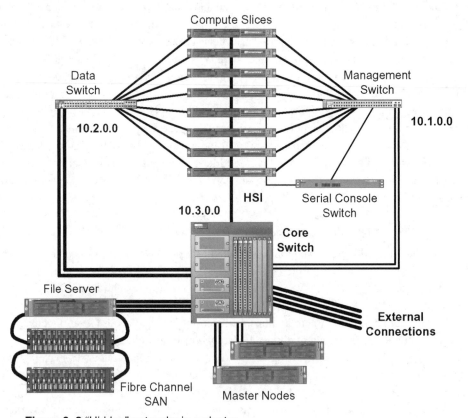

Figure 6–2 "Hidden" networks in a cluster

6.3   An Example Cluster Ethernet Network Design

Instead of talking about a design, let's do one. Our example cluster will have 1,024 nodes, and Ethernet management, data, and HSI networks. I chose 1,024 nodes because it adds some intrigue to the design.

The first thing to note is that with the IP network address (zero) and the broadcast address (all ones in the host part), we lose two addresses out of the total IP address range right out of the gate, so to speak. Also, there will be network devices like the default gateway that will take from the *available* address range. We will need to provide a host address range that provides *more than* the expected 1,024 host addresses to avoid disappointment.

Another quick note is in order with regard to this example. This configuration is more suited for a scientific cluster than for either a database or a Web serving cluster. The internal and external designs of the cluster networks are driven by the *type* of cluster and the required access to its internal components. Your application will determine the final requirements for the network design.

6.3.1   Choosing the Type of Network and Address Ranges

I like to have the network and host portions of the address readily visible without a lot of binary gymnastics. Let's choose the private, nonroutable 10.0.0.0 network format as the basis of the design, with a subnet mask of 255.255.0.0. This will give us room for 16,534 devices on each of the subnets we create.

Because our slate is clean, let's initially choose 10.1.0.0 for the management network, 10.2.0.0 for the data network, and 10.3.0.0 for the HSI network. As you can see, we are using the second octet to designate a "subnet," just to make things readable. We can now start mapping expected device addresses. The network address scheme is shown in Figure 6–3.

Notice with this scheme it is possible to add subnets to the three networks, but they will be discontinuous. Subnetting the 10.1.0.0 network would involve adding the next network at 10.4.0.0, for example. If you have to add subnets, say to support VLANs among groups of systems, it might be better to leave some "growth room" between the network addresses. For example, the management network might consist of 10.1.0.0 through 10.4.0.0; the data network, 10.5.0.0 through 10.8.0.0; and so on.

Another consideration in network design is the use of a private network for the management network. With this design choice, there must be a way for the system managers to access the management network, either through the master nodes or from a separate, multihome system that is connected to the management network. Using a separate management system, in addition to the master nodes, is a good choice, and provides multiple paths to the management network in the event of master node failures.

Thinking ahead, and working out the network design work *before* the systems need to be installed and configured, can save headaches at the last minute. Working out difficulties with subnets, host addressing, and other details is easier if you write down the addresses and draw pictures. "Measure twice and cut once" applies to other crafts besides carpentry.

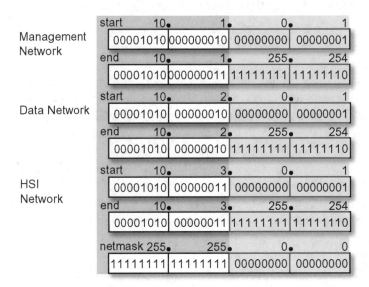

Figure 6–3 Three example cluster networks and addresses

6.3.2   Device Addressing Schemes

In our example 1,024 compute slice cluster, using the previously described example networks and net masks, we have a host address range from 1 to 65,534 in all three networks. If we assume that no subnetting is needed in those networks, there will be 1,024 host addresses necessary for the compute slices, one address necessary for the file server in the data network (possibly more if there are multiple servers), and addresses for switch management and default routes.

We will start the compute slice addresses in each network with 1 and will run up through 1,024. The default gateway and other special addresses will start at the highest address (65,534) and will work down. Knowing that the compute slice addresses in all three networks have the same host value allows us to "map" the address to a physical node in a rack, if we wish to carry the convention that far.

We can also view the addresses as being arranged by physical rack, with host 1 through 32 in the first physical rack (assuming 1U systems), host 33 through 64 in the second physical rack, and so on. Maintaining this mapping for the other networks can make physically locating the system associated with an IP address easier. Of course, some systems that are designed for racks have "locator lights" that can be activated from the management interface, but a regular IP scheme can make system administration scripts and automation easier to implement.

There are other devices that will require addresses. A cluster of this size usually has spare compute slices, administrative systems, head nodes, and test/development systems in the cluster networks. All these "extra" systems must fit into the clusterwide IP addressing scheme.

6.3.3   The Management and Control Networks

Performance in the management LAN is not as big an issue as in the Ethernet HSI or the data network. The primary need is to provide intermittent access to the devices for configuration and troubleshooting. Just having the connectivity to all the management ports, at a reasonable speed, is our goal.

The main reasons to separate the management LAN from the other cluster LANs are security and isolation from networks requiring bulk data transport and low-latency communication. Although separation is always desirable, it is possible to share the same physical network to reduce costs.

The compute slice connections to the management cards will require one IP address each, for a total of 1,024. Using 1U compute slices, with 32 systems per 42U rack, the example 1,024 compute slice cluster has 32 compute racks. If each of these racks has one 48-port 10/100 switch for the management network, then we must allocate 32 IP addresses across the cluster for the switch out-of-band management access.

The management and control network allows configuration (ports, VLANs, routes, and so forth), monitoring, and troubleshooting the switches remotely; remote console access and logging; and remote power on and off of the systems with management capability. The management LAN topology is shown in Figure 6–4.

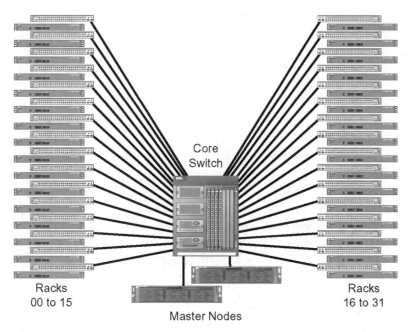

Figure 6–4 Management LAN topology

In addition to the Ethernet switches, for serial port management and console logging, there may be 32 32-port serial port switches. Each of these requires an IP address for access to the attached serial ports. These console switches will need access to an NFS server on the same network for remote buffering and console logging. The switch's out-of-band management network may be attached to a port in the 48-port management network switch.

All these management connections will need host names to match the IP addresses on the management LAN. Using a naming scheme that helps physically locate the device is a good idea. Once the IP addresses, all 64 or more of them, are assigned, a judicious choice of host name is in order. But we are getting a little ahead of ourselves.

Controlling physical access to the management LAN is important in some clusters. Keeping the management LAN connection on a completely isolated physical switch, with special external connections is a possibility, requiring access through a physically separate system is another. If physical separation is not an issue, then the head nodes may be configured to access the management LAN through the core switch. The latter configuration is shown in Figure 6–4.

6.3.4   The Data Network

In our example data network, let's choose NFS as an expedient file-serving technology. No matter what file-serving technology you choose, the data LAN needs to be optimized for bulk data transfer between the file servers and the cluster's compute slices and other clients. Switched GbE is a good low-cost choice for this connection.

Providing bandwidth with no bottlenecks will usually involve port aggregation from the server to the switch. To facilitate bulk data transport, Ethernet jumbo frames are also an option. Although link aggregation is commonly available, only certain types of switches and Ethernet interfaces support jumbo frames.

To avoid having 32 separate GbE data network connections from each rack to the master rack, it is possible to locate a properly sized GbE switch in each rack. In this configuration, the rack switches allow a "fan out" to systems in the rack, with a trunked link to the core switch. Care must be taken not to create bottlenecks (the trunk) or to oversubscribe the rack switch's backplane. An example data network topology is shown in Figure 6–5.

The network shown in Figure 6–5 uses a four-link trunk between the NFS file server and the core switch. This aggregated link provides four gigabits per second in each direction, which is a theoretical maximum throughput of 500 MB per second[1] each way (read and write) for the full-duplex link. This is roughly 488 KB per second for each node in the cluster.

Along with trunking, the configuration of Ethernet jumbo frames may introduce the need for VLANs. If a system's NIC is incapable of handling jumbo frames, it is necessary for the

---

1.   Four links at one gigabit per second each is a total of four gigabits per second. Dividing four gigabits per second by eight bits per byte yields a 500 MB per second aggregate, or 125 MB per second for each link. In reality, the link may only be 80% to 90% efficient if jumbo frames are used with a good quality switch, so a total of 400 to 450 MB per second in each direction is a more reasonable expectation.

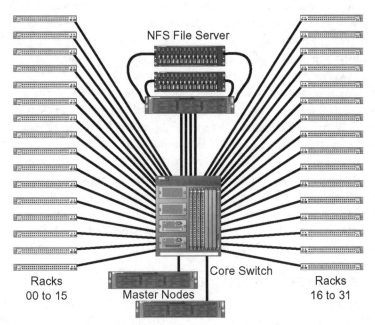

Figure 6–5 Example data network topology

switching equipment to handle fragmenting the frames into the standard size that the interface *can* handle. Some switching equipment handles this by allowing the network manager to place jumbo frame-capable systems in one VLAN, placing "normal" systems in another VLAN, and allowing the switch to route the jumbo frames to the "normal" VLAN, fragmenting them as necessary.

Designing the back-end storage to maintain this level of writes, especially synchronous (sequential) writes to RAID 5 storage, is extremely difficult and expensive. It would take multiple RAID arrays and multiple Fibre-Channel loops to permit this level of I/O to and from the cluster. It is the write performance that is the primary issue.

Sustained, high-bandwidth I/O across all nodes in the cluster is a difficult file system and storage design problem. If every node in the cluster simultaneously required a checkpoint of only two gigabytes of RAM, we would need to write more than two terabytes of data. At the 500 MB per second theoretical maximum quoted earlier, it would take one hour nine minutes to complete the checkpoint. I cover file system issues later in this book.

If each of the switches shown in Figure 6–5 had four trunks to the core switch, each of the 32 switches could simultaneously pump a theoretical 500 MB per second into the core switch while receiving an equal amount. The backplane of the core switch must be able to sustain 32 GB per second or 256 Gb per second to avoid being oversubscribed—from just the data network traffic alone.

If this switch is also used by the management and control LAN, the traffic may easily exceed the capability of a single switch chassis. It becomes necessary to split the network across multiple switches to avoid saturating the backplane. Even then, the storage backend is the bottleneck. As the cluster gets larger, the load placed on the networking equipment forces larger and more expensive switch configurations to keep up with necessary traffic.

Similar design issues occur when the back-end storage is on a SAN. The number of simultaneous Fibre-Channel fabric logins may become an issue as the number of systems accessing the data grows. It is a real good idea to calculate the theoretical maximums for the I/O media, the storage channels, and the switches to design an acceptable data network.

The design decisions you make about bulk data transport needs will depend on your characterization of the applications running in your cluster. Depending on the expected utilization of the cluster, not all compute slices may need simultaneous access to the file server or database storage. This makes the network bandwidth and design parameters somewhat easier; otherwise, partitioning the data, partitioning the network, or both may be used to reduce the aggregate burden on the file server and storage back ends.

6.3.5   Example IP Address Assignments

In each of the three IP networks in our example cluster, we have a possible 65,534 usable host addresses and 255 networks, using the `255.255.0.0` subnet mask. This range ought to be sufficient for our 1,024-compute slice cluster. There are as many different ways to assign the addresses as there are people to do the design, but an example assignment for the management network devices is shown in Table 6–1.

Table 6–1 Example Management LAN IP Address Assignments

Description	Addresses
Compute slice management ports	`10.1.0.1` to `10.1.4.0`
Rack switch addresses	`10.1.10.1` to `10.1.10.32`
Console switch addresses	`10.1.20.1` to `10.1.20.32`
Data switch addresses	`10.1.30.1` to `10.1.30.32`
Core switch address	`10.1.40.1`
Storage device addresses	`10.1.50.1` to `10.1.50.6`
Master node management ports	`10.1.60.1` to `10.1.60.4`
Default gateway	`10.1.255.254`
Broadcast address	`10.1.255.255`

Table 6–2 Example Data LAN IP Address Assignments

Description	Addresses
Compute slice data connections	10.2.0.1 to 10.2.4.0
Head node data connections	10.2.10.1 to 10.2.10.4
NFS server address	10.2.20.1
Default gateway	10.2.255.254
Broadcast address	10.2.255.255

The IP address assignments for the data network are a little easier than the assignments for the management LAN. Example data LAN IP address assignments are shown in Table 6–2. One of the reasons behind the relative simplicity of this network is the design decision to avoid adding devices that might interfere with bulk data transfer.

6.4 Cluster Network Design Summary

In this chapter's network examples we examined some of the issues surrounding the choice of an IP addressing scheme for a large cluster. Having an adequate "IP address space" for the expected connections, and an overall scheme for allocating the addresses, can save headaches as software configuration starts. The primary message is, no matter what the expected IP addressing scheme is, you should do a paper design prior to committing to it.

Because of their low cost, Ethernet switches make a good basis for these networks. In Ethernet LANs comprising this equipment, UDP and TCP protocols run over an IP base. To design the LANs involved properly, we need intimate knowledge of the features, capabilities, and limitations of the switching hardware we will use.

To keep the example figures simple, I omitted any redundancy with regard to the core Ethernet switches. For realistic cluster designs, it is essential to consider multiple core switches to provide the proper level of redundancy for your cluster. The addition of extra switches in each of the diagrams covers the potential for hardware failure or loss of power to the primary core switch.

Do not forget to plan for redundant network paths, or a single failure can disable the entire cluster. Adding the redundancy is not without its costs, however. Additional switches mean added complexity in the form of more cables and interconnections to troubleshoot, not to mention the doubling of cost for the core switch components.

Although I waved my hands over some of the issues involved in designing the data and management LANs found in clusters, I cannot possibly cover every conceivable situation, nor can I cover it to an exhaustive depth. Of course, the design and equipment considerations you must consider will depend entirely on the size and intent of your cluster networks, but my hope is that the example considerations will help you avoid some of the pitfalls.

CHAPTER 7

Life in the Fast LAN: HSIs and Your Cluster

Chapter Objectives

- Introduce the characteristics of an HSI
- Examine some basic HSI topologies
- Survey current technologies that are popular for HSIs

High-speed, low-latency interconnects are the foundation of communications for parallel applications and in clustered database solutions. Choosing the proper interconnect to match your performance needs—and your budget—is the objective of this chapter.

7.1 HSIs

You will find an HSI in clusters that have computational or communication dependencies between components in a parallel application—from parallel applications to parallel database-serving clusters. There are quite a few esoteric options available in terms of HSI technologies, ranging from Ethernet on the lower cost end of the spectrum to some of the more expensive products at the high end. Which HSI you select for your cluster will be determined by the trade-offs between bandwidth, latency, and price.

Many of the common HSIs are based on a switched network that has specialized switching equipment and a special distributed shape, or topology. The topology and switching equipment are designed to simplify node-to-node addressing, reduce the amount of time to make routing decisions, and move data rapidly across the links and through the network. They are at once familiar, and foreign, to someone who has worked with "normal" networks.

Point-to-point connectivity with a minimum number of hops, as you might imagine, is important to the performance of this type of network. Another very important feature of an HSI is that it is nonblocking. In other words, messages that need to be delivered are delivered without waiting, or blocking, if links in the network are busy. Each manufacturer has its own proprietary approach to network topology and switch configuration.

Along with using IP addressing if Ethernet is the base technology, the device drivers for the other HSI technologies will usually allow running TCP/IP over the interconnect. The advantage of this is very high-bandwidth, low-latency transport for standardized services like file-serving protocols for NFS or a cluster file system like Lustre, which I discuss later. I cover more of this topic when I discuss the cluster's "software stack" in the next section of this book.

TIP   A word of warning for those of you who might consider scrimping on the HSI portion of your compute cluster: Don't. The HSI, for clusters that require it, is a primary determining factor for overall cluster performance. You can spend lots of money on the latest, fastest compute slices for your cluster, or the biggest and fastest SAN components, and still be disappointed in the cluster's performance—if you don't pay close attention to the HSI. It is far better to build your cluster around the best HSI you can possibly afford, even if that means delaying the deployment of some of the compute resources.

7.2 HSI Latency and Bandwidth

Two fundamental characteristics of the HSI network (and most others) that are important to your cluster's design are the bandwidth of the point-to-point links and the latency in sending messages from one system to another in the network. The ability to send messages within the HSI rapidly, efficiently, and accurately is fundamental to extracting performance from a parallel application. There are many trade-offs between latency, bandwidth, and cost in the implementation of HSI technology available to you.

For example, the use of cut-through packet switching, as opposed to store-and-forward technology improves latency. The ability to deliver data at a constant rate, however, is important in a cut-through switching network to avoid the need to drop back to storing-and-forwarding (buffering) the packets. When there is a local drop in bandwidth, as from GbE speeds to 100base-TX, the switching hardware must buffer the incoming data, introducing latency in the delivery. Specialized HSI hardware is designed to eliminate this situation as much as possible.

Remember that the HSI is used by parallel software to simulate shared memory. So, the closer the latency is to local memory bus latencies, the better the potential performance available to the application. In other cluster applications, like parallel database servers, the HSI may be used to maintain locking consistency *and* to transfer data blocks from one system's cache to another system, bypassing the delay caused by a physical read from storage devices. Which parameter is more important will depend on your cluster's application. It is possible that both will be important.

The physical link bandwidth in the HSI determines how quickly bulk data may be moved across the network from one system to another. The physical link itself may be serial or parallel, and is usually full duplex. The intervening switch hardware, the number of available links in the network, and other characteristics of the HSI network determine the message latency.

There are varying measures of latency, and one has to be careful to examine the exact conditions under which latency is measured for a particular HSI technology. One measure of latency is referred to as the *ping-pong test*, which sends a message to the remote system, which receives the message and sends an equivalent-size reply. The test records the end-to-end transit time for various sizes of both the "ping" and the "pong" messages, and *usually* reports the average round-trip time. Because there are no standards for this kind of test, examine the message sizes and test setup carefully.

To a certain extent, the latency from one system to another in the HSI network is determined by the network topology and switching technology in use. The ability of an HSI network to handle traffic without blocking is another important characteristic that is tied to the topology and the switching hardware. We examine some generic topologies in the next section, followed by some real-world HSI products and their configurations.

7.3 Examining HSI Topologies

A basic understanding of some of the characteristics and topologies used in HSI networks will serve us well when we begin to look at a number of the commercially available products that are available for HSI use in clusters. In addition to the bandwidth and latency characteristics, the network topology and switching configuration for various sizes of HSI hardware are important. Reducing HSI costs by using commodity Ethernet switches is possible for some applications, provided appropriate attention is paid to the network design with regard to application performance and scaling.

Why all the fuss? Why not just connect all systems to each other equally, as with a crossbar, and be done with it? After all, it is not too difficult to visualize a square grid of connections between elements in the network (say, P systems by P systems), is it? Why not just buy a massive crossbar switch of some kind and fill it with the required number of ports?

A crossbar-based network can maintain performance levels, but it quickly becomes unsustainable from a cost standpoint. The network connections grow in complexity as the square of the number of processing elements, P^2. Imagine having to connect every telephone in the United States to every other telephone in an NxN grid. It simply is not possible (or affordable). Even with a 128-compute slice cluster, the cost of a 64x64 crossbar would be prohibitive.

By understanding traffic routing problems, bandwidth requirements, connectivity needs, and cost trade-offs, switching network designers attempt to make informed design choices for actual implementations. Continuing research into network topologies and switching methods is intended to allow maintaining the connectivity and performance without the exponential cost and complexity of this type of network. Research in this area is ongoing.

The topology of the HSI network, and the distribution of the parallel application components and data, are interrelated. The communication patterns between the application components can affect network performance if they are not evenly distributed. The HSI network, if it has bottlenecks or "blocking points," restricts traffic and impedes application performance. Developers of parallel applications must consider the mapping of their computational problem to the underlying hardware and network topology, but I will just brush the topic with a broad brush and at a very high level.

7.3.1 Some Common Topologies

We are all familiar with some of the possible network topologies: the bus and the star. And the more esoteric patterns, like a completely connected network, a mesh, or 2D and 3D toroids are possible (look ahead to Figure 7–10 for an example 3D toroidal interconnect.) These, along with a 3D hypercube, are shown in Figure 7–1. Each of these configurations has differing characteristics with regard to blocking and "network diameter," or the number of links that must be traversed, on average, in a point-to-point message path. We will see several of these configurations when we consider Ethernet and the other HSI technologies.

7.3.2 Cross-Sectional Bandwidth

You can picture drawing a line through a diagram of the network, and dividing it into two pieces across the communication link or links, with equal numbers of systems on either side of the

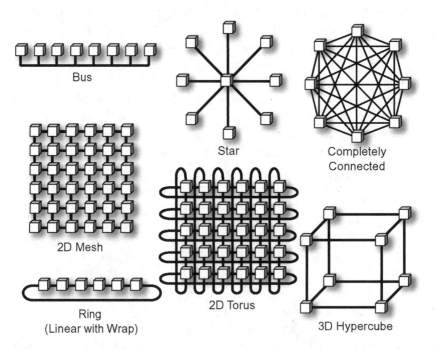

Figure 7–1 Examples of possible interconnect configurations

line. The number of links intersected is the bisection width or the cross-section width. Cross-sectional bandwidth is the minimum bandwidth possible between two pieces of the network, and it is the link bandwidth multiplied by the number of intersected links. If there is constant cross-sectional bandwidth, then the communication rate between the two portions of the network is equal. Some examples of network bisection width for common HSI topologies are shown in Figure 7–2.

As a cluster grows, it becomes more difficult and expensive to maintain constant cross-sectional bandwidth across the HSI network. When all the available ports in a switch chassis fill, instead of "splitting" the network across two separate chassis, an additional level of switch chassis is added to preserve the constant cross-sectional bandwidth and the nonblocking behavior of the HSI network. How this is done depends on the manufacturer of the HSI switching hardware.

We must pay attention to cross-sectional bandwidth because, in an ideal world, we want to maintain a constant bandwidth between any two points in the HSI. But, like other design decisions, there are times where we have to trade off the network topology, latency, bandwidth, and expense. Having a way to analyze the network, and the terminology to use in that analysis, is useful when looking at manufacturers' specifications for HSI hardware.

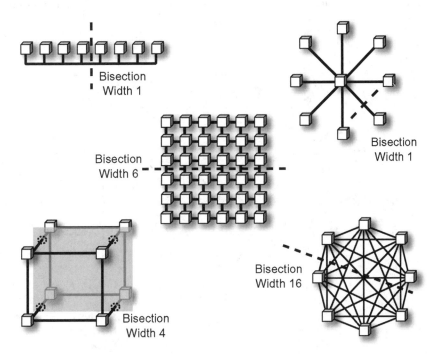

Figure 7–2 Network bisection width examples

7.3.3   Clos Networks

Investigation into generalized routing for telephone networks was performed by Charles Clos in "A Study of Non-blocking Switching Networks" [Clos 1953], and thus the name applies to HSI networks that use this configuration. There is some very in-depth theoretical analysis of multi-level, switched networks, which are all quite beyond the scope of this book. Suffice it to say that a Clos network is a multilevel network constructed in such a way as to eliminate contention for a route between inputs and outputs. A general model of a multilevel Clos network is shown in Figure 7–3.

Networks of this type are called *rearrangable* if they can route any possible combination of source and destination pairs without needing to wait for an available link, or "blocking." Theoretically, Figure 7–3 may be described as a three-stage, rearrangeable, nonblocking Clos network—let's just stick to a "Clos network." A particular implementation of a Clos network is used in the Myrinet interconnect described in a later section.

7.3.4   Fat Tree Networks

A tree topology is one possible configuration of an HSI network. There are several disadvantages to a regular tree topology, including a low cross-sectional bandwidth. Another disadvan-

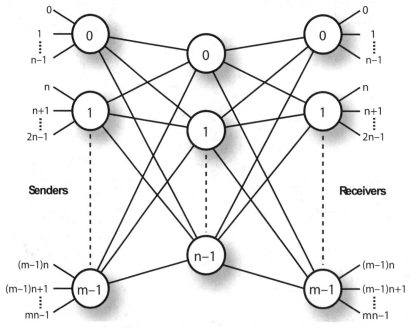

Figure 7–3 A general Clos network

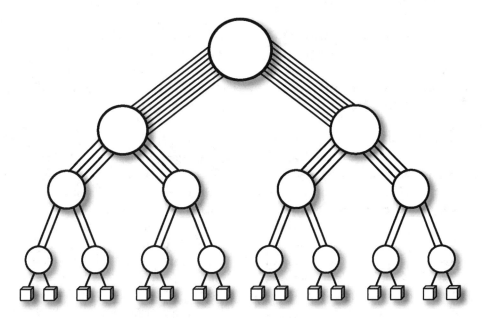

Figure 7–4 An example fat tree network

tage is the fact that messages from nodes in different leaves of the tree must traverse the tree through the root. This creates a potential bottleneck at the "top" of the tree, especially when parallel application components need to do "one-to-many" or "many-to-one" sharing of messages.

A possible topological remedy for the cross-sectional bandwidth issue is to adopt a "fat tree," as depicted in Figure 7–4. To eliminate bottlenecks in the network, the number of parallel links in a fat tree increases toward the root of the tree. The fat tree configuration eliminates the bandwidth issues, but does not address the number of switching stages (network diameter) that a message must traverse.

7.4 Ethernet for HSI

Using commodity Ethernet switches is a cost-effective way of implementing an HSI for your cluster. The fact that 10/100/1000-TX Ethernet interfaces are already built into many of the choices for compute slices means that there is no extra interface card to purchase. The cost and latency of today's Ethernet switches is quite good, and there is a wide range of capabilities from which to choose in the hardware.

In a small enough cluster, it is possible to interconnect all compute slices with an Ethernet HSI composed of a single switch. As long as the switch offers full-duplex operation, the proper link speed (100/1000 Mb) and media type (TX cable or FX fiber) of Ethernet connection, along with the appropriate number of ports, you are in business.

Ensuring that all switch ports can operate simultaneously in full duplex, without oversubscribing the backplane is another important consideration. (I repeat my previous warning here: Do not even consider using unmanaged switches in your cluster—no matter what the cost savings! The first time you have to troubleshoot a port autonegotiation problem, you will have lost any initial savings.) Remember that for full-duplex operation, the aggregate throughput per port is double the base port rate. For example, a full-duplex GbE port may require up to two Gb per second on the switch's backplane, one gigabit per second for input, and one gigabit per second for output.

Depending on your cluster's size, it may be possible to share an Ethernet switch as the HSI, management, and data connection. This topology is a star, with the "core" switch at its center. In this network configuration, there is only one level of switch to traverse, and therefore only one switch level worth of latency. Using several Hewlett-Packard ProCurve switches as a reference point the latency and backplane specifications are listed in Table 7–1.

Once the port count or switch backplane bandwidth is exceeded, or if the cluster grows to multiple racks with "embedded" switches, the "single switch for all LANs and HSI" approach is difficult to maintain. A single switch to handle 192 connections from a 64-compute slice cluster (three Ethernet connections per compute slice) can run upwards of $100,000—depending on the manufacturer and port configuration.

As a first guess, a fat tree topology appears to be the best way of extending the HSI network to multiple switches while maintaining the network's cross-sectional bandwidth. This approach, however, runs afoul of the spanning tree protocol (STP) used in switches, the maxi-

Table 7–1 Comparison of Ethernet Switch Latencies

Switch Model	Number of Ports	Port Type	Latency, microseconds[a]	Backplane, Gbps	Routing at IP Layer
HP Procurve 2824	24	10/100/ 1000-TX	100 Mbps < 11.5 1 Gbps < 5.4	48.0	2 and 3
HP Procurve 2828	48	10/100/ 1000-TX	100 Mbps < 11.8 1 Gbps < 4.4	96.0	2 and 3
HP Procurve 4108gl	128	10/100/ 1000-TX	100 Mbps < 10.5 1 Gbps < 3.2	36.6	2 and basic layer 3
HP Procurve 9315M	232	10/100/ 1000-TX	< 7	480.0	2, 3, and 4

a.   64-byte packets

mum number of links allowed in a network trunk or aggregated link, and switch backplane bandwidths. (The STP is utilized to eliminate network "feedback" from routing loops. It will disable multiple paths to the same destination.)

Trunked Ethernet links, even 10-GbE links, cannot easily aggregate enough bandwidth to "connect" two large switch domains together and maintain constant cross-sectional bandwidth.

7.4.1 An Example Ethernet HSI Network

One possible approach to solving the Ethernet bandwidth issue is to use switch "meshing," which interconnects multiple switches in a ladder-like configuration, as shown in Figure 7–5. There are two compute slice attachment schemes shown in the diagram, which are used for two example sets of latency and bandwidth calculations—direct attach and multilevel compute slice attachment.

The right half of the figure has two groups of 32 compute slices directly attached to the core switches, and the left half of the figure has two groups of 32 compute slices with an inter-

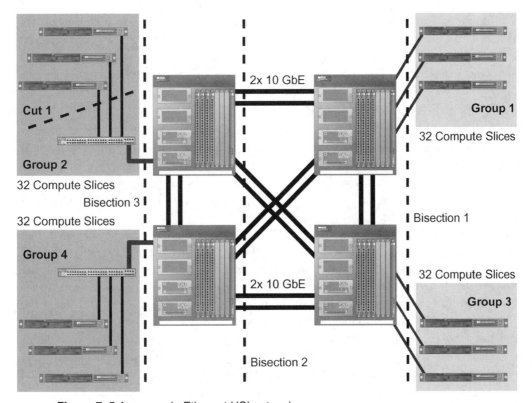

Figure 7–5 An example Ethernet HSI network

mediate level of switches trunked to the core switches. The right-side approach might be used if interrack connections are not an issue. The left-side attachment method might be used to minimize interrack cabling.

Let's assume that the compute slices are attached via a single built-in GbE interface for the sake of the examples, and that the interswitch connections for the core switches are trunks of two 10-GbE links to each of the "neighboring" switches, for a total of six 10-GbE links per switch. The first thing to notice is that, although the network is a complete switching domain, the four separate core switches effectively divide the cluster into four sections, within which all the compute slices may send and receive messages with only a single switch's latency.

In the case of the Hewlett-Packard ProCurve 9308 switches[1] shown in the diagram for the core, that latency is specified as "less than" seven microseconds for 64-byte packets. Let's use seven microseconds for this example. What about latencies for compute slices that are not on the same switch? In the case of the "direct attach" groups, the worst-case latency is double the single-switch latency: For the 64-byte packet, this would be 14 microseconds, one way. Just for comparison's sake, the local memory latency for systems is in the 120-nanosecond range, making the difference in performance about two orders of magnitude.

In the case of the groups with the intervening switches (Hewlett-Packard ProCurve 2828 switches), the worst-case one-way latency would be $8.8 + 14.0 = 22.8$ microseconds. These latencies are only for the 64-byte packet transmission listed in the switch specifications and do not include latency added by the network interfaces and operating system software.

7.4.2   Direct Attach Example Bandwidth

What about the bandwidth calculations for the direct attach example? Looking at the line marked Bisection 1 in Figure 7–5, you can see that it cuts through all 64 of the direct attach compute slice GbE interfaces in Group 1 and Group 3. This yields a *theoretical* 64 Gb per second of compute slice traffic per switch (32 Gb per second send and 32 Gb per second receive). Adding the six interswitch 10-GbE links (120 Gb per second per switch), brings the per-switch total to 184 Gb per second.

Each switch's backplane is rated at 128 Gb per second and is oversubscribed by 43% if all the GbE and 10-GbE links are fully utilized at the theoretical maximum rate. In reality, a high of 90% utilization is possible, using jumbo frames to send large messages. Utilization is typically lower than this figure. If you use the 90% utilization figure as an upper bound, the total bandwidth drops to 165 Gb per second per switch, which is an oversubscription of 28% above the 128 Gb per second backplane rating. Actual traffic and utilization will depend on the communications pattern of the applications using the cluster.

Looking at the line in Figure 7–5 labeled Bisection 2, you can see that it cuts through eight of the ten GbE interswitch connections, yielding a theoretical maximum of 160 Gb per second

---

1.   The 9308M switch has space for eight blades, the 10 GbE blades provide two ports each, and the 100/1000-TX blades have 16 ports each. There are also models with four (9304M) and fifteen (9315M) open blade slots.

between the two halves of the network if they were equally configured. Each half of the direct attach network can produce a theoretical 64 Gb per second and consume a theoretical 64 Gb per second, for a total of 128 Gb per second. The HSI network between the two halves can handle a theoretical 160 Gb per second.

Even assuming that it is possible to sustain full send and receive bandwidth (or even 90%), this is not too bad. The performance, however, comes at a price. Each of the four switches, with chassis and GbE ports, is estimated to cost approximately $100,000 US list price,[2] for a total of somewhere near $400,000. The current configuration is "maxed out" in terms of connections and bandwidth with the current switch configuration.

7.4.3   Multilevel Attach Example Bandwidth

The multilevel attach example involves Group 2 and Group 4 in Figure 7–5. Each group of 32 systems is attached to one or more Hewlett-Packard Procurve 2848 10/100/1000-TX switches, which provide 48 ports and a 96-Gb per second backplane. The switch is attached to the core network via GbE trunked ports.

Right away, we know that each 2848 switch has up to 64 Gb per second of traffic capability (examining the Cut 1 label in Figure 7–5), which does not exceed the backplane rating of the switch. We find ourselves in trouble, however, with only a four-link trunk to the core network per switch. This trunk can sustain only 8 Gbps total bandwidth.

With only four trunks in the cluster, sustaining 32 Gbps (8 Gb per second per switch trunk), there is no need for an expensive core network; the peripheral switches are the bottlenecks in the HSI. In this configuration, we may only need one core switch, which drops the overall price of the Ethernet HSI, but it also substantially drops the performance and decreases the bandwidth. What design alternatives do we have for a limited budget, other than a single core switch with direct attach from the compute slices?

In smaller clusters, the direct attach core switch approach is the simplest and easiest. As the cluster gets larger than about 128 compute slices, however, the single switch approach becomes expensive. Another issue is the 128 or more Ethernet cables coming into the switch's rack.

First, it may be possible to drop back to a 2824 switch (24 ports and a 48-Gb-per-second backplane) per group of 16 compute slices. This would give us a total of eight peripheral switches, and a 64-Gb-per-second (eight Gb per second per switch) bandwidth to and from the core network switch. Each group of 16 compute slices would produce 32 Gb per second and be linked to the core network with the same eight-Gb-per-second trunk.

You should be able to see that as we drop the number of compute slices per peripheral switch, we are approaching the "direct attach" bandwidth numbers. Using eight compute slices per switch (four switches per group of 32 compute slices) gives us a 2:1 compute slice-to-trunk

---

2.   The two-port 10-GbE blades were not priced on the Hewlett-Packard Web site as of February 13, 2004, as I was
      writing this chapter, so I estimated them at $15,000 each.

bandwidth ratio. We finally reach 1:1 when there are four compute slices per four-link trunk, which is a pointless configuration.

We have been assuming a single four-port trunk per switch up to this point. It may be possible to trade routing and configuration complexity for additional trunks by introducing port-based VLANs. In this situation, a trunk per VLAN on the switch is possible, within the manufacturer's configuration limitations. To save space, these configurations are left as an exercise for you. (The Procurve 2848 switch will support up to six trunks of up to four links each. All ports belong to the "default VLAN" unless otherwise configured. Routing between VLANs must be considered as part of the network design.)

7.4.4   A Larger Ethernet HSI Example

The 128-compute slice example shown in Figure 7–5 fully utilized the Hewlett-Packard ProCurve 9308 switches, and actually slightly oversubscribed the backplane. What would need to be done to the design to scale the cluster up to 256 compute slices? Refer back to the topologies shown in Figure 7–1 for some ideas. For the next example, let's arrange our switches in a hypercube, which is shown in Figure 7–6.

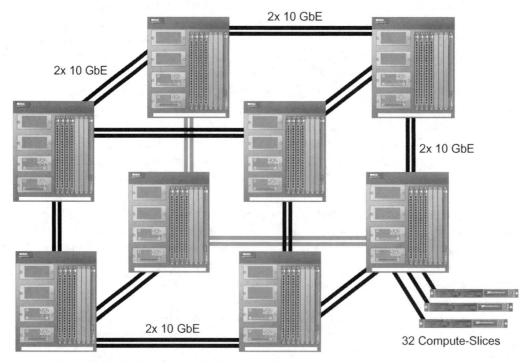

Figure 7–6 A 256 compute slice Ethernet cluster

There are now twice as many switches, but each switch still has six 10-GbE links, for a total of 120 Gb per second of bandwidth. There are still 32 compute slices per switch, with 64 Gb per second total bandwidth. The bisection of the network yields 160 Gb per second as with the switch meshing example.

The difference between this example and the switch meshing example in Figure 7–5, however, lies in the size of "half" the compute slices in the HSI network. Each HSI network half now has 128 compute slices, which can produce 256 Gb per second of traffic, exceeding the bisectional bandwidth by 60%.

Furthermore, the network diameter is now three ($\log_2 8$) rather than the previous two. The latency has increased, on the average, to 21 microseconds, one way. Even more disturbing than the increase in latency is the increase in cost from approximately \$400,000 in the previous example to the neighborhood of \$800,000. Although the previous example was in no way low cost, this is "over the top."

Even though there is another ProCurve switch chassis, the 9315M, available, we are expending more and more slots and backplane bandwidth for the interconnect. We are now into the price and performance range where the specialized HSI solutions become much more cost-effective. There are very good reasons that specialized interconnects exist. As your cluster grows, you need to start looking at different solutions for the HSI.

7.4.5   Other Ethernet HSI Configurations

Our examples up to this point have assumed a single GbE network interface card per compute slice. There are other possible configurations involving multiple interface cards that can simplify the hardware configuration of the Ethernet HSI and "flatten" the switch hierarchy. The hardware simplification, however, comes at a cost of increased interconnection complexity and custom software routing tables.

One such scheme is the flat network neighborhood (FNN) (see Dietz and Mattox [2000]) interconnect topology described at `http://aggregate.ee.engr.uky.edu/tech-pub/als2000`. The multiple NIC, single level of switch solution presented by the authors is very interesting in light of our current design issues with Ethernet. Of course, your compute slices must have the extra PCI slots to accommodate extra NICs for a multiple Ethernet LAN interconnect like the FNN setup.

We have now run out of simple, cost-effective HSI strategies for Ethernet. Certainly, small clusters may take advantage of single-switch, direct attach configurations without too much effort. Beyond the single-switch configurations, large, expensive switches can allow building special topologies, but at some point we need to admit defeat and use a more generic solution. The design effort, switch configuration complexity, software routing complexity, and other implementation difficulties may be more easily handled by abandoning Ethernet and looking at HSI solutions that are described in the upcoming sections.

7.5   Myricom's Myrinet HSI

Myrinet is an HSI solution available from Myricom Inc. Information on this commercially available product can be found at `http://www.myricom.com`. The Myrinet product consists of a choice of fiber-optic interface cards and specialized switches. Myrinet is extremely popular in the high-performance, parallel-computing world, and is well supported by message-passing and other communication software.

The Myrinet interface to a compute slice consists of an interface card (D-card), capable of sustaining 2 Gbps, full duplex (total of a theoretical 4 Gb per second), to a Myrinet switch. Also available are dual-port cards (E-card), providing "dual-rail" HSI interconnect to either a single Myrinet switching network or to two separate networks. A lot of flexibility is available with the dual-rail configuration.

Detailed performance information on these cards is available on the Myricom Web site at `http://www.myricom.com/performance/index.html`. The specific performance and configuration information is dependent on software and testing conditions, and is summarized in Table 7–2 for informational purposes only. Any information should be verified directly with the Myricom Web site and is subject to change at any time. Myricom knows their products best, and you should rely only on their information for your design or purchasing decisions.

Notice that the sustained bandwidth for the E-card is very close to the theoretical limit of a PCI-X 133-MHz interface bus. Only well-designed, high-performance systems will be able to take advantage of this type of interface. If you want to extract the very best performance from the HSI interface, the internal design of your compute slice with respect to memory bandwidth, I/O bus bandwidth, and DMA bandwidth all become very important. Picture the path from one compute slice's memory to another, through the HSI and refer to Chapter 4, for details about compute slice hardware internals.

The Myrinet HSI is a Clos network, a general example of which was depicted in Figure 7–3. There is one difference between a Myrinet HSI network and the generalized Clos network in Figure 7–3, however. The Myrinet HSI is full-duplex, so you can picture the general-

Table 7–2 Myrinet Interface Card Specifications[a]

Myrinet Interface Card Type	Number of Full-Duplex Links	Theoretical Bandwidth Send + Receive, Gbps	Theoretical Bandwidth Send + Receive, MB/s	Sustained User-level Transfer, MB/s	Latency, micro-seconds
Myrinet D-card	1	2 + 2	250 + 250	489[b]	6.5[c]
Myrinet E-card	2	4 + 4	500 + 500	950[b]	5.5[c]

a. From the Myricom web site as of February 14, 2004.

b. User-level sustained bidirectional bandwidth for large messages.

c. Small-message latency. Latency increases logarithmically with message size.

ized network "folded back" on itself, with both the sender's and receiver's sides of the network being combined in the same system.

Myrinet switches are available in chassis with 2, 3, 5, and 17 slots. Each slot in the switch chassis can hold an eight-port "line" card to connect eight Myrinet hosts, and one of the slots in the chassis may hold a management card, leaving n-1 slots in the chassis for the line cards. This means the switch chassis can handle a maximum of 8, 16, 32, and 128 connections to D-cards respectively. The switching chassis themselves may be connected together with "spine" cards to form larger networks. Information on how to do this is beyond the scope of our discussion. The Myricom Web site has an excellent document titled *Guide to Myrinet 2000 Switches and Networks* that covers details of the theory and implementation of Myrinet networks. I highly recommend downloading a copy if you are going to work with Myrinet.

Like other Clos networks, Myrinet has multiple levels of switches to provide nonblocking connections between the participating systems. Switching networks of this type may be built using common components like the 16 x 16 switching module that Myrinet literature calls an *XBar16*. The Myrinet networks are divided up into "leaf" switches and "spine" switches.

Each link in a Myrinet network comprises two Myrinet channels, as provided by the interface card or other connection types. The networks are drawn with a link represented by a single line. In each chassis configuration, even partially filled ones, a full bisectional bandwidth network is provided to the attached compute slices.

Several of the Myrinet switch chassis are shown in Figure 7–7, fully populated with the management card and line cards. The chassis contains "spine" connections that interconnect the XBar16 switches on the line cards. A diagram of a Myrinet network for 64 compute slices is shown in Figure 7–8, and represents eight slots used in the 17-slot chassis.

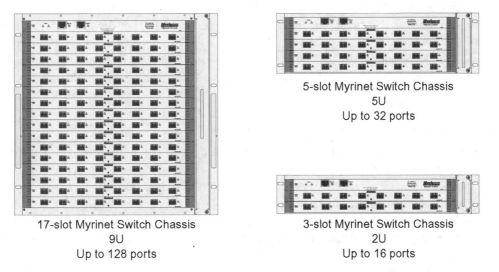

17-slot Myrinet Switch Chassis
9U
Up to 128 ports

5-slot Myrinet Switch Chassis
5U
Up to 32 ports

3-slot Myrinet Switch Chassis
2U
Up to 16 ports

Figure 7–7 Myrinet switch chassis configurations

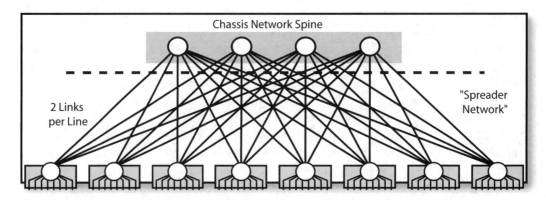

Figure 7–8 An example 64-host Myrinet Clos switching network

Because the cluster's HSI is central to its operation, features that make it highly available are very important. The Myrinet switching chassis, in addition to the switching spine, contains up to two hot-swap redundant power supplies, a hot-swap fan tray, and the "hot-swappable" monitoring and control card. The line cards themselves are also hot-swappable.

The Myrinet network maintains full bisectional bandwidth and is a rearrangeable network, so that each of the 64 factorial (64! is a huge number) possible permutations of compute slice connections in Figure 7–8 may be routed. Observe that the dashed line in Figure 7–8 intersects 32 lines, each representing two full-duplex links, for a total of 128, 2-Gb per second links (two per host). The message paths between any two hosts in the network pass through one switch in the case when both systems are connected to the same line card, and through three switches in the more complicated case.

Myrinet is capable of carrying multiple packet types in the HSI network, including TCP/IP and custom message types. There is a low-level interface API to the links, called *GM*, that may be used to implement specialized applications and routing. There are other middleware implementations over the top of the GM interface, including PVM-GM, MPICH-GM, and Sockets-GM.

7.6   Infiniband

The Infiniband technology is a relative newcomer on the HSI scene, but provides high-bandwidth, low-latency communications over high-speed serial connections. The technology was originally invented by a consortium including Microsoft, IBM, Intel, Hewlett-Packard, Compaq Computer, Dell Computer, and Sun Microsystems as a replacement for the current PCI standard for peripheral I/O. For various reasons, Infiniband has not yet lived up to the original expectations of the consortium, and both Microsoft and Intel appear to have backed away from the technology.

Table 7–3 Infiniband Specifications

Link Type	Link Raw Data Rate, Gbps	Data Bandwidth, Gbps[a]	Full-Duplex Bandwidth, Gbps	Full-Duplex Bandwidth, GB/s
Infiniband 1x	2.5	4.0	8.0	1.0
Infiniband 4x	10.0	8.0	16.0	2.0
Infiniband 12x	30.0	24.0	48.0	6.0

a. Data encoding overhead reduces the "available" data rate.

Infiniband is based on high-speed, switched serial links that may be combined in parallel to increase bandwidth. The Infiniband architecture supports a switched fabric for the traffic, in addition to the channel-based host interconnects. A single "1x" Infiniband link is rated at 2.5 Gbps, but interface and switching hardware is currently available in 10 Gbps (4x) and 30 Gbps (12x) full-duplex port configurations (20-Gbps and 60-Gbps total bandwidth, respectively). Table 7–3 details specifications for the available link types.

Infiniband seems to be catching on as an HSI choice in both scientific and commercial database clusters because of its high bandwidth and low latency (on the order of 4.5 microseconds for a 0 byte packet). A number of companies currently provide Infiniband interface cards (PCI and PCI-X) and switches, including Voltaire Inc., Topspin Communications Inc., Infinicon Systems, and Mellanox Technologies Inc. As of this writing, the number-three supercomputer in the world is the Virginia Tech Terascale cluster (more than 10 TFLOPs), comprising 1,105 Apple Computer G5 systems interconnected with Infiniband switches from Mellanox Technologies.

Infiniband physical cable lengths for copper are limited to 17 m, and for fiber are allowed up to 17 km. The Infiniband specification includes physical, electrical, and software elements of the architecture. An interesting feature of the Infiniband hardware and software architecture is the allowance for RDMA between the interface cards and a user process' address space, so that operating system kernels can avoid data copying.

The Infiniband architecture is based on a reliable transport implemented on the interface card. This allows the bypass of the kernel's TCP/IP stack by use of the socket direct protocol (SDP), which interfaces directly between an application that uses the socket API and the Infiniband hardware, providing a TCP/IP-compatible transport. With this architecture, network transport tasks that would normally occur in the software TCP/IP stack are off-loaded to the Infiniband interface card, saving CPU overhead.

The Infiniband standard allows simultaneous transport of multiple high-level protocols through the switching fabric. Additional information on the Linux implementation of the Infiniband architecture is available at `http://sourceforge.net/projects/infiniband`. A high-level representation of the Infiniband architecture is shown in Figure 7–9.

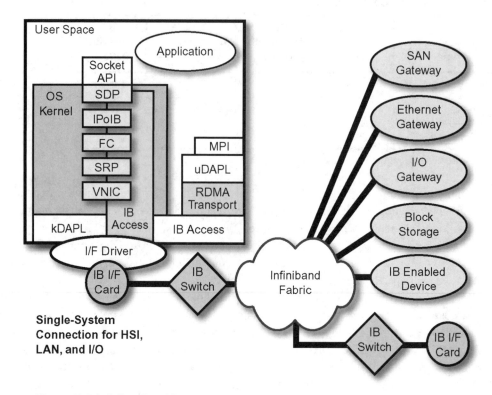

Figure 7–9 Infiniband architecture

Note that along with the Infiniband technology, we not only get the promise of a single system connection (and cable!) for the HSI, multiple LANs, and system I/O), but we also get an alphabet soup of new acronyms. Several new protocols, like IP over Infiniband (IPoIB), SCSI remote DMA protocol (SRP), and socket direct protocol (SDP) join the RDMA protocol. We also get virtual network interface card (VNIC), user direct access programming library (uDAPL), and kernel direct access programming library (kDAPL) in the bargain. Some of the preliminary relationships (some of the specifications are still being written) between these components are shown in Figure 7–9.

As an example of the current implementation state of Infiniband hardware, Mellanox Technologies[3] currently offers a dual-port, 10x PCI-X interface card and several switch configurations. A small switch, the 1U high MTS2400, with a total of 480 Gbps of backplane band-

---

3.   Information is provided from the Mellanox Web site at http://www.mellanox.com as of February 16, 2004. Information is subject to change, so check with the Mellanox Web site for the current state of their products and specifications.

width, may be configured with 24 ports of full-duplex 4x links (24 x 2 x10 Gbps) or 12 ports of 4x and 4 ports of 12x links (12 x 2 x 10 Gbps + 4 x 2 x 30 Gbps). A larger switch, the 7U high MTS9600, supports up to 96 ports of 10x links with 1.92 Tbps of backplane bandwidth.

The MTS9600 switch has eight slots for 12-port leaf boards and is configured as a two-stage fat tree to maintain constant cross-sectional bandwidth. Mellanox claims scaling to large configurations over 4000 nodes in the network. The MTS9600 switch provides redundant power supplies, a management board with provision for an additional redundant management board, and other high-availability features.

Although Infiniband pricing is not as inexpensive as a pervasive commercial-off-the-shelf solution might be, the price needs to be traded off against the performance and savings in construction costs for your cluster. Plans appear to be in place to provide 12 Gbps per link in the near term, and an aggregate of 100 Gbps sometime in the future. How Infiniband will stack up against HyperTransport and other high-speed serial technologies, only time will tell.

7.7 Dolphin

The Dolphin interconnect, from Dolphin Interconnect Solutions Inc. (also referred to as *Dolphinics*), is based on the ANSI/IEEE 1596-1992 standard scalable coherent interconnect (SCI). The link is described as a multiprocessor area network, rather than a LAN by the manufacturer, and was initially intended as a method of sharing memory access between computer hardware components.

Modular eight-port switches are available that implement 667 MB/s full duplex per link, for an aggregate bandwidth of 1.33 GB per second and a total switch backplane bandwidth of 3 GB/s. The manufacturer claims a port-to-port latency of 180 ns for this switch.[4] A latency of six microseconds for a 72-byte packet over the direct socket interface, and a peak bandwidth of 384 MB/s are listed among the benchmark information on the company's Web site.

Although the Dolphin interconnect is not as widespread as some of the others, it is used by Sun Microsystems as a high-availability clustering interconnect technology. The topology of this HSI is a 2D ring or a 3D torus, and it is interesting to note that a switch is *not* required to implement the Dolphin HSI interconnect, which saves implementation expense.

Examining the interface cards available for the Dolphin SCI interconnect reveals that there are two categories of cards—a dual-port SCI card and a six-port SCI card. The dual-port card may be used to implement directly connected 2D toroidal topologies using two axes, the six-port card may implement directly connected 3D toroidal topologies along three axes, and the switch may be employed to connect individual systems or 2D/3D topologies together.

---

4. Information is available at http://www.dolphinics.com. Information is as of February 16, 2004. Information is subject to change, so check with the Dolphin Interconnect Solutions Web site for the current state of their products and specifications

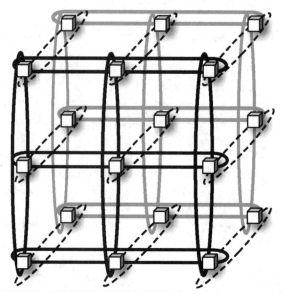

Figure 7–10 Example 3D topology with the Dolphin SCI interconnect

An example 3D topology is depicted in Figure 7–10. Shown is a 3 x 3 x 2 toroidal mesh with connections in the X, Y, and Z directions using the six-port interface card. This HSI topology is implemented without a central switch.

7.8 Quadrics QsNet

The last HSI technology we will examine in this chapter is the Quadrics QsNet and QsNet[II] networks from Quadrics[5] Ltd. The Quadrics HSI is truly an engineering marvel, providing massive amounts of bandwidth, very low latency, and high cross-sectional bandwidth. The Quadrics interconnect is used in several of the largest computers in the world, including the system at PNNL.

Interface cards for the earlier QsNet product are 64-bit, 66-MHz PCI, providing system-to-card bandwidth of 400 MB per second peak, with a card-to-network peak bandwidth of 350 MB per second (700 MB per second full duplex). QsNet[II] is based on PCI-X 133 MHz, providing a peak bandwidth of 900 MB/s unidirectional (838 MB/s bidirectional). The interface cards support direct DMA transfer of data from a process address space, providing "zero copy" transfers that improve performance and off-load processor effort.

---

5.   Information provided from http://www.quadrics.com. Information is provided is as of February 16, 2004, and is subject to change, so check with the Quadrics Web site for the current state of their products and specifications.

Quadrics supports "multiple rail" interface configurations with up to eight independent interface cards per system, providing the PCI infrastructure in the system is robust enough to provide adequate I/O performance. Networks using QsNet scale to 1,024 systems, and the newer QsNet[II] products allow scaling to 4,096 systems. Even though QsNet-based products are still available, I limit further discussion to the newer QsNet[II]-based products.

The QsNet[II] PCI-X interface implements a physical link that is 10 bits in each direction, with parallel, copper cables up to 13 m in length and ribbons of parallel fibers for increased distance—up to 100 m. The Quadrics switching hardware is built from eight-port custom switching ASICs incorporated into the standard switch chassis—available in eight-port and 64-port models.

The network topology is a multistage fat tree, and grows as a power of four, because the eight-port switch element ASICs are configured with four "up" links and four "down" links. At each stage of the network, there are four possible routes available for a packet. An example network for a 64-node three-stage fat tree is shown in Figure 7–11. Note that all switch elements in the stages are eight-port, so the "upper" stage in the diagram has four ports per switch element (64 total) available to connect "up" into a larger network.

The standard 64-port switch incorporates a three-stage fat tree network and provides 58 GB per second (`16 x 4 x 900 MB/s`) of bisectional bandwidth within the switch chassis. In this configuration, the chassis contains four 16-port switch interfaces. In larger networks, switch configurations with 64 system connections connect "up" to higher level "federated" network switches (so-called because the standard switch chassis may contain both node and top levels of switch interfaces).

A network of 1,024 nodes requires 16 64-port "node" switches and 64 16-port "top" switches, which may be housed in eight of the same chassis used for the node switch configura-

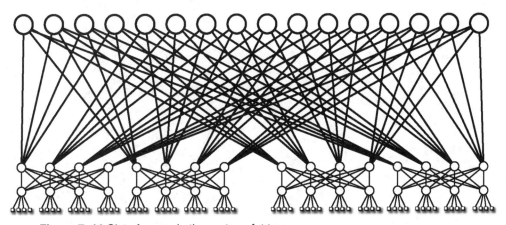

Figure 7–11 Sixty-four node three-stage fat tree

tion. Figure 7–11 shows the 64-port node switch configuration, which is the configuration for networks up to 64 systems, and is a basic building block for still larger networks.

Data routing is handled by the host adapter cards and skips busy links to avoid interference between messages. Data is routed "up" in the network until the destination port is within the available subtree, then routed "down" to the final destination. Data only changes direction in the network once, and packets maintain information about return paths to minimize return routing effort, as well as skipping faulty or disabled links.

Finally, the reported latency figure for the Quadrics QsNet^{II} interconnect is 2.95 microseconds one way for "short" MPI messages—0 bytes, to be exact. This, of course, is a *very* short message. The latency figure is for a Hewlett-Packard rx2600 Itanium 2 system, which has extremely good memory bandwidth and latency, along with a very good PCI-X I/O implementation.

7.9　HSI Technology Summary and Comparison

If your cluster needs a high-speed interconnect to support parallel program components, there are a lot of choices. Which technology you select depends on the required performance characteristics, the size of your cluster, and the total cost of implementing the HSI. You must take care to ensure that the software, in terms of MPI, PVM, or OpenMP libraries and drivers, is available for your selected HSI technology and compute slice hardware.

We examined a range of topologies and performance points for HSI technology in this chapter. We also saw that beyond a certain point, the low cost benefits of Ethernet switches may disappear as a result of the chassis interconnect requirements for maintaining cross-sectional bandwidth. If reached, this is the point at which you will need to decide whether a specialized HSI technology like Infiniband, Dolphin, Myrinet, or Quadrics QsNet^{II} is a better choice for your cluster.

## PART III

Cluster Software Architecture

The Right Stuff: Linux as the Basis for Clusters

Chapter Objectives

- Introduce some of the criteria for choosing a cluster operating system
- Describe some of the major advantages of the Linux operating system
- Explain why the Linux operating system makes a good basis for clusters
- Provide a survey of the most popular Linux distributions used for building clusters

This book is about building clusters using the Linux operating system. It should come as no surprise that we have to start describing the application of the Linux operating system to clusters at some point in our discussion. I will try to take a realistic view of the requirements for using Linux in building clusters.

8.1 Choosing a Cluster Operating System

Building a cluster's hardware from commodity pieces is only the start. To make the cluster a usable solution, it must run an operating system and applications. In short, there must be software to run *on* the cluster hardware. But which operating system forms a reasonable basis for a cluster environment?

In a book on Linux clusters, it should come as no surprise that Linux is the operating system of choice. But for fairness's sake, let's start by identifying some of the characteristics that a cluster software environment requires. This should help us understand the proper choice of operating system for our cluster.

Some attributes we want are

- Hardware support
- Stability
- Low cost
- Manageability
- Flexibility
- Scalability
- Openness
- Software availability and cost
- Multiple support options

8.1.1   Hardware Support

Support for the hardware architecture in our cluster is a must for any selected operating system. To minimize complexity, a cluster will usually consist of systems with the same processor architecture, and often the same processor speed. The operating system we choose should support the processor type we select for our cluster, and an added benefit would be support for the same functionality on multiple processor types. In this way, we can reuse our development efforts across multiple platforms.

Linux runs on a wide range of processor architectures. Currently, Linux supports systems built with IA-32, Itanium, Alpha, Opteron, PA-RISC, SPARC, and many more processors. Sometimes support for a particular processor or system configuration entails selecting a particular "flavor" of Linux, but the support *is* there.

8.1.2   Operating System Stability

Any operating system we choose must be stable and reliable, or our cluster's software environment will fail and overall reliability will suffer. Because the cluster is viewed as a single system by its users, the overall stability of that system relies, at its lowest level, on the stability of the operating system software. Note that stability in this sense refers to the operating system's ability to run long periods of time without crashing, locking up, or hanging.

Linux is very stable in both UP and multiprocessor SMP hardware configurations. Linux is increasingly used in areas in which stability and commodity costs are important. It has been used as the basis for ISPs infrastructure, provides the operating system platform for parallel Web and database servers and other business-critical systems, and has proved itself in cluster environments at many installations.

8.1.3   Software License Costs

Our cluster will comprise multiple independent hardware systems, each running a copy of the chosen operating system software. Because of this, the per-system licensing cost for the operating system and other software becomes increasingly important as the cluster grows in size.

Spending $300 or $700 or $1500 per node for the operating system and associated software licenses is very expensive (and not very practical) in a large cluster. The whole advantage of building clusters from *commodity* components is the expected cost savings over noncommodity ingredients.

Linux is available from many sources, in many different configurations. The license cost of Linux ranges all the way from free to very expensive, depending on the required support level and the vendor. Although "free is a very, very good price" (to quote a local Portland, Oregon, furniture store owner, Tom Peterson), choosing the proper distribution and associated support options will affect the cost. I will discuss this in an upcoming section.

8.1.4 Manageability

The operating system choice must provide tools for managing the multiple systems in the cluster, along with the ability to enable the automation of the custom processes that we will create. Management in this sense requires secure remote access, remote display features, robust scripting facilities, well-designed system installation and software deployment vehicles, and a strong ability to monitor system and application performance.

The individual Linux system is every bit as manageable as any other UNIX-like system, with secure remote access, scripting, software development facilities, and other essential management components. The addition of freely available tools to the base operating system enhances manageability without necessarily increasing the software license costs. The operating system provides all the features mentioned as requirements, and packages are readily available to manage networked environments like a cluster.

8.1.5 Software Flexibility

A good portion of the software infrastructure that will run in our cluster is based on client–server architectures (DHCP, DNS, NFS, and so forth). The marketing departments in some software companies feel the need to create artificial packaging for the operating system and tools. Instead of providing all functionality in a single product, the operating system is divided into "desktop" and "server" configurations. There is an extra (frequently large) charge for the server portion of the software. The fundamental assumption appears to be that there will be fewer servers than clients, so it is a better revenue-generating scheme to charge more money for server functionality.

We will avoid any operating system that follows this artificial packaging scheme. We need the flexibility to choose our own architectural configurations for our cluster's internal software. Linux provides that flexibility by allowing the system manager to choose which services run where in the cluster. Artificial marketing divisions of software functionality need not get in the way of our design choices and software costs.

8.1.6 Openness

The Linux operating system has support for multiple programming languages, multiple scripting languages, and a variety of software development tools. Its focus on providing popular development tools, along with the operating system, makes it a good choice for software development, whether your target operating system is Linux. Linux is a software developer's dream in terms of tools and environment.

The operating system specifications, and indeed the operating source code itself, is freely available. Because of the openness, the potential to run tools and applications from multiple vendors or private sources is enhanced.

8.1.7   Scalability

To borrow two terms from the current commercial IT world, we want to be able to *scale up* and *scale out* with our operating system. What this means is that we require the ability to scale "up" the number of processors inside a given compute slice, if this gives us an advantage, and at the same time our operating system should support "scaling out" by interconnecting the required number of individual systems in our cluster. This requires SMP scaling "inside" a system, and network connectivity scaling "outside" the system.

Linux supports both UP and multiprocessor SMP hardware in configurations most likely to be found in our cluster compute slices and infrastructure systems. Along with the ability to scale "up" the number of processors in a system, the operating system supports TCP/IP networking for both Ethernet and HSI hardware, along with support for other connection types to interconnect systems in the cluster and to connect the cluster to existing network infrastructure. Addition of MPI and the appropriate drivers allows parallel communication between application components on separate systems, if the cluster requires it.

8.1.8   Software Availability and Cost

In addition to the operating system, there are numerous other software packages needed to construct a cluster, including load-balancing (batch management, queueing, and so on) software, monitoring and management tools, software update and installation tools, compilers, communication libraries, and a wealth of other categories. If we choose an operating system environment that charges money for each of these tools, we face the same issues mentioned previously with regard to operating system license expense. We want a readily available selection of tools, at minimal cost.

Linux certainly provides a wealth of available software. As a matter of fact there is such a wide selection of Linux-based software that it often becomes difficult to choose between the many alternatives. Some of the software packages are available in free versions, as well as versions that cost money, but provide support, additional documentation, or other benefits.

8.1.9   Multiple Support Options

Experience levels with operating system environments vary as widely as the required availability for a particular cluster. A custom solution, with very experienced local administrators requires less support than a solution in a business-critical environment. The ability to contract for required levels of both hardware and operating system support is essential to maintaining availability of the cluster.

Support is available from the major Linux vendors, such as Red Hat or SUSE, for the components contained in their distributions. Several of the major hardware vendors, like Hewlett-Packard, also provide support for Linux through their normal support channels. It is possible to choose a level of support that matches your own specific needs and budget. You also have the option to support your Linux installation yourself and work directly with the open-source community to resolve issues.

8.2 Introducing the Linux Operating System and Licensing

A rose by any other name would smell as sweet, and Linux, no matter how you name it, is an exciting development. However, Linux, like any other technology, is only useful once we *apply* it to solving a particular problem. Building a cluster with Linux is creating just such a solution. By configuring subsystems, tuning the operating system, adding the proper software packages, and creating a final configuration for the cluster environment, we are crafting a solution from raw technology.

What is commonly referred to as Linux is actually the operating system kernel alone, originally developed by Linus Torvalds. In addition to the kernel, however, there are many tools from the GNU (an acronym for "GNU is Not Unix"[1]) project at the Free Software Foundation (FSF) *along with other* publicly available software. The kernel alone does not make up the whole of what we call Linux.

Much of Linux, in addition to the software that comes directly from the GNU project, is available from companies and software engineers that developed it under the auspices of the GNU general public license (GPL). Because a lot of the software that surrounds the Linux kernel comes from the GNU project, a more correct way to refer to Linux might be "GNU/Linux," although for simplicity we will continue to call it just "Linux." There is still some argument over this point in the community. I will take the easiest path here.

Linux is a UNIX-like operating system (a combination of the kernel and surrounding tools) that is being developed *and licensed* in a new and revolutionary way. The development method is termed *open-source software development* (OSSD), or commonly "open source." Although the FSF would prefer that everybody refer to the software as "free software," common usage still applies the term *open source*. They may not mean exactly the same thing, but it's probably too late to correct the usage at this point.

The GNU project was started in 1984 to produce an operating system that is free software. Here, the word "free" is used in a different sense than one would expect, so it is important to get

---

1. You will notice that the GNU acronym is "recursive" in that the G stands for GNU, which reintroduces the acronym "inside" the acronym. UNIX programmers, systems people, and Linux developers love this sort of "in" or tricky semantic joke.

the intention correct. Quoting from the FSF Web site `http://www.fsf.org/philoso-phy/free-sw.html`:

> Free software is a matter of the users' freedom to run, copy, distribute, study, change and improve the software. More precisely, it refers to four kinds of freedom, for the users of the software:
>
> The freedom to run the program, for any purpose (freedom 0).
>
> The freedom to study how the program works, and adapt it to your needs (freedom 1). Access to the source code is a precondition for this.
>
> The freedom to redistribute copies so you can help your neighbor (freedom 2).
>
> The freedom to improve the program, and release your improvements to the public, so that the whole community benefits (freedom 3). Access to the source code is a precondition for this.
>
> A program is free software if users have all of these freedoms. Thus, you should be free to redistribute copies, either with or without modifications, either gratis or charging a fee for distribution, to anyone anywhere. Being free to do these things means (among other things) that you do not have to ask or pay for permission.[2] [FSF 2004]

This is a very important distinction about the use of "free" software, focusing on the word "free." The software does not have to be free in terms of price, but it does have to be freely available in the sense used by the GPL and the other open-source licenses under which it is distributed. You simply cannot take free software, and convert it to proprietary, closed-source products; the GPL was written to prevent this.

For a further understanding of the GPL and other "public" licenses, like the "Artistic" license (`http://language.perl.com/misc/artistic.html`) and the Berkeley Software Division BSD-style license (`http://www.debian.org/misc/bsd.license`), nothing substitutes for *reading* them (the GPL, in several formats, is available at `http://www.fsf.org/licenses/licenses.html`).

---

2.   Copyright © 1996, 1997, 1998, 1999, 2000, 2001, 2002, 2003, Free Software Foundation, Inc., 59 Temple Place, Suite 330, Boston, MA 02111, USA. Verbatim copying and distribution of this entire article is permitted in any medium without royalty provided this notice is preserved.

There are a lot of people with a lot of ideas and misconceptions about what they really say and mean, but only some of the opinions come from actual readings of the license text. I urge you to read at least the text of the GPL if you are not familiar with it.[3]

8.3 Linux Distributions

All arguments about origins and content aside, the primary way to get Linux is by choosing and installing a particular Linux distribution. Each Linux distribution has its own selection of open-source software packages, "value-added" content like installation tools, a particular package management system, a system structure and "philosophy," and a particular version of the Linux kernel (along with applied patches, or "errata") at its center. Along with the word *distribution*, you will also hear and see *Linux distro* or just *distro* used by the community as shorthand.

As we discussed in the previous section, a Linux distribution does not have to be free. The distribution's provider may charge for documentation, packaging, support, and other content, but the free software's source code must be provided (or be freely available) as specified by whatever open-source license applies to it. The source code for the distribution may be in the commercially packaged CD-ROMs or it may be downloadable from a Web site, but it is available.

If you go to `http://www.linux.org` and use their search tool to search for Intel-compatible Linux distributions, you will find 185 separate listings. Many of these have their own particular slant on *how* the software in the distribution may be applied: embedded systems, software development, desktop computing, minimal environments, and many more design centers. You need to choose the proper distribution for your needs carefully, and it might pay to check with `http://www.distrowatch.com` for the top ten distributions and their status. In the interest of space, I cover a minimal number of the available distributions here.

Among the criteria for selecting a Linux distribution for your cluster are

- Support options, including security updates
- Software package content
- Expected longevity of the distribution
- Licensing cost per system, if applicable
- Installation tools and ease of installation
- Manageability features
- Kernel version
- Hardware architecture support
- Support software issues

---

3. This is also referred to as a *copyleft* in reference to the familiar term *copyright*, because the software is first copyrighted, then the distribution terms (free distribution, and so forth) are specifically added to the copyright. The terms of the copyleft are specified in the GPL.

You can see from this list that many of the same criteria we used to justify selecting Linux as the operating system for our cluster are also issues when choosing a particular Linux distribution to use for a cluster.

Choosing a nonmainstream distribution for your cluster may be acceptable, if you are ready to assume support responsibilities yourself. Linux distributions, especially those that are focused on narrow objectives, seem to come and go on a regular basis. It is likely that distributions that do not have wide acceptance may simply fade away. Frequently, the level of support required for business-critical clusters is only available for commercial distributions.

For these reasons it may be in your best interest to choose a commercially available Linux distribution to power your cluster. There are also several free distributions that may meet your requirements if you plan on supporting your own software environment. Some commercially available distributions include Red Hat Linux and SUSE Linux, and some free distributions include The Fedora Project and Debian Linux. We examine some of these distributions in upcoming sections.

8.4　Managing Open-Source Software "Churn"

The Linux kernel, and the open-source software packages that surround it, are under constant development. Features are added, bugs are fixed, and security vulnerabilities are patched, all of which generates revisions in the individual packages. The term *churn*, as I use it, refers to the never-ending stream of new packages that become available for a Linux environment, the effort required to install them, and the potential effects on an existing environment.

One of the great strengths of open-source development is the lack of direct financial constraints on the creativity of the programmers supporting a particular package. Bugs and issues may be very quickly resolved by contacting the developers directly via e-mail, Internet relay chat (IRC) channels, or newsgroups. The "time to resolution" for some issues is truly astounding—sometimes measured in terms of hours.

For system stability, it is normal practice to test and qualify all new software configurations before releasing them into a production environment. As new package versions are released, identifying new packages and applying the qualification process can take a substantial amount of effort, along with direct contact with the open-source developers. Your organization may not have the time or resources to sustain this level of involvement and the associated "churn."

This situation brings us back to the definition of the word *free* discussed previously. The open-source Linux-based software may be free in the sense of "unencumbered," but to apply it in your environment, and to your cluster, will have associated costs and responsibilities that match your organization's processes and requirements for reliability and stability. This is where you need to consider carefully the benefits of paying for the proper level of support for your Linux environment against expected savings for software licensing.

Your options include either assuming complete responsibility for supporting the Linux environment yourself, by hiring the appropriate people to manage the OSSD interface, buying support for Linux from your hardware vendor, or directly purchasing commercial Linux distributions that include the appropriate level of support. The message is that the use of open-source software in general, and Linux in particular, requires a different approach than you might be customary—but remember that "different" should not be equated with "bad." The good news is that you have several choices regarding how you approach the issue.

Aside from making choices about portions of your chosen environment, your independent software vendors (ISVs) will also add some constraints to the mixture. If you are using third-party software from an ISV like Oracle, you will need to choose the distribution, and version of that distribution, that supports the ISV's software. An ISV may require a particular distribution (Red Hat or SUSE), a particular version of the distribution (Red Hat 7.3 or SUSE 8.0), and specific package revisions within that version of the distribution (`glibc-2.3.2-4.80.8`, `XFree86-4.2.1-23`, and so on).

Almost every Linux distribution has a package update tool that is intended to make updating the operating system less of a chore. Currently installed versions of packages are compared with a list of available updates, selection criteria are applied, and the packages are downloaded and automatically installed. The update tools, such as Red Hat's `up2date` can mitigate the software churn in the distributions that have frequent updates.

8.5   Commercial Linux Distributions

The need to generate revenue and minimize software churn for ISVs and customers is driving some of the commercial distributions toward the same "desktop" versus "server" packaging issues we described previously, along with less-frequent updates and expanded support offerings. The packaging choices complicate our efforts to build a cluster with supported versions of Linux.

We would like to have all the server software components we might need available, without having to buy, and manage, separate operating system products for compute slices, file servers, and administrative nodes in the cluster. An alternative, buying one distribution's product and adding the necessary packages ourselves, creates extra work for us in the support area and may actually invalidate support from the vendor. We will take a quick look at the current features in two commercial Linux distributions available from Red Hat and SUSE, along with the free distribution from The Fedora Project[4] and Debian Linux.

---

4.   Please note that information provided is provided for informational purposes only and is obtained from the public Web sites for Red Hat Linux `http://www.redhat.com`, SUSE Linux `http://www.suse.com`, and The Fedora Project `http://fedora.redhat.com`. Product offerings, contents, and other specifications may change at any time. You should check with the specific Web site to verify the current information before making purchasing or design decisions.

8.5.1   Red Hat Linux

The current form of the Red Hat Linux distribution had its origins in a version of Linux that could be purchased commercially, downloaded from their Web site, and freely copied (both source and binaries) across as many systems as the customer desired. Red Hat made its money by providing optional support and update services. Today, however, the business model has changed, and you should read the Red Hat Enterprise Linux (RHEL) "frequently asked questions" list (FAQ), found at `http://www.redhat.com/software/rhel/faq`, for complete details.

The FAQ explains that the original Red Hat Linux products were primarily a vehicle for distributing the Linux operating system and open-source components to early adopters, Linux fans, and developers. As the Linux operating system matured, however, customers and ISVs began requesting a more stable, supported environment for their business-critical software. The current RHEL products are refocused on commercial, officially supported installations. The free version of Linux from Red Hat, called *Fedora*, is described later in this chapter.

The current Linux product offerings from Red Hat are purchased by yearly subscription only, and are restricted with regard to free copying. (This change occurred after the Red Hat version 9.0 software release.) The simplest way to explain the current situation is that you will need to purchase a license for every system on which you install the Red Hat software, *if you use the Red Hat binaries*. But, you ask, what about the free software (and the associated open-source licenses) upon which Red Hat is built?

The source code for the software open-source software that makes up the distribution is still downloadable from the Red Hat Web site. Most of the code contained in the Red Hat releases (with exceptions like Java) is all open source and covered by the GPL or a similar license. The source code is freely available from the Red Hat file transfer protocol (FTP) site, so the conditions of the open-source license are met.

Red Hat *does not*, however, allow you to distribute the *binaries* of RHEL freely. The system subscription that you buy from Red Hat consists of the binaries, access to upgrades, and some level of support services when you buy a particular packaging of the RHEL distribution. *Every* system on which you install RHEL *must* be properly licensed.

If you require a supported, low-churn version of Linux, and can afford to pay the subscription cost, then the Red Hat offerings are a very good choice. If you require a zero-dollar product, similar to the older Red Hat offerings like 6.x, 7.x, 8.x, and 9.x, then the Fedora distribution is probably a better choice. The primary difference will be the level of available "formal" support and the amount of "churn" you will need to manage.

As of this writing, Red Hat provides three Enterprise Linux subscriptions: WS (workstation), ES (enterprise server), and AS (advanced server). Within each of these product subscriptions, there are three possible "editions": basic edition, standard edition, and premium edition. Not all of the three subscription choices make all editions available. For example, basic and standard editions are available for RHEL WS and ES subscriptions, but not for the AS subscription.

Standard editions are available for WS, ES, and AS subscriptions, but a premium edition is only available for the AS subscription.

To make matters even more complicated, there are different availabilities and prices, depending on the processor architecture within the subscriptions. RHEL ES basic and standard editions only support the Intel x86 architecture. To get server support for Intel Itanium and AMD Opteron, customers need to select the RHEL AS subscription, with either the standard or premium editions. RHEL WS basic will support Itanium, but at an extra cost over and above the x86 price.

What used to be an easy choice for cluster environments is now fairly complex and can be expensive, particularly if you are deploying a cluster with Itanium or Opteron systems (see Table 8–1 for details). The Red Hat Web site mentions high-performance computing and recommends deploying the RHEL WS subscription in clusters, but this option is between $179 (x86) and $792 (Itanium and Opteron) at list price.[5] The Web site also mentions that Red Hat is working with partners to provide solutions specifically aimed at high performance technical computing (HPTC) clusters.

Table 8–1 RHEL Product Structure[a]

Red Hat Subscription and Processor Support	Basic Edition	Standard Edition	Premium Edition
Red Hat Enterprise Linux WS	---------------------	---------------------	---------------------
Intel 32 bit (IA-32)	Available	Available	N/A
Intel Itanium (IA-64), AMD64	N/A	Available, extra cost over IA-32	N/A
Red Hat Enterprise Linux ES	---------------------	---------------------	---------------------
Intel 32 bit (IA-32)	Available	Available	N/A
Red Hat Enterprise Linux AS	---------------------	---------------------	---------------------
Intel 32 bit (IA-32)	N/A	Available	Available
Intel Itanium (IA-64), AMD64	N/A	Available, extra cost over IA-32	Available, extra cost over IA-32

a.   As of February 24, 2004. Check the Red Hat Web site for current information.

---

5.   Price is US list price on February 23, 2004, from the Red Hat Web site. See the information listed at http://www.redhat.com/software/rhel/purchase for current details.

What we are left with, if we need a supported version of Red Hat Linux for a production cluster, is a pretty hefty set of license fees (especially if you are running on Itanium or Opteron hardware) that need annual renewal to continue support. Because all compute slices in the cluster are usually identical, one has to question the usefulness of purchasing a support subscription for every identically deployed system in a cluster. If a bug or security vulnerability shows up on one system, it will show up on all of them, and the fix for one system is the same fix that is applied to all the others.

Several possible deployment strategies, based on the current product pricing and marketing decisions about processor support and packaging from Red Hat, are as follows.

- Pay the license fee for the same version of RHEL (the greatest common denominator) and deploy it on all systems in the cluster (for example, RHEL ES basic edition for x86-based clusters).
- Deploy the WS subscription, basic edition on all compute slices (extra cost for Itanium), and ES subscription basic edition on infrastructure, administrative, and file server systems (AS subscription premium edition will be required to support Itanium servers).
- Work with your hardware vendor, or even Red Hat itself, for better pricing. Some systems come prelicensed with RHEL.
- Deploy the minimal cost Red Hat configuration (lowest common denominator) and add the required open-source functionality yourself. This will have support consequences.
- Search for distributions, like NWLinux,[6] which are based on recompiled sources from Red Hat, and are unencumbered by the Red Hat binary licenses.

One of the nice things about Linux and open source is that there are multiple places to get the same solution. Which approach you choose will depend on your individual circumstances, such as budget, ISV software, and need for business-critical support.

8.5.2   SUSE Linux

The Linux distribution from SUSE is broken down into desktop and server product offerings. The number of configurations for the server offering is only two as of this writing: SUSE Linux Standard Server and SUSE Linux Enterprise Server. The Standard Server offering supports up to two AMD32 or IA-32 (32-bit) CPUs per system and provides the server versions of subsystems that we require for our cluster infrastructure and administrative nodes. The Enterprise Server offering provides support for up to 32-way, 32-bit SMP systems or up to 64-way, 64-bit (AMD64 or Itanium) SMP systems, and provides the required server components of client–server software. The SUSE Linux desktop product structure is shown in Table 8–2.

---

6.   Information is available at http://www.emsl.pnl.gov/nwlinux. This distribution is specifically for Itanium-based systems and is based on Red Hat Advanced Server 2.1 for Itanium.

Table 8–2 SUSE Linux Desktop Product Structure[a]

SUSE Desktop Product	Personal	Professional
SUSE Linux 9.0	------------------	-----------------
Intel 32 bit (IA-32)	Supported	Supported
AMD64	N/A	Supported at extra cost

a.   Product structure as of February 24, 2004. Check the SUSE Web site for current information.

Table 8–3 SUSE Linux Product Structure[a]

SUSE Linux Server Product	Up to 2 CPUs	Up to 8 CPUs
SUSE Linux Standard Server 8	-----------------------	---------------------
Intel/AMD 32 bit (IA-32, AMD32)	Supported	N/A
AMD 64 bit, Intel 64 bit Itanium (AMD64, IA-64)	N/A	N/A
SUSE Linux Enterprise Server 8	-----------------------	--------------------
Intel/AMD 32 bit (IA-32, AMD32)	Supported	Supported
AMD 64 bit, Intel 64 bit Itanium (AMD64, IA-64)	Supported	Supported

a.   Product structure as of February 24, 2004. Check the SUSE Web site for current information.

The SUSE Linux desktop offerings are primarily aimed at providing an interactive environment for office automation. The only processors supported for the desktop versions of the SUSE distribution are the Intel x86 and AMD64 architectures. This means that a server version of the distribution must be purchased to support Itanium processors. The SUSE Linux server product structure is shown in Table 8–3.

On the surface, this would appear to be a substantially easier product structure than the Red Hat offerings. Once you get beyond the surface level of the two server products, however, the complexity of the SUSE server product offerings equals Red Hat product complexity. There are different pricing options for SUSE's Linux Standard Server and Linux Enterprise Server, based on the number (either "up to two" or "up to eight") of processors and the type of processor. Support is purchased in units of two or eight processors.

As with Red Hat products, the SUSE product's license only allows you to install their distribution on systems that have a valid maintenance agreement, even though the software packages in their distribution are covered by the GPL and other public, open-source licenses. Thus, selecting SUSE as your cluster's Linux distribution will depend more on preference and application support rather than on simplification and reduction of licensing costs. Once again, the inclusion of support substantially raises the cost of deploying a cluster solution.

8.5.3   Conclusions about Commercial Linux Distributions

To make money, remain in business, and grow, commercial Linux companies have to sell support services and their own "value-added" products along with the open-source software (which they cannot directly sell in the traditional way) in their distributions. The prices they charge are aimed primarily at commercial IT environments[7] and the replacement of existing proprietary UNIX servers, and are not easily adapted to cost savings in a cluster environment. This places cluster designers in an interesting position (some would say "catch-22") with regard to providing a supported cluster operating system environment, and yet maintaining commodity cost savings with cluster solutions.

Licenses on current commercial distributions of Linux from Red Hat and SUSE restrict the number of systems you can install with their binaries, without purchasing support, to a single system. Because a license is needed for every copy of the operating system that is installed, the cost negates part of the price savings that justified a commodity cluster approach in the first place. Although some distributions that comprise the recompiled sources from commercial distributions are available, they do not provide the level of support required for business-critical situations.

If you are not willing to produce an in-house Linux configuration from a free distribution, your option is to select a commercial version that includes support in its price. This is certainly true if you are running third-party software that was qualified against a specific distribution and version of that distribution. To provide a supported, qualified environment for your ISV software will narrow the range of your choices. Some of the commercial Linux distributions appear to be recognizing the difficulties presented for cluster solutions by the current licensing costs. Concrete solutions do not appear to be available as of this writing.

If you are running your own software, or have the resources to support a recompiled distribution yourself, then you have a wider range of choices. You may be able to deploy a freely available distribution on compute slices (the majority of the cluster members), and deploy a commercial Linux distribution only where there is a specific need for application or specialized support (file servers, administrative nodes, and so on). The next section describes two freely available distributions.

---

7.   Only time will tell how successful this approach will be. Linux is currently, by most reports, displacing mainly proprietary UNIX systems in IT departments. Many research or educational institutions are using free or special versions of Linux distributions to provide the operating system software for their clusters. We are apparently on the cusp of some changes, at least with regard to general cluster solution acceptance and commercial Linux pricing.

8.6 Free Linux Distributions

There are several free Linux distributions available. Two of them are Fedora, from The Fedora Project, and Debian Linux. Both of these distributions are free in the sense of "no charge," may be downloaded from their respective Web sites, and may be installed on as many systems as desired. The next two sections discuss these distributions.

8.6.1 The Fedora Project

If you require a freely copyable version of Linux, one that tracks the most current open-source developments and follows the standard open-source level of support (e-mail, Web, newsgroups, and IRC), you should consider the Linux distribution provided by The Fedora Project. This distribution includes all software components (client and server) in the distribution package, making no distinction between "workstations," "desktops," or "servers." As of this writing, the functionality of Fedora closely resembles Red Hat Linux version 9.0, with some changes. It is likely to move away from this resemblance in the future (particularly with the addition of the new 2.6 kernel version in the Core 2 releases).

The objectives for Fedora are also different from the commercial Linux distributions like Red Hat and SUSE, which are attempting to provide the stability required by ISVs and commercial customers. The Fedora Project is not a supported product provided by Red Hat. To see the exact definitions and goals of the project, visit The Fedora Project Web site at `http://fedora.redhat.com`. Some of the goals are

- To provide a trial environment for technologies that may become part of the RHEL products
- To provide a complete Linux operating system distribution that is built from free software
- To provide regular releases somewhere around two or three times a year

If you are willing to create your own support and qualification process, the Fedora distribution may be a potential solution, particularly if you are running your own software and do not have to rely on qualified operating system and software combinations from ISVs.

The development status of this distribution is at once an advantage and a disadvantage. As an advantage, Fedora is likely to have the new 2.6 version of the Linux kernel available before the other commercial distributions release it. As a disadvantage, the Fedora distribution will have a higher than average amount of churn because of its development and "leading-edge" focus.

As of this writing, the Fedora distribution release is currently "Core 1," which supports the Intel IA-32 (x86) processor architraves. A test version of this release is available for AMD64 processors. The Core 2 release is expected to support the 2.6 version of the Linux kernel and was released in early spring of 2004.

8.6.2   Debian Linux

One of the primary objectives for the Debian distribution is to provide a Linux environment consisting of free software. The Debian Project Web site, `http://www.debian.org/intro/about`, states:

> The Debian Project is an association of individuals who have made common cause to create a free operating system. This operating system that we have created is called Debian GNU/Linux, or simply Debian for short. [Debian 2004]

The Debian distribution is in no way compromised by providing only free software. There are more than 8,700 packages listed on their Web site. For a list of the available packages for the Debian distribution, see `http://www.debian.org/distrib/packages`. Commercial software packages are also available for Debian Linux.

The Debian distribution supports a wide range of hardware architectures. Supported architectures include Alpha, PA-RISC, Itanium (IA-64), IA-32 (x86), SPARC, ARM, and quite a few others. As of this writing, Debian does not support the AMD processor architecture. It is worth checking the Debian distribution's Web site to see if it currently supports the processor architecture you are targeting.

8.6.3   Conclusions about Free Distributions

If you are very cost conscious, you will need to consider the free Linux distributions as a way to save license expense. Of course, this will only be possible if you do not have applications that are qualified against a specific commercially supported distribution. The savings in license costs need to be weighed against the cost of supporting the Linux environment yourself.

You should not immediately dismiss the possibility of supporting a free distribution yourself, or looking for alternative support channels. There is no reason that you cannot adopt a more measured release strategy using the high-churn development distributions. Even some proprietary UNIX operating systems are infamous for the number of patches issued per unit of time.

System administrators have crafted workable release and qualification processes to deal with minimizing risk to production environments from high-churn commercial operating systems, and the circumstances with free Linux distributions are not *entirely* different. If you identify the portions of the environment that are really in use, particularly on the compute slices, you may be surprised at how minimal the Linux installation needs to be.

You should be aware of the potential difference in directory structure and package management between the two free distributions. Fedora, because it is derived from the Red Hat distributions, uses the Red Hat package manager (the `rpm` command and `.rpm` file extension for software packages) and has a similar directory structure (this may change or evolve). The Debian distribution uses a different set of package management tools (the `dpkg` command and

.deb file extension for software packages) and will have a slightly different system structure and administration approach.

8.7 Conclusions about Linux for Clusters

We have taken a pretty hard look at the product structure of two commercial Linux distributions that may be used in a cluster environment. Because of the product structure and pricing for commercial Linux distributions, there are a number of issues to overcome if you are extremely cost sensitive. I have several important points to make about using commercial versions of Linux in a cluster.

- The license costs for commercial distributions include support and updates.
- The availability of free tools may more than offset the expense of a commercial distribution (such as compilers, monitoring tools, management tools, and so forth).
- You may deploy less-capable versions of a commercial offering (for example, RHEL WS) on compute slices if your applications allow it.
- An application vendor, such as Oracle, will qualify their software against one or more specific versions of commercial distributions (for example, RHEL AS and SUSE Linux Enterprise Server 8.0), and may include specific kernel or package version requirements.
- The processor type you choose for your cluster will affect licensing costs.
- Hardware vendors may include licenses for some commercial distributions along with the system.

Some of the issues associated with using free distributions of Linux (Debian or Fedora) in a cluster are the following.

- Support is tied to communication with the open-source software developers or to providing your own Linux expertise.
- Although the acquisition of the software is free, the use and support of it within your organization still has associated costs that must be weighed against the cost of commercial distributions.
- Applications from ISVs may not be qualified and supported for free distributions.
- It is possible to manage open-source software churn by creating your own qualification and release process, thus gaining the benefits from a free distribution.

As with any design decision, choosing the proper Linux distribution will depend on your own situation and the characteristics of your cluster. Research, scientific, or experimental clusters in organizations with extensive Linux and open-source experience may have no difficulty employing free Linux distributions. Business-critical clusters with third-party software, or organizations with limited Linux and open-source experience, will have a more limited set of choices. But at least there *are* choices.

The recognition, by commercial Linux distribution vendors, that a cluster represents a special case for support, would make our selection of a distribution—commercial or otherwise—a whole lot easier. Although there is a tangible benefit to having support on all systems in a cluster, paying for the service on 256 compute slices in a cluster does not deliver 256 times the value of buying support on a single business-critical server. Scaling "up" does not currently equate with scaling "out" using commercial Linux distributions. It should not be more expensive to license eight two-CPU systems than a single 16-CPU system. Until this realization is made clear and reasonable solutions are found, cluster designers will have to weigh all operating system costs and benefits very carefully, potentially making less-than-optimum choices.

With all support issues aside, Linux still provides the most flexible operating system environment for clusters. The wide range of freely available, open-source software, like compilers, network installation tools, management tools, monitoring tools, Web servers, databases, infrastructure services, and other essential components, adds to the potential for savings. These components, along with the flexibility and openness to choose custom configurations to meet specific needs, make Linux a very cost-effective environment for cluster solutions. What we *need* is a version of a commercial Linux distribution that is targeted for compute slices, and a special support pricing scheme that acknowledges that clusters are a special case.

## CHAPTER 9

Round and Round It Goes: Booting, Disks, Partitioning, and Local File Systems

Chapter Objectives

- Cover Linux boot loaders and the initial RAM disk image
- Introduce Linux disk-partitioning processes
- Discuss the configuration and use of software RAID devices
- Introduce some popular Linux physical file systems

Disks and local file systems are an integral part of any Linux installation. The Linux boot and partition scheme is driven in part by BIOS concerns, and is central to all the systems in the cluster. Infrastructure servers in a cluster may use either hardware or software RAID devices to improve performance or availability. Once the underlying disk structures are in place, there are a number of file systems and tuning options from which to choose. This chapter provides an introduction to managing Linux disks and file systems.

9.1 Disk Partitioning, Booting, and the BIOS

The PC BIOS has been a part of commodity systems since the original IBM PC was introduced. It originally was to be found permanently "burned" into electrically programmable read-only memory (EPROM) and quite firmly attached (soldered) to the computer's motherboard. If you were *really* lucky and bought well, your hardware vendor spent the extra $0.15 to put the BIOS EPROM in a socket so it could be replaced.

Fortunately, times have changed and technology has advanced. Today, the BIOS usually lives in nonvolatile RAM (NVRAM), battery-backed complementary metal oxide semiconductor (CMOS) RAM, or "flash" programmable RAM, and may be updated by software as bugs are found and functionality is added. (As an added benefit, "flashing" the wrong BIOS version for your hardware can turn your system into a high-tech boat anchor, unless the hardware manufacturer has allocated extra NVRAM space to saving the old BIOS for later restoration.) As a matter of fact, "flashing" the BIOS is a system administration task that can consume a substantial amount of time (and risk) each time it is needed in a cluster environment.

The BIOS has continued to serve the same purpose since its introduction: providing a standardized interface between software calls in the operating system and markedly different hardware configurations available from multiple vendors. The BIOS "abstracts" some of the hardware details, such as power management and RAM detection, away from the operating system, enabling the software to operate at a higher level. This is not to say that the BIOS does not affect other important and externally visible things.

Software in the BIOS is also responsible for scanning the PCI buses, locating interface cards, and loading any specialized drivers out of NVRAM or EEPROM on the card into system memory. This makes special behavior required by the PCI device available, but also means that the "card BIOS" may need to be configured or updated. Ever see messages about "graphics BIOS loaded" or "SCSI BIOS loaded" at boot time? These messages indicate card-specific information being loaded into RAM by the system's hardware BIOS.

So, the boot process for PC-compatible hardware involves the BIOS, which makes certain demands on the structure of the boot disks and location of bootable operating system code. Modern hardware and BIOS improvements have lessened some of the restrictions, but there are still requirements, like only booting from IDE drive 0 or SCSI device 0, and only within the first 1024 *cylinders*, that you may encounter. You can almost *feel* the 10-bit field in the BIOS code that causes the boot cylinder behavior. (A cylinder made more sense in the days when there were multiple heads, each on a separate disk "platter." The heads were all positioned by a single actuator, and each head's horizontal position traced an imaginary 2D circle on the disk platter as it rotated. If you visualize connecting all the circles from multiple heads, you get a 3D "cylinder.")

9.1.1   Default Disk Partitioning

To understand the disk partitioning scheme determined by the BIOS and used by Linux, we need to start with the format for a floppy disk. Yes, really. The floppy format is the lowest common denominator as far as disk formats go.

Sector 0 on a floppy disk is called the *boot sector*. It contains the "bootstrap" code that is loaded by the BIOS start-up process, once a boot device is chosen. *Bootstrapping* is a term named after the (impossible) action of "pulling yourself up by your own bootstraps," which is one of those colorful English expressions hijacked by computer people for their own use. Resources available at boot time are limited, and at each stage of the boot process, the capabilities of the system's software increase, until finally the operating system is running, having pulled itself up "from nothing" but a small piece of executable code in the disk's boot sector.

The format of a floppy, then, may be thought of as the boot sector and "everything else," with the boot sector providing

- A jump to boot loader code located in a known place (at the front)
- A partition table that contains file system type, disk labels, and so on
- The boot loader code
- A file system

The format for a floppy disk is shown in Figure 9–1. If you examine Linux commands that create bootable floppies, for example /sbin/mkbootdisk, you will find that they use a command like mkdosfs to create a file allocation table (FAT) file system on the floppy, and then copy other higher level files to the floppy's file system. The mkbootdisk command is really a shell script, so you can examine it for details.

Although it was very common for every system to have a floppy diskette drive in the past, modern systems like laptops and servers are omitting the built-in floppy drive in favor of external USB floppy drives. A 1.4-MB floppy is just not as useful as it once was. We can still fit a Linux kernel onto a floppy, and this is done in the case of the boot disks you are prompted to make during installation.

Now we can extend the concepts from the floppy format to the format used for hard disks. The BIOS allows four "primary" partitions on a hard disk—period. There is a "master boot record" or MBR at the start of the disk, and each partition has its own boot record. It looks a little like four large floppies concatenated together, with a few differences. This layout is shown in Figure 9–2.

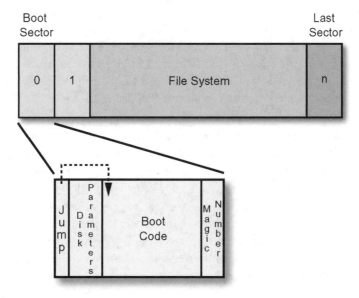

Figure 9–1 Floppy disk layout

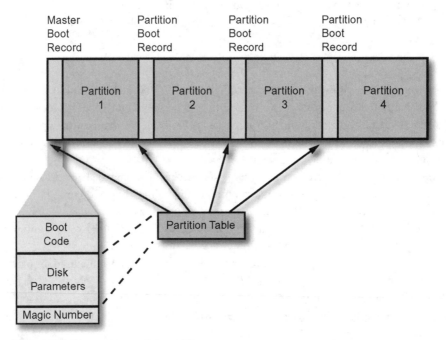

Figure 9–2 Four primary disk partitions

Because things in the compute world grow incrementally and need to maintain backward compatibility, it is not surprising to see a similar theme played over and over again. Linux assigns device names to the disk configurations, using naming conventions that depend on the type of disk. An IDE uses the device file `/dev/hda` for the whole disk device, `/dev/hda1` for the first partition, `/dev/hda2` for the second, and so on, up through the device named `/dev/hda4` for the last primary partition on the first IDE disk. This layout is shown in Figure 9–3.

Even though the partitions are shown roughly the same size in the diagram, there is no requirement to make them any particular size. There may be unallocated space on the disk, and any number of primary partitions between one and the maximum of four. One of the partitions is marked as the "active" partition to show that it is the default-bootable partition.

The BIOS scans the system for disks devices and creates numerical descriptors for them. The operating system is then able to query the BIOS to locate which devices are present and to determine how they are partitioned by reading the partition table from the disk's MBR. You can see the information for a Linux system with a dual-channel IDE controller (channels 0 and 1) on the console during the boot process, from `/var/log/messages`, or by using the `dmesg` command:

```
ide: Assuming 33MHz system bus speed for PIO modes; override
with idebus=xx
```

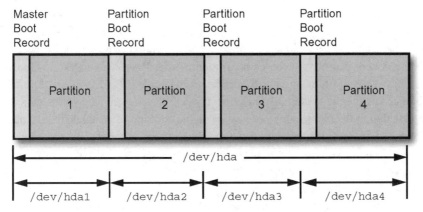

Figure 9–3 Linux devices for primary partitions

```
ICH: IDE controller at PCI slot 00:1f.1
ICH: chipset revision 2
ICH: not 100% native mode: will probe irqs later
ide0: BM-DMA at 0x1800-0x1807, BIOS settings: hda:DMA, hdb:pio
ide1: BM-DMA at 0x1808-0x180f, BIOS settings: hdc:DMA, hdd:pio
hda: WDC WD800JB-00FMA0, ATA DISK drive
blk: queue c040cfc0, I/O limit 4095Mb (mask 0xffffffff)
hdc: WDC WD800JB-00FMA0, ATA DISK drive
hdd: LG CD-RW CED-8083B, ATAPI CD/DVD-ROM drive
blk: queue c040d41c, I/O limit 4095Mb (mask 0xffffffff)
ide0 at 0x1f0-0x1f7,0x3f6 on irq 14
ide1 at 0x170-0x177,0x376 on irq 15
hda: attached ide-disk driver.
hda: host protected area => 1
hda: 156301488 sectors (80026 MB) w/8192KiB Cache, CHS=10337/
240/63, UDMA(66)
hdc: attached ide-disk driver.
hdc: host protected area => 1
hdc: 156301488 sectors (80026 MB) w/8192KiB Cache, CHS=155061/
16/63, UDMA(33)
Partition check:
 hda: hda1 hda2 hda3
 hdc: hdc1 hdc2 hdc3
```

The first IDE device found is hda, the next IDE device is hdb, followed by hdc, and so forth. SCSI disks follow a similar naming convention, starting with sda, sdb, and so on. People tend to use the device name Xda and the device file, name, /dev/Xda, interchangeably. Let's switch to just the device name from now on, unless we need to specify the device *file* explicitly for some reason.

In the previous example, the IDE slave device on channel 0 is not used, so it does not show up during the device scan. The second channel, channel 1, has a disk as the master device (hdc), and the slave device is a CD-ROM (hdd). The bus and device scanning order determines which devices are located and the assigned device file name is. (This is very important to know. Adding devices to the system can change the configuration of the device names. For example, USB devices like disks actually show up as SCSI devices [as do some IEEE 1394 disk devices]. If the device is plugged in and the system rebooted, the device file names may be reordered.)

The next step in the partitioning progression is the addition of "extended" disk partitions, which allow a primary partition to be divided into subpartitions, called *logical partitions*. As you might imagine, four primary partitions may not be enough physical divisions of the disk for some situations, so the extended partition scheme was added to cope with larger disks and more complex system disk configurations.

An example of an extended partition and the associated SCSI device names is shown in Figure 9–4. The partition table in the MBR only has enough space for four physical partition entries, which allows three primary and one extended partition. The partition table in an extended partition contains one logical partition entry, a pointer to the next extended partition, and two empty entries. This creates a linked list of partition table entries.

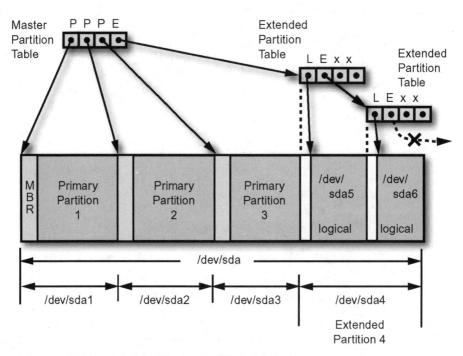

Figure 9–4 Extended partitions on a SCSI disk device

Note that the boot records in the logical partitions are not accessible as part of the device; they "belong" to an extended partition. For example, if we wanted to save a copy of the MBR, we could simply execute

```
# dd if=/dev/sda1 of=/tmp/mbr.save bs=512 count=1
```

This command accesses the first sector (512-byte block) on the device /dev/sda1 and copies it to a file. We could *not* do this for a logical partition and get what we would expect. If all this seems at once complicated *and* limiting, you are absolutely correct. The current way things are done depends on history and backward-compatible changes made at every step from MS-DOS (PC-DOS if you remember) to the present. It is entirely possible to create a partition table that confuses both humans and operating systems.

9.1.2   A Brief Note on IA-64 Disk Partitioning

In addition to the "normal" Linux partitions, an Itanium (IA-64) system adds another requirement: the extensible firmware interface (EFI) partition. The EFI environment provides the initial interaction between the hardware boot process and the hardware drivers and operating system that are loaded as the boot process continues. The "stable" storage for EFI is a disk partition, called the *EFI system partition*, that contains EFI applications and drivers.

Much of what used to be contained in the hardware and interface card BIOSs is now kept in "external" files located in the EFI partition. A standardized loading and initialization process is built into the system's NVRAM, but information that would previously have required flashing the BIOS is loaded from files by EFI at boot time. Updating the files in the EFI partition reduces (but does not eliminate) the need to update the system's firmware.

The EFI partition is a modified FAT file system, and therefore suffers from the DOS 8.3 file name format. This is the familiar DOS eight-character file name and three character file extension convention. If you look into the EFI partition on a Linux system, you will see a file, named elilo.efi, that is responsible for loading the IA-64 Linux kernel into memory and starting it. If there are other operating systems resident on the machine, other boot files will also be visible. They all will have short (or truncated) file names.

The elilo.efi file is loaded and executed by the EFI boot loader, which can also execute other EFI applications, including diagnostics, editors, shells, and network boot managers. There is a simple menu interface to the EFI boot loader that enables selection of the appropriate EFI application at boot time. The exact behavior of your EFI environment depends on the manufacturer of your hardware, so I will not go into any more detail here. Once Linux is started, its behavior is familiar, no matter what the underlying processor architecture.

The addition of the EFI partition to the list of required Linux partitions pushes the absolute minimum (EFI, "/," and swap) partition configuration to four. This virtually ensures that you will need to place additional partitions into extended partitions. Fortunately, the installation tool allows specifying the partition type ("force to be primary") or selects the best default configuration based on your partition choices.

9.1.3   Red Hat Linux Boot Loaders

The initial boot code for the system "lives" in the MBR and is loaded by the BIOS when the boot device is selected. Once activated, the boot loader has control of what happens next. There are several boot loaders that work with Intel IA-32 Linux, including the Linux loader, lilo, and the GNU grand unified boot loader, grub. For Itanium systems the boot loader is a combination of the EFI menu and elilo.efi.

lilo is a fairly simple-minded boot loader that stores information about the location of the Linux boot files inside the MBR with its boot loader code. This means that every time you make changes to the kernel or initial RAM disk configuration, you must rerun lilo to update the MBR information, or risk having an unbootable system. lilo is sometimes difficult to remove; it likes its home in the MBR and leaves only with great reluctance. (It is a good idea to save the original state of the MBR, if possible, before making changes to it.)

The default boot loader for Red Hat Linux and derivatives is now grub, although lilo is available for hardware situations that require it. I much prefer grub, for one thing, because it is possible to build an independent grub recovery disk that you can use to repair MBR problems and boot the system from a floppy if something goes wrong. All of this is possible with lilo, but it seems to be easier with grub.

Using grub has the added advantage that it can recover from errors and mistakes much more easily. As its name implies, it was designed to be flexible and to provide a unified way of booting multiple processor architectures and disk configurations. Most of the information on grub may be found by executing

```
# info grub
```

Using the info command is an acquired skill set, but there is a lot of Linux documentation for GNU tools that is only available in that facility.

The configuration information for grub is kept in /boot/grub, and includes a configuration file, boot loader stages, and file system-specific drivers. The /boot/grub/grub.conf file contains configuration information that is selectable by the user at boot time:

```
default=0
timeout=10
splashimage=(hd0,0)/grub/splash.xpm.gz
title Red Hat Linux (2.4.20-28.8)
        root (hd0,0)
        kernel /vmlinuz-2.4.20-28.8 ro root=LABEL=/
        initrd /initrd-2.4.20-28.8.img
title Red Hat Linux (2.4.20-27.8)
        root (hd0,0)
```

```
kernel /vmlinuz-2.4.20-27.8 ro root=LABEL=/
initrd /initrd-2.4.20-27.8.img
```

Each possible boot option is presented in a menu, with the first entry in the file, the 0 entry, being the default boot selection in this example. Entry 0 is the first entry at the top of the list. The splash image displayed behind the menu is a compressed X Windows pix map (XPM) file, located in the `/boot/grub` directory. Because `/boot` may be a separate partition, all file names are relative to the partition, which is `(hd0,0)`, or the first partition on the disk.

Notice that the device names used by `grub` are different from the device names used by Linux. The specification is for a hard disk and section number (partition) on that hard disk. There is a map file in `/boot/grub/device.map`, that contains the `grub` to Linux device mappings for bootable devices on the system:

```
# this device map was generated by anaconda
(fd0)      /dev/fd0
(hd0)      /dev/hda
```

The information in this file is generated by the Red Hat installation tool, called `anaconda`.

The information in each labeled boot section contains a definition for the device that contains the system's root directory, plus a kernel and RAM disk definition. The `kernel` definition line contains several parameters passed to the Linux kernel as it boots. We will examine Linux kernel parameters in an upcoming section.

You can make a stand-alone `grub` boot disk with the following commands:

```
# cd /usr/share/grub/redhat-i386
# dd if=stage1 of=/dev/fd0 bs=512 count=1
# dd if=stage2 of=/dev/fd0 bs=512 seek=1
```

Note that all data on the floppy is destroyed by this process. Once completed, you can boot `grub` from the floppy and perform useful recovery operations like searching for a bootable partition, selecting a kernel and RAM disk image, and reinstalling `grub` into the MBR.

We could write a book on just the boot loaders available for Linux. It's silly, but which Linux boot loader is someone's favorite tends to be intensely personal and a source of occasional heated "discussions." With this in mind, let's will move on to booting the kernel using your favorite boot loader.

9.2 Booting the Linux Kernel

Booting the Linux kernel involves distinct phases, and a different level of software "intelligence" is available at each step. The basic steps are

1. Hardware POST
2. Boot device selection (default or user input)
3. Boot the operating system loader from the device

4. Load the kernel and initial RAM disk into RAM

5. Start the kernel, passing parameters

6. Start the `init` process and run the `inittab` start-up

7. Run the boot scripts in `/etc/init.d`

8. Complete transition to final target run level

The hardware initialization culminates with the selection of a boot device, either from a menu or from a default value stored in NVRAM. The operating system loader is executed, and it starts the Linux kernel, passing it parameters that affect its initialization behavior. A list of some of the parameters that can be passed to the kernel is located in `/usr/share/doc/kernel-doc-<version>/kernel-parameters.txt`, if you have the kernel source Red Hat package manager (RPM) package loaded, or from `man 7 bootparam`. Both information sources have different lists of options.

First, a word about kernel files, of which there are two "flavors": compressed and uncompressed. The following listing shows the relative sizes of the kernel files on one of my systems:

```
# cd /boot
# ll vmlinu*-2.4.20-28*
-rw-r--r-- 1 root root 3175854 Dec 18 10:03 \
        vmlinux-2.4.20-28.8
-rw-r--r-- 1 root root 1122155 Dec 18 10:03 \
        vmlinuz-2.4.20-28.8
```

The compressed kernel is roughly 35% of the size of the uncompressed version. This saves space on the disk, but also makes a bootable floppy possible in the right situations (when the kernel and associated files are less than 1.4 MB total). The kernel is decompressed as it is loaded into memory by the boot loader.

The `grub` example in the previous section shows two options that are passed to the kernel: `ro` and `root=LABEL=/`. The first option initially mounts the root device read-only, and the second option specifies that the kernel should look for a file system superblock that contains a label identifying it as "/," which is the root file system. As we will see, the Linux file systems allow specifying a file system to mount by a label in addition to a device, to avoid problems caused by devices changing their association with device files resulting from "migration" in the scan order.

The initial RAM disk image is a compressed file system image that is loaded into memory, mounted as the root file system by the kernel during initialization, then (usually) replaced by the disk-based root file system. A *lot* of Linux boot activities involve manipulation of the initial RAM disk (`initrd`) contents. We examine manipulating the `initrd` image in the next section.

9.3   The Linux Initial RAM Disk Image

As with a lot of features on Linux, a little reverse engineering can help you do some interesting things. The initial RAM disk image is created manually by the /sbin/mkinitrd command, which happens to be a script. You can view the script contents to see exactly what is being done to create an initrd. Let's try running the script:

```
# mkinitrd
usage: mkinitrd [--version] [-v] [-f] [--preload <module>] \
[--omit-scsi-modules] [--omit-raid-modules] \
[--omit-lvm-modules] [--with=<module>] [--image-version] [\
--fstab=<fstab>] [--nocompress] [--builtin=<module>] \
[--nopivot] <initrd-image> <kernel-version>
(ex: mkinitrd /boot/initrd-2.2.5-15.img 2.2.5-15)
[root@ns1 tmp]# mkinitrd /tmp/initrd.img 2.4.22-1.2174.nptl
WARNING: using /tmp for temporary files
```

Okay, so we made an initial RAM disk image, by specifying the file name and the *version string* of the kernel, but what are we *really* doing?

The initrd file contains a miniature root file system, including the directory /lib, which contains the dynamically loadable kernel modules necessary to support the root file system. This is why we specify the kernel version string, because mkinitrd uses this to locate the /lib/modules/*<version>* directory. It then adds the necessary kernel modules into the initrd file system to support booting from devices and file system types that are not built into the kernel.

Notice that the mkinitrd command allows control over what kernel modules are added to the compressed file system image, along with control over how and when the modules are loaded during the kernel initialization process. We are avoiding a "which-comes-first-the-chicken-or-the-egg" issue: How do you boot the root file system if it resides on a device that requires a module in the root file system? The answer is: By using an initrd with the required module in it that is available to the kernel *before* the root file system is mounted.

Let's take an initrd apart to see what's inside. Let me warn you, I will be doing some things that appear a little magical if you haven't done them before. I promise to explain what is going on if you bear with me.

```
# gunzip < initrd.img > initrd
# losetup /dev/loop0 /tmp/initrd
# mkdir image_mnt
# mount -o loop /dev/loop0 image_mnt
# ls image_mnt
bin  dev  etc  lib  linuxrc  loopfs  proc  sbin  sysroot
```

What I just did was unzip the initrd image, associate the file with a "loop-back" device, mount the loop-back device onto a local directory, then look inside the directory. If we look at the output of the mount command

```
# mount
/dev/loop0 on /tmp/image_mnt type ext2 (rw,loop=/dev/loop1)
```

you can see that the loop-back device is mounted on the directory, as if it were an actual disk. The loop-back functionality allows us to mount a file as if it were a device, and access the data in it as if it were a file system (which it is in the case of an initrd).

You can see the directory and file structure inside the example initrd, including a file named linuxrc. This file is run by the kernel when it mounts the initrd. The file contains shell commands that are run by nash, which is a very compact command interpreter developed for just this use.

```
#!/bin/nash
echo "Loading jbd.o module"
insmod /lib/jbd.o
echo "Loading ext3.o module"
insmod /lib/ext3.o
echo Mounting /proc filesystem
mount -t proc /proc /proc
echo Creating block devices
mkdevices /dev
echo Creating root device
mkrootdev /dev/root
echo 0x0100 > /proc/sys/kernel/real-root-dev
echo Mounting root filesystem
mount -o defaults --ro -t ext3 /dev/root /sysroot
pivot_root /sysroot /sysroot/initrd
umount /initrd/proc
```

Notice that at the end of the script, the root file system (on the disk) is mounted to the /sysroot directory, then a pivot_root is executed, which switches the root directory in use by the kernel to the disk-based file system. Shortly after the root is pivoted to the disk, the kernel starts the init process (the "parent" process of everything on the system, with a process identifier [PID] of 1 and a parent process identifier [PPID] of 0) from the file system and continues the boot process.

Let's clean up the situation with the mounted initrd file from our example:

```
# umount /tmp/image_mnt
# losetup -d /dev/loop0
```

The general booting process for the Linux kernel, and the involvement of the initrd file, are important to our development activities within the cluster. The network system installation tools, network boot tools, and other Linux booting facilities (including the standard system boot from disk) all intimately involve the initrd in various forms and configurations.

Now that you know what is in the `initrd`, let's examine a few of the kernel parameters that can be passed by the boot loader. A partial list of useful kernel parameters is presented in Table 9–1.

Table 9–1 Kernel Parameters

Parameter	Values	Description	Example
`root=`	`<device>`	Sets system root directory	`root=/dev/sda2`
`nfsroot=`	`<path>`	Sets the path to an NFS root directory on an NFS server	`nfsroot=/sharedroot`
`nfsaddr=`	`<IP Address>`	Sets the NFS server address to the IP address given	`nfsaddr=192.168.0.1`
`init=`	`<path>`	Sets the name of the `init` program to be run at boot	`init=/etc/myinit`
`initrd=`	`<path>`	Sets the location of the initial RAM disk file relative to the boot directory	`init=myinitrd.img`
`mem=`	`<integer MB>`	Sets the size of system RAM to use in megabytes	`mem=128`
`load_ramdisk=`	`<0, 1>`	Enables (1) or disables (0) the loading of the initrd	`load_ramdisk=1`
`ramdisk_size`	`<integer kB>`	Sets the size of the `initrd` in kilobytes (default 4096)	`ramdisk_size=4096`
`ro`	`none`	Mounts the root directory in read-only mode	`ro`
`console=`	`<dev><com-spec>`	Sets the console output device and [speed,control, parity] value	`console=/dev/ttyS0,9600,n,8`
`vga=`	`<normal, extended, ask>`	Sets VGA mode to 80x25, 80x50, or prompts for mode	`vga=ask`

Of course, these parameters only scratch the surface of what is available. They are some of the more common ones, and we will be seeing more use of them in upcoming chapters. See the file `/usr/src/linux-<version>/Documentation/kernel-parameters.txt` for a complete list of the *documented* kernel parameters.

9.4   Linux Local Disk Storage

Administrative and infrastructure systems have varying needs when it comes to local file systems (I will cover specific information about cluster file systems and file servers elsewhere in this book). An administrative node that is responsible for performing multiple system installations at once should provide a local file system that can feed data to the network interface as rapidly as possible. An administrative node that is running an essential service and needs to be highly reliable, might trade performance for immunity from disk failure. One of my customers studied the effect of mirroring the system disk on system reliability. They concluded that, in their environment, they could attain 99.99% ("four nines") of "up" time merely by buying reliable system hardware and mirroring the system disks.

We need to consider two factors when implementing local storage: the local file system type, and the configuration of the underlying disk storage. Although many commodity servers provide hardware RAID controllers (and Linux supports the more common ones), we can also save money by using the Linux software RAID facility, provided we have configured multiple disks into the base hardware system. Linux also provides a large number of possible physical file system types—everything from DOS FAT file systems to the journaled `ext3` file system, which is the default on Red Hat Linux. Type `man fs` for a complete list of the possible (but not necessarily available) file systems.

9.4.1   Using the Software RAID 5 Facility

The Linux software RAID facility, also frequently referred to as the multiple device or `md` facility, provides striping (RAID 0), mirroring (RAID 1), striping with parity device (RAID 4), and striping with distributed parity (RAID 5). Another configuration, linear mode, creates one continuous disk device from multiple disks and provides no redundancy. Each of these behaviors is implemented in a dynamically loaded kernel module.

The `md` devices on a Linux system are defined in the `/etc/raidtab` file,[1] and are activated automatically at system boot time, either from the `initrd` file, if the system disk is on a RAID device, or from the root directory. Although it was a difficult endeavor earlier, most Linux distributions now allow installing the system partitions on RAID devices and include the proper modules in the system initial RAM disk image (`initrd`) to support this configuration. This

---

1.   This is true for devices created and managed with the `raidtools` commands, like `mkraid`, but there is now another option on some versions of Linux, the `mdadm` command which I discuss later.

means we may gain the extra reliability from mirrored system disks, even if the hardware does not explicitly have RAID capability.

The md device files themselves are located in the /dev directory and are named according to the convention for md devices: /dev/md0, /dev/md1, and so forth. These devices have their configuration and operational behavior specified in the /etc/raidtab file. Once they are initialized, each device has a persistent superblock stored on it that specifies the RAID mode and a UUID (a 128-bit universally unique identifier) for the md device to which it belongs.

It should be noted that the parity calculation is done in software (this is one reason why the facility is called *software RAID*), and so relies on the speed of the CPU. The system determines the best available parity calculation method at boot time. The following real-life example of an /etc/raidtab file contains the configuration for a RAID 5 array:

```
raiddev                      /dev/md1
        raid-level           5
        nr-raid-disks        4
        nr-spare-disks       0
        chunk-size           64
        parity-algorithm     left-symmetric
        device               /dev/sda
        raid-disk            0
        device               /dev/sdb
        raid-disk            1
        device               /dev/sdc
        raid-disk            2
        device               /dev/sdd
        raid-disk            3
```

This example RAID 5 device has four SCSI disks that are combined into a single md device. The disks that make up the RAID device are divided into 64-KB chunks. This particular RAID device does not have a spare disk, although this is possible. If a disk fails, the array will operate in degraded mode until the disk can be replaced. On repair, the data on the failed disk will be rebuilt from the parity information on the other disk drives. An example RAID 5 configuration is shown in Figure 9–5.

The /proc/mdstat file contains the current status of all active md devices on the system. The /proc/mdstat contents for the example RAID 5 array in the raidtab example is as follows:

```
# cat /proc/mdstat
Personalities : [raid5]
read_ahead 1024 sectors
md1 : active raid5 sdd[3] sdc[2] sdb[1] sda[0]
        215061888 blocks level 5, 64k chunk, algorithm 2 [4/4]\
        [UUUU]
```

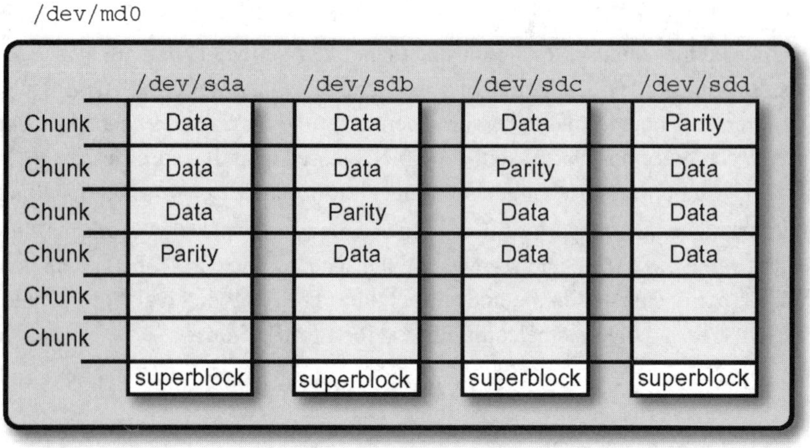

`/dev/md0`

Figure 9–5 Example RAID 5 configuration

The [UUUU] field represents each of the four disks in the array. If any of the disks are currently rebuilding, the U for that disk becomes a "_" character. The rebuilding process operates within a minimum and maximum I/O rate in kilobytes per second. These current values for these limits are available in the /proc/sys/dev/raid directory, in the files, speed_limit_min and speed_limit_max.

Creating the md device from scratch involves

1. Creating or editing the /etc/raidtab file
2. Executing mkraid /dev/md1
3. Creating a file system on the device
4. Mounting the file system and modifying /etc/fstab to remount it at boot time

The system will automatically detect the RAID array and restart it at system boot time. The RAID 5 configuration is useful for bulk data storage when immunity to disk failure is required. Because of the processing required for parity calculation, however, the performance is not optimum for writes. Aside from the parity calculation overhead, in general a RAID 5 array must wait for the parity information to be calculated and written before a given I/O transaction is complete, which has the effect of serializing the I/O to multiple disks. Hardware arrays have cache memory that helps to hide this latency from the host operating system.

The contents of the linuxrc file in this system's initrd is

```
#!/bin/nash
echo "Loading scsi_mod module"
insmod /lib/scsi_mod.o
echo "Loading sd_mod module"
insmod /lib/sd_mod.o
```

```
echo "Loading aic7xxx module"
insmod /lib/aic7xxx.o
echo "Loading xor module"
insmod /lib/xor.o
echo "Loading raid5 module"
insmod /lib/raid5.o
echo "Loading jbd module"
insmod /lib/jbd.o
echo "Loading ext3 module"
insmod /lib/ext3.o
echo Mounting /proc filesystem
mount -t proc /proc /proc
raidautorun /dev/md0
echo Creating block devices
mkdevices /dev
echo Creating root device
mkrootdev /dev/root
echo 0x0100 > /proc/sys/kernel/real-root-dev
echo Mounting root filesystem
mount -o defaults --ro -t ext3 /dev/root /sysroot
pivot_root /sysroot /sysroot/initrd
umount /initrd/proc
```

Notice that there are more modules to be loaded in this example, because the disk devices are SCSI, and modules for the SCSI interface, SCSI personality, and SCSI general disks are loaded, along with the modules for the RAID 5 devices. The RAID 5 personality module requires the parity calculation module. These modules are loaded and configured in the `initrd` even though the system's root file system is not located on the RAID 5 device. Why?

The answer to this lies in the fact that the kernel has been upgraded by loading a kernel RPM package on this particular system. Part of the installation process for the kernel RPM module is to generate a new `initrd` file by looking at the currently active kernel modules. The default behavior is to include disk-related modules in the `initrd`, regardless of whether they are directly associated with the root disk. The options to `mkinitrd` can control this behavior if it causes concern or issues, which it doesn't appear to in this case.

9.4.2   Using Software RAID 1 for System Disks

An example of a RAID 1 (mirrored) configuration is shown in Figure 9–6. The Red Hat installation tool, `anaconda`, allows configuration of RAID 1 devices through the manual disk-partitioning tool: `disk druid`. This means that you may configure the RAID 1 devices and install the operating system as part of the initial system installation process.

If you haven't configured RAID 1 devices as the system disk before, it is not as straightforward as it might be. Not that the process is difficult, but determining the correct sequence to keep the partitioning tool happy is potentially frustrating. If you do things in the wrong

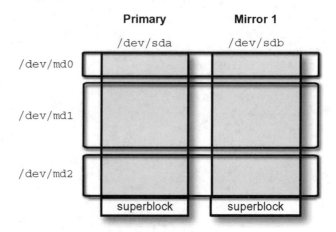

Figure 9–6 Example RAID 1 configuration

sequence, the order of your partitions gets "rearranged" for you for no apparent reason. The correct sequence is the following.

1. Locate the hardware disk devices that you want to use for RAID 1 (`/dev/sda` and `/dev/sdb` for SCSI, `/dev/hda` and `/dev/hdb` for IDE disks). There may be more than one mirror in the RAID 1 set, but this example uses one primary and one mirror.
2. Create a software RAID partition on the first drive (deselect the other potential drives from the list) for `/boot`, around 100 MB.
3. Create another software RAID partition on the second drive (deselect the first drive as a potential device from the list) that is the same size as the first (check the displayed size).
4. Now create a RAID 1 *device* using the two software RAID partitions. This will become `/dev/md0`.
5. Use the same steps to create (at least) the remaining two required RAID 1 devices for the required Linux partitions The minimal configuration requires two partitions: "/" and swap. There are other recommended configurations, such as creating a `/boot` partition, and a separate `/var` partition to keep log files from filling the root file system. Your choices will depend on your situation.

Once the partitioning and RAID creation operations are completed, the system installation will follow its normal course. When the system is booted, you can examine the current disk partition configuration to see your handiwork:

```
# fdisk -l /dev/hda

Disk /dev/hda: 80.0 GB, 80026361856 bytes
```

```
240 heads, 63 sectors/track, 10337 cylinders
Units = cylinders of 15120 * 512 = 7741440 bytes

    Device Boot    Start      End    Blocks   Id  System
/dev/hda1     *        1       14    105808+  fd  Linux raid \
autodetect
/dev/hda2             15    10268  77520240   fd  Linux raid \
autodetect
/dev/hda3          10269    10337    521640   fd  Linux raid \
autodetect
```

Besides the `fdisk` command, you can also examine (or change, or completely destroy it—always exercise great caution when using partitioning tools like these!) the partition information with `parted`:

```
# parted /dev/hda print
Disk geometry for /dev/hda: 0.000-76319.085 megabytes
Disk label type: msdos
Minor    Start        End    Type      Filesystem  Flags
1         0.031    103.359  primary    ext3        boot, raid
2       103.359  75806.718  primary    ext3        raid
3     75806.719  76316.132  primary    linux-swap  raid
Information: Don't forget to update /etc/fstab, if necessary.
```

Notice the difference in information format between the two commands. Which tool you use is a matter of personal preference, but to avoid confusion it is a good idea to be consistent. Here is an example /proc/mdstat file for a system with RAID 1 system partitions (we will use this particular layout in several examples):

```
# cat /proc/mdstat
Personalities : [raid1]
read_ahead 1024 sectors
md2 : active raid1 hda3[0] hdc3[1]
      521024 blocks [2/2] [UU]
md1 : active raid1 hda2[0] hdc2[1]
      77517632 blocks [2/2] [UU]
md0 : active raid1 hda1[0] hdc1[1]
      105216 blocks [2/2] [UU]
unused devices: <none>
```

The last `md` device in the listing, /dev/md0, is the partition used for the /boot file system. On an Itanium system, the first partition would be the EFI system partition, which should be mirrored like all other partitions. Next in the listing comes the partition used by the root file system, and then finally the `swap` partition.

The `swap` partition needs to be mirrored, just like any other essential system partition. In the event of a disk failure, if there is space in use in the failed `swap` partition, you want the operating system to be able to find the *same* data in the failed `swap` partition's mirror. If the `swap` partition data is not mirrored, this *will* cause kernel panics. This, of course, invalidates the whole use for mirroring the system disks in the first place: to *avoid* crashes resulting from disk failures. The `/etc/raidtab` for this configuration is

```
raiddev        /dev/md1
raid-level              1
nr-raid-disks           2
persistent-superblock   1
nr-spare-disks          0
    device              /dev/hda2
    raid-disk           0
    device              /dev/hdc2
    raid-disk           1
raiddev                 /dev/md0
raid-level              1
nr-raid-disks           2
persistent-superblock   1
nr-spare-disks          0
    device              /dev/hda1
    raid-disk           0
    device              /dev/hdc1
    raid-disk           1
raiddev                 /dev/md2
raid-level              1
nr-raid-disks           2
persistent-superblock   1
nr-spare-disks          0
    device              /dev/hda3
    raid-disk           0
    device              /dev/hdc3
    raid-disk           1
```

I have omitted the `chunksize` definitions that get put into the file by the configuration process. The RAID 1 personality module complains about not needing that information. Looking into the `linuxrc` file in the `initrd` for this system, we see

```
#!/bin/nash
echo "Loading raid1.o module"
insmod /lib/raid1.o
echo "Loading jbd.o module"
insmod /lib/jbd.o
echo "Loading ext3.o module"
insmod /lib/ext3.o
echo Mounting /proc filesystem
mount -t proc /proc /proc
raidautorun /dev/md0
raidautorun /dev/md1
```

```
raidautorun /dev/md2
echo Creating block devices
mkdevices /dev
echo Creating root device
mkrootdev /dev/root
echo 0x0100 > /proc/sys/kernel/real-root-dev
echo Mounting root filesystem
mount -o defaults --ro -t ext3 /dev/root /sysroot
pivot_root /sysroot /sysroot/initrd
umount /initrd/proc
```

Because the RAID 1 devices have their configuration stored in the superblock on the RAID disk members, the system is able to autodetect their presence and start them. This functionality is built into the `nash` shell that is run at start-up by the kernel. The proper `md` device files exist in the `/dev` directory inside the `initrd` file, and were created when the `initrd` was built.

9.4.3   RAID Multipath

The multipath feature in software RAID is relatively new, and appears to be barely documented. In a situation when a hardware RAID array with dual independent controllers is connected via two SCSI or Fibre-Channel interfaces, there are multiple (two) paths to the same storage inside the array. The array is configured to present one or more logical units (LUNs) from within the array to the system, as if they were individual disks. Each LUN, however, is a RAID (0, 1, 0+1, or 5) grouping of physical disk storage within the array, where the RAID behavior is handled internally by the array's hardware.

With multiple controllers, each RAID LUN may be presented to the system twice: once for the primary controller and once for the secondary controller. If one controller fails, there is an alternate path to the same device through another controller and another host interface card. This eliminates single points of failure in the path to the array hardware and its storage. Software RAID allows you to define a `multipath` device in `/etc/raidtab`:

```
raiddev/dev/md4
raid-level              multipath
nr-raid-disks           1
nr-spare-disks          1
chunk-size              32
device                  /dev/sda1
raid-disk               0
device                  /dev/sdb1
spare-disk              1
```

This configuration defines a software RAID device in such a way as to allow fail-over in the event that the primary "disk" device (really a LUN from the array) fails. Figure 9–7 shows a hardware RAID array with two controllers and two Fibre-Channel connections to a host system.

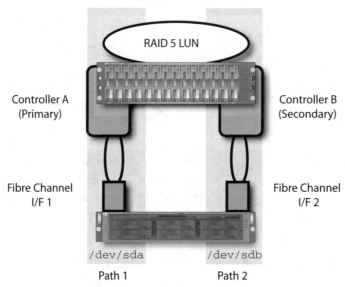

Figure 9–7 RAID multipath example

How the single RAID 5 LUN is presented to the system varies, based on the drivers and attachment method (and whether it is a built-in hardware RAID controller), but in this case two SCSI "disk" devices are presented.

The disk devices may be mounted, formatted with a file system (only once, and only with the primary path, please), and treated as if they were actually two separate disks. Both devices, however, point to the same LUN within the hardware array. The level of support and documentation for this feature varies, but is bound to increase as time passes and the functionality matures.

9.4.4   Recovering from Software RAID Failures

Both the Linux software RAID 5 and RAID 1 configurations can recover from disk failures by activating a spare or switching to a good mirror and allowing you to replace a faulty disk within the software array. If a disk failure is detected in a RAID 1 device, the process of recovery automatically involves copying a RAID 1 disk that is still operational to a spare disk in the RAID set. If the failure is on a RAID 5 device, then recovery automatically recreates the failed RAID 5 disk's data onto a spare using parity information on the operational disks.

In the event that there are no spare disks, the RAID device will continue operating with one less mirror for RAID 1 or in degraded mode (recreating data on the fly) for RAID 5. Without watching for device failures within the software RAID array, a system administrator may not realize that such a failure has occurred. (I will talk about solutions to this further on in the discussion, but the degraded performance may or may not cause user complaints, triggering the necessary investigation, discovery, and repair process.) The RAID driver will regulate the amount of system resources used for a copy or rebuild operation. If no activity is occurring on the system, then the rebuild or copy will proceed at the data rate set by `/proc/sys/dev/raid/speed_limit_max` *per device* (the default is 100,000). If activity is present on the system, the activity will proceed at `/proc/sys/dev/raid/speed_limit_min` (the default is 100).

The `raidtools` package includes `mkraid`, `lsraid`, `raidstart`, `raidstop`, `raidhotadd`, and `raidhotremove` commands. The `mkraid` command uses `/etc/raidtab` to initialize and start the `md` devices specified to it on the command line. Once the data structures on the `md` device are initialized, the system can locate and start the RAID arrays without the `/etc/raidtab` information, as we saw in the previous `initrd` example in page 185.

The `raidhotremove` and `raidhotadd` tools can remove a drive from a software array "slot" and replace it, respectively. This can be used to manipulate spares or failed drives. The basic process to replace a failed drive is to shut down the system, replace the drive, boot the system, and execute `raidhotadd /dev/md<N> /dev/<dev>`. The software RAID system will begin to rebuild the disk once it is detected. These tools may or may not still be included in your distribution.

Another tool for creating, managing, and monitoring RAID devices is the `/sbin/mdadm` command, which may partially replace the `raidtools` on your distribution. The `mdadm` tool provides similar functionality to some of the `raidtools` commands, but is a single program that stores its configuration in `/etc/mdadm.conf`. The `mdadm` tool does not use the `/etc/raidtab` information to create the `md` devices; instead, the device and configuration information is specified on the `mdadm` command line.

The `mdadm` command may run in the background as a daemon, monitoring the specified software RAID arrays at set polling intervals (the default interval is 60 seconds). If a failure is detected, `mdadm` can select a spare disk from a shared pool and automatically rebuild the array for you. The command in general is very flexible, and has Assemble, Build, Create, Manage, Misc, and Monitor or Follow modes. We will look at some examples of its use as we progress, but you should check for its existence (and `man` page) on your distribution. (You should also go locate a copy of the *Software-RAID-HOWTO* on `http://www.tldp.org/howto`. This is a great source of details that I can't include here because of space constraints.)

9.4.4.1 Saving the Disk Partition Table

Most of the Linux partitioning tools allow interactive configuration of partition parameters. It is also possible, however, to feed scripted partition definitions to the tools to recreate complex partitioning schemes automatically with a minimum of typing. Several of the automated system "cloning" or network installation tools use this method to reproduce a disk partition configuration.

One example of a tool that allows flexible partitioning operations is `/sbin/sfdisk`. The `sfdisk` tool can list partition sizes, list partitions on a device, check the partition table consistency, or apply commands from `stdout` to a specified device.

You should not underestimate the power and potential impact of this type of tool. As stated in the man page for sfdisk: "*BE EXTREMELY CAREFUL, ONE TYPING MISTAKE AND ALL YOUR DATA IS LOST.*" Notice the use of the phrase "is lost"—as opposed to "may be lost."

As mentioned in a previous section, the partition table for a disk, if it involves extended partitions, will actually be a linked list that is spread across the disk. The sfdisk tool can handle this and will dump the partition information for the specified device:

```
# sfdisk -l /dev/hda
Disk /dev/hda: 10337 cylinders, 240 heads, 63 sectors/track
Units = cylinders of 7741440 bytes, blocks of 1024 bytes,
counting from 0

   Device Boot Start     End   #cyls   #blocks  Id  System
/dev/hda1   *       0+    13     14-    105808+  fd  Linux
        raid autodetect
/dev/hda2          14  10267  10254  77520240   fd  Linux
        raid autodetect
/dev/hda3       10268  10336     69    521640   fd  Linux
        raid autodetect
/dev/hda4           0      -      0         0    0  Empty
```

This example mirrors (no pun intended) our RAID 1 example configuration. The "+" and "-" characters indicate that a number has been rounded up or down respectively. To avoid this possibility, you can specify that the size is given in sectors and in a format that may be fed back into sfdisk:

```
# sfdisk -d /dev/hda
# partition table of /dev/hda
unit: sectors
/dev/hda1 : start=        63, size=   211617, Id=fd, bootable
/dev/hda2 : start=    211680, size=155040480, Id=fd
/dev/hda3 : start=155252160, size=  1043280, Id=fd
/dev/hda4 : start=         0, size=        0, Id= 0
```

In addition to looking at partition information for the existing devices, sfdisk has a built-in list of the possible partition types (numerical labels in hexidecimal) that may be applied to disk partition table entries for Linux and other systems that use the BIOS partitioning scheme. To see that list, use

```
# sfdisk -T
```

As you will see, the list is quite long, so I will not reproduce it here. You can manually create quite complex partitioning schemes for multiple operating systems with a little knowledge and a lot of time.

You may be asking, Why would I want to save my partition information? It's on the disk, isn't it? This is a logical question. There are two very logical answers: first to be able to recover from catastrophic failures, and second to be able to use a configuration that works on multiple systems without recreating it by hand. When we begin installing systems with tools like Red Hat's `kickstart` or the `SystemImager` tool, reproducing a disk configuration becomes important.

You don't really want to type all the partition information in by hand every time you need it, do you? Having both graphical and text-based tools can be a huge advantage. Being able to use script to recreate disk configurations is extremely powerful and useful.

9.4.4.2 Determining Software RAID Array Status

If you suspect, for some reason, that you have had a disk failure in one of your software RAID arrays, you can use either the `lsraid` command or the `mdadm` command to check the status of the raid array. The `/proc/mdstat` file provides software RAID information on running arrays, but the two software tools provide a lot more options and detailed data, including on devices that may not be part of an active software array. It appears that `lsraid` is present, even if the `raidtools` package has been mostly replaced by `mdadm` on a distribution.

The `lsraid` command is very useful, because it can also be used to extract a `raidtab` format output from a functional array. If you are moving things around, or have misplaced the definition for your RAID array, this can be very helpful. An example of extracting the "`raidtab`" information for our example RAID 5 software array is

```
# lsraid -R -a /dev/md1
# This raidtab was generated by lsraid version 0.7.0.
# It was created from a query on the following devices:
#     /dev/md1
# md device [dev 9, 1] /dev/md1 queried online
raiddev /dev/md1
        raid-level   5
        nr-raid-disks   4
        nr-spare-disks   0
        persistent-superblock 1
        chunk-size   64
        device   /dev/sda
        raid-disk   0
        device   /dev/sdb
        raid-disk   1
        device   /dev/sdc
        raid-disk   2
        device   /dev/sdd
        raid-disk   3
```

You can also locate the devices in a RAID array by querying one of the member disks. This will read the superblock information written at the end of the device:

```
# lsraid -d /dev/sda
[dev 9, 1] /dev/md1 D0E77459.AD65F0FB.7D58622E.74703722 online
[dev 8, 0] /dev/sda D0E77459.AD65F0FB.7D58622E.74703722 good
```

```
[dev 8,16] /dev/sdb D0E77459.AD65F0FB.7D58622E.74703722 good
[dev 8,32] /dev/sdc D0E77459.AD65F0FB.7D58622E.74703722 good
[dev 8,48] /dev/sdd D0E77459.AD65F0FB.7D58622E.74703722 good
```

It is also possible to list failed and good disks and to perform operations on both on-line and off-line devices. Another way to locate information for the arrays is to scan all disk devices that the command can find in the /proc file system. This can also be used to generate the raidtab information:

```
# lsraid -R -p
# This raidtab was generated by lsraid version 0.7.0.
# It was created from a query on the following devices:
#       /dev/md1 /dev/sda /dev/sdb /dev/sdc
#       /dev/sdd /dev/hda /dev/hda1 /dev/hda2
#       /dev/hda3
# md device [dev 9, 1] /dev/md1 queried online
raiddev /dev/md1
        raid-level    5
        nr-raid-disks   4
        nr-spare-disks   0
        persistent-superblock 1
        chunk-size   64
        device  /dev/sda
        raid-disk  0
        device  /dev/sdb
        raid-disk  1
        device  /dev/sdc
        raid-disk  2
        device  /dev/sdd
        raid-disk  3
```

If you are fortunate, your Linux version will have both the raidtools and the mdadm command available so that you can make a choice as to which one you will use in a given situation. The raidtools are the traditional way to create and manage software RAID arrays, but there now is another option, the md administration tool (the command previously known as mdctl). The mdadm command can let you know the current operational state of your md device in addition to lots of other nifty operations. Now let's take a look at the capabilities of mdadm.

9.4.4.3   Using mdadm in Place of raidtools

Remember that creating an array involves initializing the information in the RAID superblocks stored on the devices that are members of the RAID array, including the UUID that uniquely identifies the array. Let's take a look at some of the more common uses for mdadm for similar operations to the raidtools. To create the example RAID 5 array with the mdadm command (and without the information in an /etc/raidtab file), we would use

```
# mdadm --create /dev/md1 --chunk=64 --level=5 \
```

```
            --parity=leftsymmetric --raid-devices=4 \
            /dev/sda /dev/sdb /dev/sdc /dev/sdd
```

The mdadm command is a consistent interface to the software RAID facility, instead of multiple tools, and is well documented. You can list the current status of an md device:

```
# mdadm --detail /dev/md1
/dev/md1:
          Version : 00.90.00
    Creation Time : Thu May  8 16:48:20 2003
       Raid Level : raid5
       Array Size : 215061888 (205.09 GiB 220.22 GB)
      Device Size : 71687296 (68.36 GiB 73.40 GB)
     Raid Devices : 4
    Total Devices : 4
  Preferred Minor : 1
      Persistence : Superblock is persistent
Update Time : Thu Mar  4 00:26:09 2004
            State : dirty, no-errors
   Active Devices : 4
  Working Devices : 4
   Failed Devices : 0
    Spare Devices : 0
Layout : left-symmetric
Chunk Size : 64K
Number Major Minor RaidDevice State
0        8    0        0         active sync    /dev/scsi/sdh0-0c0i0l0
1        8    16       1         active sync    /dev/scsi/sdh0-0c0i2l0
2        8    32       2         active sync    /dev/scsi/sdh0-0c0i4l0
3        8    48       3         active sync    /dev/scsi/sdh0-0c0i6l0
UUID : d0e77459:ad65f0fb:7d58622e:74703722
```

This output shows the UUID that identifies the array members along with the current state and configuration of the array. This is also one source of formatted information, besides /proc/scsi/scsi, from which you can get the full SCSI address information (host, channel, ID, LUN) for each component SCSI device in the array (if your devices are indeed SCSI).

Let's say that a friend handed you a bunch of disks in a box and told you that his system had failed, but he had managed to salvage the still-functional SCSI (or IEEE-1394) disks from a software RAID array on the system. He doesn't remember how he configured the array, and yet he wants to access the devices and retrieve their data. There are several months of work on the array that has not been backed up.

You realize that once you connect the disks to a system, you can use mdadm to query the devices, reverse engineer the array configuration, assemble the array, activate it, and mount it. You power off your system, add the four devices to your SCSI bus, power the system back on, and notice that they are assigned to `/dev/sde`, `/dev/sdf`, `/dev/sdg`, and `/dev/sdh` by the Linux boot process.

There is a conflict between the definition in the device superblocks (preferred minor number) and an existing `md` array that prevents the system from autostarting the new array. You perform the following command on the first disk, `/dev/sde`:

```
# mdadm --examine /dev/sde

/dev/sde:
          Magic : a92b4efc
        Version : 00.90.00
           UUID : d0e77459:ad65f0fb:7d58622e:74703722
  Creation Time : Thu May  8 16:48:20 2003
     Raid Level : raid5
    Device Size : 71687296 (68.36 GiB 73.40 GB)
    Raid Devices : 5
   Total Devices : 0
 Preferred Minor : 1
[... output deleted ...]
```

Each device is queried in turn, and you suddenly realize that there is one disk missing from a total RAID set of five—and your friend has gone off to a three-martini lunch. You can start the array on an unused `md` device, `/dev/md4`, with

```
# mdadm --assemble /dev/md4 --run \
        /dev/sde /dev/sdf /dev/sdg /dev/sdh
```

This command will assemble the partial array (a RAID 5 array can operate with one disk missing) from only the devices on the command line and attempt to start it. You may also specify information about UUID values or "preferred minor number" (meaning the array was built as `/dev/md1`) for the devices you want to include.

I hope this contrived example has shown you and your (still invisible) friend the value of using `mdadm` in performing recovery actions with software RAID devices. To do similar things with the `raidtools`, you would need to manipulate the `/etc/raidtab` contents as well as use multiple commands. The recovery would be possible, just not as easy or straightforward.

This example used external disks that were not previously configured on the system that was accessing them. It is possible to specify configuration information about both array component devices and arrays themselves in the `/etc/mdadm.conf` file for the current system. The `mdadm` command will search this configuration information to satisfy device lists if you also specify the `--scan` command-line option.

You can also place UUID or other device or array identification information on the command line to narrow the devices used in the request. For example:

```
# mdadm --assemble --scan --run \
        --uuid=572f9e45:22a34d0f:b6784479:9b2f25d0
```

This command will scan the device definitions in the /etc/mdadm.conf file and try to build an array out of the devices with UUIDs matching the value specified on the command line.

9.4.4.4 Monitoring Arrays with mdadm

One last piece of useful functionality from mdadm that we will cover is the ability to monitor and manage software RAID devices automatically. One problem with software RAID devices is that they can have disk members fail, and that fact may not become readily apparent until you look at the proper log file or notice degraded performance. It is more likely that your users will notice before you do.

For basic software RAID array-monitoring activity, when failure information is mailed to root on the local system, we can modify the /etc/mdadm.conf file to add the following lines for our example RAID 5 array:

```
MAILADDR root
ARRAY /dev/md1 devices=/dev/sda,/dev/sdb,/dev/sdc,/dev/sdd
```

Next we can enable and start the service:

```
# chkconfig mdmonitor on
# service mdmonitor start
```

The monitor mode will report the following events: DeviceDisappeared, RebuildStarted, RebuildNN (percent completed), Fail, FailSpare, SpareActive, NewArray, and MoveSpare. If you read between the lines, you will see that the monitor mode of mdadm is capable of managing spares for a software array. More than that, it can manage a "spare group" that is shared by multiple software RAID arrays.

If a software RAID array with a failed device and no available spares is detected, mdadm will look for another array, belonging to the same "spare group" that has available spare disks. A spare disk will only be moved from an array that has no failed disks. To configure this option, we can add the two ARRAY entries in the /etc/mdadm.conf file and define the same spare group in each entry. The complete format for the configuration file is found in the man page for madm.conf, but a short example is

```
#PROGRAM /usr/bin/log-madm-events
MAILADDR root
ARRAY /dev/md1 uuid=dae86f86:e8eb4a17:94a5dc17:c232b7c6 \
      sparegroup=group1
ARRAY /dev/md2 uuid=eaaba077:680d430e:8bb87ddb:c7bac047 \
      sparegroup=group1
```

When a spare is moved, an event is generated and is either e-mailed, as in our example, passed to a program that is specified in the configuration file (maybe the logger command to pass the event message to a remote logging server).

Although the program specified in the configuration file for madm might be a preexisting monitor from a system administration package, it might also be a simple script:

```
#!/bin/sh
# Called with up to three parameters: Event, md device,
# and component device by mdadm when something happens.
#
     EVENT="${1}"
  MDDEVICE="${2}"
REALDEVICE="${3}"
if [ -z "${REALDEVICE}" ]; then
     REALDEVICE="not specified"
fi
/usr/bin/logger -i -p daemon.err -t MDADM --\
     "Detected event ${EVENT} on md array  \
     ${MDDEVICE} component device ${3}."
###
###
```

For complete information on configuration of the many possible mdadm options for monitoring, see both man mdadm.conf and man madm.

9.5   Linux File System Types

Linux has a wide variety of available file systems, that may be categorized into several general classes. The wide variety of file systems includes many experimental or partially supported versions of file systems that are available on other operating systems. For example, there is an implementation of NT file system (NTFS) from Microsoft Windows, that is available as an experimental (read-only) implementation. The complete list of supported *physical* file systems may be had by examining the man fs output, but there are many more possibilities beyond that list.

We need to make the distinction between a "physical" file system, which dictates a specific data format on physical disk devices, and a "networked" file system. A networked file system enables remote access to physical storage, usually through some form of network RPC mechanism between clients and the file server. Somewhere in between the physical file system and a networked file system is a "cluster" file system that allows parallel access to physical storage by multiple physical machines.

At least two implementations of popular networked file systems are available on Linux, including the network file system (NFS) originated by Sun Microsystems and the SMB, also known as the CIFS, originated by Microsoft. Cluster file systems, like Lustre, GPFS from IBM, CFS from Oracle, and others, are available as add-on open-source packages or "for-dollars" products. The network and cluster varieties of file systems are covered elsewhere in this book.

Physical file systems may be built into the kernel at compile time or provided as dynamically loaded modules. Even with dynamically loaded modules, however, some modifications to code resident in the kernel may be necessary to support the file system's behavior. These modifications may require special versions of the kernel, or patches, or both. This is an activity that is best left to software experts. Try to find distributions that contain "ready-to-go" versions of these file systems if you need them.

Some of the more common physical file systems for Linux are the ext2, ext3, Reiser, vfat, iso9660 (High Sierra and Rockridge), XFS (from Silicon Graphics Inc.), DOS, and MSDOS file systems. Whew, that's a lot of choices, but variety is the spice of life—so it's said.

Because it is relatively easy to encapsulate the software that implements a file system in a loadable module, it is also relatively easy to load the behavior when you need it, and unload it when you are finished. The "standard" UNIX (and Linux) commands to manipulate file systems, like `mkfs` and `fsck`, are front-end interfaces to the file system-specific commands on Linux:

```
# ls /sbin/mk*fs*
/sbin/mkdosfs /sbin/mkfs /sbin/mkfs.ext2 /sbin/mkfs.jfs \
/sbin/mkfs.msdos /sbin/mkfs.vfat /sbin/mke2fs /sbin/mkfs.bfs \
/sbin/mkfs.ext3 /sbin/mkfs.minix /sbin/mkfs.reiserfs \
/sbin/mkreiserfs
```

This arrangement provides the same level of flexibility in the available commands as is found in the modules. Use it only when you need it.

Part of what we need to do with the design of our cluster's infrastructure nodes, administrative nodes, and file servers, is choose the proper physical storage *device* configuration (hardware or software RAID, individual disks, and so forth), build a physical *file system* configuration "on top of" the storage, and then consider how to use the file system to store and share data efficiently. This section addresses the local aspects of Linux file systems and their use by local processes and the operating system. I defer the potential to "export" them to other clients in the cluster until later.

9.6   The Linux `/proc` and `devfs` Pseudo File Systems

Another type of file system, the *pseudo* file system, is also used in the Linux environment, alongside physical and networked file system types. The primary example of this type of file system is the file system hierarchy underneath the `/proc` directory, which provides access to kernel and driver-related data for the system. The `/proc` hierarchy is at once "there" and "not there" in terms of a physical existence.

Access to the "files" in this file system actually activates underlying handlers in kernel code that receive, collect, format, and return data to the requestor through the standard file system interfaces (read, write, open, close, and so on). If you were to look for data structures for the `/proc` file system on a physical disk somewhere, you would have a hard time finding them. If you go back to the file system contents of an example `initrd` (see page 185), you will see the `/proc` file system listed and see it being mounted by the `linuxrc` script. It is an important fixture of even memory-based Linux systems.

Many of the "user space" status-reporting commands that you use daily on the system merely read information from files in `/proc`, format it, and print it to `stdout`. The `/proc` information is central to device debugging, system monitoring, and to tuning the kernel's behavior while it is running. Quite a few of the interfaces in /proc are two way—that is, both read-able *and* writable. We will be using /proc a lot in our activities with Linux.

Another pseudo file system that you may encounter on some Linux distributions (but not Red Hat-derived ones at this point in time) is the device file system, devfs. If you go to the "normal" /dev directory, you will find a lot of files that represent devices, both present and not present, on your system. As a matter of fact, on my system, counting the separate files yields

```
# cd /dev
# ls -1 | wc -1
   7521
```

Now, although not all of these are device files, most of them are. I only have, at most, 100 real devices on this system, even counting "invisible" things like PCI bus bridges. Do we really need to create all these files, manage the permissions, and search among them to find the *real* device when we plug in a USB or Firewire (IEEE-1394) device? With devfs, the answer is a resounding *no*. What is really being created with the mknod command is an inode that links the device file name and information like major and minor number to a specific device driver or "kernel space" handler that implements its behavior. Strictly speaking, there are no "real" files behind the device files in /dev.

As the kernel discovers devices and initializes their drivers, the driver can register the names of the physical devices it manages under /dev. As dynamic modules are loaded and unloaded in response to new devices, the devices may be registered and unregistered with devfs by the driver. Essentially, what is located in the new pseudo file system hierarchy cre-ated under /dev is the current set of available devices, with a reasonable naming convention.

The issue, of course, with changes like this is that of backward compatibility. This is why part of the functionality provided with devfs is the ability to create symbolic links, with the expected names, in the /dev directory. These links point to the appropriate device in the new hierarchy under the /dev directory. The links are created and managed by a daemon, devfsd, that may be configured to create the proper links as part of its behavior.

As an example of the new device names, you might expect the "old"-style disk   devices, /dev/hda and /dev/hdb, to be located at /dev/ide/hd/c0b0t0u0 and /dev/ide/hd/c0b0t1u0 respectively. These represent controller 0, bus 0, target 0, unit 0, and controller 0, bus 0, target 1, unit 0. Before you panic (or think, Is he crazy?), these are the *device* names. There are "convenience names," which are links created for   them /dev/discs/disk0 and /dev/disks/disk1. These links point to directories for the disks that contain disc for the whole   disk, and part<*N*> for the disk's partitions. The   old /dev/hda2 would   become /dev/discs/disk0/part2 under this scheme.

There is, therefore, a good mapping between being able to use reasonable human names for the devices *and* being able to find the actual physical hardware devices being used. The devfsd allows multiple schemes for mapping between old names and new names, or for the location of the devfs information (in other words, you can mount it under devfs and use hard links between the old names and the new names). If you want to experiment with devfs in your spare time, you can experiment with installing it. (Its creator, Richard Gooch, has his home page at http://www.atnf.csiro.au/people/rgooch/linux/docs/devfs.html.) It is a great example of a pseudo file system, but I do not delve into it any further here.

9.7   The Linux `ext2` and `ext3` Physical File Systems

The second extended file system for Linux, `ext2`, replaces the first `ext` file system, which was an extension of the older Minix file system used under the Minix operating system. The `ext3` file system is a journaled version of the `ext2` file system.

The `ext3` file system is the default file system for Red Hat and derivative distributions. There is still a considerable amount of confusion in some documentation (and commands) between the `ext2` and `ext3` file system. Just remember that the major difference is the presence (`ext3`) or absence (`ext2`) of a journal.

An example of this `ext2`/`ext3` confusion is that you use the `mke2fs` command to create an `ext2` *or* an `ext3` file system. There is no `mke3fs` command. Likewise, you use `e2fsadm` to shrink or grow an `ext2`/`ext3` file system within a partition (especially if it is located on a logical volume manager [LVM] partition[2], `tune2fs` performs performance tuning functions on either file system, and `e2label` changes the file system label that can be used by `mount` and `/etc/fstab` instead of a Linux device name. It's just one of those things. *C'est la vie et c'est le Linux.*

One of the first things we should do is learn to look at the parameters currently in use by an existing `ext` file system (from now on, we will be referring to `ext3` unless explicitly stated otherwise). We can dump the current file system information:

```
# dumpe2fs -h -ob /dev/md1
dumpe2fs 1.27 (8-Mar-2002)
Filesystem volume name:   BIGDATA
Last mounted on:          <not available>
Filesystem UUID:          2f191424-ffb8-4449-a6ad-6045606bff71
Filesystem magic number:  0xEF53
Filesystem revision #:    1 (dynamic)
Filesystem features:      has_journal needs_recovery
sparse_super large_file
Filesystem state:         clean
Errors behavior:          Continue
Filesystem OS type:       Linux
Inode count:              210048
Block count:              53765472
Reserved block count:     2688273
```

---

2.   The original LVM technology was donated to the OSF by IBM, for inclusion in its OSF/1 operating system. Similar functionality is available on HP-UX, Linux, and several other operating systems. If you are familiar with LVM, you will probably be right at home with Linux's version. See man lvm for details and to expand your command repertoire by about 30 to 35 Linux commands.

```
Free blocks:                  24026463
Free inodes:                  174825
First block:                  0
Block size:                   4096
Fragment size:                4096
Blocks per group:             32768
Fragments per group:          32768
Inodes per group:             128
Inode blocks per group:       4
Last mount time:              Thu Mar   4 00:26:10 2004
Last write time:              Thu Mar   4 00:26:10 2004
Mount count:                  3
Maximum mount count:          23
Last checked:                 Sun Feb   1 10:23:53 2004
Check interval:               15552000 (6 months)
Next check after:             Fri Jul 30 11:23:53 2004
Reserved blocks uid:          0 (user root)
Reserved blocks gid:          0 (group root)
First inode:                  11
Inode size:       128
Journal UUID:                 <none>
Journal inode:                8
Journal device:               0x0000
First orphan inode:           0
```

This is the information kept in the file system superblock, which normally is cached in memory if the file system is mounted (it can fall out of the cache). Notice the following from the information:

- The file system has a volume name (label) associated with it: BIGDATA.
- The file system is described by a UUID like some other objects we have encountered in Linux.
- We see that the file system has a journal (it is therefore ext3), needs recovery (has been written to), and has attributes associated with it called sparse_super and large_file.
- There is information listed about the current free inode count and other disk data structures.
- The block and fragment sizes are both 4,096 bytes (4 KB).
- Information is listed about the mount times and the next file system check to be performed.
- Finally, we see listings for journal information, such as the inode and the journal device (which can be an external disk device).

Discussing some of these points will lead us to some salient features of the Linux `ext` file systems and their operating parameters.

9.7.1 File System Volume Labels

As was mentioned in an earlier section, the Linux device file assignment scheme can result in physical devices migrating from one device file to another, say from /dev/sda to /dev/sdb, if a new device is discovered ahead of it in the chain. This spells disaster if the device contains essential system partitions, like the root file system. Let's look at /etc/fstab for guidance in the file system mounting parameters:

```
# cat /etc/fstab
LABEL=/          /          ext3    defaults    1 1
LABEL=/boot      /boot      ext3    defaults    1 2
LABEL=BIGDATA    /bigdata   ext3    defaults    1 3
```

Notice that instead of a device like /dev/hda or /dev/md1 in the first field, there is a label definition. The system will scan the superblocks on all disks to find labeled file systems to which to apply the mount commands. This can make the system immune to "device migration" issues.

The file system labels are created in the superblock with the e2label command. To change the label from BIGDATA to DATABASE, we would execute

```
# e2label /dev/md0 DATABASE
```

The label field can be at most 16 characters, or it will be truncated. The label may also be set with

```
# tune2fs -L DATABASE /dev/md0
```

and at the time of the file system's creation by the mke2fs command.

9.7.2 Creating the Example ext3 File System

The command that would create the example file system and set most of the parameters that are visible in the superblock is

```
# mke2fs -b 4096 \
                    -j -J size=400              \
                    -L BIGDATA                  \
                    -O sparse_super             \
                    -T largefile                \
        /dev/md1
```

This command sets the block size to the maximum 4 KB, creates a journal that is 400 MB in size (the maximum), sets the volume label to BIGDATA, creates the file system with fewer super-block backup copies to save space, and sets the inode-to-file ratio to one inode per 1 MB of file system space.

The file system block size is very important to overall performance. For fast I/O channels and disks, the system must be able to move enough data per I/O request to keep the channel and the disk busy transferring data, or performance will suffer. The 4 KB maximum block size for ext file systems appears to be tied more to the Intel IA-32 physical page size in memory, rather than the need for performance. Other UNIX systems allow file system blocks and transfers up to 64 KB at a time, which can keep the hardware busier transferring data. I keep hoping for larger block sizes with ext file systems, but for now we have to go to other file systems, like XFS (not to be confused with the X Windows font server: xfs), to get bigger file system blocks.

I defer the journal parameter discussion until the next section. The file system label is being set at creation time in our example, along with two other options that affect the quantity of superblock and inode data structures on the disk. Those options are sparse_super and largefile.

The sparse_super option affects how many copies of the superblock are spread over the file system. Copies of the superblock are kept in known locations, based on the block size of the file system. The first copy is found at block 8193 (1-KB file system blocks), block 16384 (2-KB file system blocks), and block 32768 (4-KB file system blocks). The alternate superblock may be specified to e2fsck if the primary is corrupted for some reason (like an aberrant dd command to the wrong location on the wrong device). The location of the superblock copies is printed when the file system is created with mke2fs, if the -n option is specified.

Specifying largefile uses a precalculated inode-to-file data ratio of one inode per 1 MB of file data. The largefile4 value specifies one inode to 4 MB of data. Using news creates one inode for every 4 KB of file data. Care must be exercised to create enough inodes, otherwise the file system will report "full," with what appears to be plenty of data space remaining. Which value is correct depends on the type of data stored in the file system. On the other hand, creating too many inodes will waste file system space that could be used for data storage rather than meta-data.

9.7.3   Linux ext3 Journal Behavior and Options

The size of the disk-based journal is important, especially if you are using the file system for heavy I/O traffic on systems like a file server. If the journal fills with data being updated to the file system, the I/O to the file system will stop until the journal is emptied. How you mount the file system will determine how the journal is used. There is a kernel process, called kjournald, that is responsible for "playing the journal" to the file system. You can watch its behavior with performance tools like top to see what is happening.

There are three options for the journal behavior that may be set in the /etc/fstab file entry for mounting the file system, in place of the defaults token. You can check the man page for the `mount` command to see all the file system-specific `mount` options for Linux file systems, including `ext3`. A lot of behavior may be determined by the mount options for the file systems.

Before I discuss the `ext3` journal options, we need to differentiate between two types of data that are written to the file system: file block data and *meta*-data. The file block data is pretty straightforward: It is the actual data that makes up the user-visible file contents. The meta-data is the information *about* the file, such as the directory information and the inode data that is not resident inside the file, but still gets written to the file system. Both sets of data must be consistent, or corruption and errors result.

The journal (or on some systems, "log") exists to ensure that if a program or the operating system is interrupted in the process of updating data in the file system, the actions are being tracked and any mismatch in state between file data and meta-data can be corrected. The level of consistency may be controlled by the journal options at mount time. The `ext3` journal options are

- `data=journal`, which writes all data destined for the file system to the journal first
- `data=ordered`, which forces all file data to the main file system before its meta-data is written to the journal
- `data=writeback`, which can write the file data and meta-data without preserving the order in which it is written

These options specify the behavior for file data; meta-data is always journaled. The default behavior, if none is specified, is `data=ordered`. You should carefully evaluate the options and their effect on the performance of your systems and the integrity of your data.

To disable journaling and drop back to `ext2` file system behavior, you can execute

```
# tune2fs -O ^has_journal
```

Other options may be cleared as well, such as `sparse_super`, but this will force changes to the file system data structures that must be performed by running `e2fsck` after the operation.

9.7.4   The `ext` File System Stride Option for RAID

The behavior and performance of a physical file system is tied to the underlying storage geometry on which is written. The `ext` file systems acknowledge the need to manage stripe sizes on underlying RAID 5 devices by providing an optional value for the "stride" of the underlying RAID array in terms of file system blocks per software RAID chunk. Figure 9–8 shows an example RAID stride configuration.

The special RAID behavior is enabled with the `-R stride=<N>` option to `mke2fs` at file system creation time. In this case the value to specify for the stride is the number of file system blocks per underlying RAID stripe. If, for example, the underlying RAID array has a 32-KB

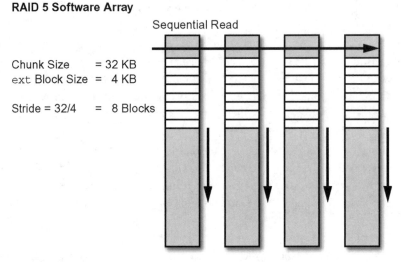

Figure 9–8 RAID stride example for the `ext` file system

stripe size and a 4-KB block size, the stride would be set to 32 KB divided by 4 KB, which equals a value of 8 blocks.

Benchmarks with tools like `iozone` (available from `http://www.iozone.org`) show that there is an increase in performance based on using this option. How large the performance gain is will depend on factors including the RAID chunk size, physical disk speed,   the I/O channel type (SCSI, IDE, and so on), and the system's I/O capabilities. Before settling on a particular configuration, you should run benchmarks to determine the optimum settings for both your RAID devices and the file system. (At the very least you should consult the software RAID HOWTO at The Linux Documentation Project [`http://tldp.org/howto/software-raid-howto-5.html`] and carefully read the performance information. There are some other underlying data structure alignment issues of which to be aware.)

9.8   Standard Mount Options for All File Systems

The `defaults` token in the `/etc/fstab` file will cause an `ext` file system to be mounted with the options listed in Table 9–2. Yet another default that is important to the performance of frequently accessed file systems is the `atime` option, which causes the inode information to be updated each time the file is accessed. Mounting a file system with `noatime` specified in the options will disable this behavior and potentially save inode updates to the disk.

Other file system mounting options affect the way that files or directories inherit the group ID on creation. The default behavior, signified by either `nogrpid` or `sysvgroups`, causes a file or directory being created to take the group ID (GID) information from the creating process, unless the `setgid` bit is set on the target directory. In this case, a file being created will take the

Table 9–2 Default Options for the `mount` Command

Default	Opposite	Description of Default
rw	ro	Allows both reading and writing to the file system
suid	nosuid	Allows creation of set user ID programs and scripts
dev	nodev	Allows interpretation of character and block special device files in the file system
exec	noexec	Allows execution of binaries from the file system on the local system
auto	noauto	Allows automatic mounting of the file system, when encountered (such as on CD-ROMs and floppies)
nouser	user	Does not allow an ordinary user to mount the file system. The user option implies nosuid, nodev, and noexec unless overridden
async	sync	Indicates all I/O to the file system is asynchronous

GID of the parent directory, and a directory being created will also inherit the `setgid` bit from the parent directory.

The opposite behavior, indicated by either `grpid` or `bsdgroups`, will cause a file or directory being created to inherit the GID of the enclosing parent directory. The options, then, may be set file system wide, or controlled on a per-directory basis. The most flexible way to allow the BSD inheritance is to maintain the default (SYSV) inheritance behavior, and use the `setgid` bit on directories that you wish to have the BSD behavior.

9.9 The Temporary File System

One file system that is useful if your systems have plenty of memory and require the equivalent of a RAM disk is `tempfs`. This file system, as you might guess, has no protection against data loss in the event of system failure or power loss. It can be used to accelerate operations that create lots of small temporary files.

The possible mount options for the temporary file system are `size=<Nbytes>`, `nr_blocks=<N>`, and `nr_inodes=<N>`. Each of the numerical values may have the suffixes `k`, `m`, or `g` for kilobytes, megabytes, or gigabytes respectively. To create and mount a 100-MB `tempfs` file system, you can use the following `mount` command:

```
# mount -t tempfs -o size=100m /dev/ram /mnt/scratch
```

There are multiple devices that match the pattern `/dev/ram*`, so there may be multiple instances of the `tempfs` active. The default size, by the way, is 50% of RAM, so be careful to specify the real amount you want.

9.10 Other Available File System Types

One file system that is readily available on Red Hat and derivative distributions is the Reiser file system. Some of the commands are: `mkreiserfs`, `reiserfsck`, `resize_reiser`, and `reiserfstune`. I have to admit that I have limited experience with implementing the Reiser file system compared with the `ext` and `XFS` file systems. Rather than appear more foolish than I already am, I will leave Reiser for my next book.

The `XFS` file system proved to be the highest performing file system I tested in one large cluster project. The difficulty with `XFS` for most situations is that it requires you to patch and rebuild the kernel to add functionality. Although the effort is well worth it, we do not have space to cover the skills needed to patch, rebuild, and test the Linux kernel.

If you are fortunate enough to have a handy kernel programmer, she can do the work in a reasonably short time, so you should not take my avoiding the subject as a negative recommendation, only an attempt at being realistic. In tests that I ran, `XFS` was 31% faster than `ext3` for a six-disk software RAID device built with ultra320 SCSI drives. (I attribute this to in-memory block caches, larger block sizes, and other `XFS` features. We benchmarked these configurations to death, so please just accept my numbers and don't send fan mail for your favorite file system.)

9.11 Advanced Performance Tuning

We do not have space to examine the finer aspects of file system tuning here. It involves lots of single changes to parameters, followed by tedious benchmarking. So, I thought it best to mention several "pointers" that can lead you to some advanced aspects of I/O tuning at the device driver level.

- At the individual hard disk level, it is possible to tune the system I/O queue latency to the device driver. At this level, you are working with the I/O "elevator," which is the Linux I/O scheduler. See the `man` page for the `elvtune` command for more (but sketchy) details.
- Investigate tagged queuing for the various disk drivers (SCSI) that may be active on your system. For heavy I/O traffic on file servers, it may be beneficial to increase the size of the request queues. Some of this tuning may be done through files in the `/proc` file system.
- It is also possible to tune the drivers that provide the disk interface support. You can get a list of a module's parameters with the `modinfo` command. Start with an `lsmod` command to list the active modules, then use `modinfo` to look for tuning opportunities.

Always remember that this level of tuning (very low level) has inherent risks. The driver may not actually work as advertised. Changes you make may damage hardware. You should never perform tuning on a production system without adequate testing. The word *adequate* is defined differently in different environments.

9.12 A Word about SMART Monitoring for Disks

SMART is an acronym that stands for self-monitoring analysis and reporting technology. This technology is built into late-model SCSI, IDE, and ATA disk drives, and collects information produced internally by the disk hardware and firmware. The software package is capable of being used to report errors, monitor temperature parameters, and examine other useful information. The SMART daemon may also have the drives run self-tests at regular intervals.

The SMART software consists of a daemon and its configuration file `/etc/smartd.conf`, along with a control program `smartctl`. The behavior of the software differs from release to release. Red Hat 8.0 had only a bare-bones daemon and the control program, but no configuration file for the daemon. The Fedora Core distributions have better documentation on the components than earlier Red Hat-derived distributions, and appears to support a lot more monitoring functionality and control over the daemon's behavior.

To determine whether your drives are supported, you can run the control program on them, as in this example on an older ATA disk drive on an IDE controller:

```
# smartctl -a /dev/hda
smartctl version 5.21 Copyright (C) 2002-3 Bruce Allen
Home page is http://smartmontools.sourceforge.net/

=== START OF INFORMATION SECTION ===
Device Model:     IBM-DAQA-33240
Serial Number:    1Y55Y0J4714
Firmware Version: R6ORA52A
Device is:        Not in smartctl database
      [for details use: -P showall]
ATA Version is:   3
ATA Standard is:  ATA-3 X3T10 2008D revision 1
Local Time is:    Sun Mar 14 00:17:02 2004 PST
SMART is only available in ATA Version 3 Revision 3 or
greater.
We will try to proceed in spite of this.
SMART support is: Ambiguous - ATA IDENTIFY DEVICE words 85-87
don't show if SMART is enabled.
A mandatory SMART command failed: exiting. To continue, add
one or more '-T permissive' options.
```

The daemon's ability to communicate with the drive depends on the command language version implemented in the drive itself. We may not be able to enable all the features fully, but let's try to enable SMART monitoring on the disk drive, despite the ambiguity noted in the previous messages:

```
# smartctl -s on  /dev/hda
smartctl version 5.21 Copyright (C) 2002-3 Bruce Allen
Home page is http://smartmontools.sourceforge.net/
```

```
=== START OF ENABLE/DISABLE COMMANDS SECTION ===
SMART Enabled.
```

Deciding to play it safe, because this system has disks on the borderline of compatibility, I only enabled the minimal checking in the `/etc/smartd.conf` configuration file. Logging goes to the `syslog` facility by default, but e-mail can also be added:

```
# A very silent check. Only report SMART health status if it
# fails. But send an email in this case
/dev/hda -H -m root@localhost.localdomain
/dev/hdb -H -m root@localhost.localdomain
/dev/hdc -H -m root@localhost.localdomain
```

Starting up the daemon is the next step:

```
# chkconfig smartd on
# service smartd start
```

Messages logged in the `/var/log/messages` file indicate that, even though the disk types are not found in the database of disk models used by the `smartd` daemon, the disks *are* being monitored by the daemon:

```
Mar 14 00:24:29 ns1 smartd[28761]: Device: /dev/hda, is SMART
     capable. Adding to "monitor" list.
Mar 14 00:24:29 ns1 smartd[28761]: Device: /dev/hdb, opened
Mar 14 00:24:29 ns1 smartd[28761]: Device: /dev/hdb, not found
     in smartd database.
Mar 14 00:24:29 ns1 smartd[28761]: Device: /dev/hdb, is SMART
     capable. Adding to "monitor" list.
Mar 14 00:24:29 ns1 smartd[28761]: Device: /dev/hdc, opened
Mar 14 00:24:30 ns1 smartd[28761]: Device: /dev/hdc, not found
     in smartd database.
Mar 14 00:24:30 ns1 smartd[28761]: Device: /dev/hdc, is SMART
     capable. Adding to "monitor" list.
Mar 14 00:24:30 ns1 smartd[28761]: Monitoring 3 ATA and
     0 SCSI devices
Mar 14 00:24:30 ns1 smartd: smartd startup succeeded
Mar 14 00:24:30 ns1 smartd[28763]: smartd has fork()ed into
     background mode. New PID=28763.
```

The default polling interval for the `smartd` process to query the drives it monitors is 30 minutes, which may not be suitable for systems that are running compute-intensive jobs that should not be interrupted. Certainly on server systems like infrastructure, administrative, or file server nodes, this monitoring is potentially worth the system overhead. The ability to predict drive failures is certainly something that we should not turn down lightly, especially on systems that are central to the operation of the cluster.

For information on the many configuration options available, see the `man` pages for `smartd`, `smartd.conf`, and `smartctl`. Also, in case you missed the Web page for the software in the earlier messages, it is located at `http://smartmontools.sourceforge.net`.

9.13 Local Disks and File Systems Summary

The information contained in this chapter should help you get a good start toward configuring the local file systems on the administrative and infrastructure nodes in your cluster. Much of what we discuss here is also useful in configuring the compute slices (local scratch file systems or system disks), file servers, or any other cluster component that uses Linux software RAID or needs to provide a local file system.

Selecting the proper RAID configuration to protect data or to provide high availability for system disks is one skill that you should take away from reading the details we discuss. There is a lot of flexibility and functionality available not only as part of the standard distributions, but as "external" open-source packages as well. We are very fortunate to have a full tool kit when it comes to file systems and the underlying use of disk resources.

TIP Software RAID on Linux is an inexpensive way to improve system reliability and data availability for infrastructure systems. For mirroring system disks, use RAID 1; for protecting data availability, use RAID 5. Order your hardware with the required multiple internal disk drives.

We did not cover some obvious disk-related features, like LVM, because there simply is not space to contain all the information on all the possible choices for file system and disk configurations in Linux. Rather than being a disadvantage, however, with a little exploring you will locate more possibilities for your Linux "bag of tricks." Don't be afraid to explore further.

## CHAPTER 10

Supporting Role: Infrastructure Services and Administration

Chapter Objectives

- Recommend general principles for cluster infrastructure implementation
- Identify common Linux infrastructure components used in a cluster
- Detail configuration options for frequently used infrastructure services

Linux, the operating system, provides a number of infrastructure services that are essential to the proper operation of a cluster. These are the services that are necessary as you begin to install the cluster from a raw hardware state, and are essential to its continued operation. This chapter covers some of the infrastructure services, their relationship to the cluster, and their basic configuration. The configuration examples focus on Red Hat or Red Hat–derived Linux distributions.

10.1 The Big Infrastructure Picture

The next several chapters cover a number of infrastructure services that support the operation of the other systems in the cluster. In many cases these services are located on dedicated systems in the cluster for both security and protection from compute-intensive interference. Which infrastructures services are necessary for your cluster is a design decision, driven by your system administration environment, the cluster's applications, and the functionality that they require.

The infrastructure services are not completely independent of one another. For example, the name resolution service is used by practically every subsystem and application that runs in the cluster—everything depends on it. Other services are used during specialized operations like cluster installation and system booting. The flow of the next several chapters is roughly in order that the services would need to be installed or activated in the cluster. A partial list of the possible infrastructure services is

- Time synchronization (NTP)
- Name services (DNS, Network Information Service [NIS], /etc/hosts)
- Authentication (Kerberos, NIS)
- Remote access (SSH, remote shell [RSH])
- Parallel command execution (parallel distributed shell [PDSH])
- DHCP
- System logging (klog and syslog)
- Log rotation
- TFTP
- Network booting (pxelinux)
- Network channel bonding
- System installation (kickstart, SystemImager)

The functional location of these services in relationship to the rest of the cluster architecture is shown in Figure 10–1. The services "ride on top of" the Linux operating system and are usually included as a standard part of the distribution, unless server-specific packages have been omitted for marketing purposes. Whether a particular distribution's packaging of Linux contains the services you want is an important fact to verify. This is when selecting the proper version of the commercial distributions is important for your cluster's infrastructure.

10.2 Initializing Your Cluster's Software Infrastructure

Your cluster hardware is completely assembled, racked, and cabled. Your racks are placed in the computer room, connected to power, and powered on. What is the next step? Where do you start? Some of the potential physical locations in the cluster architecture for the infrastructure and administrative services we will examine are shown in Figure 10–2.

There are administrative systems, master or head nodes, file servers, compute slices, and spares, all waiting to be configured. How do you install the services to bootstrap the cluster and allow the remaining installation tasks to continue? You do have a project plan and a design for the cluster's software stack, don't you? (See "Preliminary Solution Design" on page 32 for elements of the project plan and design).

Although the goal of configuring a cluster's software may be considered "creating a single system" activity, the details are similar to installing a "compressed" network environment, existing within one or more racks. Multiple networks, client–server-based services, management, routing, remote access, and other infrastructure are familiar to systems administrators working in distributed environments. The cluster requires the same sort of services that a "normal" network would require, and many of these services must be in place before the remainder of the "software stack" can be installed. They are direct dependencies for that software.

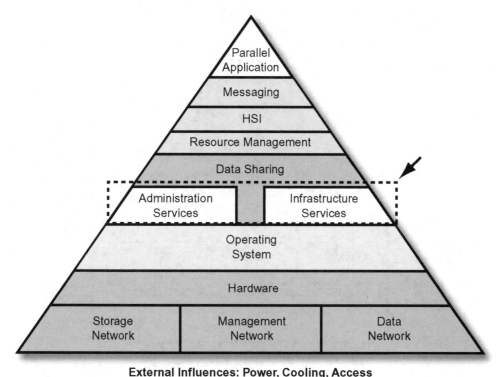

Figure 10–1 Cluster software functional relationships

In this chapter, much of the software we configure will "live" on one or more administrative nodes, head nodes, and the systems providing local storage for administrative data. These systems run the services and provide the storage necessary for supporting the compute activities that take place on the compute slices. Let's roll up the sleeves of our Linux T-shirt and begin.

10.3 Infrastructure Implementation Recommendations

There are some general principles that we should outline before we start deploying the infrastructure services for a cluster. Some basic principles that hold true in any large, complex networked environment, are

- Keep essential services separated from high-load (compute-bound or heavy user traffic) interference.
- Choose services that support multiple copies for redundancy
- Use services that have fall-back capabilities, possibly to another service for the same information.

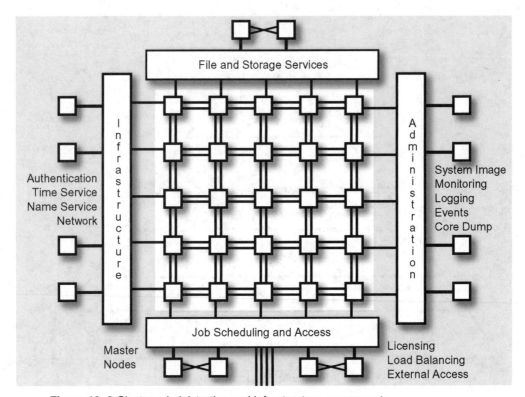

Figure 10–2 Cluster administrative and infrastructure components

- Use single-point administration techniques whenever it is possible and consistent with the other suggested approaches (for example, a single version data source, but not SPOF).
- Segregate services onto separate networks if they are high traffic or performance sensitive.
- Provide services that are efficient and that do not interfere with performance.
- Use version control and backups to protect configuration information.

Now is a good time to discuss these recommendations, before we start making software location and configuration choices for the infrastructure services.

10.3.1   Avoiding Service Interference

It is obviously a bad idea to run infrastructure services on the cluster's compute slices, because the compute-intensive nature of the parallel activities will interfere with the performance of the service. The service software may also "get in the way of" the compute slice application activities. I discuss configuration of the compute slice environment separately, but it should be considered off limits to clusterwide, essential services that would interfere with their primary function.

In some cases, it is best to run a service on an isolated system, where the software is beyond user interference, and the hardware and operating system may be tuned for maximum performance. The file server or servers are a primary example of this type of situation. Let's discuss a file server as an example of an isolated service, for just a paragraph or two.

Most file server technologies, such as NFS, rely on caching mechanisms to reduce the number of physical reads or writes required for storage media. Although disk arrays have internal caches, the operating system on the file server also caches file system blocks in the system page cache, which resides in main memory. Any activities on the file server that disturb the contents of the page cache (backups or other file system activity) cause the cache contents to be overwritten and force extra physical I/O.

In addition to the caching interference, any process on the file server that takes CPU cycles away from its file-serving activities will interfere with those activities. There is no faster way to impact *every* file server client in the cluster than to slow down the file server system with nonessential activities. The general lesson is: Dedicate the necessary resources to an essential service, and do not succumb to temptation to use the system for other purposes (including development work or compute jobs), unless you are sure that there will be no "destructive interference" between activities.

T I P   The proper location for your infrastructure services may affect the overall performance of the cluster. It is best to provide dedicated resources (separate systems) for services like file serving that are heavily used within the cluster.

10.3.2   Redundant Copies of Essential Services

Any service that is essential to the operation of the cluster should be protected by some level of redundancy or high availability. If the service becomes unavailable, you do not want the operation of the cluster impacted. There are several hardware areas, including the file server and head nodes, that are single points of failure.

Services that allow multiple copies of their server portion, coupled with client fail-over, should be configured to use that ability. Two examples of such services with built-in redundancy and fail-over are NIS and DHCP. The location of the primary and secondary copies of the services in the cluster is an important design decision.

NIS provides the ability to configure one master and multiple slave servers. Clients may be configured to bind to a specific server or to select the first server located by broadcast. If a server ever becomes unavailable, the client's binding will fail over to another master or slave server after a timeout.

The DHCP service may be configured with two servers sharing the responsibilities of managing the address pools associated with groups of clients or separate LAN segments. The two servers communicate together with a proprietary protocol, sharing the responsibility for assigning IP addresses in response to client requests. In the event of a failure, the DHCP peer protocol allows the surviving server to take over responsibilities for managing the pool, which is no longer shared with its (dead) peer.

In these two (and other) cases, implementation of redundancy requires specific planning and configuration actions. In the case of both DHCP and NIS, two servers must be configured and placed on separate systems. In both cases, the fail-over mechanism can hide any server failure from the client systems using the services.

10.3.3   Services with Fall-Back Capabilities

An example of fall-back, at multiple levels, is the client system's name resolution service. The name resolution may be configured, via the `/etc/nsswitch.conf` name service switch file, to use multiple sources for host name information, including NIS, NIS+, DNS, and the local `/etc/hosts` file. The services may be accessed in a specified order and with a specified fall-back pattern should any of the sources of the service become unavailable.

For example, the name service switch may be configured to use DNS first, followed by the local hosts file. The DNS resolver file, `/etc/resolv.conf`, may be configured to use multiple DNS servers (up to three). When a host name needs to be resolved, the client system will attempt to use the DNS service first.

If neither of the DNS servers are available, then after the appropriate time-out, the client name resolution library will fall back to using the local hosts file. This type of arrangement allows us considerable flexibility in dealing with potential failures. The more immune a client (compute slice) system is to infrastructure failures, the more reliable it will be for its users and their applications.

T I P   Using redundant services and configuring multiple copies of services will cost extra system administration effort. The effort is more than worth it if you have availability or reliability agreements to meet.

10.3.4   Single-Point Administration

Previously, we examined an example of configuring a name resolution service with multiple sources of information—namely, DNS and the local hosts file. But what is the correct (or best) order to specify the configuration of the services? Let's use this example to illustrate "single-point administration" as a design choice in a cluster.

The possible ordering of the two services in the name service switch are (1) first use the file `/etc/hosts`, followed by DNS, and (2) first use DNS, followed by the `/etc/hosts` file. The DNS service distributes its information from a single set of configuration files on the server system, with DNS replicas using identical copies of the same configuration files. The host information in the `/etc/hosts` file needs to be replicated on every system.

Comparing the two possibilities, we see that making changes or additions to the host names in the cluster would require updating all `/etc/hosts` files on every system, whereas a

DNS change involves updating the DNS configuration information and one or two replicas. The number of systems "touched" in the process is lower with the DNS approach, and the potential impact to the cluster is lower in terms of interfering with jobs that are executing.

The design choice we make depends on the type of service we are choosing and our implementation options (in other words, what are the administration characteristics of the services from which we have to choose). Some possible considerations for making this type of single-point administration design decision are

- Minimizing the number of systems touched as a result of a change
- Minimizing the amount of impact to running jobs from a change
- Minimizing the potential for configurations to get "out of sync" across the cluster
- Minimizing system administration effort required to effect the change

Careful thought and single-point administration approaches can minimize impact to the cluster *and* the amount of system administration effort needed to keep infrastructure services operational and their configurations up-to-date.

TIP   Approaching cluster management from a single-point administration angle is the best way to avoid treating the cluster as a set of pieces "flying in close formation." The same large-scale administration techniques that you would find in any large networked environment apply.

10.3.5   Choosing Efficient Services

Your choice of infrastructure services, if not carefully considered, can have unexpected performance consequences in your cluster. There are some service choices that are best avoided, if possible. One of these services, at least with regard to providing host name lookup, is NIS.

Although NIS is a very useful single-point method of distributing user login information, group information, automounter maps, and host name information, it also may have unexpected performance impacts. For example, if you are using NFS, every mount by a remote client requires a host name lookup to validate the IP address in the request. NIS can be a very slow name resolution service, sometimes taking on the order of seconds to look up and return the IP address to name mapping.

The NFS mount daemon on some UNIX implementations is single threaded, meaning that it processes a single request before moving on to the next one. Part of this processing is a name resolution request for the IP address of the mounting host, which may cause the daemon to block while waiting for the reply from the name resolution service. This is a performance bottleneck that is only made worse by slow name resolution service response for each mount request.

Although this situation may or may not be present in a given implementation of Linux (and tests in my network did not detect a problem), it serves as a good lesson for those of us designing infrastructure services: Choose services that make efficient use of resources and do not slow down the systems that depend on them. Name resolution is central to the operation of the networked services in a cluster and we better make sure it works quickly and efficiently. We should also be on the lookout for other services that are direct dependencies of other essential system services.

10.3.6   Management of Configuration Information

When making changes to system configuration information, particularly configuration files, it is a very good idea to be able to back out changes if they don't work. The ability to revert to a previous version of a configuration file set implies some form of what is called *revision control* or *configuration management* in the software development world. Fortunately, we can use Linux tools that are targeted at software development to perform this function for us.

In a large and complex environment, with multiple system administrators, version control, which usually incorporates a "checkin" and "checkout" process for files under its control, can help prevent stepping on each other's work. Check out a file, make changes to it, test it, then check it back in—and while the file is checked out, you have exclusive access to it. The check-in step creates a new version of the file within the version control software, preserving the old versions and their lineage.

TIP   Using some form of software configuration management technique to manage versions of configuration information is essential to the professional operation of a cluster. View configuration changes as software updates, and apply the same change, test, release process that software developers use.

There are two easy choices for version control tools on many Linux distributions: the revision control system (RCS) and the concurrent version system (CVS). Both tools come with the standard distributions of Linux, mainly because they are used in one form or another by the software development community. The formality of your configuration management approach depends on the requirements of your environment.

For a minimal amount of impact to your "normal" procedure, yet to add the benefits of revision control to your environment, you should consider

- Having a central repository for configuration files
- Adding revision information to a header in the files, using, at a minimum, functionality similar to Id provided by RCS
- Backing up the configuration information on a regular basis

As a simple example, adding lines to a file that consist of

```
#!/bin/sh
# $Id$
#
```

will expand to

```
#!/bin/sh
# $Id: config.sh,v 1.1 2004/02/28 17:04:34 rlucke Exp rlucke $
#
```

when the file is checked in to, and then out of, the RCS facility. Just the addition of a simple version header like this can help track down issues with configuration problems. (If you are not familiar with the operation of RCS, you can get an introductory command tutorial by issuing the `man rcsintro` command.) The larger your administration team and the more complex your cluster, the more necessary version control becomes.

10.4 Protecting Active Configuration Information

In addition to saving the version history of your configuration files, there are tools, such as `tripwire`, that can save a database of checksum information for the "active" copies of important system configuration files and programs. The database for a given system is created, and at regular intervals the tool compares the saved checksum information with that of the current system configuration files. Any changes to protected files are flagged for attention by system administrators.

Tools of this type are intended to detect intrusions and the activities of hackers that modify system files and configurations to gain control of the system. This type of protection is especially important if a system is to be connected directly to the Internet, where it is visible and potentially accessible by hackers. Tools like `tripwire` should be installed, and careful attention should be paid whenever there is the potential for a system's configuration to be modified by unwanted visitors or untrustworthy users.

10.5 Preparation for Infrastructure Installation

To prepare for loading the infrastructure services on your cluster, you need to think about the following items:

- Access to the console of the systems being loaded
- The order of installation of the administrative/infrastructure servers
- Dependencies (in other words, the need for stable storage) for loading activities, which can determine the order of installation
- Checking your activities against the plan for the cluster's infrastructure

There are a certain number of "chicken-and-egg" issues to overcome: You will likely not have all the console access facilities in place, the networks will not be "live" and configured, and the file server won't be available. You are, after all, in the process of bootstrapping the cluster's software infrastructure from "scratch."

10.5.1   Order of Installation

You have to start somewhere. I usually like to start with the file server, because that enables stable storage for the other infrastructure configuration information (Linux packages, configuration files, system images, scripts, and so on). In small clusters, this may mean starting with the master nodes, because the local storage on these systems may substitute for a file server (this is *not* the best choice of configuration).

If there is a need for downloading software to the cluster environment from the Internet, this can be a strong argument for starting with the master nodes and enabling the external connection early during the installation process. This may work in trusted network environments, but for security-conscious installations, an external connection at *any* time prior to having all security facilities in place may not be advisable. You will be able to make the proper choice based on your experience level and the local environment.

A representation of a cluster's administration and infrastructure components is shown in Figure 10–2. Although the "Job Scheduling and Access," "Infrastructure," and "Administration" functions are shown located on separate systems in the figure, in reality the separate components may be placed on shared system resources in the cluster. How these services are located is part of the overall design of the cluster's software stack. The "File Services and Storage" functionality should be located on separate resources. A recommended installation order is

  • Infrastructure services
  • Administrative services
  • File server or local storage
  • Master nodes and external access
  • Compute slices

The compute slices depend on most of the other services for their operation, which is why they are late in the installation process. Administrative services are important to the operation of the cluster and troubleshooting its operation, but the monitoring features require some compute slices to be installed with which to test. Do not make the mistake of partially installing the cluster software and then giving your users free run of the system while you are trying to complete the installation!

10.5.2   Steps for Installing Infrastructure Services

An example cluster hardware configuration with two master nodes, two infrastructure nodes, one file server, one spare node, and 16 compute slices is shown in Figure 10–3. We will use this configuration as an example of how to approach installing the software infrastructure for the cluster. We will examine a general outline, in terms of high-level steps, and future sections will outline some of the specific configuration actions for the subsystems involved. If you haven't seen the subsystems mentioned in the outline, don't worry; they are covered in upcoming sections.

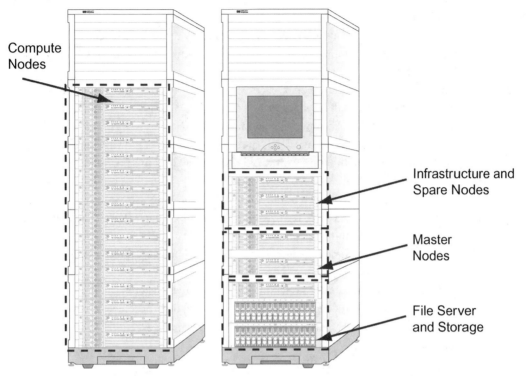

Compute Nodes

Infrastructure and Spare Nodes

Master Nodes

File Server and Storage

Figure 10–3 Example cluster for administrative and infrastructure installation

For this configuration, let's assume that the file server will provide NFS; the name services will be provided by a combination of DNS, NIS, and the `/etc/hosts` files; NTP will be used for time synchronization; user account information is provided by NIS; Kerberos is configured along with SSH for remote access and authentication; and `SystemImager` will be used for network installation of the Linux operating system.

1. Configure any networking equipment and console management equipment with their default gateway and IP address information.
2. Install and update the Linux operating system on the two infrastructure nodes, using RAID 1 to mirror the system disks.
3. Initialize SSH access for the root account between the two infrastructure nodes.
4. Install the PDSH on the two infrastructure nodes to use for executing parallel commands between the two infrastructure systems.
5. Create minimal `/etc/hosts` files containing the host information for the infrastructure nodes, master nodes, NFS server, switches, and default network gateways.
6. Configure DNS on the two infrastructure nodes with the expected cluster information, including the network addresses and names for all compute slices, infrastructure nodes,

spare nodes, master nodes, switches, and console management devices on all networks present in the cluster.

7. Configure a master and a slave NIS server on the two infrastructure nodes.

8. Build and push the minimal NIS `passwd` and `group` maps between the master and slave servers.

9. Configure the infrastructure nodes' `/etc/nsswitch.conf` file to use the NIS and DNS services, along with fall-back to `/etc/hosts`.

10. Verify proper name service operation and fall-back.

11. Configure the DHCP server and a fail-over copy on the two infrastructure nodes, and populate the configuration files with MAC address and host information.

12. Verify proper DHCP operation and fall-back.

13. Configure NTP servers on each of the infrastructure nodes.

14. Configure a master and a slave Kerberos key distribution center (KDC) and administrative server on the two infrastructure nodes.

15. Install and update the Linux operating system on the NFS server, using RAID 1 to mirror the system disks.

16. Configure channel bonding between the NFS server and the core Ethernet switch.

17. Add the NFS server's root account to the SSH information for remote access.

18. Install PDSH on the NFS server to allow parallel command execution.

19. Configure and export the NFS server's storage.

20. Perform initial tuning of the NFS server subsystem.

21. Install and configure TFTP and `pxelinux` on the infrastructure server targeted for the system installation service.

22. Replicate the TFTP and `pxelinux` installation to the second infrastructure server as a future backup.

23. Install and configure the `SystemImager` server and configuration files on both the two infrastructure servers, using the NFS server as storage for images.

24. Test the `pxelinux` network booting procedure from both infrastructure servers, one at a time.

25. Install the `SystemImager` client on both infrastructure servers and the NFS server.

26. Use `SystemImager` to capture images of both infrastructure servers and the NFS server.

27. Install and update the Linux operating system on one of the master nodes, using RAID 1 to mirror the system disks.

28. Configure channel bonding between the first master node and the external network.

29. Configure network connections between the master node, the internal cluster networks, and the external network.

30. Enable name service client (`/etc/resolv.conf` and `/etc/nsswitch.conf`) on the master node.

31. Configure the Linux firewall, if desired, on the first master node, allowing only minimal protocol access (SSH and NTP).
32. Create NFS automounter maps for user home directories, administration information, project storage, and any other required NFS data mappings.
33. Enable the NFS client and automount file system (`autofs`) on the first master node and the infrastructure nodes, if desired.
34. Install the `SystemImager` client on the master node.
35. Capture an image of the first master node with `SystemImager` and replicate it to the second master node.
36. Install and verify the second master node.
37. Create a user account and push the NIS map information.
38. Test the new user account's access to the NFS file server and other cluster resources.
39. Install and update the Linux operating system on the spare node (the image from this system will become the `SystemImager` "golden client"), using RAID 1 to mirror the system disks.
40. Configure the spare node to use the client services for Kerberos, NFS, NTP, NIS, `autofs`, and the name services.
41. Configure the spare node's network access to cluster resources.
42. Install the `SystemImager` client on the spare node.
43. Capture an image of the spare node to install on the other compute slices in the cluster.
44. Test a network installation of one of the "blank" compute slices in the second rack (remember that?).
45. Troubleshoot the network installation of the blank compute slice until it works properly (network configurations are correct, disk mirroring works, and so on).
46. Boot and install the remaining compute slices.
47. Verify all IP, host name, MAC, and other configuration information on all the clients.
48. Capture all SSH keys necessary for remote access, generate the `root` user's `authorized_keys2` and `known_hosts` files.
49. Place the two SSH files in the proper location in the `SystemImager` image for the compute slices and execute an `update-client` command on each of the clients.
50. Test remote access to all the compute slices.
51. Verify that all `SystemImager` images are up-to-date with respect to what is installed in the cluster.

These steps should put you in the position of having a cluster with a functional infrastructure and an operational starting point for loading the next layer of software, which includes monitoring tools, load balancing, HSI libraries, and applications. It is important to verify that both "normal" users and `root` have the proper access to the correct resources. Users should be prevented from accessing resources on the management network without proper authorization, but should be able to access their home directories and other permitted information on the NFS file server.

The steps outlined here are detailed in the sections on the individual services and the associated configuration steps. How long it takes you to reach a point where you have a stable infrastructure will depend on a number of factors, including

- The size of the cluster
- The stability of the operating system and hardware combination
- The number of required infrastructure services
- Your level of experience with the required administration steps
- How much preparation was done prior to the start of the installation process (in terms of design, planning, investigation, and downloading of required software)
- The readiness of the environment (power, network connections, and so on)

Ideally, an experienced cluster builder can get a hardware configuration similar in size to the example cluster to the stable infrastructure state in approximately two (long) days.

Because of the real world and the "pi Principle" (the length of time actually needed for any project is roughly 3.1415 times the predicted time), this ideal situation is almost never realized. As you dig into the upcoming sections, you will see that the amount of latitude in configuration of the subsystems leaves a lot of room for mistakes and oversights.

10.5.3   Loading the Linux Operating System Distribution

Once you have chosen the starting point for the administrative node configuration, loading an operating system goes much faster if you have a graphical point-and-click interface. Because the systems may have a minimal graphics capability built in, temporarily connecting a graphics monitor, keyboard, and mouse will get you started. The presence of a KVM switch connected to the systems being loaded will also give you a flexible way to work on several systems in parallel by sharing a graphics monitor, keyboard, and mouse.

As part of loading the Linux operating system on to the administrative nodes, you need to decide which packages to include. The server portion of services like NFS, NIS, NTP, DHCP, and TFTP are necessary to provide services to client systems. There also will be required packages for services like measurement and monitoring that will be loaded later—for example, the Apache Web server may be required for Web-based tools. Packages from outside the Linux distribution will have dependencies that you must consider.

One reason to trim unnecessary packages is to make the system footprint or image smaller. If you are going to capture a snapshot or image of the system later (I describe the methods for doing this in a later chapter), the time required for saving and restoring a system image is smaller if the system footprint is smaller. Trim unwanted packages, but be sure not to trim too far—understand the package dependencies.

Part of loading the operating system is configuring the local disks. Information and recommendations for this step are covered in Chapter 9, "Linux Local Disk Storage" on page 188. Once the disks are configured and the operating system is loaded, you can start performing the basic configuration of the administrative nodes. In the following sections, we look at some of the essential configuration steps that may be needed in your cluster.

10.6 Networking

Linux has been used for years in ISPs to create the infrastructure needed for access to the World Wide Web. Not only are the networking capabilities of Linux feature rich, but they have been thoroughly "wrung out" by demanding users. In addition to the general network availability for network services, there are several specialized capabilities of which we can make good use in our cluster.

10.6.1   Configuring Ethernet Switching Equipment

The exact configuration needs of your Ethernet switches will depend on the manufacturer of the switch and the model you are using. Most managed switches will come from the factory with a default configuration for their IP address and console passwords. You may not need to perform any configuration steps to get the switch to connect the systems in your cluster, but there will be work needed to integrate the switches into the management scheme that you will use.

Making connections from the cluster to external networks, internally configuring the file server links, and verifying management access to the switch equipment via their serial console switch (if present) connections may be necessary to prepare for infrastructure loading. After all, testing the infrastructure will require a network, at least in the management rack and with the involvement of the cores switch. Steps for configuring the switching equipment may include

- Connecting to the switch via a serial port with either the serial console switch or a laptop computer[1]
- Setting the access password for the switch's management console
- Setting the switch's management IP address
- Setting the switch's port autonegotiation behavior
- Configuring VLANs
- Configuring routing
- Configuring any port trunking that is required

Whether you install the infrastructure systems or configure the network switches first is a matter of preference (and scheduling of resources). Once the installation of the administrative nodes is started, you can attend to the switches while the operating system is loading. The net-

---

1.   Today's laptops are omitting serial ports from the standard connections that are available. There are a number of USB-to-serial port converters that are quite useful if your laptop does not have a serial port. The Linux `mini-com` application is a terminal emulator that allows you to make the connection between your laptop's serial connection and the device to which you are talking.

work interfaces on the systems being loaded may not be configured properly if a connection to network equipment is not detected.

10.6.2   Network Aliases

As we discussed in Chapter 6, an Ethernet switch will flood all frames to all ports unless VLANs or some other filtering technique is employed. This means that all traffic within the switch is presented to a system attached to one of the switch's ports, and the Ethernet interface will receive all traffic, discarding the frames that are not applicable to its MAC address.

Although the compute slices in the cluster have up to three physical interfaces—tied to the management, data, and control Ethernet networks—other systems, such as the administrative nodes, may have only one physical Ethernet interface, yet need access to all three of the networks. The particular networks and their traffic may be there, "within the switch," but we need a way to convince Linux to allow us to access the networks and their attached devices from systems that may have only a single Ethernet interface.

We can do this by creating network "aliases" to the existing Ethernet connection—for example, eth0. Remember that UNIX Ethernet interfaces are configured with the ifconfig command, which specifies details like the IP address associated with the interface, the net mask, and the broadcast address.

Example output from the ifconfig command is

```
# ifconfig eth0

eth0 Link encap:Ethernet HWaddr 00:06:25:04:DE:4E
     inet addr:192.168.0.110 Bcast:192.168.0.255 Mask:255.255.255.0
     UP BROADCAST RUNNING MULTICAST MTU:1500 Metric:1
     RX packets:20115040 errors:0 dropped:0 overruns:0 frame:0
     TX packets:26310592 errors:4 dropped:0 overruns:0 carrier:0 \
             collisions:0 txqueuelen:100
     RX bytes:3210027801 (3061.3 Mb) TX bytes:2223080970(2120.0 Mb)
      Interrupt:9 Base address:0x1400
```

To create a network alias for the eth0 interface, we would issue the following command:

```
# ifconfig eth0:0 10.0.1.1 netmask 255.255.248.0 \
        broadcast 10.0.7.255
```

What we have just done is "attached" a new IP address for a completely different network to the physical interface eth0 and called it eth0:0. The alias is added after the Linux device name by affixing a ":" character followed by a string (usually numerical, but not required to be such). (Documentation is located in /usr/src/Linux-2.4/Documentation/networking/ alias.txt if you have the kernel source RPM package installed. The possible length of the string for an alias is not specified in any documentation that I could find, and it appears that assumptions are made about the length of this field. It is best to stick with numerical alias strings for safety's sake.) We could just have easily attached another (unique) IP address in the same network as an alias—for example, `192.168.0.231`.

We can now "ping" this address from other systems and use it in the alternate network as if it were a separate physical interface with its own IP address. It is indeed, an "alias" for the existing physical interface and is handled like any other IP address by the system. The output of the `ifconfig` command shows, however, that the network alias has the same MAC address as the physical interface card that previously handled only the configuration for `eth0`:

```
# ifconfig eth0:0

eth0:0    Link encap:Ethernet HWaddr 00:06:25:04:DE:4E
inet addr:10.0.0.1 Bcast:10.0.7.255 Mask:255.255.248.0
          UP BROADCAST RUNNING MULTICAST MTU:1500 Metric:1
          Interrupt:9 Base address:0x1400
```

In addition to sharing the MAC address, which is a hardware quantity, the network alias does not have any of its own interface-level statistics (receive or transmit byte counts, and so forth) reported; these are associated with the physical interface. An example of an Ethernet alias is shown in Figure 10–4.

Another way of examining the relationship between a network alias and the physical interface is to use the Linux `ip` command. This command is frequently listed as the preferred

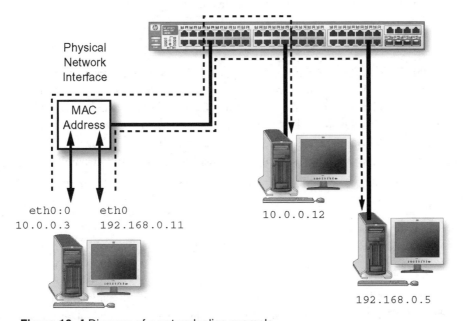

Figure 10–4 Diagram of a network alias example

method of viewing and manipulating Linux network configuration information, like ARP cache behavior, route table entries, interface configuration, and other operations that UNIX system administrators are used to performing with `ifconfig`.

It also allows access to some of the more esoteric features, like TCP/IP traffic shaping and output queue processing, but you have to work a little to find the information in the system documentation for this command. (This is not really fair. The man page for the `ip` command points to the actual documentation for the command, which is located in `/usr/share/doc/iproute-2.4.7/ip-cref.ps`. You can use the `gv` or the `ghostscript` commands to view the file. It would be nice to have a man page for it, however.) An example output from the `ip` command for our network alias is

```
# ip addr show

1: lo: <LOOPBACK,UP> mtu 16436 qdisc noqueue
    link/loopback 00:00:00:00:00:00 brd 00:00:00:00:00:00
    inet 127.0.0.1/8 brd 127.255.255.255 scope host lo
2: eth0: <BROADCAST,MULTICAST,UP> mtu 1500 qdisc pfifo_fast
    qlen 100
    link/ether 00:06:25:04:de:4e brd ff:ff:ff:ff:ff:ff
    inet 192.168.0.110/24 brd 192.168.0.255 scope global eth0
    inet 10.0.0.1/21 brd 10.0.7.255 scope global eth0:0
```

Another, more abbreviated, form for the same command that yields the same output is

```
# ip addr
```

Notice that the output from the command shows the link index ($N:$), which uniquely identifies the interface, the physical interface name (`eth0`) used by the system, followed by the physical link information (link flags, MTU size, the queuing disciplines qdisc, and then by the associated IP addresses, including the alias). This is, perhaps, a more useful and complete arrangement of the information than that provided by the `ifconfig` command.

We could have used the `ip` command to add the alias with the following format:

```
# ip addr add 10.0.0.1/21 brd + dev eth0 label eth0:0
```

or with a nonnumerical alias

```
# ip addr add 10.0.0.1/21 brd + dev eth0 label eth0:Alias0
```

The `ip` command will create the same alias, with the added benefit of automatically calculating the proper broadcast address by using the `brd +` option. This is certainly a very flexible and logical way to perform the configuration of a network alias, along with most other desired operations. I happen to like the `ip` command for this very reason. It is possible to learn a lot about the underlying functionality and capabilities of Linux networking, just by reading the documentation for the command.

A reasonable question might be: How and where would we use this feature in our cluster's implementation? This functionality may be used anywhere you need to access network traffic that may be available "on the wire," but it has different network addresses than the configured interface. An example is the administrative nodes which need to connect to the management LAN, but also need to access the file server resources which are handled by the data LAN.

Once you have decided that a particular system needs access to more than one network's traffic via one or more aliases on a single physical interface, you need to consider how to reestablish the alias at the next system boot—in other words, how to make the connection permanent. The network alias will disappear after a reboot or if you manually issue the command

```
# ifconfig eth0:0 down
```

or use the `ip` command

```
# ip addr del 10.0.0.1 dev eth0
```

The normal boot process for a Red Hat or most Red Hat–derived operating systems uses scripts and data files located in and underneath the `/etc/sysconfig` directory. Underneath this directory is the `network-scripts` directory, which contains initialization files for each network interface, such as `ifcfg-eth0`. To reinstall the alias at boot time, we only need to create `/etc/sysconfig/network-scripts/ifcfg-eth0:0` and have it contain

```
ONBOOT=yes
BOOTPROTO=static
DEVICE=eth0:0
IPADDR=10.0.0.1
NETMASK=255.255.248.0
```

The normal boot process will create the alias and attach it to the appropriate device: `eth0`. This also allows us to issue `ifup eth0:0` and `ifdown eth0:0` commands to manipulate the state of the network alias manually. Because the use of `BOOTPROTO=dhcp` appears to confuse the DHCP client, `dhclient`, it is best to assign configuration values statically to links that are network aliases.

10.6.3   Channel Bonding

There are several places within our cluster where we might wish to use port trunking for high availability and to increase network bandwidth. One of these places is between the file server equipment and the LAN that distributes the data to client systems. We discussed the theoretical concepts involved in port trunking or aggregation in Chapter 5, "Link Aggregation" on page 111. It's time to discuss how Linux handles trunking.

The Linux networking stack allows the configuration of multiple network links into a single trunked link called a *bond*. To allow bonding multiple links together, the functionality must either be compiled into the kernel or provided as a dynamically loadable module called `bonding`. In addition, there is a command, `ifenslave`, which is similar to the `ifconfig` command, that is used to assign physical devices to the bond. You can think of this as creating a virtual device, like a container with its own attributes, then assigning physical links to the container.

The process of creating a bond involves the following manual steps:

1. Creating an alias in `/etc/modules.conf` for the bonding module, with the desired device name, such as `bond0`
2. Loading the `bonding` module, with appropriate options
3. Loading the physical network "slave" interface modules
4. Configuring the bond device with `ifconfig`
5. Enslaving the slave links to the bond device
6. Verifying the bond operation

(Documentation for the process is located in the file `/usr/src/linux-2.4/Documentation/networking/bonding.txt` and is a detailed initiation into the bonding process and interfacing with Ethernet switching equipment.) Red Hat Linux and derivative distributions provide the loadable module and the `ifenslave` command to support bonding. There is no man page for the `ifenslave` command that I have been able to locate.

The source code for the `ifenslave` command is located in `/usr/src/linux-2.4/Documentation/networking/ifenslave.c` and it details the use of the parameters listed in the brief usage output presented here. This is a good example of using the presence of Linux source code to best advantage.

```
# ifenslave -?
Usage: ifenslave [-adfrvVh] <master-interface> < <slave-if> \
[metric <N>] > ...
        ifenslave -c master-interface slave-if
```

The options listed in the source are shown in Table 10–1.

Let's take an example, using four GbE links provided by Intel Pro/1000 GbE interfaces. The system[2] will probably already have detected the interfaces if the hardware is supported, and called them `eth1`, `eth2`, `eth3`, and `eth4` (assuming there is also a built-in link that is named `eth0`).

---

2.   Actually, the hardware configurator is called `kudzu`, after the pervasive vine in the South that has tendrils reaching into everything.

Table 10–1 Options for the Linux `ifenslave` command

Option	Description
`-a`	Show all interfaces
`-c`	Change active slave interface
`-d`	Detach a slave interface
`-f`	Force the operation
`-h`	How-to message
`-r`	Make receive-only slave interface
`-v`	Verbose output
`-V`	Output command version
`-?`	Usage message

First, configure the `/etc/modules.conf` entries:

```
alias eth0 3c59x
alias bond0 bonding
alias eth1 e1000
alias eth2 e1000
alias eth3 e1000
alias eth4 e1000
```

The possible module options for the bonding module may be listed:

```
# modinfo bonding
filename:    /lib/modules/2.4.22-1.2149.nptl/kernel/drivers/ \
net/bonding/bonding.o
description: "Ethernet Channel Bonding Driver, v2.4.1"
author:      <none>
license:     "GPL"
...
```

The output from the `modinfo bonding` command lists all the possible parameters that may be specified to the `bonding` module when it is loaded. These options may be specified in an "options" specification in the `/etc/modules.conf` file, or may be specified on the command line when manually loading the module. In this case, to load the module manually we would execute `modprobe bond0`, which would load the module (and any module dependencies) as specified in the `/etc/modules.conf` file, including the options.

Which options you specify for the `bonding` module will depend on the modes that your network interfaces support and the capabilities of the switching equipment to which the bond is connected. An example options specification in `/etc/modules.conf` to enable a four-link trunk to a compatible switch is

```
alias bond0 bonding
options bond0 max_bonds=4,mode=0
alias eth1 e1000
alias eth2 e1000
alias eth3 e1000
alias eth4 e1000
```

Here we specify the options for the aliased name `bond0`, as opposed to the `bonding` module itself, to allow more than one bond on the system. Once the module is loaded, the kernel will create the `bond0` network device. The next step is to configure the device with the `ifconfig` command:

```
ifconfig bond0 192.168.0.103 netmask 255.255.255.0 broadcast \
        192.168.0.255 up
```

and then finally to add the slave interfaces to the bond:

```
ifenslave bond0 eth1 eth2 eth3 eth4
```

At this point, you should be able to see the link listed in the output for the `ifconfig` or `ip` commands, and perform simple operations across the link to test it.

Now that we have manually created the bond, we can configure the Red Hat Linux networking start-up scripts to recreate the bond for us at system boot or when we issue an `ifup bond0` command, just as if it were for a "normal" network link. The contents of the configuration file `/etc/sysconfig/network-scripts/ifcfg-bond0` might be similar to the contents listed here:

```
DEVICE=bond0
IPADDR=192.168.0.103
NETMASK=255.255.255.0
NETWORK=192.168.0.0
BROADCAST=192.168.0.255
ONBOOT=yes
BOOTPROTO=none
```

For each of the slave network interfaces (`eth1`, `eth2`, `eth3`, and `eth4`) in the example bond, the interface configuration file in `/etc/sysconfig/network-scripts` should contain configuration statements similar to the example for `eth1`:

```
DEVICE=eth1
ONBOOT=yes
MASTER=bond0
SLAVE=yes
BOOTPROTO=none
```

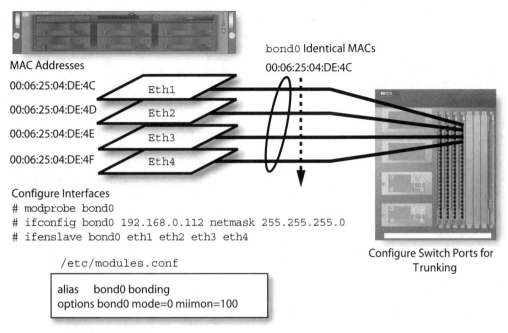

Figure 10–5 Ethernet interface bonding example

This will automatically recreate the bond at system boot time or in response to an `ifup bond0` command. Note, once again, that using DHCP for this link is likely to cause the `dhclient` program fits, so use of DHCP on the bond is disabled.

Creating trunked links, or bonds, on Linux is not too difficult. A major step in the right direction is locating the proper documentation for the process and identifying the correct commands and sequences. This overview may need to be modified, based on the network interfaces and switch equipment that you use in your cluster. Figure 10–5 shows the basic components and commands to activate a bond.

10.6.4   Setting the Ethernet Link MTU Size

The default MTU size for an Ethernet frame is 1,500 bytes. If you have the proper network interfaces and Ethernet switches to support it, you may use jumbo frames, which increase the size of the MTU to 9 KB. This functionality has to be explicitly enabled with either the `ifconfig` or `ip` commands. Examples of manually configuring this parameter for both possible commands are

```
# ifconfig eth0 192.168.0.110 netmask 255.255.255.0 \
       broadcast 192.68.0.244 mtu 9216

# ip link set eth0 mtu 9216
```

The MTU size may also be set in the /etc/sysconfig/network-scripts config-uration file for the interface device by specifying the MTU=<value> option. An example is

```
DEVICE=eth0
MTU=9216
```

This will set the MTU value as part of the device initialization at boot time or if an ifup com-mand is issued.

10.6.5   The Media-Independent Interface (MII) Tool

Ensuring that a network link is operating in the proper mode (full duplex) is sometimes difficult. If the autonegotiation process runs into difficulty, it is possible that there is a mismatch in set-tings between the switch and the client system. Linux provides a useful tool, the MII tool, or mii-tool command, that can determine the current state of the local interface *and* the switch port. This has saved me a tremendous amount of time and frustration.

An example command and the associated output are shown here for a 100base-TX inter-face:

```
# mii-tool -v eth0

eth0: negotiated 100baseTx-FD flow-control, link ok

    product info: vendor 00:10:18, model 23 rev 7

    basic mode:   autonegotiation enabled

    basic status: autonegotiation complete, link ok

    capabilities: 100baseTx-FD 100baseTx-HD 10baseT-FD \
        10baseT-HD

    advertising:  100baseTx-FD 100baseTx-HD 10baseT-FD \
        10baseT-HD flow-control
    link partner: 100baseTx-FD 100baseTx-HD 10baseT-FD \

        10baseT-HD flow-control
```

This output shows that the local interface is indeed running in 100base-TX full-duplex mode, along with the current state of the link. The command lists both the capabilities being advertised for the local interface and the switch port (link partner). This is highly valuable if you suspect autonegotiation problems.

In addition to displaying the current state of the link, it is possible to control the behavior of the link with the tool. It is not recommended to reset the link or change the duplex behavior on an active link, but sometimes errors in autonegotiation leave you no alternative. Make sure that there is no activity before doing any operations that might affect the link. Examples of restarting autonegotiation, resetting the link, and changing the duplex behavior are

```
# mii-tool -v --restart eth0
# mii-tool -v --reset eth0
# mii-tool -v --force=100baseTx-FD eth0
```

The proper operation of the network link is essential to the operation of the administrative nodes and their services. Once the operating system is installed on the administrative nodes, the mii-tool command may be used to verify link operation and to troubleshoot switch port settings.

10.7 Enabling and Starting Linux Services

Services in a Red Hat Linux or derivative distribution are controlled by a set of scripts that are located in /etc/init.d and are activated in the appropriate run level by the /etc/rc script, which is run by the init process at system boot time. Each run level has an associated directory, /etc/rc*.d, which has links to the service scripts that are to be run with the "start" or "stop" parameter when the system transitions to that run level.

Examining the scripts in /etc/init.d, you will see comments like the one found toward the top of the /etc/init.d/syslog script:

```
...
# chkconfig: 2345 12 88
...
```

This comment tells the chkconfig command where (within run level directories) to install links to the start-up script. It also specifies the priority for start-up and shutdown links. The string 2345 specifies the single-digit run levels within which to create start-up links. Shutdown links are created in the remaining run levels.

The third and fourth fields are the link "priorities" to use for the start-up and shutdown links respectively. When chkconfig --add syslog is run, the links are created, whereas chkconfig --del syslog removes the links for the service. The start-up link created is S12syslog, using the first link priority, and the shutdown or "kill" link created is K88syslog, with the second link priority.

The appropriate links are created for services at system installation time by their package installation scripts. To remove services and shorten the system boot time, links for unnecessary services may be removed. If an add-on service is not targeted for the Red Hat environment, you may have to configure the start-up script information for chkconfig manually.

Executing the command chkconfig --list will list the status of all services, including those handled by xinetd, which are configured with separate configuration files in the /etc/xinetd.d directory. Issuing chkconfig --list <service> will list the current status of the specified service's start-up and shutdown links. The chkconfig command will create and remove links and list their status, but will not actually start or shut down the service.

The `service` command will start, restart, or stop a service. Executing `service` `<service> restart` will first stop, then restart the associated service. Some services also support returning status with `service <service> status`, and saving state by executing `service <service> save`.

Both the `chkconfig` and `service` commands are frequently used when configuring services. We need to make sure that we activate the service's run-level links to ensure that they will be started at system boot time, and start the service once it is configured. Some of the services that we add later may require manual configuration.

10.8 Time Synchronization

The importance of time synchronization between networked systems is often overlooked. Accuracy and a minimum "skew" is important to some services, like Kerberos, that require all client and server systems to be synchronized within a certain time differential. There are other situations, notably software development environments, for which synchronization is also important (think about the system time as associated with software module versions and whether they are "out of date" with respect to their source).

The time service on Linux systems is handled by the NTP daemon, `ntpd`. Unfortunately, there may be no `man` pages on some of the Red Hat distributions and very little documentation on the usage of this service. The Fedora distribution seems to have remedied this situation.

The easiest way to configure the client behavior of this service is to use the `redhat-config-date` tool, which is available as part of the system installation or can be run independently after the system is installed. This is a graphical tool that requires the presence of an X Windows server to run.

You can enable the service and point it to an external server that provides the NTP service. A list of external servers is available at `http://www.boulder.nist.gov/timefreq/service/time-servers.html`. The daemon may run in multiple layers, or strata, with a client to one daemon providing server functionality to higher numbered strata. One or more NTP servers in your cluster, pointing at a highly accurate source, can service the remaining systems in the cluster.

If you wish to use an external time source, such as `time.nist.gov`, there must be a route to the external server from the chosen infrastructure node. You may need to run the daemon on a system (like a head node) that has external network routing access, and open up port 123 for UDP and TCP traffic in any firewall between the target server and the cluster's clients. A system, inside your cluster, with an accurate time source, removes the need to communicate with external NTP servers and may be necessary in high-security installations.

The majority of the data produced by NTP and its current operation is kept in `/etc/ntp`, including the `keys` file, which you should modify to contain values for your cluster's configuration. The keys provide a level of authentication that can keep malicious users from resetting your system's time. There are several cautions about using the default values for the key and password in the documentation, and you should heed the advice.

The configuration information for `ntpd` is kept in `/etc/ntp.conf`, and an example configuration file (with comments removed) created by the installation process is

```
server time.nist.gov
fudge 127.127.1.0 stratum 10
driftfile /var/lib/ntp/drift
multicastclient
broadcastdelay 0.008
authenticate no
#keys /etc/ntp/keys
```

This file points an "internal" NTP server at an external source of reliable time information. Notice that, by default, authentication is turned off between this server and all "lower level" clients. The use of multicast client capability means that all systems will listen to a multicast address, which defaults to `224.0.0.1` for time information, provided that behavior is enabled on the clients. This keeps the communications traffic between the server and the clients to a minimum.

T I P   Pay close attention to service "fan-out" and expected traffic patterns for cluster services. Multiple servers, special communication methods like multicasting, or traffic reduction may be necessary to keep performance adequate in a large cluster.

The client may also be configured to calculate the clock drift and to set the time at system boot, then exit by using the `-q` option. (Most modern systems have a hardware clock that keeps track of the time, even when the operating system is not running. This hardware clock is read at boot time by the `/etc/rc.sysinit` file and updated at shutdown by the `/etc/inittab` file.) If having the `ntpd` process continually running on client systems (compute slices) is a concern, then you can manually enable this feature in the configuration file `/etc/sysconfig/ntpd`, which contains the daemon's start-up options. Remember to enable and start the service on the appropriate systems with

```
# chkconfig ntpd on
# service ntpd start
```

The number of NTP servers you need for your cluster will depend on the number of clients to be serviced, and the mode in which the clients are operating. If you examine Figure 10–6, you can begin to see some of the "fan-out" issues for services that can occur in a cluster. For redundancy, each client will specify both NTP servers in their `/etc/ntp.conf` configuration file, resulting in 32 update messages for the whole cluster. In a larger cluster, the number of NTP servers might have to be increased, or the amount of traffic reduced or spread out in time to provide adequate performance.

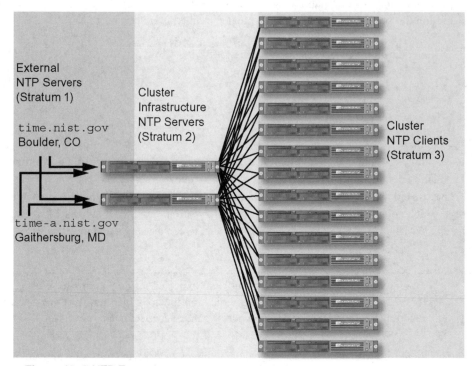

External
NTP Servers
(Stratum 1)

Cluster
Infrastructure
NTP Servers
(Stratum 2)

time.nist.gov
Boulder, CO

Cluster
NTP Clients
(Stratum 3)

time-a.nist.gov
Gaithersburg, MD

Figure 10–6 NTP Example

A very useful tool for debugging NTP, by talking to the `ntpd` daemon, is the `ntpq` command. This allows examining various parameters, including the parameters associated with peer servers. An example output from the tool is

```
# ntpq
ntpq> peers
remote        refid   st t when poll reach delay offset jitter
==============================================================
time.nist.gov 0.0.0.0 16 u - 64  0    0.000 0.000 4000.000
```

10.9 Name Services

Name resolution services are fundamental to the operation of any networked environment, and a cluster is no exception. If we adhere to the general policy of making systems internal to the cluster be "invisible" to the outside world, then there will be no direct connection between those systems and any external naming services. The required name resolution services need to be provided inside the cluster's networks, and in an efficient manner, to avoid impacting system performance.

Because the name service is so basic, it is central to the operation of every other networked service in the cluster. There are a number of ways to implement the service in a Linux environment, but the other services that you run in the cluster will have some requirements for the name service behavior. You should be aware that other services like Kerberos require an IP-to-host mapping *and* the reverse mapping, host to IP, to be available and valid.

Before I discuss the possible name resolution service configurations, we should examine the need for consistency in the *format* of the names supplied by the service—more for the system administrators of the cluster than anyone else. We have, after all, a networked environment, with tens to thousands of hosts, for which each host may have as many as three separate network connections, and each connection requires an IP address *and a separate, unique host name*. Having a convention to follow for host naming with this many systems is important for consistency, sanity, and automation of administration tasks.

10.9.1   Host Naming Conventions

Whatever your final choice of format for host names in your cluster, it is important to have alignment between the names and IP addresses for all network connections. You are free to choose whatever conventions you can dream up, and you have the opportunity to make your life easier or more difficult than necessary based on your choices. Let's talk about some ways to make your naming convention usable.

In Chapter 6 on page 123, we discussed aligning the IP addresses in the various cluster networks and allocating IP addresses in blocks of addresses for different purposes, including expansion. We associate human-readable names with the IP addresses to help make sense of a numerical IP address format that was intended more for internal use by hardware and software—even the dots in an IP address are "by convention" (including the conventions specified in the various RFC documents that originally created the notation). How names are applied to your cluster's IP addresses will determine how easy it is to locate a given system connection, sort information with host names in it, and apply automated techniques to your system administration processes. It also will affect the amount of typing you will do.

The first thing to consider is the length of the host name. Long is more descriptive, but lots of characters take more effort to type. Fewer characters are easier to type, but are less descriptive. There will be a numerical component (usually) to the host name, so the overall addition to the number of characters in the host name has to be considered.

Lexical ordering of characters needs to be considered because host1 and host10 will be sorted *ahead* of host2. When you use numbers in a host name, to get sorting algorithms to work properly, you need to include leading zeros. So the previous list of host names would be host01, host10, and host02 to get the proper sorting order. This may seem trivial, but having to change host names in a large cluster installation project is a nightmare.

As an example, let's assume we have a cluster with 128 compute slices, two head nodes, a file server, and four administrative nodes. Additionally, there are management LAN, data LAN, and HSI connections that require IP addresses and host names. There is a single management

Table 10–2 Host Naming Convention Example

Host Description	Management LAN	Data LAN	HSI
Compute slices	mcs001-mcs128	dcs001-dcs128	hcs001-hcs128
Administrative/infrastructure node	mad001-mad004	dad001-dad004	had001-had004
Head nodes	mhn001-mhn002	dhn001-dhn002	hhn001-hhn002
File server	mfs001	dfs001	N/A
Ethernet management switches	mem001-mem004	N/A	N/A
Serial console switches	mss001-mss004	N/A	N/A
Ethernet core switch	mec001	N/A	N/A

rack with a core switch, and four compute racks with 32 compute slices, one serial console switch capable of NFS, and one management switch each. A possible scheme is presented in Table 10–2.

I think the chosen host names represent a good compromise between brevity and mnemonic content. They also will sort in the proper order. Other conventions, like including the rack number are also possible. Make sure you experiment with whatever choices you make, because you will likely be stuck with them once implemented.

10.9.2   The Name Service Switch File

Linux, and indeed many UNIX systems, provides for the use of multiple name resolution services, with a search order and fall-back capability. The name resolution provided by the gethostbyname routine in the system library may search NIS, NIS+, DNS, or the local /etc/hosts file for host name information. All systems in the cluster, including head nodes, compute slices, file servers, and administrative/infrastructure nodes will need name service resolution configured.

The ordering of the search, the sources used for the search, and the fall-back behavior are all determined by the name service switch configuration file: /etc/nsswitch.conf. This file also controls the sources of information for other services and many of the system "database" files that are provided by NIS: password, group, shadow, ethers, netmasks, networks, protocols, rpc, services, netgroup, publickey, (e-mail) aliases, and the NFS automounter maps, such as auto.master. This file is a relatively new addition to UNIX systems.

In the simplest form, the configuration for the name services is a specification of a database followed by a list, in order of search, containing the sources of name resolution information. A line such as

```
hosts: files dns nis
```

would cause a host name lookup to look in the local /etc/hosts file, traverse DNS, and then finally the NIS service for an answer to the query. Besides rearranging the order or contents of the list, it is possible to exercise more control over the behavior by applying two actions—return or continue—to four possible results of the lookup: success, notfound, unavail, and tryagain.

The defaults for each action (in the format used in the file) are [SUCCESS=return], [NOTFOUND=continue], [UNAVAIL=continue], and [TRYAGAIN=continue]. The last service in the list has an implied [NOTFOUND=return] associated with it. The success result occurs if the name is located in the associated service, notfound occurs if the service cannot find the name, unavail indicates that the service is permanently unavailable or not active, and tryagain indicates a temporary service condition that may be recoverable.

It is more important for us to determine which services we are going to use for name resolution, because the default behavior of the switch suits our needs just fine. The default (implied) configuration for each name service is the same as shown for DNS in the following example:

```
hosts: files[SUCCESS=return,NOTFOUND=return,UNAVAIL=continue,\
TRYAGAIN=return] dns[...] nis[...]
```

Remember that in this example the *default* behavior for all services is specified. You do not have to configure the actions explicitly. For more information on the configuration of this file, see man nsswitch.conf. We can now move on to the configuration of the individual name resolution services.

10.9.3   The Hosts File

The /etc/hosts file was the original network host name lookup database on a UNIX system. As networked environments become larger and more complex, keeping the host files synchronized between multiple systems becomes a real chore—the more systems, the larger the chore. The networked, single-point administration tools (DNS and NIS) that are discussed later make the job easier, but they rely on network availability to operate and add complexity to the configuration process. The hosts file, however low-tech it seems, still works just fine. (It is, however, sheer lunacy to attempt to build a hosts file for large clusters by hand. By having naming conventions and host IP ranges, it is possible to script the building of the hosts files. Some of the cluster creation tools generate this type of configuration file from information stored in a cluster configuration database. There are also automated tools available to generate the DNS configuration files for you.)

If you are going to use DNS in your cluster, then you will want to provide a fully qualified host name as an alias in the /etc/hosts file. In this way, whatever form is entered for the host name, the name resolution service can return a matching format to the user or application—fully qualified or not. It can be disconcerting to enter a fully qualified host name and find just the host being used in the response.

Falling back (no pun intended) to our IP address example shown in Table 10–2, we might produce the following fragment of an `/etc/hosts` file:

```
# IP address        Host        Aliases
127.0.0.1           localhost   loopback
#
10.0.1.1            mcs001      mcs001.cluster.local
10.0.2.1            dcs001      dcs001.cluster.local
10.0.3.1            hcs001      hcs001.cluster.local
#
10.0.2.150          dfs001      dfs001.cluster.local
#
10.0.1.254          mgw001      mgw.cluster.local
10.0.2.254          dgw001      dgw.cluster.local
10.0.3.254          hgw001      hgw.cluster.local
#
10.0.1.200          mns001      mns001.cluster.local
10.0.1.201          mns002      mns002.cluster.local
10.0.1.202          mns003      mns003.cluster.local
10.0.1.203          mns004      mns004.cluster.local
```

10.9.4   The DNS

Configuration of the DNS can be a complicated endeavor. There are whole books written on just this topic.[3] The main configuration file for the Berkeley Internet name daemon (BIND) is kept in `/etc/named.conf`,[4] as in this example that I use (somewhat modified) in my network at home:

```
options {
        directory       "/var/named";
        query-source    address * port 53;
        allow-query     {
                          127/8;
                          192.168.0/24;
                        };
};

logging   {
```

---

3.   See Albitz and Lui [2001].

4.   Yes, having the service called one name (DNS) and the actual implementation, in the form of the named dae-
      mon and configuration file (BIND), called another name drives me crazy, too. I promise to try to keep it straight.

```
        category "unmatched" { null; };
        category "default"   { "default_syslog";
                               "default_debug";
                             };
        channel "default_debug" {
                             file "/var/log/named.debug";
                             severity dynamic;
        };
};

controls {
        inet 127.0.0.1 allow { localhost; } keys { rndckey; };
};
include "/etc/rndc.key";
zone    "0.0.127.in-addr.arpa" IN       {
        type master;
        file "127.0.0";
        allow-update { none; };
};
zone "cluster.local" IN                     {
        type master;
        file "cluster.local";
        allow-update { none; };
};
zone    "localhost" IN                   {
        type master;
        file "localhost.zone";
        allow-update { none; };
};
zone "0.168.192.in-addr.arpa" IN        {
        type master;
        file "0.168.192";
        allow-update { none; };
};
zone    "."              IN                  {
        type forward;
        forward first;
        forwarders{
                X.X.X.Y;        External DNS server 1
                X.X.X.Z;        External DNS server 2
                192.168.0.254; Local firewall router
        };
};
```

This is a *very basic* DNS configuration that I use as a starting point for more complex configurations. And, before we go any further, let me tell all the BIND experts out there that I am well aware that this example has holes in it. The primary reason for presenting this example is to show that without too much typing you can get a functioning DNS configuration file that resolves addresses for local "zones" and forwards everything else to external DNS servers. (If there is a DNS and BIND expert on your staff, have her create a better configuration for you.) Because of space constraints, I have to leave more complicated configuration options as an exercise for you.

The "options" and "logging" stanzas in the file set the basic behavior for the daemon in terms of the networks handled and the amount of logging output that goes to the specified files. The "controls" definition allows direct communication with the daemon by the rndc command running on the allowed hosts—in this case, the local host on which the named daemon is executing. This command allows reloading the database, turning query logging on and off, and other maintenance functions. The rndc keys file contains the value that is also specified in the /etc/rndc.conf file, so that the named daemon and the rndc command share the same key when they communicate.

The zone definitions in this example, except for the "." or root zone, have configuration files located in the /var/named directory. I may have used outdated naming conventions for these file names, so consult a DNS book or expert before casting yours in concrete. An example of the content in the cluster.local zone file is

```
$TTL     3D
@                    IN      SOA     ns2.cluster.local.
root.ns2.cluster.local. (
                             20040225            ; serial, todays date
                             8H                  ; refresh, seconds
                             2H                  ; retry, seconds
                             4W                  ; expire, seconds
                             1D )                ; minimum, seconds
                             NS      ns1.cluster.local. ;
                             NS      ns2.cluster.local. ;
localhost                    A       127.0.0.1
ns1.cluster.local.           A       192.168.0.151
                             TXT     "Primary Name Server"
ns2.cluster.local.           A       192.168.0.152
                             TXT     "Secondary Name Server"
cs01                         A       192.168.0.1
cs02                         A       192.168.0.2
cs03                         A       192.168.0.3
cs04                         A       192.168.0.4
cs05                         A       192.168.0.5
```

This file contains definitions for two name servers and five other systems in the zone that it handles. The database for DNS consists of records, and the A designator is an address record that specifies a host name-to-address association. The reverse mapping of host name to IP address is handled by the 0.168.192 file, which you will notice is named after the first three octets of the network address in reverse order:

```
$TTL 3D
@       IN  SOA  ns2.cluster.local. root.ns2.cluster.local. (
                 20040225 ; Serial
                 8H       ; Refresh
                 2H       ; Retry
                 4W       ; Expire
                 3D)      ; Minimum Time To Live (TTL)

        NS    ns1.cluster.local.
        NS    ns2.cluster.local.
1       PTR   cs01.cluster.local.
2       PTR   cs02.cluster.local.
3       PTR   cs03.cluster.local.
4       PTR   cs04.cluster.local.
5       PTR   cs05.cluster.local.
```

The addresses in this file are all relative to the `192.168.0` network. The `PTR` records are pointers back to the original records for the host names. The `NS` records represent systems that are name servers for the domain. The DNS database has many other record types to learn, in addition to the basic ones shown here.

As you can see, the BIND configuration files are a lot of repetitive information, and once you get the framework constructed, it can be relatively easy to fill in additional systems. The remaining configuration file contents are "standard" and I leave them as an exercise for you. Although the example configuration is fairly simple, BIND and DNS are moving targets, with constant security improvements and changes to the configuration syntax being made.

DNS is a hierarchical, distributed network database system. As such, it is necessarily more complex than either the hosts file or the NIS. This does not mean that minimal DNS configurations are impossible to craft. The example in this section may serve as a starting point.

Finding a good book on the subject, using a GUI-based configuration tool like `redhat-config-bind`, or having a pretrained expert, are ways to tackle a more complex DNS installation for your cluster. Do not attempt to create a secure Internet-connected DNS configuration or an intranet (internal corporate) slave configuration without consulting the proper DNS maintainers. You will save yourself potential security breaches and clashes with local (or remote) DNS administrators.

With DNS configured, do not forget to issue the required commands to create the boot-time links and start the service:

```
# chkconfig named on
# service named start
# tail /var/log/messages

Mar  1 10:55:49 ns2 named[31627]: starting BIND 9.2.1 -u \
named
Mar  1 10:55:49 ns2 named[31627]: using 1 CPU
```

```
Mar  1 10:55:49 ns2 named[31630]: loading configuration from\
'/etc/named.conf'
Mar  1 10:55:50 ns2 named[31630]: no IPv6 interfaces found
Mar  1 10:55:50 ns2 named[31630]: listening on IPv4 \
interface lo, 127.0.0.1#53
Mar  1 10:55:50 ns2 named[31630]: listening on IPv4 \
interface eth0, 192.168.0.152#53
Mar  1 10:55:50 ns2 named[31630]: command channel listening \
on 127.0.0.1#953
Mar  1 10:55:50 ns2 named[31630]: zone 0.0.127.in-addr.arpa/\
IN: loaded serial 20040225
Mar  1 10:55:50 ns2 named: named startup succeeded
Mar  1 10:55:50 ns2 named[31630]: dns_master_load:\
0.168.192:12: TTL set to prior TTL (1)
Mar  1 10:55:50 ns2 named[31630]: zone 0.168.192.in-\
addr.arpa/IN: loaded serial 20040225
Mar  1 10:55:50 ns2 named[31630]: zone cluster.local/IN: \
loaded serial 20040225
Mar  1 10:55:50 ns2 named[31630]: zone localhost/IN: loaded \
serial 20040225
Mar  1 10:55:50 ns2 named[31630]: running
```

Once you have DNS installed on at least one server, you can begin testing. I tend to "cross resolve" two DNS servers, which means that I set the /etc/resolv.conf file on one system to use the other server first, followed by itself. As an example, here is a /etc/resolv.conf file that does this:

```
domain          cluster.local #Local domain name
server          192.168.0.151 #The other server first
server          192.168.0.152 #This server last
```

You may specify up to three servers in the resolv.conf file. Client systems can use the same version of the /etc/resolv.conf file to specify the domain and DNS servers for resolution.

Testing your DNS configuration consists of verifying that all host names on all networks are resolved properly. I use the rndc command to enable query logging, which will show all DNS queries in the /var/log/messages file managed by the system logging daemon, syslogd.

```
# rndc
Usage: rndc [-c config] [-s server] [-p port]
        [-k key-file ] [-y key] [-V] command

command is one of the following:

  reload          Reload configuration file and zones.
  reload zone [class [view]]
                  Reload a single zone.
```

```
refresh zone [class [view]]
                Schedule immediate maintenance for a zone.
reconfig        Reload configuration file and new zones only.
stats           Write server stats to the statistics file.
querylog        Toggle query logging.
dumpdb          Dump cache(s) to the file (named_dump.db).
stop            Save pending updates and stop the server.
halt            Stop the server without saving updates.
trace           Increment debugging level by one.
trace level     Change the debugging level.
notrace         Set debugging level to 0.
flush           Flushes all of the server's caches.
flush [view]    Flushes the server's cache for a view.
status          Display status of the server.
*restart        Restart the server.

* == not yet implemented
Version: 9.2.1
```

So merely issuing the `rndc querylog` command will toggle the logging of client requests on and off. Also, dumping the database to a file can help with syntax issues by showing you what the daemon read and how it was interpreted. The command `rndc dumpdb` does this.

For testing purposes, you can use the Linux `host` or `dig` commands to create DNS queries against your DNS servers. The following output was from the `host` command:

```
# host 192.168.0.152
152.0.168.192.in-addr.arpa domain name pointer
ns2.cluster.local.
# host ns2
ns2.cluster.local has address 192.168.0.152
# host ns1
ns1.cluster.local has address 192.168.0.151
```

The `dig` command produces a more verbose output. Once you have "internal" cluster name resolution working, you will have to ensure that the cluster itself is visible in the "external" DNS database so that users or applications (if it is a database cluster) can access it. There are a number of issues to notice:

- Spreading login or access activities equally between head nodes with round-robin DNS resolution
- Resolving external names on the master nodes, in addition to the cluster-specific names
- Testing that "internal" names don't "leak" outside the cluster

These activities will likely take coordination with the local DNS administrator, and are beyond the scope of what we can cover here.

10.9.5   The NIS

Despite its potential issues, the NIS is a useful single-point administration tool. Although system administrators tend to think of NIS in terms of its ability to share password and group information, NIS can be used to distribute other system information from a central location, and even *custom* "maps" that drive system behavior.

In conjunction with the name service switch, /etc/nsswitch.conf, NIS can share NFS automounter maps and other system configuration information from a central copy of files located in the /etc directory on the master server: passwd, group, shadow, services, rpc, networks, netgroups, and several others. The information from NIS can either replace or augment the information in the local files. An NIS master server distributes central information to NIS slave servers, and both are capable of supporting client systems.

The NIS maps are databases that consist of gdbm (GNU dbm) files. These are simple, single-key "hashed" databases produced from a text file that is fed into the makedbm command. The first field in the text file line, up to the first whitespace delimiter, becomes the database key, and the remainder of the line becomes the database "record" associated with the key.

NIS "maps" are individual gdbm databases that are accessible via RPC requests from client systems. The client system passes the key in a request, and the NIS master or slave server looks up the key in the requested database and returns the record associated with the key. A lookup in the database takes at most two disk accesses.

10.9.5.1   NIS Server Configuration

The ypinit command[5] is used to create either an NIS master or slave server. As part of the process of creating the master server, you will specify a list of slave servers:

```
# domainname cluster.nis
# ypinit -m
-bash: ypinit: command not found
# /usr/lib/yp/ypinit -m
At this point, we have to construct a list of the hosts which
will run NIS servers.  ns1.cluster.local is in the list of NIS
server hosts.  Please continue to add the names for the other
hosts, one per line.  When you are done with the list, type a
<control D>.
        next host to add:  ns1.cluster.local
        next host to add:^D
The current list of NIS servers looks like this:
ns1.cluser.local
Is this correct?  [y/n: y]  y
We need a few minutes to build the databases...
Building /var/yp/cluster.nis/ypservers...
```

---

5.   Neither this command, nor the makedbm command are located in root's path. The commands are in the
       /usr/lib/yp directory.

```
Running /var/yp/Makefile...
gmake[1]: Entering directory `/var/yp/cluster.nis'
Updating passwd.byname...
Updating passwd.byuid...
Updating group.byname...
Updating group.bygid...
Updating hosts.byname...
Updating hosts.byaddr...
Updating rpc.byname...
Updating rpc.bynumber...
Updating services.byname...
Updating services.byservicename...
Updating netid.byname...
Updating protocols.bynumber...
Updating protocols.byname...
Updating mail.aliases...
gmake[1]: Leaving directory /var/yp/cluster.nis
ns1.cluster.local has been set up as a NIS master server.
Now you can run ypinit -s ns1.cluster.local on all slave
servers.
```

This is a relatively easy process, and it has created an NIS *domain* with the name `cluster.local` in the `/var/yp` directory. The NIS domain looks like a DNS domain, but is not the same thing—the two are separate concepts with similar formats.

The following are notes about the NIS master server creation output listed earlier.

- The domain database is kept under `/var/yp`.
- There is a `Makefile` under `/var/yp` that is responsible for creating the NIS maps from the original files.
- We set the NIS domain name, using the `domainname` command from the command line prior to creating the domain database, and the directory `/var/yp/<domainname>` contains the NIS database files.
- You will notice the prefix `yp` used a lot, because the original name for the service was "yellow pages," which is a registered trademark of a British phone company.
- A special map file, `ypservers`, contains the list of master and slave NIS servers that was created from the input during configuration.

We have built a default set of NIS maps from the system files on the master server. Before we create any slave servers, we need to make sure that the NIS services are properly enabled and started. Note that NIS master and slave *servers* also are usually NIS *clients*. Both sets of services need to be configured and enabled.

We need to get the system set up to start the NIS server software at system boot time. One necessary task is to add the `NISDOMAIN` variable definition to the `/etc/sysconfig/network` file. This will restore the proper NIS domain information globally at boot time. The settings in the file for our example would be

```
...
NISDOMAIN=cluster.nis
...
```

Once the NIS domain setting is established, and can be reestablished, we can start the NIS server (`ypserv`) software:

```
# chkconfig ypserv on
# service ypserv start
```

You should see the NIS server software start-up message. The server is now ready to respond to external requests. Any time you modify one of the files that is exported via NFS (`/etc/passwd`, `/etc/group`, or similar), you should perform the following commands:

```
# cd /var/yp
# make
```

This will recreate any maps that may be "out of date" with respect to the files you modified, and will "push" them to the slave servers. You need to realize that the files on the NIS master server are the ones being exported to the slaves and are the ones being used by the client systems. The files on the NIS master should contain the information that you want used by the other systems participating in the NIS domain. Our next step is to set up the slave servers.

10.9.5.2   Modifying the NIS Slave Server List

The `/var/yp/<domain>/ypservers` map contains a list of NIS servers that was created when the master was initialized. There are occasions when we might want to modify that list. How can we do this?

In theory, we could add a name to the `ypservers` file that gets created in the `/var/yp` directory, then use the local `Makefile` to recreate the `ypservers` map with `make ypservers`. On the Red Hat distributions I have examined, this does not appear to work. But there is another, more manual approach.

It is possible to reverse the `ypservers` map creation process using the `makedbm` command to dump the contents of the map file. For our example, the output is

```
# /usr/lib/yp/makedbm -u /var/yp/cluster.nis/ypservers
ns1.cluster.local ns1.cluster.local
YP_MASTER_NAME ns1.cluster.local
YP_LAST_MODIFIED 1078184516
ns2.cluster.local ns2.cluster.local
```

Part of the master installation process is the creation of a `/var/yp/ypservers` file. We can edit this file and use it to recreate the new `ypservers` database:

```
# /usr/lib/yp/makedbm -i /var/yp/ypservers \
```

```
-o /var/yp/cluster.local/ypservers ./ypservers ypservers
```

The first system in the file is assumed to be the master server. For more information on the creation of this file and the initialization process, you can actually examine the commands used in the `/var/yp/ypinit` command, because in Linux it is a script.

10.9.5.3   NIS Slave Server Configuration

With a master NIS server in place and operational, we now can configure the slave servers. The slave server will need to connect to the master server to download the map database, so the master must be running and available. On the slave server, we initialize NIS with the following commands:

```
# domainname cluster.nis
# /usr/lib/yp/ypinit -s ns1.cluster.local

We will need a few minutes to copy the data from ns1
Transferring shadow.byname...
Trying ypxfrd ... success

[ ... output omitted ... ]

ns2.cluster.local's NIS data base has been set up.
If there were warnings, please figure out what went wrong, and
fix it.

At this point, make sure that /etc/passwd and /etc/group have
been edited so that when the NIS is activated, the data bases
you have just created will be used, instead of the /etc ASCII
files.
```

Note that even though the command output suggests that we need to edit the `passwd` and `group` files, this is no longer necessary. The `/etc/nsswitch.conf` must be properly configured to utilize NIS for the information, but we do not have to add the infamous +::: lines to the files. (If you don't know about this antique requirement, never mind. Just rejoice that there is no more need to edit the files directly to use NIS. Unless of course you want to, then you can specify `compat` as the source of the data in place of `nis`.)

As with the master, we need to add the `NISDOMAIN` definition to the `/etc/sysconfig/network` file. When finished, we also need to enable and start the `ypserv` service, just as we did on the master server.

10.9.5.4   NIS Client Systems

Configuring NIS client systems, and which may include the NIS master and slave servers, is relatively easy. Adding the `NISDOMAIN` definition to `/etc/sysconfig/network` is necessary, just like with the master and slave servers. This restores the NIS domain information at boot time. There is one more file to configure for clients, /etc/yp.conf, which is used by the client portion of NIS, ypbind.

The /etc/yp.conf file contains information about the method to use in contacting the NIS server. This file may be created automatically by the dhclient program, based on information from DHCP, if it is active and distributing NIS server information. I cover using DHCP as a single-point administration tool in the next chapter. An example of the /etc/yp.conf file is

```
domain cluster.nis server ns1.cluster.local
domain cluster.nis server ns2.cluster.local
```

This file will be used by ypbind to attempt a direct connection to the first server in the list, for NIS information, and will not use broadcasting. It is possible to add a line domain cluster.nis broadcast to enable server location for the desired domain via a broadcast. Broadcasting is inherently unsafe because of the ability for systems to replace, or "spoof," the real NIS server. In the event that the first server does not answer, ypbind will try the second server.

To ensure that the NIS client, ypbind, is enabled and operational, you should execute

```
# chkconfig ypbind on
# service ypbind start
```

The ypbind process running on an NIS client will send "keep alive" messages to the master server every 20 seconds. In the event that the master does not respond, ypbind will attempt to locate and connect to an alternate server. The exact fail-over behavior is documented in the man page for ypbind.

10.9.5.5   Special NIS Configuration Options

The /var/yp/Makefile file contains make commands that will create the NIS maps from the standard set of system files. There are some configuration options that affect the NIS map contents. A section of the /var/yp/Makefile is listed here:

```
# The lowest gid that will be included in the group maps.
MINUID=500
MINGID=500

# Don't export this uid/guid (nfsnobody).
# Set to 0 if you want to
NFSNOBODYUID=65534
NFSNOBODYGID=65534

# Should we merge the passwd file with the shadow file ?
# MERGE_PASSWD=true|false
MERGE_PASSWD=false

# Should we merge the group file with the gshadow file ?
```

```
# MERGE_GROUP=true|false
MERGE_GROUP=false
```

The low-order GIDs and UIDs in the `/etc/password` and `/etc/group` files are usually reserved for system entities. It is not desirable to export these values to all systems, so it is possible to set a threshold below which the NIS map will not contain the UIDs or GIDs. Remember that the exported values could *override* the local values, depending on the settings in the name service switch file. A similar situation occurs with the `NFSNOBODY` UID and GID values, which are defined to prevent unauthenticated users from accessing files on the local system via NFS.

Linux has the ability to use shadow password and group files to address the security issues caused by the permitted access to `/etc/passwd` and `/etc/group`. Because the user and group passwords are visible in these files, Linux can utilize separate files, with more restricted access, that "shadow" the information in the publicly readable files. The options to merge the password and group shadow information into the NIS maps allows sharing the information across the NIS domain, but also subverts the additional security provided by the shadow files.

10.9.5.6   Adding Custom NIS Maps

The `/var/yp/Makefile` for NIS that creates the map database will create some default maps for the NFS automounter. The `auto.master`, `auto.home`, and `auto.local` maps are created from the associated files in the `/etc` directory. If you want to add maps, then you must modify the `Makefile` to add the processing necessary.

Modifications are necessary in four places in the file to add a map. Let's look at an example, adding the `auto.indirect` map, which will be created from the `/etc/auto.indirect` file. First, we need to add a definition for the new map to the list of files that are built:

```
AUTO_MASTER  = $(YPSRCDIR)/auto.master
AUTO_HOME    = $(YPSRCDIR)/auto.home
AUTO_LOCAL   = $(YPSRCDIR)/auto.local
AUTO_INDIRECT= $(YPSRCDIR)/auto.indirect
```

If you examine the file, you will find that the `YPSRCDIR` variable is defined as `/etc`, so the definition `$(YPSRCDIR)` will be replaced by that string. Next, we add the target to the list of targets to be created:

```
# If you don't want some of these maps built, feel free to
# comment them out from this list.

all:  passwd group hosts rpc services netid protocols mail \
      auto.indirect \
        # netgrp shadow publickey networks ethers bootparams \
        # printcap \
        # amd.home auto.master auto.home auto.local \
        # passwd.adjunct \
        # timezone locale netmasks
```

Lines ending with the "\" character are continued on the next line, in true UNIX format. Now we can locate a section of rules that create the `auto.local` map, clone it, and modify it for our `auto.indirect` map:

```
auto.indirect: $(AUTO_INDIRECT) $(YPDIR)/Makefile
        @echo "Updating $@..."
        -@sed -e "/^#/d" -e s/#.*$$// $(AUTO_INDIRECT) | \
            $(DBLOAD) -i $(AUTO_INDIRECT) \
            -o $(YPMAPDIR)/$@ - $@
        -@$(NOPUSH) || $(YPPUSH) -d $(DOMAIN) $@
```

This rule says: If ever the `auto.indirect` target is out of date with respect to the file specified by the variable AUTO_INDIRECT or the `/var/yp/Makefile`, then execute the commands below. This will read the `/etc/auto.indirect` file, remove leading and trailing comments using the `sed` command, and feed the results to the `makedbm` command, which will create a new map file in `/var/yp/<domain>/auto.indirect`.

These changes to `/var/yp/Makefile` are prototypical for adding any new map to the NIS domain's database, provided no specialized processing is required for the text in the source file. You may notice that the `awk` command is used in some of the rules to alter the order of tokens on the text lines (recall that the first token on the line becomes the database key for `gdbm`).

We can now add map information to the cluster's NIS domain, but why would we want to? Certainly, if we are going to use the NFS automounter facility, we may need to add more maps to the default set. But we can apply the general NIS map distribution and lookup mechanism to other goals, such as using NIS as a general-purpose database for our own system administration purposes.

Once NIS is started, we can access any map that it distributes, using the information there to affect system configuration and behavior. Say, for example, that we create an NIS map that contains host name-to-time server assignments. By accessing the NIS map, finding its host name, and extracting the associated time server IP addresses, a system could configure its own NTP server associations at boot time.

The system administrator could manage this information in a single place—the NIS map—and have the individual client system alter its behavior as part of the normal start-up. This assumes, of course, that NIS is operational at the time the configuration file needs to be generated. Although this particular example may not be earthshaking, I have seen this approach put to very good use in large environments.

10.9.5.7   NIS Testing

Testing for proper operation of NIS is fairly straightforward, and uses several commands that are available. Some of the useful commands are

- `domainname`—to list the current NIS domain

- ypwhich—to list the current NIS server we are using
- ypmatch *<key> <mapname>*—to find data that matches a given key in the map
- ypcat -k *<mapname>*—to list the data from an NIS map, including the key

The first step in debugging a suspected NIS problem is to verify the operation with the tools listed here. Verify that the domain name is properly set, that the client is bound to an NIS server, and that information may be extracted from the map in question. If things don't work at this level, you may need to troubleshoot network configuration as well.

If the underlying NIS and network interactions appear to be correct, it is a good idea to take a look at the contents of the /etc/nsswitch.conf file to verify that it contains the proper configuration. NIS may be functioning properly, but if the hostname, automount, passwd, or other services are not configured to get their information from NIS, it could be the culprit.

10.9.5.8 NIS Summary

The use of NIS is certainly optional in your cluster. I rarely find anyone who is neutral on the subject of whether to use NIS. I believe NIS can be extremely useful if your environment is not strictly focused on absolute security. There are security features available in the form of access control, but they do not address the inherently unencrypted design of the software's data transfer.

Even if you do not choose to use the NFS automounter, NFS, or /etc/passwd style authentication, NIS can provide useful facilities for name resolution and general data distribution. NIS certainly deserves consideration as part of your system administration suite if it can save you time and effort. For a more complete treatise on NIS, see Stern [1992].

10.9.6 Name Resolution Recommendations

Linux provides you with the choice of (at least) three sources for name resolution: the local /etc/hosts file, DNS, and the NIS hosts map. All three of these services may be tied together with the name service switch configuration file, /etc/nsswitch.conf, to provide access to multiple sources of host name information. As a system architect, you can choose the ordering of the services and their fall-back behavior.

The name service switch is implemented in the main system library, A schematic representation of the name service switch is shown in Figure 10–7. The routines in the main system C library are dynamically linked to applications that make lookup requests. The routines, like gethostbyname, in turn cause the /etc/nsswitch.conf file to be read, and a set of dynamic libraries to be loaded that handle the communications with the name services according to the configuration information in /etc/nsswitch.conf. (The dynamically loaded libraries in Linux have the .so suffix, which indicates a "shared object." These libraries are loaded when referenced [explicitly or implicitly], and may be shared by multiple applications on the system. These libraries may also be called *shared libraries* on other operating systems.)

In addition to the flexibility of the name service switch, you have the ability to configure the behavior of the individual services. NIS may be configured to use DNS if a host query is not

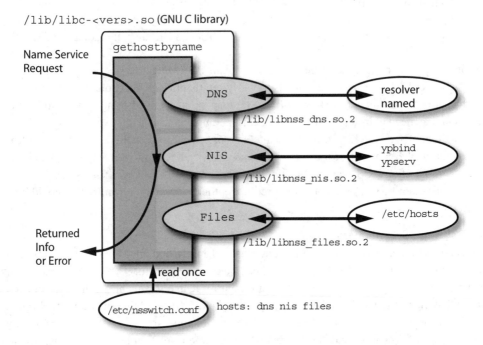

Figure 10–7 Name service switch functional diagram

in its databases, and DNS may be configured to use multiple local servers and to forward unknown requests to external DNS servers. This is a lot of flexibility, and making the proper choices for flexibility, reliability, and ease of administration can be challenging.

In a small cluster it may be easier to manage just the /etc/hosts file, and the lack of dependency on the network can be a plus. In the long run, however, it is less error prone and more efficient with respect to updates to use one or both of the network-based services, once you invest in the work of setting up the service. The local hosts file may then contain only the absolutely essential IP addresses and names, like the file server and default gateways. Striking a balance between maintaining and distributing the data is the issue: If the network is not there, how much real work will you be getting done, anyway?

NIS is an optional service for name resolution, particularly if you are performance and security conscious. However, the ability to distribute automounter maps and other information from a single point is very useful. Using it as a fall-back service to DNS provides some additional redundancy. My tendency is to implement local DNS servers for the cluster "domain," with fall-back to NIS via the name service switch, and a minimal amount of information in a local system's /etc/hosts file for each system in the cluster. This provides a local file as a final backstop for failures.

For the "fixed" resources in the cluster, like the administrative and infrastructure servers, static network configurations may be reasonable. In this case, the systems are not making DHCP requests and so will need their own host name and IP addresses in the local /etc/hosts file and network configuration files in /etc/sysconfig. Also, the NIS master, if you choose to use NIS, will by default distribute the /etc/hosts file from the system that on which it resides, so we are back to maintaining at least one complete copy of the /etc/hosts file if you choose to enable NIS.

A minimal hosts file, with default gateways and server system definitions, provides sufficient information to handle the system boot process in conjunction with DHCP. With a minimal configuration of /etc/nsswitch.conf, and the DNS, NIS, and "files" order of search, we can have reasonable flexibility and immunity to failure. Another strategy is to specify the host file first in the list, with a fall-back to DNS and finally NIS. Your selection depends on need and your level of comfort with the available name service options.

The choices are not always easy, and sometimes you have to pick an initial path and adjust it later. This is all the more reason to consider implementing several of the name resolution methods during the initial cluster installation. You can enable, disable, or reorder them with the name service switch configuration file to make changes. The rules of the system administration game are the following: You can't win, you can't break even, and you have to play. Anyone who tells you differently is probably selling something.

10.10 Infrastructure Services Summary

In this chapter we examined a number of general recommendations for the design and implementation of infrastructure services. How big your cluster is will determine how many systems you need to dedicate to infrastructure service, but for availability's sake you should dedicate two systems to this purpose. Your software requirements will determine which of the services are needed, and your design choices determine *how* the services are installed.

The discussion of common infrastructure services and configuration techniques, like network aliases, channel bonding, starting and stopping Linux services, time synchronization with NTP, and several name resolution services are intended to point to individual areas where you can do further research, if needed. Infrastructure services, such as time synchronization, are often overlooked in favor of more glamorous, software-like parallel applications. The services we are deploying, however, are required for the operation of the higher level software packages.

We will continue to build a strong foundation for our cluster's software environment in the upcoming chapters.

## CHAPTER 11

Reach Out and Access Something: Remote Access Services, DHCP, and System Logging

Chapter Objectives

- Continue introducing necessary cluster infrastructure services
- Detail configuration options for remote access, Kerberos, SSH, PDSH, DHCP, and system logging (`klog` and `syslog`)

The previous chapter introduced a number of important infrastructure services provided by Linux. In this chapter we continue the coverage with more infrastructure services, including remote access services, local file system configuration, logging, console management, and authentication.

11.1 Continuing Infrastructure Installation

As part of your cluster's design process, you had to make choices about the infrastructure services that are necessary. Let's continue implementing the cluster infrastructure by giving configuration considerations and procedures for some of the more common services. Bootstrapping the cluster to prepare for installation of compute slices, administrative tools, monitoring tools, and other higher level software layers involves activating the required infrastructure services *first*.

Examples of required infrastructure services (along with some configuration and design options) that are covered in the upcoming sections are

- Authentication services (allowing administration staff to log in and work together)
- Remote access services (to allow network administration)
- Stable storage (for administrative software, scripts, and installation of packages)

- Local and remote administrative file systems (sharing data necessary for the installation process)
- Boot-time configuration (preparing for automatic system installation)
- Logging and console management (for testing and error detection)
- Core dump capture (for system debugging)
- Licensing (for any licensed software in the cluster)

It is essential to understand the relationships, or dependencies, between the individual services to pick the proper installation order. If the work of installing and configuring the services is to be shared between multiple administrators, *physical* access to the systems for multiple people at once becomes an important consideration. The number of administrative and infrastructure nodes in a cluster is small in relationship to the compute slices, but the few support the many in this case.

11.2 "Traditional" User Login and Authentication

The default Linux authentication and privilege scheme, like that of most UNIX and UNIX-like operating systems, is based on two numerical values, the UID and GID. With the default scheme, users authenticate themselves to the system with a combination of their user name and a password, and they are given system identifiers that are represented by the associated UID and GID values.

These values are then checked when users attempt to access resources to determine whether they are authorized to access a particular resource. Ensuring that the authorizations granted to specific users on the system are correct is a major task for a UNIX administrator.

Things have evolved to the point where users and processes may actually possess multiple UIDs and GIDs as well as specific "capabilities." Finding information on Linux capabilities requires persistence. They do not appear to be fully implemented and they are not very well documented in many of the kernel releases. Later versions of the Linux kernel are extending the authorization features to capabilities, access control lists (ACLs), and other facilities.

The UNIX user and group information is traditionally kept in the /etc/passwd and /etc/group files, which are "world readable." The open access to these files led to scripts and applications directly parsing the information in them (primarily to translate the numerical UID and GID values to their equivalent ASCII representations—in other words, translating the GID 0 to its human-readable name root)—changing that approach promised to break existing software, so the situation remains on today's system. This use of the files, by the way, is equivalent to a directory service: looking up information given a key like the user name or a UID.

With the advent of programs like crack, which can use "brute-force" techniques to determine passwords, the visibility of the encrypted password field in the files becomes a real liability (because it is only the equivalent of a 56-bit encryption key) in public environments. crack and similar programs use dictionaries of words and common user password choices (like the user name backward), encrypt them in all possible combinations, and check them against the values in a user's password field. If a match is found between the password field and the "cracked" password value, the user's account may be easily compromised.

Again, the Linux approach to this situation is similar to that of other UNIX-like systems: use larger password fields and optionally place "sensitive" information in files that have "tighter" security associated with them (they are only readable by `root`). These files on Linux are `/etc/shadow` and `/etc/gshadow`, and there are routines to convert to and from the formats with and without shadow files—for example, `pwconv`, `grpconv`, `pwunconv`, and `grpunconv`. Linux can use MD5 password encryption, with up to a total of 30 usable bytes, not including delimiters—a 210-bit key. (This could more accurately be described as a passphrase, rather than a password.)

The distribution of Linux MD5 password fields via NIS or other services may cause compatibility issues with versions of UNIX that use the older password encryption scheme and expect at most 8 bytes in the password field. Interoperability with existing authentication systems is a strong consideration when picking your cluster's authentication mechanism. The MD5 and shadow functionality are separate options. They, along with the authentication mechanism, can be configured from the `authconfig` tool.

TIP If interoperability is not an issue and you choose to use the "traditional" `/etc/passwd` and `/etc/group` files as the authentication database, enable either MD5 passwords, the shadow files, or both for additional security. You should also consider password aging and password strength checking to augment security.

The actual authentication process on Linux is implemented with pluggable authentication modules (PAM), a system based on stackable, dynamically loaded modules which may be configured into a multi-layered authentication process. A brief survey of the `/etc/pam.d` directory will show PAM-enabled applications, and examining the `/lib/security` directory (where the PAM libraries are kept), shows quite a number of PAM libraries, handling a number of authentication sources (Kerberos, lightweight directory access protocol [LDAP], SMB, rhosts) in addition to the libraries that implement the "standard" Unix authentication. Configuration information for PAM is kept in the file `/etc/pam.conf`. (I do not have space to delve into the intricacies of security in general, or PAM in particular. See Garfinkel and Spafford [1994] for a good treatise on UNIX security.)

The authentication scheme you choose for your cluster will determine which infrastructure issues you face. In some cases, the standard UNIX authentication mechanism is sufficient; in others, you may be required to interface to existing Kerberos, Microsoft Windows authentication mechanisms (SMB or Active Directory), or other services. Whatever the choice, you must be able to authenticate users and control their access to resources.

11.2.1   Using Groups and Directory Permissions

The standard Red Hat Linux installation procedure creates the `root` user account and gives it access to a dedicated home directory in `/root`. The default permissions on that directory, shown in the output from an `ls -ld /root` command, are

```
drwxr-x---    26 root       root         4096 Mar  2 22:49 /root
```

These permissions prevent anyone except the `root` user and members of the `root` group from accessing (including viewing) the directory's contents. The minute that someone who is not either the root user or in the root group needs to access files in that directory, the "world" permissions on the directory need to be "opened up."

This action points out one of the major weaknesses of the directory access scheme used by UNIX. Changing the access permissions to make files accessible to users other than the owner and the group makes the contents of the directory visible to any user on the system. Of course, this situation needs to be avoided, particularly for sensitive information that might be kept in `root`'s home directory.

Linux attempts to make management of directory access permissions easier, using the following approach.

- Each user has his own unique UID and matching GID (for example, user `rob1`, UID 500, group `rob1`, GID 500) created in the `passwd` and `group` files.
- Default home directory permissions are initially set to `700` (`rwx------` indicating read, write, and execute for the directory's owner only) on that directory.

Let's say we have several users configured in a similar manner. What would be needed for them to share information in a central project directory?

Permissions on the files created in a shared directory like this require special attention. The UNIX heritage has left us with two inheritance schemes for group ownership of files. In the first scheme (from SYSV UNIX), the group ownership of a file comes from the GID of the process creating the file. But what about the BSD situation, when a user or process may be a member of more than one group at the same time? (Just try typing `id` to see to which groups you belong. There are more than you think.) In this case, the files group comes from the directory in which the file is created.

The default behavior on Linux is to create a file with the group inherited from the process or user that creates it, irrespective of the directory group permissions. To get the "inherit from the directory" behavior, we must set the set group ID (or SGID) bit on the directory. This is done with the command `chmod g+s <directory>`.

With the SGID bit set, files created in the directory will retain the UID of the creating user or process, but will inherit the group ownership from the directory. Judicious use of the user mask can make the files available to the original user *and* the group that owns the directory. One additional trick is to set the "sticky" bit on a directory (`chmod o+t <directory>`) to

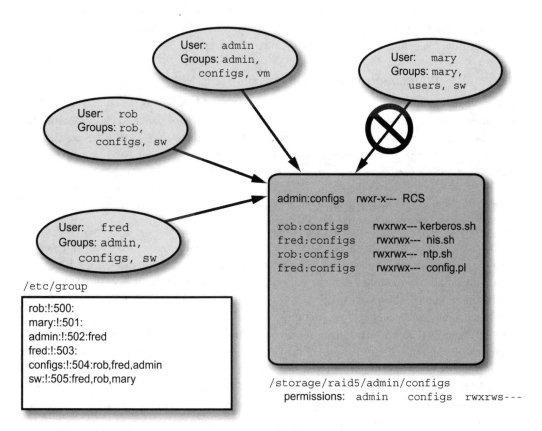

Figure 11–1 Shared project directory with SGID

enable restricted deletion behavior: Only `root` or the file's owner may unlink or rename it. An example configuration is shown in Figure 11–1.

T I P   Use group ownership to manage the access to shared directories and files. It is far easier to add and remove users from a group to control access to shared resources, than to change ownership and permissions on individual files or directories with every change to a project team.

When protecting the contents of a shared directory, rather than opening the permissions up "to the world," it is far easier to use assign project members to the directory's group owner. The directory's owner permissions then designate full rights for an individual who manages the data in the directory, while the group rights on the directory apply to all of the users of the data. Setting the SGID permission on the directory, in conjunction with the proper `umask` value, will properly handle the owner and group permissions on shared files in the directory. In this way, instead of changing permissions on the directory when users are added to or deleted from the project—or fighting with the "world visible" problem—access is managed by adding or removing users from the definition of the group that owns the directory.

11.2.2   Distributing Password Information with NIS

If you are using the `/etc/passwd` and `/etc/group` information as the sole authentication mechanism for your cluster, you can use NIS to distribute this information to client systems that must use it to authenticate users and their processes. If you want to use NIS to distribute `/etc/passwd` and `/etc/group` information, you should refer to Chapter 10 for information on configuring NIS servers and clients.

11.2.3   Introducing Kerberos

A number of software environments, including the DCE and the Andrew file system (AFS) use Kerberos as the central authentication mechanism. The current version of the software is Kerberos 5, and you should be aware that there are at least three major implementations of the daemons, including the versions from the Massachusetts Institute of Technology (MIT) and for Microsoft Windows. (See Garman [2003] for a complete treatise on the Kerberos protocol, implementations, and system administration.)

To support Kerberos inside the cluster you will need to set up at least one key distribution center (KDC) and the client software on the other systems. The KDC provides for redundancy, and it is a very good idea to have a replicated KDC available to your cluster systems. The Kerberos KDC comprises the principal database the authentication server, and the ticket-granting server. Slave KDC servers have a copy of the database, and are capable of authentication and ticket operations, but cannot make changes to the database information.

Once your system's Kerberos client authenticates you, you are granted a "ticket-granting ticket" (TGT) that maintains a record of your authentication and may be used to obtain other tickets for access to Kerberos-enabled services in the environment. A domain of Kerberos administration is referred to as a *realm*. Your cluster may be its own Kerberos realm or it may be required to take part in an existing realm, in which case you will need to interoperate with the existing KDCs. An example of a "Kerberized" interaction is shown in Figure 11–2.

The Kerberos service is very secure (provided it is properly installed and configured), in that all communications in the network are encrypted and therefore are not subject to prying eyes looking at network traffic with packet sniffers. (It is also important to control physical access to KDCs to prevent tampering.) The protocols involved for authentication, ticket granting, and service access are designed to prevent issues like "man-in-the-middle" attacks and other tricks that sneaky hackers might try to eavesdrop on conversations or to hijack system resources.

The fact that your initial ticket (or TGT) expires after a preset interval (configurable, but usually eight hours to a full day) helps ensure that by the time someone could use brute-force decryption techniques to determine your conversation's contents, the information would do them no good.

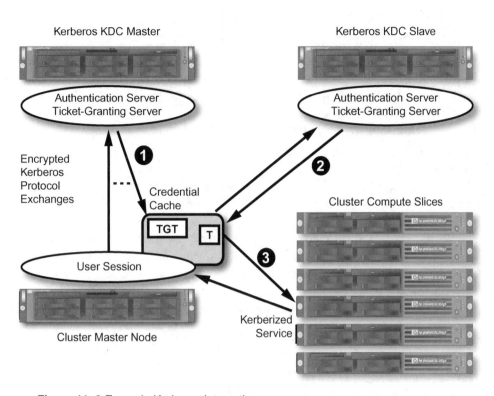

Figure 11–2 Example Kerberos interaction

Kerberos requires each entity, or communication point, in a conversation to be authenticated. These entities are called *principals*, and may be a service, a host (system), a user, or a special entity within the Kerberos system itself. The requirement that all parties be authenticated means that each principal that can participate in a conversation needs to be authenticated, with an identity and an encryption key.

A brief introduction to the terminology used to describe entities in Kerberos is in order at this point. There are three types of principals and two formats for a principal "name" or just "a principal" in Kerberos 5 (the format differs slightly from previous versions). The first format is used for both users and host principals:

> `user[/instance]@REALM`

In the case of a host principal, the `user` portion of the principal is the string "`host`." Examples of two user principals and a host principal respectively are:

```
rob/admin@CLUSTER.LOCAL
kadmin/admin@CLUSTER.LOCAL
host/ns1.cluster.local@CLUSTER.LOCAL
```

For services, the principal format is

> *service/fully-qualified-domain-name@REALM*

Now that you can recognize principals, you will see them used in the output examples in the next section. We will be doing minimal work with principals in this section, because we have limited space. You may need to locate a Kerberos expert if your installation is complex.

11.2.4   Configuring a Kerberos KDC on Linux

The Red Hat distribution includes the Kerberos version 5 server software in the ES versions, and the server is also a standard part of the Fedora distribution. The configuration files for the KDC are /etc/krb5.conf and /var/kerberos/krb5kdc/kdc.conf. Let's call our local Kerberos realm CLUSTER.LOCAL, which is the upper-case form of our DNS domain.

The systems in a Kerberos realm must have their times synchronized within a five-minute window. When running Kerberos in your cluster, it is a very good idea to use a time synchronization service, such as NTP, to keep the system clocks within the required tolerance. This is a very good example of a dependency between two infrastructure services.

We can use the skeleton /etc/krb5.conf file on the first KDC machine (assuming that we will do at least two), filling in the appropriate system names, domain names, and Kerberos realm:

```
[logging]
 default = FILE:/var/log/krb5libs.log
 kdc = FILE:/var/log/krb5kdc.log
 admin_server = FILE:/var/log/kadmind.log

[libdefaults]
 ticket_lifetime = 24000
 default_realm =  CLUSTER.LOCAL
 dns_lookup_realm = true
 dns_lookup_kdc = true

[realms]
 CLUSTER.LOCAL = {
  kdc = ns2.cluster.local:88
  admin_server = ns2.cluster.local:749
  default_domain = cluster.local
 }

[domain_realm]
 .cluster.local. =  CLUSTER.LOCAL
 cluster.local = CLUSTER.LOCAL

[kdc]
 profile = /var/kerberos/krb5kdc/kdc.conf
[appdefaults]
```

```
pam = {
  debug = false
  ticket_lifetime = 36000
  renew_lifetime = 36000
  forwardable = true
  krb4_convert = false
}
```

Next, modify the `/var/kerberos/krb5kdc/kdc.conf` file, again using our system, domain, and realm names:

```
[kdcdefaults]
 acl_file = /var/kerberos/krb5kdc/kadm5.acl
 dict_file = /usr/share/dict/words
 admin_keytab = /var/kerberos/krb5kdc/kadm5.keytab
 v4_mode = nopreauth

[realms]
 CLUSTER.LOCAL = {
  master_key_type = des-cbc-crc
  supported_enctypes = des3-cbc-sha1:normal des3-cbc-
sha1:norealm des3-cbc-sha1:onlyrealm des-cbc-crc:v4 des-cbc-
crc:afs3 des-cbc-crc:normal des-cbc-crc:norealm des-cbc-
crc:onlyrealm des-cbc-md4:v4 des-cbc-md4:afs3 des-cbc-
md4:normal des-cbc-md4:norealm des-cbc-md4:onlyrealm des-cbc-
md5:v4 des-cbc-md5:afs3 des-cbc-md5:normal des-cbc-md5:norealm
des-cbc-md5:onlyrealm des-cbc-sha1:v4 des-cbc-sha1:afs3 des-
cbc-sha1:normal des-cbc-sha1:norealm des-cbc-sha1:onlyrealm
 }
```

Once the configuration files are modified, we need to create the initial Kerberos database files and enter the master database key. These are located in `/var/kerberos/krb5kdc`. The `/etc/init.d/krb5kdc` start-up script explicitly looks for a file named `principal` that gets created in that directory as part of the database initialization, and exits silently if the file does not exist:

```
# kdb5_util create -s
Initializing database '/var/kerberos/krb5kdc/principal' for
realm 'CLUSTER.LOCAL',
master key name 'K/M@CLUSTER.LOCAL'
You will be prompted for the database Master Password.It is
important that you NOT FORGET this password.
Enter KDC database master key:
Re-enter KDC database master key to verify:
```

We are now ready to start the service and make sure it gets restarted at system boot time:

```
# chkconfig krb5kdc on
# service krb5kdc start
```

If there are errors, you can look in the `/var/log/krb5kdc.log` file for diagnostic messages. The local administration tool, `kadmin.local` is designed to operate only on a KDC server and will not allow remote connections. Once the KDC is operating, we can use the local administrative tool to authenticate to it and add a user as an administrative principal to the database:

```
# kadmin.local
Authenticating as principal root/admin@CLUSTER.LOCAL with
password.
kadmin.local:  listprincs
K/M@CLUSTER.LOCAL
kadmin/admin@CLUSTER.LOCAL
kadmin/changepw@CLUSTER.LOCAL
kadmin/history@CLUSTER.LOCAL
krbtgt/CLUSTER.LOCAL@CLUSTER.LOCAL
kadmin.local:  addprinc rob/admin
WARNING: no policy specified for rob/admin@CLUSTER.LOCAL;
defaulting to no policy
Enter password for principal "rob/admin@CLUSTER.LOCAL":
Re-enter password for principal "rob/admin@CLUSTER.LOCAL":
Principal "rob/admin@CLUSTER.LOCAL" created.
kadmin.local:  quit
```

Now we want to start the Kerberos administrative daemon, which is the service that handles remote administration requests and allows users to change their passwords. We need to modify the `/var/kerberos/krb5kdc/kadm5.acl` file to allow our administrative user to perform administrative operations. The ACL options are complex, so for this simple example we will edit the file to contain

```
*/admin@CLUSTER.LOCAL *
```

This allows any principle name that matches the instance and realm `/admin@CLUSTER.LOCAL` to perform all operations. In real life, this is probably neither safe nor smart.

Next we need to create the `/var/kerberos/krb5kdc/kadm5.keytab` file. This file contains principal information for the two principals specified in the `ktadd` command, which appends the information to the specified file, along with new, random passwords generated during the process:

```
# kadmin.local
kadmin.local: ktadd -k /var/kerberos/krb5kdc/kadm5.keytab \
kadmin/admin kadmin/changepw

kadmin.local# quit
```

The key tab information is used to authenticate remote connections to the `kadmin` server, which we can now start:

```
# chkconfig kadmin on
# service kadmin start
```

When the daemon (which is named `kadmind`) starts, you should see a long list of messages detailing the administrative principals it is using. If everything went as expected, you should be able to use the `kadmin` command, either locally or remotely:

```
# kadmin
kadmin: listprincs
K/M@CLUSTER.LOCAL
kadmin/admin@CLUSTER.LOCAL
kadmin/changepw@CLUSTER.LOCAL
kadmin/history@CLUSTER.LOCAL
krbtgt/CLUSTER.LOCAL@CLUSTER.LOCAL
rob/admin@CLUSTER.LOCAL
kadmin: quit
```

The `kadmin` command authenticates the user with the KDC and encrypts the traffic between it and the `kadmind` process, which makes remote administration safe.

Now that you have a functional KDC, you should be able to authenticate yourself and get a TGT with the `kinit` command. If you see an error message like

```
kinit(v5): Client not found in Kerberos database while \
getting initial credentials
```

It means that Kerberos cannot find a principal in its database that matches your UNIX user name. Notice that I used my administrative principal in this request. I got the error message when I tried a `kinit` without specifying the principal on the command line, and the principal name defaulted to `rob`. We have not added any other principals at this point. I leave this as an exercise for you.

```
$ kinit rob/admin
Password for rob/admin@CLUSTER.LOCAL:
$ klist
Ticket cache: FILE:/tmp/krb5cc_1000
Default principal: rob/admin@CLUSTER.LOCAL
Valid starting     Expires               Service principal
03/03/04 22:25:20  03/04/04 08:25:20  \
          krbtgt/CLUSTER.LOCAL@CLUSTER.LOCAL
Kerberos 4 ticket cache: /tmp/tkt1000
klist: You have no tickets cached
```

One final note on the tickets you obtain: They are stored in the credentials cache in the `/tmp` directory and stay around until destroyed with the `kdestroy` command (or until they expire). You need to put the `kdestroy` command in your shell's logout script to ensure that they are not left hanging around after you log out.

11.2.5   Creating a Kerberos Slave KDC

If you want to replicate the Kerberos database to a slave KDC server, you need to initialize two KDCs following the procedure outlined in the previous section: One will become the master and one will become the slave KDC. This next section shows the steps for creating the slave KDC. We are *almost* finished with the Kerberos server configuration!

In this example, we have two KDC servers, `ns1.cluster.local` and `ns2.cluster.local`. The `ns2.cluster.local` system will be the slave KDC and `ns1.cluster.local` will be the master KDC.

To begin, we need to create host principals on the master and the slave KDC systems. The principal is added to the key tabs for the KDC machines for use in the replication process, once it is created. This example is for the master:

```
# kadmin
Authenticating as principal rob/admin@CLUSTER.LOCAL with
password.
Enter password:
kadmin:  addprinc -randkey host/ns2.cluster.local
WARNING: no policy specified for host/
ns2.cluster.local@CLUSTER.LOCAL; defaulting to no policy
Principal "host/ns2.cluster.local@CLUSTER.LOCAL" created.
kadmin:  ktadd host/ns2.cluster.local
Entry for principal host/ns2.cluster.local with kvno 3,
encryption type Triple DES cbc mode with HMAC/sha1 added to
keytab WRFILE:/etc/krb5.keytab.
Entry for principal host/ns2.cluster.local with kvno 3,
encryption type DES cbc mode with CRC-32 added to keytab
WRFILE:/etc/krb5.keytab.
kadmin: quit
```

After repeating the operation on the slave, we will create a `/var/kerberos/krb5kdc/kpropd.acl` file on the slave KDC system, that contains the host principals that we just created:

```
host/ns1.cluster.local@CLUSTER.LOCAL
host/ns2.cluster.local@CLUSTER.LOCAL
```

Only the master KDC is required in the file, but if we ever have to flip roles (because the master is lost for some reason), we will be prepared. The Red Hat distributions provide the `kpropd` service, which needs to be started on the slave KDC:

```
# chkconfig kprop on
# service kprop start
```

Note that if the `/var/kerberos/krb5kdc/kprop.acl` file exists, the start-up scripts will silently refuse to start the `kadmin` service. Apparently this should be running on only the master KDC. Once the `kpropd` daemon is running on the slave, we can dump the master's database to a file and send it to the slave, using the default file names

```
# kdb5_util dump /var/kerberos/krb5kdc/slave_datatrans
# kprop -f /var/kerberos/krb5kdc/slave_datatrans \
      ns1.cluster.local
Database propagation to ns1.cluster.local: SUCCEEDED
```

The database is extracted from the master KDC server with the `kdb5_util` command and is copied across a secure, encrypted channel to the slave KDC, where the database is loaded into the slave, again using the `kdb5_util` command. We have one last operation to perform before we can rest on our Kerberos laurels: We need to enable the slave KDC to read the database, which is encrypted by the master password we entered oh so long ago.

```
# kdb5_util stash
Enter KDC database master key:
#
```

This command simply stores the master database password in a local file that is used by the slave KDC to "open" the database for use. You should enter the master password you used when you created the master database. The last remaining task, which I leave to you, dear reader, is to create a `cron` job that transfers the database from the master KDC to the slave KDC at regular intervals.

11.2.6   Kerberos Summary

Kerberos allows users to authenticate themselves once, receive a TGT, and then use that TGT to access "Kerberized" services. In addition to the manual authentication process, Linux provides a PAM module that can perform the user's authentication as part of the normal system login. See the documentation in `man pam_krb5` for information on setting up the PAM service for Kerberos. The integration of the two services simplifies ticket management issues for the user, obtaining the TGT and releasing tickets in the credential cache on logout, among other features.

Once a user is authenticated and granted a TGT, Kerberized clients for services are available, including `telnet`, `ftp`, `rlogin`, `rsh`, and `rcp`, which are all located in the `/usr/kerberos/bin` directory. There are also other clients and services, like SSH, that are Kerberos aware. Kerberos is one way to solve the "clear text password" security issues within a networked environment.

The Red Hat distributions, and Fedora, provide an MIT-based version of Kerberos 5. The configuration steps in this section are based on that version of the software. A diagram of the interactions and files involved in master and slave KDCs is shown in Figure 11–3. Administrative information for the server portion of Kerberos is available in Hypertext Markup Language (HTML) format in the `/usr/share/doc/krb5-server-<version>` directory. Documentation for the Kerberos "workstation" package, which contains the Kerberized servers (`klogind`, `krb5-telnetd`, `kshd`, and so forth) is located in `/usr/share/doc/krb5-`

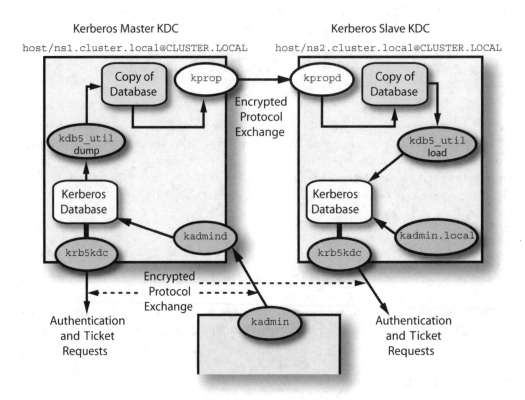

Figure 11–3 Kerberos 5 slave KDC components

`workstation-<version>`. (I discuss configuration of these services in the next section, primarily because they are required for remote access to the administrative servers that we are discussing.)

You will find Kerberos to be very good about logging the actions being taken in the `/var/log/krb5kdc.log` and `/var/log/kadmind.log` files. With the addition of auditing capabilities to the Kerberos features, we can complete the three basic "A" components in a secure environment: authentication, authorization, and auditing. If your environment warrants it, using Kerberos provides a level of security that is difficult to get without it.

11.3 Remote Access Services

For a system administrator, remote access to systems in the network is an important part of the day-to-day administration activities, as well as the initial installation operations. For users, access to the cluster will be primarily through some form of secure connection to the master nodes (if it is a computational cluster) or through an application front end (if the system is a parallel Web or database server).

In the case of direct remote access for the user or administrator, some form of authentication is required to prove identity and to control the level of permission. Within the cluster, as well, access to the resources needs to be tightly controlled to prevent issues with system stability and to cut down on the potential for users to "go around" the job-scheduling mechanisms. (They find enough ways to do this, even if there are no "gaping" holes in the access.) Although the level of required security can narrow the available choices for remote access to a system, there are two major groups of remote access services that can meet our needs.

Both of the service groups, the BSD remote shell (the BSD offering is really a set of separate services) and SSH (several commands with the same transport), can interact with the Kerberos service, which we discussed in the previous section. This gives us a lot of flexibility regarding which choice we make.

The BSD services are turned off by default, because the non-Kerberized versions transmit passwords and data "in the open," with an unencrypted transport. SSH (really "Open SSH") is enabled and is seen as the default Linux remote access method because of its security and flexibility.

11.4 Using BSD Remote Access Services

Most UNIX administrators and a lot of UNIX users are aware of the network services introduced to UNIX by the BSD4.2 distribution: `rsh`, `rlogin`, `rcp`, `telnet`, and `ftp`. We have all configured `${HOME}/.rhosts` files and `/etc/hosts.equiv` files to allow easy access to remote systems. Ah, those were simpler days. As easy and convenient as these services are for users and system administrators, they all rely implicitly on the integrity of the systems involved and the network between them.

Except in very special circumstances, this level of trust is a dangerous thing in today's networks, especially if you are connected directly to the Internet. If you are used to using the previously mentioned clients and their equivalent servers—`in.rlogind`, `in.rexecd`, `in.rshd`, `in.telnetd` (even with the   benefit of the TCP wrapper files `/etc/hosts.allow` and `/etc/hosts.deny`)—you should think strongly about "moving on." Likewise, you should consign the `.rhosts` file and `/etc/hosts.equiv` to the dust bin, unless you want to invite network intrusions and all the other problems that come with unencrypted communications and passwords in "clear text" on the network. You should know that one of the applications included with every Linux distribution, or freely available, is a software packet sniffer that is capable of trapping user passwords in clear text.

You should not use the BSD remote access services in your cluster. Period. If you going to give in to user pressure to enable these services in their raw, nonsecure form, then at least consider this a transition period and set a date by which you will start using the more secure replacements. Fortunately, Kerberized versions of these services exist, so the transition need not be nightmarish in proportion (rewriting administrative scripts, retraining users, and so on).

T I P   The BSD remote access services are nonsecure and should not be used. The SSH services are a better replacement for the BSD remote access tools, but should not have the fall-back to BSD operation enabled. Using a secure service with a fall-back to an nonsecure one is a terrible idea from a security standpoint.

If you have the luxury of breaking with the past and are willing to set up Kerberos, you will want to examine the secure Kerberized "replacement" services. The best option is to take a look at SSH, which is covered in an upcoming section. I do not discuss the older, nonsecure services any further.

11.5 Kerberized Versions of BSD/ARPA Remote Services

As previously mentioned, there are client replacement versions of the BSD/Advanced Research Projects Agency (ARPA) remote services that use Kerberos authentication, and most are located in the /usr/kerberos/bin directory. The server portion of these services must be explicitly enabled on the system being accessed by the client, and are located in the /usr/kerberos/ sbin directory. The BSD/ARPA services and their Kerberized equivalents are listed in Table 11–1.

One of the disadvantages of using the Kerberized versions of the BSD services is that, if the Kerberos authentication fails, the service will drop back to the old-style login behavior, with unencrypted passwords. Additionally, to get the secure behavior, the user must explicitly request encryption. The use of ticket forwarding and other features requires the user to be aware of the operation of Kerberos and to be familiar with its terminology. This may be useful in a transitional mode, but it still leaves room for insecure communications if users don't properly invoke the service client.

Table 11–1 Kerberized Equivalents for BSD Remote Services

Service Description	"Standard" Service	Kerberized Server
Remote login, BSD style	in.rlogind	klogind
Remote login, Kerberos authentication		eklogind
Remote terminal session	in.telnetd	krb5-telnet
Remote shell	in.rshd	kshd
File transfer	in.ftpd, in.wuftpd	gssftp

For example, instead of simply issuing a `telnet <target system>` command, the user would specify `telnet -a -x -f <target system>`. The options to the Kerberized `telnet` tell the client to log in on the remote system as the current principal (`-a`), to encrypt all conversations (`-x`), and to forward all "forwardable" Kerberos tickets (`-f`) to the remote system. Users may tend to fall back to old habits, without the options, which will result in nonsecure behavior.

The server portion of the services are started by the `xinetd` process in response to an incoming client request. The `xinetd` process configuration is `/etc/xinetd.conf` is essentially a skeleton with a few global definitions and a directive that includes all files located in the `/etc/xinetd.d` directory. (This is an interesting administration paradigm that you will find in several places on the system. It allows a package requiring an `xinetd` service to install itself, drop the configuration file in the `/etc/xinetd.d` directory, and cause `xinetd` to reload its configuration. No `grep`, `sed`, or `awk` is required, and the possibility of disturbing other services is minimized. Removal of a package is the reverse set of operations.) These files need to be modified to enable the appropriate servers for the Kerberos versions of the BSD/ARPA clients.

For instance, to enable the `eklogin` server on a client system, you need to modify the `/etc/xinetd.d/eklogin` file:

```
# default: off
# description: The encrypting kerberized rlogin server accepts
# rlogin sessions authenticated and encrypted with Kerberos 5.
service eklogin
{
        flags    = REUSE
        socket_type    = stream
        wait    = no
        user    = root
        server  = /usr/kerberos/sbin/klogind
        server_args    = -e -5
        disable = no
}
```

A brief note on the contents of the `xinetd` configuration files may save some confusion. Sometimes the default value for line in the reads, `disable = yes`, as in this example. Other times, the line may specify, `enable = no`, which is an inverted specification for the same result. You need to watch closely for the difference, particularly in scripts.

After modifying the service files, you must cause the `xinetd` daemon to reread its configuration files:

```
# service xinetd reload
```

Perform similar configuration changes and the system will now handle incoming requests from the Kerberized clients for the services you enable. For debugging purposes, and to verify

that the service is talking to the Kerberos KDC, you can look at the `/var/log/`
`krb5kdc.log` file for the tickets that are issued to the clients:

```
Mar 04 22:38:40 ns2 krb5kdc[757](info): AS_REQ (3 etypes {16 3
1}) 192.168.0.152(88): ISSUE: authtime 1078468720, etypes
{rep=16 tkt=16 ses=16}, host/ns2.cluster.local@CLUSTER.LOCAL
for host/ns1.cluster.local@CLUSTER.LOCAL
```

You should be able to see the KDC issue a ticket for the client as it tries to access the service. Even if the ticket is properly issued, the access could fail, as shown in the following encrypted `telnet` request:

```
# telnet -x ns1
Trying 192.168.0.151...
Connected to ns1.cluster.local (192.168.0.151).
Escape character is '^]'.
Waiting for encryption to be negotiated...
[ ... output deleted ...]
[ Kerberos V5 refuses authentication because telnetd:
krb5_rd_req failed: Decrypt integrity check failed ]

Authentication negotation has failed, which is required for
encryption.  Good bye.
#
```

What is happening? To find out, we need to enable debug output on the server side of the connection for the service we are using. This can be done by modifying the `xinetd` configuration file, in this case for `krb5-telnet`, adding the `server_args` option to pass the debug flags:

```
# default: off
# description: The kerberized telnet server accepts normal
# telnet sessions, but can also use Kerberos 5 authentication.
service telnet
{
        flags   = REUSE
        socket_type  = stream
        wait   = no
        user   = root
        server = /usr/kerberos/sbin/telnetd
        server_args = -D report
        log_on_failure += USERID
        disable  = no

}
```

This will dump lots of information on the *client's* side of the conversation. We can watch the negotiation process occur, see what the supported encryption types are for both the client and server, and look for something going amiss. With the server-side debug option installed and activated, we see

```
# telnet -x ns1
Trying 192.168.0.151...
Connected to ns1.cluster.local (192.168.0.151).
Escape character is '^]'.
Waiting for encryption to be negotiated...
td: send do AUTHENTICATION
[... output deleted ...]
td: send suboption AUTHENTICATION SEND KERBEROS_V5
CLIENT|MUTUAL|ENCRYPTKERBEROS_V5
CLIENT|MUTUAL|ENCRYPTKERBEROS_V5 CLIENT|ONE-WAY|ENCRYPT
td: recv do ENCRYPT
td: send will ENCRYPT
td: recv will ENCRYPT
td: send do ENCRYPT
td: send suboption ENCRYPT SUPPORT DES_CFB64 DES_OFB64
[... output deleted ...
[ Kerberos V5 refuses authentication because telnetd:\
        krb5_rd_req failed: Decrypt integrity check failed]
```

The error message, it turns out, is confusing the issue. What is *really* happening is a mismatch in the encryption capabilities that can be handled between the service daemon and the host principal. Kerberos will always try to use the strongest encryption available to it, and some clients can't handle the stronger type of encryption, especially if they are compiled to be used outside the United States (a clue to this can be found in man -k cfb64, which returns the man page for DES_CRYPT).

We need to regenerate the key tab entry for the host principal involved:

```
# kadmin
Authenticating as principal root/admin@CLUSTER.LOCAL with
password.
Enter password:
kadmin: ktrem host/ns1.cluster.local
Entry for principal host/ns1.cluster.local with kvno 3 removed
from keytab WRFILE:/etc/krb5.keytab.
Entry for principal host/ns1.cluster.local with kvno 3 removed
from keytab WRFILE:/etc/krb5.keytab.
kadmin: ktadd
Usage: ktadd [-k[eytab] keytab] [-q] [-e keysaltlist]
[principal | -glob princ-exp] [...]
kadmin: ktadd -e des host/ns1.cluster.local
Entry for principal host/ns1.cluster.local with kvno 4,
encryption type DES cbc mode with RSA-MD5 added to keytab
WRFILE:/etc/krb5.keytab.
kadmin: quit
```

This example shows the commands necessary to create a key tab entry with just the lowest common denominator between the host and the service, which is date encryption standard (DES)
encryption. Now we can try connecting again:

```
# telnet -x ns1
Trying 192.168.0.101...
Connected to ns1.cluster.local (192.168.0.151).
Escape character is '^]'.
Waiting for encryption to be negotiated...
[ Kerberos V5 accepts you as "root@CLUSTER.LOCAL" ]
done.
Last login: Fri Mar  5 14:43:17 from ns2
#
```

We are finally able to connect, using `telnet` with an encrypted communication path and
a new ticket generated for us from the Kerberos KDC's ticket-granting service (TGS):

```
Mar 05 14:43:37 ns2 krb5kdc[5716](info): TGS_REQ (1 etypes \
{1}) 192.168.0.110(88): ISSUE: authtime 1078526609, etypes \
{rep=16 tkt=16 ses=1}, root@CLUSTER.LOCAL for \
        host/ns1.cluster.local@CLUSTER.LOCAL
```

The Kerberos login facilities allow a user to create a `${HOME}/.k5login` file, which
contains the names of principals that are allowed to access the account. The file must be owned
by the account owner and contains the familiar `principal[/instance]@realm` format,
one per line. An example `.k5login` file is

```
rob/admin@CLUSTER.LOCAL
rob@CLUSTER.LOCAL
freebie@CLUSTER.LOCAL
```

Any authenticated Kerberos principal listed in the `.k5login` file is allowed access to the
account. This finishes our introduction to configuring and using Kerberos. Now, onward to SSH.

11.6 The Secure Shell

Although SSH sounds as if it should be a general-purpose scripting language, like the Korn shell
(`ksh`) or the Bourne shell (`sh`), or even the Borne-again shell (`bash`), it is not a shell in the
sense of a "command shell" that is the local user interface to the operating system's kernel or
user applications. Instead, SSH is a transport, or protocol, that defines a method of secure, network-based communication using encryption and mutual authentication. Adding to the confusion, there are various versions and implementations of the SSH protocol.

The implementation of SSH that is included with Linux, and that I will discuss, is really
OpenSSH from the OpenBSD project (see `http://www.openssh.com` for more details).
This particular SSH implements both the SSH version 1 and version 2 (SSH1 and SSH2) *proto-
cols* with a client–server architecture. For our purposes, I will refer to the OpenSSH implemen-

tation when I use the term *SSH,* along with the SSH2 protocol, which is now used as the default transport.

Red Hat Linux, and derivatives, include the SSH client and server software as part of the Linux distribution. In general, SSH is well integrated into the Linux environment, and the default configuration is usable once the operating system is installed. This is good, because it means that with minimal work we have a mechanism to log in to remote systems securely and to transfer files via a secure channel.

Just when you thought that things could not get better, they can. SSH is also capable of forwarding TCP/IP network traffic through secure "tunnels." This process is also called *port forwarding*, because a numerical TCP/IP port on one machine may be securely connected to an entirely different port on another machine via secure communications through an SSH tunnel. As complicated as this may sound, it really isn't.

The flexibility of SSH allows secure communications in any number of situations that do not require modification of client or server software, as needed with Kerberos. The administration of SSH is also somewhat less involved than that of Kerberos. The transition from using BSD remote access (for example, `rsh`) may be as easy as setting up SSH and substituting the `ssh` command for `rsh` in existing scripts.

The SSH transport also is optionally used by quite a few Linux installation, monitoring, and system administration tools, which optionally use encrypted transport and authentication to guarantee secure communications between their components. If SSH sounds like a good thing, it is—without a doubt. It is for good reason that SSH is enabled by default, and the BSD-style services are *disabled* by default. (For more complete coverage of SSH features and its administration than I can cover here, see Barrat and Silverman [2001].)

11.6.1   SSH and Public Key Encryption

Like Kerberos, SSH uses mutual authentication to verify that the participants in a communications channel are who they claim to be. Public key encryption is heavily used by SSH for user authentication and data transport. Unfortunately, we don't have space or time to delve heavily into encryption in general, or public key encryption (as used in SSH) in particular. I will simplify the details without losing too much information in the process. (Aside from the SSH-specific introduction in Barnett and Silverman [2001], you should also read *The Code Book: The Science of Secrecy from Ancient Egypt to Quantum Cryptography* [Singh 2000].)

One way to understand what public key encryption is, and how SSH uses it, is to examine the contents of the `/etc/ssh` directory. There you will see the following files containing the string "key" in their names:

```
ssh_host_dsa_key
ssh_host_dsa_key.pub
ssh_host_key
ssh_host_key.pub
ssh_host_rsa_key
ssh_host_rsa_key.pub
```

These are the keys that are used by the `/usr/sbin/sshd` process to identify the local host. They are generated when the system boots for the first time, and by default are created to be unique to the host on which they reside. The `ssh_host` and `ssh_host.pub` files are the private and public keys, respectively, that belong to the host "key pair" that is used by the SSH1 protocol. The other files belong to host key pairs that are used by the SSH2 protocol.

The two files that compose the key pair are generated by the `/usr/bin/ssh-keygen` command using a particular algorithm (either Rivest, Shamir, Adelman [RSA] or Digital Signature Algorithm [DSA]). The public key may be shared or published openly, but the private key should *never* be shared. The private key files are only accessible by `root`, whereas the public key files are readable by everyone.

The magic about public key systems is that data encrypted with the public key from a key pair may be decrypted with the private key. It is not practical to create the private key from the public key. The private key becomes the "proof of identity," or the credential associated with a particular "agent" involved in the authentication process. Among other things, the agent may be a user, an application, or a host.

SSH uses a fairly complex protocol to authenticate an agent, establish an encrypted channel, and exchange data. The protocol ensures that both ends of the conversation are authenticated and that they can exchange the encryption keys necessary to pass data in both directions. This protocol, and the exact way that the public keys are used for authentication, are beyond the scope of this discussion.

In addition to generating keys with the RSA and DSA algorithms, the `ssh-keygen` program can output the "fingerprint" of a key, which is useful in comparing the contents of two key files:

```
# ssh-keygen -l  -f ssh_host_rsa_key.pub
1024 dc:b6:4d:e4:92:84:20:0e:a0:8f:f6:53:0f:0e:7d:35 \
ssh_host_rsa_key.pub
```

Key files may also be protected by a pass phrase, when they are generated, to keep them from being used if the file is stolen. The `ssh-keygen` command will allow a user with the proper pass phrase to change the pass phrase protecting the key file. An example of generating a 1,024-bit RSA key pair is

```
# ssh-keygen  -b 1024 -t rsa -f /tmp/foo
Generating public/private rsa key pair.
Enter passphrase (empty for no passphrase):
Enter same passphrase again:
Your identification has been saved in /tmp/foo.
Your public key has been saved in /tmp/foo.pub.
The key fingerprint is:
33:c0:68:00:fe:60:dc:12:db:70:99:0b:16:eb:6a:07 root@nec2
```

Notice from this example that it is possible to specify an empty pass phrase for the key file. It is more secure to specify a pass phrase (10 to 30 characters). However, to use the key files, you must specify the pass phrase. For this reason, host keys are created with no pass phrase.

11.6.2   Configuring the SSH Client and Server

Configuration files for SSH are located, along with other important information, in the `/etc/ssh` directory. The server portion of the software is `/usr/sbin/sshd`, and the local client programs `ssh`, `ssh-add`, `ssh-keygen`, `ssh-keyscan`, and `ssh-agent` are located in the `/usr/bin` directory.

Although it is not usually necessary to alter the server or client configurations radically from the default, there are some local preferences that might need to be enabled, as in this server configuration file example:

```
#X11Forwarding no
X11Forwarding yes
#X11DisplayOffset 10
#X11UseLocalhost yes
#PrintMotd yes
#PrintLastLog yes
#KeepAlive yes
#UseLogin no
#UsePrivilegeSeparation yes
#Compression yes
#MaxStartups 10
# no default banner path
#Banner /some/path
#VerifyReverseMapping no
# override default of no subsystems
Subsystem       sftp    /usr/libexec/openssh/sftp-server
```

In this configuration example, the server allows X Windows forwarding, and the `sftp` subsystem is enabled for use by clients.

The client SSH configuration is kept in `/etc/ssh/ssh_config`, and the server configuration is located in the `/etc/ssh/sshd_config` file. Both files are populated with comments that represent the default values for the full set of the software's configuration options:

```
# Host *
#   ForwardAgent no
#   ForwardX11 no
#   RhostsAuthentication no
#   RhostsRSAAuthentication no
#   RSAAuthentication yes
#   PasswordAuthentication yes
#   BatchMode no
#   CheckHostIP yes
#   StrictHostKeyChecking ask
```

```
#   IdentityFile ~/.ssh/identity
#   IdentityFile ~/.ssh/id_rsa
#   IdentityFile ~/.ssh/id_dsa
#   Port 22
#   Protocol 2,1
#   Cipher 3des
#   Ciphers aes128-cbc,3des-cbc,blowfish-cbc,cast128- \
        cbc,arcfour,aes192-cbc,aes256-cbc
#   EscapeChar ~
    ForwardX11 yes
```

This example, from the client configuration file, /etc/ssh/ssh_config, shows X Windows forwarding enabled for the associated client. Note the default values for the port, user identity files (key pairs), and protocols. The ${HOME}/.ssh/identity file is used by SSH1 only.

11.6.3   Configuring User Identity for SSH

Each user needs to have an RSA and DSA key pair to use for authentication purposes. These files are created in the ${HOME}/.ssh directory, which also contains other user-specific SSH configuration information. The following command creates the RSA keys:

```
# ssh-keygen -b 1024 -t rsa -f id_rsa
Generating public/private rsa key pair.
Enter passphrase (empty for no passphrase):
Enter same passphrase again:
Your identification has been saved in id_rsa.
Your public key has been saved in id_rsa.pub.
The key fingerprint is:
c1:a3:3e:07:e5:80:83:31:38:36:af:ff:09:c6:82:31 root@ns2
```

Next we create the DSA keys:

```
# ssh-keygen -b 1024 -t dsa -f id_dsa
Generating public/private dsa key pair.
Enter passphrase (empty for no passphrase):
Enter same passphrase again:
Your identification has been saved in id_dsa.
Your public key has been saved in id_dsa.pub.
The key fingerprint is:
b4:07:05:51:96:23:59:a2:92:fa:06:1c:c0:a2:99:d9 root@nec2
```

The number of bits in the key is specified in these examples for illustration purposes only. The default number of bits—1,024—is the recommended length for the keys.

In environments where the user's home directory is shared, and potentially open to access by other users, the SSH identity files in the ${HOME}/.ssh directory should be protected by a pass phrase to prevent unauthorized use if they are copied. Typing the pass phrase every time the key is required, however, can lead to strong objections from users. If too much effort is required with regard to supplying pass phrases, the users will simply stop using them, thus compromising security.

To solve this issue, SSH provides a "helper" program, ssh-agent, that allows the user to specify the identity key's pass phrase once, when the key is loaded into the agent with ssh-add. The agent is started as the parent of all processes in the user's session, and it creates well-known environment variables (SSH_AUTH_SOCK and SSH_AGENT_PID) that specify information about how to contact the agent. All SSH-aware programs will use the communication path defined (temporary sockets in /tmp) to contact the agent. This is shown in Figure 11–4.

The agent may execute a subcommand, in which case the environment variables are exported to the child process, or it may be run with command-line options to generate csh or sh (Bourne shell) formatted definitions for the environment variables. (In this case, the command is run with the shell's eval command, which causes the output of the ssh-agent program to be interpreted as shell commands. For example, use 'eval ssh-agent -s' for Bourne shell environments.) In this mode, the agent will terminate when the subprocess exits. When ssh-add is executed, it will load the SSH1 identity and SSH2 id_dsa and

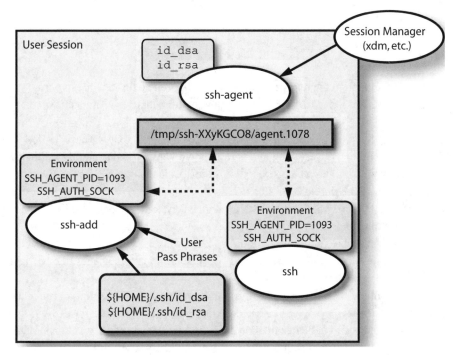

Figure 11–4 The SSH authentication agent

id_rsa private key files by default. The X Windows display manager, xdm, is set up to run the ssh-agent program as part of a GNU Network Object Management Environment (GNOME) or K Desktop Environment (KDE) session, or if X Windows is started with startx.

If the identity key files are protected by pass phrases, the user is prompted for the pass phrase, with either a text or X Windows-based prompt. The private identity keys are never made directly available; instead, the agent performs operations requiring them and sends the results over the communication channel. This preserves the integrity of the private keys.

11.6.4   SSH Host Keys, and Known and Authorized Hosts

Once the identity keys are created, we may connect to any remote hosts that might be available with SSH servers:

```
# ssh ns1
The authenticity of host 'ns1 (192.168.0.151)' can't be
established.
RSA key fingerprint is
dc:b6:4d:e4:92:84:20:0e:a0:8f:f6:53:0f:0e:7d:35.
Are you sure you want to continue connecting (yes/no)? yes
Warning: Permanently added 'ns1,192.168.0.151' (RSA) to the
list of known hosts.
Last login: Fri Mar  5 09:28:27 2004 from ns2.cluster.local
#
```

The process of logging in to the remote system via SSH has created a new file in our ${HOME}/ .ssh directory: the known_hosts file. Every unique host that we visit causes an entry to be placed in this file.

The known_hosts file contains information for the hosts that we have visited with the SSH client. These entries are very long and aren't shown here, but you should examine the file, just to see what they look like. Each entry contains the host name, the IP address, the type of key (ssh_rsa), and the RSA *public* key value itself.

The full set of hosts that are known to a given system is contained in all the user's known_hosts files, and in a global /etc/ssh/known_hosts file that is used system wide. Populating the global file with commonly accessed hosts will eliminate the need for the user files to maintain separate information, and will help eliminate messages like we saw when first connecting in the previous example.

In an environment like a cluster, with a fixed number of systems and a regular network configuration, an identical /etc/ssh/known_hosts file, containing the RSA *public* host keys from every system, might be installed on every system. However, to avoid invalidating user and system known_hosts key values, the host key sets themselves must be preserved across new system installations. (This can happen when spare nodes are swapped into the cluster as a result of a hardware failure. Also, to "reimage" a node with some of the installation tools may involve the tool running the key generation sequence as part of a standard postinstall script. This, of course, will result in different host keys for the system.) Collecting the host keys from the cluster's hosts and replacing them in /etc/ssh after a system is reinstalled can avoid messages warning of altered host keys as a possible result of man-in-the-middle attacks.

The error messages that are output when a host key does not match the expected value are intended as a security feature. This behavior is controlled by the configuration option StrictHostKeyChecking, which may be set to values of yes to output error messages and fail the connection on a mismatch, no to ignore mismatches and automatically update the database, or ask to prompt the user for the appropriate action. The ask setting is the default, but the correct setting for your cluster depends on your security requirements.

TIP   Collect the SSH host keys from all systems in your cluster and maintain them in a secure location. If a system is reinstalled, you can replace the original host key files to avoid invalidating clusterwide "known hosts" information.

11.6.5   Using the Authorized Keys File

Now that we have some idea of the role that keys play in the SSH authentication scheme, we can take advantage of another useful feature that allows users to log in to an account on another machine without reauthenticating. This ability is useful for system administrators using the root account on machines in the cluster, or for parallel tools (like PDSH, discussed in the next section) that use SSH as a transport to execute commands on multiple systems.

This feature involves the use of the ${HOME}/.ssh/authorized_keys2 file, which may contain the RSA *public* identity keys for multiple users. (Although the documentation does not mention it, the authorized_keys2 file appears to be available for use only with the SSH2 protocol version, whereas the authorized_keys file was the original name used by SSH1.) The SSH server on the remote system will allow connections to the local account by users whose identity key matches an entry in the account's authorized_keys2 file. A user whose identity is already authenticated with a particular key will not have to reauthenticate to access the remote system.

Setting up this access for the root account (or others) involves the following steps:

1. Generating the identity keys for the user account on each system
2. Adding the *public* RSA identity key for each system's user account into the an authorized_keys2 file
3. Distributing the authorized_keys2 file containing all user keys to the ${HOME}/.ssh directory on each system
4. Authenticating as the user in question and connecting to the remote systems

A simple example, involving the root accounts on two systems, follows:

```
login: root
password:
[root@ns1 root]# cd .ssh
```

```
[root@ns1 .ssh]# ssh-keygen -t dsa id_dsa

[ ... output deleted ...]

[root@ns1 .ssh]# ssh-keygen -t rsa -f id_rsa

[ ... output deleted ...]

[root@ns1 .ssh] scp id_rsa.pub root@ns2:/root/.ssh/rsapub_ns1
root@ns2's password:
rsapub_ns1 100% |************************|   219        00:00
[root@ns1 .ssh] ssh ns1
root@ns2's password:
[root@ns2 root] cd .ssh
[root@ns2 .ssh]# ssh-keygen -t dsa id_dsa

[ ... output deleted ...]

[root@ns2 .ssh]# ssh-keygen -t rsa -f id_rsa

[ ... output deleted ...]

[root@ns2 .ssh]# cat id_rsa.pub rsapub_ns1 > authorized_keys2
[root@ns2 .ssh]# chmod g-rwx,o-rwx authorized_keys2
[root@ns2 .ssh]# exit
[root@ns1 .ssh]# scp root@ns2:/root/.ssh/authorized_keys2 .
authorized_keys2 100% |************************|   438 00:00
[root@ns1 .ssh]# chmod g-rwx,o-rwx authorized_keys2
```

In this example we use the SSH secure copy (scp) command to move files back and forth via SSH. Notice that once the remote authorized_keys2 file was created, it was no longer necessary to authenticate ourselves as root to the remote system.

By logging in to an account that has SSH identity keys available, a user has authenticated himself to the local system and gained access to the SSH credentials (keys) for that account, contained in the ${HOME}/.ssh directory. With the user's RSA public identity key installed in the remote system's authorized_keys2 file, the user's identity is proved to the remote SSH server when the local private key successfully decrypts the challenges produced by the remote SSH server using the user's public key. If the process works properly, then no reauthentication is required.

Although the ability to save authentication operations and the associated password entry can save an immense amount of work and make automation of administration tasks easier, there are risks involved. If the root account is compromised on one system, then the "keys to the kingdom" are readily available. You should carefully evaluate the security risks associated with using this feature.

11.6.6   Fine-Tuning SSH Access

There are a number of SSH server configuration options, in `/etc/ssh/sshd_config`, that allow you to allow access selectively to the system that runs the server. You can control the hosts, users, and groups (primary groups only) that are allowed to connect to the server from remote clients. Example configurations for the `/etc/ssh/sshd_config` file on an administrative node are provided as follows:

```
AllowHosts        *@cluster.local
DenyHosts         *@10.0.2.* *@10.0.3.*
AllowUsers        root
AllowGroups       *
DenyGroupsusers
```

If any line denies access to a host, user, or group, then that line takes precedence over an `Allow*` configuration line. So even though the `AllowGroups` configuration line specifies a wildcard that matches all groups, the `DenyGroups` specification disables any user whose primary group is `users`. (It is unfortunate that the checking is limited to primary groups [the group specified in the `/etc/passwd` file], which limits the use of the group as an access control entity.) Another example is the `AllowHosts` configuration, which enables access for any system within the `cluster.local` domain, followed by the `DenyHosts` specification, which limits the host access to only a single network (the management network).

The SSH server allows the lists of strings to contain up to 256 members for the `Allow*` and `Deny*` lists. See the documentation for the SSH server for further information about configuring these options.

Finally, there are ways to execute customized commands and change SSH behavior in a user's session or globally. Those options include

- A per-user SSH client configuration file in `${HOME}/.ssh/config`
- A systemwide SSH client configuration file in `/etc/ssh/ssh_config`
- A per-user SSH client-executed file, `${HOME}/.ssh/rc`, which is executed just before the user's shell is started
- A systemwide SSH client-executed file, `/etc/ssh/sshrc`, which is executed just before the user's shell is started, but not if `${HOME}/.ssh/rc` exists
- A per-user environment variable definition, `${HOME}/.ssh/environment`
- The per-user `${HOME}/.shosts` file and `/etc/ssh/hosts.equiv`, which allow behavior similar to the BSD `rhosts` authentication, but do not use the `rlogin/rsh` authentication

With all this user-level behavioral modification for SSH, the system administrator needs an upper hand. If the `/etc/nologin` file exists, then only the `root` user is allowed access to the system. A cluster-wide `nologin` script can sometimes be a very useful thing. I discuss the implementation of such a thing, along with parallel command execution, in an upcoming section.

11.6.7 SSH `scp` and `sftp` Commands

SSH transport does not define file transport behavior, but there are two useful utilities that use the transport to do secure file copy and file transport operations: `scp` and `sftp` respectively. The `scp` and `sftp` commands both use a subsystem that is defined in the `/etc/ssh/sshd_config` file: `sftp-server`. The definition for this service is

```
Subsystem        sftp     /usr/libexec/openssh/sftp-server
```

Although `sftp` subsystem is a special case, it does use a general-purpose facility provided by the SSH server for creating subsystems, which allows the execution of a remote command. The command line

```
ssh -s <subsystem> ns1.cluster.local
```

executes the named subsystem on behalf of the user.

The `scp` command behaves in a fashion similar to the BSD `rcp` command, but uses the SSH transport to perform secure copies. The command will prompt the user for password information if it is required as part of the authentication process. The `scp` command, along with `ssh` and `sftp`, allows an option (`-i`) that specifies an alternate identification file (key) to be used for the operation.

We used `scp` in a previous example to move a *public* key file between systems. Please refer to this example for the command format. The `sftp` command operates in a manner similar to the familiar `ftp` utility. The major difference between these utilities lies in the ability to specify the remote user and system as part of the target file parameter, as in `root@ns2:/tmp/myfile`.

11.6.8 SSH Forwarding

With the SSH transport successfully installed and operating, it is possible to forward a TCP/IP port on one system to another port, either locally or on another system. The uses for this tend to be complex, so I touch only briefly touch on the capability here. SSH port forwarding, or tunneling, tends to be more of an issue for master nodes that must connect the cluster to the outside world, servicing users that want potentially unsecure services, such as X-Windows, available outside the cluster.

The forwarding operations take place outside the applications that are doing the communicating, so the applications themselves do not need to be modified. The system administrator may design and produce an environment that uses secure SSH transport without the implicit knowledge of the applications using it. This makes SSH a better choice than some other mechanisms like Kerberos, which require applications to "participate" in the infrastructure by explicitly calling library routines (requiring recompilation).

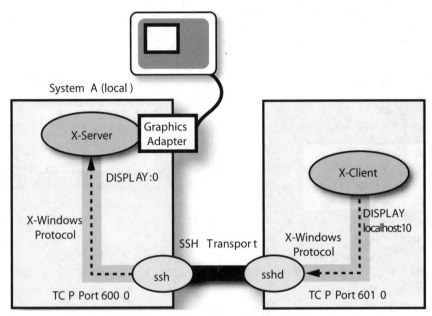

Figure 11–5 X-Windows protocol forwarding with SSH

First, for X-Windows forwarding, the option must be enabled on the server, and the Linux version disables it by default. In this case, the server will create a proxy connection to the user's local X Windows server. This is conditional on the DISPLAY variable being set in the local user's environment. Using this feature of SSH makes the communication between the X-Windows client on the remote host and the local X-Windows server secure, which is not normally the case. See Figure 11–5 for an example X-Windows forwarding configuration.

X-Windows forwarding is a special case of port forwarding, providing special support for the X-Windows system architecture and features like X authentication. The more general case of port forwarding with SSH allows you to create a secure connection from a local port to another port, either local or remote. It is also possible to create a secure connection from a remote port to a local port using another option.

The SSH command format for local port forwarding, when the client TCP port to be forwarded is on the local machine, is

```
ssh -L<Listen>:<host>:<port> <system>
```

Thus, if we wanted to connect the local port 2105 to the sendmail port (TCP port 25) on the local host, we could use

```
# ssh -L2501:localhost:25 localhost
```

```
Last login: Sun Mar  7 14:02:57 2004 from localhost
# netstat -an | grep 2501
tcp   0   0   127.0.0.1:2501    0.0.0.0:*              LISTEN
# ps -ef | grep L2501

root      16152 15946  0 14:02 pts/1    00:00:00 ssh \
-L2501:localhost:25 localhost

# exit
Connection to localhost closed.
#
```

As the netstat output from the previous command example shows, the SSH client is listening on the specified local port and will forward traffic to the SSH daemon on the specified target port—in this case, on the local system.

The connection will persist until the SSH client is terminated, which you can do with the kill command or, as shown in the example, by exiting the interactive session. The SSH client provides a -f option that instructs it to fork into the background, but this is intended for executing a remote command that has no output. If we try to use the option without a command, we get the following error message:

```
# ssh -f -L2501:localhost:25 localhost
Cannot fork into background without a command to execute.
#
```

This is annoying. To get around this behavior, we have to specify a command to satisfy SSH, but we want the command to do nothing for the duration of the connection. This is an example:

```
# ssh -f -L2501:localhost:25 localhost sleep 100000
# ps -ef | grep 2501 | grep -v grep
root      16377    1  0 14:56 ?        00:00:00 ssh \
        -f -L2501:localhost:25 localhost
# kill 16377
Killed by signal 15.
```

The nature of the interactive forwarding operation is such that we have to deal with "back-grounding" the SSH client in our sessions if we want to use forwarding as a user. If we attempt to log out of our session with active port forwarding, SSH will wait for the forwarded connections to terminate before exiting. The port forwarding configurations may be specified in the SSH configuration files if they are of a permanent, systemwide nature, so that they are reestablished and available for all users at system boot time.

SSH also allows forwarding ports "off system" to a remote target. This is still called *local* forwarding, because it is a *local* port that is forwarded for a *local* client. Any local program that connects to the "listen" port will have its traffic transparently and securely forwarded to the destination port on a remote system. As before, we need to deal with the backgrounding issue:

```
# ssh -f -L2501:localhost:25 ns1.cluster.local sleep 100000
# netstat -an | grep 2501
tcp       0       0   127.0.0.1:2501     0.0.0.0:* LISTEN
# ps -ef | grep 2501 | grep -v grep
root     16425     1  0 15:13 ?          00:00:00 ssh \
         -f -R2501:localhost:25 ns1.cluster.local
#
```

It is also possible to forward a remote port to a port on the local system using the -R option instead of the -L option. This is called *remote port forwarding*, and it creates a connection between a listen port on the remote system and the specified port on the local system:

```
# ssh -f -R25:ns2.cluster.local:2501 ns1.cluster.loal \
      sleep 100000
[root@ns2 root]# ssh ns1
Last login: Sun Mar  7 15:23:19 2004 from ns2.cluster.local
[root@ns1 root]# netstat -an | grep 25
tcp   0      0       127.0.0.1:25     0.0.0.0:* LISTEN
#
```

Configuration of SSH with regard to forwarding is quite complex, and I do not cover any more details here. See the man pages for ssh, sshd, ssh_config, and sshd_config for more details, including the creation of "gateway" systems.

11.6.9   SSH Summary

The main point of the discussion about SSH is that it provides a secure transport that you can use for remote access, remote command execution, and generalized remote services. This functionality is available inside the cluster, but may also be provided for *external* connections to the cluster's master nodes. Any number of previously unsecure services may be provided in a secure manner, with only one open port on the master nodes: the SSH port, 22.

The transition from BSD remote access services is made easier by similar functionality in SSH that is disabled by default. Once users are used to working with SSH, there is no need for the potentially insecure access services. The SSH transport forms a secure backbone for implementing both user and system-level access, and configuration options allow the system administrator great latitude in controlling the availability and behavior of the environment.

For use in your cluster, SSH is probably the best choice for remote access, because of its integration into the Linux distributions. The "out-of-the-box" configuration with Red Hat and derivatives is quite usable. You can add to SSH's usefulness for system administration by

- Populating /etc/ssh/known_hosts files inside the cluster
- Setting the appropriate value for the server's StrictHostKeyChecking option in your cluster's environment
- Collecting and restoring system host keys when systems are reinstalled
- Creating and distributing the root account's .ssh/authorized_users file

You will find that SSH is already assumed, or supported as an option, in a number of open-source system administration and monitoring tools that are available.

T I P   Use SSH as the basis for remote access to any new cluster installations. You can make any necessary transition from unsecure BSD services to SSH as slow as necessary, or choose the "total immersion" method—whatever fits your needs.

11.7 The Parallel Distributed Shell

A cluster may comprise several to several thousand systems. Performing the same operation manually on each system in a cluster can take a lot of time, and even automation or scripting of remote tasks can also suffer scaling issues. Unless you have worked in a cluster environment before, this problem might not even occur to you.

Consider, as an example, an automated process of getting the date from 100 systems in a cluster with a shell script. The script performs a remote login, gets the date information, then logs out and proceeds to the next system. Each `get` operation takes approximately three seconds (one second for login, one second for the `date` command, and one second to log out). If you believe my numbers, it will take a total of 300 seconds (five minutes) to get the date information from 100 systems—if no errors occur.

By the time a cluster reaches 500 or more systems, it will take 25 minutes for even the simplest operations to complete, and much longer for commands that require more time. Obviously, there needs to be a cluster-specific solution for this kind of system administration operation. We have a parallel environment, what about a parallel command tool that can execute a single command on multiple systems at the same time?

The PDSH is just such a solution. I automatically include it in my cluster environments. If someone hasn't seen it before, they immediately take a liking to it once they see its capabilities.

11.7.1   Getting and Installing PDSH

The PDSH software was written by Jim Garlick at Lawrence Livermore National Laboratory, and the home page for PDSH software has a brief description of its capabilities (`http://www.llnl.gov/linux/pdsh`). You may download PDSH from a public FTP site (`ftp://ftp.llnl.gov/pub/linux/pdsh`). Because PDSH is a relatively simple application, let's take the time to install the source RPM file and take a brief look at compiling RPM packaged software for the Red Hat environment.

PDSH is available from the FTP site in three forms: a compressed "tar ball"[1] (`pdsh-1.7-6.tgz`), a binary RPM package (`pdsh-1.7-6.i386.rpm`), and a source RPM-package (`pdsh-1.7-6.src.rpm`). One of the big contributions Red Hat has made to the Linux

---

1.   A reference to the tape archiver (tar) and a sticky little blob of files. The `.tgz` suffix indicates a tar archive compressed with GNU zip.

world is the Red Hat package manager or RPM software. This allows installation of binary packages, but also can easily configure, compile, and install *source* packages.

To install the PDSH source package, `pdsh-1.7-6.src.rpm`, all we need to do is execute the following command:

```
# rpm -ivh pdsh-1.7-6.src.rpm
```

The i option to `rpm` indicates an install operation, the v option indicates verbose output, and the h option causes the command to output a progress bar composed of "hash" marks or "#" as it performs the installation.

Installing the PDSH source RPM package as outlined here will place the package contents under the directory `/usr/src/redhat`. The `/usr/src` directory also contains the Linux kernel source tree, if it is installed. A diagram of the directory structure is shown in Figure 11–6. The directory structure shown is for the Fedora distribution, which has a kernel with a "native POSIX threads library," and thus the `.ntpl` suffix on the kernel source directory version.

The installation of the source RPM package places the `pdsh.spec` specification file under the `/usr/src/redhat/SPECS` directory and the `pdsh-1.7-6.tgz` file under the `/usr/src/redhat/SOURCES` directory. Up until a recent release, the source package building capability was part of the `rpm` command, but now it is located in a separate `rpmbuild`

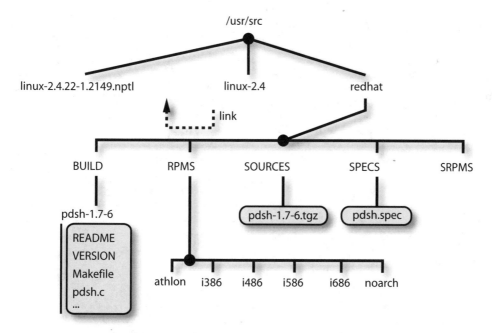

Figure 11–6 The `/usr/src` directory contents

command. To extract the source files from the archive `pdsh-1.7-6.tgz` to `/usr/src/redhat/BUILD`, execute the `rpmbuild` command with the `prep` option:

```
# rpmbuild -v -bp /usr/src/redhat/SPECS/pdsh.spec
```

This will create the source files from the tar archive.

If you examine the `pdsh.spec` file, you will see that it contains information about how to configure, build, install, and manage the PDSH software package using the standard environment provided by the package manager. The file contains sections that define the actions taken in each step (in the `%prep`, `%build`, `%install` portions of the file) along with other information used by the package manager. To execute the `prep` and `build` steps (but not `install`), you can use

```
# rpmbuild -v -bc /usr/src/redhat/SPECS/pdsh.spec
```

Finally, you can do the whole process, `prep`, `compile`, and `install` in one `rpmbuild` command line:

```
# rpmbuild -v -bi /usr/src/redhat/SPECS/pdsh.spec
```

The fact that a binary package is available for PDSH removes the need for you to compile the source package yourself, unless you want to make changes to the software's configuration.

The source packages do not show up in the RPM package database for the system on which they are installed. If you were to install both the `pdsh-1.7-6.i386.rpm` file and the `pdsh-1.7-6.src.rpm file`, executing

```
# rpm -qa | grep pdsh
pdsh-1.7-6
```

produces output that shows the installed *binary* package is the only one visible in the RPM package database. The files installed by the binary package are

```
# rpm -q --filesbypkg pdsh
pdsh                          /usr/bin/dshbak
pdsh                          /usr/bin/pdcp
pdsh                          /usr/bin/pdsh
pdsh                          /usr/man/man1/dshbak.1.gz
pdsh                          /usr/man/man1/pdcp.1.gz
pdsh                          /usr/man/man1/pdsh.1.gz
pdsh                          /usr/share/doc/pdsh-1.7
pdsh                          /usr/share/doc/pdsh-1.7/ChangeLog
pdsh                          /usr/share/doc/pdsh-1.7/DISCLAIMER
pdsh                          /usr/share/doc/pdsh-1.7/README
pdsh                          /usr/share/doc/pdsh-1.7/README.KRB4
```

It is possible to get the `rpmbuild` command to build a binary version of the RPM package, build both source and binary RPMs, and build only the source RPM version of the package with the following commands:

```
# rpmbuild -bb /usr/src/redhat/SPECS/pdsh.spec
```

```
# rpmbuild -ba /usr/src/redhat/SPECS/pdsh.spec
# rpmbuild -bs /usr/src/redhat/SPECS/pdsh.spec
```

The source RPM, if created, is placed under /usr/src/redhat/SRPMS and the binary RPM is placed under /usr/src/redhat/RPMS/<arch>, where <arch> is, by default, the processor architecture of the machine doing the compiling.

To save effort, you can install the source RPM; perform the prep, build, and install steps; create the binary RPM packages; and remove all the BUILD, SOURCE, and SPEC files with a single command:

```
# rpmbuild --rebuild pdsh-1.7-6.src.rpm
```

The RPM facility makes it fairly easy, although not necessarily trivial, to get software packages installed that are not part of the standard Red Hat Linux distribution and are not compiled for the hardware architecture that you are using. Be aware, however, that not all packages are available in RPM format. Most packages have dependencies that must also be installed, and not all packages are as simple to handle or as readily configured as PDSH.

11.7.2   Compiling PDSH to Use SSH

It turns out that we have to make some modifications to the "stock" PDSH package to get it to use SSH as the default remote shell. The default remote shell type is RSH, which means we have to enable the associated security risks. To use SSH, the necessary steps are

1. Installing the pdsh-1.7-6.src.rpm package
2. Configuring the pdsh.spec file to enable SSH as the remote shell
3. Compiling PDSH and producing a binary RPM package
4. Installing the new binary RPM package

Don't worry. This will be easy, and it is a great introduction to working with source RPM files. Locate the section in the specification file that matches

```
%build
%if %chaos
./configure --prefix=/usr --with-readline --with-elan
%else
./configure --prefix=/usr --with-readline \
        --with-machines=/usr/local/etc/machines
%endif
make
```

We want to change the line between %else and %endif to read

```
./configure --prefix=/usr --with-ssh=/usr/bin/ssh \
        --with-machines=/usr/local/etc/machines
```

Note that this is a single line—make the change with your favorite editor and save the file. The change is essentially replacing the `--with-readline` with `--with-ssh=/usr/bin/ssh`. Next, we want to build the binary RPM file, using

> # **rpmbuild -bb /usr/src/redhat/SPECS/pdsh.spec**

This will produce the new binary RPM file in `/usr/src/redhat/RPMS/i386`, with the original package's name.

Next, install the new binary RPM on the systems in your cluster that you wish to run PDSH. You might want to change the package name to differentiate it from the original `pdsh-1.7-6.i386.rpm` file. You can tell which remote shell is the built-in default, with

> # **pdsh -w foo -q | grep RCMD**
> RCMD_SSH

If the answer from this command comes back `RCMD_BSD`, then the changes did not "take" and PDSH is still using the BSD RSH remote shell mechanism, which is the original behavior. Make sure you installed the correct binary RPM file. I cover the options and use of PDSH in the next section. This example specifies a dummy system (`foo`) and tells PDSH to print current settings and exit without performing any actions.

11.7.3   Using PDSH in Your Cluster

The `pdsh` command will create multiple threads in its process, each of which will attempt to connect to a remote system specified in the command's options. The number of system connections at any one time is called *fan out*, and is specified by the `-f` option to the shell. It defaults to 32. Output from each system is prefixed with the system's host name:

> # **pdsh -w cs[01-02] date**
> cs02: Tue Mar 2 17:45:04 PST 2004
> cs01: Tue Mar 2 17:44:42 PST 2004

This output can, in turn, be piped to the `dshbak` command, which will sort the output from the client systems into blocks of adjacent output, removing the system tag from the front:

> # **pdsh -w nec[01-02] date | dshbak**
> ----------------
> cs02
> ----------------
> Tue Mar 2 17:45:23 PST 2004
> ----------------
> cs01
> ----------------
> Tue Mar 2 17:45:01 PST 2004

PDSH supports the specification of a set of systems, using ranges for the numerical suffixes. We discussed host naming conventions in Chapter 10. Choosing a consistent host name scheme can make it easier to use commands like `pdsh`, which rely on consistency in the host

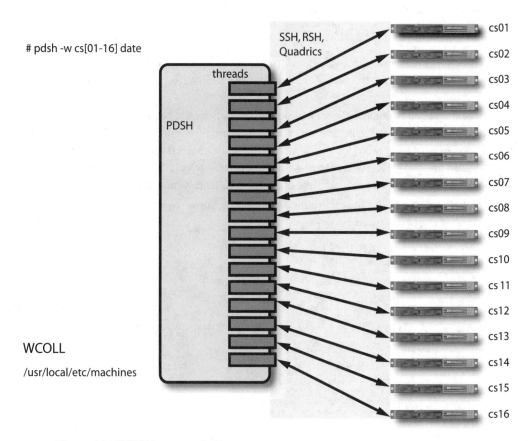

Figure 11–7 PDSH communication

name format. It is worth the initial design effort to save system administration effort on an on going basis. A diagram of PDSH is shown in Figure 11–7.

In the previous example, we specified a host range with the -w option—specifically, -w cs[01-02], which expands to the host names cs01 and cs02. Other range examples are -w cs[0-9] and -w cs[001-143,145,176]. It is also possible to specify more complex ranges, such as cs[01-05,09-20], and to exclude systems from the range with the -x option, as in -w cs[01-20] -x [06-09], which produces the equivalent to the range -w cs[01-05,10-20].

There are a number of ways to specify a default set of machines, so that you can issue the pdsh command with an associated remote command without specifying system name ranges with the -w option. The facilities are

1. Specifying the `-a` options, and the list of systems in `/usr/local/etc/machines` will be used; the `-x` option may be used in conjunction with the list from the `machines` file

2. Setting the environment variable `WCOLL` to point to a file containing a list of systems; the `-x` option may be used in conjunction with the list from the associated file

I usually set up shell command aliases that point to predefined files containing classes of cluster nodes: administrative nodes, compute slices, name servers, file servers, and so forth. In this way I can choose a base class of systems on which to execute a command, exclude any special cases with `-x`, and fire away. (The ability to make major mistakes in parallel is an exhilarating experience. This is a comment on my typing and error-checking ability, not on PDSH.)

PDSH can also run in interactive mode, prompting for a sequence of commands that are executed on the remote systems:

```
# pdsh -w cs[01-02]
pdsh> date
cs02: Tue Mar  2 19:27:01 PST 2004
cs01: Tue Mar  2 19:26:37 PST 2004
pdsh> cat /etc/issue
cs02: Red Hat Linux release 8.0 (Psyche)
cs02: Kernel \r on an \m
cs02:
cs01: Fedora Core release 1 (Yarrow)
cs01: Kernel \r on an \m
cs01:
pdsh>exit
```

This interactive mode proves useful for extended sessions on multiple systems.

11.7.4   PDSH Summary

PDSH is a very useful tool in any environment in which you want to execute identical commands on multiple systems at once. With a little adjustment to use SSH as the default shell (making note of the disclaimers in the PDSH documentation about SSH prompting for passwords and creating other output), PDSH can allow `root` to access any node in the cluster without explicit authentication. I think the extra work needed to use SSH is worth it.

The PDSH package includes the `pdsh` command, the `dshbak` output formatting tool, and a parallel version of the copy command, called `pdcp`, that uses the same mechanism as PDSH. If you are using a Quadrics QsNet interconnect with the Quadrics resource management software (RMS) package, PDSH will also interface to and use the QsNet interconnect, and will get system (resource) information from the RMS package. See the PDSH installation instructions and documentation for details on how to set up this feature.

11.8 Configuring DHCP

DHCP can automatically assign IP addresses to hosts at boot time based on broadcast requests from the DHCP client on those systems. In addition to dynamically assigning IP addresses, which can drive system administrators and network monitoring applications crazy, DHCP can statically assign IP addresses *and* distribute networkwide configuration information to the clients it services. The service is based on UDP datagrams, using UDP port 68 by default.

When properly configured, DHCP is an essential single-point administration tool for a cluster environment. In addition to the benefits we have already mentioned, the DHCP server can handle the boot-time installation requests from client system's boot ROMs supporting pre-execution environment (PXE) and Internet Bootstrap Protocol (BOOTP) standardized requests. The DHCP server initially responds to a client's broadcast request for information, and manages initial boot information requests and the assigned IP address "lease" given to the client thereafter.

The Red Hat DHCP server-side implementation is the daemon `/usr/sbin/dhcpd`, and the client-side is implemented by `/sbin/dhclient`. The configuration files are `/etc/dhcpd.conf` and `/etc/dhclient.conf` respectively. The DHCP server, once a configuration file is created, may be enabled and started in the traditional manner:

```
# chkconfig dhcpd on
# service dhcpd start
```

Once started, you can check for error messages from the daemon in the `/var/log/messages` file.

11.8.1   Client-side DHCP Information

DHCP client information is kept under `/var/lib/dhcp`, particularly the `dhclient-<device>.leases` file, which contains useful information about the client's current lease for a given Ethernet interface (in this case, the file is `/var/lib/dhcp/dhclient-eth0.leases`):

```
lease {
    interface "eth0";
    fixed-address 192.168.0.103;
    filename "pxelinux.0";
    option subnet-mask 255.255.255.0;
    option routers 192.168.0.1;
    option dhcp-lease-time 86400;
    option dhcp-message-type 5;
    option domain-name-servers 192.168.0.151,192.168.0.152;
    option dhcp-server-identifier 192.168.0.151;
    option nis-domain "local.cluster";
    option nis-servers 192.168.0.151,192.168.0.152;
    option ntp-servers 192.168.0.151,192.168.0.152;
    option broadcast-address 192.168.0.255;
```

```
option host-name "cs01";
option domain-name "cluster.local";
renew 0 2004/3/7 17:13:47;
rebind 1 2004/3/8 05:02:33;
expire 1 2004/3/8 08:02:33; }
```

Although looking at a client's information assumes that there is a functional server to distribute it, we put the cart before the horse here to see just what kind of information DHCP can distribute to clients.

Notice the information contained in the listing of the client's lease file, along with the information about the lease times: IP address, host name, subnet mask, default gateway (router), NIS domain, NIS servers, NTP servers, and DNS servers. Additionally, a file is specified (pxelinux.0) that will be supplied to this system if it makes a PXE boot request to the DHCP server. I cover more about system installation using this feature in an upcoming chapter, but suffice it to say that this file will be loaded and executed by the local system in response to a PXE request.

To enable the use of DHCP on a given interface, the interface's network initialization file, /etc/sysconfig/network-scripts/ifcfg-eth0 in this case, eth0 needs to contain a BOOTPROTO=dhcp definition:

```
# Accton|SMC2-1211TX
DEVICE=eth0
BOOTPROTO=dhcp
HWADDR=00:10:B5:7C:70:42
ONBOOT=yes
TYPE=Ethernet
```

This tells the network start-up script that the DHCP client, dhclient, should be invoked as part of the network initialization.

The DHCP client will receive information from the DHCP server, and will *automatically generate system configuration file information from it.* The dhclient process executes the /sbin/dhclient-script file, which can generate configuration files like /etc/resolv.conf, /etc/yp.conf, and /etc/ntp.conf. In addition to generating system configuration files from the DHCP server's reply, the script can run the domainname and hostname commands, and install default network routes.

The DHCP client may need configuration information provided so that it can properly deal with multiple network interfaces. For example, a system may wish to have the DHCP information from one interface take precedence over information from other interfaces. Certain system parameters, like the host name, can only have one value. Controlling which parameters are accepted from the DHCP server by the DHCP client is allowed. If you are having issues resolving the DHCP information on a client system, see the man page for dhclient and dhclient.conf.

The dhclient-script itself is called from dhclient with an environment containing variables that may be used by the script in the configuration of the network services, including the reason the script was called, the interface name, and the IP address assigned to the client. The behavior of the dhclient-script may be extended by rewriting the script or creating the files /etc/dhclient-enter-hooks and /etc/dhclient-exit-hooks, which are executed before and after the DHCP configuration is performed respectively. See man dhclient-script for details. Figure 11–8 depicts the major components of the DHCP subsystem on the server and the client.

The Linux dhclient has some limited support for dynamic DNS updates, which are necessary to maintain host name-to-IP address mappings if you allow IP addresses to be dynamically assigned. In general, you should probably avoid using dynamic IP addresses in your cluster, but this is no reason to forego DHCP itself. See the man page for dhclient.conf for more information on configuring dynamic DNS.

Now that we have examined the client-side information distributed by DHCP (and even more is possible), we need to discuss configuring the DHCP server and making the information available to the clients. This is done in the next section.

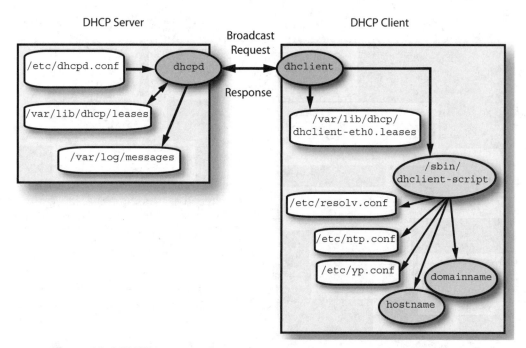

Figure 11–8 DHCP components

11.8.2   Configuring the DHCP Server

Configuration of the DHCP server may be quite involved, but it doesn't have to be. A single server may listen to multiple subnets, clients may be gathered into groups that share configuration information, and global parameters may be specified for each subnet and group of clients. This minimizes the amount of typing necessary to get a functional configuration file.

Once the basic functionality is tested, the remaining systems in the cluster may be added to the appropriate portions of the configuration file. A skeleton example of the /etc/dhcpd.conf file is

```
authoritative;
ddns-update-style                    none;
default-lease-time                   2592000;
use-host-decl-names    =             true;
boot-unknown-clients  =              true;


shared-network cluster {

        subnet 10.1.0.0 netmask 255.255.248.0 {

                option domain-name-servers   10.1.0.151,10.1.0.152;
                option domain-name           "cluster.local";
                option nis-domain            "local.cluster";
                option subnet-mask           255.255.248.0;
                option nis-servers           10.1.0.151,10.1.0.152;
                option ntp-servers           10.1.0.151,10.1.0.152;
                option routers               10.1.0.254;
                option broadcast-address     10.1.7.255;

                group physical-hosts {

                    host ns1 {
                            option host-name "ns1";
                            hardware ethernet 00:06:25:04:FF:4C;
                            fixed-address 10.1.0.151;
                    }
                    host ns2 {
                            option host-name "ns2";
                            hardware ethernet 00:06:25:04:DE:4E;
                            fixed-address 10.1.0.152;

                    }
                }

                group PXE-clients {

                    allow booting;
                    allow bootp;
```

```
filename "pxelinux.0"; # Relative to /tftpboot!

host cs01 {
        option host-name "cs01";
        hardware ethernet 00:20:78:11:3C:F1;
        fixed-address 10.1.0.101;
}
host cs02 {
        option host-name "cs02";
        hardware ethernet 00:01:02:03:EB:9B;
        fixed-address 10.1.0.102;
}
}

}

subnet 10.2.0.0 netmask 255.255.248.0 {
        option routers          10.2.0.254;
        option subnet-mask      255.255.248.0;
        option broadcast-address 10.2.7.255;

        host dn01 {
                option host-name "dn01";
                hardware ethernet 00:20:78:23:32:FF;
                fixed-address 10.2.0.101;
        }
        host dn02 {
                option host-name "dn02";
                hardware ethernet 00:20:78:23:31:FC;
                fixed-address 10.2.0.102;
        }

}

subnet 10.3.0.0 netmask 255.255.248.0 {
        option routers          10.3.0.254;
        option subnet-mask      255.255.248.0;
        option broadcast-address 10.3.7.255;
}

}
```

This configuration file is a slight modification from the configuration file that I use in my home network. The global definitions for the entire DHCP server are outside this "block." The authoritative definition in the global parameters allows the DHCP server to send negative acknowledgments (NAKs) to clients—something that your local IT department would frown upon if this server were on a corporate network. (Make sure that there is no "leakage" from your cluster's networks into the external networks. If there is, someone will eventually come knocking at your cubicle. You also want to make sure there is no leakage *into* your cluster for DHCP, especially from Microsoft DHCP servers, which have the nasty habit of answering all requests on the subnet, regardless of whether they "own" the client. If I had a nickel for every time this has happened ...) The global parameters also allow booting unknown clients (without a MAC address entry in the configuration file) and force the use of the declared host names (`use-host-decl-names`).

There are three subnets, all sharing the same physical, switched Ethernet network. Hosts may belong to any of the networks by configuring their Ethernet interface or interfaces with a "primary" network, and then adding any necessary network aliases. The infrastructure services, like DNS, NIS, NTP, and boot installation, are all provided on the `10.1.0.0` management network. It turns out, by the way, that the current `dhclient` does *not* handle aliased network interfaces properly. I am still investigating this.

The enclosing `shared-network` definition is required to allow the DHCP server to deal with having only one physical interface, but being able to access three subnets (a "shared" interface). Inside the `shared-network` block are three `subnet` blocks, each with their own parameter definitions. The first `subnet` block has two client `group` definitions. The first group is a set of hosts that is not expected to be doing remote network-based installations—they are the infrastructure servers. The second group, `PXE-clients`, is configured to return the file `/tftpboot/pxelinux.0` to the client's PXE boot requests.

The client definitions contain declarations of the host name, hardware (MAC) address, and IP address associated with each system. Because the initial DHCP requests are based on broadcasts, it is the client's MAC address that identifies the specific interface that is making the request. This means that all MAC addresses for all interfaces must be collected and entered into the configuration file before you can expect DHCP to assign IP addresses and host names properly in a "fixed" configuration like this.

Although the DHCP service is important to the cluster's operation, it is not critical as long as the address allocation scheme is not dynamic. Even if a server fails, clients will hang on to their previous lease information, and because this is static, failure to renew a lease will not result in bad configuration data. It may be desirable to distribute the DHCP service between two or more servers if a cluster gets large enough.

The DHCP servers may be put into "partner" mode to provide fail-over between a primary and a secondary server, but configuration of that functionality is beyond the scope of this discussion. See the `man` page for `dhcpd.conf` for more information on configuring fail-over between two DHCP servers.

DHCP can make our system administration life a lot easier by automatically specifying the "personality" for systems in the cluster. When we begin to discuss installation of compute slices, we will need a way to clone systems, yet ensure that the unique information that makes them separate network entities can be easily managed. DHCP will help with this task.

11.9 Logging System Activity

In any single-system environment, the use of activity and error logging is essential to managing the system effectively. The word *managing*, in this case, means both debugging problems and monitoring system activities for patterns that may need attention or corrective action. In a cluster environment, the amount of log information that gets generated is proportional to both the default log levels *and* the number of systems in the cluster.

Now, anyone who has managed more than two systems knows it is just not practical to go running back and forth between systems, manually comparing log files and error messages. If you agree that the model of a cluster operation involves creating a single, integrated system solution, then you must realize that a reasonable goal is managing all the log information from the cluster's individual systems in a cohesive, central manner. This discussion covers ways of using the software packages that are supplied "out of the box" with Linux distributions. "Add-on" tools from the open-source community for system management are discussed in a later chapter.

The Red Hat distributions and derivatives supply the standard Linux system logging daemon, `syslogd`, and two useful tools—`logrotate` and `logwatch`—to help with log file management. There are a number of other more specific tools, such as Web-server log analyzers, that are available from the open-source community. Integrating the `syslog` facility on multiple systems in a cluster, and using the standard log management tools, is the goal for the current discussion.

The architects of the BSD version of the UNIX operating system realized that there was a need for a standardized and *central* system facility that allowed the operating system, subsystems, applications, and users to generate and log informative messages. At the same time, they realized that any central system logging facility needed to be flexible enough to handle different message priorities and permanent log file destinations for the messages. The Linux system logging daemon, `syslogd`, is compatible with the behavior of the familiar UNIX subsystem.

One useful change made to the logging architecture under Linux is the addition of a separate daemon, `klogd`, to handle logging of messages generated by the kernel. These messages are a special case, because they require special processing to deal with converting numerical addresses from the kernel to symbolic output readable by humans. The combined logging daemons are collectively called the `sysklogd` system. Indeed, the manual page for `syslogd` and `sysklogd` are synonymous, whereas the newer `klogd` has a separate entry.

The output files from both of these daemons are essential in debugging software issues with the kernel and subsystems of Linux. The flexibility of the system is such that the level of information available may be adjusted up or down depending on the operating needs of the system manager. Under default operation, the `klogd` output is disabled. Let's examine the basic operation of the system and put it to use in our cluster.

11.9.1   Operation of the System Logging Daemon

The behavior of the `syslogd` daemon is controlled by its configuration file, `/etc/sys-log.conf`. This file contains "rule" specifications with the general format *<selector> <action>*, with the two fields being separated by one or more whitespace characters. The *<selector>* field is further defined as two tokens separated by a "." character: *<subsystem>.<priority>*.

Currently allowed literal values for the *<subsystem>* token are `auth`, `authpriv`, `cron`, `daemon`, `kern`, `lpr`, `mail`, `mark`, `news`, `syslog`, `user`, `uucp`, and the values `local0` through `local7`. Possible literal values for the *<priority>* token are `debug`, `info`, `notice`, `warning`, `err`, `crit`, `alert`, and `emerg`. The subsystem tag specifies the subsystem that produced the message, and the priority specifies the importance level of the message.

The default behavior of the `syslogd` daemon is to log all messages for a given rule and associated priority or higher, and the others are ignored. In addition to simple rule format, multiple selector fields for a given action may be separated by a ";" character, and multiple facility values for a single priority are separated by a "," character.

The *<action>* token may be either a file (full pathname, starting with a "/" character), a named pipe (a path to the `fifo` file, with "|" as the first character), a terminal device (such as /dev/console), a comma-separated list of users who will receive the message if they are logged in, every user that is logged in (specified with an "*" character), or a remote machine ("@" character followed by the name of the remote host with remote logging enabled). At this point, an example will serve us well. The default `/etc/syslog.conf` file included with the Fedora distribution contains the following definitions:

```
# Log all kernel messages to the console.
# Logging much else clutters up the screen.
#kern.*         /dev/console

# Log anything (except mail) of level info or higher.
# Don't log private authentication messages!
*.info;mail.none;authpriv.none;cron.none /var/log/messages

# The authpriv file has restricted access.
authpriv.*      /var/log/secure

# Log all the mail messages in one place.
mail.*          /var/log/maillog

# Log cron stuff
cron.*          /var/log/cron

# Everybody gets emergency messages
*.emerg              *
```

```
# Save news errors of level crit and higher in a special file.
uucp,news.crit          /var/log/spooler

# Save boot messages also to boot.log
local7.*        /var/log/boot.log
```

Several notes about the rules specified in this default configuration file will help clarify the use of selectors, priorities, and actions.

1. The logging of kernel messages to the console is disabled (contained in a comment line), but would normally go to the system console.
2. Everything at info level or higher is logged to /var/log/messages, except for mail, authpriv, and cron messages, which are excluded by using none for the priority level in the selector's priority value.
3. The information from authpriv, cron, and mail is separated into three separate log files via three separate rules that specify the log file target as the action.
4. Any emerg messages are sent to all users that are currently logged in to the system.
5. Critical messages generated by the uucp and news subsystems are directed to the /var/log/spooler file.
6. Messages from the system boot process are directed to /var/log/boot.log by the start-up scripts, which use the initlog command and a default logging level of local7, as specified in the /etc/initlog.conf file.

The last note is interesting. The start-up scripts in /etc/init.d use a common definition of shell functions that is sourced from /etc/init.d/functions. This file defines success and failure functions that the init scripts can use to log start-up messages via the initlog command, which defaults to the local7 facility and a notice priority. This is a great example of Linux system architects using the syslog facility in a creative way enabled by its designers.

Although the initlog command is primarily intended for use by the system start-up scripts, there is another facility that we can use to our advantage: the /sbin/logger command. This command provides a -i option to add the PID to the log message, the -p option to specify a numerical or subsystem.level value, and a -t option to allow specifying a tag that is placed in the message. Let's see what an example command does:

```
# logger -i -p local0.info -t TAG-YOURE-IT 'Test message!'
# tail -1 /var/log/messages
Mar  8 21:29:20 ns2 TAG-YOURE-IT[19958]: Test message.
```

We can certainly use this facility in the custom scripts that we create if we ever need to generate a permanent record of the script's actions.

11.9.2   Kernel Message Logging

Now that we have a brief understanding of how the `sysklogd` system works, we can put it to use tracking the system activities in our cluster. Before continuing on to the configuration of remote logging with `syslogd`, we need to attend to one detail that we have neglected: the kernel logging daemon, `klogd`.

The kernel produces error messages in the `/proc/kmsg` file, which is an interface to the kernel message buffer. It is the job of the `klogd` process to detect and read any messages, properly format them by translating numerical addresses to   symbolic values using the appropriate `/boot/System.map-<version>` file, and finally directing the output to either a file, the system console, or `syslogd`.

Kernel error messages, or recoverable failures called *oops*, are most likely to occur when new functionality is added to the kernel, either by patches or by software from sources other than the Linux current operating system distribution version. You might need to add new driver modules, enable an experimental kernel feature, or patch a portion of the kernel to meet user-specific needs. All of these activities disturb the status quo and add the potential for kernel error messages. In this situation, it is a good idea to be able to capture any messages and debug information generated by the kernel software failures. (This is especially true if you are working with an ISV or a software developer who will want feedback on their software.)

Configuring and enabling `klogd` will enable you to log the messages generated by the kernel and choose exactly how much information is generated, along with where it ends up, either on the local system console, in a log file, or both. If one of the targets is a serial console, and you have serial port switches, such as those made by Cyclades, that are capable of logging serial console output to central files via NFS, then it may not be necessary to direct the output to a log file on the local system as well. But then kernel crashes, panics, and oops behave in mysterious ways.

To enable `klogd`, you must modify the contents of the `/etc/sysconfig/syslog` file, which contains two variable definitions that set the daemon start-up options for the `ksyslogd` subsystem—one for `syslogd` and one for `klogd`:

```
# Options to syslogd
# -m 0 disables 'MARK' messages.
# -r enables logging from remote machines
# -x disables DNS lookups on messages received with -r
# See syslogd(8) for more details
SYSLOGD_OPTIONS="-m 0"
# Options to klogd
# -2 prints all kernel oops messages twice; once for klogd
# to decode, and once for processing with 'ksymoops'
# -x disables all klogd processing of oops messages entirely
# See klogd(8) for more details
KLOGD_OPTIONS="-x"
```

As you can see from the variable definition for KLOGD_OPTIONS, the processing of kernel oops messages is disabled by default. If you alter the definitions of the variables, you must execute

    # **service syslog restart**

to get the new options passed to the daemon. This action will stop and restart both the syslogd process and the klogd process.

11.9.3   Enabling Remote Logging

As mentioned previously, to enable sending logging information to a remote system, you may replace the "action" portion of the rule in /etc/syslog.conf with a token of the form @*<system>*—for example, @ns1 to send the messages associated with a particular rule to ns1. The remote logging feature uses UDP port 514 (see the definition in /etc/services).

But sending the messages out into the ether is only half of the required action. After all, this is a *client–server* software architecture. You must configure the remote syslogd to *listen* for and accept network messages. This is easy to do, by adding the -r option to the definition for the SYSLOGD_OPTIONS variable in the /etc/sysconfig/syslog file (as listed earlier). Once the changes are made, restart the syslogd daemon (and by default its klogd daemon brother) with

    # **service syslog restart**

A diagram of the ksyslogd subsystem and its components is shown in Figure 11–9.

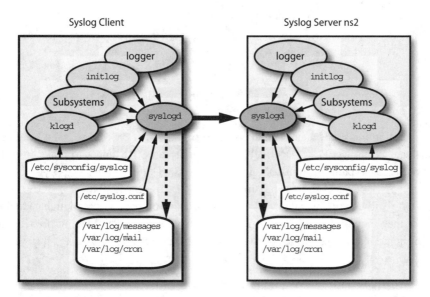

Figure 11–9 ksyslogd subsystem components

There are a number of design choices you must make with regard to providing remote logging services for the cluster's logging client systems.

- What logging information is important to me?
- How much disk space do I need on the logging servers?
- Do I need to enable kernel messages?
- How many remote logging servers are necessary?
- How is the log data divided between the servers?
- What is the mixture between remote and local message logging?

Once you have decided which messages to log remotely, you can craft the client's /etc/syslog.conf file to send the appropriate messages based on subsystem and priority. An example client configuration might be

```
# Log kernel messages to the remote server, 'klogd -c 4'
# will also display messages above this level to the console.
kern.err        @ns1.cluster.local
# Log anything (except mail) of level info or higher locally.
# Don't log private authentication messages!
*.info;mail.none;authpriv.none;cron.none /var/log/messages
# The authpriv file has restricted access.
authpriv.*      @ns2.cluster.loal
# Log all the mail messages in one place.
mail.*          /var/log/maillog
# Log cron stuff
cron.*          /var/log/cron
# Everybody gets emergency messages
*.emerg         @ns2.cluster.local
# Save news errors of level crit and higher in a special file.
uucp,news.crit      /var/log/spooler
# Save boot messages also to boot.log
local7.*        @ns1.cluster.local
```

This configuration file sends client kernel errors to ns1.cluster.local and local authorization messages (this would be a perfect place to apply an SSH tunnel to make sure that all information is encrypted in transit), and boot messages to the remote syslog server ns2.cluster.local. Configuring the KLOGD_OPTIONS variable in /etc/sysconfig/syslog with the option value -c 4 sends kernel error messages (and higher) to the console, where they may be logged by a serial port console switch. The logging priority "name" maps to the numerical values extracted from /usr/include/sys/syslog.h (lower values are higher priority):

```
#define LOG_EMERG    0        /* system is unusable */
#define LOG_ALERT    1        /* immediate action */
#define LOG_CRIT     2        /* critical conditions */
```

```
#define LOG_ERR       3              /* error conditions */
#define LOG_WARNING 4                /* warning conditions */
#define LOG_NOTICE    5              /* normal but significant */
#define LOG_INFO      6              /* informational */
#define LOG_DEBUG     7              /* debug-level messages *
```

As you can see from the example, it is relatively easy to set up remote logging on a large number of clients and collect gigabytes of log information on the logging servers. The design decision was made to separate the kernel messages from the other logging output by sending them to a separate remote `syslog` server. This may not be necessary on a production cluster that is running qualified applications on fully supported operating system releases.

11.9.4   Using `logrotate` to Archive Log Files

Once you begin collecting log information from remote systems, the storage requirements on the logging servers will increase, often dramatically. (This is when having a separate /var partition for the Linux system can pay off. If, for some reason, there is a runaway client that is logging large amounts of messages, the associated log file will grow to fill the partition. With a separate /var partition, the full file system may not stop other essential system activities.) The amount of log information you need to keep will depend on the stability and security posture of the environment in which you work. A useful tool for managing log file revisions is /usr/sbin/ logrotate, which automates the rotation, compression, and removal of log file information once it is collected.

The /etc/logrotate.conf file contains the configuration information for logrotate, and in the same manner as the xinetd facility, has an include statement for a directory that contains individual configuration files for separate log information.

```
# see "man logrotate" for details
# rotate log files weekly
weekly
# keep 4 weeks worth of backlogs
rotate 4
# create new (empty) log files after rotating old ones
create
# uncomment this if you want your log files compressed
#compress
# RPM packages drop log rotation information into this
# directory
include /etc/logrotate.d
# no packages own wtmp -- we'll rotate them here
/var/log/wtmp {
    monthly
    create 0664 root utmp
    rotate 1
}
# system-specific logs may be also be configured here.
```

The configuration information in /etc/logrotate.d is added by individual packages that require log management. This is the *real* location to examine for examples of log management configuration files. The configuration information for syslogd log files is contained in /etc/logrotate.d/syslog:

```
/var/log/messages /var/log/secure /var/log/maillog          \
/var/log/spooler /var/log/boot.log /var/log/cron            \
{
    sharedscripts
    postrotate
      /bin/kill -HUP `cat /var/run/syslogd.pid 2> /dev/null` \
                    2> /dev/null || true
    endscript
}
```

The default configuration file for the named daemon, /etc/logrotate.d/named is

```
/var/log/named.log {
    missingok
    create 0644 named named
    postrotate
        /bin/kill -HUP `cat /var/run/named/named.pid 2> \
                    /dev/null` 2> /dev/null || true
    endscript
}
```

These two configuration files illustrate some of the features of logrotate: the ability to execute scripts before and after the log is "rotated," control over how the log file gets created, and the ability to handle multiple files (or wild cards) in a single configuration. Normally, the prerotate and postrotate command scripts are executed for each file specified or for those that match the wild card for the configuration. The sharedscript definition indicates that the two scripts, if present, should only be executed once for the entire set of files associated with the configuration.

In both these examples, the postrotate script executes a command that causes the daemon to close open files and restart. For modern daemons, this will cause open files, like the log, to be closed, the daemon configuration to be reread, and the log file to be recreated. Some older daemons may not behave in such a civilized manner, and so there are a number of configuration options that can help deal with custom situations. (In this case, the procedure might be to stop the daemon completely, rename the log file to the new name, then restart the daemon. It may be necessary to create the default log file for the daemon before restarting it.) See the man page for logrotate for more details.

In the default files, the rotation takes place on a weekly basis, as specified in the main configuration file, /etc/logrotate.conf, which governs the behavior of the tool *once it is run by some external scheduler* (see information on cron that follows). In a busy cluster, this can result in huge log files for logs associated with frequently performed activities, like DNS lookups or user authentication information. You may need to consider dropping back to a daily rotation.

The activities of `logrotate` are scheduled by the `cron` subsystem,[2] out of the `/etc/cron.daily` directory, which is specified along with hourly, weekly, and monthly directories in the `/etc/crontab` file. The `/etc/cron.daily/logrotate` file merely calls the `logrotate` command with its configuration file on the command line. The `logrotate` command keeps its state information (when files were last rotated) in the `/var/lib/logrotate.status` file, which contains entries similar to

```
logrotate state -- version 2
"/var/log/messages" 2004-3-7
"/var/log/secure" 2004-3-7
"/var/log/boot.log" 2004-3-7
"/var/log/cron" 2004-3-7
```

A diagram of the "`logrotate`" facility and associated components is shown in Figure 11–10.

11.9.5   Using `logwatch` Reporting

The `/usr/sbin/logwatch` tool allows general-purpose reporting generated by scanning log information. It is highly configurable and is able to scan the currently active log files, as well as the compressed archives. The configuration information for `logwatch` is located in the `/etc/log.d` directory, and the configuration file, `/etc/log.d/logwatch.conf`, is a link to the file in the `/etc/log.d/conf` directory. The default configuration information for the reporting is

```
LogDir = /var/log
MailTo = root
Print = No
#Save = /tmp/logwatch
Range = yesterday
Detail = Low
Service = All
```

The default configuration settings will search log files in the specified directory, generate and mail the report to `root`, will not print the report to `stdout`, will not save the report output, will search only the prior day's information, and will produce a low-resolution report for all defined services. The entire system is implemented in Perl, and may be extended to meet your specific needs.

---

2.   One note on the default `cron` configuration is needed. The default is to mail the output of `cron` jobs to the user specified in the `MailTo` clause in `/etc/crontab`. This, of course, depends on having `sendmail` activated to handle the mail, which will *silently* stack up waiting for delivery otherwise. This dependency on local mail operation, and by association the `sendmail` daemon, is a problem with a lot of UNIX and Linux subsystems.

Logging Server

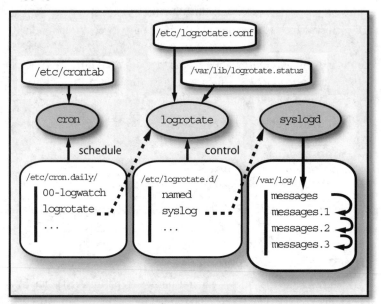

Figure 11–10 Software components for the `logrotate` facility

The `logwatch` utility seems to work with varying degrees of success on different versions of the Red Hat and Fedora distributions. An example of using `logwatch` follows:

```
# logwatch --service sshd --range all --archives --print

################### LogWatch 4.3.2 (02/18/03) ##############
        Processing Initiated: Wed Mar 10 00:33:38 2004
        Date Range Processed: all
      Detail Level of Output: 0
          Logfiles for Host: ns1
##############################################################
--------------------- SSHD Begin -----------------------
SSHD Started: 1 Time(s)
Users logging in through sshd:
   root logged in from hpxw4100.lucke.home (192.168.0.111)
using password: 1 Time(s)
**Unmatched Entries**
RSA1 key generation succeeded
RSA key generation succeeded
DSA key generation succeeded
--------------------- SSHD End ------------------------
##################### LogWatch End #######################
```

Several other open-source log-watching and analysis tools are available. One such tool is `wots` (`http://www.vcpc.univie.ac.at/~tc/tools/`) and another is `swatch` (`http://swatch.sourceforge.net`).

11.9.6   An Example Subsystem Logging Design

Without looking too hard, you might notice that configuration information is not provided for managing either the Kerberos `kadmind` or `krb5kdc` log files, and `/var/log/kadmind.log` and `/var/log/krb5kdc.log` respectively. This is an important point to remember: `logrotate` configuration files may not be specified for all subsystems that you enable as part of your cluster. Let's pick on our old friend Kerberos and craft a logging configuration for the two daemons as a final exercise.

First, we need to research the logging and control behavior of the associated Kerberos daemons. Second, we need to adjust the behavior of the system logging facility to meet our needs for this information. Third, we need to create the `/etc/logrotate.d/krb5kdc` and `/etc/logrotate.d/kadmind` configuration files with our favorite text editor (one of the 436 different editors available on Linux).

On investigation, we notice that the default logging behavior of the Kerberos daemons is specified in `/etc/krb5.conf`:

```
[logging]
 default = FILE:/var/log/krb5libs.log
 kdc = FILE:/var/log/krb5kdc.log
 admin_server = FILE:/var/log/kadmind.log
```

The fact that the `syslog` facility is not being used may or may not represent a security decision, because we don't see any warnings in the Kerberos documentation, let's decide to go ahead with the changes. The man page for `krb5.conf` shows that the subsystem does allow for configuration of `SYSLOG` as a target for logging instead of `FILE`.

Now we need to determine what `syslogd` subsystem and priority we want to use for logging, and whether we want to separate the information into one or more log files that are distinct from `/var/log/messages`. The man page for `krb5.conf` tells us that if we use `syslogd` and do not specify a subsystem and priority, the defaults are `auth` and `err` respectively. Let's make the choice to use the "Local0" subsystem, so that we can separate the Kerberos information into a separate file.

Before we completely commit the systems to these changes, we need to ensure that the `Local0` service is not in use for something already (like the `Local7` subsystem is used for Linux boot messages). Once we have verified the safety of using `Local0`, we may proceed. The information in the Kerberos configuration file is changed to

```
[logging]
 default = SYSLOG:INFO:LOCAL0
 kdc = SYSLOG:INFO:LOCAL0
 admin_server = SYSLOG:INFO:LOCAL0
```

The next step is to add the following information to the `/etc/syslog.conf` file on the KDCs:

```
# Kerberos specific logging to remote server
Local0.* @logserver.cluster.local
```

Don't forget to restart the `syslog` service on the KDCs to activate the changes:

```
# service syslog restart
```

This will now route the client's `Local0` messages to the remote log server. On the logging server, we need to direct the Kerberos messages into a log file by adding a configuration rule to the `/etc/syslog.conf` file:

```
# Kerberos messages get their own local log file
Local0.* /var/log/Kerberos
```

Again, don't forget to restart the `syslog` service on the log server:

```
# service syslog restart
```

Now we need to set up the `logrotate` subsystem on the log server to handle the new file. Because we are adding a file to the `syslogd` suite, we can just modify the `/etc/logrotate.d/syslog` file to add the new log file to the standard processing:

```
/var/log/messages /var/log/secure /var/log/maillog        \
/var/log/spooler /var/log/boot.log /var/log/cron          \
/var/log/Kerberos {
    sharedscripts
    postrotate
        /bin/kill -HUP `cat /var/run/syslogd.pid 2> \
            /dev/null` 2> /dev/null || true
    endscript
}
```

We can also test the path between the remote client and the logging server before we restart the Kerberos daemons:

```
# logger -i -t KERBEROS_TEST -p local0.err 'Message from KDC1'
```

If the message comes through on the remote log server, we can restart the Kerberos daemons to start using the new logging target:

```
# service krb5kdc restart
# service kadmin restart
```

This is a simple walk-through for adding remote logging streams into your cluster's central logging scheme. You should carefully design the additions to the logging facilities before committing the changes. Design twice and implement once.

11.9.7 Linux System Logging Summary

Utilizing the default Linux logging tools involves specifying options to the individual subsystems that implement a specific logging strategy for your cluster. The facilities provided by `syslogd` and `klogd` allow either local or remote logging of messages from subsystems or custom scripts. In this way you can capture whatever informational messages you might require to manage or debug your cluster.

Once the log information is captured to log files, Linux provides the ability to manage the log files by compressing them and maintaining a predetermined number of on-line versions. The `logrotate` facility allows daily, weekly, or monthly rotation of individual log files, with or without compression, so you can adjust the management frequency to meet the specific needs of your cluster. Further archival actions are left as an exercise for the system administrator.

The amount of information accumulated in the log files is too much to analyze manually. The `logwatch` tool may be used to scan the information and summarize it. Customizing the scanning behavior allows you to pick and choose the messages to include in the summary information.

A logging strategy should include the configuration of the basic tools to implement the system administration policies for log information. The design information for your cluster should include information about the configuration of the standard log management subsystems and additional log management software.

11.10 Access and Logging Services Summary

This chapter has been an infrastructure marathon. We covered user and group permissions, remote access with SSH, parallel commands with PDSH, installing and building source RPM packages, Kerberos authentication, configuring DHCP, system logging strategies, and system log file management. This is a wide range of possible services and configuration examples, but we have still only scratched the surface of what Linux has to offer.

There are still as many infrastructure design possibilities as there are system architects to create them. This is one of the beauties of Linux—that there is always more than one way to solve a problem. The more familiar you are with the offerings, and the more you are able to expand your knowledge base, the more creative the solutions that are open to you.

The infrastructure services discussed in this chapter and the previous one are the basis for the higher level services that I cover in the chapters to come.

Installment Plan: Introduction to Compute Slice Configuration and Installation

Chapter Objectives

- Discuss the requirements for configuring software on a cluster's compute slices
- Describe choices for cluster compute slice operation
- Compare network-based system installation tools
- Introduce the `pxelinux` boot tool
- Describe the installation and use of Red Hat `kickstart` for installation
- Introduce some of the concepts necessary for NFS diskless clusters

With infrastructure nodes firmly in place, available storage for saving system configuration information, and active networks, we are ready to begin installing the cluster's compute slices. Because the compute slices (or "worker" nodes) usually far outnumber the other system types in the cluster, we need to be efficient and apply large-scale administration tactics to the effort. This chapter discusses several of the tools and methods for installing several to several hundred compute slices.

12.1 Compute Slice Configuration Considerations

If you ever discuss the integration of a cluster with someone who has never worked in a large-scale system environment, there are two possible reactions that frame the spectrum. When you try to describe the task at hand, you may encounter the "that-doesn't-sound-so-hard" reaction. On the other hand, if the person has *any* system administration experience at all, they may be able to relate their experience to what you are doing. In that case, you will get the "are-you-crazy?" reaction.

327

As with most things, the truth lies somewhere between the two extremes. Building a cluster is not easy, but neither is it impossible. A lot of people have done it, have done it successfully, and continue to do it year after year. You can too.

If you are already a cluster expert, I don't expect that you will be reading this book. If you are building your first cluster, you may not know how or where to start the process, once you have made some guesses about the infrastructure you might need. As you gain experience, you will know the technologies and methods that work, and you will continue to use and adapt them.

The best thing to realize is that you *will* discover things of which you were unaware or that don't work as planned as the project progresses. It is best to resign yourself to that, up front, and recognize that you may need to adopt an incremental approach to building the cluster environment. There isn't (yet) an all-in-one software environment that allows the complete construction of a cluster's software environment without some custom system engineering effort.

When I mention an "incremental approach," I am suggesting that you implement the various software components in "layers," adding functionality (and complexity) one step at a time. Once the current environment is verified and the configuration is captured, then add another component, verify it, and continue. Eventually, you should run out of components. (Do not take the approach of "stacking cubes of Jello," which is so tempting. In other words, don't install the software, light it up, and move on with no testing. Following this procedure is somewhat like stacking Jello cubes—you might get a temporarily stable configuration, but the slightest jolt will jiggle the whole stack back to randomness.)

For example, once the expected infrastructure services are in place, move on to getting the system installation process for the rest of the cluster implemented. Once you can install (replicate) systems easily, begin to add and activate the other required functionality to the core configuration. This is the approach I will take in this chapter toward installing the compute slice operating system configuration.

12.2 One Thousand Pieces Flying in Close Formation

In Chapters 8, 9, and 10, I presented low-level Linux services that enable us to support the compute slices we are preparing to install. The obvious starting point is to enable the infrastructure servers that will be needed to bring up the rest of the cluster's systems. We need to have the basic infrastructure—like shared storage, networking, remote access, authentication, and other "enablers"—in place to continue. Refer back to Infrastructure Implementation Recommendations on page 221 for a recommended installation order.

It is much the same as building a good-size, client–server desktop environment. The same level of detail is necessary, and the same level of complexity (plus a little) is present. As we choose software components and administration practices, we need to have some goals in mind. It also doesn't hurt to have some pretty sound large-scale system administration philosophies in place.

Some possible targets for the overall cluster's final software environment might be

- *Reliable*—The system behavior must be predictable.
- *Scalable*—Software systems must scale to support the final number of cluster systems. This includes the infrastructure and administrative tools, as well as the applications that we expect the cluster to run.
- *Verifiable*—We must be able to confirm that the system is working properly and to pinpoint areas that are affecting the other goals.
- *Manageable*—We must be able to administer all the components of the environment to meet the other goals for the cluster.
- *Supportable*—We must choose software components that fit our organization's support requirements.

We are attempting to meet some of these requirements with the installation of replicated infrastructure services and mirrored disk resources. We have to consider the infrastructure and administrative nodes as "support" for the remainder of the cluster, and they are necessarily different in some ways from the compute slices.

But what is it that we are really doing when we choose a software configuration for the compute resources that make up the majority of the cluster? The answer is, we are trying to create a group of systems that behaves as if it is a *single system* to the users and the applications that utilize it. Let's focus on the word "single" for a while.

12.3 The Single-System View

Current industry terminology refers to *scaling up* versus *scaling out* for expanding a set of compute resources. *Scaling up* refers to adding CPUs, memory, and capability to a single system to increase its resources and response to its user's needs. *Scaling out* refers to a multiple-system approach—adding individual systems to a shared resource pool. A cluster of systems expands the available resources that would previously have been limited by a single system's maximum configuration, but still should provide a "single-system view" of those resources, at a potentially lower cost.

If we need to provide a single-system view of a particular set of resources, we might expect that the solution's behavior in terms of performance, availability, and management might need to imitate a single system. Whenever we make choices about implementing portions of our cluster, we need to have this "single-system view" in mind. This is actually one of the most difficult concepts to understand and apply to the type of large-scale system administration efforts required in clusters.

In a perfect world, the operating system and software that we select for a cluster environment would allow us to have

- A single installation process
- A single boot process
- A single, identical set of infrastructure services

- A single system administration process
- A single view of common storage
- A single, consistent set of user accounts
- A single set of shared devices
- A single unified view of the network
- A single application environment

In other words, we need to pursue our cluster with single-minded resolve, engineering the whole solution to appear as if it were a single system from the outside.

Although there is continuing research into an integrated environment like this, and there is a preliminary release of software available, this environment still takes a level of software development expertise to implement that is beyond our capabilities as beginning cluster builders. The environment to which I am referring is the single system image (SSI) for Linux clusters, which may be found at http://openssi.org. For now, the principles involved are exactly what we want to use, but the software is still in a preliminary state.

You should carefully examine the overview information from the OpenSSI Web site. It details some of the developments that are included in the OpenSSI environment—developments that we have to "emulate" with our cluster's software configuration. The beauty of Linux is the ability to create environments like OpenSSI from open-source components, and to make them available to the general community at no cost. I can assure you that I will continue to watch this Web site with high hopes.

Until the OpenSSI environment matures a little more, however, it is just tantalizingly out of our reach. Let's continue on and examine what needs to be present in our compute slices to approximate a unified, single-system environment.

12.3.1   Shared System Structure, Individual System Personality

From a practical standpoint, we can view our multiple cluster compute slices as absolute copies of one another—clones. Sharing operating system software structure (a common set of installed packages) across identical hardware configurations allows us also to share administrative processes and be assured that the systems will behave the same. After all, within a set of systems with an identical hardware configuration, the operating system configuration and management process should be identical. If they are not, then we need to correct the situation or create a new category.

This is not quite true. If you install an operating system on a particular hardware configuration, then copy it to another identical piece of hardware, they may be identical *until you need them to boot and be present in a network*. At some point, the identical software structure needs to be given a small but unique set of configuration information to differentiate it from all other systems in the network. This is minimal information, such as a host name and IP addresses, but the system is no longer 100% identical to its clone. (I will avoid the annoying trend to assign human traits and behaviors to collections of hardware and software. This is not a matter of soft-

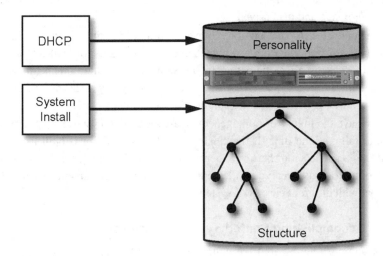

Figure 12–1 System personality and structure

ware "nature versus nurture.") This relationship of "personality" to "structure" is shown in Figure 12–1.

One way to think of this situation draws on terminology from the object-oriented programming world. In that view, there are "classes" of objects—in this case, systems—that share a set of base-level characteristics. Objects are created, or "derived," from base classes possessing the basic characteristics shared by all members of the class, then are extended with any special characteristics required by the application that is using the object. The object is part of a cohesive whole that exists to perform some useful function for its users.

Like the software objects in our analogy, our compute slice systems have a basic software structure and a set of inputs and outputs that we may consider an "interface" to the cluster environment. Understanding the requirements of our system objects, and their interface to the environment, gives us a model for replicating them and creating automated processes for managing them. It also defines the set of services that must be present to support the required inputs and make use of the outputs.

The custom data, or "personality," of each system is minute when compared with the overall quantity of data in the system's operating system software. After all, how many configuration files would need to be changed, by how much, on a system to make it participate in the network? If you consider the client-side configuration data necessary to use the network and infrastructure services like `ksyslogd`, NTP, DNS, NIS, and SSH, it is really quite small.

A compute slice should be able to boot, get most of its personality from a central service, like DHCP, and immediately begin participating in the cluster environment. We might have to install some custom scripts manually that automatically adapt the configuration based on the system's host name or IP addresses, but our goal is to make the changes identical on each node.

By using single-point administration techniques, we can keep the adjustments to the system's configuration automatic and data driven.

This is a good time to point out that your goal, if at all possible, is to have identical hardware and identical software on *all* the compute slices and spares in your cluster. If you have different classes of systems all participating in the same cluster environment, the management complexity and the chance of "interesting" failure modes go up. This is one place where a homogeneous solution is a simpler, safer solution.

You may have the luxury of homogeneous hardware in your cluster if you are allowed to build the entire thing at one time. If the cluster is built in phases, or is built from "reclaimed" hardware, having a single set of hardware across the cluster is unrealistic. If you do have a mix of hardware configurations, then you will need to use system management and installation techniques that deal with different classes of systems.

12.3.2   Accomplishing Shared System Structure

One way to accomplish the "shared" structure for a compute slice is to copy the complete configuration on each node from a "golden" or prototype system. The systems behave as if they were sharing a common set of information, but there are multiple local copies, not a single, central version. As you might recognize, there are version control issues with this approach. All copies of the data *must* remain synchronized.

Linux supports a number of system installation tools that can address creating identical configurations at the initial system installation. These tools may be package based, like Red Hat's `kickstart` tool, or they can be file-based, like the more general-purpose `SystemImager`. There are advantages and disadvantages to both types of tools.

A package-based installation method like `kickstart` provides a nice, modular way to install software—provided the software is already part of a package. One little-realized flaw is the repeated execution of the package installation and configuration scripts on *every* system at *every* installation. This overhead takes time and may create scaling issues. This installation approach is flexible; works well in small, simple clusters; and can be modified to avoid some of the negative issues mentioned.

The "system image" installation methods, like `SystemImager`, can copy and replicate existing system installations. The approach is extremely flexible, but still can suffer from scaling issues on the installation server. It is possible to copy, store, and replicate any system configuration (including faulty ones) easily once it is initially built on a "golden" system. It is even possible to make changes to a configuration tree and update associated systems without a complete reinstall.

Another approach to shared structure that is used in some clusters truly shares a single system structure between multiple compute slices: a diskless configuration. Linux readily supports a remote root file system, shared via a networked file system such as NFS. The compute slices boot the Linux kernel over the network and then share an NFS file system that contains the system libraries, executables, and configuration information needed by the individual systems.

Advantages to this approach include reliability improvements resulting from no local disks, a single-system image to manage with no local copies, and true single-point administration. Disadvantages include possible scaling issues, lack of "standard" Linux diskless environments (requiring custom work to adapt and implement), and reliance on Linux's NFS server implementation (which is still lacking features).

12.3.3   Compute Slice Software Requirements

The trick to keeping compute slice installation manageable is using tools that allow automated installation. There is really no way that we can justify performing a manual installation on multiple compute slices, even if we managed to kick off multiple installations in parallel. There is still the matter of feeding floppies, CD-ROMs, and user input to the installation process.

One issue that we must address is the question: Just what needs to be loaded on a compute slice? The answer to this is: Only the necessary software, and nothing more. The reasons for this are (1) keeping the installation time short, (2) reducing the amount of network traffic required on a per-node basis, (3) reducing the load on the installation servers, and (4) reducing the complexity (and therefore the possible failure modes) on the compute slices.

Each application environment is different, but the software set needs to include the kernel, specialized hardware drivers (HSI, network, and so on), the required system libraries, system commands (shells, `ls`, `grep`, `awk`, and so forth), system monitoring tools, system management tools, application components (libraries, scripts, executables), HSI libraries, and any other specifically identified packages (licensing software, data access, authentication, and so on). It takes a concerted effort to trim the unnecessary software to keep the system "footprint" small, but it is worth it.

Along with automating the installation, we need a facility to allow booting the system and kicking off an unattended installation—running diagnostics—when we specifically need a special system boot (and *only* if requested). If a compute slice fails, we need to "reimage" it quickly to determine whether it was a hardware failure or a software issue. If the system fails again, it needs to be replaced, repaired, and reimaged.

The less time the installation process takes, the faster the cluster can be upgraded. Many commercial clusters have maximum installation time specified in their contractual requirements. The more flexible the boot environment, the easier it is to use some of the network-based installation and diagnostic tools at our disposal.

12.4 A Generalized Network Boot Facility: `pxelinux`

Systems that have either BOOTP or DHCP capabilities built into their system start-up ROMs can broadcast a request on a network connection for boot service. (The Linux `dhcpd` server implements both BOOTP and DHCP boot protocols. Another protocol, PXE, is also frequently available in client boot ROMs.) A DHCP server listening on the local LAN receives the request and returns client information, including the name of a boot file and the client's IP address, to the requestor. Also included in the response packet is the IP address of the DHCP server, and potentially the IP address of another server that actually handles the boot request file transfer.

For an example of the information that is returned to the client by the DHCP server, see Client-side DHCP Information on page 307. This example DHCP client information contains the boot file name `pxelinux.0` provided by the DHCP server, which is the `pxelinux` network bootloader file. The `pxelinux` bootloader is part of the `syslinux` package (available at `http://syslinux.zytor.com`) that is used to create compact Linux bootable floppies, and includes `isolinux` for creating bootable Linux CD-ROMs. This utility allows us to create a general-purpose network boot menu for selecting different network-based installation mechanisms.

Although you may not need something this general, it can allow selecting between Red Hat's standard installation utility, the Red Hat `kickstart` service, or `SystemImager`. The ability to select different boot processes is ideal if you are trying to choose a boot installation method for your cluster. Instead of limiting the boot choice to a single file specified by DHCP, `pxelinux` enables either a default boot or selection of the method from a menu.

An example of the DHCP server configuration necessary to support booting is shown in the example `dhcpd.conf` file listed in Configuring the DHCP Server on page 310. The PXE client group in the configuration file contains the necessary configuration information, including the bootloader file. Once the file is specified to the client, the client requests the file from the `tftpd` server, loads it into the client's memory, and executes it.

The bootloader then handles the user interaction, allowing selection of a kernel and `initrd` to use for the remainder of the boot process. The bootloader is responsible for passing the specified parameters to the kernel. Once the kernel and `initrd` are loaded into memory, the bootloader jumps to the kernel to start system execution and Linux takes it from there. The `pxelinux` bootloader replaces the disk-based bootloaders like `lilo` and `grub`. The DHCP network boot process and its components is shown in Figure 12–2.

12.4.1   Configuring TFTP for Booting

First, it is important to understand that TFTP, in general, is a large security hole. It can allow arbitrary, unauthenticated access to any file on your system unless properly configured. You should restrict access to the `tfpd` daemon on the boot servers to the management LAN only. (You can do this with the `/etc/hosts.allow` and `/etc/hosts.deny` files, which control the TCP wrapper behavior. You may also restrict the access via the `xinetd` configuration file with the `only_from` configuration option. This allows you to specify a network address or a range of hosts that will be accepted for access.) Another feature that increases the security level is to use the `chroot` feature of the TFTP server, which limits the daemon's access to the directories below a prespecified point in the file system hierarchy.

The `tftpd` daemon is started by `xinetd`, but the service is disabled by default. The configuration file is `/etc/xinetd.d/tftp`. I usually make two modifications to the configuration file: (1) enable the service and (2) increase the verbosity of output to the `syslogd` process.

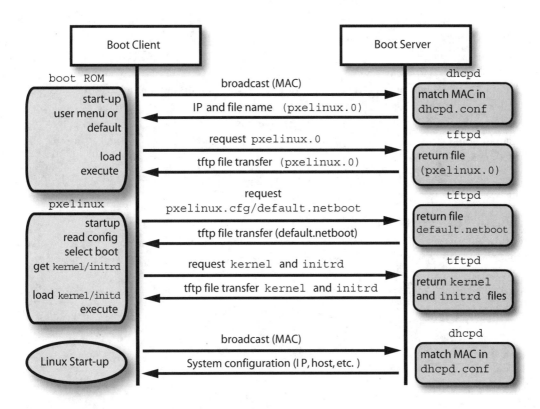

Figure 12–2 The network boot process with `pxelinux`

The increased message level allows me to track the files and activity being handled by the daemon. The modified configuration file is

```
# default: off
# description: The tftp server serves files using the trivial
# file transfer protocol.  The tftp protocol is often used to
# boot diskless workstations, download configuration files to
# network-aware printers, and to start the installation
# process for some operating systems.
service tftp
{
        socket_type       = dgram
        protocol          = udp
        wait    = yes
        user    = root
        server            = /usr/sbin/in.tftpd
        server_args       = -v -v -v -s /tftpboot
        disable           = no
```

```
per_source        = 11
cps      = 100 2
flags             = IPv4
}
```

Enabling additional message output from tftpd is important, not only for tracking normal activity, but because the file names that are requested will all be relative to the /tftpboot directory, which is where the daemon is constrained by the -s /tftpboot option in the configuration file. Even understanding that this is the case, it can be difficult to make sure that the files are actually available and that you are specifying the correct path to DHCP.

Don't forget to restart the DHCP daemon after making the changes to the configuration file:

```
# service dhcpd restart
```

The best way to ensure that you are accessing the correct files is to test from a potential client using the TFTP client software:

```
# cd /tmp
# tftp ns2
tftp> get pxelinux.0
Received 10205 bytes in 0.4 seconds
tftp> get pxelinux.cfg/default.netboot
Received 1289 bytes in 0.3 seconds
tftp> quit
```

Once you are sure that TFTP allows you to access the files properly, you can add DHCP to the mixture and start testing a client boot.

12.4.2   Configuring the pxelinux Software

The pxelinux package requires you to place the pxelinux.0 file somewhere that tftpd can find it, and to specify the proper path to it in the dhcpd.conf file. In addition to the boot file, there is a configuration directory, pxelinux.cfg, that pxelinux will access once it is started. This directory contains configuration information that determines the behavior of pxelinux with respect to a particular system or group of systems by linking a system identifier to a configuration file unique to the particular system, or group of systems, being booted.

To differentiate the booting behavior for clients, the pxelinux package searches for links (or files) in the configuration directory that match some portion of the hexidecimal IP address of the requesting system. The link names must be 8.3 compatible (in other words, no more than eight characters in the file and three in the extension), which is why the configuration directory is named pxelinux.cfg, for example. I choose to use soft links, because it is possible to have a single configuration file that the links target, reducing the chance of version mismatches between separate files.

The pxelinux bootloader looks first for the whole network address in hexidecimal. If the link is not found, then it removes one character from the right of the hex address and looks again. This process continues until a match is found or the search fails. As an example, let's take the host address 192.168.0.111. This would convert to hexidecimal C0.A8.00.6F if we preserve the octet-based formatting. The link for this file would be named C0A8006F after removing the dots.

You can see from the searching order that the pxelinux software first looks for C0A8006F, followed by C0A8006, C0A800, C0A80, C0A8, and so on, until it runs out of characters. (You can see this process by watching the verbose output from TFTP in the /var/log/messages file.) This allows you to specify a single link that would match only the network portion of the address. For searching efficiency, I choose to create a link for every system, and use a script named make_links to create them from a list of addresses:

```
#!/bin/bash -x
SCRIPT="default.netboot"
if [ -n "${1}" ]; then
        SCRIPT="${1}"
fi
for HEXIP in $( sed 's@#.*$@@' < IPS.hex )
do
        ln -s "${SCRIPT}" "${HEXIP}"
done
```

A partial list of the client's hexidecimal addresses fed to the script is in a file I call IPS.hex:

```
C0A80067     # 103
C0A8006D     # 109
C0A8006F     # 111
```

This is, admittedly, a simple-minded approach, with a minimum of error checking. Some industrious person could write a Perl script that does the whole operation and performs the proper amount of error checking without too much trouble.

12.4.3   The pxelinux Configuration Files

Now we have DHCP pointing to TFTP, pointing to the pxelinux.0 file, which will try to access /tftpboot/pxelinux.cfg to find the links that we have been discussing. The next step is to create the configuration files that drive the bootloader behavior. The bootloader will drop back to a default file, called default in the configuration directory, if it cannot find a match for a hexidecimal IP address. The contents of my default file simply specifies a boot from the local disk:

```
default linux
label   linux
        localboot 0
```

The links in the configuration directory all point to a file called `default.netboot` (only the link name needs to be 8.3 compatible). This file contains the following:

```
#  Remember everything is relative to /tftpboot !
#
default local    #  Uninterrupted network boot does this label
serial  0,38400n8       #  Serial port at 38400 Baud
                        # 8 bits no parity 1 stop bit
prompt  0      #  Will stop if Ctrl and Alt is held down or
                # <Caps Lock> or <Scroll Lock> enabled
F1       help.txt          # Will display help if a function
F2       help.txt          # key is pressed at the boot: prompt
F3       help.txt
F4       help.txt
F5       help.txt
F6       help.txt
F7       help.txt
F8       help.txt
F9       help.txt
F0       help.txt


label    linux9.ks
         kernel rh9.0/vmlinuz
         append vga=extended load_ramdisk=1 \
             initrd=rh9.0/initrd.img \
             ks=nfs:192.168.0.110:/kickstart9.0/

label    linux9.in
         kernel rh9.0/vmlinuz
         append vga=extended load_ramdisk=1 \
             initrd=rh9.0/initrd.img
label    linux.fedora
         kernel fedora/vmlinuz
         append vga=extended load_ramdisk=1 \
             initrd=fedora/initrd.img
label    linux.si
         kernel si/kernel
         append vga=extended load_ramdisk=1 prompt_ramdisk=0 \
             initrd=si/initrd.img root=/dev/ram rw \
             ramdisk_blocksize=4096
label    linux.pxes
         kernel pxes/vmlinuz
         append ramdisk_size=32768 ro video=vesa vga=0F0F \
             initrd=pxes/initrd.img root=/dev/ram rce=1 pd=1 \
             csn=192.168.0.110

label    local
         localboot 0
```

When a system makes a DHCP or BOOTP boot request, it gets the `pxelinux.0` file, which will continue to a local disk boot unless the `Ctrl` or `Alt` key is held down when `pxelinux` gains control. If the boot is interrupted, a prompt is output, which waits for a selection matching one of the labels in the configuration file. If a link is missing for a particular hexidecimal address, the default behavior is to perform a boot from the local disk.

Pressing `F0-F8` will output a nice color menu that lists the options. The menu information, with color attributes (control characters are prefixed with "^"—for example ^L is `Ctrl-L`) flanking the text, is located in a separate text file called `/tftpboot/help.txt`:

```
^L
^O79
  Available options for the boot are:

    linux9.ks    Do a kickstart installation of Red Hat 9.0
    linux9.in    Do a manual Red Hat 9.0 installation
    linux.fedora Do a manual Red Hat Fedora installation
    linux.si     Do a system image installation of Red Hat 9.0
    linux.pxes   Boot PXES thin client
    local        Boot from local disk

  Enter a selection to continue the boot process.
^O09
```

Because I am continually experimenting with new operating system versions and diskless environments (such as `pxes`), this facility serves me well. I can easily add a new boot option to the menu, plug in a new directory underneath `/tftpboot`, populate the kernel and `initrd` for my boot option, and be up and running in a very short time.

Even if someone stumbles into the network boot option by accident, the normal behavior is to boot from the local disk unless the process is interrupted. This helps prevent accidental installations. I can choose between `kickstart`, `SystemImager`, or the standard Red Hat network installation process from the `pxelinux` menu. The configuration of the TFTP directory and the `pxelinux` bootloader files is shown in Figure 12–3.

You may notice that none of the RPM packages for either the interactive Red Hat installation or the `kickstart` installation are present under this directory tree. If you go back to the `linux9.ks` label in the `pxelinux` configuration file, you can see that a kernel parameter specifies `/kickstart9.0` as the `kickstart` directory for this installation method. See the following section for details on this installation method and the contents of this directory.

The `SystemImager` directory, `si`, contains the special kernel and `initrd` file for that installation method. Another file, `boel_binaries.tar.gz`, provides the RAM-based operating system with tools used in the installation. See Using the SystemImager Software on page 351 for coverage of the configuration and operation of `SystemImager`.

The `pxelinux` bootloader may be viewed as adding another "layer" to the boot installation process. This extra step provides the ability to interface to other installation methods that

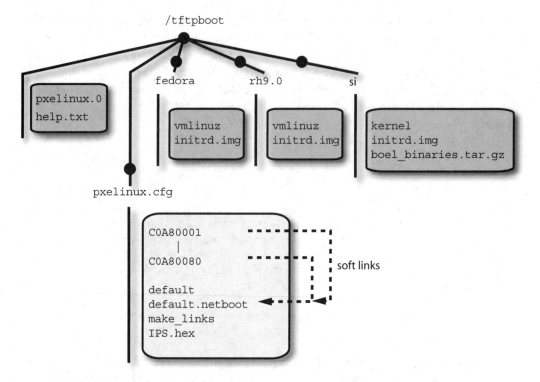

Figure 12–3 The /tftpboot directory with pxelinux configuration

might be used in your environment. If you settle on one installation method for your cluster, the intermediate step may be unnecessary. The basic configuration of the DHCP and TFTP server software is similar, no matter whether you choose to use pxelinux or go directly to SystemImager or kickstart.

12.5 Configuring Network kickstart

The Red Hat installation tool, anaconda, provides a cohesive way for the user to use a point-and-click interface (or a VGA text-based one) to step through the Linux installation process. The tool saves the configuration information for a system installation in the /root/anaconda-ks.cfg file. This file may be used to automate the installation process for other systems.

In addition to the kickstart file that is produced by anaconda, it is possible to create a configuration file manually with a text editor or to use the Red Hat tool called redhat-config-kickstart if a graphical interface is desired. The graphical tools, including anaconda, do not expose the full functionality of the kickstart configuration file. An example kickstart file from a system with a RAID 1 system device is

```
install
cdrom
lang en_US.UTF-8
langsupport --default en_US.UTF-8 en_US.UTF-8
keyboard us
mouse generic3ps/2 --device psaux
xconfig --card "Intel 810" --videoram 16384 --hsync 30-80   \
      --vsync 56-85 --resolution 1024x768 --depth 24         \
      --startxonboot  --defaultdesktop gnome
network --device eth0 --bootproto dhcp
rootpw --iscrypted $1$CvYYIEvU$2dTwrsY7nJ9JALZrKmia7.
firewall --disabled
authconfig --enableshadow --enablemd5
timezone America/Los_Angeles
bootloader --location=partition --append hdd=ide-scsi rhgb
clearpart --linux
part raid.8 --size=100 --ondisk=hda --asprimary
part raid.9 --size=103 --ondisk=hdc --asprimary
part raid.12 --size=75701 --ondisk=hdc
part raid.11 --size=75701 --ondisk=hda --asprimary
part raid.15 --size=509 --ondisk=hdc
part raid.14 --size=509 --ondisk=hda
raid /boot --fstype ext3 --level=RAID1 raid.8 raid.9
raid / --fstype ext3 --level=RAID1 raid.11 raid.12
raid swap --fstype swap --level=RAID1 raid.14 raid.15
%packages
@ everything
kernel
grub
%post
```

Note that the partitioning statements in the file have been uncommented from the automatically generated file. They would normally be set up to preserve the existing partitions on the target disks. This file may be fed to the installation process via a floppy, CD-ROM, or a network access.

12.5.1 The `kickstart` File Format

If you look at the example `kickstart` file, you will see several statements that divide the file into sections: a "command" section, followed by `%packages`, `%pre`, and `%post`. The ordering of the sections is important, although certain information may be specified in any order. The `%pre` and `%post` sections may be defined in any order, as long as they are at the end of the file, following `%packages`.

The command section has a large number of options possible, and in the example file we have specified an `install`, which will reload the system from the specified source: `cdrom`. (The possible source media are CD-ROM, local disk, NFS, FTP, and HTTP. You may need to provide a network driver diskette to the installation process for your network interface hardware.) All the options, and then some, that are available from the graphical or text interfaces may be specified in the commands and options. We will not cover the details here, see the documentation for the `redhat-config-kickstart` command, which is in HTML format under `/usr/share/doc/redhat-config-kickstart-<version>`. The Red Hat Linux documentation also does a good job of introducing the capabilities.

Following the command section, is the `%package` section, which specifies which software packages are to be loaded from the source media. Lines that begin with "@" signify package groups, and lines without the "@" designate individual package names. Our example file specifies `@ everything`, which loads all available packages. You do *not* want to do this for the final configuration of your compute slices. (The installation time is proportional to the number of packages that you load. If you want to keep the `kickstart` installations short, specify only the packages you need. This may take some trial and error, along with close attention to the packages that are getting loaded [and the dependencies that are automatically selected].)

If you want to see the definitions for the packages on the Red Hat media, they are contained in an extensible mark-up language (XML) file named `comps.xml` on the CD-ROM media. This file is normally located in the `RedHat/base` directory relative to the root of the install media. This file is in a format that is "mostly" readable by text editors, if you want to examine it. It drives the list of available languages, packages, and other options in the installation tool.

The `%pre` section allows you to specify commands to be run immediately after the `kickstart` file has been interpreted by the installation kernel. It is important to understand the environment in which this script executes, especially the limitations on available commands and resources. The target system hardware being installed has been scanned by the Linux installation kernel, the network is available without name services, and the installation kernel is operating out of RAM disk with the local disks mounted under a special directory (not the root directory.)

The `/proc` file system will contain useful information about the target hardware that your installation script can use to make decisions and adjustments. You can examine the exact configuration of this environment during an interactive installation by pressing `Ctrl-Alt-F2`, which will switch to an X-Windows virtual display running a VGA text-mode shell prompt. The entire environment is sitting there to be examined. Type `Ctrl-Alt-F7` to get back to the `anaconda` installation screen.

Fortunately, the environment for the `%post` script is a little more civilized. This script executes once the installation process is completed and before the system is rebooted. The operations in the script are all relative to the new system's root file system, unless you specify otherwise. If you are using DHCP, then the name resolution will still not be working, but you can use IP addresses, just like in the `%pre` script environment.

If you specify an NFS source for the installation files, that server directory is mounted under `/mnt/source` in the installation environment. Your `%post` script can mount other NFS file systems, and access RPM files, compressed tar balls, prototype configuration files, or any other information you may require. It is entirely possible to install a minimal environment with `kickstart`, then perform the majority of the system software configuration and loading in the `%post` script. I have seen some powerful installation processes implemented in exactly this way.

12.5.2   Making the Install Media Available for `kickstart`

One of the easiest ways to make the installation media available for network installs is to place the files on a server (NFS, FTP, or HTTP) and allow the installation kernel to access the data at the remote location. For NFS, the path to the files must be exported via the `/etc/exports` file, and NFS clients must be able to access the NFS service without interference from TCP wrappers.

The installation media may be unloaded to a directory structure or provided as International Organization for Standards ISO CD-ROM images to the installation process. (Note that ISO is not an acronym, it is the word *iso*, which is the Greek word meaning "equal.") To unload the binary RPM packages to the target local directory `/export/RedHat/9.0`, issue the following commands for all the CD-ROMs in the install set (usually three or four):

```
# mount /mnt/cdrom
# cp -var /mnt/cdrom/RedHat /export/RedHat/9.0
# umount /mnt/cdrom
# eject
```

You may see some warnings about overwriting `trans.tbl` files, and these can be safely ignored. If you want to make the release notes and image files available, you may also copy the whole top-level directory from the CD-ROM to the target directory. If you use these commands, the target directory for the remaining CD-ROMs becomes `/export/RedHat/9.0/RedHat`.

In addition to the installation media, which contain the RPM packages used by the install, you need to make the bootable kernel and `initrd` files available for booting by the client systems. These files are located in the `/images/pxeboot` directory on the first CD-ROM in the media set for Red Hat and derivative distributions (like Fedora). The files are called `vmlinuz` and `initrd.img`, and they need to be placed in the `/tftpboot` directory hierarchy so they can be found by the client TFTP requests. Figure 12–3 shows the placement of these files, as used by `pxelinux`.

12.5.3   The Network `kickstart` Directory

We now have the ability to boot the `kickstart` installation kernel via the network and supply it with the installation media via an NFS server. What is left is providing the custom configuration file that drives the installation process. If you go back to the example `default.netboot` configuration file for `pxelinux`, you will see the following definitions for the network `kickstart` installation:

```
label   linux9.ks
        kernel rh9.0/vmlinuz
        append vga=extended load_ramdisk=1 \
          initrd=rh9.0/initrd.img \
          ks=nfs:192.168.0.110:/kickstart9.0/
```

This definition passes the proper kernel and initial RAM disk, but also specifies a special parameter that determines the location to search for the kickstart configuration file by passing the ks= kernel parameter to the installation kernel. In this case, we are specifying an NFS directory that contains the configuration file.

This directory contains soft links with a name of the form <client-IP-address>-kickstart, which point to the kickstart configuration file for the client with the associated IP address. An example link name is 192.168.0.111-kickstart. The target file name in my example directory is RedHat9.0-ks.cfg. As with the pxelinux example, I have a data-driven script that creates the appropriate links.

The kickstart file contains information that points the install kernel to the NFS-mounted RPM packages and some other useful customizations:

```
text

#Install Red Hat Linux instead of upgrade
install

#Use NFS installation media
nfs --server 192.168.0.151 --dir /export/RedHat/9.0/RedHat

#System bootloader configuration
bootloader --location=mbr

#Clear the Master Boot Record
zerombr yes

#Clear all partitions from the disk
clearpart --all --initlabel

#Disk partitioning information
part /boot --fstype ext3 --size 100 --asprimary
part / --fstype ext3 --size 1 --grow --asprimary
part swap --size 512 --asprimary

#Use DHCP networking
network --bootproto dhcp

#System authorization information
auth  --enablenis --nisdomain cluster.local
```

```
#Firewall configuration
firewall --disabled

#XWindows configuration information
#Probe for video card
#Probe for monitor
xconfig  --depth 24 --resolution 1280x1024 --
defaultdesktop=KDE --startxonboot

%packages --resolvedeps
@ Everything

%post
/sbin/chkconfig sendmail     off
/sbin/chkconfig ypbind       on
```

This configuration file loads "everything" on one of my experimental systems. I would explicitly trim the configuration from this point on for compute slice installation.

In general, it may not be a good idea to have the DHCP server and the NFS server be the same machine. In this case, the `kickstart` kernel can use the DHCP server's information from the `next-server <system>` option to mount and use the installation media from an alternate system. There are many, many different configuration options possible with `kickstart` and you should carefully consider all of them before settling on your cluster's configuration.

You may need to be able to install using the Red Hat package-based installation tools to create a "golden" image for a tree-based installation tool like `SystemImager`. Once the system is configured to your liking, you can capture the configuration with `SystemImager` and use that image to install the cluster's compute slices. At some point in the process of loading a Red Hat or derivative system, you will need to do the initial installation from the RPM-based media, and you may as well automate that process as much as possible.

12.6 NFS Diskless Configuration

The use of an NFS diskless configuration for a cluster's compute slices removes the need for local storage and a local, permanent copy of the operating system. This can do wonders for removing the requirement to install an operating system on every node, and it simplifies keeping all versions synchronized, because there is only one *shared* copy. A diskless cluster simplifies the compute slice configuration, but complicates the software configuration on the NFS `root` server.

The good news is that an NFS diskless configuration can eliminate the multiple system administration issues associated with local copies of the operating system on each compute slice. The bad news is that there is not a comprehensive cluster NFS diskless package available. You will have to engineer one from existing knowledge and packages that may not be aimed at clusters. This is not necessarily an impossible task. Linux has the features necessary to implement a diskless environment, but it will take a lot of engineering.

At the very simplest level, an NFS diskless client boots a kernel and an `initrd` over the network and mounts its system root file system from a remote NFS server. Multiple clients share the same root directory on the NFS server, so care must be taken to ensure that client-specific data is separated from data shared by all clients. Often this is done by keeping volatile files in a RAM disk on the client and mounting the root as read-only. Beyond this simple description, there are many other hidden details. It is best to start with an example environment as a basis.

As a starting point, the kernel for your diskless clients must have the ability to use an NFS root file system enabled. The addition of this ability requires the kernel configuration option to be set and the kernel recompiled to incorporate the functionality. If you are not comfortable with recompiling your kernel, it is best to start with an environment that provides the NFS root ability.

Rather than take the space to run through a complete implementation, let's survey several of the available components for implementing diskless clusters. Many of the available environments are experimental and will require modifications to the kernel or other system components. Unless you are comfortable with undertaking this type of activity, it is best to stick with "sharing by copying"—a local operating system on each compute slice.

12.6.1   The Linux Terminal Server Project (LTSP)

There are a number of environments available for implementing Linux diskless thin-client environments. Most are aimed at creating shared X Windows environments, and several of those are based on NFS. One of which is the LTSP. I have considerable experience with version 3.0 of the LTSP software (version 4 has just been released), and I think it makes a good starting point for someone who wants to understand the creation of an NFS diskless environment, even though this is not its primary intent.

The really great thing about LTSP is that it is very well documented compared with similar open-source projects. The documentation explains each step of the boot process, and it makes a great prototype for a diskless cluster. It *is* a diskless cluster, so it is not a stretch to use it as a starting point for your own diskless cluster. Information about this software is available from `http://ltsp.org`.

If you take the LTSP `initrd` file apart, you will see that a file named `linuxrc` runs in place of the `init` process. This script is well documented, and does much of the same initialization that we saw in `initrd` for the `SystemImager` tool. The major difference is that an NFS directory is mounted and the system's root directory is "pivoted" to it. This directory is exported from the NFS `root` server, and is passed in the DHCP information:

```
        option root-path          "192.168.0.103:/opt/ltsp/i386";
```

Once the root directory is mounted, the `init` process from the shared NFS root is run and references `/etc/inittab`, just like a disk-based system. The `/etc/inittab` file references `/etc/rc.sysinit`, which performs the initialization of the client, including building the RAM disk and creating local files in the memory-based file system. Although this initialization process is similar to what happens on a regular system, all the executables, shared libraries, and data files being accessed are on the NFS server.

The behavior of an LTSP client is controlled by a global configuration file under the NFS root—`/opt/ltsp/i386/etc/lts.conf`—which contains stanzas with client-specific configuration information. The path just mentioned is in relation to the *server's* root directory. On the client, the behavior is as if the client had done a `chroot` to the `/opt/ltsp/i386` directory. You need to get used to thinking in terms of the perspective from the *client* and from the *server*.

If you take a look in the `etc/` directory (this is a relative path), you will see that several of the files there, like `resolv.conf`, `hosts`, and `syslog.conf` are actually links that point to `/tmp`. The `/tmp` directory is in the RAM disk on the client. At a higher level in the directory tree, both the `var/` and the `mnt/` directories are links to `/tmp/var` and `/tmp/mnt` respectively. This is a paradigm that you will find repeated over and over with diskless environments. An example of an NFS diskless client and server relationship is shown in Figure 12–4.

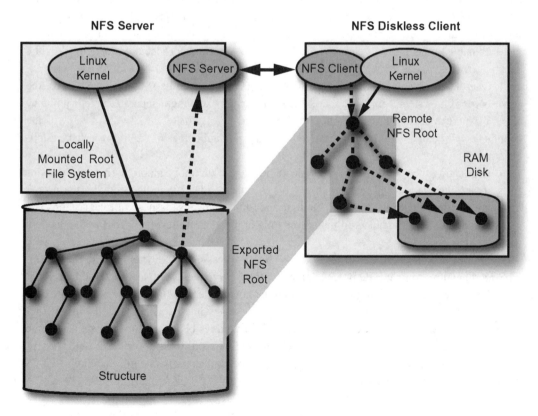

Figure 12–4 Diskless client and an NFS root server

12.6.2   Cluster NFS

Although the LTSP project uses soft links and local RAM disks to give a diskless client local copies of volatile files, the Cluster NFS package implements a different approach. This software package involves modifications to the server's NFS daemons that translate specially formatted file names on the server to the file request generated by the remote client. The file names that are translated have the format <*filename*>$$<*identifier*>=<*value*>$$, where the identifier field is a host name, IP address, UID, GID, or a tag that matches any access from a client system over NFS (as opposed to a local access).

As of this writing, the package is available from `http://clusternfs.source-forge.net` and is released with a 3.0 version available. It consists of replacing the server's NFS daemon (NFSD) module, which implement NFS server I/O operations on behalf of the clients. The intent is to allow clients to share an NFS root that is readable *and* writable, without destructive interference.

Instead of having local copies of volatile files stored in RAM disk, the client systems actually access the file on the NFS server. This keeps all the files for all clients in one place, and allows managing the individual client information in static files. The client "thinks" it is accessing a "well-known" file name like `/etc/hosts`, but instead is getting a translated version of the file named `hosts$$IP=192.168.0,151$$` or another specially tagged file, like `hosts$$hostname=ns1.cluster.local$$`.

One of the advantages of using the Cluster NFS modifications is that you can share the server's root file system with the client systems, instead of keeping a separate directory hierarchy for export to clients. For example, the LTSP package exports `/opt/ltsp/i386` as the client's root directory, which means that you have to maintain copies of the files for diskless clients there.

Replicating the root directory underneath a different directory hierarchy has implications for software installation and maintenance. This is because identifying and copying the proper application libraries, executables, and configuration files can cause issues with versioning. The software first has to be installed on the server's hierarchy, then it must be copied to the diskless root hierarchy.

Figure 12–5 shows three cluster diskless clients accessing an NFS server with the Cluster NFS modifications to its NFSD process. Because the NFS request contains the IP address, UID and GID of the user performing the access, and the host name, the NFSD process may look for matching file names that are client specific. Clients share any file that is not tagged with the special file name format. In this example, the client host name is being used to provide a separate copy of `/etc/sshd_config` file per client, in addition to the server's `/etc/ssh/sshd_config` file. To provide a file for the local server and *one* separate file shared by all NFS clients, the system administrator would specify `/etc/ssh/sshd_config$$client$$`.

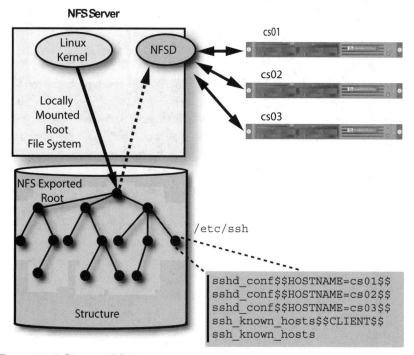

Figure 12–5 Cluster NFS file access

12.7 Introduction to Compute Slice Installation Summary

Producing the compute slice operating system configuration is an iterative process. To support installation and replication of so many systems, it is absolutely necessary to have an automated tool that allows unattended installation and configuration of the systems. Both tools introduced in this chapter, the Red Hat `kickstart` and `SystemImager`, are very capable installation facilities "out of the box."

Which tool you use will depend on your previous experience, whether you want a package-based installation process, and how frequently you expect to install or reinstall the systems in your cluster. How quickly a complete reinstallation of the cluster must occur is determined by a number of factors, including the type of network used for installations and the scaling ability of the installation server. The degree of scaling that you require from the installation tool may also require you to make choices about using the tools as they are, creating multiple installation servers, or making modifications like we examine in the upcoming prototype multicast installation example.

As I mentioned, the installation of the systems in a cluster is an iterative process, especially as software packages, libraries, and other components are added to the compute slices to support the cluster's applications. The more flexible and scalable the installation facility, the less effort and time required to alter the system configurations via reinstallation or file updates. The maximum flexibility requirements tend to tilt the balance in favor of SystemImager, in my opinion (I know there are kickstart fans out there who will argue with me), mainly because of its ability to synchronize minor changes that do not require a complete reinstallation of the compute slice software.

This, by the way, is an important point. You do not want to reinstall the complete operating system from scratch, just to update a three-character change to a configuration file. There is, however, a threshold beyond which it is better just to reimage the nodes. The installation tools described here do not enforce any system administration process. They *enable* you to create your own—and you need to think about how to *use* the tools in your own processes.

## CHAPTER 13

Improving Your Images: System Installation with SystemImager

Chapter Objectives

- Describe installation, configuration, and standard operation of `SystemImager`
- Detail extending `SystemImager` to use multicast compressed archives
- Introduce the `SystemImager flamethrower` facility for multicast installation

T he `SystemImager` tool is one of the most flexible and versatile installation tools available—at any price. This chapter covers the information necessary to start using `SystemImager` in your cluster. We will prototype an extension of the standard `SystemImager` tool to multicast compressed tar archives to client systems to show the inner workings of the tool. Finally, I introduce the `flamethrower` extension to `SystemImager` that provides an integrated multicast capability.

13.1 Using the `SystemImager` Software

The `SystemImager` package allows you to capture and replace system images in the form of a system's complete directory hierarchy and its contents. The server stores an identical tree structure to be placed on a target system, complete with every file captured from the original "golden" system used as a prototype. The `SystemImager` tool consists of both client and server software packages, and supports several of the more popular processor architectures, and Itanium.

Actually, `SystemImager` is part of and uses the components of the System Installer Suite (SIS) (available at `http://sisuite.org`; `SystemImager` software is available at `http://systemimager.org`,) which comprises `SystemImager`, `SystemInstaller`, and `SystemConfigurator`. From this point on, we will refer to `SystemImager` as `SI` for simplicity's sake. When I say SI I am really referring to the complete set of SIS tools that are necessary to make SI function.

The SIS is the installation and management tool set for the open-source cluster application resources package (OSCAR), which is produced by the Open Cluster Group (information available at http://openclustergroup.org). I consider OSCAR in a later chapter, along with other integrated "complete" cluster environments. For now, let's focus on just SI.

The high-level steps to follow for installing and using the SI software in your cluster are

- Choose one or more administration servers to provide SI services
- Configure the proper storage and network resources on the SI servers to support simultaneous image loading by multiple client systems
- Install and configure the SI server software
- Install and configure compute slice operating system and software
- Install SI client software on a "golden" system, which serves as the prototype for cloning
- Capture the client system image to the SI server
- Boot and install other clients using the captured image
- Fine-tune the image contents and client configuration
- Replicate your configurations as necessary

The hardware and I/O capabilities of the SI servers are important to the overall performance of the imaging service. The number of simultaneous client installations is affected by the network and disk I/O performance of the server system. I cover ways to improve performance (multicasting) later in this chapter, but for now let's assume that multiple systems will "hit" the SI server at the same time.

13.1.1   Downloading and Installing SI

The SI developers provide us with a really nice tool and procedure to get the SI code, as contained in the RPM packages for Red Hat distributions. A script, using the wget command[1] will download the proper packages for us:

```
# cd /tmp
# wget http://sisuite.org/install
--23:02:04--  http://sisuite.org/install
           => install
Resolving sisuite.org... done.
Connecting to sisuite.org[66.35.250.210]:80... connected.
HTTP request sent, awaiting response... 200 OK
Length: 13,573 [text/plain]
```

---

1.   The wget and curl commands are very useful for scripting access to remote HTML-provided files.

```
100%[===================>] 13,573          109.54K/s     ETA 00:00

23:02:06 (109.54 KB/s) - install saved [13573/13573]
# chmod +x install
```

We have the `install` script (note there is already a command by that name on the system, so make sure you run the local one), now let's follow directions and see what's available for download:

```
# ./install --list
Packages available for download and/or install:
  perl-AppConfig
  perl-MLDBM
  systemconfigurator
  systemimager-client
  systemimager-common
  systemimager-i386boot-standard
  systemimager-ia64boot-standard
  systemimager-ppc64-iSeriesboot-standard
  systemimager-ppc64boot-standard
  systemimager-server
  systeminstaller
  systeminstaller-x11
To install packages, do a:
        ./install --verbose PKG1 PKG2 ...
For example:
        ./install --verbose systemconfigurator perl-AppConfig
```

Okay, so the packages we want are picked up with the following command:

```
# ./install systemimager-client \
                systemimager-server \
                systemimager-common \
                systemimager-i386boot-standard
```

The results are dropped into the `sis-packages` directory. Wow, this is easy! Let's go ahead and install the packages:

```
error: Failed dependencies:
        perl-XML-Simple is needed by
           systemimager-server-3.0.1-4
```

Uh, oh. We have some package dependencies missing. A quick check of the Web site instructions lists the following packages that have to be installed:

```
rsync
perl-DBI
```

```
perl-Tk
perl-XML-Simple
```

So, we have to track down these dependencies before we can continue. This actually turns out to be a fairly common activity on Linux systems. Packages are shared by multiple projects, distributions, and software tools, so there are common repositories and "natural" places to look for the required pieces. Let's start by eliminating packages that are already loaded:

```
# rpm -q rsync
rsync-2.5.7-0.8
```

The `rsync` package is already loaded on my system. If you have not loaded it on yours, it is available on the Red Hat installation media. The `perl-DBI` package is also available on the installation media. No such luck for the other two packages. They are *not* included in Red Hat and derivative releases (Fedora Core 1 is missing the files, also).

Off to our trusty friend, `http://rpmfind.net`, where we can search for the missing packages. Drat. The files are there, but no Red Hat or Fedora versions, just Mandrake, Debian, and PLD Linux, which are different package schemes. Off to another place mentioned on the Web site—the comprehensive Perl archive network (CPAN).

At `http:/search.cpan.org` we can look for the modules. Ah, the pain. There must be at least 20,195 hits to the search for `perl-Tk` on the CPAN site. Which one do we want? Oh, I guess I am specifying the wrong format, I need to speak `perl` module syntax—but forgot my phrase book. Let's try `::Tk` and see what we get. This narrows it down to only 520 hits. Forget that.

Next let's try a `Google` search for `perl-Tk`. This comes up with `http://www.perl-tk.org/binaries/index.htm` as one of the hits. Success! We have finally located some Red Hat–compatible RPM packages, even though they are for Red Hat release 7.0. It will have to do.

The `perl-XML-Simple` module is available off the `SI` site, but the note says there is no guarantee that it will install on our system. Let's settle on using that one, because we are tired of grunging around the Internet, looking for the right pieces. This could be a little easier for first-time users, couldn't it?

Everything has to be properly installed, in the correct order. On my system, the `perl-DBI` package was already installed. Installing the dependencies yields

```
# rpm -ivh perl-AppConfig-1.55-1.7.3.noarch.rpm \
       perl-Tk-800.024-2.i386.rpm                 \
       perl-XML-Simple-1.08-1.noarch.rpm
Preparing... ################################# [100%]
   1:perl-XML-Simple ######################### [ 33%]
   2:perl-AppConfig ########################## [ 67%]
   3:perl-Tk ################################# [100%]
```

I have found it somewhat easier to install the dependencies separately from the rest of the packages. Don't forget to include the `systemconfigurator` package, because it is a dependency for the rest of the `SI` packages. Deal with any package dependencies, ordering, or version issues before continuing with the installation.

Once we have all of the packages and understand the dependencies, we can complete the installation of the proper `SI` pieces at the top of the dependency tree. Installing the actual `systemimager` and `systemconfigurator` packages goes smoothly, once the dependencies are in place:

```
# rpm -ivh system*.rpm
Preparing... ################################### [100%]
   1:systemconfigurator ####################### [ 25%]
   2:systemimager-common ####################### [ 50%]
   3:systemimager-i386boot-standard ############# [ 75%]
   4:systemimager-server ####################### [100%]
```

On the client we install the `client` and `common` RPMs (along with dependencies), and on the server we install `common`, `server`, and the `i386boot-standard` packages (along with dependencies). If, for some reason, you want to capture the server (for example, to clone it to an identical system), you will need to install all the packages to make it both a client *and* a server.

Once we have all the necessary packages and have slogged through at least one attempt, `SI` installation is easy. (Once you know how to do something, knowing how to do it is easy.) I actually create three directories that contain *all* the necessary pieces: `SiClient-<version>`, `SiServer-<version>`, and `SiClientServer-<version>`. In this way, I don't have to think about the installation dependencies; I can just change to the proper directory and perform

```
# rpm -ivh *.rpm
```

I also make sure that I have the directories backed up and included in my CD-ROM-based cluster tool kit. I don't want to have to go through the whole package and dependency discovery process "on-site" during a cluster installation.

Let me state right here: The work necessary to get `SI` installed is well worth it. It is my tool of choice when it comes to cluster installation. Hopefully the information about satisfying dependencies will get you over the initial frustration of dealing with this wonderful tool.

Before we close the section on installing `SI`, there is one more dependency that you may encounter (yes, I know it seems like there is *always* one more). In Itanium installations, there is a special version of TFTP that must be installed for proper operation. This package is `tftp-hpa` and may be found at `http://rpmfind.net` or at `http://www.kernel.org`.

13.1.2   Configuring the SI Server

The SI software, once loaded, has components in several system locations: /etc/sys-temimager, /var/lib/systemimager, and /usr/lib/systemimager. Configuration files are placed in /etc/systemimager to control the behavior of the software, including a special configuration file for rsyncd. Log files are created under the /var/log/systemimager directory, but no logrotate configuration is installed, so you need to provide that file yourself.

Documentation packages are available in the /usr/share/doc/systemimager-client-<version> and /usr/share/doc/systemimager-server-<version> directories. As of this writing, the most recent value for <version>" is 3.0.1. Manuals for the software are available in PDF or HTML format at http://systemimager.org/documentation, and they are quite good.

T I P   Plan on storing SI images on an external file system that has at least 2 GB available for every expected image. The actual size will depend on the number of revisions you keep and the operating system footprint of the systems being imaged.

The manuals cover all the possible options in the configuration files in /etc/sys-temimager, including settings in client.conf, rsyncd.conf, systemim-ager.conf, and updateclient.local.exclude. The last file is important, because it contains a list of files *not* to update on client systems when using the updateclient command. This prevents altering system information, like device files, that may be client specific.

A brief note about the /etc/rsyncd.conf file. This configuration file is automatically generated as image information is added to the server. The information for the file is kept in the rsync_stubs directory and is used by the mkrsyncd_conf command. If the SI server seems to know about image or override directories that don't exist, you have probably gotten this information out of "sync." Always use rmimage to remove images from the SI server; it keeps the data properly up-to-date. (Although I do not cover the details here, clients that share a common structure with only some differences may apply an "override" directory to the installation to create the unique content. See the SI manual for details about using this feature.)

Probably the most important directory, from the standpoint of local server hardware and storage configuration choices, is the /var/lib/systemimager directory. There is a subdirectory, called images, under /var/lib/systemimager that contains the system image "trees" from the systems that you wish to clone. This directory can grow to be quite large, exhausting even the largest /var partition you might create on the imaging server.

I usually end up linking this directory to an external storage device that has the space to contain the multiple tens of gigabytes of image data. This involves creating an image directory somewhere   else,   moving   the   README,   ACHTUNG,   CUIDADO,   and DO_NOT_TOUCH_THESE_DIRECTORIES files (containing warnings about messing with the images) to that directory, then replacing the `/var/lib/systemimager/images` directory with a soft link to the new location.

Now that we have the `SI` server software installed, we need to configure the start-up links, enable the service, and start it:

```
# chkconfig --add systemimager
# chkconfig systemimager on
# service systemimager start
```

This will start the `rsync` service as a daemon, using the custom configuration file in the `/etc/systemimager` directory. After the daemon is started, the `SI` client systems may open connections to it.

You need to consider the security issues involved with running the daemon carefully. Constrain the `rsync` activities to the management network, limit the client access with TCP wrappers, or otherwise ensure that a random system may not access the `rsync` daemon. It is also possible to use SSH as the installation transport, but that currently requires special modifications to `SI` components.

13.1.3 The `SI` Cold Installation Boot Process

The installation of the `systemimager-i386boot-standard-<version>` package (or the other possible boot support packages) will place information in `/usr/share/systemimager/boot/<arch>/standard`, which contains the files necessary to support network booting and installation with the `SI` software. In this case, the `<arch>` component of the directory name is `i386`. There is support available for `ia64` and other architectures as well.

The network boot support directory contains files named `kernel`, `initrd.img`, `boel_binaries.tar.gz`, and `config`. The first three files need to be placed into the `/tftpboot` directory on the DHCP server, as shown in the `pxelinux` example in Figure 12–3 on page 340. This assumes that you will be using `pxelinux` to boot things other than `SI`. If this is not the case, then you can use the default `SI` boot configuration and information, which is in `/etc/systemimager/pxelinux.cfg`. The components of the SI cold-installation environment are shown in Figure 13–1.

The file `config` is the configuration information used to build the `SI` boot kernel, so you can produce your own boot kernel if necessary. If you are familiar with this process, then substituting the `SI` configuration information into the build, and rebuilding a kernel, is a trivial process. I do not cover how to do this here.

We can examine the contents of the `boel_binaries.tar.gz` file with

```
# tar tvzf boel_binaries.tar.gz
```

This shows a list of files, relative to the file system root, that are made available to the `SI` install kernel at boot time. This takes care of making resources like commands and kernel modules available to a boot environment that does not have everything included in the initial configuration. If we once again practice our skills at taking an `initrd` file apart

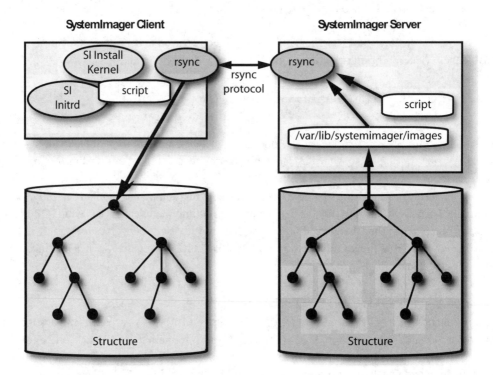

Figure 13–1 `SI` "cold" installation

```
# cp initrd.img /tmp
# cd /tmp
# gunzip < initrd.img >initrd
# losetup /dev/loop0 initrd
# mkdir image
# mount -o loop /dev/loop0 image
```

we will find a slightly different structure than that with which we are accustomed, however, following the information in `/etc/inittab`, we can locate the start-up script in `/etc/init.d/rcS`. (We know that the first program to be executed at system start-up is `init`. This usually, but not always, makes `/etc/inittab` the center of initial system activity.) This is fairly involved, and I won't go deeper into it at this point. If you are willing to explore, you can use this as an example of how to create your own custom installation environment.

The kernel, once loaded into memory by the bootloader and activated, will load its binary package, install it in the RAM disk, and continue with the installation process. This involves preparing the disk partitions and then using `rsync` to replicate the directory tree from the `SI` server to the local disk. Once the installation completes, the system is rebooted to its new configuration.

Table 13–1 Some `SI` Server-side Commands

Command Name	Description
`getimage`	Capture a system image from a golden client
`updateclient`	Update a client's image by synchronizing files or reinstalling
`mkautoinstallscript`	Create an `autoinstall` script from an image's information
`mkdhcpserver`	Create a DHCP server configuration from network parameters
`mkdhcpstatic`	Create a DHCP server configuration file from dynamically leased IP addresses

The installation process is guided by a system-specific script that is loaded from the `SI` server. The `/var/lib/systemimager/scripts` directory contains the scripts that may be shared between groups of identical systems by (you may have guessed it) creating soft links. We will look at the contents of a client script in an upcoming section. First we need to install the client software and capture an image.

13.1.4   `SI` Server Commands

A number of useful server-side commands are available with `SI`. Some of them are listed in Table 13–1.

13.1.5   Installing and Configuring the `SI` Client Software

Once you have an `SI` server installed, configured, and started, it is time to prepare for capturing your first client image. Obviously you need to install the operating system software and configure the system for proper operation before capturing the image. Remember, anything that is on the "golden" system will be replicated on each of its clones—this includes good things as well as bad.

An example client software installation (after the dependencies) is

```
# rpm -ivh system*.rpm
Preparing... ################################### [100%]
   1:systemconfigurator ####################### [ 33%]
   2:systemimager-common ####################### [ 67%]
   3:systemimager-client ####################### [100%]
```

This has installed a number of commands on the client, including `prepareclient`, `updateclient`, and `lsimage`.

The `prepareclient` command performs the local operations necessary for the `SI` server to take a snapshot of the local system's disk format and contents. Running the command will make some modifications to the client, which are reversed once the image is captured. Check the man page for `prepareclient`, and the SI manual for complete details on using the command.

The `updateclient` command will perform a "pull" update from the SI server of only the changes to the client's image tree that have occurred since the system was imaged or last updated. I discuss this command in more depth in an upcoming section.

One way of testing the client-to-server connection for SI is to use the `lsimage` command from the client to connect to the `rsync` daemon on the server. This will list the available images:

```
# lsimage -server ns2
-------------------
Available image(s):
-------------------
```

As we might expect, there are no "captured" images yet, so none show up in the list. This command does not accomplish much at this stage of the installation, besides verifying that the local system can connect to the SI server.

13.1.6   Capturing a Client Image

Executing `prepareclient` will create the necessary information on your client, start the local `rsync` daemon, and wait for the SI server to issue a `getimage` command to copy the client's information. Two files are placed into a "known location"—that is, `/etc/systemimager`—so that the SI server can find them in its local image directory. The files include `mounted_filesystems`, which contains the following information for the example client:

```
/dev/hda2 on / type ext3 (rw)
none on /proc type proc (rw)
none on /dev/pts type devpts (rw,gid=5,mode=620)
usbdevfs on /proc/bus/usb type usbdevfs (rw)
/dev/hda1 on /boot type ext3 (rw)
none on /dev/shm type tmpfs (rw)
```

Additionally, a file named `autoinstallscript.conf` is created, which contains local partition information (in XML format):

```
<!--
   This file contains partition information about the disks on
your golden client.  It is stored here in a generic format
that is used by your SystemImager server to create an
autoinstall script for cloning this system. You can change the
information in this file to affect how your target machines
are installed. See "man autoinstallscript.conf" for details.
-->
<config>
```

```
<!--
This disk's output was brought to you by the partition tool
"sfdisk". And by the numbers 4 and 5 and the letter Q.
-->
<disk dev="/dev/hda" label_type="msdos"
unit_of_measurement="MB">
<part  num="1"  size="101"  p_type="primary"  p_name="-"
flags="boot" />
<part  num="2"  size="9029"  p_type="primary"  p_name="-"
flags="-" />
<part  num="3"  size="*"  p_type="primary"  p_name="-"
flags="-" />
</disk>

<fsinfo  line="10"  real_dev="/dev/hda2"  mount_dev="LABEL=/"
mp="/"  fs="ext3"  options="defaults"  dump="1"  pass="1" />
<fsinfo  line="20"  real_dev="/dev/hda1"  mount_dev="LABEL=/
boot"  mp="/boot"  fs="ext3"  options="defaults"  dump="1"
pass="2" />
<fsinfo  line="30"  real_dev="none"  mp="/dev/pts"  fs="devpts"
options="gid=5,mode=620"  dump="0"  pass="0" />
<fsinfo  line="40"  real_dev="none"  mp="/proc"  fs="proc"
options="defaults"  dump="0"  pass="0" />
<fsinfo  line="50"  real_dev="none"  mp="/dev/shm"  fs="tmpfs"
options="defaults"  dump="0"  pass="0" />
<fsinfo  line="60"  real_dev="/dev/hda3"  mp="swap"  fs="swap"
options="defaults"  dump="0"  pass="0" />
<fsinfo  line="70"  real_dev="/dev/cdrom"  mp="/mnt/cdrom"
fs="udf,iso9660"  options="noauto,owner,kudzu,ro"  dump="0"
pass="0"  format="no" />
<fsinfo  line="80"  real_dev="/dev/sda"  mp="/mnt/floppy"
fs="auto"  options="noauto,owner,kudzu"  dump="0"  pass="0"
format="no" />
</config>
```

The next step is to go to the SI server and issue a getimage command:

```
# getimage -golden-client cs01 -image cs01_20040316 \
        -ip-assignment dhcp -post-install reboot          \
        -exclude '/scratchdir/*'
```

The options to this command first assign the name cs01_20040316 to the image being collected, use DHCP as the address assignment method, cause the client to reboot automatically when the installation terminates, and exclude the directory contents of /scratchdir from the image, but include the empty directory. We are now prompted to make sure that we wish to continue. The message output is

```
This program will get the "cs01_20040316" system image from
"cs01"making the assumption that all filesystems considered
part of the system image are using ext2, ext3, jfs, FAT,
reiserfs, or xfs.This program will not get /proc, NFS, or
other filesystems not mentioned above.

****************** WARNING *************************************
All files retrieved from a golden client are, by default, made
accessible to anyone who can connect to the rsync port of this
machine.  See rsyncd.conf(5)for details on restricting access
to these files on the imageserver.  See the systemimager-ssh
package for a more secure (but less efficient) method of
making images available to clients.
****************** WARNING *************************************

See "getimage -help" for command line options.

Continue? ([y]/n): y
```

The next message is

```
Retrieving /etc/systemimager/mounted_filesystems from cs01 to
check for mounted filesystems...
------ cs01 mounted_filesystems RETRIEVAL PROGRESS ---------
receiving file list ... done
/var/lib/systemimager/images/cs01_20040316/etc/systemimager/
mounted_filesystems
wrote 132 bytes  read 709 bytes  560.67 bytes/sec
total size is 595  speedup is 0.71
------ cs01 mounted_filesystems RETRIEVAL FINISHED ---------
Retrieving image cs01_20040316 from cs01
------ cs01_20040316 IMAGE RETRIEVAL PROGRESS ----------
```

There is a pause in activity while the rsync daemon calculates the information it needs to do the transfers. During this time, there is *some* content under the SI image directory. Indeed, the /etc/systemimager directory is the first location fetched for the client-specific information underneath it.

Once the rsync calculations are completed and the imaging begins, you will see all the file names flying by on the screen, unless you selected the -no-listing option to getimage. After debugging is completed, specifying -no-listing speeds up the imaging process by not printing the file paths being received to stdout. The -quiet option will suppress questions (like "Overwrite existing image on the server?"), but will report errors if they occur.

Although it is tedious, you should watch the files being saved to the image. You may notice all kinds of things being put into the image that you will want to remove in the next iteration. The absolute first time you get an image from the golden client, just treat it as a learning and debugging experience. It is unlikely that you will keep the first image's configuration without additional trimming of the software footprint.

You will learn about `/usr/lib/local`, `/usr/share`, and other system directories with contents that your compute slice will probably not need. Remember a *small* compute slice system footprint is your goal! Every 100 MB of size you save is one second on a GbE link. You can use the `-exclude` option to exclude a single location (in a variety of ways) or to read the excluded locations from a file with `-exclude-file` `<file-with-list>`. However you trim things from the system tree, you will eventually see the messages

```
wrote 1438312 bytes read 2118609960 bytes 1047195.99 bytes/sec
total size is 2112589544  speedup is 1.00
------ ns1_20040316 IMAGE RETRIEVAL FINISHED -------------

Press <Enter> to continue...
Would you like to run the "addclients" utility now?(y/[n]): y
```

Proceeding on to the `addclients` utility allows you to link the system name (or a set of system names following a convention) to the proper installation script in the `/var/lib/systemimager/scripts` directory. In this case, we are specifying only one system in the range, which will create a single link. It is also possible to create the links manually if they are "sparse."

```
addclients -- Section 1 (hostname information)
------------------------------------------------------------

The next series of questions will be used to create a range of
hostnames.You will be asked for your domain name, the base
host name, a beginning number, and an ending number.

For example, if you answer:
  domain name      = systemimager.org
  base host name   = www
  starting number  = 7
  ending number    = 11

Then the result will be a series of hostnames that looks like
this:
  www7.systemimager.org
  www8.systemimager.org
  www9.systemimager.org
  www10.systemimager.org
  www11.systemimager.org
What is your domain name? []:
What is the base host name that you want me to use? [ns]:
What number should I begin with? []: 1
What number should I end with? []: 1
I will work with hostnames: ns1 through ns1
            in the domain:
```

```
Are you satisfied? (y/[n]): yes, very
```

We've created the `autoinstall` script, and there is now a link named `ns1` pointing to it. This is the installation behavior that will be applied to the `ns1` client when it boots the `SI` install kernel.

```
addclients -- Section 2 (soft links to master script)
------------------------------------------------------------
Would you like me to create soft links to a "master" script so
that hosts:

ns1 through ns1

can be autoinstalled with that image? ([y]/n): y
Here is a list of available autoinstall scripts:

ns1_20040316

Which script would you like these hosts to be installed with?
[ns1_20040316]:

Your soft links have been created.
Press <Enter> to continue...
```

Okay, now the installation process wants to run `addclients`. Because we already have DNS working, let's skip this operation.

```
addclients --Section 3(adding or modifying /etc/hosts entries)
------------------------------------------------------------
Your target machines need to be able to determine their host
names from their IP addresses, unless their host name is
specified in a local.cfg file.

The preferred method for doing this is with DNS.  If you have
a working DNS that has IP address to hostname resolution
properly configured for your target machines, then answer "n"
here.

If you don't have a working DNS, or you want to override the
information in DNS, then answer "y" here to add entries to the
"/etc/hosts" file on your image server.  After adding these
entries, the /etc/hosts file will be copied to "/var/lib/
systemimager/scripts" where it can be retrieved by your target
machines.

I will ask you for your clients' IP addresses one subnet at a
time.
```

Would you like me to continue? (y/[n]):**n**

There is now a master script in the /var/lib/systemimager/scripts directory named ns1_20040316.master, after the name of the image. There is a single soft link in that directory named ns1, after the system's host name, pointing to the master script. This is how SI automatically maps the installation behavior to a particular image for a particular system. Simple and elegant.

If you examine the master script, you will see that it runs under the memory-based install kernel. Environment variables are passed from the memory-based kernel's start-up script via a file: /tmp/variables.txt. The script will install kernel modules for the disk devices, partition the disks, create and mount the file systems, and will then "fill" the disk with the image contents from the SI server using rsync.

Once the image tree is installed to the local disk, the master script invokes SystemConfigurator to configure the local system's network interfaces. The commands to System-Configurator are read right from the body of the master script, and are contained in a shell "here document" (between the EOL markers in the following example excerpt). You can find the documentation for the possible commands at http://sisuite.org/systemconfig/man/systemconfig.conf.html. The portion of the master script for our example system is

```
### BEGIN systemconfigurator ###
# Configure the client's hardware, network interface, and boot
# loader.
chroot /a/ systemconfigurator --configsi --stdin <<EOL ||
shellout

[NETWORK]
HOSTNAME = $HOSTNAME
DOMAINNAME = $DOMAINNAME

[INTERFACE0]
DEVICE = eth0
TYPE = dhcp
EOL
### END systemconfigurator ###
```

This is where you can perform more complicated initialization of network and system parameters by editing the script. The [INTERFACE0] block is always the default gateway interface, but otherwise there is no mapping between the [INTERFACE<N>] blocks and the actual ordering of the interfaces (it took quite a while to figure this out).

When all actions are completed, the system will then will either spin and beep until rebooted, automatically reboot, or halt—based on the choice made with the -post-install <action> option. Let's chose reboot for the action, so the system will automatically reboot when the installation completes. These behaviors are built into the master script, so to change the option requires regenerating the master script, editing it, or using `mkautoinstall-script`.

13.1.7   Forcing Hardware-to-Driver Mapping with `SystemConfigurator`

One note, based on experience with systems that have multiple network interfaces, and several possible modules to drive the interface, is in order here. The `SystemConfigurator` portion of the SI software has its own database that maps the `VendorID:CardID` returned from the PCI hardware scan to the proper kernel module containing the driver. I have seen the wrong driver installed in some cases. Although the documentation tantalizingly mentions the ability to use an "order" directive in the `[HARDWARE]` section to force the order of the driver loading, this did not solve the problem that I encountered.

To override the `SystemConfigurator` choice of driver for a particular `VendorID:-CardID` pair, you need to place a file named `hardware.1st` underneath `etc/systemconfig` *in the client image tree* to force the proper mapping. The `VendorID:CardID` information may be found in the distribution's `/etc/sysconfig/hwconf` file, which is produced by the hardware scanning utility `kudzu` at system boot time. The `kudzu` tool uses the databases in `/usr/share/hwdata` to look up the proper driver for the hardware.

These are both four-digit hexadecimal numbers—for example, `14E4:1645` for the Broadcom GbE hardware used in the particular Hewlett-Packard rx2600 Itanium 2 systems we were using. The `etc/systemconfig/hardware.list` file *in the image tree* contains lines like this example:

```
#VendorID  CardID   Type        Module
14E4       1645     ethernet    tg3
```

The sketchy information about this configuration file is contained in the man page at `http://sisuite.org/systemconfig/man/systemconfigurator.html`. This specific example occurred on a cluster I helped build that was headed for Qatar (during the War in Iraq). We lost about a day's time locating the problem and reverse-engineering this information. Use the information wisely.

13.1.8   Installing a Client Image

The `SI` server is properly configured and functioning, there are images resident on the server, and we have blank-slate compute slices to install. In our example `pxelinux` environment, we can follow these steps to install a compute slice.

- Reboot the system.
- Hold down the `Ctrl` and `Alt` keys together to activate `pxelinux`.
- Type `linux.si` to the `boot:` prompt from `pxelinux`.
- Confirm the installation.

• Do the next client, repeating these steps.

These steps require connecting to the console of each system. There is another way to "fire off" client installations, without interacting with the console. We can use our old friend SSH and the `updateclient` command:

```
# ssh ns2
Last login: Tue Mar 16 21:38:03 2004 from ns1.cluster.local
# updateclient -server ns1 -image ns2_20040316 \
        -autoinstall -reboot
```

This will move the SI boot kernel and `initrd` into place on the client and will reboot into the installation process. No boot media or console interactions are necessary with the client, as long as it is accessible via the network and has a "live" operating system on it. It is also possible to use the `pdsh` command to do the same operation on multiple nodes at the same time:

```
# pdsh -w cs[01-24] updateclient -server ns1 \
        -image cs_20040316 -autoinstall -reboot
```

Clients may also be installed from an SI boot floppy created with `mkautoinstall-diskette` or a boot CD-ROM created with `mkautoinstallcd`, in case the client system does not support PXE, BOOTP, or DHCP booting.

13.1.9 Updating Client Software without Reinstalling

Using the `rsync` as the central update engine in SI allows some very powerful system administration processes. The `rsync` daemon detects any files on the client that are out of date with respect to a reference tree and updates them, without reinstalling the whole tree. Only the differences are transferred between the reference tree and the client tree.

This means that for most minor changes to the client systems—that is, changes that don't involve disk partition structure—the SI server's use of `rsync` allows the clients to synchronize with the server's image without copying any more data than necessary. The proper form of the SI `updateclient` command is all that is needed. This is shown in Figure 13–2.

In practice, this means you can update the *<image-directory>*/etc/hosts file relative to a stored image tree on the SI server, say with the file's full path being /var/lib/systemimager/images/ns1_20040316/etc/hosts, then cause the clients to "pull" the update from the server to the local file. Again, we can use SSH or, better yet, PDSH to cause the clients to update themselves:

```
# pdsh -w cs[01-29] updateclient -server ns1 \
        -image ns2_20040316
```

In the event of a major change, say the update of a large software package, the update may be performed to the golden client, the image recaptured (it will update the image stored on the server), and then pulled to all clients. We can write scripts to detect the clients linked to a partic-

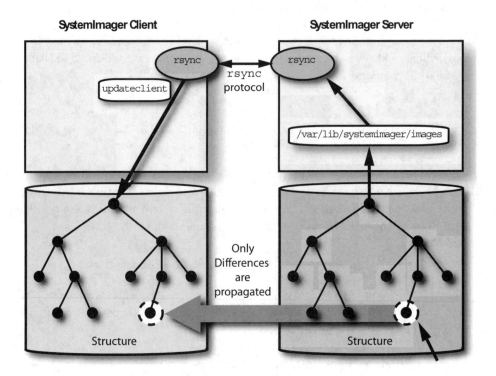

Figure 13–2 Client "pull" update from the `SI` server

ular image by looking at the links in the `/var/lib/systemimager/images` directory, and perform the update.

13.1.10   Image Management and Naming

Although `SI` is very flexible, it does not implement or enforce any system administration practices or processes. It is up to us to decide *how* to use the tool and what features to use. As you can see from some of the examples so far, it is important to have naming conventions for the systems in the cluster to help differentiate between the various classes of systems.

It is also important to have a naming convention for the system images that are maintained for the `SI` clients, and a versioning scheme to make sure that we can track changes to images. It is entirely possible to push an out-of-date or experimental image to the cluster, and to wreak havoc with the users and their applications. For this reason, I strongly suggest that you have a naming convention that identifies the target type of system, a class (production, experimental, obsolete, and so on), and a date string as part of the image name.

This, of course, means more typing when you execute `SI` commands, but it will save putting the right image in the wrong place, or at least reduce the chances. An example image name might be, `ComputeSlice-Experimental-Version01-20040627`. There is nothing to stop you from being as verbose as strikes your fancy with image names.

13.1.11   Avoiding the Big MAC-Gathering Syndrome

Before we finish with this introduction to `SI`, I should mention one other procedure that may save a lot of time, but is not necessarily obvious: How to deal with gathering the MAC addresses necessary to use DHCP in the cluster. We could call this the *big MAC debacle*, because each system may have as many as three MAC addresses (associated with data, management, and HSI network connections) for us to gather and manage in the DHCP server configuration file.

This is a lot of tedious, error-prone hand copying of multiple-digit hexidecimal numbers, followed by a lot of typing. We all have better things to do with our time. Several of the `SI` tools, notably `mkdhcpserver` and `mkdhcpstatic` can help with this task.

The process, in theory, follows these steps:

1. Generate a dynamic DHCP configuration for the networks with `mkdhcpserver`.
2. Configure the DHCP server to have a long lease time, so that once a dynamic address is assigned to a client, it will remain in use for several days.
3. Boot the cluster's systems in the order that you want IP addresses assigned from the pools.
4. Verify that the current client has the appropriate address assigned before moving to the next client.
5. When all clients are booted, run the `mkdhcpstatic` command, which will take all assigned IP and MAC information and modify the DHCP configuration file to contain the static MAC-to-IP address mapping.

Now, in practice, it may not be easy to get all systems booted properly and assigned the correct IP addresses, but the "theoretical" process can still help save a lot of collecting and typing of MAC addresses. This works better in smaller, less complex clusters.

13.1.12   Summary

`SystemImager` is a very powerful tool that can help with the installation and system administration of a cluster's software. In this section we examined a representative section of the `SI` functionality, but there is still more to learn. Even with concrete examples, as provided here, the specific configuration and adaptation of `SI` to your cluster's environment and your system administration practices will take time.

Practical experience with `SI` in large clusters tells us that there are potential scaling issues with the network, the `SI` server, the disk subsystems on the servers and clients, and the file systems used for storing the images. All these issues may be addressed to the best of Linux's ability, and the `SI` approach still may not scale well beyond about 500 to 700 systems, and this number will require multiple servers. There is ongoing research into the area of multicasting and other special techniques to break through the scaling barriers.

The following is an overview of details relating to several of the `SI` server performance issues that were just mentioned.

- Network performance—The `SI` server needs to have the network bandwidth to handle multiple client installations at the same time. The theoretical maximum for a GbE link is 125 MB/s. Network bonding can provide additional scaling, but only if the switching equipment can handle it.
- Server disk performance—If the network link out of the system represents one bottleneck, then the ability to feed data from the image storage file system to the network can also limit the number of clients that an `SI` server can feed. RAID 5 disk storage is immune to failure, is cheaper than striped (RAID 0) file systems, but does not perform well for writes. The image installation process can be primarily reads (read-mostly), so the capture of images may be the major issue.
- Server I/O performance—Using high-performance disks in an `SI` server can help performance, but the number of I/O channels and their maximum bandwidth are important to keeping the client systems "fed" with outgoing data. Striping across multiple devices and multiple I/O channels can keep the back-end storage from becoming a bottleneck. If hardware RAID is in use, multiple SCSI or Fibre-Channel interfaces may be necessary to remove single-channel I/O bottlenecks.
- Server memory configuration—The `SI` server needs a substantial amount of memory to allow caching of disk information destined for clients. The time offset between clients' access to a given file can mean that the page cache is not able to keep the data long enough to prevent physical reads for multiple installation streams.
- File system configuration—The more images you keep on the back-end file system, the larger the requirement for storage *and* meta-data, like inodes. It is quite common to get file system "full" error messages during image capture, even when there appears to be substantial free space within the file system. Check the inode information with `dumpe2fs -h <device>` to determine whether the file system is out of free inodes. It is extremely painful to have to unload multigigabytes of image data, rebuild the file system with more inodes, then restore the images.
- Dedicated resources—The amount of RAM, CPU, and I/O necessary during the installation of multiple clients makes the server unsuitable for other activities without destructive interference with services that share the system. Care is required to ensure that the `SI` activities do not impact clusterwide performance.

These issues have more to do with the configuration of the server used to run `SI`, than with the software itself. You should treat these issues as design recommendations, intended more as suggestions to help you avoid performance issues, than as criticism of `SI` itself. I think that

SI is currently the *best* choice for a network-based cluster system installation tool, especially if you want something that is ready to use and has been proved to work with multiple architectures.

13.2 Multicast Installation

Some of the installation server scaling issues discussed in the last section are the result of the nature of cloning multiple nodes at the same time, by simultaneously streaming separate image data to every node. The same scaling issues affect package-based installation methods, resulting from multiple systems accessing the package repository on the server.

If we were able to send a single data stream to all nodes being installed, as if it were being broadcast, it would reduce the load on the installation server to approximately that of one system being installed. Broadcasting, however, will flood frames to every switch port in the network, regardless of whether a system needs the data. Casting about for solutions, we find there is a better answer: multicasting.

Multicasting is a one-to-many data transmission scheme, but unlike the recipients of a broadcast, a multicast client specifically subscribes to a multicast group to receive the multicast traffic for that group. (Actually, systems that are not recipients of the multicast traffic may send data "into" the multicast group. They cannot, however, receive any data out of it until they register their interface with the multicast group.) With multicasting, we have the one-to-many benefits of a broadcast, but with the ability for the client to determine which data streams it sees. Switches that are multicast capable will make the multicast data available to all LAN segments that have a subscribed client. Care must be taken not to eradicate the performance gains that switching equipment gave us by controlling broadcast traffic flooding to switch ports.

There are protocols like the Internet Group Management Protocol (IGMP), the Generic Attribute Registration Protocol (GARP), and the GARP Multicast Registration Protocol (GMRP; built on top of GARP) that attempt to control the flooding of multicast information to all ports on a switch. Simply put, these protocols allow clients to tell switching equipment to which ports to send multicast traffic based on entries in the switch's filtering tables. The level of support for these features is network interface and switch dependent.

13.2.1   Multicast Basics

Multicast data is transported by the TCP/UDP layer; it is not a connection-oriented stream like the TCP/IP transport. Multicast data may have greater scope than the local LAN (segment or switch domain), and the "time to live" (TTL) values in the packets determine how "far" the data is allowed to travel. Switches and routers that are multicast capable look at the TTL value to determine whether to forward the packet. Scoping values for TTL are listed in Table 13–2.

In our discussion in Chapter 5 about IP addressing, we showed some of the fixed TCP/IP address formats (classes A, B, and C) that are commonly used, along with subnetting and supernetting examples with the associated net masks. The address format reserved for multicasting is a "class D," in which the first 4 bits of the 32-bit IP address are 1110. This scheme has no "net-

Table 13–2 Multicast Scoping Based on TTL Values

TTL Value	Multicast Datagram Scope
0	Local host only, not transmitted
1	Local subnet only, not forwarded
2–32	Same site, organization, or department
33–64	Same region
65–128	Same continent
129–255	Unrestricted

work" and "host" portions; instead, there is the 4-bit portion necessary to identify a class D address, followed by a 28-bit multicast group identifier.

Figure 13–3 shows the class D address range for multicast groups, along with the net mask format and two reserved address ranges. The first reserved address range is for local use. For example, all hosts subscribe to the *all hosts* address 224.0.0.1 when they initialize multicast-capable interfaces. If you ping that address, you will get a reply from every multicast-capable interface connected to the LAN. Linux systems are fully multicast capable. Other addresses in this range include the *all routers* address, 224.0.0.2, and addresses belonging to several other classes of devices.

The address range reserved for "administrative scoping" allows determining scope in more flexible ways than the TTL values. Switching and routing equipment may be configured to contain multicast packets and frames with "administrative scope" addresses to specific zones. There are protocols, like the Multicast Scope Zone Announcement Protocol (MZAP), that handle sharing zone information among network devices. Thankfully, this is all I'll mention about this topic here.

Once they reach their target LAN segment, IP multicast addresses must be converted to MAC addresses by the network equipment for delivery to Ethernet interfaces. One little issue needs to be resolved: What is the correct destination MAC address (because there are potentially multiple target MAC addresses and this is *not* a broadcast frame)? There is a formula for converting the incoming multicast group address to a local MAC address: The first 24 bits of the MAC address are set to 0x01005E, the next bit is a 0, and the last 23 bits of the multicast address are copied to the last 23 bits of the multicast MAC address.

This is the pattern that local Ethernet interfaces detect if they are registered to the associated multicast group. As an example, let's use a multicast group address of 230.3.2.1 as the destination multicast group. The destination MAC address would be 0x01005E-030201.

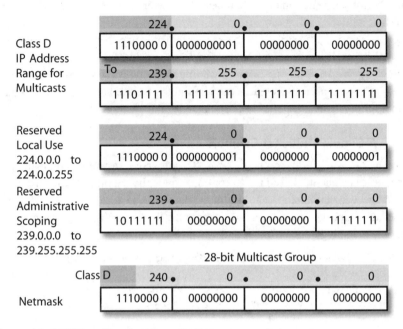

Figure 13–3 TCP multicast address formats

13.2.2 An Open-Source Multicast Facility: `udpcast`

Now that we have some of the basic information about the mechanics of multicasting out of the way, we can move to more practical matters. What can we do with multicasting, and how do we do it? Fortunately, there is an available open-source implementation of multicast sender and receiver software that may be useful in crafting multicast installation tools. (As a matter of fact, the administrators at the PNNL have reportedly modified `SystemImager` to use a multicast approach for their cluster. The work is available in NWLinux, compiled for Itanium 2 systems, from their Web site at `http://www.emsl.pnl.gov/nwlinux`. I don't know if they used the particular software I am using as an example.) This software is `udpcast`, available from `http://udpcast.linux.lu`.

The `udpcast` package consists of a sender program (`/usr/sbin/udp-sender`), a receiver program (`/usr/sbin/udp-receiver`), and `/usr/lib/udpcast/makeImage`, which takes files from a template under `/usr/lib/udpcast/templ` and creates an `initrd` file. There are manual pages installed for the sender and receiver components.

By installing the `kernel-udpcast` package, you also get a prebuilt kernel (`/boot/vmlinuz-2.4.25-udpcast`) and a matching set of kernel modules under `/lib/modules/2.4.25-udpcast`. When you install both RPMs, you get a do-it-yourself kit that allows you to build bootable environments that use the multicast software on your hardware to do one-to-many system installations. The boot kernel environment needs to have its driver components tailored for your target hardware, unless you use another framework for booting (more on this in a short while).

The `udp-sender` and `udp-receiver` commands may be used on the command line or as part of the bootable environment. In the simplest case, data from a file (or `stdin`) may be sent from the `udp-sender` to one or more waiting `udp-receiver` programs over a multicast "channel." This has usefulness that is not just limited to installation. Any data that needs to be sent to multiple systems in parallel is a candidate for this method.

13.2.3   A Simple Multicast Example

Let's test the `udp-sender` and `udp-receiver` software in a simple command-line example. On the multicast "client," I used the `-p` option to pipe the output of the receiver to the standard input of the `tar` command. The multicast data will be received by `udp-receiver`, decompressed and unpacked by `tar`, and written to the local disk. The receiver gets started and will wait for the incoming data from the sender, which we run here:

```
# udp-receiver -log /tmp/multi.log -p "tar xvzf -"
Udp-receiver 2004-02-22
Compressed UDP receiver for (stdout) at 192.168.0.109 on eth0
received message, cap=00000019
Connected as #0 to 192.168.0.110
Listening to multicast on 232.168.0.110
Press any key to start receiving data!
root/.ssh/     10 240   ( 8.32 Mbps) 73 709 551 615
root/.ssh/known_hosts
root/.ssh/id_dsa
root/.ssh/id_dsa.pub
root/.ssh/authorized_keys2
bytes=         10 240   ( 0.16 Mbps) 73 709 551 615
Transfer complete.
```

The output on the receiver side is

```
# tar cvzf - /root/.ssh | udp-sender
Udp-sender 2004-02-22
Using mcast address 232.168.0.110
UDP sender for (stdin) at 192.168.0.110 on eth0
Broadcasting control to 192.168.0.255
New connection from 192.168.0.109  (#0) 00000019
Ready. Press any key to start sending data.
tar: Removing leading / from member names
root/.ssh/
root/.ssh/known_hosts
root/.ssh/id_dsa
root/.ssh/id_dsa.pub
root/.ssh/authorized_keys2
Starting transfer: 00000019
```

```
bytes=          10 240 re-xmits=000000 (  0.0%) slice=0202   73
709 551 615 -    0
Transfer complete.
Disconnecting #0 (192.168.0.109)
```

Notice that I made a "boo-boo" in this example. I sent the /root/.ssh SSH keys, which are the identity of one root account on a specific system, to *all* the multicast receivers. Darn. Now I have to regenerate all the root DSA keys. So much for creative demonstrations.

These multicast tools have a number of options that are quite useful, including the ability for the sender to group UDP packets into "slices" and ensure that all clients have successfully received the whole slice before continuing on. There are forward error correction (FEC) packets sent with each slice, and the size of the "slice" and number of FEC packets can be configured. The maximum transmit bit rate may also be controlled to keep from overrunning slower network equipment.

13.2.4   A More Complex Example

If we wanted to implement a system installation tool based on udpcast, how would it function? One approach might be to use the SystemImager boot and capture framework, and add udpcast as an optional replacement for the rsync installation. How would we package the data sent to the clients?

Our first instinct might be to use a tool, like tar, to save a tree, compress it, and send it to the clients, for whom the archive stream would be unpacked in real time to the disk, as in our simple previous example. Something would need to prepare the disk partitions on the client, just like SI and its bootable kernel and scripting, prior to installing the file system contents. It turns out that as a cluster gets larger, the differences in the disk access times across systems can cause the installation to fail using this method. We want to do something that scales.

A better approach might be to send either a prepackaged, compressed "tar ball" or to create the archive on the fly from the local system image. The multicast receivers would stuff the compressed archive into a RAM disk and unpack it to the local disk only when the whole archive is received. In this way nobody has to wait for retries as a result of disk timing issues. The issue then becomes the size of the compressed image archive versus the size of the available RAM disk on the installation clients. Keeping the image small and compressed addresses the memory issues.

We should consider using SI commands and as much of the existing infrastructure to capture the image tree from the golden client, and to manage the images on the server. This model would entail just using the udpcast tools to perform the initial multicast installation of the clients from the image tree. In other words, we should add multicasting as an option to the existing behavior of SI to minimize the amount of development work needed to get "on the air" (on the ether?) with a multicast solution.

After handling the boot modifications, one remaining issue is the synchronization of the sender and the receivers. The sender should wait until all the receivers are ready before launching into its multicast conversation. The `udp-sender` program has facilities to support this by waiting for a predetermined minimum number of clients to connect before proceeding, or for a period of time. There also are controls over how long to wait for all clients to connect, and how long to wait *after* all clients have connected.

13.2.5   Command-line Prototyping with Multicast

Let's run some experiments with the `udpcast` software from the command line to determine some of the possibilities for time savings. We will also get some experience with using the options to the sender and receiver commands.

In this example, let's send to only two clients and create a compressed archive file from the SI image tree on the fly. We are also specifying some FEC and a maximum bit rate that is 90% of the local 100baseTx switched network's maximum throughput:

```
# cd /var/lib/systemimager/images/ns1_20040316
# tar czf - * | udp-sender --full-duplex --nokbd \
        --min-clients 2 --max-bitrate 90m --fec 8x8
Udp-sender 2004-02-22
Using mcast address 232.168.0.110
UDP sender for (stdin) at 192.168.0.110 on eth0
Broadcasting control to 192.168.0.255
[ ... output deleted ... ]
Transfer complete.
Disconnecting #0 (192.168.0.109)
```

One of the issues with this approach is that the efficiency is limited by the back-end speed of reading the directory tree (and lots of little files) from a software RAID 5 device, creating the archive blocks, compressing the blocks, then piping them to `udp-sender`, which transmits the data as packets. We find that the transfer of the image data takes roughly 30 minutes for a tree captured from a full Fedora installation (@ `everything`). We used the following receiver command once the sender was started:

```
# udp-receiver --nokbd --nosync --file /tmp/localarchive.tbz
```

The image tree is roughly 2,342,828,000 bytes (2.2 GB), and the network throughput observed was roughly 1.3 MB/s average, substantially below the capabilities of 100base-TX (theoretical, 12.5 MB/s). The numbers work out if you divide the size by the data rate: The transfer time is 30 minutes. I watched carefully and saw that the network data rate improved markedly when a large file was transferred. It kept the "channel" from the server's disk to the client busier.

A more efficient approach might be to produce the compressed archive from the tree and send that. It is a smaller amount of data to send (773,051,480 bytes or 737 MB), and the compute bottleneck is moved away from the on-the-fly archive creation. This transfer completed in three minutes at just more than 4.1 MB/s. We have to conclude that distributing a precompressed archive is the route to take.

Looking at the sender output from your test, you might notice that there are a substantial number of retransmissions, probably because of data overruns in the switch path. Note that some vendor's switches do *not* buffer UDP traffic if they get congested. They throw it away. By using the `--max-bitrate` option on the sender, you can determine the maximum transmission rate without retries and limit the data rate to this value or less.

13.2.6 Prototyping a Network Multicast Installation

We have tested the `udpcast` software on the command line and liked what we saw. Now how do we put what we know about `initrd` files, booting, and the `udpcast` tools to work? First we decide on an architecture for our installation tool using multicast. We want the individual system to

- Boot a modified `SI` environment with `pxelinux`
- Set up a large RAM disk to hold a compressed `tar` archive containing a system image
- Use the `SI` master script to prepare the partition information on the disk
- Run the multicast receiver from the master script to get the compressed `tar` archive into the RAM disk
- Execute `tar` to unpack the archive to the disk, instead of the `rsync` command, when the receiver finishes
- Reboot the system to its new configuration

The multicast sender needs to be waiting for the client systems to connect as they boot. We will start the sender, then boot the individual clients to be installed. A diagram of this is shown in Figure 13–4.

We need to start somewhere and with some minimal debugging capability to track the software's actions. Let's set up a separate boot for a test client, boot a system, execute a shell, and look at the memory-based environment. Steps involved in this are as follows.

1. **Copy an existing master script**. Make a copy of an existing `SI` master installation script in the `/var/lib/systemimager/scripts` directory and create a soft link to it, named with a test system's host name and a `.sh` extension—for example, `test-sys.sh`.

2. **Edit the master script**. Delete everything in the *copy* of the master script that you just linked, below the comment line that says

   `### BEGIN Stop RAID devices before partitioning begins ###`

3. **Add an escape to a shell in the master script**. There is a function defined in the master script named `shellout` that is intended to exit the master script and execute a command shell when an error occurs during normal operation. Let's use this to "take a look around" once the installation kernel is booted. Add a line to the end of the master script that says `shellout`.

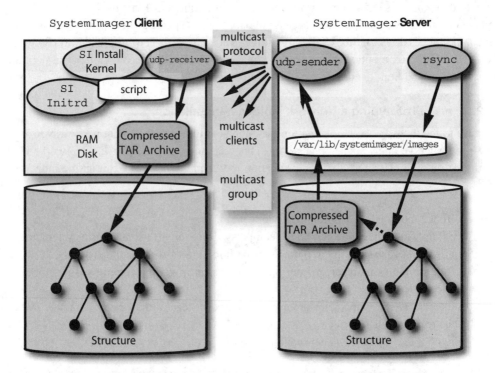

Figure 13–4 Multicast prototype architecture for SI

4. **Add a boot option to `pxelinux`.** Using the `pxelinux` facility allows us to add a new booting option while maintaining the normal SI booting. Replicate a configuration clause with a new kernel and new `initrd` path information in the `/tftpboot/pxelinux.cfg/default.netboot` file that reads

```
label    linux.udp
         kernel udp/kernel
         append vga=extended load_ramdisk=1 prompt_ramdisk=0  \
         initrd=udp/initrd.img root=/dev/ram rw               \
         ramdisk_blocksize=4096
```

5. **Create the `/tftpboot/udp` directory.** Create the directory referenced by the kernel and `initrd` files in the previous step, and place a copy of the SI kernel and `initrd` in the directory. We may not need the copy of the files (the master script modifications might be enough to differentiate the installation method), but let's play it safe.

6. **Create a statically bound version of `udp-receiver`.** Download the source package for `udpcast` from `http://udpcast.linux.lu`. "Untar" the archive in `/tmp` and modify `Makefile` to create a statically bound version of the executable that requires no shared libraries. (Otherwise, we get into the realm of needing to identify the

proper shared libraries used by the application [easy with the `ldd` command], and matching them to the kernel version being used in the boot framework [hard].) You can do this by changing the `LDFLAGS` option by adding `-static` to the end of the line. Typing `make` will recompile the programs and create static versions.

7. **Add the static `udp-receiver` program to the binary tools package**. The RAM-based installation kernel uses tools from `/usr/share/systemimager/boot/` `<arch>/standard`, which are in the `boel_binaries.tar.gz` file. This is loaded by the master script, via `rsync`, as part of the start-up. Because this package is in one place, we cannot create a duplicate; we have to unpack the archive, add the `udp-receiver` program, and then recreate the archive file. To create an enhanced version of the `tar` archive, follow these steps (assuming you are on an i386 architecture):

```
# cd /usr/share/systemimager/boot/i386/standard
# mkdir new
# cp boel_binaries.tar.gz boel_binaries.tar.gz.SAVE
# cd new
# tar xvzf ../boel_binaries.tar.gz.SAVE
# cp /tmp/udpcast-<version>/udp-receiver bin/
# tar cvzf ../boel_binaries.tar.gz *
```

8. **Boot the `SI` install kernel**. Boot to the `pxelinux` prompt and enter `linux.udp`, which is the label of our experimental environment. This will boot the install kernel, discover the hardware, initialize the network interface, load the master script, copy the `boel` archive, install the modified binary tools, and then exit to a shell. We can then use the console to look around at the environment and investigate using the `udp-receiver` command from the command line. We have not modified the local disk on the test machine, everything is in RAM *only*.

13.2.7   Making More Modifications

Now that we have the install kernel booting and have verified the operation of the statically bound `udp-receiver` in the RAM-based environment, we can start to automate the process a little more. My philosophy when making modifications like this is to keep the additions separate and modular. There will be another release of `SI` coming along, and we need to be able to upgrade without too much effort.

Fortunately, because the authors of the tool also have a good philosophy about their use of infrastructure like `rsync`, we can extend things without hacking up the original intent or operation of the tool. Once we have a base of understanding, we can extend the software for our own needs. This, by the way, is the very heart of what open-source software is all about. If we had no access to sources (scripts, programs, and so on), we could not find out how the system works, nor could we modify or extend it.

Next, I will outline the modifications that I undertook to get an experimental multicast capability into the SI tool. There are a few more extensions and discoveries necessary in our next step.

1. **Create a separate "depot" for multicast information accessible with rsync.** This involves creating a directory in /usr/share/boot/systemimager, called multicast and then allowing rsyncd to pick up information from it. This will also provide a base path that rsync will understand, and that we can use to pick up configuration information for the multicast installation inside the modified SI scripts. Add the following configuration lines to the /etc/systemimager/rsync_stubs/99local file and then run mkrsyncd_conf to create the new /etc/systemimager/rsyncd.conf file and restart the daemon:

   ```
   [multicast]
   /usr/share/boot/systemimager/multicast
   ```

2. **Consider how to pass information into the multicast install.** The SI tool uses shell environment variables at various points in the process to direct the installation. One source of the configuration information may be the local.config file that is created in the installation target's root directory by some of the scripts (options that mention "create a local configuration file"). This file is sourced, if it exists, by the installation kernel's start-up script. Network configuration information may be provided by DHCP, if it is present. Examine the etc/dhclient.conf file in the initrd.img file for the information that SI requests from DHCP (including options). There are two other available methods of getting parameter information: (1) get the kernel command line, passed by the bootloader, from /proc/cmdline after the /proc file system is mounted; and (2) test for environment variables passed from the kernel to the init process and on to rcS.

3. **Passing /etc/init.d/rcS information on to the master script.** Information is passed *from* the rcS script to the master script in the /tmp/variables.txt file in the RAM file system. The rcS script defines variables named ARCH, FLAVOR, SCRIPTS, VERSION, and a PATH value at the very top of the script.

4. **Use rsync to get information.** In addition to the shell variables, the rsyncd daemon understands "module" definitions that are placed in its configuration file, like the [multicast] definition used previously. This allows us to reference the modules (directory paths) in rsync commands in our scripts. See the man pages for rsync and rsyncd.conf for details. You will find command lines in the SI scripts of the form

   ```
   # Get a file from the rsync server under the path defined
   # as [scripts] in the /etc/systemimager/rsyncd.conf file. Put
   # the file in /tmp, follow links, and be verbose.
   rsync -avL ${IMAGESERVER}::${SCRIPTS}/${SCRIPTNAME} /tmp
   ```

5. **Precedence of master scripts**. In the version of SI that I have installed, 3.0.1, the rcS script implements a hierarchy of master scripts. If there is an image name specified by the IMAGENAME variable in a /local.config file, then the install script will load (with the get_script subroutine) and will execute the *<ImageName>*.master script; otherwise, the *<HostName>*.sh script is attempted, followed by *<Base-HostName>*.master (which is the host name stripped of any numerical suffix). We could modify this logic in the script to test whether the multicast-specific script exists, and to load it if it does. This would allow us to preserve the "standard" SI installation process as much as possible and yet add our specific steps and data.

6. **Create a modified boot environment start-up**. We need to modify the start-up script, rcS, in the boot kernel's initrd file to contain the changes we make to the rcS script. If we have separate pxelinux boot directories for the "standard" SI and our multicast experiment, we can place the modified initrd.img file into /tftp-boot/udp. Without the flexibility of a network bootloader, we would have to replace the "standard" boot files for our experiments.

7. **Consider how to handle different hardware architectures**. We need to remember that we might be dealing with different hardware architectures in our installation facility, so let's add a hierarchy under the new /usr/share/systemimager/boot/multicast directory to handle this. The SI rcS script defines variables called ARCH and FLAVOR that can be used to generate the proper paths in relation to an rsyncd known location. An example command line for rsync, to pick up the boel_binaries.tar.gz file would be

```
#
# Must define appropriate variable values in rcS script
#
rsync -avL ${IMAGESERVER}::${BOOT}/${ARCH}/${FLAVOR}/${BOEL} \
        /tmp
```

8. **Make changes to the rcS script**. You should know how to mount and examine the initrd.img file's contents by now, but we need to modify the contents. You will find that you cannot change anything within the loop device mounted file system, because it is "full"—the maximum size it can be. The file system is mounted as a cramfs, if you look at the output of the mount command, so we need to use mkcramfs to create a new one. Investigating mkcramfs leads to the following commands if the initrd file system is mounted under /tmp/image (I use tar to preserve any existing links during the copy). If you keep the copied directory and contents, you don't have to unpack the initrd file repeatedly, just make the changes, recreate the file, compress it, and move it into place:

```
# cd /tmp
# mkdir newimage
# tar cvf - image/* | (cd newimage; tar xf -)
```

```
# vi newimage/etc/init.d/rcS
# mkcramfs newimage newinitrd
# gzip < newinitrd > newinitrd.img
# cp newinitrd /tftpboot/udp/initrd.img
```

9. **Make modifications to the `rcS` script to catch kernel parameters.** The bootloader can pass parameters to the kernel and the kernel will pass them on to `init`, which will pass them on to the `rcS` script in its environment. By modifying the start of the `rcS` script, we catch two options that affect the script's behavior. Setting the FLAVOR variable will pick up a different `boel_binaries.tar.gz` file:

```
# Passed in from kernel command line -RwL-, set a multicast
# installation, and possibly enable simple debug
#
if [ -n "${simulti}" ]; then
    FLAVOR="multicast"
    MULTICAST=yes
    if [ -n "${simulti_debug}" ]; then
       MULTICAST_DEBUG=yes
    fi
fi
```

10. **Add the kernel command-line parameters to the `pxelinux` configuration.** To pass parameters "through" the kernel to `init` and `rcS`, the parameters must be declared as *<name>=<value>* on the bootloader line. If the parameters have no values associated with them, they will not be passed. We also need to add another parameter definition, `tempfs_size=173m`, to the bootloader command line (this will be explained a little further on). Edit the `/tftpboot/pxelinux.cfg/default.netboot` file and modify the `linux.udp` boot stanza to read

```
label   linux.udp
        kernel udp/kernel
        append vga=extended load_ramdisk=1 prompt_ramdisk=0 \
            initrd=udp/initrd.img root=/dev/ram rw            \
            ramdisk_blocksize=4096                            \
            tempfs_size=173m simulti=1 simulti_debug=1
```

11. **Make another modification to the `rcS` script**. This modification is to determine which master script is grabbed by `rsync` from the image server by the `rcS` script. We will show the section to be modified in the `/etc/init.d/rcS` script inside the `initrd` image (see page 185 if you need a refresher on how `initrd` works). There is a function called `get_script` that uses `rsync` to pick up a script from `/var/lib/systemimager/scripts`. The last actions that `rcS` performs is to select a

master script name, get it from the boot server, save the local variable definitions, and
then execute the master script.

```
if [ ! -z $IMAGENAME ]; then
    # If IMAGENAME is specified, then the IMAGENAME.master
    # script takes precedence over the HOSTNAME.sh script.
    # -BEF-
    echo
    echo "This host will be installed with image:${IMAGENAME}"
    SCRIPTNAME="${IMAGENAME}.master"
    get_script || shellout
else
    # Try to get an autoinstall script based on $HOSTNAME.
    SCRIPTNAME="${HOSTNAME}.sh"
    get_script
    SCRIPTFAIL=$?
    # Try for a multicast script name
    if [ ${SCRIPTFAIL} != 0 ]; then
        echo "Trying ${HOSTNAME}.mcast"
        SCRIPTNAME="${HOSTNAME}.mcast"
        get_script
        SCRIPTFAIL=$?
    fi
    if [ ${SCRIPTFAIL} != 0 ]; then
        echo "$CMD failed!"
        # Try to get a master file based on the "base
        # hostname".  For example,if the hostname is
        # compute99, then try to get compute.master. -BEF-
        #
        BASE_HOSTNAME=`echo $HOSTNAME | sed "s/[0-9]*$//"`
        echo "Trying ${BASE_HOSTNAME}.master"
        SCRIPTNAME="${BASE_HOSTNAME}.master"
        get_script
        SCRIPTFAIL=$?
    fi

    [ ${SCRIPTFAIL} != 0 ] && shellout

fi

echo
echo write_variables               # Save variable values to
write_variables || shellout        # to /tmp/variables.txt

echo
echo run_autoinstall_script        # Execute the master script
run_autoinstall_script
exit 0
```

12. **Adjust the RAM disk size**. We would like the RAM disk used by the install kernel to encompass all the available RAM to make room for the compressed archive containing the system image. The `rcS` script mounts the / directory to a `tempfs` device, which by default will take only 50% of the system's available RAM. This may be fine for a fully operational system that wants to use `tempfs` as scratch, but we need to have as much space as is available to contain the compressed archive with the system image in it. One way to pass an adjustment is as a kernel parameter on the kernel command line from the bootloader. The whole kernel command line shows up in the special `/proc/cmdline` file after `/proc` is mounted, which it isn't when this subroutine is executed. We must rely on the variables being set from the `init` environment from the kernel, with a definition of `tempfs_size=<size>` used to set the `mount` option. As mentioned in The Temporary File System on page 213, an option may be specified to `mount` for the size of the file system, with k, m, or g as a suffix to a numerical value. Note that the `mount` command has a slightly different syntax here. Modifications to `rcS` for this behavior are in the `switch_root_to_tmpfs` subroutine:

```
switch_root_to_tmpfs() {
# Switch root over to tmpfs so we don't have to worry about
# the size of the tarball and binaries that users may decide
# to copy over. -BEF- (mods to control tempfs size -RwL-)
#
    if [ -n "${MULTICAST}" ]; then
        RAMFS_OPTS=""
        if [ -n "${tempfs_size}" ]; then
            RAMFS_OPTS="-o size=${tempfs_size}"
            echo -e "Options for tempfs are\"${RAMFS_OPTS}\"."
            [ -n "${MULTICAST_DEBUG}" ] || sleep 10
        fi
    fi
    mkdir -p /new_root || shellout
    mount tmpfs /new_root -t tmpfs ${RAMFS_OPTS} || shellout
    cd / || shellout
    rsync -a bin etc lib my_modules root sbin tmp usr \
          var /new_root/ || shellout
    cd /new_root || shellout
    mkdir -p old_root || shellout
    pivot_root . old_root || shellout
}
```

We are finally ready to boot our configuration all the way through to the `shellout` that we added in the master script for our test system. We boot to the `pxelinux` prompt, type `linux.udp`, and watch the output stream by on the console. We are rewarded with a shell prompt when we hit `Enter`. We should probably test to determine whether our interface is multicast enabled by pinging the multicast "all hosts" address (you should see responses from your host and all multicast-enabled systems on the network:

```
# ping 224.0.0.1
```

Now it's time to test the whole thing up to the unpacking of the archive on the client. We have to make sure that the following configuration tasks are completed:

- Ensure the `/tftpboot/pxelinux.cfg/default.netboot` file contains the proper boot stanza and variables. Remove `simulti_debug` and increase the value of `tempfs_size` to the maximum your system will support.
- Ensure that the `boel_binaries.tar.gz` file with `udp-receiver` added is in the correct location for the installation client. This is in the `/usr/share/systemimager/boot/<ARCH>/multicast` directory.
- Check that the `/var/lib/systemimager/scripts/udp.master` file is in place, and the test system link is present: `<system>.mcast`.
- Make sure the `/tftpboot/udp/initrd.img` file contains the modified `rcS` script.
- Create the entry in the `/etc/systemimager/rsync_stubs/99local` file for `/etc/systemimager/multicast` and recreate the `/etc/systemimager/rsyncd.conf` file from it. (We will use this in the next section.)
- Make sure that the `systemimager` service has been restarted if the `rsyncd` configuration file was changed:

  ```
  # service systemimager restart
  ```

- Add the following line to the `udp.master` file to run the `udp-receiver` program from the script:

  ```
  udp-receiver --nokbd --file /tmp/localarchive.tgz
  shellout
  ```

With all this in place, you can start the `udp-sender` program on the image server, with the following command line:

```
# udp-sender --nokbd --min-clients <N> --fec 8x8 \
        --max-bitrate <N>m --file <ImageArchive>
```

Keep the number of clients you reboot to a minimum, unless you want to go for the "smoke factor." Debugging information for files transferred to the client via `rsync` will be in `/var/log/systemimager/rsyncd`. When the basic modifications are working, we can move on to the next phase of improvement.

The first issue I had was forgetting to start the `udp-sender` manually on the image server, which caused the `udp-receiver` on the clients to exit with no debugging messages. I modified the `udp.master` script to add a logging option for the receiver:

```
# udp-receiver --nokbd --log /tmp/receiver.log \
      --file /tmp/localarchive.tgz
```

It was smooth sailing after the initial issue. The next section makes some final adjustments to the prototype configuration.

13.2.8   Generalizing the Multicast Installation Prototype

We have a proof-of-concept prototype for multicast system installation, using `SI`. The basic framework is in place, now we need to think a little more about what we are doing and generalize the process that we are automating. Once we do that, we can apply some finishing touches to our handiwork and get on with other cluster software issues. Some design questions for us to consider include the following.

- The `udpcast` tools are currently using the default administrative and multicast network addresses. How can we control the client and server usage of the network resources?
- Will we have different images for different clients (most certainly for testing and debugging), and will we need to perform multiple installs at the same time?
- How do we automatically schedule the `udp-sender` program on the `SI` server prior to initiating the client installations?
- How do we apply tuning parameters to the `udpcast` tools to utilize the network and minimize errors best?
- How do we continue to use the benefits of `SI` to capture system images, and provide client updates without reinstallation, but maintain the advantage of multicasting?

The best answer I can think of to most of these questions begins with a model in which an installation image and a group of clients are associated with a specific multicast group and set of administrative settings. In this model, one set of installation parameters, primarily a compressed archive and a set of `udpcast` sender and receiver options, are associated with a group of systems. We can pick one client or all clients in a particular "multicast install group" to participate in an installation, but all clients and the sender have the same set of configuration parameters and the same target image.

The `udpcast` sender supports a kind of barrier operation, where it starts and waits either for a predetermined minimum number of clients to connect, a fixed period of time, or for a fixed period of time after a minimum number of clients connect. (All processes or tasks rendezvous at a the "barrier", and will not continue until a preset condition is met. In our case, this is the arrival of the number of expected installation clients.) We need to think about starting the sender, then getting all clients rebooted to the receiver program. At that point the installation starts automatically.

I decided to create two files in the `/etc/systemimager/multicast` directory that is accessible from the `rsyncd`: an `mcast.default.defs` file that contains common variable definitions and an `mcast.default.list` file that contains a list of systems that participate in the multicast group `default`. The general format is `mcast.<mcastgroup>.<file>`, which allows us to make name assumptions in scripts based on the multicast group name.

The first file allows us to share information between the clients and the server, and the second file allows us to set up the number of clients to install for the `udp-sender` program when we write a script to start the installations automatically. The definitions file contains

```
# Default multicast group parameters for sender and receiver.
# Use the command-line options for "udp-receiver" and
# "udp-#sender". See the man pages for these commands for
# details. 20040317 -RwL-
#
SIMCASTGROUPNAME="mcast.default" # File names driven from this
         MYPID="$$"
UNARCHIVECOMMAND="tar xvzf "
   ARCHIVESUFFIX="tbz"
     LOGSUFFIX="${MYPID}.log"
    UDPRECEIVER="/sbin/udp-receiver"   # Different on client!
     UDPSENDER="/usr/sbin/udp-sender"

# ------ Common values for both sender and receiver
# Send and receive file name
  AFILENAME="${SIMCASTGROUPNAME}.${ARCHIVESUFFIX}"
LOGFILENAME="${AFILENAME}.${LOGSUFFIX}"
     NOUSER="--nokbd"                     # No user prompts

# ------ Values for receiver only -------
RFILEPATH="/tmp"
    RFILE="${RFILEPATH}/${AFILENAME}"
 RLOGFILE="${RFILEPATH}/${AFILENAME}.${LOGSUFFIX}"
RSYNCOPT="--nosync" # Set if writing to mounted file system
RFILEOPT="--file ${RFILE}"   # File name for local file
  RLOGOPT="--log ${RLOGFILE}" # Local log file for transfer
# Single quote holds off substitution until "eval"
 RCMDLINE='${UDPRECEIVER} ${RFILEOPT} ${RLOGOPT} ${NOUSER}'

# ------ Values for sender only   -------
  BITRATE="70m"           # Numeric, can have "k" or "m" suffix
SFILEPATH="/var/lib/systemimager/images"
   SFILE="${SFILEPATH}/${AFILENAME}"   # File to send
 SLOGPATH="/tmp"
```

```
SLOGFILE="${SLOGPATH}/${AFILENAME}.${LOGSUFFIX}"
BITRATEOPT="--max-bitrate ${BITRATE}"    # Limit bit rate
DUPLEXOPT="--full-duplex"    # For switched network
MCASTADDR=""                     # Default 232.<27 bits of IP>
  SFILEOPT="--file ${SFILE}"       # File to send
   SLOGOPT="--log ${SLOGFILE}"    # Local log for transfer
# Expect value to be set in environment for ${NMCLIENTS}
# then "eval ${SCMDLINE}"
 CLIENTOPT='--min-clients ${NMCLIENTS}'
# Single quote holds off substitution. Order of the options
# matters!
  SCMDLINE="${UDPSENDER}\
       ${SFILEOPT}       \
       ${BITRATEOPT}     \
       ${DUPLEXOPT}      \
       ${NOUSER}         \
       ${SLOGOPT}        \
       ${CLIENTOPT}      \
    "
```

When a shell sources this file, it defines the shared variables for the sender and receivers in a multicast installation group. Several variable values are quoted to prevent evaluation until the shell `eval` command is used to execute the command line. This allows a script to set a value in the environment for the number of expected clients, then execute `eval ${SCMDLINE}` to start the `udp-sender` or `udp-receiver` program.

We can tune both the sender and receiver behavior with the common definitions file. The client's master script gets the definitions with `rsync`, sources the variable definitions, and executes the `udp-receiver` command line:

```
. /tmp/variables.txt || shellout

MCASTGROUP="mcast.default"
MCASTDEFS="${MCASTGROUP}.defs"
MCAST=multicast

[ -z $OVERRIDES ] && OVERRIDES="${MCASTGROUP}"

# Pull in remote definitions for this mcast group
echo "Getting multicast group definitions"
rsync -aL ${IMAGESERVER}::${MCAST}/${MCASTDEFS} /tmp/ \
      >/dev/null 2>&1
[ $? != 0 ] && shellout

[ ... disk partitioning and file system init ... ]
#Fill it up

echo "Sourcing multicast group definitions"
```

```
. /tmp/${MCASTDEFS} >/dev/null
[ $? != 0 ] && shellout

echo "Starting the multicast receiver ..."
echo -e "Command line \"${RCMDLINE}\" ..."
eval ${RCMDLINE}

echo "Unpacking archive to disk ..."
cd /a/
${UNARCHIVECOMMAND} ${AFILENAME}
[$? != 0 ] && shellout

[ ... System Configurator Operations ... ]

# Tell the image server we're done.
rsync $IMAGESERVER::scripts/imaging_complete > /dev/null 2>&1

# Take network interface down
ifconfig eth0 down || shellout

# reboot the autoinstall client
shutdown -r now
```

We very carefully preserve all the operations that would take place if this were a "normal" installation with rsync, but replace the rsync operations from the image tree with the multicast receiver and archive unpacking. The disk partitions are made, file systems are formatted, and the file systems are mounted under /a by the unmodified portions of the script.

When the disk is ready, we schedule udp-receiver to get the compressed tar archive to the /tmp directory. Once the archive is received, we unpack it to /a, run the override directory processing, and allow the SystemConfigurator to run on the new system structure. The actual modifications to the master script are minimal, so we can capture the image normally and then run mkautoinstallscript on the system image to produce a script we can modify.

13.2.9   Triggering a Multicast Installation

Up to this point, we have been using the pxelinux bootloader and manual intervention to test our multicast installation modifications. We are now ready to start using the autoinstallation tools provided with SI. This will eliminate the need for manual intervention and physical presence to boot the clients.

Running the updateclient script *on the clients*, with the -autoinstall and the -reboot options will cause the install kernel and initrd to be installed, and the client will be rebooted to the installation process. The kernel and initrd.img files are found and installed by updateclient from the /usr/share/systemimager/<ARCH> directory on the SI server. We can use the -flavor option to updateclient to trigger an installation of the kernel and `initrd.img` from `/usr/share/systemimager/i386/multicast` instead of the `/usr/share/systemimager/i386/standard` directory.

Just make sure that the modified boot files and `boel_binaries.tar.gz` file are in the proper location under the `flavor` directory `multicast`. The client will automatically reboot with our modified kernel and `initrd`, and will locate the proper autoinstall script in `/var/lib/systemimager/scripts`, which will guide its installation. Synchronizing all of this is the next step.

To perform the installations automatically, we need to run `updateclient` on all the clients in the multicast install group and make sure that the `udp-sender` process is running on the image server. The automatic install process should do the rest for us. A rough prototype script, using PDSH to launch the `updateclient` command remotely, follows:

```
#!/bin/sh
# Start up a multicast installation on the passed group name
  PDSH="/usr/bin/pdsh"
DSHBAK="/usr/bin/dshbak"
MGROUP="default"
if [[ -n "${1}" ]]; then
    MGROUP="${1}"
fi
MULTIPATH="/etc/systemimager/multicast"
MULTIPREF="mcast.${MGROUP}"
 MDEFFILE="${MULTIPATH}/${MULTIPREF}.defs"
MLISTFILE="${MULTIPATH}/${MULTIPREF}.list"
#Check that all files are there
[ -f ${MDEFFILE} ]  ||   exit 1
[ -f ${MLISTFILE} ]  ||   exit 2
# Source the common definitions
. ${MDEFFILE}
[ $? != 0 ] &&    exit 3
#Count systems in the list
typeset -i SYSCOUNT
SYSCOUNT=$( sed -e '/^#.*$/d' < ${MLISTFILE}  | wc -l )
[ ${SYSCOUNT} -gt 0 ] ||   exit 4
# Start the reboots with PDSH, using the group list
export WCOLL="${MLISTFILE}"
${PDSH} updateclient -server ${HOSTNAME} \
        -flavor multicast          \
        -autoinstall               \
        -reboot           |        \
${DSHBAK}
# Start the sender and wait for the clients
export NMCLIENTS=${SYSCOUNT}
eval ${SCMDLINE}
[ $? != 0 ] &&    exit 9
exit 0
```

Obviously, if you don't want to update all the clients in the multicast installation group list at once, this script would need modification. There is little or no error checking, but if a client fails to reboot, the sender will wait for the full complement of clients, so there is time to fix the problem manually. This is still a prototype, and will be improved as we gain experience with this installation method.

13.3 The SI flamethrower Facility

Now that we have trundled through a custom implementation of multicast installation, we can take a look at a multicast installation tool that is integrated with SI: flamethrower. The software for the tool is available on the SI download site. The most current version as of this writing is 0.1.6-1.

The documentation describes the tool as a general-purpose multicast installation facility that is capable of stand-alone operation or integration with SI. The flamethrowerd daemon is started on the server and uses information in a configuration file to determine where the multicast information source is located. This is the SI image directory in the case of integration with SI.

The first client initiates a multicast session by contacting the flamethrowerd daemon, which will wait for a preset length of time before initiating the multicast session. Clients that miss the starting window will wait until the next session is started on their behalf. This looks like it fills the void in our previously described prototype. Let's take a closer look.

13.3.1   Installing flamethrower

The package is a noarch type, which is an indication of architecture-independent code, usually scripts or Perl code. The first step is to download the flamethrower package from http://sourceforge.net/projects/systemimager. To take a look at the package requirements, use the following command:

```
# rpm -qp -requires flamethrower-0.1.6-1.noarch.rpm
/usr/bin/perl
udpcast
/bin/sh
res flamethrower-0.1.6-1.noarch.rpm
rpmlib(PayloadFilesHavePrefix) <= 4.0-1
rpmlib(CompressedFileNames) <= 3.0.4-1
```

If you examine the content listings, you will see that it requires Perl and the udpcast package that we discussed in the previous section. The udpcast package is also available from the SourceForge site. Thankfully, there are no more dependencies that we saw previously.

We can also look at what files the package provides to the system when it is installed:

```
# rpm -qp -filesbypkg flamethrower-0.1.6-1.noarch.rpm
flamethrower /etc/flamethrower/flamethrower.conf
flamethrower /etc/init.d/flamethrower-server
```

```
flamethrower /usr/bin/flamethrower
flamethrower /usr/bin/flamethrowerd
flamethrower /usr/lib/flamethrower/Flamethrower.pm
flamethrower /usr/share/doc/flamethrower-0.1.6
flamethrower /usr/share/doc/flamethrower-0.1.6/COPYING
flamethrower /usr/share/doc/flamethrower-0.1.6/CREDITS
flamethrower /usr/share/doc/flamethrower-0.1.6/HOWTO
flamethrower /usr/share/doc/flamethrower-0.1.6/README
```

When I installed this version of the package on an already installed SI server, I found the HOW-TO file empty. I thought this was a little odd.

13.3.2   Activating `flamethrower`

Examining the `/etc/flamethrower/flamethrower.conf` file installed by the RPM package, we see some global options that may be configured, including the base port for the `flamethrower` daemon (9000) and some other `udpcast`-related items. I decided to stick with the default values for the initial tests. The service for `flamethrower-server` needs to be added with `chkconfig`:

```
# chkconfig --add flamethrower-server
```

Once this is done, the next step is to try to "light up" the daemon:

```
# service flamethrower-server start
```

This results in an error message about `/var/state/systemimager/flamethrower` not being present, so let's create it:

```
# mkdir -p /var/state/systemimager/flamethrower
```

The daemon starts up without any problems this time and creates the file `/var/log/messages/flamethrower.flamethrower_directory`, and two process PID files in the `/var/state/systemimager/flamethrower` directory named `flamethrowerd.flamethrower_directory.pid` and `flamethrowerd.flamethrower_directory.udpsender.pid`. Let's see just what is running on the system. In addition to a process for `flamethrowerd`, there is

```
# ps -ef | grep \
      $( < ./flamethrowerd.flamethrower_directory.pid )
root     21631 21630  0 16:48 ? 00:00:00                          \
      udp-sender --pipe tar -B -S -cpf
```

So `flamethrowerd` starts a subprocess that runs the `tar` command from a pipe, with commands to make handling sparse files and reading from a pipe more efficient. So far, so good. Now for the interface to SI.

The documentation mentions that three commands—`mvimage`, `cpimage`, and `getimage`—will make appropriate entries in the `/etc/systemimager/flamethrower.conf` file. We find no such linkage in the Perl code for the commands, so this is where we really start scratching our heads.

What we find when we retrace our steps is that we completely missed downloading the newest version of the SI tools before installing the *latest* version of `flamethrower`. So, hoping the dependencies have not changed, let's download

- `systemimager-client-3.2.0-4.noarch.rpm`
- `systemimager-common-3.2.0-4.noarch.rpm`
- `systemimager-flamethrower-3.2.0-4.noarch.rpm`
- `systemimager-i386boot-standard-3.2.0-4.noarch.rpm`
- `systemimager-server-3.2.0-4.noarch.rpm`

After we've updated the packages, let's decide to keep this as an example of "if things don't add up, check your assumptions." We had downloaded the stand-alone copy of `flamethrower` and were trying to get it to work with an old copy of `SI`. We will find that the new commands, configuration files, directories, and other components were added to the system during the package update.

The following services were added by the update:

- `/etc/init.d/systemimager-server-flamethrowerd`
- `/etc/init.d/systemimager-server-netbootmond`
- `/etc/init.d/systemimager-server-rsyncd`

The configuration file contents for `flamethrowerd` have changed only minimally, but SI keeps its own copy of the file, `/etc/systemimager/flamethrowerd.conf`. After performing the configuration, adding the new services (to be certain the links are in place), and restarting the services (to see which ones are already there), we are rewarded with operating daemons.

One addition that is necessary to get clients to use the new multicast installation is to modify the DHCP configuration (if you use that rather than a `local.cfg` file). The addition places some "custom" parameters in the DHCP response packet that the SI clients will pick up and use. This sets the base port for the client's `udp-receive` multicast client to match the server's base port:

```
option option-143 code 143 = string;                          \
        # (only for ISC's dhcpd v3)
option option-143 "9000";
```

This value is set into the `FLAMETHROWER_DIRECTORY_PORTBASE` variable by the DHCP client in the installation `initrd` file. This will trigger the client's use of the multicast installation process. You can control which clients are fed this option by properly placing it in a group or pool definition in the DHCP configuration file. This allows multicast installation for specific systems to coexist with "normal" installations.

The `flamethrower` daemon manages multicasts of the various modules (scripts, overrides, and so forth) associated with an installation by multicasting directory information to the clients that have requested a multicast installation. After receiving the directory information, the client locates its installation script and executes it, which processes the directory information and uses it to join the appropriate multicast "sessions."

Images that are added to the server by the `getimage`, `mvimage`, and `cpimage` commands are entered into the `/etc/systemimager/flamethrower.conf` file. The file is dynamically read by the daemon as images are added, so there is no need to restart the daemon manually after making changes. The daemon can manage multicast sessions to multiple groups of clients simultaneously.

As usual, the `SI` folks have done a wonderful job of providing system installation functionality that we can all use. Thanks to their efforts, our prototype multicast installer can remain just an experiment. The concepts are directly applicable to understanding the new `flamethrower` facility.

13.3.3   Additional `SI` Functionality in Version 3.2.0

This version of SI has several new and very useful features.

- The ability to change the default boot behavior from a network installation to a local boot, using the `netbootmond`. This functionality is configured in the file `/etc/systemimager/systemimager.conf` with the `NET_BOOT_DEFAULT` variable, which may have the values `net` or `local`. The daemon monitors installation completion and changes the default behavior for the client.
- `flamethrower` multicast capabilities.
- The ability to control access to images (lock them) to prevent interference or bad installations if an image is being modified. See the `/etc/systemimager/imagemanip.conf` and `/etc/systemimager/imageman.perm` files, along with the `imagemanip` command. Information is still a little sketchy on this feature.

13.4 System Installation with `SI` Summary

In this chapter I have introduced multicasting concepts and the `udpcast` tools that implement multicast communications protocol between a sender and receiver. We used these tools to modify an existing open-source solution, `SI` to use multicasting instead of `rsync` to replicate system structure. The expectation is that the scaling for cluster installation will be much better with multicast tools.

We applied an iterative approach to extending the `SI` tool, gaining understanding of its operation one step at a time, then modifying its behavior to meet our needs. The modifications have been kept to a minimum to allow the normal imaging process and use of the standard tools.

This type of modification and approach would not be possible if SI were not an open-source tool, with its sources readily available to us.

Along with the specific application to multicast installation, we have covered a lot of the booting process and mechanics for Linux in general. There is a wide range of this knowledge that may be applied elsewhere, and this was an ulterior motive in spending so much time on this example. The end result is a fairly functional multicast installation tool, but it is still in a prototype stage.

The flamethrower facility for SI, of course, removes the need for further work in the area of the prototype, unless there are still enhancements required for your particular installation. Thanks again, SI team!

CHAPTER 14

To Protect and Serve: Providing Data to Your Cluster

Chapter Objectives

- Introduce the concept of a cluster file system
- Explore available file system options
- Present examples of cluster file system configurations

The compute slices in a cluster work on pieces of a larger problem. Without the ability to read data and write results, the cluster's computation is of little value. Whether the cluster is a database cluster or a scientific cluster, the compute slices need coordinated access to the shared data that is "behind" their computations. This chapter introduces some of the design issues associated with providing data to multiple compute slices in a cluster and presents some of the currently available solutions.

14.1 Introduction to Cluster File Systems

When talking about cluster file systems we have to be careful about how we define the phrase. One simple definition might be: "a file system that is capable of serving data to a cluster." Another more complex definition might be: "a file system that allows multiple systems to access shared file system data independently, while maintaining a consistent view of that data between clients."

There is a subtle difference in the two definitions to which we need to pay close attention. The first definition might include network-based file systems like the NFS, which has only advisory locking and can therefore allow applications to interfere with each other destructively. The second definition tends to imply a higher level of parallelism coupled with consistency checks and locking to prevent collisions between multiple application components accessing the same data. Although the first definition is somewhat vague, the second definition might be said to refer to a "parallel file system."

14.1.1   Cluster File System Requirements

Because the I/O to a cluster's file system is being performed by multiple clients at the same time, there is a primary requirement for performance. Systems that run large parallel jobs often perform data "checkpointing" to allow recovery in the event that the job fails. There may be written requirements for a "full cluster checkpoint' within a given period of time. This has very direct requirements in terms of file system throughput.

If one assumes that the compute slices in the cluster must simultaneously write all memory to the disk for a checkpoint in a given length of time, you can compute the upper boundary requirement for the cluster file system's write performance. For example, 128 compute slices, each with 4 GB of RAM, would generate 512 GB of checkpoint data. If the period of time required for a clusterwide checkpoint is ten minutes, this yields 51.2 GB/min or 853 MB/s.

This is an extraordinarily high number, given the I/O capabilities of back-end storage systems. For example, a single 2-Gbps Fibre-Channel interface is capable of a theoretical maximum throughput of 250 MB/s. Getting 80% of this theoretical maximum is probably wishful thinking, but provides 200 MB/s of write capability. To "absorb" the level of I/O we are contemplating would take (at least) five independent 2 Gbps Fibre-Channel connections on the server. This ignores the back-end disk array performance requirements. Large, sequential writes are a serious performance problem, particularly for RAID 5 arrays, which must calculate parity information.

This example assumes a compute cluster performing sequential writes for a checkpoint operation. The requirements for database applications have different I/O characteristics, but can be just as demanding in their own right. Before we get too much ahead of ourselves, let's consider the general list of requirements for a cluster's file system. Some of the attributes we seek are

- High levels of performance
- Support for large data files or database tables
- Multiuser and multiclient security
- Data consistency
- Fault tolerance

One might also add "consistent name space" to this list. This phrase refers to the ability for all clients to access files using the same file system paths. Some file systems provide this ability automatically (AFS, the DCE distributed file system [DFS], and Microsoft's distributed file system [dfs]), and others require the system administrator to create a consistent access structure for the clients (NFS, for example). We will need to watch for situations that might affect the client's view of the file system hierarchy.

There are some standard questions that we can ask when we need to analyze the architecture of a given cluster file system solution.

How is the file system storage shared?

How many systems can access the file system simultaneously?

How is the storage presented to client systems?

Is data kept consistent across multiple systems and their accesses, and if so, how?

How easy is the file system to administer?

What is the relative cost of the hardware and software to support the file system?

How many copies of the file system code are there and where does it run?

How well does the architecture scale?

These questions, and others, can help us to make a choice for our cluster's file system. Two primary types of file system architectures are available to us: network-attached storage (NAS) and parallel access. As we will see in the upcoming sections, each has their own fans and detractors, along with advantages and disadvantages.

14.1.2   Networked File System Access

Both NFS and CIFS are client–server implementations of "remote" network-attached file systems. These implementations are based on client-to-server RPC calls that allow the client's applications to make normal UNIX file system calls (open, close, read, write, stat, and so on) that are redirected to a remote server by the operating system. The server's local, physical file systems are exported via an Ethernet network to the server's clients.

The server's physical file systems, such as `ext3`, `jfs`, `reiser`, or `xfs`, which are exported via NFS, exist on physical storage attached to the server that exports them. The I/O between the network, system page cache, and the file blocks and meta-data on the storage is performed only by a single server that has the file system mounted and exported. In this configuration, the physical disks or disk array LUNs, and the data structures they contain, are modified by a single server system only, so coordination between multiple systems is not necessary. This architecture is shown in Figure 14–1.

Figure 14–1 shows two disk arrays that present a single RAID 5 LUN each. Because each array has dual controllers for redundancy, the NFS servers "see" both LUNs through two 2-Gbps (full-duplex) Fibre-Channel paths. (It is important that the two systems "see" the same view of the storage, in terms of the devices. There are "multipath I/O" modules and capabilities available in Linux that can help with this task.) The primary server system uses the LUNs to create a single 2.8-TB file system that it exports to the NFS clients through the network. The secondary server system is a standby replacement for the primary and can replace the primary system in the event of a server failure. To keep the diagram from becoming too busy, the more realistic example of one LUN per array controller (four total) is not shown.

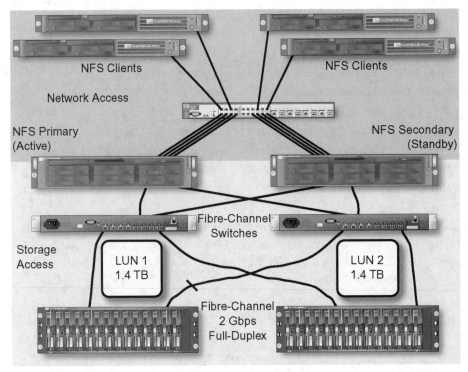

Figure 14–1 A network-attached file system configuration

The NAS configuration can scale only to a point. The I/O and network interface capabilities of the server chassis determine how many client systems the NFS server can accommodate. If the physical I/O or storage attachment abilities of the server are exceeded, then the only easy way to scale the configuration is to split the data set between *multiple* servers, or to move to a larger and more expensive server chassis configuration. The single-server system serializes access to file system data and meta-data on the attached storage while maintaining consistency, but it also becomes a potential performance choke point.

Splitting data between multiple equivalent servers is inconvenient, mainly because it generates extra system administration work and can inhibit data sharing. Distributing the data between multiple servers produces multiple back-up points and multiple SPOFs, and it makes it difficult to share data between clients from multiple servers without explicit knowledge of which server "has" the data. If read-only data is replicated between multiple servers, the client access must somehow be balanced between the multiple instances of the data, and the system administrator must decide how to split and replicate the data.

In the case of extremely large data files, or files that must be both read and written by multiple groups of clients (or all clients) in a cluster, it is impossible to split either the data or the access between multiple NFS servers without a convoluted management process. To avoid splitting data, it is necessary to provide very large, high-performance NFS servers that can accommodate the number of clients accessing the data set. This can be a very expensive approach and once again introduces performance scaling issues.

Another point to make about this configuration is that although a SAN may appear to allow multiple storage LUNs containing a traditional physical file system to be simultaneously accessible to multiple server systems, this is not the case. With the types of local file systems that we are discussing, only one physical system may have the LUN and its associated file system data mounted for read *and* write at the same time. So only one server system may be exporting the file system to the network clients at a time. (This configuration is used in active standby high-availability NFS configurations. Two [or more] LUNs in a shared SAN may be mounted by a server in read–write mode, whereas a second server mounts the LUNs in read-only mode, awaiting a failure. When the primary server fails, the secondary server may remount the LUNs in read–write mode, replay any journal information, and assume the IP address and host name of the primary server. The clients, as long as they have the NFS file systems mounted with the `hard` option, will retry failed operations until the secondary server takes over.)

The SAN's storage LUNs may indeed be "visible" to any system attached to the SAN (provided they are not "zoned" out by the switches), but the ability to read and write to them is not available. This is a limitation of the physical file system code (not an inherent issue with the SAN), which was not written to allow multiple systems to access the same physical file system's data structures simultaneously. (There are, however, restrictions on the number of systems that can perform "fabric logins" to the SAN at any one time. I have seen one large cluster design fall into this trap, so check the SAN capabilities before you commit to a particular design.) This type of multiple-system, read–write access requires a parallel file system.

14.1.3 Parallel File System Access

If you imagine several to several *thousand* compute slices all reading and writing to separate files in the same file system, you can immediately see that the performance of the file system is important. If you imagine these same compute slices all reading and writing to the *same file* in a common file system, you should recognize that there are other attributes, in addition to performance, that the file system must provide. One of the primary requirements for this type of file system is to keep data consistent in the face of multiple client accesses, much as semaphores and spin locks are used to keep shared-memory resources consistent between multiple threads or processes.

Along with keeping the file data blocks consistent during access by multiple clients, a parallel cluster file system must also contend with multiple client access to the file system meta-data. Updating file and directory access times, creating or removing file data in directories, allocating inodes for file extensions, and other common meta-data activities all become more complex when the parallel coordination of multiple client systems is considered. The use of SAN-based storage makes shared *access* to the file system data from multiple clients easier, but the

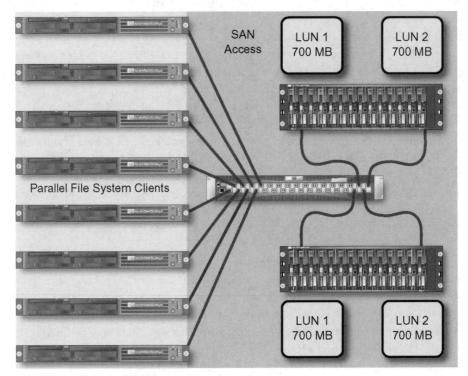

Figure 14–2 A parallel file system configuration

expense of Fibre-Channel disk arrays, storage devices, and Fibre-Channel hub or switch interconnections must be weighed against the other requirements for the cluster's shared storage.

Figure 14–2 shows a parallel file system configuration with multiple LUNs presented to
the client systems. Whether the LUNs may be striped together into a single file system depends
on which parallel file system implementation is being examined, but the important aspect of this
architecture is that each client has shared access to the data in the SAN, and the client's *local*
parallel file system code maintains the data consistency across all accesses.

A primary issue with this type of "direct attach" parallel architecture involves the number
of clients that can access the shared storage without performance and data contention issues.
This number depends on the individual parallel file system implementation, but a frequently
encountered number is in the 16 to 64 system range. It is becoming increasingly common to find
a cluster of parallel file system clients in a configuration such as this acting as a file server to a
larger group of cluster clients.

Such an arrangement allows scaling the file system I/O across multiple systems, while still
providing a common view of the shared data "behind" the parallel file server members. Using
another technology to "distribute" the file system access also reduces the number of direct attach
SAN ports that are required, and therefore the associated cost. SAN interface cards and switches

are still quite expensive, and a per-attachment cost, including the switch port and interface card, can run in the $2,000- to $4,000-per-system range.

There are a variety of interconnect technologies and protocols that can be used to distribute the parallel file system access to clients. Ethernet, using TCP/IP protocols like Internet SCSI (iSCSI), can "fan out" or distribute the parallel file server data to cluster clients. It is also possible to use NFS to provide file access to the larger group of compute slices in the cluster. An example is shown in Figure 14–3.

The advantage to this architecture is that the I/O bandwidth may be scaled across a larger number of clients without the expense of direct SAN attachments to each client, or the requirement for a large, single-chassis NFS server. The disadvantage is that by passing the parallel file system "through" an NFS server layer, the clients lose the fine-grained locking and other advantages of the parallel file system. Where and how the trade-off is made in your cluster depends on the I/O bandwidth and scaling requirements for your file system.

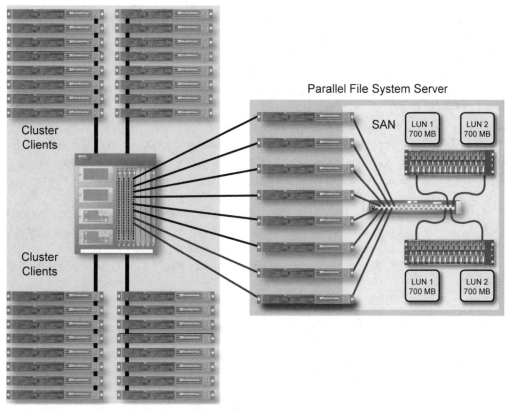

Figure 14–3 A parallel file system server

The example in Figure 14–3 shows an eight-system parallel file server distributing data from two disk arrays. Each disk array is dual controller, with a separate 2-Gbps Fibre-Channel interface to each controller. If a file system were striped across all four LUNs, we could expect the aggregate write I/O to be roughly four times the real bandwidth of a 2 Gbps FC link, or 640 MB/s (figuring 80% of 200 MB/s).

Dividing this bandwidth across eight server systems requires each system to deliver 80 MB/s, which is the approximate bandwidth of one half of a full-duplex GbE link (80% of 125 MB/s). Further dividing this bandwidth between four client systems in the 32-client cluster leaves 20 MB/s per client. At this rate, a client with 8 GB of RAM would require 6.67 minutes to save its RAM during a checkpoint.

Hopefully you can begin to see the I/O performance issues that clusters raise. It is likely that the selection of disk arrays, Fibre-Channel switches, network interfaces, and the core switch will influence the actual bandwidth available to the cluster's client systems. Scaling up this file server example involves increasing the number of Fibre-Channel arrays, LUNs, file server nodes, and GbE links.

The examples shown to this point illustrate two basic approaches to providing data to cluster compute slices. There are advantages and disadvantages to both types of file systems in terms of cost, administration overhead, scaling, and underlying features. In the upcoming sections I cover some of the many specific options that are available.

14.2 The NFS

A primary advantage of using NFS in your cluster is that it is readily available and part of most Linux distributions. Its familiarity also is an advantage to most UNIX or Linux system administrators, who are able to deploy NFS almost in their sleep. The knowledge needed to tune and scale an NFS server and the associated clients, however, is not as readily available or applied as you might think.

The implementation of features in NFS also varies between Linux distributions, the version of a particular Linux distribution, and between the NFS client and server software components. Some of the features that we may be used to having on proprietary UNIX systems are not yet available on Linux, or are in a partially completed state. NFS on Linux can be a moving target in some respects.

One example of this type of incomplete functionality lies in the area of NFS read and write block sizes, which may default to 1 KB on some versions and may not be set larger than 8 KB on others—limiting potential performance. Another area is the support of NFS over TCP, which is enabled for Fedora Core 1, but not for some earlier versions of Red Hat, like 8.0.

Because NFS is a client–server implementation of a networked file system, setup and tuning is necessary on both the client and the server to obtain optimum performance. Understanding the major NFS software components and the complete NFS data path can help select the best operating parameters for your installation. I will cover these topics in upcoming sections.

14.2.1   Enabling NFS on the Server

Once the local physical file systems are built on your NFS server, there are several steps necessary to make them available to NFS clients in the network. Before starting the NFS server subsystem, there are a number of options that we need to consider for proper operation. We also
need to pay attention to potential security issues.

The NFS server processes are started from the `/etc/init.d/nfs` and `/etc/`
`init.d/nfslock` files. Both of these files may be enabled with the customer `chkconfig`
commands:

```
# chkconfig nfs on
# chkconfig nfslock on
```

The behavior of NFS on your server may be controlled by the `/etc/sysconfig/nfs` file.
This file contains the options used by the `/etc/init.d/nfs` file, and usually does not exist
by default.

The `/etc/init.d/nfs` file uses three programs that are essential to the NFS server
subsystem: `/usr/sbin/rpc.mountd`, `/usr/sbin/rpc.nfsd`, and `/usr/sbin/`
`exportfs`. The `rpc.mountd` daemon accepts the remote mount requests for the server's
exported file systems. The `rpc.nfsd` process is a user space program that starts the `nfsd` kernel threads from the `nfsd.o` module that handles the local file system I/O on behalf of the client systems.

The `exportfs` command is responsible for reading the `/etc/exports` file and making the exported file system information available to both the kernel threads and the mount daemon. Issuing the `exportfs -a` command will take the information in `/etc/exports` and
write it to `/var/lib/nfs/xtab`.

The number of `nfsd` threads that are started in the kernel determine the simultaneous
number of requests that can be handled. The default number of threads started is eight, which is
almost never enough for a heavily used NFS server. To increase the number of `nfsd` threads
started, you can set a variable in the `/etc/sysconfig/nfs` file:

```
RPCNFSDCOUNT=128
```

The exact number of threads to start depends on a lot of factors, including client load, hardware
speed, and the I/O capabilities of the server.

The `nfsd` threads receive client requests on socket number 2049 for either UDP/IP or
TCP/IP requests. Which transport is used as a default depends on the Linux distribution and version. Some versions do not have NFS over TCP available. Performance is better over UDP, provided the network is robust.

One way to tell if you need more `nfsd` threads is to check for NFS socket queue overflows. Unfortunately, this method will tell you only if some socket on the system has over-
flowed, not the specific NFS socket. If the system is primarily an NFS server, you can infer that
the most likely socket to overflow is the NFS socket. Check for this situation with

```
# netstat -s | grep overflow
    145 times the listen queue of a socket overflowed
```

If you are seeing socket overflows on the server, then try increasing the number of nfsd threads you are starting on your server. If the NFS server's input socket queue overflows, then a client request packet is dropped. This will force a client retry, which should show up in client NFS statistics available with the nfsstat command (on a client system):

```
# nfsstat -rc
Client rpc stats:
calls       retrans       authrefrsh
20          0             0
```

The number of hits in the retrans counter would potentially reflect any server issues with socket overflows, although there are other reasons for this number to increase, such as the end-to-end latency between the client and server or the server being too busy to reply within the time-out period set by the client. I discuss setting the client request time-out values when I talk about mount parameters.

You can easily tell how many nfsd threads are currently running on the system with the ps command. For example,

```
# ps -ef | grep nfs| grep -v grep
root        855     1  0 Mar18 ?        00:00:00 [nfsd]
root        856     1  0 Mar18 ?        00:00:00 [nfsd]
root        857     1  0 Mar18 ?        00:00:00 [nfsd]
root        858     1  0 Mar18 ?        00:00:00 [nfsd]
root        859     1  0 Mar18 ?        00:00:00 [nfsd]
root        860     1  0 Mar18 ?        00:00:00 [nfsd]
root        861     1  0 Mar18 ?        00:00:00 [nfsd]
root        862     1  0 Mar18 ?        00:00:00 [nfsd]
```

This shows the eight *default* nfsd threads executing on a server system. Oops. The fact that daemons are kernel threads is indicated by the brackets that surround the "process" name in the ps output.

14.2.2   Adjusting NFS Mount Daemon Protocol Behavior

The rpc.mountd process provides the ability to talk to clients in multiple NFS protocols. The most recent protocol, NFS protocol version 3 (NFS PV3) is supported, along with the older protocol version 2 (NFS PV2). Which protocol is used is selected based on the NFS client's mount request, or on the options supplied to the nfsd threads when they are started. The rpc.nfsd command is used to pass the protocol options to the kernel threads when they are started.

If you examine the man page for rpc.nfsd, you will see two options that control the available NFS protocols: --no-nfs-version and --nfs-version. Either of these options may be followed by the value 2 or 3 to disallow or force a particular NFS protocol version respectively. The `/etc/sysconfig/nfs` file provides two variables that translate into these options.

The `MOUNTD_NFS_V2` variable and the `MOUNTD_NFS_V3` variable may be set to the values `no`, `yes`, or `auto`. A value of `no` disallows the associated protocol version, a value of `yes` enables the associated protocol version, and a value of `auto` allows the start-up script to offer whichever versions are compiled into the kernel. An example `/etc/sysconfig/nfs` file that disallows NFS PV2 and enables only NFS PV3 would contain

```
MOUNTD_NFS_V2=no
MOUNTD_NFS_V3=yes
```

It is better to offer the available mount types, and control which one is used with the client `mount` parameters, unless there are issues between the client and server.

It is possible to determine which version of the NFS protocol a client system is using by looking at statistics from the `nfsstat` command. This command, in addition to providing retry information, will show the number of NFS PV3 and PV2 RPC requests that have been made to the server. An example output from this command is

```
# nfsstat -c
Client rpc stats:
calls        retrans      authrefrsh
20           0            0
Client nfs v2:
null    getattr setattr root lookup readlink
0 0%    0 0%     0 0%     0 0%    0 0%    0 0%
read         wrcache      write        create      remove      rename
0 0%         0 0%         0 0%         0 0%        0 0%        0 0%
link         symlink      mkdir        rmdir       readdir     fsstat
0 0%         0 0%         0 0%         0 0%        0 0%        0 0%
Client nfs v3:
null         getattr      setattr      lookup      access readlink
0 0%         14 70%       0 0%         0 0%        0 0%   0 0%
read         write        create       mkdir       symlink     mknod
0 0%         0 0%         0 0%         0 0%        0 0%        0 0%
remove       rmdir        rename       link readdir readdirplus
0 0%         0 0%         0 0%         0 0% 0 0%   0 0%
fsstat       fsinfo       pathconf     commit
0 0%         6 30%        0 0%         0 0%
```

The statistics kept by `nfsstat` are reset at each reboot or when the command is run with the zero-the-counters option. This command is

```
# nfsstat -z
```

It is also possible to use the `nfsstat` command to examine the server statistics for all clients being serviced. If there are clients using one or the other or both protocol versions, this is visible in the command's output, because the RPC calls are divided into groups according to protocol version. An example of the server statistics from `nfsstat` follows:

```
# nfsstat -s
Server rpc stats:
calls       badcalls     badauth      badclnt      xdrcall
1228        0            0            0            0
Server nfs v2:
null        getattr      setattr      root lookup      readlink
1 100%      0 0%         0 0%         0 0% 0 0%         0 0%
read        wrcache      write        create       remove       rename
0 0%        0 0%         0 0%         0 0%         0 0%         0 0%
link        symlink      mkdir        rmdir        readdir      fsstat
0 0%        0 0%         0 0%         0 0%         0 0%         0 0%

Server nfs v3:
null        getattr      setattr      lookup access      readlink
1 0%        212 17%      0 0%         83 6% 141 11%      0 0%
read        write        create       mkdir        symlink      mknod
709 57%     0 0%         0 0%         0 0%         0 0%         0 0%
remove      rmdir        rename       link readdir      readdirplus
0 0%        0 0%         0 0%         0 0% 22 1%         38 3%
fsstat      fsinfo       pathconf     commit
3 0%        18 1%        0 0%         0 0%
```

As you can see from the output of `nfsstat`, the server and client are both using NFS PV3 to communicate. Furthermore, by looking at the server, you can see that all clients are using NFS PV3, because there are no RPC calls listed for the PV2 categories. I am getting just a little ahead, because the `nfsstat` statistics are available only after NFS has been started. We aren't quite ready for this situation yet.

On an NFS server with a considerable number of clients, the maximum number of open file descriptors allowed by the NFS mount daemon may need to be adjusted. The `rpc.mountd` process uses the `--descriptors` option to set this, and the default number is 256. This value has to be passed with the RPCMOUNTD_OPTS variable in `/etc/sysconfig/nfs`:

```
RPCMOUNTD_OPTS='--descriptors=371'
```

This number represents the number of file handles allowed by the server; one is maintained per NFS mount. It is not the number of files that may be opened by the clients.

14.2.3   Tuning the NFS Server Network Parameters

The `/etc/sysconfig/nfs` file allows tuning the input queue size for the NFS sockets. This is done by temporarily altering the system default parameters for the networking subsystem, specifically the TCP parameters. To understand how this is done, we need to look at the general parameter tuning facility provided by the /sbin/sysctl command.

This command reads the contents of the /etc/sysctl.conf file and applies the parameters listed there to the appropriate system parameters. The application of kernel parameter changes is usually done at start-up time by the init scripts, but may also be done on a "live" system to alter the default kernel parameter values.

Using the sysctl command, temporary changes may be applied to the system's kernel parameters, and these "tunes" may be permanently applied by adding them to the /etc/ sysctl.conf configuration file. The NFS start-up script allows us to tune only the NFS socket parameter, instead of making global changes. The commands to do this are listed from the /etc/init.d/nfs start-up file:

```
# Get the initial values for the input sock queues
# at the time of running the script.
if [ "$TUNE_QUEUE" = "yes" ]; then

    RMEM_DEFAULT='/sbin/sysctl -n net.core.rmem_default'

    RMEM_MAX='/sbin/sysctl -n net.core.rmem_max'

    # 256kb recommended minimum size based on SPECsfs
    # NFS benchmarks

    [ -z "$NFS_QS" ] && NFS_QS=262144

fi
[... intermediate commands deleted ...]
case "$1" in

  start)

# Start daemons.
        # Apply input queue increase for nfs server
        if [ "$TUNE_QUEUE" = "yes" ]; then
            /sbin/sysctl -w net.core.rmem_default=$NFSD_QS \
                >/dev/null 2>&1
            /sbin/sysctl -w net.core.rmem_max=$NFSD_QS       \
                >/dev/null 2>&1
        fi
[... intermediate commands deleted ...]
# reset input queue for rest of network services
        if [ "$TUNE_QUEUE" = "yes" ]; then
            /sbin/sysctl -w                                  \
                net.core.rmem_default=$RMEM_DEFAULT \
                >/dev/null 2>&1
            /sbin/sysctl -w                                  \
                net.core.rmem_max=$RMEM_MAX                \
                >/dev/null 2>&1
        fi
```

The script temporarily modifies the values of the `net.core.rmem_max` and `net.core.rmem_default` parameters, starts the `nfsd` threads, then replaces the old values of the parameters. This has the effect of modifying the receive memory parameters for only the socket that gets created by `nfsd` threads for receiving NFS requests, socket 2049.

These network parameter values are also available in the files `/proc/sys/net/core/rmem_max` and `/proc/sys/net/core/rmem_default`. Note the similarity between the file path name in `/proc` and the parameter names used with the `sysctl` command. They are indeed the same data; there are just several methods of modifying the parameter value. We could alter the values (globally!) for these parameters by executing

```
# echo '262144' > /proc/sys/net/core/rmem_default
# echo '262144' > /proc/sys/net/core/rmem_max
```

Any changes we made this way would alter the defaults for all new sockets that are created on the system, until we replace the values.

You can crash or hang your system by making the wrong adjustments. Exercise caution when tuning parameters this way. It is, however, best to try values temporarily before committing them to the `/etc/sysctl.conf` file or to `/etc/sysconfig/nfs`. To enter parameters prematurely in this file can render your system unbootable (except in single-user mode). To perform these tuning operations when NFS is started, we can set the following values in the file `/etc/sysconfig/nfs`:

```
TUNE_QUEUE=yes
NFS_QS=350000
```

14.2.4   NFS and TCP Wrappers

If you use TCP wrappers (`/etc/hosts.deny` and `/etc/hosts.allow`) to tighten security in the cluster's networks, you need to make special provisions for NFS. There are a number of services that must be allowed access for proper NFS operation. One of the standard ways to use TCP wrappers is to deny any service that is not explicitly enabled, so if you use this approach, you need to modify the `/etc/hosts.allow` file on the NFS server to contain

```
mountd:      .cluster.local
portmap:     .cluster.local
statd:       .cluster.local
```

The client systems must be able to access these services on the server to mount the server's exported file systems and to maintain information about the advisory locks that have been created. Even though the binary executables for the daemons are named `rpc.mountd` and `rpc.statd`, the service names must be used in this file.

14.2.5   Exporting File Systems on the NFS Server

The format of the `/etc/exports` file on Linux systems is a little different than that of other UNIX systems. The file provides the necessary access control information to the NFS mount daemon, determining which file systems are available and which clients may access them. The `exportfs` command takes the information from the `/etc/exports` file and creates the information in the `/var/lib/nfs/xtab` and `/var/lib/nfs/rmtab` files, which are used by `mountd` and the kernel to enable client access to the exported directories.

The `/etc/exports` file contains lines with a directory to export, and a whitespace-separated list of clients that can access it, and each client may have a list of export options enclosed in parentheses. The client specifications may contain a variety of information, including the specific host name, wild cards in a fully qualified host name, a network address and net mask, and combinations of these elements. An example file for our cluster might be

```
/scratch        cs*.cluster.local(rw,async)
/admin          10.3.0.0/21(rw)
/logs           ms*.cluster.local(rw) cs*.cluster.local(rw)
```

An entry in the `/var/lib/nfs/xtab` file for an exported directory with no options specified is listed (for each system with a mount) as

```
/kickstart      cs01.cluster.local(ro,sync,wdelay,hide,        \
secure,root_squash,no_all_squash,subtree_check,secure_locks,\
mapping=identity,anonuid=-2,anongid=-2)
```

This shows the default values for the options in the `/etc/exports` entry:

- Read-only access.
- Synchronous updates (don't acknowledge NFS operations until data is committed to disk).
- Delay writes to see if related sequential writes may be "gathered."
- Require file systems mounted within other exported directories to be individually mounted by the client.
- Require requests to originate from network ports less than 1024.
- Map `root` (UID or GID 0) requests to the `anonymous` UID and GID.
- Do not map UIDs or GIDs other than `root` to the `anonymous` UID and GID.
- Check to see whether accessed files are in the appropriate file system *and* an exported system tree.
- Require authentication of locking requests.
- User access permission mapping is based on the identity specified by the user's UID and GID.
- Specify the `anonymous` UID and GID as the value `-2`.

14.2.6   Starting the NFS Server Subsystem

Now that we have all the various files and configuration information properly specified, tuning options set, and file systems built and ready for export, we can actually start the NFS server subsystem and hope that the clients can access the proper file systems. This is done in the normal manner:

```
# service nfs start
# service nfslock start
```

You should be able to verify that the [nfsd] and [lockd] kernel threads are shown by the ps command. Entering the command

```
# exportfs
```

should show the exported file systems on the server with the proper export options. You should also be able to locate processes for rpc.mountd, rpc.statd. portmap, and rpc.rquotad in the ps output. With the configuration parameters and required processes in place, we may proceed to mounting the server directories from a client system.

14.2.7   NFS Client Mount Parameters

The client mount parameters for NFS can control the behavior of the client and server interaction to a large degree. These parameters are shown in Table 14–1.

Several important points need to be made about NFS mount parameters and their default values.

- The default size for rsize and wsize (1,024 bytes) will almost certainly have an adverse impact on NFS performance. There are a number of points where these settings can impact the performance of NFS servers and clients: file system read and write bandwidth, network utilization, and physical read/modify/write behavior (if the NFS block size matches file system fragment size). In general, the 8-KB maximum for NFS PV2 is a minimum size for efficiency, with a 32,768-byte block being a better option if supported by the NFS PV3 implementation.

- The values for timeo and retrans implement an exponential back-off algorithm that can drastically affect client performance. This is especially true if the NFS server is busy or the network is unreliable or heavily loaded. With the default values, timeo=7 and retrans=3, the first sequence will be 0.70 second (minor time-out), 1.40 second (minor time-out), 2.80 seconds (minor time-out), and 5.60 seconds (major time-out). The second sequence doubles the initial value of timeo and continues.

- The default behavior for a mount is *hard* and should be left that way unless the remote file system is read-only. NFS is meant to substitute for a local file system, and most applications are unaware that the data they are accessing is over a network. When *soft* mounts return errors on reads or writes, most applications behave badly (at best) and

Table 14–1 Important NFS Client Mount Parameters

NFS Mount Parameter	Default	Description
rsize	rsize=1024	The number of bytes to request in an NFS read operation (maximum for NFS PV2 is 8,192 bytes)
wsize	wsize=1024	The number of bytes to write in an NFS write operation (maximum for NFS PV2 is 8,192 bytes)
timeo	timeo=7	Tenths of a second between RPC retries (NFS minor time-outs); value is doubled each time-out until either 60 seconds or the number of minor time-outs specified in retrans is reached
retrans	retrans=3	The number of minor time-outs that can occur before a major NFS time-out
soft		If a major time-out occurs, report an error and cease retrying the operation (*This can result in data corruption! Soft is bad, bad, bad!*)
hard		If a major NFS time-out occurs, report an error and continue to retry; this is the default and the only setting that preserves data integrity
intr		Similar behavior to *soft*, do not use unless you have good reasons!
nfsver=<2/3>	nfsver=2	Allow mounting with either NFS PV2 or PV3; PV2 is the default
tcp		Mount the file system using TCP as the transport; support may or may not be present for the TCP transport
udp		Mount the file system using UDP as the transport, which is the default

can lose or corrupt data. The *hard* setting causes the client to retry the operation forever, so that a "missing" NFS server resulting from a crash or reboot will pick up the operation where it left off on returning. This is extremely important NFS behavior that is little understood.

- The default NFS transport is UDP. This transport is nonconnection oriented and will perform better than TCP in stable, reliable networks. NFS implements its own error recovery mechanism on top of UDP (see the `retrans` and `timeo` parameters), so unless the mount is over a WAN connection, the preferred transport is UDP. Some proprietary UNIX operating systems, like Solaris, default to using TCP as the NFS transport.

• The default mount protocol is NFS PV2, which is less efficient than NFS PV3. The NFS PV3 protocol supports large files (more than 2 GB), larger block sizes (up to 32 KB), and safe asynchronous writes (acknowledgment of physical commit to disk not required on every write operation). Using NFS PV3 is extremely important to overall NFS performance.

The mount parameters for NFS file systems, whether in `/etc/fstab` or specified in automounter maps, need to have the following options specified for best performance:

```
rsize=32768,wsize=32768,nfsvers=3
```

14.2.8   Using `autofs` on NFS Clients

Maintaining the NFS mounts in a `/etc/fstab` file on multiple systems can become an exercise in frustration. A more centralized method of maintaining this information is to use the NIS subsystem to distribute the `auto.master` map and other submaps to the client systems. The NFS client system may then be configured to use the `autofs` subsystem to mount file systems automatically when required and unmount them when idle.

Unmounting the NFS file system when idle removes the direct dependency between the client and server that can cause retries if the remote file system's server becomes unavailable. This behavior is supported by "indirect" maps, unlike the direct map entries that simulate an NFS mount created by an entry in the `/etc/fstab` file. A side benefit is that indirect mounts can be changed without rebooting an NFS client using them. This level of indirection allows the system manager to change the location (server, directory path, and so on) of the data without affecting the client's use of the data.

An `auto.master` map from either NIS or a local file provides the names of pseudo directories that are managed by a specific map and the `autofs` subsystem on the client. The settings in the `/etc/nsswitch.conf` file for the `automount` service define the order of precedence for locating the map information—for example,

```
automount: nis files
```

Thus, `autofs` will examine the NIS information for the maps first, then local files located in the `/etc` directory. A simple example of a master map would be

```
/data      auto.data        nfsvers=3,rsize=32768,wsize=32768
/home      auto.home        nfsvers=3,rsize=32768,wsize=32768
```

Notice that the mount options in the master map, which override the submap options, are in the third field in the master map data. This is different from the options in the submaps, which are the second field in the data. I use the convention `auto.<directory>` to name the map that instructs `autofs` how to mount the information under the pseudo directory named `<directory>`. An example `auto.data` map might contain the entries:

```
scratch          fs01:/raid0/scratch
proj             fs02:/raid5/projects
bins             fs02:/raid5/executables
```

Any time a client system references a path, such as `/data/proj`, the `autofs` subsystem will mount the associated server directory at the appropriate location. When the directory is no longer in use, it is dismounted after a time-out.

Once the `autofs` configuration in `/etc/nsswitch.conf` is complete, and the NIS or local map files are present, the `autofs` subsystem may be started with

```
# chkconfig autofs on
# service autofs start
```

You should be able to `cd` to one of the directories controlled by the indirect maps to verify their proper operation. I do not cover direct maps here, because I consider them to be evil.

14.2.9   NFS Summary

Although NFS is not a parallel file system, its ease of implementation can make it a choice for smaller clusters. With proper tuning and attention to the NFS data path between client and server, NFS can offer adequate performance. Certainly, most UNIX or Linux system administrators have experience with implementing NFS, but tuning this network file system is not always trivial or obvious. ("You can tune a file system, but you can't tune a fish," as stated by the UNIX man page for `tunefs`.)

There are a number of areas that can be tuned on an NFS server, and the examples that we covered in this section illustrate a general method for setting Linux kernel parameters. The use of the `sysctl` command and its configuration file `/etc/sysctl.conf` allow any parameters to be modified at boot time. A cautious approach to tuning is to set the parameter values temporarily with either `/proc` or the `sysctl` command before permanently committing them.

In general, NFS mounts in the `/etc/fstab` file, and direct mounts using `autofs` are a bad idea because they create direct dependencies between the client systems and the server that is mounted. If you decide to service the NFS server, the client RPC retry behavior for hard mounts will preserve data integrity, but will cause infinite retries until the server returns. It is better to let `autofs` unmount unused file systems and avoid the direct dependencies.

14.3 A Survey of Some Open-Source Parallel File Systems

This section provides an overview of some of the available parallel file systems. This is not an exhaustive list, just some of the options that I have come across in my research and experience. I cover several open-source parallel file systems, and one commercially available one in the overviews.

A common issue with open-source parallel file systems is that they may require kernel reconfiguration expertise to install and use. Some of the functionality may be available in the form of premodified kernels and modules, precompiled kernel modules for a particular kernel version, or a do-it-yourself kit in the form of patches. If you are not running a production environment, or are open to experimentation and have the necessary kernel hacking skills, several of the file systems covered here might be options for you. Otherwise, a commercially available and supported solution is a better choice.

Many of the possible choices will require you to work with a minimum amount of documentation, other than the source code. This is a normal occurrence in the Linux and open-source world. The projects that we are examining are still works in progress, although some of the functionality is being included in the next release of Linux version 2.6 of the kernel.

You should note that most of the parallel file systems we are examining use TCP/IP as a transport. This means that the parallel file systems may be run over Ethernet, but there are other choices. Recall that the HSIs like Myrinet and Quadrics allow transport of TCP/IP along with the other message formats needed by MPI or OpenMP. This means that very fast transport is available for the parallel file system, provided that your cluster has an HSI in place.

14.3.1   The Parallel Virtual File System (PVFS)

The first cluster file system we will examine is the parallel virtual file system, or PVFS. There are currently two versions of this file system, PVFS1 and PVFS2. The newest version, PVFS2, requires the Linux 2.6 kernel, so for the purposes of this introduction, we will concentrate on PVFS1. Both versions are currently being maintained.

The PVFS1 software is available from `http://www.parl.clemson.edu/pvfs` and the PVFS2 software is available from `http://www.pvfs.org/pvfs2`. I chose the PVFS1 software as the first example, because it requires no modifications to the kernel to install, just compilation of the sources. The architecture of PVFS is shown in Figure 14–4.

Figure 14–4 shows an application talking to PVFS through a dynamically loaded kernel module that is supplied as part of the PVFS software. This module is provided to allow normal interaction between the application, the Linux virtual file system (VFS) layer, and the PVFS daemon, which performs I/O on behalf of the application. Applications may be recompiled to use a PVFS library that communicates directly with the meta-data server and the I/O daemons on the server nodes, thus eliminating the kernel communication (and one data copy).

The server nodes store data in an existing physical file system, such as `ext3`, to take advantage of existing journaling and recovery mechanisms. The PVFS `iod` process, or I/O daemon, performs file operations on behalf of the PVFS client system. These operations take place on files striped across the PVFS storage servers in a user-defined manner.

You may download the source for PVFS1 from `ftp://ftp.parl.clemson.edu/pub/pvfs` and perform the following steps:

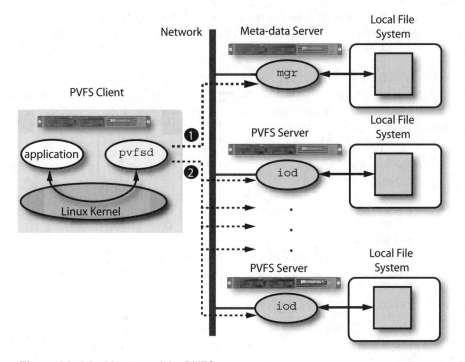

Figure 14–4 Architecture of the PVFS

```
# tar xvzf pvfs-1.6.2.tgz
# cd pvfs-1.6.2
# ./configure
# make
# make install
```

The installation unpacks /usr/local/sbin/iod, /usr/local/sbin/mgr, the application library /usr/local/lib/pvfs.a, and a host of utilities in /usr/local/bin, such as pvfs-ping and pvfs-mkdir. The default installation includes auxilliary information, like the man pages and header files for the development library under /usr/include. The entire operation takes approximately three minutes.

If you wish to use the kernel module to allow access to the file system for existing programs, you may download the pvfs-kernel-1.6.2-linux-2.4.tgz file and build the contents:

```
# tar xvzf pvfs-kernel-1.6.2-linux-2.4.tgz
# cd pvfs-kernel-1.6.2-linux-2.4
# ./configure
# make
# make install
```

```
# cp mount.pvfs /sbin/mount.pvfs
# mkdir /lib/modules/2.4.18-24.8.0/kernel/fs/pvfs
# cp pvfs.o /lib/modules/2.4.18-24.8.0/kernel/fs/pvfs
# depmod -a
```

Let's install the software package on five nodes: one meta-data server and four data servers. For this example, let's install the kernel package on a single node that is to be the PVFS client. For the meta-data server, install and configure the software, then started the meta-data manager daemon, `mgr`:

```
# mkdir /pvfs-meta
# cd /pvfs-meta
# mkmgrconf
This script will make the .iodtab and .pvfsdir files
in the metadata directory of a PVFS file system.
Enter the root directory (metadata directory):
/pvfs-meta
Enter the user id of directory:
root
Enter the group id of directory:
root
Enter the mode of the root directory:
777
Enter the hostname that will run the manager:
cs01
Searching for host...success
Enter the port number on the host for manager:
(Port number 3000 is the default) <CR>
Enter the I/O nodes: (can use form node1, node2, ... or
nodename{#-#,#,#})
cs02, cs03, cs04, cs05
Searching for hosts...success
I/O nodes: cs02 cs03 cs04 cs05
Enter the port number for the iods:
(Port number 7000 is the default) <CR>
Done!
# /usr/local/sbin/mgr
```

On each of the data servers, configure and install the I/O server daemon, `iod`:

```
# cp /tmp/pvfs-1.6.2/system/iod.conf /etc/iod.conf
# mkdir /pvfs-data
# chmod 700 /pvfs-data
# chown nobody.nobody /pvfs-data
# /usr/local/sbin/iod
```

Then test to make sure that all the pieces are functioning. A command that is very useful is the `pvfs-ping` command, which contacts all the participating systems:

```
# /usr/local/bin/pvfs-ping -h hpepc1 -f /pvfs-meta
mgr (cs01:3000) is responding.
iod 0 (192.168.0.102:7000) is responding.
iod 1 (192.168.0.103:7000) is responding.
iod 2 (192.168.0.104:7000) is responding.
iod 3 (192.168.0.105:7000) is responding.
pvfs file system /pvfs-meta is fully operational.
```

Wahoo! We can now go and mount the file system on a client. There are a few minor steps before we can mount the file system on the client. First we need to create the /etc/pvfstab file, which contains mounting information:

```
cs01:/pvfs-meta      /mnt/pvfs  pvfs      port=3000        0 0
```

Next, we can actually mount the parallel file system, which involves installing the kernel module and starting the pvfsd to handle communication with "normal" programs and commands:

```
# insmod pvfs
# /usr/local/sbin/pvfsd
# mkdir /mnt/pvfs
# /sbin/mount.pvfs cs01:/pvfs-meta /mnt/pvfs
# /usr/local/bin/pvfs-statfs /mnt/pvfs
blksz = 65536, total (bytes) = 388307550208,                        \
        free (bytes) = 11486298112
```

We are now ready to start using the file system. Let's load a copy of iozone, which is a handy file system performance tool, available from http://www.iozone.org, and start running tests. Things should work just fine within the limits of your test network and systems. For performance and scaling information, see the PVFS Web site.

The version of PVFS that we are testing, PVFS1, although it is still maintained, is likely to be superseded by the PVFS2 version when the Linux 2.6 kernel becomes generally available. There have been a number of noticeable improvements in the tools for configuring and managing the file system components, along with more documentation. Download and try PVFS1 for your cluster, but keep your eyes on PVFS2.

14.3.2   The Open Global File System (OpenGFS)

The Open Global File System, also known as OpenGFS and OGFS, is another file system that provides direct client access to shared storage resources. The systems that use OpenGFS access the storage devices through a Fibre-Channel SAN (Figure 14–5). Some of the features of OpenGFS are

- Individual journals for separate systems
- Pluggable locking services based on LAN connections

- Management of cluster "participation" to manage journaling and locking actions
- "Fencing" of storage access to prevent corruption by failed nodes[1]
- Support for volume manager aggregation of multiple devices, with volume managers like the enterprise volume management system (EVMS; available at `http://evms.sourceforge.net/docs.php`)

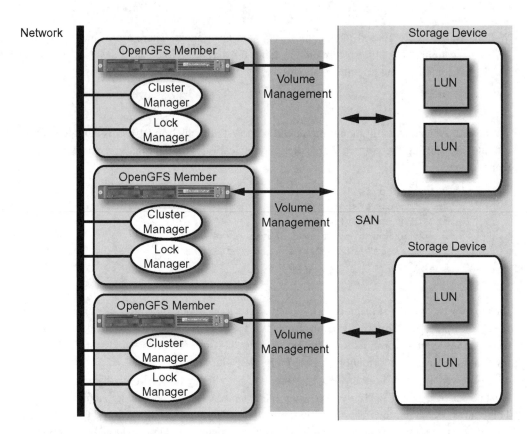

Figure 14–5 OpenGFS architecture

The OpenGFS software requires compilation and patching of the kernel as part of the installation process. This means that only certain versions of the kernel are acceptable for use

---

1.   If you have not heard of STOMITH, then this is a good time to learn that it stands for "shoot the other machine in the head." This is a common, somewhat humorous, term in parallel file systems, and it refers to the collective cluster's ability to modify access for a given system to the SAN devices. A misbehaving cluster member is voted "off the island" by its partners.

with OpenGFS. If you choose to use EVMS in conjunction with OpenGFS, additional patching is required. The current release version, as of this writing, is 0.3.0.

Because the level of modification to the kernel requires specific software development and kernel-patching expertise, it is beyond the scope of this discussion. If you are interested in experimenting with OpenGFS, there is plenty of documentation available for obtaining the software, compiling it, patching the kernel, and installing it (go to `http://opengfs.source-forge.net/docs.php`). Among the HOW-TO information on this site are documents on using OpenGFS with iSCSI, IEEE-1394 (Firewire), and Fibre-Channel storage devices.

14.3.3   The Lustre File System

The name *Lustre* is a melding of the words *Linux* and *cluster*, with a tweak of the last two letters. Although the vision of the final Lustre file system is far from realized, version 1.0 (actually version 1.04 as of this writing) is now available for download and demonstration purposes. Information on Lustre is available from `http://www.lustre.org`. Before we actually try Lustre, let's enumerate some of the target design attributes:

- Object-oriented storage access (hundreds of object storage servers [OSSs])
- Scalable to large numbers of clients (tens of thousands)
- Scalable to huge amounts of storage (petabytes)
- Scalable to large amounts of aggregated I/O (hundreds of gigabytes per second)
- Manageable and immune to failures

As you can tell from the descriptive items, the word *scalable* comes up a lot with reference to Lustre. So do the words *huge* and *large*. Although the end goal is a parallel file system that scales for use in very large clusters, there is nothing to prevent us from using Lustre for our own, albeit, smaller clusters.

Storage in Lustre is allocated at a higher level than the physical hardware blocks that are associated with disk sectors. File objects may be spread over multiple "object storage servers," with a variety of flexible allocation and access schemes. The internal architecture of Lustre is quite complex, and to start even a high-level description we should examine a diagram. Figure 14–6 shows a high-level collection of Lustre components.

Lustre clients access meta-data servers (MDSs) and OSSs using a message-passing library called "Portals" from Sandia National Laboratories (see `http://www.sandiaportals.org` and `http://sourceforge.net/projects/sandiaportals`.) This library, among other things, provides a network abstraction layer that allows message passing over a variety of physical transports, including TCP, Infiniband, SCI, Myrinet, and Quadrics ELAN3 and ELAN4. The specification includes provisions for RDMA and operating system bypass to improve efficiency.

Lustre clients create files from objects allocated on multiple OSS systems. The file contents are kept on the OSS systems, but the meta-data is stored and maintained by a separate

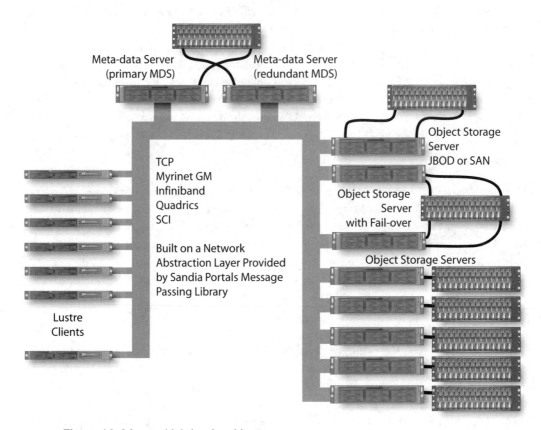

Figure 14–6 Lustre high-level architecture

meta-data server. The later versions of Lustre are to allow many MDS systems to exist, to scale the meta-data access, but the current implementation allows for only one MDS (and possibly a fail-over copy, but the documentation is unclear about this).

Lustre OSS systems use the physical file systems of a Linux host to store the file objects. This provides journaling and other recovery mechanisms that would need to be implemented "from scratch" if a raw file system is used. It is entirely possible that manufacturers will create special OSS hardware with the Lustre behavior captured in firmware, thus providing an OSS appliance. This does not appear to have happened yet.

To try Lustre, you can download two packages from the Web site:

```
kernel-smp-2.4.20-28.9_lustre.1.0.4.i586.rpm
lustre-lite-utils-2.4.20-28.9_lustre.1.0.4.i586.rpm
```

There is also a kernel source package and an all-inclusive package that contains the kernel *and* the utility sources. The precompiled packages are easy enough for a quick trial. As you can see by the names, the packages are based on a version of the kernel from Red Hat 9.0. The two packages and the HOW-TO at `https://wiki.clusterfs.com/lustre/lustrehowto` can help us get started.

First, install the two packages. Make sure that you use the `install` option to the `rpm` command, *not* the `update` option, or you might replace your current kernel. We want to install the software in addition to the current kernel:

```
# rpm -ivh kernel-smp-2.4.20-28.9_lustre.1.0.4.i586.rpm          \
        lustre-lite-utils-2.4.20-28.9_lustre.1.04.i586.rpm
```

This will place the kernel in `/boot`, update the bootloader menu, and install the required modules in `/lib/modules/2.4.20-28.9_lustre.1.0.4smp`. When you reboot your system, you should see a menu item for `2.4.20-28.9_lustre.1.0.4smp`. Select it and continue booting the system.

The configuration information for Lustre is kept in a single file that is used by all members of the cluster. This file is in XML format and is produced and operated on by three main configuration utilities in `/usr/sbin`: `lmc`, `lconf`, and `lctl`. There is a rather large PDF document (422 pages) describing the architecture and setup of Lustre at `http://www.lustre.org/docs/lustre.pdf`. It is not necessary to understand the whole picture to try out Lustre on your system. There are example scripts that will create a client, OSS, and MDS on the same system, using the loop-back file system.

The demonstration scripts are located in `/usr/lib/lustre/examples`. There are two possible demonstrations. The one we are using activates `local.sh` as part of the configuration:

```
# NAME=local.sh; ./llmount.sh
loading module: portals srcdir None devdir libcfs
loading module: ksocknal srcdir None devdir knals/socknal
loading module: lvfs srcdir None devdir lvfs
loading module: obdclass srcdir None devdir obdclass
loading module: ptlrpc srcdir None devdir ptlrpc
loading module: ost srcdir None devdir ost
loading module: fsfilt_ext3 srcdir None devdir lvfs
loading module: obdfilter srcdir None devdir obdfilter
loading module: mdc srcdir None devdir mdc
loading module: osc srcdir None devdir osc
loading module: lov srcdir None devdir lov
loading module: mds srcdir None devdir mds
loading module: llite srcdir None devdir llite
NETWORK: NET_localhost_tcp NET_localhost_tcp_UUID tcp cs01 988
OSD: OST_localhost OST_localhost_UUID obdfilter            \
        /tmp/ost1-cs01 200000 ext3 no 0 0
MDSDEV: mds1 mds1_UUID /tmp/mds1-cs01 ext3 no
recording clients for filesystem: FS_fsname_UUID
Recording log mds1 on mds1
```

```
OSC: OSC_cs01_OST_localhost_mds1 2a3da_lov_mds1_7fe101b48f
OST_localhost_UUID
LOV: lov_mds1 2a3da_lov_mds1_7fe101b48f mds1_UUID 0 65536 0 0\
[u'OST_localhost_UUID'] mds1
End recording log mds1 on mds1
Recording log mds1-clean on mds1
LOV: lov_mds1 2a3da_lov_mds1_7fe101b48f
OSC: OSC_cs011_OST_localhost_mds1 2a3da_lov_mds1_7fe101b48f
End recording log mds1-clean on mds1
MDSDEV: mds1 mds1_UUID /tmp/mds1-cs01 ext3 100000 no
OSC: OSC_cs01_OST_localhost_MNT_localhost
986a7_lov1_d9a476ab41 OST_localhost_UUID
LOV: lov1 986a7_lov1_d9a476ab41 mds1_UUID 0 65536 0 0          \
      [u'OST_localhost_UUID'] mds1
MDC: MDC_cs01_mds1_MNT_localhost
91f4c_MNT_localhost_bb96ccc3fb mds1_UUID
MTPT: MNT_localhost MNT_localhost_UUID /mnt/lustre mds1_      \
      UUID lov1_UUID
```

There are now a whole lot more kernel modules loaded than there were before we started. A quick look with the `lsmod` command yields

```
Module                      Size  Used by      Not tainted
loop                       11888  6  (autoclean)
llite                     385000  1
mds                       389876  2
lov                       198472  2
osc                       137024  2
mdc                       110904  1  [llite]
obdfilter                 180416  1
fsfilt_ext3                25924  2
ost                        90236  1
ptlrpc                    782716  0                                    \
      [llite mds lov osc mdc obdfilter ost]
obdclass                  558688  0                                    \
      [llite mds lov osc mdc obdfilter fsfilt_ext3 ost ptlrpc]
lvfs                       27300  1                                    \
      [mds obdfilter fsfilt_ext3 ptlrpc obdclass]
ksocknal                   81004  5
portals                   144224  1                                    \
      [llite mds lov osc mdc obdfilter fsfilt_ext3 ost              \
        ptlrpc obdclass lvfs ksocknal]
```

These are the Lustre modules that are loaded in addition to the normal system modules. If you examine some of the Lustre architecture documents, you will recognize some of these module names as being associated with Lustre components. Names like `ost` and `obdclass` become familiar after a while. Notice the number of modules that use the `portals` module.

The output of the `mount` command shows that we do indeed have a Lustre file system mounted:

```
local on /mnt/lustre type lustre_lite                              \
     (rw,osc=lov1,mdc=MDC_cs01_mds1_MNT_localhost)
```

There are also a lot of files under the `/proc/fs/lustre` directories that contain state and status information for the file system components. Taking a look at the `local.xml` configuration file created by the example, we can see lots of Lustre configuration information required to start up the components (I have used bold type for the major matching XML tags in the output):

```
<?xml version='1.0' encoding='UTF-8'?>
<lustre version='2003070801'>
  <ldlm name='ldlm' uuid='ldlm_UUID'/>
  <node uuid='localhost_UUID' name='localhost'>
    <profile_ref uuidref='PROFILE_localhost_UUID'/>
    <network uuid='NET_localhost_tcp_UUID' nettype='tcp'    \
      name='NET_localhost_tcp'>
      <nid>hpepc1</nid>
      <clusterid>0</clusterid>
      <port>988</port>
    </network>
  </node>
  <profile uuid='PROFILE_localhost_UUID'                    \
      name='PROFILE_localhost'>
    <ldlm_ref uuidref='ldlm_UUID'/>
    <network_ref uuidref='NET_localhost_tcp_UUID'/>
    <mdsdev_ref uuidref='MDD_mds1_localhost_UUID'/>
    <osd_ref uuidref='SD_OST_localhost_localhost_UUID'/>
    <mountpoint_ref uuidref='MNT_localhost_UUID'/>
  </profile>
  <mds uuid='mds1_UUID' name='mds1'>
    <active_ref uuidref='MDD_mds1_localhost_UUID'/>
    <lovconfig_ref uuidref='LVCFG_lov1_UUID'/>
    <filesystem_ref uuidref='FS_fsname_UUID'/>
  </mds>
  <msdev uuid='MDD_mds1_localhost_UUID'                     \
      name='MDD_mds1_localhost'>
    <fstype>ext3</fstype>
    <devpath>/tmp/mds1-cs01</devpath>
    <autoformat>no</autoformat>
    <devsize>100000</devsize>
    <journalsize>0</journalsize>
    <inodesize>0</inodesize>
    <nspath>/mnt/mds_ns</nspath>
    <mkfsoptions>-I 128</mkfsoptions>
    <node_ref uuidref='localhost_UUID'/>
```

```
      <target_ref uuidref='mds1_UUID'/>
    </mdsdev>
    <lov uuid='lov1_UUID' stripesize='65536' stripecount='0'  \
        stripepattern='0' name='lov1'>
      <mds_ref uuidref='mds1_UUID'/>
      <obd_ref uuidref='OST_localhost_UUID'/>
    </lov>
    <lovconfig uuid='LVCFG_lov1_UUID' name='LVCFG_lov1'>
      <lov_ref uuidref='lov1_UUID'/>
    </lovconfig>
    <ost uuid='OST_localhost_UUID' name='OST_localhost'>
      <active_ref uuidref='SD_OST_localhost_localhost_UUID'/>
    </ost>
    <osd osdtype='obdfilter'                                   \
        uuid='SD_OST_localhost_localhost_UUID'                \
        name='OSD_OST_localhost_localhost'>
      <target_ref uuidref='OST_localhost_UUID'/>
      <node_ref uuidref='localhost_UUID'/>
      <fstype>ext3</fstype>
      <devpath>/tmp/ost1-cs01</devpath>
      <autoformat>no</autoformat>
      <devsize>200000</devsize>
      <journalsize>0</journalsize>
      <inodesize>0</inodesize>
      <nspath>/mnt/ost_ns</nspath>
    </osd>
    <filesystem uuid='FS_fsname_UUID' name='FS_fsname'>
      <mds_ref uuidref='mds1_UUID'/>
      <obd_ref uuidref='lov1_UUID'/>
    </filesystem>
    <mountpoint uuid='MNT_localhost_UUID' name='MNT_localhost'>
      <filesystem_ref uuidref='FS_fsname_UUID'/>
      <path>/mnt/lustre</path>
    </mountpoint>
  </lustre>
```

I believe we are seeing the future of configuration information, for better or worse. Although XML might make a good, easy-to-parse, universal "minilanguage" for software configuration, it certainly lacks human readability. If this means we get nifty tools to create the configuration, and nothing ever goes wrong to force us to read this stuff directly, I guess I will be happy.

The example script calls `lmc` to operate on the XML configuration file, followed by `lconf` to load the modules and activate the components. As you can see from the configuration, an MDS and object storage target (OST) are created along with a logical volume (LOV) that is mounted by the client "node." Although this example all takes place on the local host, it is possible to experiment and actually distribute the components onto other systems in the network.

Cleaning up after ourselves, we perform the following:

```
# NAME=local.sh;./llmountcleanup.sh
MTPT: MNT_localhost MNT_localhost_UUID /mnt/lustre mds1_UUID
lov1_UUID
MDC: MDC_cs01_mds1_MNT_localhost
21457_MNT_localhost_4aafe7d139
LOV: lov1 d0db0_lov1_aa2c6e8c14
OSC: OSC_cs01_OST_localhost_MNT_localhost
d0db0_lov1_aa2c6e8c14
MDSDEV: mds1 mds1_UUID
OSD: OST_localhost OST_localhost_UUID
NETWORK: NET_localhost_tcp NET_localhost_tcp_UUID tcp cs01 988
killing process 3166
removing stale pidfile: /var/run/acceptor-988.pid
unloading module: llite
unloading module: mdc
unloading module: lov
unloading module: osc
unloading module: fsfilt_ext3
unloading module: mds
unloading module: obdfilter
unloading module: ost
unloading module: ptlrpc
unloading module: obdclass
unloading module: lvfs
unloading module: ksocknal
unloading module: portals
lconf DONE
```

To try the multinode example, you will need to install the Lustre kernel on multiple nodes, reboot, and feed a common XML configuration file to the `lconf` command on each node. Because this is relatively intrusive, we will not attempt the nonlocal demonstration here. The multinode example is left as an exercise for you, when you feel ambitious.

One of the interesting things about Lustre is the abstraction of the file access. There are what might be called "pseudo" drivers that implement access patterns (striping, RAID, and so on) across the multiple OSS devices. This architecture appears to be substantially different from some of the other parallel file systems that we will encounter in terms of the "back-end" storage and SAN configurations. The I/O requests (object accesses) may be spread across multiple SANs or physically attached devices on the OSS systems to produce the promised level of scaling.

Lustre development continues today, so many of the architectural promises have not yet been realized. The level of support for this project from major corporations like Hewlett-Packard, however, shows a potential for realizing the goals, and the project is on a stepwise approach to the full vision (what we have today is "Lustre Lite"). We need to keep our eyes on Lustre as it matures and extends its features.

14.4 Commercially Available Cluster File Systems

In addition to the open-source cluster file systems that are readily available for free, there are a number of commercial parallel file system implementations on the market. The primary advantage of the commercial packages is the available support, which can include bug fixes and updates to functionality. Although I do not have time or space to delve deeply into all these products, three will serve as a representative sample of what is available.

There is a set of common requirements that you will find in all parallel file systems used in Linux clusters. The first requirement is POSIX semantics for the file system, which allows UNIX and Linux applications to use the file system without code modifications. The set of operations, the behavior, and the data interfaces are specified in the POSIX standard. For database use, you will find that the file system needs to provide some form of direct-access mode, in which the database software can read and write data blocks without using the Linux system's buffer or page cache. The database software performs this caching itself and removes the associated overhead.

For use with Oracle 9i RAC installations, a parallel file system allows sharing of the Oracle home directory with the application binaries and associated log and configuration files. This means a single software installation (instance) instead of one install per node participating in the cluster. This is one of the general benefits of using a file system of this type for clusters—the shared data *and* shared client participation in the file system can mean less system administration overhead.

14.4.1   Red Hat Global File System (GFS)

Red Hat has recently completed the purchase of Sistina Software Inc. and their GFS technology (information at `http://www.sistina.com`). On a historical note, the OpenGFS software described earlier is built on the last open-source version of GFS before the developers founded Sistina Inc. Red Hat offers a number of cluster "applications" for their Linux offering, including high availability and IP load balancing, and GFS adds a parallel cluster file system to that capability. The Sistina Web site mentions that the GFS software will be open source soon.

The GFS product provides direct I/O capabilities for database applications as well as POSIX-compliant behavior for use with existing UNIX and Linux applications. Both Red Hat and SUSE Linux are supported. The Red Hat Linux versions supported as of April 2004 are RHEL 3.0, RHAS 2.1, and Red Hat version 9.0. The SUSE SLES 8 release is also supported. GFS supports up to 256 nodes in the file system cluster, all with equal (sometimes referred to as *symmetric*) access to the shared storage.

As with other parallel cluster file systems, GFS assumes the ability to share storage devices between the members of the cluster. This implies, but does not require, a SAN "behind" the cluster members to allow shared access to the storage. For example, it is quite possible to use point-to-point Fibre-Channel connections in conjunction with dual-controller RAID arrays and Linux multipath I/O to share storage devices without implementing a switched SAN fabric.

Another way to extend the "reach" of expensive SAN storage is to use a SAN switch with iSCSI or other network protocol ports. The Fibre-Channel switch translates IP-encapsulated SCSI commands, delivered via the iSCSI protocol, into the native Fibre-Channel frames. High-performance systems may access the SAN via the switch Fibre-Channel fabric, and other, potentially more numerous systems may access the storage via GbE.

In addition to shared access to storage in an attached SAN fabric, Red Hat provides GFS server systems the ability to access a storage device via a local GFS network block device (GNBD), which accesses devices provided by a GNBD server. This type of interface on Linux (there are several, including the network block device [nbd] interface) typically provides a kernel module that translates direct device accesses on the local system to the proper network-encapsulated protocol. The GNBD interface allows extending storage device access to the server systems via a gigabit (or other) low-cost Ethernet network transport. This arrangement is shown in Figure 14–7.

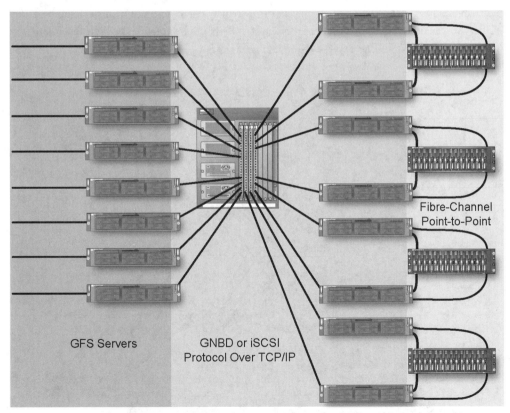

Figure 14–7 GNBD and iSCSI device access to Red Hat GFS

This approach provides more fan-out at a lower cost than a switched SAN, but at a potentially lower performance. A key factor is the ability to eliminate expensive back-end SAN switches by using direct attach Fibre-Channel storage and either GNBD or iSCSI over lower cost GbE, thus decreasing costs. An entire book could be written on the design issues and implementation approach for this type of solution—I am hoping that somebody will write it soon. We will stop here before we get any deeper.

14.4.2   The PolyServe Matrix File System

The Matrix Server product is a commercially available cluster file system from PolyServe Inc. The product runs on either Microsoft Windows or Linux systems and provides a high availability, no SPOF file-serving capability for a number of applications, including Oracle databases. Red Hat and SUSE Linux distributions are supported by the software. See `http://www.polyserve.com` for specific information.

Access to the file system is fully symmetric across all cluster members, and is managed by a distributed lock manager. Meta-data access is also distributed across the cluster members. The Matrix Server product assumes shared storage in a SAN environment. The high-level hardware architecture is shown in Figure 14–8.

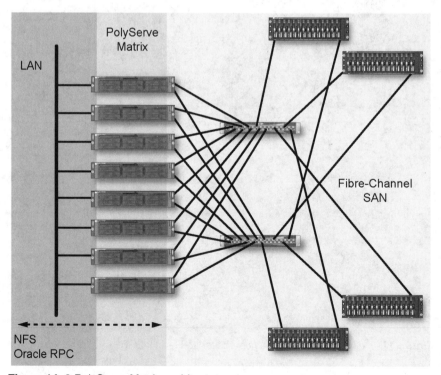

Figure 14–8 PolyServe Matrix architecture

The file system is fully journaled and provides POSIX semantics to Linux applications, so they do not need to be specially adapted to cluster environments. The high-availability package provides a number of features, including multiple fail-over modes, standby network interfaces, support for multipath I/O, and on-line addition or removal of cluster members.

An interesting management feature provided by the PolyServe file system is the concept of "context-dependent symbolic links" or CDSLs. A CDSL allows node-specific access to a common file name (for example, log files or configuration files like `sqlnet.ora`) in the file system. The CDSLs allow the control of which files have one instance and are shared by all members of the cluster, and which files are available on a node-specific basis. The PolyServe file system allows creating CDSLs based on the node's host name.

The PolyServe file system may be exported via NFS or made available to database clients with Oracle RPC, via the network. In this situation, the PolyServe nodes also become NFS or Oracle 9i RAC servers to *their* clients, in addition to participating in the cluster file system. Their common, consistent view of the file system data is available in parallel to NFS or Oracle clients. Other applications, like Web serving, Java application serving, and so forth, also benefit from exporting a single, consistent instance of the data in the cluster file system.

14.4.3   Oracle Cluster File System (OCFS)

The Oracle cluster file system (OCFS) is designed to eliminate the need for raw file access in Linux implementations of Oracle 9i RAC. The OCFS software is available for download free, and it is open source. It is intended only for supporting the requirements of the Oracle RAC software and is not a general-purpose cluster file system.

Because the Oracle database software manages the required locking and concurrency issues associated with data consistency, this functionality is not provided by the OCFS implementation. Other restrictions exist with regard to performing I/O to the OCFS, so its use should be limited to Oracle 9i RAC implementations only. It can help reduce the cost of implementing an Oracle 9i RAC cluster by eliminating the need to purchase extra cluster file system software.

Although OCFS removes the requirement to use raw partitions to contain the database, there are other side effects of which you should be aware. For this reason, you should investigate the system administration consequences, such as no shared Oracle home directory (implying multiple instances of log files and other information), before committing to OCFS as the file system for your database cluster.

14.5 Cluster File System Summary

We examined a number of cluster file systems and their architectures in this chapter. Although there is a lot of promise in PVFS, OpenGFS, Lustre, and the plethora of other open-source cluster file systems, the current developmental state of these file systems may not be appropriate for production environments. There are many more parallel file systems available from the open-source and research communities, and more are becoming available every day.

An alternative to the experimental nature of some of the parallel open-source file systems is good old NFS. We are mostly familiar with NFS and its characteristics, and should have a fairly good instinct about whether it is up to the challenge presented by our cluster. Like the other open-source cluster file systems, the price is right, but NFS has the advantage of being thoroughly wrung out by a large number of users who are familiar with it.

The commercially available file systems, like the Red Hat GFS and the PolyServe Matrix file system, are potentially viable alternatives to the open-source file systems for production environments that require scaling, resiliency, and availability of professional support. The support and feature set from the commercial cluster file systems makes them attractive for database, Web-serving, and high-availability cluster file system applications. It is unclear whether these file systems will scale into the many hundreds or thousands of clients.

Which choice you make for providing data to your cluster will depend on your ability to deal with software development issues, scaling, implementation details, and the availability of support. I recommend a thorough investigation before selecting a cluster file system for your environment. The good thing is that we have a wide range of choices.

## CHAPTER 15

Stuck in the Middle:
Cluster Middleware

Chapter Objectives

- Introduce the parallel program execution environment
- Discuss the installation of the MPI infrastructure
- Define the environment for monitoring a cluster's resources
- Survey common monitoring and event generation software packages

The HSI hardware and software infrastructure required to support low-level cluster operations was introduced in previous chapters. We now cover the environment necessary to support the execution of parallel jobs and cluster software, along with the system management tools required to monitor the cluster's health.

15.1 Introduction to Cluster Middleware

Up to this point in the book, we have discussed the lower levels of the cluster's software hierarchy: authentication, name services, file systems, and so on. Once these components are active, we need to move "up the food chain" to start addressing the needs of the applications that will be running in the cluster. Allocating the resources necessary for a cluster's parallel applications, scheduling the application components, providing the necessary communication paths over the HSI, and monitoring the performance and health of the cluster is the concern of the cluster's middleware.

To help us recall where we are in the scheme of things, examine the area enclosed by the dotted box in Figure 15–1. Although I have repeatedly stressed that this book is not intended as a tutorial on parallel programming, we still need to understand a certain amount of the requirements of a parallel application environment to get our arms around what services we must

433

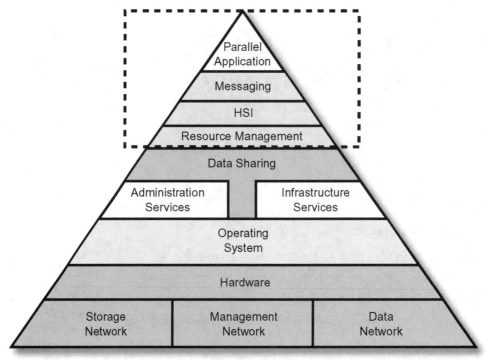

Figure 15–1 Cluster middleware architecture

design and configure. From the application's viewpoint, the cluster's software needs to provide the necessary infrastructure to support the resources required for the application's execution.

15.1.1   Describing the Parallel Application Execution Environment

If our cluster is running a parallel database, then much of the application environment may be considered "external" to the cluster itself. The application clients contact the database instances on the compute slices, handle authentication, and deal with retrying query operations in the event of a failure. The cluster's database instances must handle balancing request loads, keeping data consistent, recovering from failures, and monitoring the state and performance of the cluster's components.

In a general-purpose scientific cluster that is running parallel applications, the cluster infrastructure must schedule parallel jobs on behalf of the users, efficiently allocate the resources for a given job's requirements, schedule the individual components of the application, and monitor the health of the parallel application and its environment.

The monitoring of cluster parameters and node status is an important aspect of the overall behavior of the cluster. Detecting whether a targeted node in the cluster is dead, for example, has a profound impact on the success of launching the whole application. Fortunately there are a number of really good open-source tools for performing this type of monitoring.

15.1.2 The HSI Message-Passing Facility

The parallel application may be thought of as a group of programs that are communicating via the HSI hardware by passing messages. The message-passing operations are programmed into the application code using library calls from the message-passing libraries that support a particular set of standard semantics. One such common standard is the MPI.

The MPI standard describes the communication operations necessary to tie parallel program components together, but does not specify the environment that initiates the program components. Initialization actions that must be performed to start the parallel program across the cluster are allocating the "virtual computer" resources to execute the program (for example, the correct number and type of CPUs), scheduling the program components on multiple compute slices, enabling command-line parameter passing, redirecting the component's standard I/O (`stdin`, `stdout`, and `stderr`) in a consistent way, and permitting the proper access to cluster resources by the application's individual pieces. (The systems that are selected for the parallel application may need to be "close" together in the HSI mapping to prevent frequent operations like "broadcast all" or "reduce all" from impacting performance. The scheduling mechanism must take the topology of the HSI and the application into account when choosing the cluster resources.)

There are tools, such as the `mpirun` command, that are available with the MPI package to handle basic parallel program scheduling, parameter passing, and I/O redirection, but there may need to be adaptation to whatever load-balancing mechanism is in use in the cluster. This functionality may be handled by custom scripts or by entirely separate commands that are provided with the load-balancing software. I discuss this issue and the issue of allocating parallel processing resources in the upcoming sections.

15.1.3 Load Balancing or Job Scheduling

We need to be careful how we use the phrase *load balancing* with respect to both clusters running multicomponent parallel jobs and other more service-oriented types of clusters. In Web-serving, database, or other service or transaction-oriented types of clusters, the cluster is handling individual, immutable transactions or streams of independent requests. In this configuration, the phrase *load balancing* may actually refer to "traffic distribution" or "transaction directing" between the compute slice systems. The individual transactions are directed to compute slices in a "round-robin," "fair-share" or some other real-time priority distribution scheme, determined by a facility that may be external to the cluster. (*Fair share* has a number of definitions, but usually refers to a scheduling algorithm that attempts to allocate a fixed percentage of resources to a given user or process over time.)

In a cluster running parallel applications, *load balancing* or *load sharing* may refer to allocating and assigning the parallel resources for an application, as well as maintaining "batch" queues of jobs that are waiting for the required resources to execute. Users in this type of environment submit their jobs to the *load balancer, scheduler,* or *batch queuing* system through some form of client interface that allows them to define the necessary resources to run their application, and to identify the location of the executables, the job environment, and the sources of data for the job. Usually, the software performing the load balancing runs on administrative nodes that are considered part of the cluster.

Once a job is submitted, the load-balancing software applies a set of predetermined rules to the requested resources, determining priority and execution order in relationship to other requests. At submission time, the batch system may allocate the necessary resources and immediately execute the program, if the required resources are available, or it may queue the job until the required resources are available. Staging the job's I/O data files may also be performed as part of the execution of the job.

In both example uses of the phrase *load balancing*, the cluster compute slices represent available resources that need to be efficiently scheduled to perform work on behalf of the cluster's users. The load is "balanced" between the available compute slices, or "shared" with other jobs according to resource allocation rules. Whether the work is scheduled in real time, based on individual transactions, or by using a batch-queuing model, there are a set of predetermined priorities and rules for managing the workload.

The cluster's system administrator needs to be able to set the rules, monitor the cluster's performance, and adjust the resource allocation behavior to meet the user's needs according to the business objectives of the cluster's owner. In a cluster running parallel applications, allowing users to schedule their own resources whenever they want may only work if the number of users is small and the contention for resources is infrequent. This type of "free-for-all" or "ad hoc" scheduling, however, can cause resource issues, contention, and large-scale conflict in larger and more complex groups (proportional to the size of the egos involved).

In both senses, the phrase *load balancing* denotes software that allows a system administrator to implement and enforce policies for the use of cluster resources. The services that are making the resource allocation or direction decisions may be considered part of the cluster management software, because they make decisions about the use and distribution of the cluster's resources between multiple competing users of the cluster. It should go without saying that the load-balancing services must be treated as critical to the operation of the cluster.

Setting up the load-balancing software involves installing the necessary software services, configuring the client and server software elements for the service, and creating the rules for resource allocation. Which specific load-balancing software is installed, such as the LVS package or batch-queueing software like Altair Grid Technologies' commercial PBS Pro, the open-source OpenPBS, or Platform Computing's commercially available load-sharing facility (LSF), will depend on whether the cluster is a transaction-based cluster or is running general parallel applications. (Information on both PBS Pro and OpenPBS is available at `http://open-`

`pbs.org`. OpenPBS was developed by the NASA Ames Research Facility, Lawrence Livermore National Laboratory, and Veridian Information Solutions, Inc.)

The interface between the job submission facility and a particular "resource management system" in your cluster may need to be customized. It is possible, for instance, to issue `mpirun` commands from job scripts that are submitted to the batch-queuing software, with no checking for live versus dead resources other than that provided by the batch-scheduling facility. This additional level of resource checking and management may be handled by another facility that interfaces to the load-balancing software: a cluster resource manager.

15.1.4 Cluster Resource Management

The nodes that are live or available at the time that a parallel job is submitted to a batch-queuing system may be dead, catatonic, or unavailable when the job actually starts to execute. If the load-balancing system must check all available resources before starting each job, it needs to understand some cluster-specific information to make the checks. This functionality may be abstracted to a RMS that maintains the current resource information about the cluster's member systems along with their health and availability.

Some of the more common features and informational items that are found in cluster resource management software are

- Node state (up, down, assigned, unavailable)
- Node resource configuration (disk, memory, CPUs, and so on)
- Node membership in a partition assigned to parallel jobs
- Node HSI position information (network rank)

The amount and type of information available varies from resource manager to resource manager, but much of it is very useful for allocating the resources to execute a parallel job. There are certain parallel functions (like barriers and broadcasts) that are more efficient if the nodes participating in a parallel application's partition are adjacent to one another in the HSI network.

Specialized HSI hardware vendors, such as Quadrics, may provide their own resource management facility that is closely tied to their specific HSI hardware. The Quadrics RMS, for example, maintains information about the current cluster "membership"—that is, the currently allocated or available compute resources in the cluster. Some load-balancing software, such as Platform Computing's LSF product, have an interface to the optional RMS software to help identify available (and unavailable) resources in the cluster's compute slice pool.

15.1.5 Custom Scheduling

We also need to be careful about the use of the word *scheduling*. This may indicate merely that the job has been assigned a set of resources and a time to run (it is "scheduled"), or it could indicate special software that runs to optimize ("schedule") the resource allocations in the cluster.

There are several RMSs available, and it can be quite difficult to tell where the term *resource manager* leaves off and the term *scheduling* begins.

Most modern load-balancing services provide APIs allowing access to status and custom management of their policies, queues, and general behavior. These programmatic interfaces may be used to implement custom behaviors that might be desirable in some cluster environment, but are not implemented in the load-balancing facility itself. An example of this type of feature is "backfilling"—the ability to execute jobs out of order to maximize efficient use of the cluster's resources. (For example, assume a batch queue for a 128-CPU cluster contains jobs that required 100, 64, and 20 CPUs respectively. A scheduler that was capable of backfilling would run the jobs out of order: executing the 100- and 20-CPU jobs concurrently, followed by the 64-CPU job. This would presumably get the 20-CPU job finished faster, without impacting the 100-CPU job or delaying the 64-CPU job.)

The RMS client may be a separate daemon or a kernel module that runs on the system being monitored. Periodic checks are made from a central point of control, on an administrative server, into the current state (live or dead) of a compute slice and state may be maintained in a database. System administrators may be allowed to kill job components, enable debugging messages, form or dissolve parallel partitions, or remove systems from the available pool of compute resources in the cluster. The system administrator can thus alter the behavior or availability of specific groups of compute slices to the general load-balancing and job dispatch service.

Some resource managers implement the concept of a resource "bank," endowed with a certain amount of resource "currency." This currency is doled out to specific users, groups of users, or may remain unallocated. The amount of currency that is "charged" to a given user's bank account is related in some way to the amount of resources used by their jobs, based on resources like CPU cycles, CPU performance, memory usage, and so forth.

Resource management software, in addition to providing currency to spend on allocations of cluster resources, may log the actual resource utilization for the purpose of charging *real* money for the use of the cluster. Users may be given the option to use high-priority resources at a higher charge rate, or to use lower priority resources, all depending on their goals and currency allocation. The tracking of resource usage must be accurately tied to the user's account and the actual logged resources consumed by the user's jobs.

There are both commercial and open-source versions of resource management and scheduling systems available from a variety of sources. This level of control and detail, of course, has its cost in terms of configuration and system management effort required—not to mention the level of user sophistication required. Whether you use this type of RMS to administer the use of your cluster is dependent on your specific environment.

As an example, the Maui scheduler interfaces with LSF, Sun Grid Engine (SGE), Open-PBS, PBS Pro, and several other load-balancing facilities through their APIs, implementing custom scheduling *and* what could be considered resource management functionality. To complicate the picture, the simple Linux utility for resource management (SLURM) resource manager provides information about the state of nodes in the cluster and other attributes that are useful for scheduling decisions, but it also interfaces with the Maui scheduler. I talk specifically about the features of the Maui scheduler and SLURM in upcoming sections.

15.1.6 Monitoring, Measuring, and Managing Your Cluster

It is essential to the effective management of a cluster to have access to the current state of all hardware and associated software resources. Measuring the parameters from the hardware and operating system on each system in the cluster is only part of the picture, however. Once you have collected the data, you must also be able to recognize and take action on any parameters that are out of normal operating range.

Sorting through the mountains of data that get generated every minute (second?) in a cluster is very impractical without a high level of automation. To take corrective action when an issue occurs, you must be notified of any abnormal conditions that exist within the hardware or software components across the whole cluster. It is not humanly possible to sift through the thousands of individual parameters manually. This is why we have computers and software to help us.

We need to be able to collect the data, set the expected operational ranges, and generate the proper notification if an exceptional event occurs. Fortunately, there are some very good packages available to aid our efforts. For software services, we also need to be notified of failures or malfunctions so that we can correct the situation before it becomes a cascading nightmare. One can think of monitoring "internal" parameters and "external" services, and there is just such a functional division in the available packages.

Several very good open-source measurement packages exist for cluster environments. One of the packages, Ganglia, is a very powerful collection and visualization tool for "internal" system performance parameters. In addition to the monitoring of low-level performance parameters with Ganglia, both the `nagios` and `mon` tools allow generation of events and notification in response to exceptions to normal operational limits or disappearance of services from the "outside." I introduce and cover these tools further on in this chapter.

15.2 The MPICH Library

As we have seen, the acronym MPI stands for "message-passing interface"—the software facility that allows parallel application components to communicate with each other. The specific open-source version of the MPI library and utilities that you will frequently encounter is called MPICH (information and downloads are available at `http://www-unix.mcs.anl.gov/mpi/mpich`). The CH stands for the word *chameleon*—in reference to the software's ability to adapt to a wide variety of hardware and software environments. Indeed, it was designed specifically for this purpose.

15.2.1 Introduction to MPICH

The MPICH software is available on Microsoft Windows, Linux, and in a variety of UNIX "flavors." In addition to the version that is available from Argonne National Laboratory, you may find HSI-specific versions that have been tuned by a particular hardware vendor. For example, Myricom makes a version of MPICH available for the Myrinet GM interconnect (see information at http://www.myricom.com). If you cannot find a prebuilt version for your environment, you will need to download and build the software yourself.

MPICH implements the MPI version 1.1 standard, and MPICH2, which implements the MPI 2.0 standard, is currently in beta test. More general information on the MPI standards is available from the MPI forum Web site (at http://www.mpi-forum.org). This is a really good time to remind you that this book is not intended to be a tutorial on parallel application development. I cover MPI elements only in enough detail to show their interaction with the general cluster software environment—specifically, starting parallel applications.

The MPICH software includes commands for executing MPI and non-MPI programs on remote compute slices in the cluster. This service presupposes the existence of a clusterwide remote access service, like RSH (or SSH), to authenticate the user and allow access to the remote nodes for starting the application components. Additionally, the execution service must be able to authenticate the user on the remote machine and locate the executable to run.

15.2.2   Downloading and Installing MPICH

The MPICH software is available as a tar ball that may be downloaded, compiled, and installed on every node that will run an MPI program. One way to do the installation is to unpack the tar ball on the cluster's file server in a directory that is mounted on every compute slice. Compile the software then perform the installation step on each compute slice. An alternative is to install the software on the "golden client," capture a system image, then push the image to all compute slices.

You can download the MPICH software by executing

```
# wget ftp://ftp.mcs.anl.gov/pub/mpi/mpich-1.2.5.2.tar.gz
```

Once you have the tar ball, you can unpack it, configure the software, then compile and install MPICH for your system:

```
# tar xvf mpich-1.2.5.2.tar.gz
# cd mpich-1.2.5.2
# ./configure --prefix=/usr/lib/mpich-1.2.5.2
# make
# make install
```

On starting the software build, you will be rewarded with the normal output from the make command. The build will take anywhere from a few minutes to up to an hour, depending on your environment. On the average, it takes about 15 minutes to complete the configure, build, and installation steps.

In addition to the base software, which is now installed under /usr/lib/mpich-1.2.5.2, after the build and install are complete,   several software utilities are placed in the /usr/lib/mpich/bin directory. (Your users' PATH environment variables will need to be modified to incorporate the proper directory for running the MPI commands. This can be considered part of the required configuration for the MPICH software.) These utilities include the `mpirun` command and tools for linking C++ (`mpiCC`), C (`mpicc`), and FORTRAN (`mpif77` and `mpif90`) programs with the appropriate libraries. I do not cover the details of developing, compiling, and linking MPI programs in this book; there are several good texts available. A minimal programming manual is available in HTML by opening `/usr/lib/mpich-1.2.5.2/www/index.html` with your browser, or by using the `mpiman` command.

We can test the compilation and installation on the current machine with the example programs that are located in `/usr/lib/mpich-1.2.5.2/examples`. Let's compile the `cpi` example, which calculates the value of pi, log in as a nonroot user, and execute the program with `mpirun` on the local system:

```
# cd /usr/lib/mpich-1.2.5.2/examples
# make cpi
# su - rob
# cd /usr/lib/mpich-1.2.5.2/examples
[rob@cs01 examples]$ ./mpirun -np 1 cpi
Process 0 on cs01.cluster.local
pi is approximately 3.1416009869231254, Error is
0.0000083333333323
wall clock time = 0.000418
```

Information about the systems that will be participating in the MPICH executables needs to be entered into `/usr/lib/mpich-1.2.5.2/share/machines.<ARCH>`. This file is called `machines.LINUX` on my system and contains lines with host names or host names followed by: `<number_of_cpus>` for SMP machines with multiple CPUs.

15.2.3   Using `mpirun`

Using `mpirun` is a useful way to test the installation of the MPICH software. In general, however, your cluster may use some of the other execution facilities that are part of batch-queuing software like OpenPBS or Platform Computing's LSF. It is a good idea to run some simple tests across the cluster to verify the MPICH installations, so we will cover a little of the `mpirun` capabilities and some of the steps needed to set up the test. More information about the many options is available in the MPICH documentation.

As was previously mentioned, the `mpirun` command assumes an underlying remote-access service for starting the parallel application components. Obviously, using the standard BSD RSH service is an insecure and undesirable option. This means that you should use either the Kerberized version of the RSH service or SSH as the remote-access shell. Configuring these services was covered previously in the software infrastructure chapters of this book.

Let's use SSH in our example tests, because it is a service that is present on all the systems and will take a minimum of effort to set up for the initial testing. The remote-access service used by `mpirun` may be configured at compile time or may be chosen with the `P4_RSHCOMMAND` environment variable to override the default, so we can force SSH no matter what the installation specified as the default. The list of steps necessary to enable the "quick" test is as follows.

1. Install MPICH on all compute slices that will run the MPI software.
2. Configure the `/usr/lib/mpich-1.2.5.2/share/machines.LINUX` files to contain the list of each machine participating in the MPI environment.
3. Log in as the test user (some of the test or example programs warn against running them as the `root` user) or use `su - <user>` to assume the user's login identity and home directory. (One assumption in this step is that the user's directory is available on all systems participating in the test.)
4. Generate the `${HOME}/.ssh/authorized_keys2` file for the user performing the test and ensure that it contains a key for every host that will participate. (If you are using pass phrases on your keys [a good idea], then configuration of the `ssh-agent` to manage the key pass phrases is a real time-saver.)
5. Set the `P4_RSHCOMMAND` environment variable to `ssh` to use the SSH service.
6. Run the `/usr/lib/mpich-1.2.5.2/sbin/tstmachines` command to test the consistency of the installation.

This test, and `mpirun` in general, require that the systems in the cluster all have access to a shared file system, have consistent user identifications and permissions, and have executables that are located in the same place on the target machines. The `testmachines` program attempts to access files and commands from all the machines that are listed in the `/usr/lib/mpich-1.2.5.2/share/machines.LINUX` file to test the remote access and the file consistency. In fact, this "program" is actually a shell script, and you can observe its tests by running it as `tstmachines -v` or by looking at the commands in the script.

We can now try a more general test of the configuration with one of the MPICH example programs, called `cpi`. On each of the machines with MPICH installed, perform

```
# cd /usr/lib/mpich-1.2.5.2/examples
# make cpi
```

This will create the executable we wish to run in a common location on all clients. Additionally, you can compile the example executable and push it out to the compute slices. `SystemImager`, for example, would allow you to update only the executable file in the `examples` directory on "golden client," then push the changes to the associated clients.

Once the example is compiled and installed on all of the compute slices under test, we may proceed. We will perform a simple test of the MPICH installation by running `cpi`, which we just compiled, to calculate the approximate value of pi[1]:

---

1.   This example is a fairly simple program and it is a good introduction to the MPI programming environment. Its accuracy increases with the number of parallel components doing the calculations.

```
# su - <testuser>
$ cd /usr/lib/mpich-1.2.5.2/examples
$ ./mpirun -np <N> cpi
```

The example output from a four-node run is:

```
$ cd /usr/lib/mpich-1.2.5.2/examples
[rob@cs01 examples]$ ./mpirun -np 4 cpi
Process 0 on cs01.cluster.local
Process 1 on cs02.cluster.local
Process 2 on cs03.cluster.local
Process 3 on cs04.cluster.local
pi is approximately 3.1416009869231245, Error is
0.0000083333333314
wall clock time = 0.007258
```

With a test such as this, we have verified the installation of the MPICH software on the target nodes. The fact that the application ran to completion shows that we must be doing something right.

The mpirun command has to do a remote login for each of the remotely scheduled components. These logins must verify the user's ID or credentials by looking up the proper information on each of the remote clients. Proper configuration of the login process and start-up files in the user's home directory is a prerequisite to successful launching of parallel jobs with mpirun. For example, if X11 forwarding is enabled by SSH, there may be extraneous messages about X11 authorization failures generated by the login process. The remote access should be properly configured to handle interactive and noninteractive connections.

MPICH offers another scheduling mechanism for the ch_p4 device in the form of "secure daemons." These daemons use the BSD ruserok routine to check that a user is allowed access to the system, which may not be allowed in your environment if security is an issue. Additionally, the secure daemons only work with the ch_p4 device and the underlying TCP/IP transport.

This scheduling method is neither very general purpose nor secure, but it does save scheduling time over the individual RSH accesses to remote systems by allowing direct access to the daemons from mpirun. The daemons must be started on the target systems, either manually or with a script that is provided: /usr/lib/mpich-1.2.5.2/sbin/chp4_servs. Once the daemons are started, the mpirun command is told to use the secure daemon access either with a command-line option specifying the port to contact the daemons or with two environment variables:

```
$ mpirun -p4ssport <port-number> -np 4 cpi
$
$ export MPI_USEP4SSPORT=yes
$ export MPI_P4SSPORT=<port-number>
$ mpirun -np 4 cpi
```

As mentioned, this method has security issues associated with the authentication mechanism, it provides no protection from users trying to run simultaneous jobs on the same targets, and it requires manual setup to function. For this reason, unless the cluster environment is extremely simple (a single user or application instance), other methods are necessary. The positive aspect of the service is that it is free and included with the MPICH software.

15.2.4   Special Versions of MPICH

Specialized versions of the MPICH library are available from HSI vendors like Myricom that have specially tuned the underlying device drivers to work with their hardware. (There are usually low-level direct-access libraries that are available for programmers or application developers who wish to create their own specialized interconnect software.) The Myrinet-enabled version of MPICH, MPICH GM, uses the Myrinet low-level communication libraries to pass messages, reducing the time that would be spent in a high-level software "stack" such as TCP/IP. This reduces the overall end-to-end latency for messages sent over the specialized HSI hardware.

Obtaining the special versions of MPICH (and other libraries) supported by your HSI vendor will usually require access to the vendor's download site and specialized instructions. There may also be different configuration requirements based on the underlying HSI hardware. You should obtain the specialized MPICH library software and carefully follow your vendor's documentation for compilation, installation, configuration, and testing of the combined HSI hardware and MPICH software.

Another specialized MPICH implementation that you may encounter is the MPICH G2 (grid-enabled) library. This version of the MPICH library allows parallel application components to communicate together across (potentially) widely separated cluster boundaries. This may involve a transition from a specialized HSI message-passing transport within the cluster to wide area TCP/IP transport that can span the network between the participating clusters.

15.2.5   MPICH Summary

We looked at the MPICH software early in this chapter because it is fundamental to the execution of MPI programs. It also serves as a good example of the services required for parallel execution. Similar functionality is required for programs that are built around the PVM libraries. There are quite a few open-source, commercial, and hardware-specialized versions of MPI libraries, and MPICH is only one particular implementation. A generalized diagram of an MPICH environment is shown in Figure 15–2.

The default installation used in our MPICH testing examples, uses the ch_p4 device. This device uses Ethernet and TCP/IP as the underlying transport. (You will see the term *LAM* used frequently in the documentation for MPICH. This is an acronym for "local area multicomputer.") Adjustment in the installation and testing process is required for the specialized versions of MPICH. In all cases, the underlying transport hardware and software layers must be properly installed and configured for the MPICH communications to be successful.

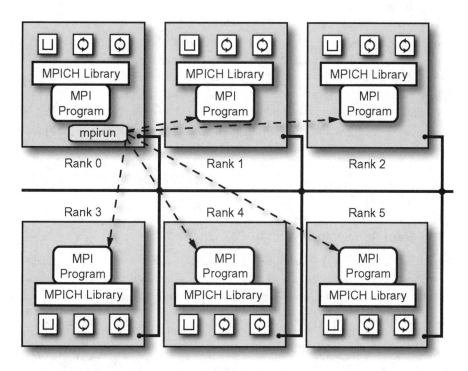

Figure 15–2 The `mpirun` and MPICH library software

The example parallel program that we launched as a test serves to underscore the important point: The MPICH software enables the creation and launching of parallel applications, but it does nothing to ensure that the cluster resources are available to the applications. It is important to realize that unless you have only one user on your cluster, you will need services to manage the allocation of the cluster's parallel resources and keep users from walking on each other as they schedule parallel jobs. The requirement for shared storage "behind" the jobs is another important requirement.

15.3 The Simple Linux Utility for Resource Management

An open-source resource management system called the simple Linux utility for resource management, or SLURM, is available (first quarter of 2004) from `http://www.llnl.gov/linux/slurm/slurm.html`. The SLURM system is under development by the Lawrence Livermore National Laboratory and Linux NetworX. (There apparently are several SLURM projects in the open-source community, including one that is a general-purpose network monitor. SLURM is also the largest brand of carbonated cola in the universe, manufactured on the planet Wormulon. See `http://www.gotfuturama.com/information/encyc-66-slurm`

for details.) SLURM consists of a control daemon `slurmctld`, the `slurmd` client daemon, and a PAM module to control user access to resources.

One method of ensuring that a user has dedicated access to a compute slice is to "lock out" all other users' access, with the exception of the `root` user, while the node is allocated for a user's job. This is the method chosen for the PAM module that is included in the SLURM package. The SLURM system will provide node status and job scheduling when the software is released, augmenting the minimal functionality available from MPI environments like MPICH.

The preliminary documentation indicates that all communications by SLURM are authenticated, and that it is designed to manage resources for large, complex clusters. Because SLURM is a hypothetical solution at the time of this writing, we won't spend any more time covering it. It can, however, serve as an example of the services required to provide resource management beyond that provided by MPICH or MPI-LAM software.

15.4 The Maui Scheduler

The Maui scheduler software is an open-source package, written in Java, that manages and schedules parallel MPI jobs over Myrinet and Ethernet. The Maui scheduler interfaces with a number of available load-balancing and batch-queueing facilities, enabling special functionality that those packages may not be capable of providing by themselves. The software may be found at `http://mauischeduler.sourceforge.net` and is designed to run on POSIX-based operating systems, including FreeBSD and Linux.

The feature set of the Maui scheduler is quite complex and could fill an entire chapter of this book with details of the various configuration options and behaviors. I only have space for a brief overview of this package, but it makes a good example of this class of software. The version we are examining is the Maui scheduler, Molokini Edition. I refer to the software generically as "Maui" as we continue.

15.4.1   Maui Scheduler Software Architecture

The Maui software is divided up into "server," "client," and "drone" packages that are installed on an administrative control node, head or master nodes, and compute slices respectively. Because the software is written in Java for portability, each system will require a Java virtual machine (JVM).

Along with the Maui package itself, there are three software dependencies required for installation on your cluster:

- A Java 1.3 (or later) virtual machine from `http://java.sun.com` or also available from `http://www.blackdown.org`
- Cryptix Java security software from `http://www.cryptix.org`, version 3.2.0 or later
- The MySQL database from `http://www.mysql.org`

Examining the software architecture for Maui will enable us to understand most of the other available batch-queuing, load-balancing, and scheduling facilities that we may encounter. An overview of the software architecture of Maui is shown in Figure 15–3.

Clients submit requests to the scheduler in XML format, encrypted by the Blowfish block cipher algorithm, provided by the Cryptix software package. (See the documentation at http:/ /www.schneier.com/blowfish.html for information on this algorithm.) The commands submitted to the Maui software and the documents received in response are all formatted according to the Maui-specific document type definitions. The communications are encrypted with the Blowfish symmetric key, which both the clients and the server share.

The cluster resources are represented as "nodes" and "slots" for the purpose of scheduling jobs. There are two types of reservations that are available: job reservations for a job that is to be executed, and sys reservations created by a system administrator on behalf of a specific user, group, or account. A job is given exclusive use of the nodes and slots for a specific length of time, at a particular scheduled time, as dictated by an associated reservation.

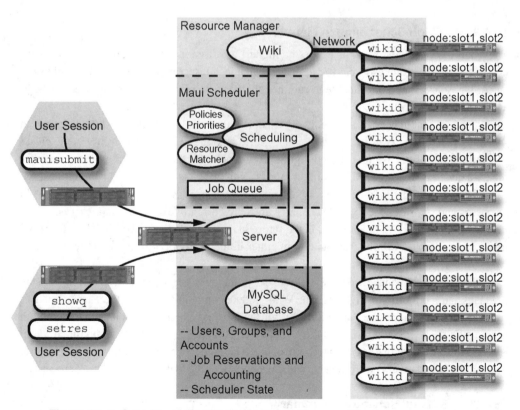

Figure 15–3 Overview of the Maui scheduler software architecture

A node in the Maui scheme of things is a container for resources like CPU, disk, and RAM. A slot represents the ability to perform one unit of computation on a node, using resources like the CPU. There is at least one slot per node, and it does *not* have to correspond to per-CPU resources, although this is a normal situation.

As you might expect, the Maui software allows full control of the job scheduler and its behavior. User jobs may be submitted, canceled, held, released, and may have their status checked. Reservations may be created, canceled, and have their status checked. Users may check the status of the job queue and examine cluster resources managed by the scheduler and their availability. System administrators may start and stop the job scheduler and alter the attributes of jobs, reservations, and the scheduler itself.

Most of the components in Maui have general-purpose interfaces that allow substitutions of functionality. For example, the scheduler and resource manager may be replaced by other modules written to the interface specifications. This is how other software packages are able to use the Maui scheduler, while replacing the job submission, resource management, and other pieces of the Maui distribution.

15.4.2   Job Scheduling in Maui

The Maui job scheduler attempts to run the highest priority job from the queue as soon as it is possible to do so. If the resources for a job are available, a reservation is made and the job is executed. If resources are not available to run the job, then a reservation is made to execute the job at some time in the future.

For jobs that may not be immediately executed, the scheduler will "backfill" them into the schedule, making reservations based on their priority and the resource availability in the cluster. The number of jobs to examine is a configurable parameter for the scheduler. An example schedule for a cluster with 12, two-CPU compute slices (with two slots each) is shown in Figure 15–4.

The scheduling module's job is to run jobs as soon as possible given the available resources and priority as set by the scheduler. Jobs are currently executing, and reservations are in place for jobs that will be executed in the future in the example in Figure 15–4. The process of making reservations for jobs that can be run either immediately or at some future time is called *backfilling*.

The resource manager module, called *Wiki* in the documentation, is responsible for starting tasks and monitoring their status. The Wiki module communicates with the `wikid` daemons running on the client nodes. Authentication for the jobs and communications is handled by the secure start shell (SSS), which uses the UID and GID values of the user that submitted the job (or `root`) to execute the application component. The authentication information is sent to the SSS on the client systems over the encrypted channel between Wiki and the `wikid` process.

15.4.3   Maui Scheduler Summary

The Maui package contains a very powerful batch submission and scheduling package at a very good price (free). The ability to backfill jobs from the queue into cluster resources and its flexi-

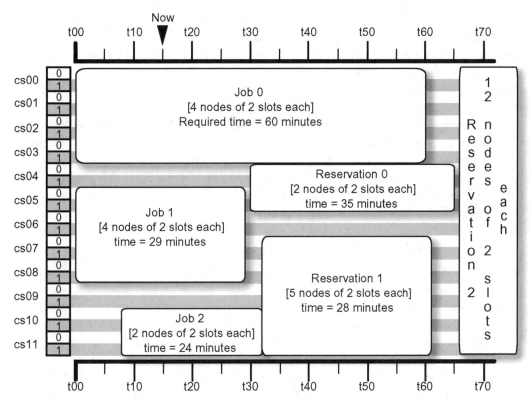

Figure 15–4 Example Maui schedule

ble software APIs makes Maui a widely used software resource, even with other queuing and load-balancing packages. The components and operation of the Maui software make a good prototypical example for our examination of other batch-queueing and scheduling software.

Note that the software we have examined so far, the default MPICH utility `mpirun` and the Maui scheduler, provide similar functionality in terms of the ability to schedule parallel application components on multiple compute slices. The Maui scheduler's ability to queue jobs, control job execution, authenticate user job components, and backfill resources, makes it a more powerful option than the minimal facility provided with most MPI implementations. Configuration of Maui in your cluster environment is left as an exercise.

15.5 The Ganglia Distributed Monitoring and Execution System

Ganglia is an open-source cluster monitoring and execution package that is designed to scale to very large clusters. It also has the ability to summarize monitoring information from physically separated clusters that are part of a computing grid. (For now, I will defer the definition of a "grid" computing environment.) Installation and configuration of the default software is quite simple and it is possible to get useful information within a very short time.

There are three major software components in the monitoring package: two making up the Ganglia monitoring core and the third being the Ganglia Web front end. The monitoring core comprises the Ganglia monitoring daemon, gmond and the Ganglia meta-daemon, gmetad. Together these daemons collect and share the clusterwide parameters displayed by the Ganglia Web-front end. The databases used by the Ganglia monitoring system are based on the "round-robin database" (RRD) and associated rrdtool package, which I discuss later in this section.

You can view Ganglia as making "internal" system parameters available for monitoring across the cluster. The tool kit allows visualization of the current state of the monitoring parameters across a single cluster or a grid, but at the current time does no thresholding or alarming. The Ganglia package is absolutely essential for your cluster if you want to show guests (or the boss) an impressive view of your cluster's current state.

15.5.1   The Ganglia Software Architecture

A set of operating system-dependent parameters is gathered from the /proc file system by gmond, which extracts information from the UNIX or Linux system (soon Windows, too) on which it runs. The gmond on each node collects the local parameters and shares them with other gmond daemons in the cluster, maintaining the state of all cluster parameters and summary information across the cluster. Information is shared between the gmond daemons via a multi-cast channel that "hides" the traffic from unsubscribed nodes. (The availability of a complete set of cluster parameters on each node can simplify the job launching process. Knowing the state of the target nodes for a parallel job eliminates the need to poll the nodes before job launch. This helps the gexec daemon, which is not technically a part of Ganglia, to determine the state of its targets from the local node's database.)

The Ganglia software package also provides the facility to extend the default parameter database by adding custom parameters with the gmetric command-line tool. It is a simple matter to write scripts that collect the desired information and call the gmetric command, which make the parameters available to the gmond instances in the cluster via the shared multi-cast channel.

The Ganglia meta-daemon, gmetad, collects data that is multicast from gmond instances in a cluster being monitored and produces RRD files for individual system parameters, as well as a summary database for the entire set of entities being monitored. A very efficient multicasting channel is used, along with XML and external data representation formats to gather the information from the client systems. The gmetad process may also "federate" clusters, collecting summary information from multiple clusters running gmetad and providing an overview of a grid. This architecture is shown in Figure 15–5.

The Web front end provides a graphical, Web-based display capability that handles the default parameter set, but is also extensible as new metrics are monitored. Graphs of the parameter values and summaries are produced using the rrdtool command's built-in capabilities.

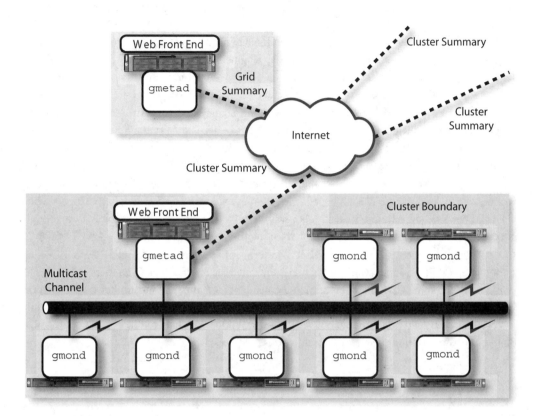

Figure 15–5 Ganglia monitoring system architecture

The Ganglia Web front end is built using a compact but powerful set of hypertext preprocessor (PHP) language scripts and the Apache Web server.

In addition to the Ganglia monitoring components, the developers provide an authentication mechanism for parallel applications and a parallel execution facility for scheduling application components. The authd daemon implements the parallel authentication mechanism and the gexec daemon allows users to schedule parallel application components on compute slices in the cluster. Monitoring of the authd and gexec services may be built into the Ganglia monitoring facility, providing an integrated way to schedule parallel application components and to monitor the progress and usage of the cluster's resources.

15.5.2 Introducing RRD Software: rrdtool

The rrdtool package contains a single tool that allows the creation and manipulation of RRD files. The tool, called rrdtool, provides subcommands such as create, info, and even graph, and is a direct dependency for the other Ganglia packages that use it. The software for this package is available from several sources, primarily from the author's Web site at `http://people.ee.ethz.ch/~oetiker/webtools/rrdtool`. (The author of this package is Tobi Oetiker, who is a senior system manager for the IT support group of the Department of Information Technology and Electrical Engineering at the Swiss Federal Institute of Technology in Zurich, Switzerland.) It may also be located for your version of Linux from `http://rpmfind.net` or from the archive at `http:/freshrpm.net`.

RRDs are a little different from what we are accustomed to with relational databases. When you create an RRD file, it is a fixed size, and it really is a "circular" container for a specific number of "primary data points" that belong to "data sources" in the file. When the file becomes "full," new data will overwrite the existing data, thus the "circular" nature of an RRD.

When you create the database, you tell the `rrdtool` how often the primary data point will be entered into the database by specifying a `step` value. The RRD database expects a primary data point to be entered for each data source in the file every `step` seconds. If a value is not entered for a specific time step, the software interpolates a value.

Time is always expressed to `rrdtool` in terms of seconds since the UNIX epoch (which started at 00:00:00 on January 1, 1971) and is referred to as *universal coordinated time*, or UTC. This seems like somewhat of a pain, until you consider that Linux and most other UNIX systems keep the internal time in this format. A minimum of internal conversion is necessary when time is stored this way, and it is portable between UNIX systems. You can get the current value of the time in this format using the `date` command:

```
$ date '+%s'
1081713876
$
```

For convenience, the `rrdtool` allows you to use time values that are more convenient than the UTC value. For example, you can use `now`, `now-1h`, or absolute times like "12:00:01" for specifying start and end times to the tool. See the `man` page, section "time reference specification," for the `rrdfetch` variation of the command for more information on how to specify times.

The `rrdtool` command has several subcommands available: `create`, `dump`, `restore`, `update`, `fetch`, `tune`, `last`, `info`, `rrdresize`, and `xport`. Instead of one huge `man` page for the whole tool, there are separate `man` pages for the individual subcommands. You can find the `man` page by prefixing `rrd` to the subcommand. For example, `man rrdcreate` will yield the information on how to create your own RRD file.

Let's create an example RRD database to contain the NFS operations collected from an NFS server node in our cluster:

```
rrdtool create nfs_ops.rrd --step 60                          \
    DS:ops:GUAGE:120:0:100000                                 \
    RRA:AVERAGE:0.5:1:60                                       \
    RRA:AVERAGE:0.5:1:1440
```

This example creates an RRD file named `nfs_ops.rrd` in the current directory. The file expects to collect a data point every 60 seconds for this metric. The DS definition names the data set within the file, and the RRA definitions define two archive areas where hourly and daily averages will be stored (60 * 60 seconds = 1 hour and 1440 * 60 seconds = 24 hours).

The type of data set specified in the DS information may be one of GUAGE, COUNTER, DERIVE, or ABSOLUTE. The specification determines how the data is stored, and GUAGE will store the actual value given to `rrdtool`. See the man page for `rrdcreate` for information on the other specification types. The data value will be set to `unknown` if the time interval exceeds 120 seconds, and the minimum value is zero, whereas the maximum value is 100,000.

After creating the file, we can examine its parameters (or that of other RRD files) with the `rrdtool info <RRD-file-name>` command. Output from the `rrdtool info` command for our newly created NFS I/O operations RRD database is

```
# rrdtool info nfs_ops.rrd
filename = "nfs_ops.rrd"
rrd_version = "0001"
step = 60
last_update = 1081719530
ds[ops].type = "GAUGE"
ds[ops].minimal_heartbeat = 120
ds[ops].min = 0.0000000000e+00
ds[ops].max = 1.0000000000e+05
ds[ops].last_ds = "UNKN"
ds[ops].value = 0.0000000000e+00
ds[ops].unknown_sec = 50
rra[0].cf = "AVERAGE"
rra[0].rows = 60
rra[0].pdp_per_row = 1
rra[0].xff = 5.0000000000e-01
rra[0].cdp_prep[0].value = NaN
rra[0].cdp_prep[0].unknown_datapoints = 0
rra[1].cf = "AVERAGE"
rra[1].rows = 1440
rra[1].pdp_per_row = 1
rra[1].xff = 5.0000000000e-01
rra[1].cdp_prep[0].value = NaN
rra[1].cdp_prep[0].unknown_datapoints = 0
```

Now we need to feed data into the RRD file from our chosen source at the proper intervals. The NFS information for server RPC operations is kept in `/proc/sys/rpc/nfsd`, and is the same information displayed by the `nfsstat` command. The second field in the line that starts with `rpc` is the information we want:

```
# cat /proc/net/rpc/nfsd
rc 0 1150 18583
fh 0 19773 0 22 14
```

```
io 20688842 540264
th 8 0 16.839 0.074 0.031 0.000 0.039 0.044 0.000 0.000        \
        0.000 0.000
ra 16 2559 44 6 11 10 12 20 10 15 5 50
net 19733 19733 0 0
rpc 19733 0 0 0 0
proc2 18 1 0 0 0 0 0 0 0 0 0 0 0 0 0 0 0 0 0 0
proc3 22 1 7813 75 6215 1254 0 2742 662 153 3 0 0 185 3        \
        26 43 64 112 37 24 0 320
```

We can write a small test script to update the information in the RRD file we created. Later we can add the script to the `cron` definitions to run at set intervals. This is actually less than desirable, since there is a lot of overhead involved with scheduling the script from `cron`. We need to look at alternate possibilities for collecting the information and updating the RRD databases.

The default behavior for the `rrdtool update` subcommand is to use the current UTC time for the update. We can collect the information from the `/proc` file and add the value to the RRD file without the extra overhead of getting the current time from the system. The simple test script might resemble

```sh
#!/bin/sh

NFS_SOURCE="/proc/net/rpc/nfsd"
   NFS_TAG="rpc"
  RRD_FILE="/tmp/nfs_ops.rrd"
  INTERVAL=60

while true
do
        NFSOPS=$( grep ${NFS_TAG} ${NFS_SOURCE} |              \
            awk '{ print $2 }' )
        rrdtool update ${RRD_FILE} N:${NFSOPS}
        sleep ${INTERVAL}
done
```

The last thing with which to experiment is extracting the data from the RRD file. This can be a relatively complex operation, depending on the type of data you are collecting and its attributes. You can get the raw data from the file with a command similar to this:

```
# rrdtool fetch nfs_ops.rrd AVERAGE --start -720 --end now
1081723080: 2.0000000000e+00
1081723140: 2.0000000000e+00
1081723200: 1.7300000000e+01
1081723260: 5.2809500000e+03
1081723320: 9.8327166667e+03
1081723380: 1.7634500000e+04
1081723440: 2.5198000000e+04
```

```
1081723500: 2.5198000000e+04
1081723560: 2.5198000000e+04
1081723620: 2.5198000000e+04
1081723680: 2.5198000000e+04
1081723740: 2.5198383333e+04
```

As an alternative to the raw data, you can try graphing the information with `rrdtool graph`. Generating either graphics interchange format or portable network graphics format graphs is a relatively complex operation. This introduction to RRD will allow us to understand how Ganglia uses the tool, and from this point we will let Ganglia do the work of manipulating RRD files for us.

15.5.3 Downloading and Installing Ganglia Software

Software for the Ganglia tool is available from `http://ganglia.sourceforge.net`. In addition to the Ganglia packages, you will need to download and install the `rrdtool` package on the system that will run the `gmetad` process and the Ganglia Web front-end package. In addition to the author's Web site, `rrdtool` is available from the usual suspects: `http://rpmfind.net` and `http://freshrpms.net`.

If your version of Linux supports RPM packages, these are available on the Ganglia project Web site for download. If you will be installing the `authd` and `gexec` packages along with Ganglia, you can download them at the same time. The installation is simple, quick, and trouble free.

15.5.4 Ganglia's `gmond` and `gmetad` Daemons

The database information collected by the `gmetad` process for Ganglia is kept in RRD files in `/var/lib/ganglia/rrds`. Underneath this directory are separate directories for each system in the case of a cluster monitoring configuration, or for individual clusters in a grid environment. The `gmetad` process exists to allow collecting the clusterwide multicast data and also to share the summary information across federated collections of clusters (also known as a *grid*).

On each compute slice or other system to be monitored by the `gmond`, install the software, configure the `/etc/gmond.conf` file, and then start the daemon:

```
# rpm -ivh ganglia-monitor-core-gmond-2.5.6-1.i386.rpm
# chkconfig --add gmond
# chkconfig gmond on
# vi /etc/gmond.conf
      #
      # The name of the cluster this node is a part of
      # default: "unspecified"
      # name   "My Cluster"
      name   "Local Cluster"
# service gmond start
```

Once you have chosen the location for your gmetad and the Web front end, you need to install the Ganglia components:

```
# rpm -ivh ganglia-monitor-core-gmetad-2.5.6-1.i386.rpm
# rpm -ivh ganglia-webfrontend-2.5.5-1.noarch.rpm
# chkconfig --add gmetad
# chkconfig gmetad on
```

Once the components are installed, you need to configure the minimal amount of information in the /etc/gmetad.conf file before you start the daemon:

```
# vi /etc/gmetad.conf

    # data_source "my cluster" 10 localhost                \
            my.machine.edu:8649  1.2.3.5:8655
    # data_source "my grid" 50 1.3.4.7:8655 grid.org:8651 \
            grid-backup.org:8651
    # data_source "another source" 1.3.4.7:8655  1.3.4.8

    data_source "Local Cluster" 10 localhost

# service gmetad start
```

The Apache Web daemon, httpd will be needed by the Web front end. If you are in a safe environment, all you need do is start the daemon:

```
# chkconfig httpd on
# service httpd start
```

If your system will be exposed to the Internet, or if there are other security concerns, carefully consider the configuration you use for the Web-server software. I do not address the security issues with starting httpd here. At this point, you should be able to start your Web browser and point it to the Web server:

```
$ mozilla http://localhost/ganglia
```

You should be rewarded with the Ganglia main page for your cluster, as shown in Figure 15–6. The PHP scripts that produce the web output are remarkably compact and are located in /var/lib/www/html/ganglia. The PHP language resembles the shell scripting languages with which we are all familiar, so it is not hard to read the graph.php file that contains the commands to produce the graphs on the Ganglia Web pages.

Clicking on one of the systems on the main page will reward you with individual parameter information for that system. In the same way, you can "drill down" from a site that monitors a grid until you are viewing specific cluster or system information. This is all done in a hierarchical manner, keeping the cluster and system-specific information within the minimum sphere of influence, much like DNS domains. An example of node-specific details is shown in Figure 15–7.

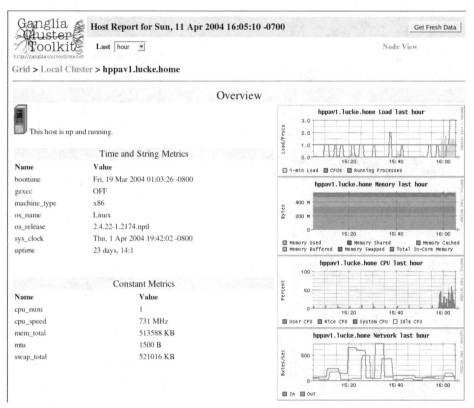

Figure 15–6 Ganglia Web front-end main page

15.5.5   Adding Your Own Ganglia Metrics

The basic method for adding a Ganglia metric is to collect the required information and use the `gmetric` command to make it known to the local `gmond` processes. The `gmetric` command uses the multicast channel to make the particular data in which you are interested available to all the `gmond` processes. This will automatically make the parameter information available on the system that is running the `gmetad` process that is performing the global collection for the cluster.

As if by magic, the parameter that you send via `gmetric` will show up in its own RRD on the system running the `gmetad` daemon, associated with the system that sent it. The Web front end will also display the metric on the page for the associated systems. Ganglia has eliminated the need for us to create and manage our own RRD databases and reports, especially if we

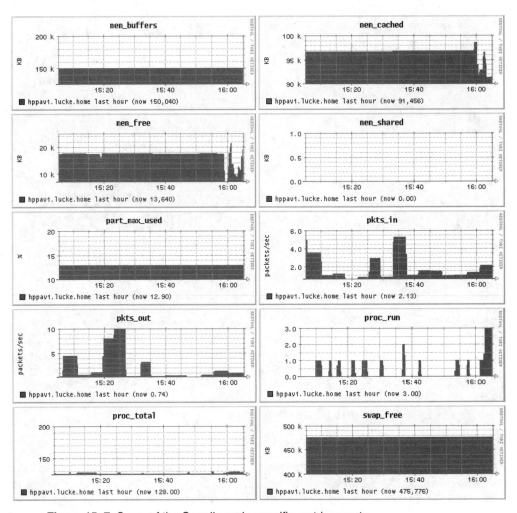

Figure 15–7 Some of the Ganglia node-specific metric reports

want to monitor some custom parameters. Our monitoring script for NFS I/O operations becomes

```
#!/bin/sh
NFSOPS_TAG="rpc"
  NFSFILE="/proc/net/rpc/nfsd"
   NFSOPS=$(grep ${NFSOPS_TAG} ${NFSFILE}|awk '{print $2 }' )
/usr/bin/gmetric --name=nfsops --value=${NFSOPS}              \
        --type=uint32 --units=IOPS --slope=both --tmax=60
```

This makes a good first approximation for the data-gathering script. The first thing we need to notice is that the values in the `/proc/net/rpc/nfsd` file will "stick" at the last value recorded. Another item to notice is that `cron` has a minimum resolution of one minute.

A little adjusting is needed to make the script handle this situation. We can make the script repeat its execution twice or more before exiting, to increase the number of samples. Additionally, we can check to see whether the value that is being reported is the same as the last value and return zero if no change is detected (the ability to zero the NFS counters is not yet implemented).

The example script can be started from `cron` every midnight, and will check to see whether it has crossed a day boundary. If it is the next day, it will terminate to "get out of the way" of the new script that `cron` will launch. The script becomes:

```
#!/bin/sh

NFS_SOURCE="/proc/net/rpc/nfsd"
  NFS_TAG="rpc"
  GMETRIC="/usr/bin/gmetric"
 INTERVAL=30                     # Seconds to sleep
     SDOY=$( date '+%j' )        # Save Julian date we started
  LASTVAL=$( grep ${NFS_TAG} ${NFS_SOURCE} | \
              awk '{ print $2 }' )

while true
do

    NFSOPS=$( grep ${NFS_TAG} ${NFS_SOURCE} | \
              awk '{ print $2 }' )
    [[ ${NFSOPS} -eq ${LASTVAL} ]]    && NFSOPS=0
    ${GMETRIC} --name=nfsops --value=${NFSOPS} \
        --type=uint32 --slope=both --tmax=60
    [[ ${NFSOPS} -gt 0 ]]             && LASTVAL=${NFSOPS}
    sleep ${INTERVAL}
    [[ ${SDOY} -ne $( date '+%j') ]] && break

done

exit 0
```

Running the script and generating a little NFS loading on my NFS server populated the RRD file with data. The resulting graph from the Ganglia Web front end is shown in Figure 15–8.

This simple example shows how to add metrics to the default list that is supported natively by the Linux `gmond`. There is a repository of scripts that add metrics to the Ganglia database at `http://ganglia.sourceforge.net/gmetric`. It is a good idea to check the repository for existing scripts before reinventing the wheel (like I did with the example NFS script).

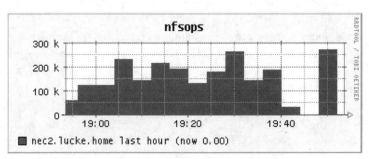

Figure 15–8 Example graph from custom Ganglia metric

15.5.6   Parallel Authentication with `authd` and `gexec`

Both `authd` and `gexec` work together to allow users to execute parallel commands or jobs on cluster nodes. The `authd` package allows verification of user credentials with an RSA public key signature. In a cluster environment, `authd` is typically installed on every node that wishes to authenticate users, and it uses a single, clusterwide public and private RSA key set. Applications or services such as `gexec` may obtain credentials and authenticate the user clusterwide, without the need for each user to obtain and manage their own set of keys.

The `authd` package may be obtained from the Ganglia Web site, or from the author's (Brent N. Chun at the California Institute of Technology's Center for Advanced Computing Research) Web site at `http://www.theether.org/authd`. A prerequisite for `authd` is the `openssl` package, which is used extensively by Web servers, browsers, and Web applications for encrypted socket communication. Installing the `authd` package consists of generating the key set, copying it to all nodes, installing `authd`, and starting the daemon. The steps are as follows:

```
# cd /etc
# openssl genrsa -out auth_priv.pem
Generating RSA private key, 512 bit long modulus
..+++++++++++++
..+++++++++++++
e is 65537 (0x10001)
# chmod 600 auth_priv.pem
# openssl rsa -in auth_priv.pem -pubout -out auth_pub.pem
writing RSA key
# ls *.pem
auth_priv.pem  auth_pub.pem
# scp *.pem root@cs01:/etc
# rpm -ivh authd-0.2.1-1.i386.rpm
Preparing...
########################################### [100%]
   1:authd
########################################### [100%]
```

```
Shutting down authd: [FAILED]
Starting authd: [  OK  ]
```

Once `authd` is installed and operational, you may install the `gexec` RPM package. Installing the `gexec` package will load the `gexec` client, the `gexecd` daemon, and will install the `/etc/xinetd.d/gexec` file. The `gexec` package may be obtained from either `http://ganglia.sourceforge.net` or the author's web site located at `http://www.theether.org/gexec`.

Before installing and configuring `gexec`, a configuration line for the service must be added to the `/etc/services` file. The line must read

```
gexec        2875/tcp               # Caltech gexec service
```

Because the package is contained in a single RPM file, the command to install `gexec` is simply

```
# rpm -ivh gexec-0.3.4-1.i386.rpm
```

The service is started from `xinetd`, so there are no permanently running daemons.

15.5.7   Starting Parallel Programs with `gexec`

The `gexec` client, when running independently of Ganglia, will take a list of target hosts on which to run a parallel command from the environment variable `GEXEC_SVRS`. To execute the `hostname` command on several nodes, use the commands

```
# export GEXEC_SVRS="cs01 cs02 cs03 cs04"
# gexec -n 4 hostname -f
0 cs01.cluster.local
2 cs03.cluster.local
3 cs04.cluster.local
1 cs02.cluster.local
```

Theoretically, `gexec` can use Ganglia information to locate least-used compute resources in the cluster on which to run jobs. Alas, I could not get the integration between Ganglia and `gexec` to work in my environment. By specifying several systems running `gmond`, the `gexec` command should be able to query the daemons and create a list of least-loaded nodes on which to execute the specified number of commands. The commands should resemble

```
# export GEXEC_GMOND_SVRS="cs01 cs02 cs03"
# gexec -n 4 hostname -f
```

We should be able to see the available hosts by using the `gstat` command-line tool to list all the live nodes in the cluster:

```
# gstat --all
CLUSTER INFORMATION
       Name: Local Cluster
```

```
        Hosts: 4
  Gexec Hosts: 0
   Dead Hosts: 0
    Localtime: Sun Apr 11 23:26:07 2004

CLUSTER HOSTS
Hostname                        LOAD                      CPU
  CPUs (Procs/Total) [   1,     5, 15min] [  User,   Nice,
System, Idle]Gexec

cs01.cluster.local
    1 (    0/ 107) [  0.00,  0.00,  0.04] [   1.7,   0.0,
0.4,  96.7] OFF
cs02.cluster.local
    1 (    0/ 107) [  0.02,  0.23,  0.72] [   4.8,   0.0,
0.8,  94.6] OFF
cs03.cluster.local
    1 (    0/ 123) [  0.34,  0.08,  0.02] [   8.7,   0.1,
0.7,  90.6] OFF
cs04.cluster.local
    1 (    0/ 125) [  0.37,  0.18,  0.24] [   2.5,   0.3,
1.4,  95.9] OFF
```

You can see that the gexec function is listed as disabled on all the nodes. The metric is being collected by the gmond daemons, but as of this writing, I cannot figure out how to enable the link between the gmond and the gexec client. I am not sure how the software was compiled for the standard distribution, but the functionality may be disabled in this version.

15.5.8   Ganglia Summary

The Ganglia monitoring package is a flexible, scalable way to monitor "internal" parameters in your cluster's systems. If the standard set of metrics does not fit your needs, extend the set with the gmetric tool. The parameter collection, coupled with the Web front-end reporting gives us a good way to visualize the activities in your cluster, and to share that view with managers and other nontechnical personnel. Ganglia is an essential addition to your cluster's middleware.

15.6 Monitoring with Nagios

There are several general purpose "external" monitoring packages available for general system environments. Two that come to mind are mon and nagios commands. Both packages, and their relatives, are general-purpose scheduling frameworks that can run a test at a specified time and generate "events" when the test returns a failure. The more general-purpose the framework, the greater the amount of work that seems to be associated with setting it up.

Because Nagios is Web based and is more of a ready-to-use solution than mon, it is the tool that I have chosen to introduce here. This is not to say that another choice, like mon, might not be better for your cluster environment, it's just that I do not have space to spend on in-depth configurations and installations of the type required by mon. There are at least 14 system monitoring tools available at http://sourceforge.net—all in various states of completion.

15.6.1   Explaining Nagios

Nagios can monitor environmental conditions, services, and host parameters, generating logs and notifications in response to failures or out-of-bounds conditions. The checks are implemented as plug-in modules to make Nagios extensible. Current status information, reports, and log files are accessible via a Web-based front end, making Nagios easier to use than text-based tools.

The Nagios main Web window is shown in Figure 15–9. There is a considerable amount of installation necessary to get to the point that this window can be displayed, but the documentation is fairly good.

15.6.2   Downloading and Installing Nagios

The software for Nagios may be downloaded from either http://nagios.org or from http://nagios.sourceforge.net. Nagios comes as a compressed tar ball (for example, nagios-1.2.tar.gz) and as a tar ball containing the plug-ins (nagios-plugins-1.3.2.tar.gz). There are also RPM packages for the software, but I had trouble downloading these for some reason.

Along with the two major packages, there are also "extras" available, which consist of icons, plug-ins, and add-on tools. There is a substantial list available for download underneath the main site at http://www.nagios.org/download/extras.php. Let's concentrate only on the main package because a stable installation of this is required for the add-ons to function. Fairly specific instructions for configuration of Nagios are on the Web site located at http://nagios.sourceforge.net/docs/1_0/installing.html.

There are also a number of package dependencies that must be satisfied before we can install Nagios. First, httpd must be installed on the target system, and I used the same system on which Ganglia was installed with no problems or adverse interactions. In addition to the Web server, the nagios package requires the zlib, png-devel, jpeg-devel, and gd packages to be installed first.

I found the png-devel, zlib, and jpeg-devel packages either as part of the RPMs included with my Linux distribution or from http:/rpmfind.net and the alternate opensource RPM site: http://freshrpm.net. The gd package was available as a tar ball from the author's site (http://www.boutell.com/gd). Let's start by installing the gd package from the tar ball, followed by the RPM files:

```
# tar xvzf gd-2.0.22.tar.gz
# cd gd-2.0.22
# ./configure
# make
```

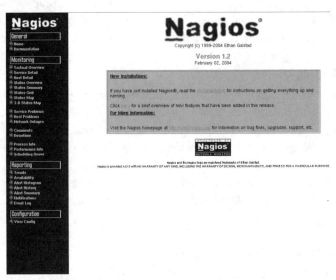

Figure 15–9 Nagios main Web window

```
# make install
```

When adding shared libraries to a Linux system, you must let the shared library loader know where they are. This configuration step is usually handled as part of the RPM packages that contain the libraries, but in this case we need to add the information about the location of the gd libraries (/usr/local/lib) to the system configuration file, /etc/ld.so.conf, and to run the ldconfig utility to update the systemwide information. Once these operations are complete, applications using the libraries, like Nagios, will be able to load them.

Once the gd software is installed, along with the other dependencies, it is possible to install the nagios package. You need to add a nagios user and group to the system before proceeding. This UID and GID will be used for file protection. Let's use the tar ball to install the main software, because when I did it the RPM package kept getting corrupted during download.

```
# tar xvzf nagios-1.2.tar.gz
# cd nagios-1.2
# ./configure --with-gd-lib --with-gd-inc
# make
# make install
# make install-init
# make install-commandmode
# make install-config
```

Once we have all the software installation for the main package out of the way (installed in /usr/local/nagios), we can begin installing Nagios plug-ins downloaded from http://

`nagiosplug.sourceforge.net`. The easiest way to do this is to install the RPM package containing the plug-in software. The plug-ins will be installed under the `/usr/local/nagios/libexec` directory by default, and most of the files will be named `check_<item>`, where `<item>` is a service or entity that is monitored by the plug-in.

15.6.3   Configuring the Web Server for Nagios

Because Nagios uses a Web interface, it is only natural that it must be configured into the Web server on the system on which it executes. This is not an involved process, fortunately, unless you have special requirements for the Web server on the Nagios home system in addition to running Nagios.

Specific information on configuring the Web server is available at `http://nagios.sourceforge.net/docs/1_0/installweb.html`. Let's use the generic instructions, which add a stanza for the common gateway interface (CGI) script directory to the `/etc/httpd/conf/httpd.conf` file:

```
#
# "/var/www/cgi-bin" should be changed to whatever your
# ScriptAliased CGI directory exists, if you have that
# configured.
#
<Directory "/var/www/cgi-bin">
    AllowOverride None
    Options None
    Order allow,deny
    Allow from all
</Directory>

# Add Nagios stuff -RwL-

ScriptAlias /nagios/cgi-bin/ "/usr/local/nagios/sbin/"
<Directory "/usr/local/nagios/sbin/">
        AllowOverride AuthConfig
        Options ExecCGI
        Order allow,deny
        Allow from all
</Directory>
Alias /nagios/ "/usr/local/nagios/share/"
<Directory "/usr/local/nagios/share/">
        Options none
        AllowOverride AuthConfig
        Order allow,deny
        Allow from all
</Directory>
```

Oh, by the way, I think there is a typo in some of the directions on the Web page. I had to modify the entries to appear like those just presented to get the software to work properly. One last configuration step remains: setting up the access control for the Web site.   Instructions for this are located at `http://nagios.sourceforge.net/docs/1_0/cgiauth.html`. Let's use the very basic steps, as outlined.

First, we need to create the file `.htaccess` in the `/usr/local/nagios/sbin` and the `/usr/local/nagios/share` directories with the following contents:

```
AuthName "Nagios Access"
AuthType Basic
AuthUserFile /usr/local/nagios/etc/htpasswd.users
require valid-user
```

Although the permission information for these files is left out of the instructions, experimentation (and subsequent failure) shows that the file should be owned by `nagios:nagios` and have a 644 mode. The last step is to create passwords for the users that will be authenticating to the `nagios` package (including the `nagiosadmin` user):

```
# htpasswd -c /usr/local/nagios/etc/htpasswd.users nagiosadmin
# htpasswd /usr/local/nagios/etc/htpasswd.users rob
```

These commands will create the required entries in the password file. Note that the `-c` option creates the file. Don't make the mistake of using it on more than the first command instance.

15.6.4   Configuring and Using Nagios

Although you may have the installation and Web configuration portion of Nagios completed, you will not be able to start the software until you configure the files in `/usr/local/nagios/etc`. The installation process will create sample configuration files, all named `<file>.cfg-sample`, but these serve only as examples. You will need to produce files that match your cluster's environment.

Take my advice and create a `/usr/local/nagios/etc/Samples` directory and copy all the sample files to it *before* you start modifying anything. I actually moved the sample files to the subdirectory and copied and edited them one by one. Information on the configuration process is located at `http://nagios.sourceforge.net/docs/1_0/config.html`, and it is quite involved.

There are somewhere around six or seven configuration files that need to be populated with interrelated information before we can start the Nagios software. At start-up, Nagios will check the validity of the configuration information and steadfastly refuse to start until it is "happy" with your configuration. My advice is to prune things back to a minimal level and build from there.

The files contain template information for the example configuration clauses, so it is fairly easy to create a basic configuration. You will need to identify information like services to check, people to have access, groupings of system types, contact methods, and escalation information.

This information is used to define the checks that are made, define the proper operating conditions, and identify the people to be notified in case of issues.

The files that must be configured contain a lot of cross-references, so allow plenty of time to configure Nagios. Several features, like issuing sounds and displaying fancy icons, can be added later, once the configuration is stable. The files and some of the relationships will resemble those shown in Figure 15–10.

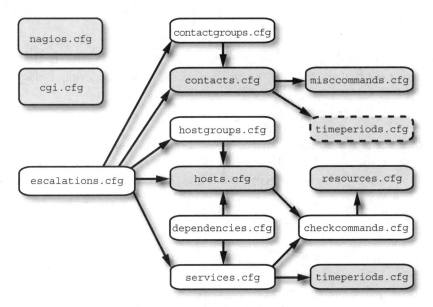

Figure 15–10 Nagios configuration file relationships

The relationships between the data in the configuration files are what makes the configuration difficult. It is an all-or-nothing configuration operation before you can actually start the Nagios service. I tend to start at the "bottom" of the dependency list (shaded boxes in Figure 15–10), for example, with the hosts.cfg file. An entry in that file resembles

```
# 'cs01' host definition
define host{
        use generic-host         ; Name of host template to use
        host_name                cs01
        alias                    Compute Slice #1
        address                  192.168.0.101
        check_command            check-host-alive
        max_check_attempts       10
        notification_interval    120
        notification_period      24x7
        notification_options     d,u,r
```

```
        }
```

Notice that the host entry references the information in the `checkcommands.cfg` file.
That particular entry is

```
# 'check-host-alive' command definition
define command{
        command_name    check-host-alive
        command_line    $USER1$/check_ping -H $HOSTADDRESS$ \
            -w 3000.0,80% -c 5000.0,100% -p 1
        }
```

The definition of `$USER1` is set in the `resource.cfg` file, which enables the definition of
macros used in other configuration files. An example definition from the default file is

```
# Sets $USER1$ to be the path to the plugins
$USER1$=/usr/local/nagios/libexec
```

The `hostgroup.cfg` file aggregates individual hosts into functional groups for reporting and notification purposes. Examples of the types of groups that you might have in your cluster are file servers, administrative nodes, compute slices, head nodes, and so forth. An example
host group definition is

```
# 'file-servers' host group definition
define hostgroup{
        hostgroup_name  file-servers
        alias           File Servers
        contact_groups  fileserver-admins
        members         fs01,fs02
        }
```

This entry contains a pointer to the contact group `fileserver-admins`, which is
defined in the `contactgroups.cfg` file. This configuration file aggregates user definitions
from the `contacts.cfg` file into logical groups. An example contact group definition is

```
# 'fileserver-admins' contact group definition
define contactgroup{
        contactgroup_name       fileserver-admins
        alias                   File Sever Administrators
        members                 nagios
        }
```

We have followed the chain of definition dependencies almost all the way down to the
base information. The next level of information is contained in the `contacts.cfg` file. This
file contains definitions with information about the individual users that make up the contact
groups. An example entry is

```
# 'nagios' contact definition
```

```
define contact{
        contact_name                       nagios
        alias                              Nagios Admin
        service_notification_period        24x7
        host_notification_period           24x7
        service_notification_options       w,u,c,r
        host_notification_options          d,u,r
        service_notification_commands      notify-by-email
        host_notification_commands         host-notify-by-email
        email root@localhost.localdomain
        }
```

The host and service notification definitions are in the `misccommands.cfg` configuration file. They define the system commands used to effect the notification. The command definition executes a system mail command, filling in a message template. A definition for this is

```
# 'notify-by-email' command definition
define command{
        command_name     notify-by-email
        command_line     /usr/bin/printf "%b" "***** Nagios   \
        *****\n\nNotification Type:                            \
        $NOTIFICATIONTYPE$\n\nService:                         \
        $SERVICEDESC$\nHost:                                   \
        $HOSTALIAS$\nAddress: $HOSTADDRESS$\nState:            \
        $SERVICESTATE$\n\nDate/Time:                           \
        $DATETIME$\n\nAdditional Info:\n\n$OUTPUT$" |          \
        /bin/mail -s "** $NOTIFICATIONTYPE$ alert -            \
        $HOSTALIAS$/$SERVICEDESC$ is $SERVICESTATE$ **"        \
        $CONTACTEMAIL$
        }
```

There are a number of other services defined, such as the `notify-by-pager` service. For specialized notification operations, you may create your own services in this file or modify the existing ones.

You may have noticed a number of specialized time periods being used in the example definitions. These are specified in the `timeperiods.cfg` file. An example definition for the `24x7` time period is

```
# '24x7' timeperiod definition
define timeperiod{
        timeperiod_name 24x7
        alias           24 Hours A Day, 7 Days A Week
        sunday          00:00-24:00
        monday          00:00-24:00
        tuesday         00:00-24:00
        wednesday       00:00-24:00
        thursday        00:00-24:00
```

```
friday              00:00-24:00
saturday            00:00-24:00
}
```

Once all the configuration files are created and filled in, you can attempt to start the `nagios` service:

```
# chkconfig nagios on
# service nagios start
```

Be prepared to work on the configuration files iteratively to get your base-level configuration to start up. It took about eight tries for me to get my initial configuration to pass the syntax and dependency checking that Nagios performs on start-up.

When the `nagios` service finally starts correctly, you may point your browser to `http://localhost/nagios/index.html` to see the initial screen in Figure 15–9. You will notice that the service checks will show "pending" as the status at first. This indicates that the scheduler has not yet run the checks associated with them. We can examine the status of the systems being monitored (this example uses my home network) with the Nagios tactical monitoring overview page shown in Figure 15–11.

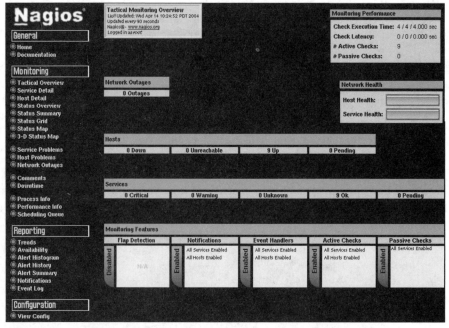

Figure 15–11 Nagios tactical monitoring overview page

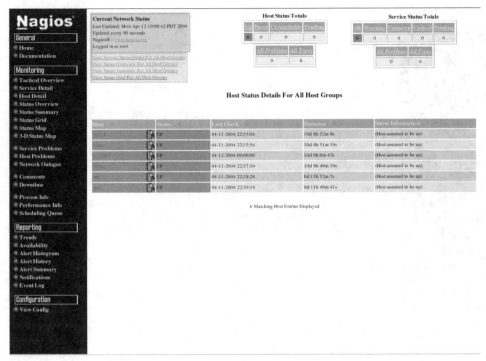

Figure 15–12 Nagios host detail information page

The tactical monitoring overview page gives us a high-level picture of the events, services, hosts, and other Nagios monitoring points that are available. For specific information about the status of the individual hosts being monitored by Nagios, we can select the host detail page, which is shown in Figure 15–12.

Another way of looking at this information is the host status map, which shows a 2D map of the hosts on a common Nagios server. The map has several formats, but Figure 15–13 shows a the default map of the hosts being monitored. The options at the upper right of the page allow selecting host groups and other information to include in the map.

Nagios allows associating icons with specific hosts to differentiate them visually from other host types. This information is not configured by default, and is part of the hostextinfo definitions that are in the cgi.cfg file. There are numerous icons available to describe different system types. A description from the configuration file

```
# EXTENDED SERVICE INFORMATION
# This is all entirely optional.  If you don't enter any
# extended information, nothing bad will happen - I promise...
# Its basically just used to have pretty icons and such
# associated with your services.You can also specify an URL
# that links to a document containing more information about
```

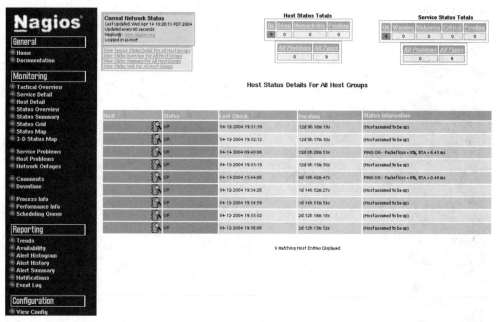

Figure 15–13 Nagios host status map page

```
# the service (location details, contact information,# etc).
# serviceextinfo[<host_name>;<svc_description>]=<notes_url>;\
        <icon_image>;<image_alt>
```

allows you to specify URL information for the host and notes, along with the icon images.

The icon files themselves are located by default in the `/usr/local/nagios/share/images/logos` directory. There are currently about eight contributed logo packages available in the "extras" section of the Nagios Web site for download. The URL for these downloads is `http://www.nagios.org/download/extras.php`. If you get tired of seeing the "?" icon on the page, you should download these packages and configure the information in `cgi.cfg`. An example of this page is shown in Figure 15–14.

As an example of the graphical information available in Nagios, let's examine the services status detail page, which is shown in Figure 15–15. This page allows us to examine all the services defined for the various hosts in the network, along with the current status of that service. This gives a good overview of services that might need attention. Services that are not available are highlighted in red, and services that are functioning normally are shown in green (this is hard to show in a grayscale book.)

Nagios also can generate uptime, trending, and a number of other useful reports. Obviously, the accuracy of these reports depends on how well (and correctly) you configure the service checks for your environment. It may take some time to track down reporting or event

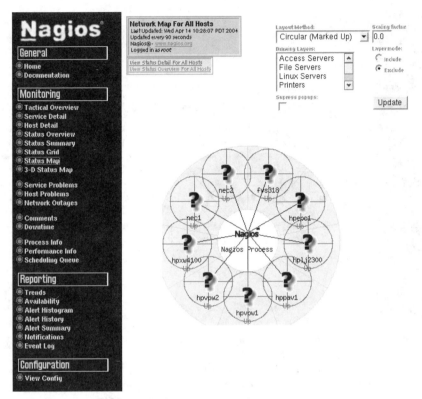

Figure 15–14 Nagios circular host status map

generation problems and correct them. Plan on a period of debugging and adjustment after you first install Nagios.

As a final example, consider the host state trends report shown in Figure 15–16. This report shows the availability (or unavailability) of the associated host over the time period specified for the report. In this case, I generated the report for a system that was available 100% of the time during the last week—just the type of report you want to show your boss.

15.6.5   Nagios Summary

Nagios is very good at external monitoring of hosts and services. Its ability to depict failures graphically, generate reports, and notify system administrators in case of events is very useful, particularly if you have service-level agreements or contractual uptime requirements to fulfill. Once properly configured, the Web front end provides a good method to access the current status of your cluster, even from home.

If there is one downside to Nagios, it is the amount of initial configuration work that is necessary to get the software running. You should carefully plan the implementation of Nagios

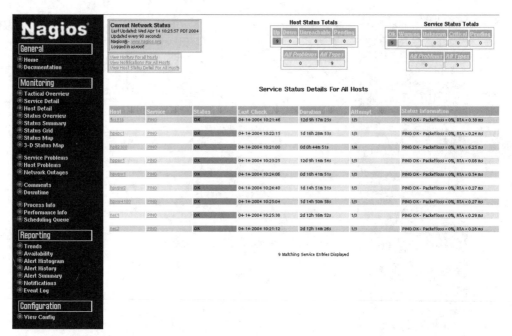

Figure 15–15 Nagios service status page

with this in mind, starting with simple services (like `ping`) and adding capabilities when you are sure that the installation is stable. Nagios is essential for generating and monitoring events in your cluster.

15.7 Cluster Middleware Summary

This chapter touched the surface of the available middleware packages for your cluster. There are hundreds or thousands of choices available, many of which are open source and are therefore free. As we have seen, being free of charge does not necessarily mean "you get what you pay for." The Maui scheduler, Nagios, and Ganglia are all world-class applications that you should consider for your cluster.

Part of what might be called *middleware* is the software responsible for monitoring and profiling parallel applications that use MPI. As you might imagine, profiling the behavior of a parallel, distributed application can be difficult without the proper tools. There are several tools that are worth mentioning.

First is the TotalView parallel debugger. It is a commercial debugger that handles multiple languages (C, C++, FORTRAN, and so on), multiple compilers, and multiple parallel programming paradigms such as threads, MPI, and OpenMP. Information on this debugger is available from the manufacturer at `http://www.etnus.com/products/totalview`. The only thing more difficult than *writing* a parallel application is *debugging* a parallel application.

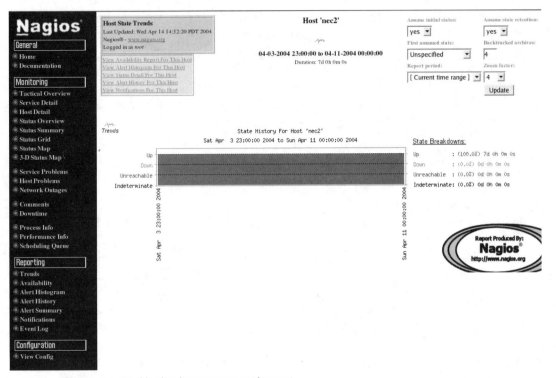

Figure 15–16 Nagios host state trend report

As of this writing, it appears that the Pallis HPC Products, Vampir, Vampirtrace, and others, have been acquired by the Intel Software and Solutions Group. The two products Vampir and Vampirtrace allow the tracing and analysis of parallel applications based on MPI, MPI/ MPICH, LAM-MPI, and other messaging facilities. A graphical analysis of the software's call behavior allows performance tuning the application. (A real-world, multicolored Vampir graphical analysis of a complex parallel application is a sight to behold.) See the Pallas Web site (for how long is unclear) at `http://www.pallas.com/e/products` for information.

The general availability for Linux middleware is excellent, particularly in the open-source arena. This is because the open-source development process is based on the same standing-on-the-shoulders-of-giants approach that is used in the scientific community: Results are openly published, shared, and made available for inclusion into new projects. This approach builds the knowledge (or software) pool that is available for use by the community.

15.8 An Afterword on Linux High-Availability and Open-Source

Because of space constraints, I have not covered many of the open-source, high-availability packages that might be needed for your cluster. Protecting services like the cluster master nodes,

NFS servers, Kerberos, DNS, and others may require active–standby or active–active system configurations—along with the software to monitor and fail over between the instances of the service. There is a whole boatload of open-source software to do this for Linux systems, most of which is pointed to or available from the `http://linux-ha.org` Web site.

Commercial packages such as Oracle 9i RAC have built-in, high-availability monitors distributed as part of the vendor's software package. Other commercially available high-availability packages include Hewlett-Packard's ServiceGuard package, which has been ported to Linux. If you want to investigate the high-availability packages, the following Web sites are useful.

- The Fake package for IP address fail over, at `http://www.vergenet.net/linux/fake`. There are a number of very useful tools available at `http://www/vergenet.net` that are applicable to high-availability or load-balanced environments.
- A full-featured highly available, load-balanced server project, which is featured at `http://www.ultramonkey.org`.
- The LVS project, which allows scalable, highly available configurations for Web servers, FTP servers, and other TCP/IP services, which is available at `http://www.linuxvirtualserver.org`.
- Web sites `http://sourceforge.net` or `http://freshmeat.org` for projects that pertain to high availability.

If you do a little research, you are almost guaranteed to find a package suitable for your particular need.

## CHAPTER 16

Put Tab A in Slot C: OSCAR, Rocks, OpenMOSIX, and the Globus Toolkit

Chapter Objectives

- Introduce a cluster installation tool called OSCAR
- Use the OSCAR installation process as a prototype for general cluster installation
- Introduce the Rocks cluster installation tool
- Briefly discuss the OpenMOSIX Project
- Examine the Globus Toolkit for grid-enabled applications

The previous chapters in this section of the book have introduced a number of the standard infrastructure subsystems that may be used to build a cluster. What is lacking, up to this point, is a broad overview of the *order* that you install the software and subsystems. This chapter covers two cluster-building toolkits that will lead you through the process. Finally, I discuss the concept of a "grid" of clusters, and introduce the Globus grid toolkit, which enables the creation of grid applications.

16.1 Introducing Cluster-Building Toolkits

Although there are quite a few projects that attempt to simplify various pieces of cluster creation, there are two tools that automate the entire process: the open-source cluster application resources (or OSCAR) and the National Partnership for Advanced Computational Infrastructure (NPACI) Rocks. Both tools take a different approach to building and managing a cluster, but both allow you to create a functional cluster "out of the box." Which tool you use will depend on the type and size of cluster you are building, as well as your particular system administration preferences.

It will be instructive to list the characteristics of both tools so that you can understand the differences. First, OSCAR

- Does not contain Linux distribution software
- Supports Red Hat 8.0/9.0, SUSE 8.0, and Mandrake 9.0 distributions (Red Hat ES 3.0 and Debian are "in the works")
- Can automatically download other packages
- Supports Intel x86 and Opteron (x86_64) architectures
- Is targeted at small to medium clusters
- Uses `SystemImager` as the installation mechanism
- Is intended for installation only
- Supports Ethernet networks; multiple networks require manual intervention

Now for NPACI Rocks (hereafter referred to as just "Rocks").

- Contains its own license-free Linux distribution
- Is based on Red Hat release sources (the included Linux distribution)
- Can be downloaded as a series of ISO CD-ROM images, with the install disk being bootable
- Supports Intel x86, Itanium (IA-64), and AMD Opteron (x86_64)
- Is intended to be scalable on large clusters
- Uses Red Hat `kickstart` as the installation mechanism
- Includes installation along with monitoring and management processes as part of the model
- Supports Ethernet and Myrinet networks

Which of the two tools you select will depend on the size of your cluster, your selected Linux distribution (and hardware support), and the desired system management "approach." The best way to understand the process and the differences is for us to examine an install using the tools.

Both tools need to save the current "state" information about the cluster. This information is kept in a MySQL database that maintains the data about the compute slices, network configuration, and other architectural components. (Open-source software for MySQL is available at `http://sourceforge.net/projects/mysql`, and the commercial package is available a `http://www.mysql.com`.) The cluster-building tools insert, remove, and update the information in the database as you work with the cluster and the GUI-based commands. In most cases, you don't even need to know that the database is "underneath" the surface.

In addition to the open-source tools, there are a number of commercially available cluster installation and management tools. Most notably, there are tools available from Scyld, IBM, and Linux Networx on their commercial cluster implementations. I concentrate only on the open-source tools in this chapter.

16.2 General Cluster Toolkit Installation Process

The previous chapters in this book introduce the Linux subsystems that are likely candidates for cluster environments. There almost certainly will be custom additions to your cluster's environment, no matter what tool or approach you take. My experience has shown that the 80/20 rule applies: Roughly 80% of the work is reusable and 20% will be custom for a given cluster.

We can use tools like OSCAR and Rocks to create the initial 80% (or more) of the cluster software environment, then use custom software integration to extend the cluster's environment after the installation tool is finished. You may find that just using the choices made by OSCAR and Rocks will create an environment that is sufficient for your needs. If you need to add functionality, it is possible to use the information that has been provided up to this point on Linux subsystems.

So, now you know—there *was* a method to my madness. We have covered seemingly disconnected software configuration operations, but now we will tie things together. To understand what OSCAR and Rocks are doing with the cluster environment, and how to extend their results, we *had* to wave our hands over the basics. The overview of installing a cluster's software environment involves

- Installing a base system from which to operate, usually an administrative or master node
- Activating the base management network on the master or administrative node
- Downloading installation tools, packages, and other software to the master
- Installing and configuring the installation tools (OSCAR, Rocks, or `System Imager`)
- Creating the infrastructure to support compute slice installation (DHCP, DNS, and so on)
- Building and capturing a compute slice image from a "golden" system
- Testing and refining the compute slice image
- Completing the software configuration of the HSI, if present
- Installing and configuring job launching and queuing software
- Performing application testing

You will find that as we go through OSCAR and Rocks, the approach and process is slightly different. OSCAR allows you to choose the structure of the master node, then assumes that you will use it to create images and install the base compute slices. Rocks, on the other hand, will impose a particular structure on the master node, because it completely installs from a bootable CD-ROM. Both tools capture cluster "structure" information like node names, IP addresses, MAC addresses, and so forth in a database that is used for system management.

The best way to tell which tool is best for your needs is to do an installation with both, compare the results, and choose. If you look closely underneath the surface, you will find that the tools will handle many of the manual configuration steps that we have covered up to this point. Understanding what OSCAR and Rocks do, and why they do it, is essential to deciding what to do about extending the software environment that they provide. With any luck at all, we are prepared for this task.

16.3 Installing a Cluster with OSCAR

OSCAR actually has several "flavors" of clusters that it can install, and there are different sub-projects to support these cluster types. As of this writing, there are several variations: Thin-OSCAR (an environment for diskless clusters), HA-OSCAR (an environment for high availability), and several more. I concentrate on the "normal" diskful flavor of OSCAR here.

The OSCAR software may be downloaded from `http://oscar.opencluster-group.org` in the form of a tar ball. The most current version, as of this writing, was version 3.0. After downloading the OSCAR software, we need to configure and install it on the future master node for the cluster.

The master node should be a fresh install of the supported Linux distribution to be used in the rest of the cluster. Some basic configuration of the `/etc/hosts` file and the network interfaces will make the installation process easier. You should also create at last one nonroot user to allow testing benchmark code further during the installation process.

16.3.1   OSCAR Initial Software Installation and Configuration

Here are the steps required to unpack and configure the OSCAR package on the selected master system:

```
# cd /tmp
# tar xvzf oscar-3.0.tar.gz
# cd oscar-3.0
# ./configure
# make install
```

Because OSCAR does not have its own built-in Linux distribution, the next step is to copy the RPM files from a supported distribution into the `/tftpboot/rpm` directory:

```
# mkdir /tftpboot/rpm
< Insert Red Hat 9.0 Installation CD #1 >
# cp /mnt/cdrom/RedHat/RPMS/*.rpm /tftpboot/rpm
# eject
< Insert Red Hat 9.0 Installation CD #2 >
# cp /mnt/cdrom/RedHat/RPMS/*.rpm /tftpboot/rpm
# eject
< Insert Red Hat 9.0 Installation CD #3 >
# cp /mnt/cdrom/RedHat/RPMS/*.rpm /tftpboot/rpm
# eject
```

Now we have the entire RPM set from the distribution underneath `/tftpboot/rpm`. I tend to apply my Red Hat update RPMs to this set of files, so I have the most current software

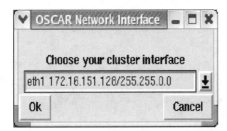

Figure 16–1 OSCAR cluster network dialog

available for the clients. I also make sure that the master node is properly updated. If you are not running in X-Windows mode, then issue a `startx` command to fire up an X-Windows desktop. We next invoke the OSCAR installation script from a terminal window:

```
# cd /opt/oscar
# ./install_cluster <internal_network_device>
```

If you don't specify the network interface (`eth1`) for the cluster network on the `install_cluster` command line, you should be rewarded with a request to choose which network interface on the master node to use for the *internal* cluster network. This is shown in Figure 16–1.

16.3.2   The OSCAR Installation Wizard

You will be asked to enter the password to use on the cluster configuration database after a number of text-based configuration steps are completed. Once you have entered the password, more configuration occurs and, eventually, the OSCAR installation "wizard" will launch. This window is shown in Figure 16–2. Now you can view the high-level set of steps that the wizard will guide the rest of the installation.

OSCAR supports the addition of a number of "extra" packages, including two MPI implementations (MPICH and LAM-MPI), Ganglia, `clumon` (a cluster monitoring package), Open-PBS, the Maui scheduler, and quite a few more "third-party" packages. The supported packages will be added to your cluster environment for you by the installation process. Each package may be configured to a certain extent from dialogs in the package configuration step. Figure 16–3 shows the OSCAR package downloading tool's interface.

Of course, the use of the automated package downloading tool assumes that one of the network interfaces on the master node being installed has an Internet connection and is active. To make your job easier, it is best to plan on using an Internet connection to download packages. Providing the connection is part of the "prep work" you must accomplish prior to starting the installation.

The next logical step is to select the packages you want to download in the package downloader window. Each package has a nice set of information that includes a description and where

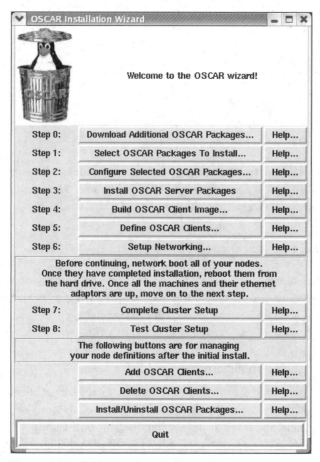

Figure 16–2 OSCAR installation wizard

it originates. Checking the box next to the package will select it for installation into the OSCAR environment. When all your package shopping needs are met, you merely need to click on the Download Packages button to start the process.

Needless to say, this makes the process of selecting third-party packages for your cluster much easier. The catch is that the package has to be supported by OSCAR, or you will have to add the software later. With a stable cluster and the ability to push new images to nodes, this becomes much easier. A little structure to the process helps make the next step clearer. Figure 16–4 shows the package downloader at work.

If you follow along in the terminal window where you started the installation script, you can watch the transcript of the installation while it is being performed. This type of information is very useful for troubleshooting or gaining the knowledge you will need to extend the OSCAR environment, should you desire to do so.

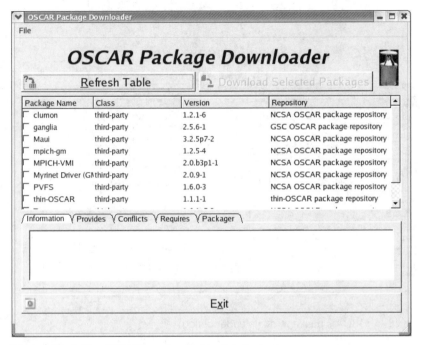

Figure 16–3 The OSCAR package downloader tool

16.3.3   OSCAR Package Configuration

Once the packages are downloaded, the installation wizard provides you with the ability to configure the package behavior when it is installed. The information required will differ based on the package with which you are working, but each supported package has a dialog box that allows you to configure its parameters. The package configuration dialog box is shown in Figure 16–5.

One feature of OSCAR that is very useful is the ability to switch the MPI environment being used in the cluster between MPICH and the LAM-MPI packages. Part of the package configuration step for the MPI packages is the selection of the default systemwide MPI package. This configuration dialog is shown in Figure 16–6. In this example, I have selected MPICH Ethernet as the systemwide default.

OSCAR allows you to install multiple versions of the MPI software, but only one may be active at any given time for a given user. We are setting the systemwide default with this configuration option. Users later have the option to choose their own version of the installed MPI packages. The environment switcher, which is the tool that performs the configuration changes, alters the environment variables such as PATH that determine which MPI executables and libraries are used.

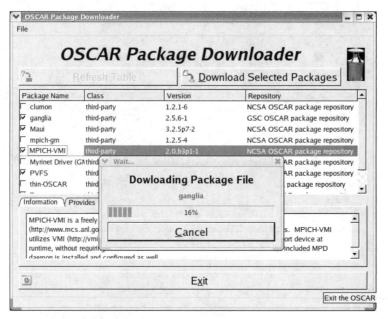

Figure 16–4 OSCAR package downloader dialog

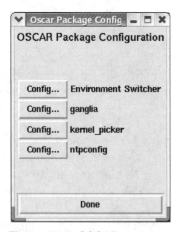

Figure 16–5 OSCAR package configuration dialog

Another example of package configuration is shown in Figure 16–7, for the Ganglia package. Note that the manual configuration of Ganglia involves entering information into two files. The `/etc/gmond.conf` file and the `/etc/gmetad.conf` file detail the name of the cluster and the interface to use for the Ganglia multicast traffic. You can easily see how the information in the form is translated into the configuration lines in the files.

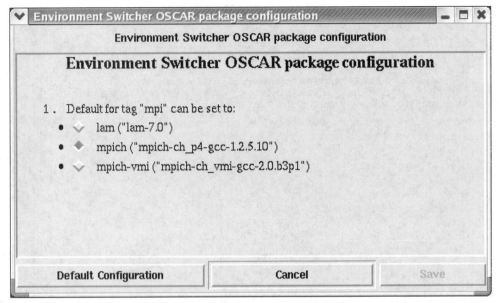

Figure 16–6 OSCAR configuring the default MPI package for your cluster

After all the software packages are configured, the next step in the installation is to configure the OSCAR server packages (refer to Step 3 in the OSCAR Installation Wizard dialog shown in Figure 16–2). This step will initialize the services required to support the rest of the cluster's client systems. Configuring the services on the master node can take a considerable amount of time and will eventually result in a dialog box indicating success or failure of the operation.

16.3.4   Building an OSCAR Compute Slice Image

With the server packages installed, including the System Installation Suite, it is time to build an image for the compute slices in your cluster. OSCAR has an interesting approach to building the image for you: It happens on the server, without the need to install a "golden system" first. This actually saves some steps and ensures that the image that is pushed to the compute slices is absolutely consistent across the cluster (at least the first time).

The image is built in the location with which we are familiar: /var/lib/systemimager/images. The OSCAR software builds the images in place by judicious use of the chroot command in conjunction with the RPM packages we loaded into /tftpboot/rpm. You can build as many images as your disk will hold, to accommodate the different system types in your cluster.

Before you go crazy and build a whole bunch of images (simply because you can), it is a good idea to think about the configuration of the compute slice disks and the extra (custom) software that you might want to install. As you can see from the image-building dialog box, you

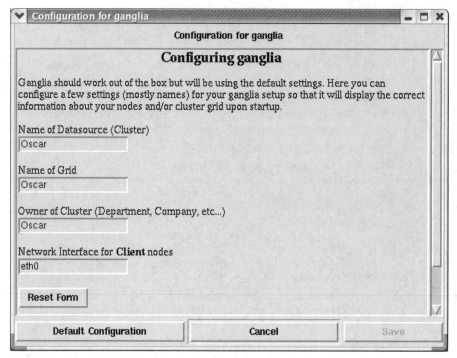

Figure 16–7 OSCAR Package Configuration for Ganglia

have the opportunity to select which packages you want to include in the image, as well as how the disk is to be configured.

The package information file contains a list of RPM packages and dependencies that you want included in the image. OSCAR requires only the package name, not the version information, to specify the package (for example, Perl). The required partition information should also look familiar, because it is very close to the information you would enter into the Red Hat disk configuration tool. Example files are in the /opt/oscar/samples directory. The default selections in the top-level dialog box are shown in Figure 16–8.

Notice that there are options in the dialog that correspond directly to behaviors implemented in the SI master script. This version of SI also includes the ability to multicast the installation. The SI multicast facility, flamethrower was discussed in a previous chapter.

My SI installation option selections are shown in Figure 16–9. Minimal documentation for the flamethrower functionality is available on the SI web site. Of course we should use the facility, because it is provided in a ready-to-use state. Once again, the SI folks produced a winning installation tool for us, and OSCAR makes it easy to use in our cluster.

This step hides the behind-the-scenes actions which build the image and an associated master script for SI installation. As you will recall, to "autoinstall" a client with SI, there are links created in the /var/lib/systemimager/scripts directory that will point to this

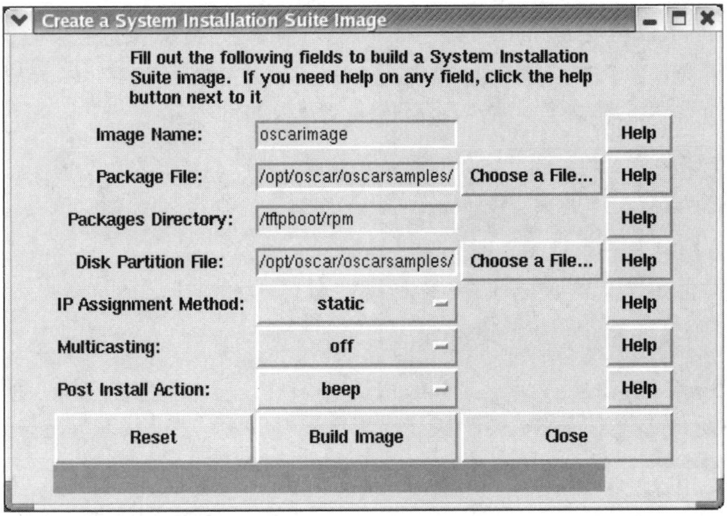

Figure 16–8 OSCAR image creation dialog

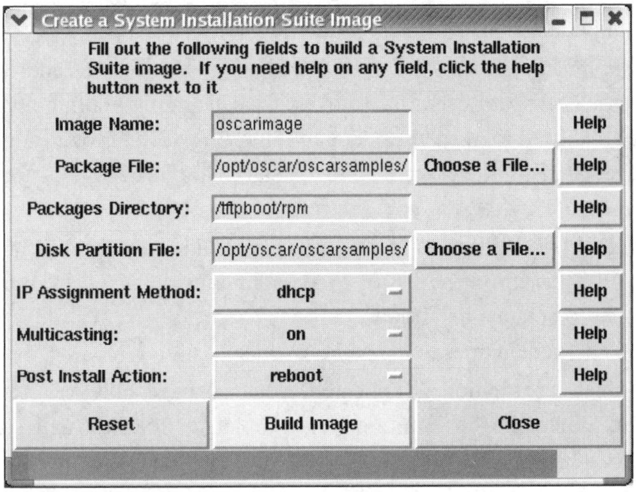

Figure 16–9 Selecting nondefault OSCAR image options

master script. Creating these links, and associating the client systems with the master script, is accomplished by the next step in the OSCAR process.

16.3.5   Defining and Installing OSCAR Clients

We now get to define a block of compute slices or other systems that share a particular image. This step involves defining a range of TCP/IP addresses that will share the same SI image. The

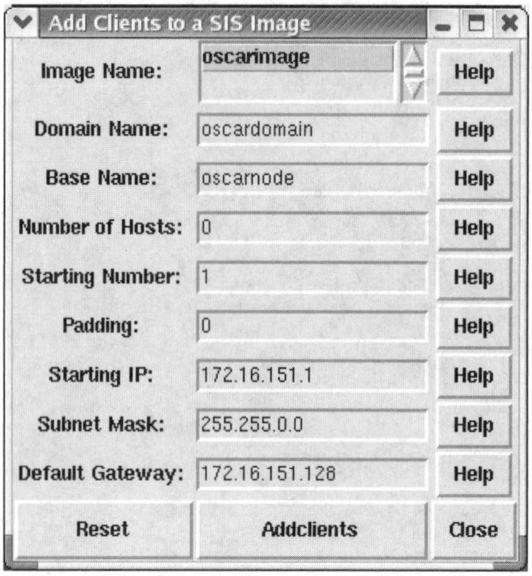

Figure 16–10 Add clients to an OSCAR image

form OSCAR uses to do this is shown in Figure 16–10. The client information is entered into the OSCAR database, as you will notice if you are watching the text transcript.

Once we have created the IP addresses for the clients, we need to associate an address with a specific client's MAC address. There are several ways to do this, including booting nodes one by one and manually matching the IP to MAC addresses, and importing a list of MAC addresses. Which method you use will depend on the size of your cluster. The OSCAR tool for MAC address collection is shown in Figure 16–11.

The manual collection of MAC addresses is possible in smaller clusters, but managed switches and other devices will show up in the list of MAC addresses collected from the network. Sometimes it is just easier to create a list, import the MAC addresses from a file, and *then* assign the proper IP addresses and node names to the MAC address.

Once all the MAC address information is collected, you can have OSCAR create the DHCP configuration for you. When the configuration is completed, OSCAR will start the DHCP server for you on the master node. We won't go further into this process at this point.

With the MAC and IP address mapping completed, the next step is to boot the compute slices. Because `SI` is set up to autoinstall the clients, they should all install the associated image and reboot to the local hard disk. After this is completed, we can verify the overall operation of the cluster.

16.3.6   Completing the OSCAR Installation

Let's review where we are in the process of the OSCAR install by looking at the installation wizard once again. We are just about to start Step 7 in the wizard (Figure 16–12). Once this button is

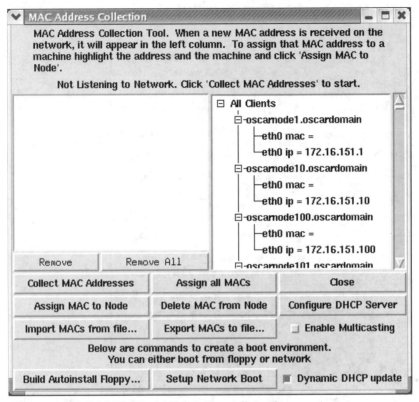

Figure 16–11 OSCAR Client MAC Address Collection

selected, the installation process will set up the job scheduler queues, set security, and clean up various temporary files. When the cluster is completely set up successfully, you will be rewarded with a pop-up window that says "Done!" Maybe the OSCAR authors should add, "Whew!"

OSCAR provides some rudimentary tests to check the cluster's functionality. Selecting the Test Cluster Setup button will check OpenPBS node and server installations, check the mail service and /home NFS mounts, and proceed to user-level tests. Some of the user-level tests include checking SSH server and client connections, and testing MPICH along with LAM-MPI, if installed.

16.3.7   Adding and Deleting OSCAR Clients

If your cluster has more than one type of node in it, or if you decide to expand (or shrink) the number of compute slices in it, you will need to use the OSCAR Add Nodes or Delete Nodes functions. These tools update the database information (which is kept in MySQL files located in /var/lib/mysql/oscar) regarding the state and configuration of your cluster. The dialog for adding nodes is shown in Figure 16–13.

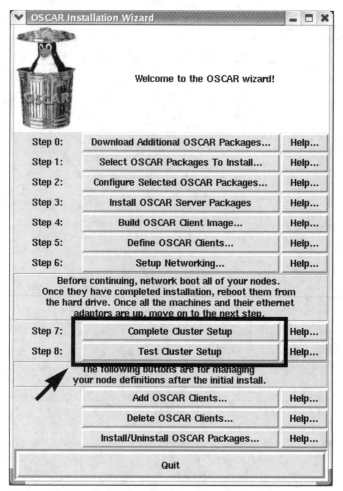

Figure 16–12 Completing the OSCAR installation

Notice that the dialog is similar to the final portion of the installation wizard process. Once your initial execution of the installation wizard is complete, you may run it exactly as before, specifying the network device of the internal cluster network on the command line:

```
# cd /opt/oscar
# ./install_cluster <internal_network_device>
```

To add (or delete) nodes from the cluster, select the appropriate button from the wizard and follow the steps in the dialog box.

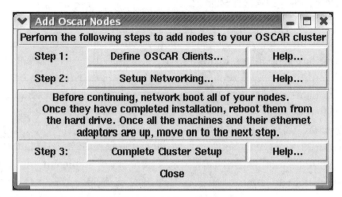

Figure 16–13 OSCAR add nodes dialog

16.3.8 OSCAR Summary

OSCAR can help automate the installation of an Ethernet-based cluster. Once the cluster is installed, OSCAR wants to step out of the way and let you do the managing of the cluster software. If you change too much from the baseline installation, however, you may find that the automated processes don't work.

We can use OSCAR as a general outline of the process required for installing a simple cluster. If you carefully examine *how* and *what* OSCAR does (watch the transcript), you will find that it configures many of the same software subsystems we have discussed in the previous chapters of this book. It is possible to work within the OSCAR framework to configure the subsystems further, or to extend the environment with your particular needs once OSCAR is finished installing the cluster software.

Although OSCAR is a good starting point for learning to create a simple cluster, it has some shortcomings of which we need to be aware:

- No direct support for Itanium Linux[1]
- Assumes a single Ethernet network inside of the cluster
- Places most infrastructure services on a single master node

These shortcomings are easy to get around if you use OSCAR as a starting point, and I highly recommend spending time with OSCAR to understand cluster architecture. Using OSCAR to install your first cluster, and investigating the configuration choices, is a good way to get the feel for any custom installations you may wish to perform.

---

1. As of this writing, there is a beta version of "OSCAR Gold" software for the Itanium platform available at `http://sponge.ncsa.uiuc.edu/oscar-gold` in the form of a single ISO CD-ROM image. In general, there is a lot of Linux for Itanium software available at `http://www.gelato.org/software/index.php`.

16.4 Installing a Cluster with NPACI Rocks

The National Partnership for Advanced Computing Infrastructure Rocks cluster-building toolkit (hereafter called just *Rocks*) allows the creation of larger, more complex clusters than the OSCAR tool. Because it also has support for Itanium systems, it may be a natural choice for clusters based on that hardware. The native architecture for a Rocks cluster is also more complex, allowing multiple front-end (master) systems, and assuming a management network, an external network, and an HSI network.

The high-level architecture for a Rocks cluster is shown in Figure 16–14. Note that the HSI switch may be Ethernet or Myrinet; they both are officially supported (primarily in the MPI packages that are included with the tool) as HSI networks. The network architecture is divided between "internal" or "private" network connections, and "external or "public" network connections. Access to services inside the cluster is protected by firewall rules on the front-end nodes, and other security measures are in place inside the cluster, such as use of SSH for access and the "411" secure directory service to distribute account and management files.

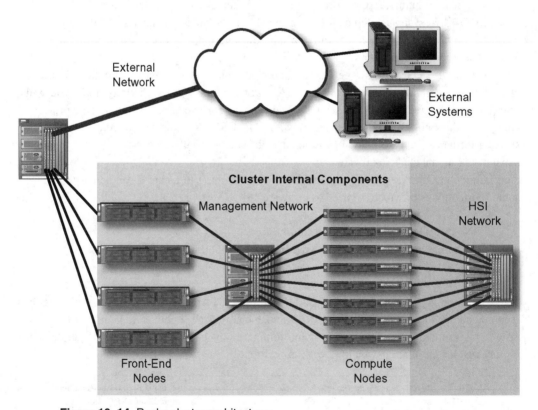

Figure 16–14 Rocks cluster architecture

The cluster members consist of one or more front-end nodes, multiple compute nodes, and external systems. These "classes," along with the ability to do an "update" while preserving the current cluster configuration, are the install operations supported by the installation software. Software for Rocks is available for download as ISO CD-ROM images.

A single bootable "base" CD-ROM performs the installation of the node classes and is augmented by software "rolls," on separate CD-ROMs, that contain additional functionality. You may view these rolls as allowing class-based management of the software environment for the different node types. The Rocks rolls consist of the following:

- The Rocks base image (`rocks-base-<version>.<architecture>.iso`), comprises the Red Hat Linux operating system RPMs and installation tools. The CD image is bootable once burned onto media.
- The HPC roll (`roll-hpc-<version>-<architecture>.iso`) contains HPC software like Ganglia and MPICH, along with Rocks-specific packages.
- The grid engine roll, (`roll-sge-<version>.iso`) contains the Sun Grid Engine (SGE) software.
- The grid roll (`roll-grid-<version>.any.iso`) contains the Globus grid tool kit software.
- The Java roll (`roll-java-<version>.any.iso`) contains a JVM.
- The Intel roll (`roll-intel-<version>.any.iso`) contains Intel compilers and development tools.

Software installation uses the Red Hat `kickstart` facility, so it is package based. The creators of Rocks, however, have made extensive use of class-based administration techniques, dividing functionality into groups of packages and enabling you to install the rolls that you want for your cluster. This is very well designed and implemented!

16.4.1 Getting the Rocks Software

The Rocks ISO images are available for download from `http://www.rocksclusters.org`. A word of caution is needed: The files are large, with the Rocks base and Java rolls taking 650 MB or more. This can take a substantial amount of time to download.

Once you have the ISO images, you can take a look at their contents with the following commands:

```
# mkdir /mnt/iso
# losetup /dev/loop0 rocks-base-3.1.0.i386.iso
# mount -o loop -t iso9660 /dev/loop0 /mnt/iso
# cd /mnt/iso
# ls
< ... explore the CD image ... >
# cd
# umount /mnt/iso
```

```
# losetup -d /dev/loop0
```

Examine as many of the images as you wish. Familiarity with the contents of the various rolls can help you decide which to install.

The next step is to use your favorite CD-burning software to create the actual CD-ROMs that you will use for installing Rocks. I do not cover a complete tutorial on how to do the CD burning, but if you have a CD burner installed on your system, it is fairly easy to create the CDs from the ISO images that we just downloaded. You can use the cdrecord software to scan for CD recorders:

```
# cdrecord -scanbus
Cdrecord-Clone 2.01a19 (i686-redhat-linux-gnu) Copyright (C)
1995-2003 Jörg Schilling
Linux sg driver version: 3.1.25
Using libscg version 'schily-0.7'
cdrecord: Warning: using inofficial libscg transport code
version (schily - Red Hat-scsi-linux-sg.c-1.75-RH '@(#)scsi-
linux-sg.c 1.75 02/10/21 Copyright 1997 J. Schilling').
scsibus0:
        0,0,0    0) *
        0,1,0    1) *
        0,2,0    2) *
        0,3,0    3) *
        0,4,0    4) *
        0,5,0    5) *
        0,6,0    6) 'iomega  ' 'jaz 2GB          ' 'E.17'    \
            Removable Disk
        0,7,0    7) *
scsibus1:
        1,0,0  100) 'HP       ' 'CD-Writer+ 7200 ' '3.01'    \
            Removable CD-ROM
        1,1,0  101) *
        1,2,0  102) *
        1,3,0  103) *
        1,4,0  104) *
        1,5,0  105) *
        1,6,0  106) *
        1,7,0  107) *
```

This scan shows the devices on my two SCSI buses (yes, this CD-burning hardware is kind of old). The CD-ROM burner is at device address 1,0,0 in the language required by cdrecord. To burn the Rocks base software CD, we would issue:

```
# cdrecord -v speed=2 dev=1,0 rocks-base-3.1.0.i386.iso
```

For the burning process to work properly, all the hardware and software on the system must be properly installed and configured. If you have issues with burning the CDs, then drop back to your favorite troubleshooting methods. Once the CD set is created, you can move on to the Rocks installation.

16.4.2 Installing a Cluster Front-End Node Using Rocks

The Rocks installation process is fairly straight forward. The first step is to boot the base CD on your system. This will produce the window shown in Figure 16–15. When the window appears, you will need to select the type of installation you are performing *quickly*. The default is the "cluster node" installation, and (as I said) it flies by quickly. (This default behavior is intended to minimize the amount of time waiting to install the most numerous systems in the cluster, the compute slices.) Select frontend as the installation type, and you are on your way.

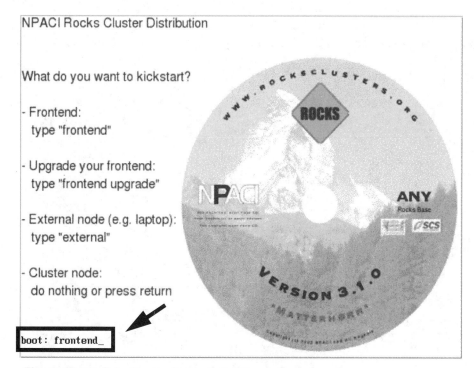

Figure 16–15 Selecting the Rocks installation type

Once the installation type is selected, you will eventually be presented with a dialog that asks you if there are additional roll CDs to be installed. Answering yes to this dialog will cause you to be prompted to insert each of the roll CDs in turn. When they have all been inserted, you respond no to the request for additional CDs, and you will be prompted to re-insert the base CD-

ROM to continue. The installer is just registering the disks and their contents; it will not load the packages quite yet. The start of this dialog is pictured in Figure 16–16.

Next you'll be prompted by the install tool to fill in general cluster information, such as the name of this cluster, the owning department of the cluster, and contact information. This is shown in Figure 16–17. This information is used in several ways in the new cluster (for example, to set Ganglia Web front-end site information).

The next step is to partition the disk in preparation for installation. This step will be familiar if you have installed Red Hat Linux before. Hopefully you have experience with the VGA-based installation screens (lots of blue). The disk layout for the Rocks front-end node requires three partitions: the root partition (/), the swap area, and another partition that will be mounted on /export. Note that there is no separate /boot partition used.

The partitions will be set up with 4 GB in the root partition, the normal (although mostly arbitrary) two times system RAM for swap, and the remainder will be placed into the /export partition. The Rocks installer tries to select a reasonable partition layout, but you must be sure to provide enough disk space for the base installation and all the rolls. My recommendation is to not scrimp on the disk space for front-end nodes *and* to use software or hardware RAID 1 to mirror the system disks.

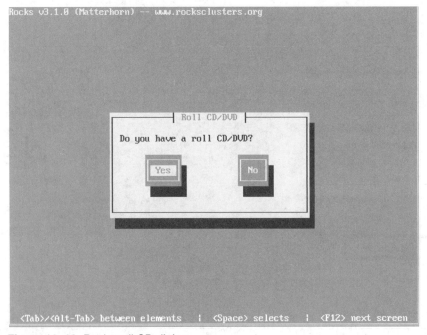

Figure 16–16 Rocks roll CD dialog

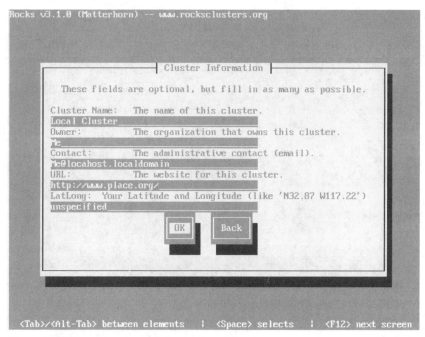

Figure 16–17 Rocks cluster information dialog

Whatever the underlying disk hardware configuration, it is important to use the layout that Rocks proposes to you, unless you have specific experience with changing the partitioning. My reasoning for this recommendation is based on the update process that Rocks supports. The existing state information for your cluster is preserved across new installations (updates) of the Rocks software, and the roll software is stored in the /export/home/install directory. It is best to stick to defaults until you have experience with the effects of altering the disk layout.

With disk partitioning out of the way, you will be prompted to enter the DNS server information for the front-end node you are installing. Remember that the front-end node will have two interfaces, one "facing" the public world and another "facing" the internal structure of the cluster. Without connections to the outside world, your cluster would not be terribly useful.

Once the DNS configuration is entered, you will need to configure the two interfaces on the front-end node. The eth0 interface will be the cluster-facing network interface and the eth1 device will be the public interface (this example assumes that you are using Ethernet as the HSI as well as the management network). The cluster's services and security will be configured to support the internal usage and to be unavailable to the external world.

Configuration for the two networks is straightforward, as long as you have done the necessary design work for your cluster. You should know the network configurations, the host addresses, net masks, and other details at the point you begin the installation. You do not want to try to modify the information later, especially if you are not familiar with the Rocks configura-

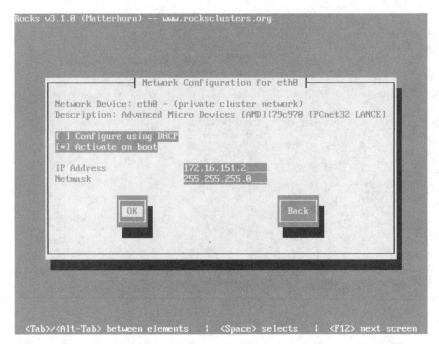

Figure 16–18 Configuring the Rocks private cluster network

tion process or the subsystems that it uses. Figure 16–18 shows the configuration dialog for the private cluster network interface.

The next step is to choose a name for the front-end node. There is a small difficulty with the normal Linux host name situation: It is only possible to have a single host name assigned to a system, even if there are multiple network interfaces. The names that are looked up via the local DNS server in the cluster use the domain .local to avoid confusion. It turns out that some software requires the node name to be the public name (visible in external DNS servers), and some software requires the node to be named with the internal name. Rocks resolves this issue (no pun intended) by strictly separating the public and local "name spaces."

The first front-end machine name can be set manually or from DHCP. If you select manually, the name is configured in the /etc/sysconfig/network file. If you select DHCP, then the name is automatically configured by dhclient when the public interface (eth1) is brought up (Figure 16–19). If you have access to the DHCP and DNS service configurations in your external network, then use DHCP to define the host name; otherwise, you will need to (maybe temporarily) use the manual method until you can get the network administrators to make the changes for you.

When the network information is filled in, you will be prompted for the system's root password. Following this, the installation process will begin with packages from the Rocks base CD. You will also be prompted during the installation to insert the roll CDs that were registered

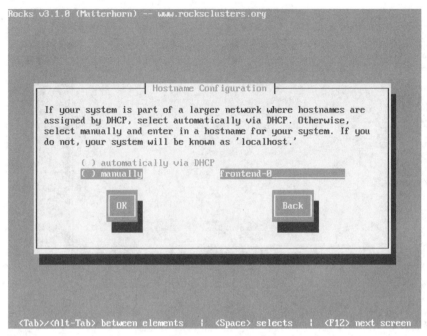

Figure 16-19 Setting the initial Rocks front-end system name

during the initial portion of the installation. This time, their contents will be added to the RPM package library on the front-end node. The front-end node installation requires the Rocks base CD and the HPC roll CD as the minimum software set to configure—everything else is optional.

Once the package loading starts, it will look just like normal Red Hat system installation, interspersed with prompts to insert the roll CDs. This is shown in Figure 16-20. It does not take a long time to complete the software installation, particularly if you are not adding a lot of the roll software. Once the software is all loaded, the system will reboot. Make sure you have removed the installation CD from the drive.

16.4.3   Completing the Installation

Naming conventions in Rocks are based on the rack and system number. For example, the first compute node is named `compute-0-0` by default, indicating node 0 in rack 0. This information is entered into the database by the `insert-ethers` command. The help output for this command is:

```
# insert-ethers -h
Insert Ethernet Addresses - version 3.1.0
Usage: insert-ethers [-h] [-d database] [-u username]
     [-p password] [--help]
     [--list-rcfiles] [--list-project-info] [--update]
```

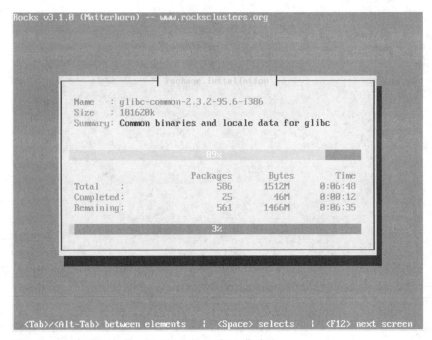

Figure 16–20 Rocks front-end package installation

```
[--staticip] [--db database]
[--host host] [--user username] [--password password]
[--cabinet number]
[--rank number] [--replace hostname] [--remove hostname]
```

Notice that this command allows you to modify the information in the cluster's database regarding the individual node.

Once the front-end node is booted and you have logged in as root, you must run insert-ethers to capture MAC addresses for the Ethernet switches, Myrinet switches, compute nodes, and other hardware devices in the network.

The default device type in the insert-ethers menu is compute, and the rack number will start with 0. The compute nodes in rack 0 need to be booted in order using the Rocks base CD (or one or more copies of it). The compute nodes should be booted sequentially from the bottom of the rack (remember that equipment is usually loaded into the bottom of the rack first because of weight) to the last system in that rack. Once the first rack is complete, you can move on to the next by rerunning insert-ethers with the --cabinet 1 option and so forth.

When a MAC address is captured by insert-ethers, the tool will enter the MAC address, host name, IP address, and other configuration information into the MySQL cluster database, along with generating new configuration files for DHCP, OpenPBS, Maui, PVFS, and the `/etc/hosts` file. The beauty of having a database-driven environment is that the configuration files may be regenerated from the database whenever necessary. If you accept the naming conventions and approach, the job may be quite easy. The nodes still have to boot in order. This can be a problem if you have managed devices making DHCP calls to get their IP address. They can insert themselves into the discovery process. You either have to hand configure the switches making the request and have `insert-ethers` waiting with the proper menu selection (Myrinet switches, Ethernet switches, and so on) or keep the particular device from making a DHCP request until you are ready for it. Knowing the MAC addresses of the switches and doing them first can help avoid issues, but it is impossible to control the order or timing.

Once the compute nodes and other devices are installed, you may move on to testing the cluster's basic operation. This process can be quite involved, but Rocks provides some precompiled parallel applications to test the cluster's mettle (metal?).

One of the first things you need to do to start the process is to add a non-`root` user account from which to run the jobs. You will want to have the Rocks user's guides for the base software and the various rolls handy when you start testing. I leave off at this point, because the testing process could take a separate chapter by itself. It depends on the specific software that you have installed.

16.4.4   Rocks System Administration

The front-end node in a Rocks cluster has a central point of management available: a Web site provided by the Apache Web server. This is installed and configured as part of the standard environment. You can access it by logging into the front-end node and running the Mozilla Web browser over a secure SSH connection. As an alternative, you can enable the cluster's Web server for direct access.

If you decide to enable the cluster's Web server for public access, there is a "table of contents" page provided to access the cluster resources. You should limit the systems and users that have direct access to this information if you want to maintain security. You will need an Apache system administrator's manual handy for configuration tips and information.

Some of the information you can access via the table of contents page is

- Database contents and administration (if enabled, private network only)
- Current cluster performance statistics from Ganglia
- Cluster `top`, which shows detailed system statistics extracted from `/proc` on each system
- Current contents of the cluster distribution tree under `/home/install`
- The Rocks user's guide
- An application to generate a PDF label file for your cluster nodes

Linux subsystems that are in use in Rocks are

- The MySQL database
- The Apache Web server
- The Ganglia monitoring system
- The 411 secure information service (a replacement for NIS)
- The SSH
- The Linux IP filter (`iptables`) facility
- The DNS
- OpenPBS and Maui
- SGE (optional roll)
- MPICH
- NFS and autofs
- NTP
- Java (optional roll)
- Intel development environment (optional roll)
- The Globus Toolkit (optional roll)

You will notice that this list contains many of the individual subsystems that we have examined in the last few chapters.

This gives us a way to use all the knowledge of Linux subsystems that we have so laboriously covered prior to this chapter. By understanding the Rocks approach to building clusters, it is possible for you to extend or add functionality to the base Rocks cluster architecture. If you desire to do this, or just want to learn more about how the tool is implemented, there is help in the Rocks user's guide for modification of the standard software and node configurations.

16.4.5   Rocks Summary

The Rocks environment represents a major head start on a fully functional cluster. As a matter of fact, with very little effort you already *have* a functional cluster after the initial installation is completed. Customization and day-to-day administration will take a substantial amount of investment in learning the architecture and the tools that are available, but you have a known, good starting point. For medium to large cluster environments and for learning how to implement solid cluster architectures, Rocks is a great choice.

16.5 The OpenMOSIX Project

OpenMOSIX adds extensions to the Linux kernel that allow transparent migration of processes to other systems participating in the cluster. Because the addition of these extensions requires an advanced level of knowledge (specifically, how to patch and configure a Linux kernel), the environment may not be suitable for all cluster users (unless you can use the preconfigured kernel versions). The capabilities of OpenMOSIX, however, offer hints regarding the future of mainstream cluster solutions.

One of the interesting design features is the fact that the OpenMOSIX extensions are inside the Linux kernel, which means that software running on the cluster does not need to be "cluster" aware to benefit from the extra functionality. The cluster will transparently migrate processes and dynamically load balance across its member systems. The cluster mimics a large SMP system, but comprises many potentially smaller physical systems.

16.5.1   Getting and Installing OpenMOSIX

There are only two packages to download: the kernel patch and the user tools, if you are using the plain kernel source from `http://kernel.org`, or two RPM packages, if you are installing to a specific release of Red Hat (as of this writing, the latest RPM packages support the version 2.4.22-3 kernel). These are available from `http://openmosix.sourceforge.net`.

The good news is that once the kernel is built and installed, a lot of the work of building the cluster is finished. This, of course, is somewhat of a simplification, but I think you can see that it might be immediately possible to get useful work from the basic configuration—for certain types of applications.

In addition to the kernel extensions, there is a single archive of "user space" tools that are compiled and installed. The minimal features that the installation process (for patching the kernel) suggests enabling in the kernel configuration file are

- OpenMOSIX process migration support
- Stricter security on OpenMOSIX ports
- Direct file- system access
- OpenMOSIX file system
- Poll/select exceptions on pipes

These features give us some clues regarding what OpenMOSIX is doing "under the hood."

Aside from the pipe and port security options, there are three features of immediate interest. The process migration support allows the Linux kernel to migrate processes *transparently* between nodes in the cluster, dynamically balancing the load just as an SMP system would across local processors. The direct file system access option allows these remote processes to perform some file system access locally, instead of needing to forward them to the "unique home node," where the process was initially created. The OpenMOSIX file system is a clusterwide file system that is described as being similar to NFS, but with cluster-wide consistency features.

The absolute easiest way to get started with OpenMOSIX is to choose at least two machines and download the RPM packages for the user space tools and the appropriate kernel.

16.5.2   Configuration of OpenMOSIX Clusters

The OpenMOSIX HOW-TO, available at `http://howto.x-tend.be/openmosix-howto`, lists three configurations that may be used for planning an OpenMOSIX cluster:

1. *Single-pool*—In this configurations all machines (your desktop workstation included) are part of the cluster. All machines may be targets for processes.
2. *Server-pool*—Client desktops are not part of the cluster and must log in to a cluster node to launch jobs.
3. *Adaptive-pool*—Servers are members of the cluster, and workstation clients join and leave the pool as they wish to make their resources available to the cluster.

There are a number of administrative steps that must be performed to create the cluster. First, as you might expect, the UIDs and GIDs must be consistent across the cluster. Likewise, networking must be properly set up. It is possible to run an automatic discovery daemon on each of the nodes to allow them to join the cluster when they boot.

16.5.3   OpenMOSIX Summary

The cluster environment provided by OpenMOSIX reminds me, in a lot of ways, of the Apollo Computer DOMAIN/OS workstation environment. Autodiscovery of nodes, the clusterwide file system, and the ease of management all are characteristics that are familiar, and much beloved, by anyone who has experience with the Apollo software. Any nodding similarity, however, comes to a screeching halt at the more advanced features like transparent process migration and dynamic load balancing.

In addition to the environment itself, there is also an OpenMOSIX programming API that allows creation of programs specifically for the OpenMOSIX environment. There are example tools built with this API on the Web site. One tool of specific interest is `openMosixview`—a system administration and performance monitoring tool for OpenMOSIX clusters.

OpenMOSIX, because it is relatively simple to install and manage, makes a great place for you to start with your cluster experience. There are a number of environments and add-ons that are built on top of OpenMOSIX, including a version of the LTSP, a checkpointing facility, a complete wallet-size CD-ROM version of OpenMOSIX that allows booting a computer into the cluster without touching the local disk, and a number of other interesting applications.

If you want to experiment with an easy-to-install, easy-to-administer, load-balancing cluster, here is probably the easiest way available to do it.

16.6 Introduction to the Grid Concept

The word *grid* has reached critical mass with regard to "buzz" status in the current computer industry. It seems that everything having to do with software (and some hardware) is "grid-capable" or "grid-enabled." Let's be clear: A grid is a very useful concept, but there is still considerable ongoing research into the problem sets that can use grid technology. Moreover, as of this writing, the frameworks and tools for creating a grid-aware application are only starting to become standardized.

If we have been spending more than a little time on individual clusters, actually, *the* individual cluster that possibly represents your first attempt at cluster building, the concept of a grid may seem difficult to define and hard to grasp. Think of it as extending *your* cluster's resources out across the public TCP/IP network to allow it to participate in running *other* cluster's jobs or to provide storage or other resources to members of the grid. Step back to a higher level and see your cluster as a very complex compute slice in another widely distributed, linked-with-WAN-technology cluster.

As a more concrete example, think of the Ganglia architecture that we have already examined. Within a cluster, the Ganglia `gmond` processes gather performance information that is aggregated by a `gmetad` on the master node. The `gmetad` may use one or more `gmond` daemons for its data source, or the aggregated data from other `gmetad` daemons. One system running the Ganglia Web front end, then, may display data collected from individual *clusters*, just as if they were separate systems.

This is a "grid" view of the monitoring data provided by Ganglia. I can already hear some potential protests: "That isn't a grid!" "A grid is more than just monitoring data." "You are limiting the definition of the term!" I answer that we don't quite yet know *what* a grid is, or *how* to use it. The technology is still young and searching for the "killer application." We have to start thinking about the concept somewhere—especially if we are just starting out.

The grid-related marketing hype is just slightly ahead of reality at this point, but a particular technology always leads solutions applying it. Grids are already in use for certain types of situations: HPC, large-scale data analysis, and distributed collaboration. You might think of the SETI@Home project as being a type of grid that manages data and compute resources across a broad number of participating computer systems.

There is at least one specific example of an attempt to build a general-purpose toolkit for producing "grid-aware" applications and environments. That toolkit is the Globus Toolkit from the Globus Alliance, currently available from `http://www.globustoolkit.org`. Before closing out this chapter, I briefly cover the toolkit and what it is trying to accomplish.

16.7 The Globus Toolkit

If you think for a moment about distributing parallel jobs or applications across widely separated clusters, you may start to understand why a grid application is not an easy thing to produce or manage. There are a number of problem areas that must be coordinated across multiple organizations and "clumps" of globally separated resources:

- Distributed security
- System monitoring and management for widely separated systems
- Compute and other resource allocations
- Managing and moving data
- Networking performance and connectivity

Imagine the difficulty of managing a single system. Now consider the complexity of managing a cluster of systems that must behave as a single system for its users. Next consider what it must take to manage a grid of clusters within your own organization. Finally, consider managing multiple clusters of clusters, all of which may be owned by people you don't know or trust (from a security point of view, that is). You might consider it difficult enough to get your own cluster household in order, let alone linking it to other clusters that have different procedures, approaches, and constraints.

The Globus Toolkit exists to help deal with these issues and to enable the creation of grid applications. It is essential to realize, before proceeding, that we are using the term *toolkit* intentionally. This is *not* an out-of-the-box solution that is ready to go once it is installed. It is more like glue for existing off-the-shelf components.

By downloading and installing the Globus Toolkit, you are creating a grid development environment along with a basic set of grid services. This means, for example, that you have a set of Java, C, and C++ APIs for interacting with grid services, you have grid services that are able to authenticate users with Web-based security certificates, and you have examples of grid-aware applications.

To extend the functionality of a cluster across the Internet, a set of grid-aware services is needed that is analogous to the existing local services in a cluster. Some of these grid services include

- Grid job submission and management services (batch queueing)
- Grid file transfer service
- Grid access to database information
- Grid-aware date replication and management services
- Grid-based data indexing and monitoring service
- A grid-aware implementation of the message-passing interface (MPICH-G2)

Unless you are an application developer, these services will not do you much good. They all need to be glued together with the APIs to produce the grid application. This is why the word *toolkit* is applied to Globus.

As a parting comment, I would like you to understand that grid computing *does* exist and *is* solving real problems today. Most of the application areas are currently in the research community, but as general-purpose solutions become available, I expect them to appear in the sphere of every day use. For an example of a functioning grid for computationally-intensive physics, pay a visit to the Web site at http://www.ivdgl.org/grid2003/. You'll see our old friend Ganglia at work, along with a number of other grid tools.

An example of a grid-distributed job is shown in Figure 16–21, with a single job running across multiple cluster resources. You should note that this is only an example of distributing compute resources across a grid. There are other types of resources (like storage) that may be managed and used across a grid environment. If you think about the logistics of actually doing this, it may become apparent why a lot of grid-associated hype may be premature.

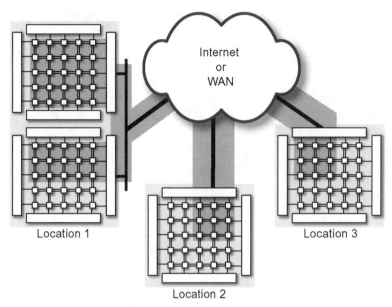

Figure 16–21 A grid-distributed parallel job

16.8 Cluster-Building Toolkit Summary

This chapter covered two existing cluster-building toolkits—OSCAR and Rocks—and used them to provide some structure to the creation of a cluster. Although the target design for a particular cluster is driven by the applications it will run and the users it services (along with the 80/20 rule of standard versus custom functionality), it is possible to get a good strong architectural foundation using both of these tools. The information in previous chapters covered some of the most likely subsystems for extending the default cluster environments, but there will always be additions (and subtractions) in the area of available tools.

OSCAR's strengths lay in its simplicity and its attempt to "get out of the way" after the initial installation. Its single-network, Ethernet-only architecture, and limited support for Itanium, are a potential issues, but its support of commercial and open-source versions of Linux allows it to be a basis for supported cluster environments. For its target cluster audience (small to medium-sized systems) OSCAR is a strong tool and certainly belongs in your "bag of tricks."

Rocks is targeted at a more complex environment, and because of this takes more control over the architecture and management aspects of its target clusters. For clusters of all sizes, its support for Myrinet and Ethernet make it a good choice, particularly if a free, unsupported version of Linux is required. Rocks provides a rich subsystem and system management environment, along with a very flexible, extensible software structure.

Our brief introduction to Globus Toolkit served to discuss the current state of grids and grid-aware applications. I am a firm believer that continued research into this area will produce mainstream grid-aware applications that will become part of our everyday Internet life. It is exciting to see the Globus technology today and it will be even more exciting to watch it develop to its full potential.

Building and
Deploying Your
Cluster

## CHAPTER 17

Dollars and Sense:
Cluster Economics

Chapter Objectives

- Examine the costs associated with cluster hardware
- Look for trends in cluster hardware costs

T his chapter discusses the hardware expenses associated with building small to midsize clusters. Analysis of the costs is presented, based on list hardware prices for three compute slices and two HSI technologies.

17.1 Initial Perceptions

When I first became involved with clusters, it was on a rather huge implementation, by anyone's standards. The complexity of the environment was familiar to me, and neither I nor anybody else on the team thought that the job would be easy. By the time the target installation was complete, more than two years had elapsed. Even with our initial presumptions of difficulty, the job turned out to be more complex, difficult, and expensive than we expected.

Working on smaller clusters for other customers, I encounter the attitude that clusters are automatically cheaper than other comparable solutions, merely because they use commodity hardware and software. (I have come to call this the *pile o' hardware syndrome*.) As with any complex solution, there are a *lot* of details requiring attention when building a cluster, and I wondered whether the rosy assumptions were actually true. After all, I had worked on an exceptional project. Maybe the economies of scale *were* different for different-size clusters. I decided to see if there was an economic analysis available for clusters comprising 8 to 128 compute slices.

To date, I have found lots of agreement across the industry that clusters are a growing solution and that they can save money for certain types of applications. This opinion is repeated over and over again in articles and whitepapers. What is not discussed, however, are the actual cost breakdowns associated with building a cluster, with regard to hardware, software, or labor. Because labor costs are so variable, such an analysis is beyond the scope of this book. (Indeed, I frequently run into clusters that are built "for free" by graduate students or interns at educational institutions. In these cases, somebody is paying, I'm just not sure who.)

17.2 Setting the Ground Rules

As part of my job, I analyze and recommend new technologies that may be turned into solutions for my company's customers. Because application-specific clusters are of particular interest to our customers, I started researching the topic. Because I was unable to find an analysis of the hardware costs associated with the size of clusters that we target, I decided to build my own model clusters and analyze the hardware component cost.

Building even a model cluster from scratch involves generating a design, researching the available components, generating a parts list, and finally producing a hardware cost estimate. Starting the analysis, I made some discoveries fairly quickly.

- There is a difference between using 1U compute slices and 2U compute slices in the cluster. A cluster of a given size will take twice as many compute racks with 2U compute slices as with 1U systems.
- The complexity of a cluster is a function of the number of active components and the required number of interconnections. Minimizing the number of interconnections can improve reliability, but will increase cost.
- Cluster interconnect switches tend to provide a number of ports that is a power of two, whereas Ethernet switches follow different rules. This is important because once you run out of ports on a switch, you need to add another one or move to the next bigger model, driving up the costs.

Each of these discoveries plays a part in the overall cost of the cluster's hardware.

Our example configurations have 8, 16, 32, 64, and 128 compute slices in 1U and 2U packages. Three HSI technologies are used in the designs: Ethernet, Myrinet, and Quadrics QsNet. All price calculations are based on published US list prices from the companies' Web sites. The cost of the HSI interface card for the compute slice is included in the HSI cost breakdown.

The systems considered were all dual-processor servers from Hewlett-Packard, the DL-360 G3, the zx6000, and the rx2600. The DL-360 is a dual-processor 3.2-GHz Intel Pentium 4 Xeon system, whereas both the zx6000 and rx2600 systems are dual-processor 1.5-GHz Intel Itanium 2 systems. The zx6000 is a workstation system, with graphics capability and an optional management card, whereas the rx2600 is intended as a commercial server and has management functionality included standard.

All systems were configured with similar configurations: two processors, 2 GB of system RAM, and one 36.4-GB SCSI disk. The zx6000 system was configured with the optional management card to match the functionality of the DL-360 and rx2600. The list prices were generated from this set of configurations.

17.3 Cluster Cabling and Complexity

There is a size beyond which a cluster's complexity skyrockets. Ask anyone who builds clusters and they will tell you it is somewhere between 128 compute slices and 512. If you take a look at the number of cables in the configurations, you can see an exponential increase in the number of cables, and therefore interconnections in a cluster as it gets larger.

Figure 17–1 shows the total number of cables in a cluster based on a 1U compute slice for various sizes of clusters, up to 128 compute slices. The figure shows cable configurations for a cluster using Infiniband as the HSI, along with a management LAN and data LAN. Also depicted is a cluster that has only Ethernet management and data LANs, and finally a "full configuration" with Ethernet being used for management and data LANs, and a separate HSI.

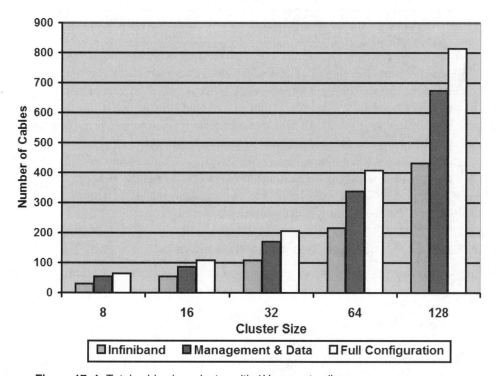

Figure 17–1 Total cables in a cluster with 1U compute slices

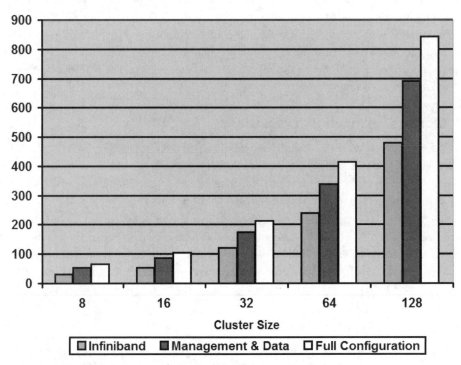

Figure 17–2 Total cables in a cluster with 2U compute slices

Figure 17–2 shows the number of cables for a cluster based on 2U compute slices. There is a slight increase in the number of cables resulting from the increased number of racks. The number of connections per system increases with 2U compute slices, but if the designer uses switches inside the racks, there is still an increase in connections over the cluster built with the 1U compute slices—mainly because there are more racks to connect.

Infiniband allows connecting systems with a single cable that provides high-bandwidth and low-latency multiplexed communications. It is possible to run the HSI, the management LAN, and the data LAN over a single cable. This can drastically reduce the number of cables per system, and therefore the overall system complexity.

17.4 Eight-Compute Slice Cluster Hardware Costs

Starting with the least expensive cluster configuration, one with eight compute slices, let's examine the contribution of the various hardware elements. The costs are broken into

- Compute slice hardware
- HSI
- Infrastructure (management and data LANs)

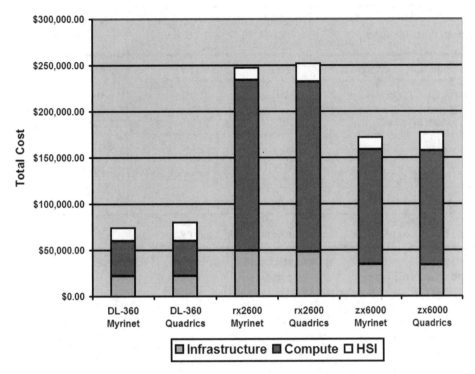

Figure 17–3 Hardware component cost, eight-compute slice cluster

Figure 17–3 shows that the major component of the total cost is the compute slices. The networking components and HSI are implemented with the smallest possible switches, which lowers the overall cost. When multiple switches, or multiple levels of HSI switches, are required, as for larger clusters, the cost increases substantially.

Both 1U (DL-360) and 2U (rx2600 and zx6000) systems are included in the graphs. The infrastructure costs, as a percentage of the total, are expected to increase for the 2U systems over the 1U systems, because more racks and switches are required as the cluster gets larger. The associated cost percentages with the first graph are listed in Table 17–1.

17.5 Sixteen-Compute Slice Cluster Hardware Costs

Table 17–2 lists the cost breakdowns for a 16-compute slice cluster. At 16 systems, the compute slices still will fit into a single rack. The infrastructure costs are slightly larger than the eight-node cluster, and the HSI costs, which include interface cards and cables, are higher because of the increased number of rsystems.

Note that as the size of the cluster grows, the cost of the infrastructure tends to drop as a percentage of the total costs. Part of this is the result of the more efficient filling of the acks. Six-

Table 17–1 Eight-compute Slice Hardware Cost Percentages

System and HSI Type	infrastructure Cost, %	Compute Cost, %	HSI Cost, %
HP DL-360 G3, Myrinet	29.57	51.80	18.63
HP DL-360 G3, Quadrics	27.20	47.65	25.16
HP rx2600, Myrinet	20.05	74.39	5.55
HP rx2600, Quadrics	19.06	72.95	8.00
HP zx6000, Myrinet	20.17	71.85	7.98
HP zx6000, Quadrics	19.00	69.65	11.36

Table 17–2 Sixteen-Compute Slice Hardware Cost Percentages

System and HSI Type	Infrastructure Cost, %	Compute Cost, %	HSI Cost, %
HP DL-360 G3, Myrinet	18.76	62.84	18.40
HP DL-360 G3, Quadrics	14.91	51.40	33.68
HP rx2600, Myrinet	7.19	87.50	5.32
HP rx2600, Quadrics	10.07	82.47	7.46
HP zx6000, Myrinet	11.59	73.53	14.88
HP xz6000, Quadrics	11.42	77.97	10.61

teen 1U compute slices require only one compute rack and one master rack, whereas 16 2U compute slices require two compute racks and one master rack. Hardware costs for this configuration are shown in Figure 17–4.

Network switches tend to have ports in units of eight or 12, so moving to 16 compute slices means that one switch will be filled and a second is needed—increasing the cost. The HSI switches also begin to fill up, either requiring additional chassis or blades *in* the chassis to support the additional systems.

17.6 Thirty-two-Compute Slice Hardware Costs

As the cluster grows to 32 compute slices, the smaller Quadrics HSI switch chassis needs to be replaced with a larger size. This increases the cost for the HSI for this size of cluster, but leaves additional capability for expansion. The compute slice portion of the cluster's cost continues to

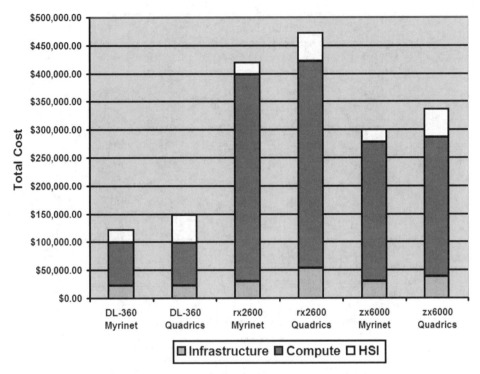

Figure 17–4 Hardware component cost for a 16-compute slice cluster

grow in relationship to the infrastructure and HSI costs. This cost relationship is shown in Figure 17–5.

At 32 compute slices, the cluster is producing close to 274 MFLOP peak for the Intel Pentium Xeon systems and roughly 378 MFLOP peak for the Itanium 2 systems. This calculation is the sum of the capabilities of individual systems, and does not take into account the scaling across the cluster of the parallel Linpack benchmark. Producing 70 to 80% scaling is considered very good.

The infrastructure costs of our 32-compute slice clusters are dropping toward the single-digit percentages as the total number of compute slices increases. A 32-compute slice cluster requires two compute racks and one master rack for the 2U compute slices. The 1U compute slices require one compute rack and one master rack.

The total cost for the 32-compute slice clusters range from a low of $224,000 to a high of $903,000. The cost percentages for this cluster configuration are shown in Table 17–3.

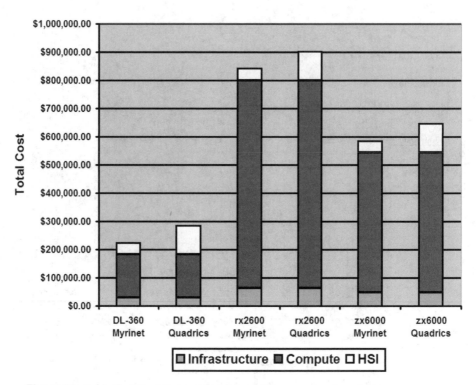

Figure 17–5 Hardware component cost for a 32-compute slice cluster

Table 17–3 Thirty-two-Compute Slice Hardware Cost Percentages

System and HSI Type	Infrastructure Cost, %	Compute Cost, %	HSI Cost, %
HP DL-360 G3, Myrinet	13.47	68.11	18.42
HP DL-360 G3, Quadrics	10.66	53.40	35.94
HP rx2600, Myrinet	7.69	87.40	4.91
HP rx2600, Quadrics	7.17	81.45	11.38
HP zx6000, Myrinet	8.51	84.43	7.05
HP xz6000, Quadrics	7.70	76.41	15.88

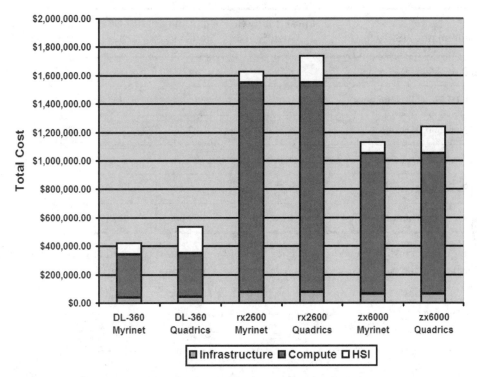

Figure 17–6 Hardware component cost for a 64-compute slice cluster

17.7 Sixty-four-Compute Slice Hardware Costs

At 64 compute slices, the cluster now requires two compute racks for 1U compute slices and four compute racks for 2U systems. Sixty-four ports of HSI does not fill either the Myrinet or the Quadrics switch chassis. The cost breakdown is shown in Figure 17–6.

Because the HSI chassis do not require expansion, the overall percentage contribution to the cluster cost stays in a range similar to the 32-compute slice cluster. The cost of the compute slices dwarfs the infrastructure and HSI expenses (Table 17–4) .

17.8 One Hundred Twenty-eight-Compute Slice Hardware Costs

Our final example hardware configuration is 128 compute slices (Figure 17–7). This cluster requires four compute racks for 1U compute slices and eight racks for 2U systems. The number of interrack cables begins to grow and there may be a need for additional management racks to hold HSI or other switch equipment.

With 128 compute slices in the cluster, the HSI switch chassis for both Myrinet and Quadrics are completely full. To expand the HSI would require additional levels of switches to ensure

Table 17–4 Sixty-four-Compute Slice Hardware Cost Percentages

System and HSI Type	Infrastructure Cost, %	Compute Cost, %	HSI Cost, %
HP DL-360 G3, Myrinet	8.54	72.62	18.84
HP DL-360 G3, Quadrics	8.01	56.91	35.08
HP rx2600, Myrinet	4.73	90.40	4.87
HP rx2600, Quadrics	4.43	84.72	10.84
HP zx6000, Myrinet	5.50	87.49	7.01
HP xz6000, Quadrics	5.01	79.80	15.19

the required connectivity and low latency. Beyond this point, specialized HSI clusters begin to add substantial cost to this area. The cost percentages are shown in Table 17–5.

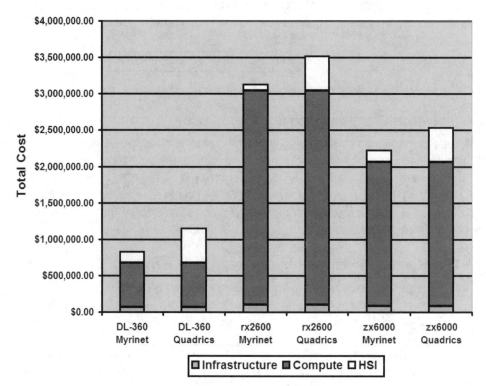

Figure 17–7 Hardware component cost for a 128-compute slice cluster

Table 17–5 One Hundred Twenty-eight-Compute Slice Hardware Cost Percentages

System and HSI Type	Infrastructure Cost, %	Compute Cost, %	HSI Cost, %
HP DL-360 G3, Myrinet	7.90	73.46	18.65
HP DL-360 G3, Quadrics	5.75	53.29	40.96
HP rx2600, Myrinet	3.31	94.15	2.54
HP rx2600, Quadrics	2.95	83.70	13.36
HP zx6000, Myrinet	3.99	89.03	6.98
HP xz6000, Quadrics	3.50	77.99	18.51

As we might expect, the majority of the cost is still in the compute slice hardware, ranging from a low of 74% to a high of 94%. In the clusters with a specialized HSI, the cost percentage ranges from a low of 3% to a high of 41%. The low value is the lower cost IA-32 systems with Myrinet, and the high-end cost is for the more expensive Itanium 2 systems with Quadrics. The performance and latency that you require will affect the hardware cost relationships in your cluster.

17.9 The Land beyond 128 Compute Slices

I mentioned earlier in this chapter that there is a point at which most cluster builders expect the complexity to become very difficult to manage. Certainly, if you look at the cost breakdown for the 128-compute slice cluster and compare it with the smaller clusters you can see that the hardware costs are following an exponential curve as the cluster gets larger. This is shown in Figure 17–8.

Part of this exponential rise in cost is due to the fact that we are using (exponential) powers of two for the number of compute slices in the cluster. Some of the cost increase, however, is the result of the limits in the number of available ports on the HSI and Ethernet switches. When one chassis is filled, it will take multiple identical switches (in the case of Ethernet) or multiple layers of switches (in the case of the HSI) to provide the necessary connections and to maintain bandwidth.

I am not considering software complexity here, but that tends to rise exponentially in relation to the number of interconnected systems. Along with the software and hardware costs, the amount of labor required to build the cluster also follows a similar complexity. When taken together, these factors all seem to indicate that the next major step—to 256 compute slices—is the point where organizations with limited time and budget will have to start making trade-offs in cluster size and hardware selection.

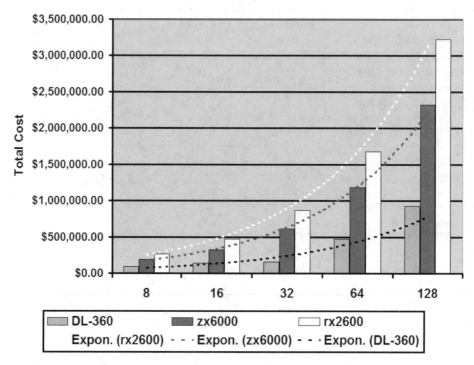

Figure 17–8   Growth of total cluster hardware costs (list prices)

Buying the cheapest possible "white box" system for your compute slices may not be the correct answer to the cost increases. (A "white box" system is brandless hardware, from cottage-industry manufacturers that have no high operating overheads and can therefore offer the lowest possible prices.) The systems must be manageable, must be properly designed for rack heating situations, must have the proper chip sets to allow memory and CPU performance, and, finally, the company manufacturing the systems has to stay in business long enough to support your cluster's hardware. Initial hardware price is not the only consideration for your cluster's success.

Another way to look at the compute slice expenses is in terms of cost per GFLOP for scientific and engineering clusters or in terms of cost per transaction for commercial application clusters. Many of the industry-standard transaction benchmarks also include the cost per transaction in the reporting. An example of the cost per GFLOP is shown in Figure 17–9.

17.10 Hardware Cost Trends and Analysis

The preceding sections presented information on the cost breakdown percentages of several cluster configurations, from 8 to 128 compute slices. It is possible to analyze the hardware costs in terms of "cost per system" for racking hardware, or "cost per port" for networking equipment.

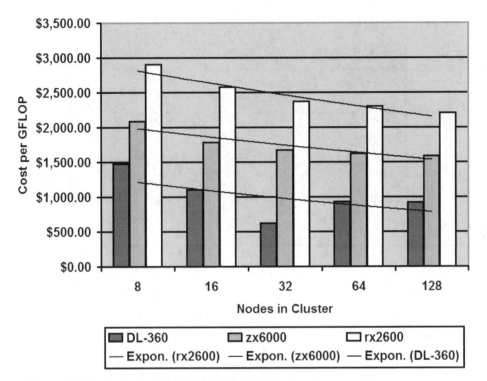

Figure 17–9 Cost per GFLOP based on cluster size

An example of cost-per-system calculations for the Hewlett-Packard Proliant racks is shown in Figure 17–10, broken down per 1U and 2U compute slice.

The increase in price at the 2U 16-system point is the result of the need for two racks instead of one. For configurations that are small enough, rack sizes other than the 42U racks are possible. This is reflected in the expenses for the smaller 1U and 2U clusters.

For Ethernet data and management LAN costs, see Figure 17–11, which details the per-system cost for a GbE data LAN and a 10/100 management LAN. All equipment used was Hewlett-Packard ProCurve network switches.

Total cost for these LANs includes the required switches in the individual compute racks and the core switching equipment in the master rack. Note that in Figure 17–11 a single switch with a higher port count may be used in the 32-compute slice example, in which there are 1U systems, because there is only one compute rack. In the 32-compute slice cluster, with 2U systems, there are two compute racks.

The number of unused or "wasted" ports is calculated into the total cost. A very useful feature of the compute slices is multiple, built-in LAN interfaces. The built-in interfaces reduce cost by eliminating the need for added PCI interfaces. In systems with limited PCI connectivity, this leaves room for the HSI interface card.

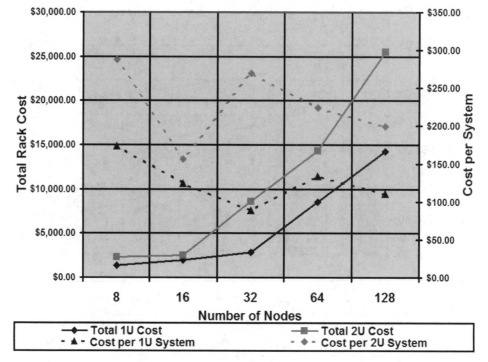

Figure 17–10 Hewlett-Packard Proliant rack costs per system (list prices)

When making a choice of HSI technology, the per-port cost is a useful way of looking solely at price differences. The per-port costs for Myrinet and Quadrics are shown in Figure 17–12, for the 8-, 16-, 32-, 64-, and 128-compute slice clusters. The total cluster cost of the HSI technologies go up exponentially in the number of compute slices, because they try to maintain complete connectivity and constant latency across the network.

At 128 ports of either Myrinet or Quadrics, the first chassis is completely filled, with all ports in use. To expand the network beyond this point requires additional levels of switch chassis, which increases the HSI cost considerably. This would be reflected in an increase in the total cost per port.

17.11 Cluster Economics Summary

In this chapter we analyzed a limited set of hardware across a limited set of cluster sizes. Additionally, we used the list prices for all of the hardware, although there are usually quantity or "special" discounts available from the hardware vendors. Dealing with "street price" for the components, however, is very tricky, because the street price varies with the source, situation, and vendor relationship.

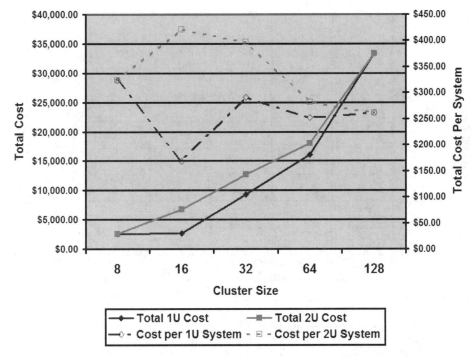

Figure 17–11 Per system cost for data and management LANs (list price)

By using list prices, we have been able to draw some conclusions to use as a baseline for making hardware configuration and purchasing projections, even if discounts *are* involved. It is likely that different components will be discounted at different rates in a real-world situation (for example, RAM, disk, system processing units, networking equipment, and HSI equipment).

To account for all the permutations here is beyond the scope of our discussion. To maintain some level of sanity in your situation, use the published list prices as a starting point, but allow for discount percentages in whatever hardware purchasing models you build. You can then adjust total costs as the quotations come in from your vendors.

Based on our tables, graphs, and observations, we have a somewhat better idea of what to expect for hardware costs in a given-size cluster:

- Constantly increasing hardware cost, with the total percentage contribution from compute slices increasing as the cluster grows, as shown in Figure 17–8
- Decreasing cost per GFLOP or transaction, approaching a constant value, as shown in Figure 17–9, provided scaling is linear across the cluster
- Increased complexity, associated with the overall size of the cluster and the number of interconnections between active elements

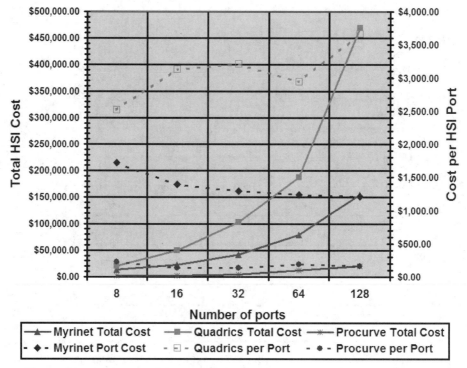

Figure 17–12 Per-port HSI costs (list prices)

- Infrastructure costs that increase in step with the cluster size, but decrease toward a constant value on a per-system basis

Taking all these observations into account, it is difficult to see how the automatic impression that "clusters are cheaper" has taken hold, until you consider the cost of a similar-sized SMP server, as shown in Table 17–6.

The costs for large SMP systems escalate with memory capacity and total number of available CPUs. By the time an SMP server can support 64 CPUs, it must have an internal crossbar and possibly a special interconnect. Using smaller SMP systems to build a cluster, then, can improve performance and reduce cost, provided the application you are using supports a cluster environment.

Figure 17–13 shows a hardware-only comparison between large SMP configurations and equivalent compute slice-only hardware costs for a number of standard CPU configurations. All systems were configured with 4 GB of RAM per CPU. Prices are based on US list price as of May 14, 2004, and will change. Before making any assumptions about your particular situation, you should seek updated information.

Table 17–6 Comparison of Four-Way SMP Server versus Two-Way Compute Slices

Qty	System Description	Number of CPUs	Total RAM, GB	Total Cost[a]
2	HP Proliant DL-360 G3, 3.2-GHz Pentium 4 Xeon	4	8	$14,494.00
1	HP Proliant DL-580, 2.8-GHz Pentium 4 Xeon	4	8	$28,046.00
2	HP rx6000, 9 GB RAM	4	18	$63,020.00
1	HP rx5670, 17 GB RAM	4	17	$83,694.00

a.   All prices are US list price as of January 31, 2004.

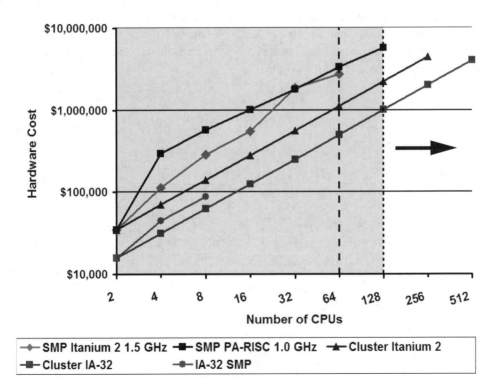

Figure 17–13 Comparison of large SMP configurations and cluster hardware

There are several labels on the graph to notice. The leftmost dotted line on the graph marks the largest SMP configuration available for an Itanium 2 processor configuration at the time of this writing. The rightmost dotted line marks the largest SMP configuration available for a Hewlett-Packard PA-RISC processor, the PA-8800. This processor has a dual-CPU core, which allows two CPUs per module. This allows expansion of the system CPU capacity without necessitating a hardware design refresh.

The bottom two lines in Figure 17–13 show a compute slice configuration with equivalent numbers of CPUs built with dual-CPU systems: one line representing Itanium 2 and the other, IA-32 processors. The arrow to the right indicates the ability of the cluster solutions to scale the number of processors beyond the limits of the SMP configuration. For applications that can take advantage of this scaling, there is a potential cost advantage *and* it is possible to scale out beyond 128 processors, something the SMP configurations cannot do.

The commodity IA-32 processor also suffers from scaling issues in SMP configurations. The line representing the IA-32 SMP configurations stops at eight processors because that is the largest configuration I could find in the configuration guides. To scale the IA-32 solution, one *has* to adopt a cluster approach.

As a final note, the price scale on the left of the graph is logarithmic, so be sure to take that into account when reading the prices from the graph. This comparison is an artificial exercise, but it does illustrate the potential scaling and hardware cost savings provided by cluster configurations. A realistic model would take all aspects of the final solution into account, but such a model is beyond the scope of this discussion.

## CHAPTER 18

Racking Your Brains: Example Cluster Rack Assembly Steps

Chapter Objectives

- List some of the manual steps necessary to rack and install a cluster
- Examine the manual steps, looking for ways to improve efficiency
- Perform some simple time estimations for an example cluster

Each cluster is unique in its own way. The size of the cluster, the selection of individual components, and the target environment all affect the amount of effort needed to implement the cluster. Many of the steps involved, however, such as racking and cabling, require similar efforts in every cluster project. This chapter quantifies some of the actual steps required in the physical construction of a cluster.

18.1 Examining the Cluster Assembly Process

The best way to find and take advantage of the parallelism involved in the process of physically assembling a cluster is to build one serially, detailing all the manual steps involved along the way. (Your first cluster will be an experiment in creating a process from scratch, and opportunities for improving the process may not occur to you until you are finished with the effort or have discovered "beginner's" mistakes.) The more analytical, detail-oriented, and fanatical you are about recording the steps, the more likely you will be to identify areas of improvement. This is assuming that you will be building more clusters, and that applying the information from this exercise will help you later.

If opportunities for improving the process or speeding it up exist, then looking for patterns or more efficient ways of allocating your team among the individual operations will help. For systems consisting of a single rack, you will not have to pay as much attention to details as long as you have all the correct parts and tools available. The larger the cluster, the more that overlooking small details can bite you.

18.2 Assembly Assumptions

There are some basic requirements for assembling racks of systems, both in terms of facilities and available tools. A partial list, based on experience, is

- Static controlled area for installation of RAM and interface cards, consisting of static control mats and bench tops or, minimally, wrist straps
- Ladders for safely installing or working on equipment off the ground
- Power torx drivers or screwdrivers, chargers, and extra batteries
- Well-equipped tool kit with screwdrivers, wrenches, hammers, and crowbars
- Power connection for individual node assembly and checkout
- Rack power connection for rack checkout
- Laptop and serial cables for switch/management/console configuration
- USB-to-PS/2 convertor for keyboard and mouse
- USB-to-serial convertor for systems without built-in serial ports
- Serial or graphics console, graphics monitor preferred
- Pallet jacks, hand trucks, and other equipment for handling heavy items
- Label-making tools
- Cable manufacturing and test tools
- Complete design documentation, including rack design, cable design, system documentation, switch documentation, rack positioning documentation, and so forth

Note that last-minute changes to the "final" design details, like physical placement of multiple cluster racks, will also change the length of the cables required to make connections between racks. Any changes to the physical placement of the racks may well ripple through the rest of the cluster. The amount of up-front design that you do can help to minimize assembly surprises. No matter what you do, however, there are sure to be multiple trips to the local hardware and electronics stores before you are finished.

18.3 Some "Rules of Thumb" for Physical Cluster Assembly

A lot of the details of the physical assembly of your cluster will depend on the rack systems that you end up using, the mounting hardware provided by your system vendor, and the facilities you have available. Some rules of thumb you can use right away are the following:

- Do not "tie-wrap" anything permanently into place until the entire installation is complete.
- Be sure to check the cable clearance with the systems in and out of the rack on their slides.

- Heavy things go in the bottom of the rack.
- To avoid tipping, load the rack from the bottom up.
- Always use the antitipping safety devices provided by the rack manufacturer.
- System or device numbering starts from the bottom of the rack.
- Devices with many connections are best racked higher in the rack to avoid tight cable bends or clearance issues with cable entry/exit to the rack.
- Each rack needs a unique number or ID that is tied to the floor plan.
- A numbering scheme that maps physical rack location to system ID is desirable.
- Minimize interrack connections at all costs.
- Run power cables separately from all others, if possible.
- Check, double-check, and triple-check. It will save time in the long run.
- Anyone who changes cable positions or labels without updating documentation dies a slow and painful death.

Some of these recommendations may seem obvious at first, but you would be surprised how many times I have seen the assembly process start down the wrong path, only to need expensive correction later. It is far better to have an established, well-thought-out approach ahead of time for things like cable management. The best-case remedy to changes is to update the design or documentation. The unappealing alternative is to rerack or recable to correct design issues that are discovered during assembly. See Chapter 19 for recommendations on cable labeling and documentation.

18.4 Detailed Cluster Assembly Steps

Many of the assembly steps for a cluster with multiple racks involve lots of repetition. There are individual rack-specific steps and steps that are only necessary if your cluster has multiple racks. What follows is a detailed description of a hypothetical assembly process. It must be modified for your specific situation.

See Figure 18–1 for a rack diagram of our example cluster. (This diagram was produced using Microsoft Visio 2000 and was exported to Adobe Illustrator. The hardware objects are from a set of Hewlett-Packard-specific stencils from `http://www.visio-cafe.com`.) Our example assembly process will assume the following.

- There are multiple racks in the cluster.
- Each rack contains an Ethernet switch and a serial port console switch.
- Each compute node has a management LAN connection, a data LAN connection, a serial port console connection, and an HSI connection.
- A "management" rack will contain the HSI switch and the core Ethernet switch.
- The vendor's rack system includes cable management arms as part of the mounting kit.
- One lucky person with a lot of time and a very strong back is doing the assembly for the entire cluster.

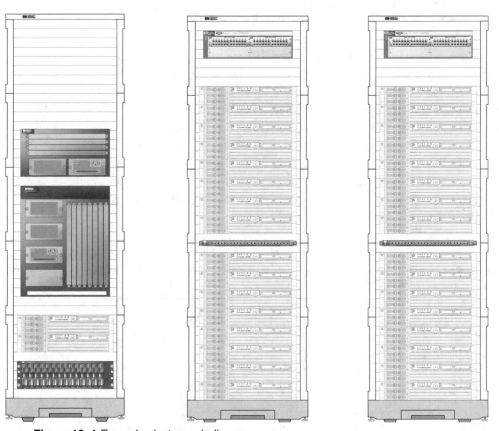

Figure 18–1 Example cluster rack diagram

The step-by-step assembly process is listed in the following subsections. I know this is a very verbose set of steps, but to understand the nature of the assembly process, you must first understand as many of the details as possible. I will note any potential parallelism and manufacturing efficiencies in the next section.

18.4.1   Physical Rack Assembly

- If all racks are unpacked and configured, flip ahead to page 537, Physical Rack Positioning.
- Unpack the rack, sides, power distribution units, power cord, and so forth.
- Remove the packing material. (Save the packing material for shipping if the rack is to be shipped as a unit once full.)
- Install the power distribution units (PDUs) into the rack.

- Assemble the rack frame, if necessary (this is different for each manufacturer and rack type).
- Add feet/tip protection devices.
- Add sides, doors, rack height extensions, and so forth. (Sides and doors may be left off until assembly is complete, depending on access needs.)
- Add the power cord to the rack. (The wiring of the rack's PDUs may require a certified electrician.)
- Check that the rack power cord is the correct one for the final installation location. (Nothing is more embarrassing than to assemble a rack of equipment, ship it, and then discover that the plug does not match the customer's power receptacles. Well, that's almost true. To do the same thing with ten racks is more embarrassing.)
- If this is a compute rack, then flip ahead to page 534, Physical Compute Rack Assembly.
- If this is the management rack, then continue with the next section, Physical Management Rack Assembly.

18.4.2   Physical Management Rack Assembly

- Unpack the core Ethernet switch for the cluster.
- Install the mounting hardware for the core switch equipment.
- Install the core switch into the management rack.
- Place labels on both ends of the power cords for the core switch.
- Route the power cords from the core switch to the rack PDUs.
- Make note of cable serial number and type, and the attachment codes for each end onto the cabling spreadsheet.
- Plug the cords in at both ends.
- Unpack the HSI switch (or switches) for the cluster.
- Install the mounting hardware for the HSI equipment.
- Install the HSI switch equipment into the management rack.
- Place labels on both ends of the power cords for the HSI switch.
- Route the power cords from the HSI switch to the rack PDUs.
- Note the cable serial number and type, and the attachment codes for each end onto the cabling spreadsheet.
- Plug the power cords in at both ends.
- Place the proper labels on the HSI switch management LAN cable.
- Route the HSI management LAN cable to the core Ethernet switch.
- Note the cable serial number and type, and the attachment codes for each end into the cabling spreadsheet.
- Plug in the cable at both ends.
- Place the proper labels on the serial console switch management LAN cable.

- Route the serial console switch LAN cable to the Ethernet switch.
- Note the cable serial number and type, and the attachment codes onto the cabling spreadsheet.
- Plug in the cable at both ends.
- Unpack and install the cluster management nodes.
- Unpack and install storage for the cluster management nodes.
- "Cable" the management nodes and storage.
- Flip ahead to Physical Rack Cleanup on page 536.

18.4.3   Physical Compute Rack Assembly

- Unpack the Ethernet switch for the data and management LANs.
- Power on the Ethernet switch and configure it via the serial port.
- Make note of the Ethernet switch configuration and passwords.
- Make note of the Ethernet switch MAC address and assigned IP address.
- Install the mounting hardware for the Ethernet switch in the rack.
- Rack the Ethernet switch in the assigned rack location.
- Unpack the HSI switch for this rack, if present.
- Power on the HSI switch and configure it via the serial port.
- Install mounting hardware for HSI switch in the rack.
- Rack the HSI switch (this operation is different for each switch and manufacturer).
- Make note of the HSI switch configuration and passwords.
- Make note of HSI switch MAC address and assigned IP address.
- Power on the serial port console switch and configure it via the serial port.
- Install the mounting hardware for the serial port console switch.
- Rack the serial port console switch, if present.
- Make note of configuration and passwords.
- Make note of switch MAC address and assigned IP address.

18.4.4   Physical Compute Rack System Installation

- Unbox the system and dispose of the packing material.
- Make note of system serial number, configuration, and all MAC addresses.
- Apply a system label to the system enclosure where it will be visible in the rack.
- Unpack the RAM and interface cards to be added, and dispose of the packing materials.
- Open the system case which may or may not require tools.
- Install extra RAM into the system using appropriate static discharge protection.
- Install the HSI interface card (Quadrics, Myrinet, and so on) into the system.
- Install any additional interface cards into the system
- Power up the system and run self-tests to check the RAM and interface installation.
- Close the system case.

- While the system is still powered up, set the IP address and the password for the management card (if present) via the serial connection.
- Make note of the management card's MAC address and IP address assignment.
- Correct any problems with added RAM or interface cards.
- Perform any firmware or BIOS upgrades that may be necessary.
- Power down the system.
- Add the mounting rails to the system (this is usually about four screws).
- Add the mounting rails for this system to the rack (this may be another four screws, and four screw "keepers" in the rack itself).
- Place the system into the mounting rails in the rack (this may be a two-person operation because of safety latches).
- Slide the system into the rack, making sure it does not bind or catch.
- Check that the rails are properly aligned and that the system is securely latched into them.
- Place the proper labels on the power cords, one at each end. The proper location of the cable labels will be determined by the type of labels used and the construction of the rack's cable management hardware.
- Go to the back of the rack and attach the cable management arm for the system (this is as many as four screws or thumbscrews) to the rack.
- Plug the power cable into the system and thread it through the cable management arm and up/down to the PDU.
- Check the power cord path for kinks, twists, or binding.
- Note the cable serial number and type, and the attachment codes for each end onto the cabling spreadsheet.
- Plug in the power cord at both ends.
- Place the proper labels on the management LAN (10/100base-TX) cable.
- Thread the management LAN cable through the cable management arm and to the Ethernet switch.
- Check the cable path for kinks, twists, or binding.
- Note the cable serial number and type, and the attachment codes for each end into the cabling spreadsheet.
- Plug the management LAN cable in at both ends.
- Place the proper labels on the data (GbE LAN or SAN) cable.
- Thread data LAN cable through cable management arm and to Ethernet (or Fibre-Channel) switch.
- Check the cable path for kinks, twists, or binding.
- Note the cable serial number and type, and the attachment codes for each end onto the cabling spreadsheet.
- Plug in the data LAN cable at both ends.
- Place the proper labels on the serial port console cable.

- Thread the serial port console cable through the cable management arm to the serial port switch.
- Note the cable serial number and type, and the attachment codes for each end onto the cabling spreadsheet.
- Plug in the cable at both ends.
- If the rack is not fully populated, return to page 534, Physical Compute Rack System Installation.
- If the rack is fully populated with the required equipment, continue on to the next section, Physical Rack Final Assembly and Checkout.

18.4.5   Physical Rack Final Assembly and Checkout

- Verify all physical connections for the rack against the cable connection spreadsheet and other documentation.
- Verify the position of all systems and equipment in the rack against documentation.
- Verify the MAC addresses and IP assignments against the system labels.
- Power on the rack and verify proper operation.
- Power on the infrastructure equipment in the rack (Ethernet, Myrinet, console management, and so forth).
- Check the status of the switches via the serial connection or the Ethernet management port with a laptop.

18.4.6   Individual System Checkout

- Verify the management port connection to the bottommost system that has not been tested (this is usually powered on even if the system is not booted).
- Power on the system via the management console or front panel switch.
- Verify hardware POST.
- Correct any issues.
- If an operating system image is present, verify that the devices and RAM are found.
- Shut down the operating system if it is running.
- Power off the hardware via the management card.
- Continue with the next section Physical Rack Cleanup if all systems in the rack are checked out.
- Return to the beginning of this section if there are more systems in this rack remaining to be checked out.

18.4.7   Physical Rack Cleanup

- Dispose of all packing material and extra manuals.
- Ensure that all systems are powered off.

- Ensure that all infrastructure equipment is powered off.
- Power off the rack.
- Carefully bundle all interrack cables and place them in a safe location inside the rack.
- Carefully "cable tie" all cables into place, ensuring that they are not kinked and that they allow the systems to slide on their rails.
- Install rack sides and doors.
- Install blank panels in the rack front for any empty spaces.
- Install a copy of the rack and cable documentation inside the rack door so that it does not block the air flow.
- Remove any feet or antitip equipment from the rack.
- Move the rack to the proper cluster installation location or prepare it for shipping.
- If all racks are configured and verified, continue with Physical Rack Positioning (next section).
- If there are more unassembled racks, return to Physical Rack Assembly on page 532 for the next physical rack.

18.4.8   Physical Rack Positioning

- Ensure that the current rack is properly placed according to the cluster floor plan.
- Check that there is proper access to the rack and that all doors can open.
- Install any antitip devices for this rack.
- Remove any necessary raised floor tiles to access cable troughs or runs.
- Connect the rack to its power receptacle.
- If there are no more racks to position, continue with the next section, Interrack Configuration.
- Continue on to the next rack using the steps just listed.

18.4.9   Interrack Configuration

- If there are no more racks to interconnect (or no interrack connections in the cluster), move on to the next section, Final Cluster Hardware Assembly and Checkout.
- Remove the rear door to the rack that must be interconnected, to access the bundled interrack cables.
- Carefully feed the interrack cables through the cable access area in the rack.
- Align the cables with the access holes in the raised floor tiles.

18.4.10   Interrack Cabling

- Using the cluster cable documentation, identify the cable serial number along with the destination rack, device, and port/connection identifier.
- Carefully route the cable to the destination rack.

- Keep the cable types segregated, if possible.
- Check cable for binding or kinking.
- If there are more interrack cables for this rack, repeat these steps once more.
- Verify the proper connection of each interrack cable for this rack against the documentation and design documents.
- If there are more racks, repeat the steps in this section for the next rack.
- Continue on to the Final Cluster Hardware Assembly and Checkout.

18.4.11   Final Cluster Hardware Assembly and Checkout

18.4.11.1   Master Rack Power-on

- Power on the management rack.
- Power on the console management switch in the management rack.
- Power on the core network switches in the management rack.
- Power on the HSI switch.
- Power on the master nodes and associated storage devices.

18.4.11.2   Compute Rack Power-on

- Power on the console management switch.
- Power on the data and management LAN switches.
- Power on each system in the rack.
- Verify that all devices in the rack powered on successfully.

18.4.11.3   Clusterwide Hardware Verification

- When all devices are successfully powered up, take a moment to watch the pretty lights and congratulate the team.
- Verify console access to all switches in the cluster.
- Correct any cabling issues with the console management switches.
- The vast majority of the cable verification must now wait for some level of operating system to be installed on the master nodes.
- It is easier to verify proper "location" of the systems and devices in the cluster's networks when it is possible to ping them. The HSI is often the last network to be verified, because it requires libraries and drivers that are usually not part of the operating system and must be loaded "on top of" the operating system software.

I presented the preceding steps as a "straw man" for further examination of dividing the cluster hardware assembly process and to allow us to predict some of the activities. The specific amount of time necessary for any cluster depends on the size of the cluster, the number of people available to construct it, and numerous other parameters. No matter how much you plan, reality will intervene. In the next section, we will take a look at some of the ways we might be able to improve the serial process by locating parallel operations and potential efficiencies.

18.5 Learning from the Example Steps

If one person is doing all the work detailed in the example process then, by definition, all the operations are serial—one after the other. This will take a very long time for even small clusters. Adding extra people to the project does not always speed up the process, however, unless you can keep the activities separate, so they do not interfere with one another, and properly sequenced so they do not hold each other up.

Basic decisions about how to do the simple assembly operations may have drastic effects on what other members of the team are able to do. For example, if you wait until after all hardware is installed in the rack to do the cabling, then the addition of any network switches in the rack may be done at any point. If you are going to rack a system, then connect it to the infrastructure, the devices must be in the rack first.

The first time you try to build a cluster with multiple people, you will find yourself tripping over your team members as you try to find a successful physical working arrangement and a logical division of labor. Let's look for some parallelism in the example process that can save some effort in that area.

18.5.1   Finding Efficiencies in Cluster Construction

Starting at the beginning of the process, we can see that there are several areas in building individual racks that may be performed independently of one another. One of these is unpacking the systems and another is the installation of RAM and interface cards. Some operations that fit this description are

- Unpacking and assembling the racks
- Unpacking the systems and optional interfaces
- Installing the options into the systems
- Performing the firmware or BIOS updates
- Installing mounting rails onto the system
- Installing mounting rails into the rack

T I P   Look for repetitive operations that are independent of one another. These are opportunities to apply multiple people to the activities at the same time.

The longest single operation in this list is the firmware or BIOS updates and configuration, because it may involve multiple system reboots. The next longest is the initial installation of

RAM and cards into the systems. Both of these steps involve one or more system reboots.

T I P   Try to minimize the number of system reboots required. A ten-minute per-system operation turns into 21 hours when there are 128 systems in the cluster.

These two steps are examples of two logically disconnected operations that may be combined into one to save time. If the system's POST is to be used to check for proper RAM and interface installation, then at least one system reboot may be saved if the firmware update is done at the same time. Even with the operations combined, however, the system and optional hardware have to be unpacked before they may be installed into the system.

The unpacking operation "feeds" the second installation and checkout step, and they are therefore dependent on each other. Additionally, the option installation and firmware update is much slower than the unpacking operation. If you have enough space for the unpacker to continue unpacking all the systems, then you don't need to worry about overrunning the system option installation or having the unpacker standing around waiting.

T I P   Look for slow operations that are fed by faster ones. They are an opportunity for multiple people or teams in parallel.

There are several different ways to arrange the tasks, but how they are arranged depens on the number of people and the space available. Let's assume we have three identical racks, three equally skilled people, and unlimited space. Three possible arrangements are the following.

1. Each person unpacks and assembles one rack. Each person unpacks the mounting rails for their rack and installs the mounting rails into the rack. When the racks are completed, one person begins unpacking systems and options, feeding the results to two system installers. When one system is assembled, the installers help each other install the system into the rack. (To avoid injury, putting a system into rails is a two-person operation. This is especially true if the system is located above shoulder height in the rack, or if the system is heavy or unwieldy.) The BIOS/firmware upgrades are deferred until all racks are completely populated, then one person does each rack. If the unpacker finishes before the rackers, he may begin doing the BIOS/firmware upgrades.

2. Each person is responsible for all installation work for their own rack. Each rack is assembled completely independently, with the exception of installing systems into the rack.

3. Divide the task into one unpacker, one installer, and one floater. Only one rack is assembled at a time. The floater unpacks the rack while the unpacker is unpacking a single system and options. The floater installs rails into the rack, then helps the unpacker or the installer with whatever tasks are available.

The best way to know how to divide the work is to have experience with the rack systems and mounting hardware that you are using. If you start to assign time values to the list of operations that are detailed in our example steps, you will find several areas that consume massive amounts of time. To produce realistic time estimates, there is no way to avoid or prevent many repetitive operations from adding up quickly.

One such activity is cable labeling. As a matter of fact, almost anything that has to do with cables will consume a disproportionate amount of time, because there can be a *lot* of cables in a cluster. (Don't even think about making your own cables unless there are few of them and you have lots of spare time on your hands.) It takes time to label cables, run cables, connect cables, and verify cables. Even with a conscious effort by the cluster designers to minimize cables, it is impossible to do.

T I P   Labeling the rack's mounting posts with the EIA unit numbers, or buying racks that already have the unit locations labeled, can speed up the racking process.

In our previous task assignments, number 3 may be the best option if there are "downstream" steps that are to operate in parallel. Once a rack is completed, it may be cabled by a separate team, if one is available. In this case, the goal is to keep feeding the cabling team completely assembled racks. In smaller cluster assembly jobs, this type of consideration is not an issue.

Even with small clusters, managing people and job assignments can be an issue, particularly in the cable-labeling area. Taking time out to generate labels and attach them to each cable slows down the racking or cabling portion of the process. Having the cables prelabeled and sorted by length and type can save a lot of time. This, of course, becomes a separate part of the process.

If each system in the cluster has five intrarack cable connections (power, HSI, management LAN, data LAN, and serial console), that is a total of 80 cables for a 16-system rack (each system is two EIA units) or 160 cables for a 32-system rack (each system is one EIA unit). If it takes five minutes to generate labels and apply them to a single cable, it would take almost seven hours to finish 80 cables and a little more than 13 hours to finish 180.

For a large system, you need to keep the rack building going as described previously, and make sure that the rack placement and integration keeps moving forward. So you could have three people per rack doing the hardware assembly, and at least two people doing the rack placement and interrack cabling.

T I P   For clusters involving a large number of cables, buy premade cables of the proper lengths and have someone label them for you ahead of time. This speeds up the racking and assembly process.

18.5.2   Parallelism in Rack Verification and Checkout

Once the racks are populated with hardware and cabled internally (intrarack cabling), it is a good idea to double-check the documentation against the actual cabling results in the rack. Because the racks are independent entities at this point, they may be verified in parallel by multiple teams. Once the verification is completed, the same team can perform the final tie-down of the cables in the rack.

T I P   When verifying cables in a single rack, two people can speed up the process: one person to verify the documentation, and one person to locate and call out the cable information. For interrack cables, two callers (one on each of two racks) and one document checker works well.

18.5.3   Parallelism in Interrack Cabling

Our example cluster not only has cables inside the racks, but because the HSI switch is located in the management rack, each compute rack has 16 HSI connections and 9 Ethernet connections that go outside the rack (interrack cabling). Although the designers placed Ethernet switches for the data and management LANs in each rack, these switches still need connections to the core switches in the management rack. The serial port console switch eliminates 16 interrack cables by plugging into the management LAN switch.

If the management LAN requires one connection and the data LAN requires eight in a single "trunk" or "channel," this is a total of nine interrack cables per compute rack in addition to the 16 HSI connections. This is a good trade-off if possible, because there are 25 interrack cables per compute rack instead of 64 (HSI, management LAN, data LAN, and serial console).

For interrack cabling, the management rack needs to be completed and placed before compute racks may be connected to it. It is a good idea to have as many compute racks placed as possible before beginning the interrack cabling. If a separate team is used for this activity, they may require that all compute racks are placed and verified before beginning. (Now is not the time to lift the floor tiles and discover that the cable troughs are full, the racks have the wrong power plugs, the power is improperly located, or the incorrect length of cables was specified.)

There is not much parallelism available in this part of the assembly process. The core switches in the management rack are only physically accessible to two or so people at a time. It is important to keep the cables from the various racks separately identifiable, if possible, so only one compute rack at a time may be connected. If there are cables between the various compute racks, they may be installed in parallel.

18.5.4   Types of Teams and Specific Skills

For small clusters, (less than 128 nodes), a single group of very dedicated people may perform the design, physical assembly, software integration, and final checkout work for a cluster. Who you have work on your cluster will depend on your budget and what kind of labor is available to you. People with available graduate students or interns tend to like to assign them to cluster projects.

For larger clusters, it is likely that specialized vendors or contractors will perform much of the physical assembly work for you. This is especially true if you have little experience with building clusters. A company that specializes in building large clusters may have several types of teams and several instances of each type of team. This allows them to schedule the teams properly between different cluster implementations to keep them busy.

T I P   In large cluster projects, plan on paying for a dedicated project manager to deal with scheduling and coordination issues.

Table 18–1 lists some common divisions of labor in a cluster project. Each stage of the implementation is handled by a specialized group of people that completes its task, hands the cluster to the next team, and moves on to the next cluster "engagement." Note that the types of teams and division of work outlined in Table 18–1 lend themselves to the cluster manufacturing process outlined in Chapter 2.

Table 18–1 Large Cluster Construction Activities, Assignments, and Locations

Activity	Team Type	Location
Hardware integration	Hardware technicians	Vendor integration center
Rack placement and integration	Hardware technicians	At cluster site
Software integration	System engineers, system managers, and technicians	At cluster site
Acceptance testing	System engineers, system managers, and application specialists	At cluster site
Project management	Experienced technical project manager	Works at all locations of the project

18.6 Physical Assembly Conclusions

A good portion of a cluster's physical complexity is the result of the many pieces that must be assembled. These pieces include systems, racks, interface cards, and cables. There is a lot of manual repetitive labor involved in physically assembling a cluster.

Communication, documentation, and project management are essential to the success of large cluster projects, and they certainly don't hurt in smaller efforts. Each stage of the construction must flow smoothly into the next. Efficient use of your resources can mean that the physical assembly of your cluster takes less time and effort than a scattered, ad hoc approach.

## CHAPTER 19

Getting Your Cluster Wired: An Example Cable-Labeling Scheme

Chapter Objectives

- Describe two classes of cables present in a cluster
- Examine a system for labeling and tracking cables and connections

The number of cables present in a cluster, and the amount of work they present to a cluster builder, is frequently underestimated. Along with so many cables comes the burden of tracking (and later debugging) the connections made by the cables. This chapter presents a prototype cable labeling and tracking approach that may be adapted to your cluster construction efforts.

Any cluster you build will have cables; it is an inevitable fact. Cables interconnecting the individual components in a cluster represent a large potential source of interesting failure modes and system management headaches. When a compute slice fails, it needs to be uncabled, repaired or replaced, and then recabled. If a cable fails, which does happen, it is necessary to locate and replace it with a minimum amount of impact to the entire cluster, which may continue running while the replacement is taking place.

How well you can manage your cables and troubleshoot the connections when something goes wrong will affect the total time-to-solution and inevitably your cluster's reliability. (This is especially important if you have contractual uptime requirements for your cluster.) This chapter discusses a potential approach to labeling and tracking the many cable connections in your cluster.

19.1 Defining the Cable Problem

How many and what type of cables are involved depends on the size and nature of your cluster. Managing cables during the construction and ongoing operation of a cluster can become a major chore if you do not have a flexible and understandable approach. It can be a total disaster if you have no approach at all. Some typical cable types found in clusters are

- Power cords or cables
- Network cables or fibers
- HSI cables
- Storage cables or fibers
- Serial console cables

Let's take a single compute slice from a hypothetical cluster as an example. The customer requirements for a cluster dictate that each compute slice has one serial port connection for console management, an HSI using Myrinet, one GbE LAN for data access, one 10/100 Mb LAN for monitoring and management data, 300 GB of local storage (two Ultra-320 SCSI enclosures with four, 73-GB disks each, two SCSI buses), and dual power supplies. These requirements yield 12 cables (or fibers) per compute slice (two power and four SCSI for the disk enclosures, two power for the compute slice with redundant power supply, serial console, management LAN, data LAN, and HSI).

Assuming that each compute slice and its disk enclosures take four EIA standard units (each EIA unit is 1.74 inches), this allows space for nine compute slices and associated storage in a standard 41U rack. This leaves 5U unused in the example compute rack. Why I decided to use only nine systems, instead of the maximum possible ten in the compute rack, will become apparent as we proceed. A picture of the example compute and management rack arrangement is shown in Figure 19–1.

19.2 Different Classes of Cabling

Using our example rack, how many of the cables must pass outside the single compute rack to the switches that are located in the management rack? With the current design, there are 108 total cables in the compute rack if you ignore external power connections to the compute rack's PDUs. There is a total of 81 cables connected to devices inside the compute rack and 27 passing outside to equipment in the management rack. Figure 19–1 shows this cabling arrangement.

As mentioned, the cabling example has 108 cables in the compute rack and at least 26 in the management rack. But all cabling is not created equal—some cables are easier to trace, install, and manage than others. Cluster cables may be broken down into two distinct groups according to whether the interconnected devices are located in the same rack. The next sections discuss the two "classes" of cables that we encounter in building a cluster.

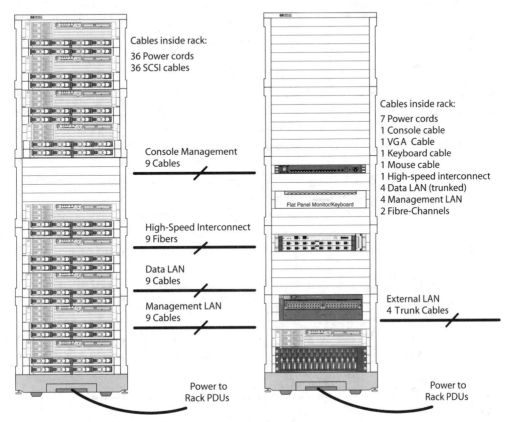

Cables inside rack:

36 Power cords
36 SCSI cables

Console Management
9 Cables

High-Speed Interconnect
9 Fibers

Data LAN
9 Cables

Management LAN
9 Cables

Flat Panel Monitor/Keyboard

Cables inside rack:

7 Power cords
1 Console cable
1 VGA Cable
1 Keyboard cable
1 Mouse cable
1 High-speed interconnect
4 Data LAN (trunked)
4 Management LAN
2 Fibre-Channels

External LAN
4 Trunk Cables

Power to
Rack PDUs

Power to
Rack PDUs

Figure 19–1 Example for cluster compute rack cabling

19.2.1 Intrarack Cables

Let's call cables that are contained inside a single rack *intrarack cables*. This class of cable connects to one device in a rack, passes through the rack's cable management system, to a second device in the same rack. Tracking the connections for intrarack cables may not be easy, but at least we do not have to lift floor tiles or sort through the contents of a cable trough to trace *this* class of cable.

19.2.2 Interrack Cables

The simplest type of cluster cable, ignoring loop-back cables, is the intrarack cable, but there is another class of cable with which all cluster designers must deal. These cables will pass through the cable management system in one rack, out through an access area in the rack, through an access hole in a floor tile, through a cable trough under the raised floor, up through another floor tile, up into the second rack, through the cable management system in the second rack, and finally attach to the second device. Cables that pass between two or more racks are called *inter-*

rack cables. (There are specialized SCSI cables, called *Y-cables* that may connect to three devices. The cable has a single SCSI connector on one end and splits into two separate cable ends and connectors on the other.)

19.3 A First Pass at a Cable-Labeling Scheme

Table 19–1 details the type, class, and number of each cable connection in our example cluster. We would like any cable labeling or identification scheme to enable us to find the correct connection in both racks, without physically following the cable for its entire length. A method that we select should handle both inter- and intrarack cables equally and should minimize the chance of getting the wrong cable.

The first thing we need is a unique way of identifying and locating the end connections for a given cable. To make the information unique within the cluster, the individual racks in the cluster must be individually identified, followed by the piece of equipment, and finally the type and number of the connection. Remember that some equipment will have multiple connections of the same type, like redundant power supply power cords on network switches and compute slices.

Uniquely numbering the racks in your cluster is not a difficult thing. Once the unique rack numbers are chosen (starting from 00 or 01, depending on whether you are a programmer or not), we need a way of uniquely identifying individual devices in the rack. One way to do this is to select the starting EIA Unit for the device in question. Let's start our numbering at the bottom of the rack from 00 and go upward. Most racks have between 41U and 49U as a maximum

Table 19–1 Example Compute Rack Cabling

Each Compute Rack Item	Type of Cables	Class of Connection	Cluster Total
Redundant power for compute slice	Two power	Intrarack	18
Disk storage unit	Two SCSI and one power each	Intrarack	54
Management LAN	One category 5e cable	Interrack	9
Data LAN	One category 5e cable	Interrack	9
Myrinet HSI	One fiber-optic cable	Interrack	9
Console	One serial	Interrack	9
Per-compute slice connections	Compute slice connections	Intra-/Interrack	108

height, The tallest rack you can use will probably be set by the height of your computer room ceiling and local fire or earthquake codes.

T I P   When numbering items with your cable-labeling system, remember that you may want to be able to use spreadsheets and other text-processing tools to sort the items. Because of the differing column widths for rack 1 and rack 999, you may want to use leading zeros in your numbers to keep the columns of equal width. This can make your documentation neater looking.

So with a rack number between 00 and 99, and locations within the rack between 00 and 41, you can uniquely select a rack and the starting location of a device. For the next portion of the connection identifier, start at the top left and number identical connection types from top to bottom, left to right. You may also need to account for connections either to the front or to the back of a given device (some systems, instead of having keyboard and mouse connections on the back, have USB connections on the front of the system) or special connections like PDUs that run from front to back in the rack.

Let's take all of this information into account, and use the example configuration of devices shown in Figure 19–2. If the management rack is 00 and the compute rack is 01, then an example connection point identifier for the second power connection on the third system in the first compute rack is: `rack01-sys02-pwr01`. You may wish to designate two- or three-letter codes for the various types of connections on the devices to save extra typing and space in the documentation. Remember that the cost of shortening the type field in this way is a mental translation or a lookup in a table of values, so try to make them mnemonic.

Now, if you think about the other end of the example power cable's connection, you will discover a potential flaw in the system: Some devices, like PDUs are not mounted in the "regular" portion of the rack. (There are other exceptions with which you may have to deal. Most racks have kits that allow you to bolt them together into a single unit, called *baying* kits. If you are going to do this, you should think about the ramifications to whatever documentation process you have chosen.) This may be dealt with as an exception to the use-the-EIA-unit-as-a-device-label approach. You may have to try different schemes to find one that works for your equipment and preferences. The important characteristic is clarity.

Whatever numbering scheme you choose, whether zero based or one based, be consistent throughout the cluster documentation. Be sure to note any exceptions, like PDUs that do not fit the rest of the scheme prominently. Make sure you keep the exceptions to a minimum. Someone else will have to read and use the documents.

19.4 Refining the Cable Documentation Scheme

Being able to identify the connection points uniquely for a cable is very useful, but it is only part of what we need to manage the cables in a cluster successfully. We also need to choose a way to

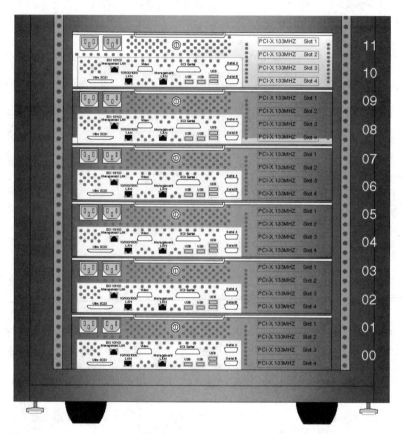

Figure 19–2 Rack close-up for example device connection identifiers

label the cables themselves, and to ensure that we have the correct cable, even when it spans multiple racks. So let's build on our connection ID approach in the next sections.

19.4.1   Labeling Cable Ends

Now that we have determined a scheme for identifying the end points of a cable, we need to choose a method of labeling the cables themselves. Just looking at a bundle of cables, trying to tell which one is which doesn't work very well, even if the cables are neatly done. (A well-constructed and maintained cluster should not have cabling that looks as if it were done by a rat on LSD.) A visible label affixed to the cable is a big help in verifying that you have the correct connection and cable *before* you unplug the server's SAN connection instead of the 1000base-FX GbE line on which you are working.

A logical approach to putting labels on cables is to place the target connection point identifier on each end of the cable. For example, using the previous information, you might label the power cable `rack01-sys02-pwr01` on the end connected to the system, and `rack01-pdu02-pwr05` on the end connected to the PDU itself. This way you know where the cable is *supposed* to be connected on each end. As long as you don't have to move the cable, or change the connection, you will not have to relabel the cable.

This approach may work okay for intrarack cables, but what happens when the cable is an interrack cable? You might have an Ethernet cable labeled `rack01-sys02-gbe01` in one rack, and at the other end, in another rack, is the label `rack09-swtch16-gbe24`. How do you match the first label to the second to make sure that you have the correct cable, without tracing the entire length of cable? With the connection-ID-on-the-ends scheme, there really is no way to identify the *specific cable* on which you are working, or to ensure that you have the correct one in both racks by examining the connection point IDs. This is a recipe for mistakes and cluster downtime.

A better approach is to "serialize" the individual cables. That is, assign a unique serial number to the cable, based on its type. By locating the connection point ID in one rack, matching it to the cable's serial number and to the connection point ID in the other rack, you are absolutely sure you have the correct cable in *both* racks. This approach also does not require you to relabel the cable when the connections change—just update the documentation.

19.4.2 Tracking and Documenting the Connections

Using the connection identifiers to describe the cable end points and a cable serial number for the connection, based on type, makes it possible to track cables between racks quickly. This approach is shown in Figure 19–3. An example table for documentation is shown in Table 19–2.

The examples in Table 19–2 show a number of different connection types and connection point IDs: GbE, power, high-speed Myrinet interconnect, and an entry for a SCSI Y-cable with one "left" end and two "right" ends. (Left and right will depend on how you are standing in relationship to the cluster. Take this into account.) How creative you get with the serial numbers and connection point IDs will depend on how much label space you have, among other things. The

Table 19–2 Example Cable Documentation

Left Connection Point ID	Cable Serial Number	Right Connection Point ID
`rack01-sys02-gbe01`	`ngbe-cat06-40ft-00001`	`rack00-msw01-gbe0121`
`rack03-sys16-pwr01`	`powr-c13xx-002m-00341`	`rack03-pdu04-pwr0015`
`rack81-sys32-hsi01`	`myri-fibxx-020m-00128`	`rack00-hsw01-myr0122`
`rack01-sys02-scs01`	`scsi-ycabl-010m-00015`	`rack00-arr01-scs0002`
		`rack00-arr02-scs0002`

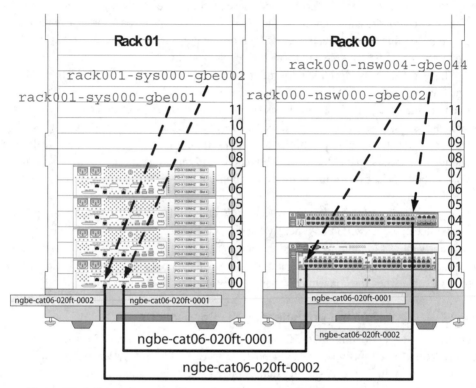

Figure 19–3 Example connection point IDs and serialized cables

important thing is picking a system. sticking to it consistently, and always keeping the documentation up-to-date.

A spreadsheet with the cable information may be made more readable with the addition of colors for the various cable types. The color may substitute for characters in the serial number or connection point IDs. (You may need to be sensitive to system managers or other personnel who are color blind when you consider using color in the documentation and cable labels. Don't rely on color to encode too much information.)

19.5 Calculating the Work in Cable Installation

Given the cable-labeling system in this chapter, just how much work should we expect to invest in both inter- and intrarack cabling? A rough estimate of the total number of cables in our example cluster, with one compute rack and one master rack, is 134, not counting any rack power connections.

Of those cables, a total of 36 are interrack, leaving 98 intrarack connections in the compute rack and the master rack. See Interrack Configuration on page 537 for information on specific assembly activities involved in interrack cabling and configuration.

Table 19–3 Example Cabling Tasks and Time Estimates: First Design

Task Description	Estimated Time, min	Number of Tasks	Total Time, min
Serialize cables	5 [a]	134	670
Make intrarack connection	5	98	490
Verify/document intrarack connection	2	98	196
Make interrack connection	15	36	540
Verify/document interrack connection	2	36	72
Verify entire compute rack	2	134	268
Total time			2236

a.   Assuming that the labels are already made and there are two labels per cable.

Interrack cabling is more than just another class of cables, it is an extra source of work in the cluster assembly and checkout phases. Because this type of cabling must be run under the computer room floor, every interrack cable adds substantial time to the process of getting the cluster up and running. There are two rack cable management systems to negotiate for each cable, along with the under-the-floor situation.

The time values for the intrarack cabling assume negotiation of the rack's cable management system along with making the actual connection. The information in Table 19–3 details some estimated times based on our example cluster in Figure 19–1. The interrack time values include time for negotiating the cable management systems in two racks as well as installing the cable under the raised flooring. Your actual times will vary depending on the distance between racks, the state of your cable troughs, and other physical constraints.

19.6 Minimizing Interrack Cabling

In the example compute rack pictured in Figure 19–1, part of the rack was left unfilled, even though we could have racked another compute slice and associated storage devices. Let's revisit that decision. It was made in the hope that we could minimize the interrack cabling.

One way of minimizing interrack cabling is to convert as many interrack cables into intrarack cables as is possible. You can do this by adding extra switch hardware to each rack. The systems in the rack connect to the local switch, and that switch uses network "trunking" or link aggregation to attach to the core switch.

Care must be taken to ensure that the performance requirements of the various networks are still met with this approach. For management LANs, the bandwidth requirements are not critical, it is possible to replace 18 interrack connections with two by the addition of a serial port switch and a 10/100baseT switch in the compute rack. This design is shown in Figure 19–4.

Keeping the data network and HSI at full bandwidth is more difficult. In most cases, the HSI switches are too expensive to replicate, and the additional latency added by a layer of switches may become a performance problem. Likewise, if the data LAN is required to run "full tilt" without bottlenecks, the cluster designer must pay close attention to the backplane (gigabits per second) rating of the switches and their trunking capability. It may be necessary to replicate the switch to keep it from becoming a bottleneck to the bandwidth.

The second design example, in Figure 19–4, shows the changes resulting from the addition of the extra "edge" switches in the compute rack. Table 19–4 shows adjustments to the task time estimates based on the changes in the design. The overall cabling time for the two racks

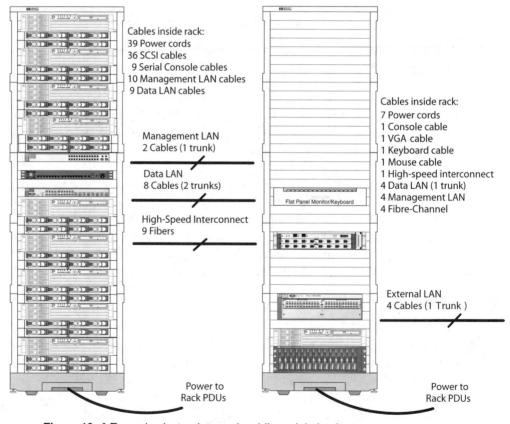

Figure 19–4 Example cluster, interrack cabling minimized

Table 19–4 Example Cabling Tasks and Time Estimates: Second Design

Task Description	Estimated Time, min	Number of Tasks	Total Time, min
Serialize cables	5 [a]	150	750
Make intrarack connection	5	127	635
Verify/document intrarack connection	2	127	254
Make interrack connection	15	19	285
Verify/document interrack connection	2	19	38
Verify entire compute rack	2	150	300
Total time			2262

a.   Assuming that the labels are already made and there are two labels per cable.

increased by approximately 30 minutes. The hardware changes also increase the amount of switch configuration time necessary during the next phase of the installation.

The reduction of interrack cables may not seem worth the effort in our example cluster. Consider, however, a cluster comprising four compute racks and a single management rack. Reducing the number of interrack cables from 144 to 76 not only saves labor installing interrack cables, it saves ports on the core switches for the management and data LANs, and reduces the under-the-floor time installing the cluster's cables.

Because of the increased hardware cost for the extra switches, whether the economy is really there will depend on the extra cost versus your labor rates and expected reduction in complexity, reduction in the interrack cabling tasks, and potential increases in overall cluster reliability. The increased troubleshooting efficiency and decreased time-to-solution also need consideration.

TIP   In addition to labeling the cables, it is useful to have a labeling scheme for the hardware units in the cluster, including things like configuration, MAC addresses, purchase date, purchase order number, and other useful facts. Bar-coded labeling is another innovation that could be worth its weight in gold. Imagine being assigned to take physical inventory of the cluster hardware for your asset management group.

19.7 Cable Labeling System Summary

This chapter presented a prototype cable labeling and documentation scheme for an example (very small) cluster. Along with identifying two classes of cables present in a cluster, variations of the connection point identifier and cable serialization recommendations are proved in real-world clusters. This approach may be adapted to your own design and implementation efforts. Any choice of cable documentation system should be carefully evaluated to ensure that it "scales" to whatever size cluster you are designing or building.

## CHAPTER 20

Physical Constraints: Heat, Space, and Power

Chapter Objectives

- Identify the physical constraints for cluster design
- Show simple examples of power ratings and calculations
- Discuss heat generation and removal
- Provide floor layouts for example clusters

An example is presented of a real-world design situation with space, power, and cooling for a medium-size cluster.

20.1 Identifying Physical Constraints for Your Cluster

Any cluster has to have a home, a place to exist during its useful lifetime. Ensuring that the cluster design process takes physical constraints into account is an important detail. It would do no good to build a cluster that cannot function properly in its intended location. This chapter identifies the physical constraints placed on clusters by budget and location, and shows a simple example dealing with heat, space, and power requirements.

The cluster design and physical parameters used here are from a proposed design for use in the facilities at the company where I work. The building space, cooling, and power figures were all taken from the plans for the computer room in our facility. The design parameters are

- 188,000 BTUs (18 tons at 87% efficiency) of cooling installed, and another 188,000 BTUs available
- Two 220-V three-phase, 100-Amp circuits for power distribution
- A lab that is 38 feet by 24 feet, with 874 square feet of space available

Figure 20–1 Cluster hardware used for example calculations

The facility was "built out" with cluster equipment in mind, so there was additional cooling available and, we hope, adequate power.   We will examine each of the design considerations in the upcoming sections.   The front view of the example cluster equipment is shown in Figure 20–1.

20.2 Space, the Initial Frontier

Perhaps the easiest constraint to satisfy appears to be the required square footage and placement for the equipment racks in your facility. There either is enough space or there isn't. This is easy, right?

In actuality, there are a number of considerations about the placement of racks, and the larger the cluster, the more important and difficult they become. These details include planning for proper airflow, access to the racks and equipment, and requirements that may be dictated by local building codes, such as maximum height with respect to the ceiling or aisle widths. Before you place rows of racks too close to obstacles, think about access to the front and rear of the racks and the ability to place service equipment, like "crash carts," close to the system on which you are working. It is also important to be aware of your local building codes.

For a large number of racks, a standard practice is to create "cold aisles" and "hot aisles" to aid delivery of cooling to the equipment. This is done by placing the front of the rack rows (air intake) facing each other with perforated floor tiles in front of the racks. Cold air is forced out from under the raised floor, through the perforated tiles, into the cold aisle and is allowed to flow into the equipment in the racks.

The fans in the equipment racks draw the cool air into the equipment and exhaust it out the back, into the hot aisle. The air rises to the ceiling and is removed by the cooling system. There must be enough space available to place the racks in this arrangement, and proper placement of perforated tiles and racks can be important.

We examine the cooling situation a little closer in a future section. It takes specialized expertise to properly design a large-scale cooling approach. Although there are simulation programs that can help in this task, it is better to seek professional help for large, complex cases. We now return to placing the example installation's racks.

The example rack placement for our five-rack cluster is shown in Figure 20–2. In this particular case, the racks will be placed against a wall, with the hot-air exhaust (backs of the rack) toward the wall. Note the clearance for the rear door in the diagram. What is not shown is the requirement for space in front of the rack for stabilization plates, and for the equipment's slide rails to extend out the front of the rack.

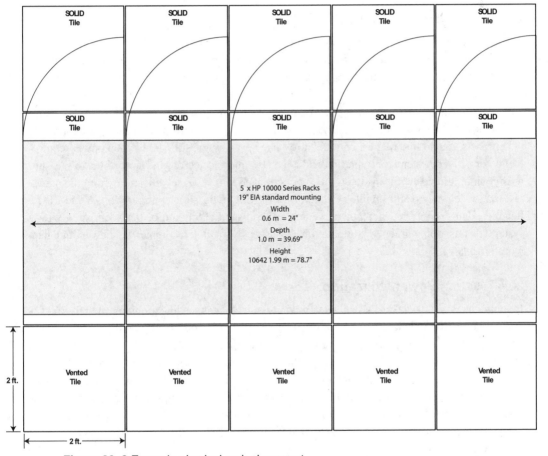

Figure 20–2 Example physical rack placement

Although the space considerations are not overly complex for our example installation, be sure not to underestimate the needs for your installation. Front and back clearance for the racks, and placement to help cooling are all important. The power receptacles, of course, also must be within reach of the racks.

The cluster takes five standard (each tile is two feet square) floor tiles by four tiles, for a total of 96 square feet. This area does not count any spacing between the racks and adjacent racks, which might require another row of tiles on either side, or another 32 square feet.

While we are on the subject of space, let's touch on height for a minute. Any preassembled racks are going to need to fit through doors, hallways, and possibly freight elevators (if the computer room is on the second floor). You do *not* want to be confronted with disassembling your nicely built cluster racks to make them fit through a constricted space on the way to their final home. (I am reminded of a tape subsystem error from the Apollo Computer DOMAIN/OS software which read, "Unit does not fit through 36-inch hatch," that was jokingly added to the message catalog in reference to attempting to install a tape unit on board a ship.)

20.3 Power-Up Requirements

It is important to ensure that your power infrastructure can support the additional equipment you will be adding. Any calculations you do should be checked by a professional electrician and you should check that any work that requires a licensed professional is done by one. To do otherwise is risky business.

To determine the total power used by the racks of equipment, you must turn to the manufacturer's specifications. Unfortunately, there may be a lack of information that you require, or the numbers you do find may be contradictory. The best way to estimate the total power requirements for a given system configuration (RAM, disks, interface cards, and so forth) is to measure it. If you don't have the means to do this, you will need to rely on specifications from the manufacturer, which may be for an idle system, or for maximum possible configurations. (The CPU's floating-point processor, when active, generates a substantial amount of heat compared with a system that is doing integer computations. It is easy to underestimate the power and heat requirements.)

20.4 System Power Utilization

If you go to Hewlett-Packard's Web site and find the technical specifications for the DL-360 G3 system, you will immediately see a number like 325 W per system. Until you dig a little deeper, you will have no idea what configuration this number represents. Make sure that you understand what the number represents before you use it in your calculations.

Searching most major manufacturers' Web sites will lead you to a power calculation tool that allows picking a system configuration and generating a power figure for it. This is the next-best way to generate a power utilization number without actually measuring it. For our cluster's compute slice configuration, I came up with 445 W. The power utilizations for the other devices are shown in Table 20–1.

Table 20–1 Device Wattage Ratings for Example Cluster Configuration

Device Description	Number in Cluster	Watts per Device	Total Watts
HP DL-360 G3, Dual 3.2-GHz Pentium Xeon CPU, 2 GB RAM	128	445	56,960
HP DL-380 NFS Server, Dual 3.2-GHz Pentium Xeon CPU, 6 GB RAM, dual power supply	1	800	800
HP StorageWorks 4454R storage enclosure	3	754	2,262
HP Procurve 2848 switch	8	100	800
HP Procurve 2650 switch	4	100	400
Cyclades TS2000 serial port switch	4	37	148
Integrated keyboard/video/mouse	1	50	50

These numbers are still estimates, so it is important to design with a safety margin that is adequate to protect from underestimates. The total wattage for the cluster's active devices is estimated at 62,040 W. To convert this to kilowatts, which is a common way of expressing power (a lot of the calculations we will do are expressed in kilowatts instead of Watts), we use the following equation:

$$kW = \frac{W}{1,000} = \frac{62,040\ W}{1,000} = 62.04\ kW$$

Our next job is to calculate the available power, given the two 100-Amp, 220-V, three-phase service entrances in our target facility. Some very useful conversion factors may be found on the Web site at http://www.abrconsulting.com/conversions/elec-con.htm. Let's calculate the available kilowatts using the following conversion:

$$kW = \frac{Volts\ x\ Amps\ x\ PF\ x\ 1.73}{1,000} = \frac{220\ x\ 200\ x\ 0.85\ x\ 1.73}{1,000} = 64.70\ kW$$

where the PF in the equations stands for the power factor, which measures the efficiency of power conversion by the equipment. This value is very rarely specified by the manufacturer, so the value of 0.85 is an estimate used in the examples on the previously mentioned Web site.

As you can see from the calculations, our power requirements are within 2 kW of the available power distribution. This is possibly too close for comfort. It would be best to consult with the local electrician.

20.5 Taking the Heat

Power flows into the computer room in the form of electrical energy and is supplied to the cluster's equipment, which converts it to heat in the process of doing work. To prevent the buildup of heat in the computer room, which can lead to equipment overheating and failure, the cooling system must have the appropriate capacity to remove the excess heat. A simple model of a computer room, with heat, power, and airflow is shown in Figure 20–3.

The example in Figure 20–3 shows an uninterruptable power supply (UPS) providing power to the cooling system and two racks of equipment. The racks are arranged to pull cold air from the cold aisles through the rack and exhaust it into the hot aisle. The hot air rises to the ceiling, where it is pulled through the cooling unit.

The cool air is pulled through the cooling units and is forced under the raised floor. (Notice that there is a pressure drop across the length of the under-the-floor duct. There is also flow constriction because of cable troughs and PDUs that block airflow under the floor.) The

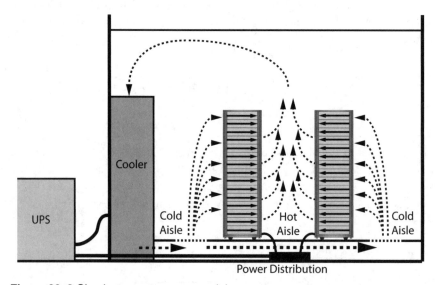

Figure 20–3 Simple computer room model

cool air is then fed to perforated tiles that supply air to the racks. The racks are fed power, which gets converted into heat. The equipment is rated in terms of Watts. We can also convert the power usage into British thermal units (or BTUs[1]) with the following equation:

$$\text{BTUs} = \text{kW} \times 3{,}413 = 62.04 \times 3{,}413 = 211{,}743 \text{ BTUs}$$

The conversion factor, 3,413 is obtained by dividing the number of joules in a kilowatt (1 kW is equal to 3.6×10^6 joules) by the number of joules per BTU. Oops, as you can see from the numbers, it looks like we have exceeded the 188,000-BTU capacity available from our single, existing cooling unit. We need to have the second one installed to cope with the extra 23,743 BTUs. Good thing we did the calculations before we put in the equipment!

Whenever you see the term *tons* used in reference to cooling capacity, it refers to a *refrigeration ton*. A refrigeration ton[2] is defined as

$$1 \text{ Refrigeration Ton} = 2{,}000 \text{ lb} \times \frac{144 \text{ BTUs}}{1 \text{ lb} \times 24 \text{ hour}} = 12{,}000 \text{ BTUs}/\text{Hour}$$

Notice that this is in terms of units of work over time. Also notice that it takes 144 BTU to raise one pound of water one degree. Our existing 18 tons of capacity yields 216,000 BTU/hour. Assuming 87% efficiency (based on temperature differences and other factors) yields the documented 188,000 BTU in the plans for our facility.

Another useful conversion is

$$1 \text{ Refrigeration Ton} = 4.72 \text{ Horsepower} = 3{,}516 \text{ W}$$

---

1. A unit of energy, equivalent to the heat required to raise one pound of water by one degree Farenheit, from 58.5 degrees F. to 59.5 degrees F. A BTU is equal to 1054.4 joules. The metric equivalent, a thermodynamic calorie, is the amount of energy required to raise the temperature of one gram of water from 14.5 degrees Celsius to 15.5 degrees Celsius. This is equal to 4.184 joules.

2. The amount of heat required to melt one ton of ice at 32 degrees farenheit in a 24-hour period. Can you guess that this is a hold-over from the days when ice was the only cooling source?

Table 20–2 Device BTU Ratings for Example Cluster Configuration

Device Description	Number in Cluster	BTUs per Device	Total BTUs
HP DL-360 G3, Dual 3.2-GHz Pentium Xeon CPU, 2 GB RAM	128	1,519	194,432
HP DL-380 NFS Server, Dual 3.2-GHz Pentium Xeon CPU, 6 GB RAM, dual power supply	1	1,475	1,475
HP StorageWorks 4454R storage enclosure	3	1,232	3,696
HP Procurve 2848 switch	8	341	2,728
HP Procurve 2650 switch	4	341	1,464
Cyclades TS2000 serial port switch	4	126	504
Integrated keyboard/video/mouse	1	170	170

This equation allows us to convert between refrigeration tons, Watts, and horsepower, and when coupled with the previous equation, allows us to convert to and from BTUs as well.

As a check, let's take a look at the manufacturer's specifications for the equipment BTU ratings. Note that the BTU rating for most equipment is really expressed as BTUs per hour, although they are rarely labeled that way. Table 20–2 lists the BTU ratings for our example equipment.

The total BTUs, based on the manufacturer's information, is 204,469. Notice this number is close to that obtained from the wattage ratings, with the difference being 7,224 BTUs (2.12 kW). This discrepancy is very close to the difference between the predicted wattage and the available power, so it bears further investigation. This type of discrepancy is not unusual when using manufacturer's figures for BTUs and Watts. It does serve as a check on our previous calculations.

20.6 Physical Constraints Summary

As a final note, each compute rack weighs 1,479 pounds and the management rack weighs 517 pounds. It is important that your raised floor is strong enough to support the cluster's racks. The weights are also important if you are going to ship the cluster racks.

Ensuring that your cluster's expected home meets its requirements is important. Designing for the proper power, cooling, and space to support your cluster will not only help during the eventual operation of the cluster, but can help eliminate implementation delays. This chapter covers only the very basic approach to designing your cluster's new home; you should consult with experienced professionals when you have further questions.

Acronym List

ACL	Access control list
AFS	Andrew file system
AGP	Accelerated graphics port
AMD	Advanced Micro Devices
API	Application program interface
ARP	Address Resolution Protocol
ARPA	Advanced Projects Research Agency
ASCII	American standard code for information interchange
ASIC	Application-specific integrated circuit
ATA	Advanced technology attach
AutoFS	Automounted file system
BIND	Berkeley internet name daemon
BIOS	Basic input output subsystem
BOOTP	Internet Bootstrap Protocol
BSD	Berkeley Software Design, Inc.
BTU	British thermal unit
ccNUMA	Cache-coherent nonuniform memory access
CDMA/CD	Carrier detect multiple access with collision detect
CDSL	Context-dependent symbolic link
CIDR	Classless internet domain routing
CPAN	Comprehensive Perl archive network
CPU	Central processing unit
COTS	Commercial off-the shelf
2D	Two-dimensional

3D	Three-dimensional
DCE	Distributed computing environment
DHCP	Dynamic Host Configuration Protocol
DIMM	Dual in-line memory module
DDR	Double data rate
DMA	Direct memory access
DNS	Domain name system
DSA	Digital signature algorithm
DVI	Digital visual interface
ECC	Error check and correct
EFI	Extensible firmware interface
EIA	Electrical Institute of America
EMSL	Environmental Molecular Science Laboratory
EPIC	Explicitly parallel instruction-set computing
EPROM	Electrically programmable read-only memory
ES	Enterprise server
EVMS	Enterprise volume management system
FAQ	Frequently asked questions
FAT	File allocation table
FEC	Forward error correction
FLOP	Floating-point operation
FNN	Flat network neighborhood
FPP	Floating-point processor
FSB	Front-side bus
FSF	Free Software Foundation
GARP	General Attribute Registration Protocol
GbE	Gigabit Ethernet
GFLOP	Giga-floating-point operation
GFS	Global file system
GID	Group identifier
GUI	Graphical User Interface
GNBD	GFS network block device
GNU	GNU is not UNIX
GPL	GNU public license
HPC	High-performance computing
HSI	High-speed interconnect
HTML	Hypertext markup language
IA	Instruction architecture
IC	Integrated circuit

IDE	Integrated drive electronics
IEEE	Institute of Electrical and Electronic Engineers
iLO	Integrated lights-out
ILP	Integer, long, pointer
I/O	Input/output
IP	Internet Protocol
IPoIB	IP over Infiniband
IRC	Internet relay chat
IPv4	Internet Protocol version 4
IPv6	Internet Protocol version 6
iSCSI	Internet SCSI
ISO	International Standards Organization
ISP	Internet service provider
ISV	Independent software vendor
IT	Information technology
JVM	Java virtual machine
kDAPL	Kernel direct-access programming library
KDC	Key distribution center
KVM	Keyboard, video, mouse
LAM	Local area multicomputer
LAN	Local area network
LDAP	Lightweight Directory Access Protocol
LP	Long, pointer
LSF	Load sharing facility
LTSP	Linux terminal server project
LUN	Logical unit
LVM	Logical volume manager
LVS	Linux virtual server
MAC	Media access control
MBR	Master boot record
MDS	Meta-data server
MII	Media independent interface
MIT	Massachusetts Institute of Technology
MPI	Message-passing interface
MPICH	MPI chameleon
NAS	Network attached storage
NAT	Network address translation
NFS	Network file system
NFSD	Network file system daemon

NIC	Network interface card
NIS	Network information service
NPACI	National Partnership for Advanced Computing Infrastructure
NTP	Network time protocol
NVRAM	Non-volatile RAM
OCFS	Oracle cluster file system
OSCAR	Open-source cluster application resource
OSF	Open Software Foundation
OSI	Open systems interconnect
OSS	Object storage server
OST	Object storage target
OSSD	Open-source software development
OUI	Organizationally unique identifier
PAM	Pluggable authentication module
PBS	Portable batch system
PC	Personal computer
PCI	Peripheral component interconnect
PCI-X	Peripheral component interconnect extended
PDF	Portable document format
PDSH	Parallel distributed shell
PDU	Power distribution unit
PHP	Hypertext preprocessor
PID	Process identifier
PNNL	Pacific Northwest National Laboratory
POST	Power-on self test
PVFS	Parallel virtual file system
PVM	Parallel virtual machine
PXE	Preexecution environment
RAC	Real application cluster
RAID	Redundant array of (independent) inexpensive disks
RAM	Random access memory
RCS	Revision control system
RDMA	Remote direct memory access
RFC	Request for comment
RHEL	Red Hat enterprise Linux
RMON	Remote monitoring
RMS	Resource management service
ROM	Read-only memory
RPC	Remote procedure call

RRD	Round-robin database
RSA	Rivest, Shamir, Adelman
RSH	Remote shell
SAN	Storage area network
SCI	Scalable coherent interconnect
SCSI	Small computer system interconnect
SDP	Socket Direct Protocol
SDRAM	Synchronous dynamic random access memory
SETI	Search for extraterrestrial intelligence
SGE	Sun Grid Engine
SGID	Set group identifier
SIS	System installer suite
SLURM	Simple Linux utility for resource management
SMART	Self-monitoring, analysis and reporting technology
SMB	Server message block
SMP	Symmetric Multiprocessor
SPEC	Standard Performance Evaluation Corporation
SPOF	Single point of failure
SRP	SCSI RDMA Protocol
SSH	Secure shell
SSI	Single system image
SSL	Secure socket layer
SSS	Secure start shell
3TCS	Three-tier client–server
STP	Spanning Tree Protocol
TCP	Transmission Control Protocol
TCP/IP	Transmission Control Protocol/Internet Protocol
TFTP	Trivial file transfer protocol
TGT	Ticket-granting ticket
TTL	Time to live
uDAPL	User direct-access programming library
UDP	User datagram protocol
UID	User identifier
UP	Uniprocessor
UPS	Uninterruptable power supply
URL	Universal resource locator
USB	Universal serial bus
UTC	Universal coordinated time
UUID	Universal unique identifier

VGA	Video graphics array
VLAN	Virtual local area network
VNIC	Virtual network interface card
WAN	Wide area network
WS	Workstation
XML	Extensible mark-up language

List of URLs and Software Sources

B.1   Cluster Construction Tool Kits

Itanium OSCAR
> http://sponge.ncsa.uiuc.edu/oscar-gold

Linux Terminal Server Project
> http://ltsp.org

NPACI Rocks Cluster Builder
> http://www.rocksclusters.org

OpenMOSIX
> http://openmosix.sourceforge.net

OSCAR Cluster Builder
> http://oscar.openclustergroup.org

Single System Image
> http://openssi.org

B.2   Cluster Design Tools

Microsoft Visio Stencils for Hewlett-Packard Equipment
> http://www.visio-cafe.com

Netzoom Visio Stencils
> http://www.netzoomstencils.com

B.3   Conversion Factors

Electrical and Heat Conversion

```
http://www.abrconsulting.com/conversions/elec-con.htm
```

B.4   File Systems and Volume Management

Cluster NFS

```
http://clusternfs.sourceforge.net
```

The Device File System

```
http://www.atnf.csiro.au/people/rgooch/linux/docs/
    devfs.html
```

Enterprise Volume Management Service

```
http://evms.sourceforge.net
```

File System Performance

```
http://www.iozone.org
```

Intermezzo File System

```
http://www.inter-mezzo.org
```

Lustre File System

```
http://www.lustre.org
```

OpenGFS

```
http://opengfs.sourceforge.net/docs.php
```

PolyServe Matrix File System

```
http://www.polyserve.com
```

PVFS Version 1

```
http://www.parl.clemson.edu/pvfs
```

PVFS Version 2

```
http://www.pvfs.org/pvfs2
```

Sistina (Red Hat) GFS

```
http://www.sistina.com
```

B.5   General Linux Software

Itanium Linux Software

```
http://www.gelato.org/software/index.php
```

Linux Documentation Project

`http://www.tldp.org/howto`

Linux Software

`http://freshmeat.org`

Perl Tk Toolkit

`http://pww.perltk.org/binaries/index.htm`

RPM Package Repository

`http://rpmfind.net`

RPM Package Repository

`http://freshrpms.net`

UDP Multicast Tool

`http://udpcast.linux.lu`

B.6 Grid Tool Kits and Software

Grid Example for Physics

`http://www.ivdgl.org/grid2003/`

Grid Software Toolkit

`http://www.globustoolkit.org`

B.7 Hardware Vendors

Cyclades Serial Port Switch

`http://www.cyclades.com`

Hewlett-Packard

`http://www.hp.com`

Opteron Processor Data

`http://www.amd.com`

B.8 High-Availability Software

Fake IP Takeover Package

`http://www.vergenet.net/linux/fake`

Linux High Availability

`http://linux-ha.org`

Linux HA and Load Balancing

http://www.ultramonkey.org

Linux Virtual Server

http://www.linuxvirtualserver.org

B.9   High-Performance Graphics

Nvidia Quatro FX Graphics

http://www.nvidia.com/page/quadrofx.html

Panoram Display Technology

http://www.panoramtech.com

Parallel Display Software

http://www.modviz.com

B.10   HSI Technologies

Dolphin HSI Networking

http://www.dolphinics.com

Linux Infiniband Project

http://sourceforge.net/projects/infiniband

Mellanox Infiniband Switches

http://www.mellanox.com

Myrinet HSI Networking

http://www.myricom.com

Quadrics HSI Networking

http://www.quadrics.com

B.11   Java Software for Linux

Cryptix Java Security

http://www.cryptix.org

Java SDK and JRE for Linux

http://java.sun.com

Java SDK and JRE for Linux

http://www.blackdown.org

B.12 Linux Distributions and Open-Source License Examples

Free Software Philosophy

http://www.fsf.org/philosophy/free-sw.html

Debian BSD License

http://www.debian.org/misc/bsd.license

Debian Linux

http://www.debian.org/intro/about

GNU Public License

http://www.fsf.org/licenses/licenses.html

Linux Distribution List

http://www.linux.org

Linux Distribution List

http://www.distrowatch.com

NWLinux

http://www.mscf.emsl.pnl.gov

Perl Artistic License

http://language.perl.com/misc/artistic.html

Red Hat Fedora Linux

http://fedora.redhat.com

Red Hat Linux

http://www.redhat.com

SUSE Linux

http://www.redhat.com

B.13 Monitoring and Event Generation Software and Dependencies

Ganglia Add-ons

http://ganglia.sourceforge.net/gmetric

Ganglia Monitoring Tool

http://ganglia.sourceforge.net

gd Library

http://www.boutell.com/gd

Nagios Extras

http://www.nagios.org/download/extras.php

Nagios Monitoring Tool

http://nagios.org

Nagios Plugins

http://nagiosplug.sourceforge.net

Round-Robin Database

http://people.ee.ethz.ch/~oetiker/webtools/rrdtool

SWATCH Log Monitor

http://swatch.sourceforge.net

SMART Monitor Tool

http://smartmontools.sourceforge.net/

WOTS Log Monitor

http://www.vcpc.univie.ac.at/~tc/tools/

B.14 Networking Software, Hardware, and Examples

Flat Network Neighborhood

http://aggregate.ee.engr.uky.edu/techpub/
als2000

Network Address Calculations

http://www.telusplanet.net/public/sparkman/
netcalc.htm

Network Subnetting

http://www.learntosubnet.com

NTP Server List

http://www.boulder.nist.gov/timefreq/service/
time-servers.html

Syslinux and Pxelinux

http://syslinux.zytor.com

B.15 Open-Source Databases

Commercial MySQL Database

http://www.mysql.org

Free MySQL Database

http://sourceforge.net/projects/mysql

B.16 Parallel Applications and Development Tools

Vampir and Vampirtrace

http://www.pallas.com/e/products/

B.17 Parallel Application Examples

Folding@Home

http://foldingathome.stanford.edu

Genome@Home

http://genomeathome.stanford.edu

NWChem

http://www.emsl.pnl.gov/docs/nwchem/
nwchem.html

SETI@Home

http://www.olympus.net/personal/dewey/
mandelbrot.html

B.18 Performance Benchmarks and Lists

Linpack Performance

http://performance.netlib.org/performance/
html/pdsbrowse.html

Top 500 Supercomputers

http://www.top500.org

B.19 Protocols and Messaging Libraries

MPICH

http://www-unix.mcs.anl.gov/mpi/mpich

MPI Specification

http://www.mpi-forum.org

Sandia Portals Protocol

http://www.sandiaportals.org

B.20 Resource Management, Parallel Execution, and Scheduling

Authd

        http://www.theether.org/authd

Gexec

        http://www.theether.org/gexec

Maui Scheduler

        http://mauischeduler.sourceforge.net

OpenPBS

        http://evms.sourceforge.net

Parallel Distributed Shell

        http://www.llnl.gov/linux/pdsh

SLURM

        http://www.llnl.gov/linux/slurm/slurm.html

SLURM Cola

        http://www.gotfuturama.com/information/
            encyc-66-slurm

B.21 Security and Encryption

Blowfish Encryption

        http://www.schneier.com/blowfish.html

Open SSH

        http://www.openssh.com

B.22 System Installation and Management Tools

System Imager

        http://systemimager.org

System Installation Suite

        http://sisuite.org

Glossary

active cluster elements
Components of the cluster architecture that have an interactive ability, including device management interfaces. Examples include network switches, computer systems, serial port concentrators, and remote-access management cards.

administrative node
A system in a cluster that runs performance monitoring or other system administrative services.

API
An acronym for "application programming interface"; a set of subroutine calls and data types that define an interface to a software service.

application-specific cluster
A cluster configuration that runs only a single application. This may drastically simplify the scheduling and system management aspects of a cluster when compared with a general-purpose cluster that must run multiple applications.

batch job scheduling
A service that manages access to shared (and often scarce) resources by prioritizing and queueing user job requests until the required resources are available. A user submits a request to the scheduling service which determines where and when the request will be serviced.

bisectional bandwidth
The minimum volume of communication possible between any two halves of the network with an equal number of processors. Bisection bandwidth equals the bisection width times the link bandwidth.

bisection width
The minimum number of network links that must be removed to divide the network into two equal halves.

British thermal unit (BTU)
The amount of energy required to raise the temperature of one pound of water from 58.5° F. to 59.5° degrees F.

broadcast

A network frame that is sent from one system to all systems on the attached LAN. This is a one-to-many transmission.

ccNUMA

An acronym for "cache-coherent nonuniform memory access," where all memory in a system is directly addressable but may be nonlocal to a particular processor bus. The memory (and processor) hierarchy allows avoiding the bus scaling issues inherent in SMP systems. Although the hardware allows applications to access all memory as if it were local, maintaining cache coherency, there is a performance penalty for nonlocal memory.

channel bonding

Also referred to as *teaming* and *link aggregation*, this operation creates a single logical network link from multiple physical links, providing increased performance, increased availability, or both.

Clos network

A multistage, switched network architecture that eliminates contention for a route between the network's inputs and outputs.

cluster

A closely coupled, *scalable* collection of interconnected computer systems, sharing a common hardware and software infrastructure, providing a parallel set of resources to services or applications for improved performance, throughput, or availability.

cluster file system

A file system that provides a consistent view of a shared storage area across a group of independent systems while maintaining access and data consistency between them.

collapsed network computing

An architecture that moves the majority of compute resources and high-speed network connections into racks located in a central location. The hardware resources that would normally be located at a user's desk are "collapsed" into the computer room and shared by their users as a central pool.

compute rack

A physical rack in a cluster that contains compute slices and associated hardware. Compute racks are normally connected to management racks.

compute slice

An individual computer member of a cluster that performs computational work. A compute slice is similar in nature to the preengineered integrated circuit components called *bit slices*, that electrical engineers ganged together in parallel to create computer architectures. Each computational system is a *slice* of the total compute resources in the cluster.

directory services

A generic term referring to a service providing the ability to locate information like network port numbers, user names, or general system information by sending an inquiry to a directory agent with the appropriate lookup key. The LDAP allows a standard way of accessing a directory server to obtain information.

diskless system

A system that has no root directory on its local disk. The system root is either in a RAM disk or is provided by a networked file server (an NFS server in the case of an NFS diskless system). Diskless systems may use a local disk (for swap or temporary storage), if present; they just don't boot from it.

disk partition

A physical division of a disk drive, usually used to segregate operating systems or other physical data types from each other. Partition tables are maintained on the disk in areas accessible by the BIOS. The software entity (operating system) "owning" the partition determines its specific usage and format.

distributed application

A program with components running on more than one system, interconnected by a network.

EIA Unit

A unit of measurement set by the Electronic Industries Alliance for standardized equipment racks. One EIA unit, or commonly "U," is equal to 1.75 inches of height. A 2U device would take up a space 3.5 inches in height in a standardized rack.

extensible firmware interface

A facility that provides initial interaction between the BIOS boot process, hardware drivers, the user, and the operating system. EFI represents an attempt to minimize the requirement to update firmware when hardware configurations change.

fat tree

A network topology, arranged in a tree structure, that provides higher cross-sectional bandwidth toward the root of the tree to eliminate bandwith issues.

file server node

A system in a cluster that provides file services to client nodes.

full duplex

A data communications term indicating a channel that is able to send and receive data simultaneously.

half duplex

A data communications term indicating a channel that is able to send data in only one direction at a time.

high-availability cluster

A cluster that provides parallel *redundant* resources to guarantee availability of an important service or application.

high-speed interconnect

A specialized high-bandwidth, low-latency network connection between multiple systems in a cluster. The HSI hardware is specially optimized to speed point-to-point communications, and is used by message passing and other subsystems to allow parallel applications and services to simulate a single, large SMP machine.

high-throughput cluster

A cluster that provides parallel resources to multiple *independent* jobs, to execute as much work in as little time as possible.

infrastructure node

A system in a cluster that runs important services that support the cluster's operation, such as license servers, authentication servers, name services, or time services.

initial RAM disk

A compressed file that contains an image of a Linux file system. The `initrd` is loaded by the bootloader and is initially mounted by the kernel during the Linux boot process. The `initrd` contains drivers and start-up processes that are needed to access the system's root directory, whether it is on hard disk, in RAM disk, or mounted via NFS.

interrack cable

A cable that connects two or more devices in two or more separate racks.

intrarack cable

A cable that connects two or more devices in the same rack.

I/O node

A system in the cluster that performs I/O functions like file system serving, data transfer, or interfacing to other I/O-intensive devices.

jumbo frames

A term referring to the proprietary ability of some network interfaces and switching equipment to increase the maximum transmission size of an Ethernet frame from 1,500 bytes to 9 KB. This adjustment decreases the number of network requests that are made to send bulk data transfers and can improve the performance of bulk data transfers.

kernel parameter

A value passed to the Linux kernel by the bootloader. The value may be used by the kernel, passed to drivers in the kernel, or passed on to the `init` system process.

link bandwidth

The total volume of communication across a communication link. Link bandwidth may be expressed in a number of different ways, including bits per second or bytes per second.

Linux

A freely available, open-source kernel implementation pioneered by Linus Torvalds.

Linux distribution

A specific packaging of the Linux kernel, GNU, and other open-source tools, and value-added components like a system installer, package manager, documentation, and a system management philosophy. The contents of a distribution are chosen by the distribution's architect or maintainer, usually to meet a specific set of goals or needs.

load balancing

A service that attempts to keep resource usage (CPU, RAM, and so on) constant across a group of systems by selecting the most advantageous system to execute a particular request. The selection process may be quite complex or may be based on a simple parameter like current system load-level averages (how many processes are waiting in the run queue on a given system). The "least-busy" resource may be selected, although this alone does not guarantee "balance."

management rack

A physical rack in a cluster that contains common elements like master nodes, core switches, and global storage.

master node

A system in a cluster that is an access point for cluster resources. Users log in to a master node to submit jobs, compile applications, or use other cluster resources. There may be (and should be) more than one master node in a cluster to provide high availability for user access.

maximum transmission unit

The maximum amount of data payload that may be sent across a physical network link. The default MTU for Ethernet is 1,500 bytes, but may be adjusted if the networking equipment can handle it. See "jumbo frames."

memory access hierarchy

The path taken by a unit of data, when accessed by the processor, may span multiple levels of cache memory, local memory, remote memory, or storage. In this hierarchical relationship, each step or level is usually slower the farther it is from the processor.

memory bandwidth

The total throughput, in terms of bytes per second, available to transfer data to and from a system's memory controller and other system units.

memory interleaving

The dividing of memory accesses between two or more memory controllers or channels. Memory interleaving can increase the rate that memory information may be supplied to the system processors.

Moore's Law

An often misquoted relationship first expressed by one of the founders of Intel, Gordon Moore. Moore's Law proposes that the density of devices on integrated circuits follows the curve described by $2^{(year - 1962)}$. The period for doubling is closer to 18 months today.

multicast

A network communication frame that is sent from a single source to all subscribers on a particular multicast channel. This is a one-to-only-those-that-want-it transmission.

name services

A generic term referring to the ability to map host names to IP addresses and vice versa. There are a number of name services, including DNS and NIS.

network alias

A logical network device, with its own separate IP address and management information, that is "attached" to a physical network device, such as eth0. An alias, which might be named eth0:0, might have a completely different IP addressing scheme, net mask, and routing information from the physical device, allowing the system to see multiple networks or to have multiple IP addresses with only a single interface card.

NUMA

Nonuniform memory access. Refers to a memory hierarchy in which memory access times may differ depending on the location's position in the hierarchy.

open-source software

A software development and distribution philosophy that is similar in nature to the scientific research community's information-sharing process. Software is created and shared openly, allowing programmers to "stand on the shoulders of giants." To generate new solutions using novel integrations of previously released or published libraries, programs, tools, and operating systems components. In other words, software implementations and their source code are freely available without proprietary licensing to inhibit their free and open use.

parallel application

A program that distributes code and data to multiple systems, breaking up a problem into smaller problems that may be simultaneously solved.

passive cluster elements

Elements of the cluster architecture, such as racks, cables, and mounting rails that do not actively participate in the operation of the cluster.

/proc

A Linux pseudo file system that provides readily accessible information from the kernel, processes, and drivers running on an active system. In many cases, this file system implements a two-way communication path between the system software and applications.

public-key encryption

An encryption scheme that employs two keys: a private key and a public key. Data encrypted with the public key may be decrypted with the private key. It is not computationally practical to recreate the private key from the pubic key, so information may be shared securely without the danger of eavesdropping by a third party. Only public keys from the key pair should be shared with others!

refrigeration ton

The amount of energy required to melt one ton of ice at $32°$ F. in a 24-hour period. Although historical in nature, the term is used frequently in relation to air-conditioning design.

remote procedure call

A communication method that allows program components distributed in a network to pass data between systems in a natural call–return mechanism. Details of data translation, network connection, and error recovery may be hidden from the program component by the associated library, simplifying application development.

software churn
Rapid changes in the available software packages in a product distribution, causing a frequent change in the operating system or application software environment.

software RAID
An implementation of RAID algorithms that utilize the system processor to manage the RAID device. Parity calculation, error recovery, and array rebuilding are performed by the local processor. Software RAID is a low-cost method of creating and managing redundant arrays of independent disks on Linux.

software stack
The set of interrelated software subsystems and components required to operate a cluster. Because the components are often dependent on each other, they are referred to as being "stacked."

solution
The application of a technology to solve a particular problem. If you are not part of the solution, you are part of the precipitate.

symmetric multiprocessor
A computer system, with two or more processors, in which all processors have equal access to a globally shared memory.

unicast
A network frame that is sent from a system to a single destination. This is a one-to-one transmission.

uniprocessor system
A computer system that contains a single CPU.

virtual address space
The range of memory addresses provided to a process by an operating system with virtual memory management capabilities. Virtual addresses are transparently mapped to physical memory addresses by the virtual memory system. A process' virtual address space may be larger than available physical memory.

worker node
A system in a cluster that executes one or more portions of a parallel job or service.

BIBLIOGRAPHY

Albitz, P., and C. Liu. (2001) *DNS and BIND.* 4th ed. Sebastopol, CA: O'Reilly & Associates.

Ault, M., and M. Tumma. (2003) *Oracle9i RAC—Oracle Real Application Clusters—Configuration and Internals.* 1st ed., Kittrell, NC: Rampant Techpress.

Barrett, Daniel J., and Richard E. Silverman. (2002) *SSH: The Secure Shell.* 1st ed. Sebastopol, CA: O'Reilly & Associates.

Clos, Charles. (1953) A Study of Non-blocking Switching Networks. *The Bell System Technical Journal,* vol. 32, no.2:406-424.

H. G. Dietz, and T. I. Mattox. (2000) *Compiler Techniques for Flat Neighborhood Networks.* Proceedings of the 13th International workshop on Languages and Compilers for Parallel Computing, IBM Watson Research Center, Yorktown, New York, August 10-12, 239-254.

Debian. (2004) Available at `http://www.debian.org/intro/about`. Accessed March 32, 2004.

Feit, Sidnie. (2000) *Local Area High Speed Networks.* 1st ed. Indiananapolis, IN: Macmillan Technical Publishing.

Feit, Sidnie. (1999) *Wide Area High Speed Networks.* 1st ed. Indianapolis, IN: Macmillan Technical Publishing.

Free Software Foundation. (2004) *The Free Software Definition.* Available at `http://www.fsf.org/philosophy/free-sw.html`. Accessed May 31, 2004.

Garfinkel, S., and G. Spafford. (1994) *Practical Unix Security.* 1st ed. Sebastopol, CA: O'Reilly & Associates.

Garman, J. (2003) *Kerberos: The Definitive Guide.* 1st ed. Sebastopol, CA: O'Reilly & Associates.

Grama, A., A. Gupta, G. Karypis, and V. Kumar. (2003) *Introduction to Parallel Computing.* 2nd ed. Essex, UK: Pearson Education Limited.

Koniges, Alice E. (2000) *Industrial Strength Parallel Computing.* 1st ed. San Francisco, CA: Morgan Kaufmann Publishers.

Loshin, Pete. (2004) *IPv6: Theory, Protocol, and Practice.* 2nd ed. San Francisco, CA: Morgan Kaufmann Publishers.

Lucke, Robert W. (1999) *Designing and Implementing Computer Workgroups.* 1st ed. Upper Saddle River, NJ: Prentice Hall PTR.

Mancill, Tony. (2002) *Linux Routers: A Primer for Network Administrators.* 2nd ed. Upper Saddle River, NJ: Prentice Hall PTR.

Mosberger, David and Eranian, Stéphane. (2002) *IA-64 Linux Kernel—Design and Implementation.* 1st ed. Upper Saddle River, NJ: Prentice-Hall PTR.

PNNL EMSL. (2004) Pacific Northwest National Laboratory Environmental Molecular Science Laboratory. Available at `http://mscf.emsl.pnl.gov/hardware/config_mpp2.shtml`. Accessed January 10, 2004.

PNNL MSCF. (2004) Pacific Northwest National Laboratory Molecular Science Computing Facility Computer Hardware. Available at `http://www.emsl.pnl.gov/docs/nwchem/nwchem.html`. Accessed January 10, 2004.

Rich, David and J. Cownie. (2003) *AMD Opteron: Performance Issues, Application Programmers View,* Cern Computing Colloquia 2003. Available at `http://computing-colloquia.web.cern.ch/computing-colloquia/talks/Boris%20Software%20Talk.ppt`, Accessed May 31, 2004.

Schimmel, Curt. (1994) *Unix Systems for Modern Architectures.* 1st ed. Boston: Addison-Wesley.

Singh, Simon. (2000) *The Code Book: The Science of Secrecy From Ancient Egypt to Quantum Cryptography.* 1st ed. New York: Anchor Books.

Stern, Hal. (1992) *Managing NFS and NIS.* 1st ed. Sebastopol, CA: O'Reilly & Associates.

INDEX

A